BATMAN BLACK and WHITE

VOLUME FOUR

WRITERS

NEAL **ADAMS**
RAFAEL **ALBUQUERQUE**
MICHAEL **ALLRED**
LEE **ALLRED**
JOHN **ARCUDI**
LEE **BERMEJO**
IVAN **BRANDON**
BLAIR **BUTLER**
CLIFF **CHIANG**
DAN **DIDIO**
PAUL **DINI**
NATHAN **EDMONDSON**
SEAN **GALLOWAY**
KEITH **GIFFEN**
RAFAEL **GRAMPÁ**
ADAM **HUGHES**
RIAN **HUGHES**
DAVE **JOHNSON**
CHIP **KIDD**
JEFF **LEMIRE**
DAVID **MACHO**
HOWARD **MACKIE**
OLLY **MOSS**
DUSTIN **NGUYEN**
JIMMY **PALMIOTTI**
DAMION **SCOTT**
DAVE **TAYLOR**
MICHAEL **USLAN**
LEN **WEIN**
MARIS **WICKS**
MARV **WOLFMAN**

ILLUSTRATORS

NEAL **ADAMS**
RAFAEL **ALBUQUERQUE**
MICHAEL **ALLRED**
LEE **BERMEJO**
DAVE **BULLOCK**
RICCARDO **BURCHIELLI**
CLIFF **CHIANG**
MICHAEL **CHO**
BECKY **CLOONAN**
SEAN **GALLOWAY**
RAFAEL **GRAMPÁ**
ADAM **HUGHES**
RIAN **HUGHES**
VICTOR **IBÁÑEZ**
DAVE **JOHNSON**
J.G. **JONES**
DEREK **LAUFMAN**
SEAN **MURPHY**
DUSTIN **NGUYEN**
ALEX **NIÑO**
RUBÉN **PELLEJERO**
JAVIER **PULIDO**
JOE **QUINONES**
PAOLO **RIVERA**
JOE **RIVERA**
KENNETH **ROCAFORT**
ANDREW **ROBINSON**
STÉPHANE **ROUX**
CHRIS **SAMNEE**
DAMION **SCOTT**
DAVE **TAYLOR**
CHRIS **WESTON**

LETTERERS

MICHAEL **ALLRED**
DAVE **BULLOCK**
SAL **CIPRIANO**
TAYLOR **ESPOSITO**
JARED K. **FLETCHER**
JOHN J. **HILL**
RIAN **HUGHES**
DAVE **JOHNSON**
TRAVIS **LANHAM**
ROB **LEIGH**
CARLOS M. **MANGUAL**
JACK **MORELLI**
JAVIER **PULIDO**
CLEM **ROBINS**
ERICA **SCHULTZ**
DAVE **SHARPE**
DEZI **SIENTY**
DAVE **TAYLOR**
STEVE **WANDS**
CHRIS **WESTON**

Cover art by MARC **SILVESTRI**

B A T M A N C R

AN

ACK

and

HITE

T E D   B Y   B O B   K A N E

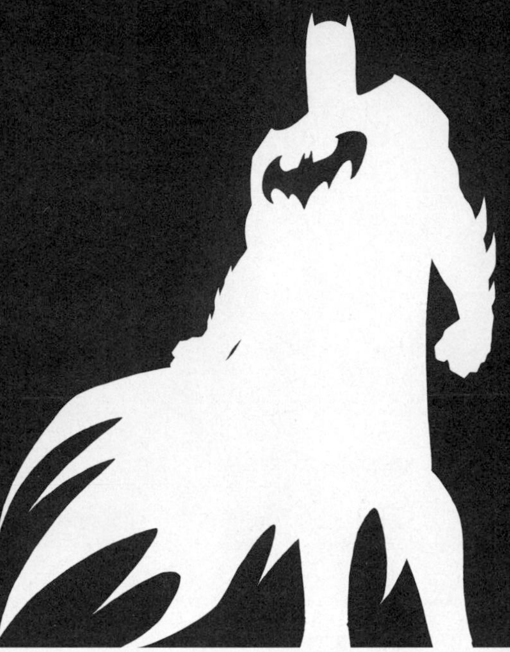

MARK CHIARELLO EDITOR – ORIGINAL SERIES **CAMILLA ZHANG** ASSISTANT EDITOR – ORIGINAL SERIES
ROBIN WILDMAN EDITOR **ROBBIN BROSTERMAN** DESIGN DIRECTOR – BOOKS

BOB HARRAS SENIOR VP – EDITOR-IN-CHIEF, DC COMICS

DIANE NELSON PRESIDENT **DAN DIDIO** AND **JIM LEE** CO-PUBLISHERS **GEOFF JOHNS** CHIEF CREATIVE OFFICER
AMIT DESAI SENIOR VP – MARKETING AND FRANCHISE MANAGEMENT
AMY GENKINS SENIOR VP – BUSINESS AND LEGAL AFFAIRS **NAIRI GARDINER** SENIOR VP – FINANCE
JEFF BOISON VP – PUBLISHING PLANNING **MARK CHIARELLO** VP – ART DIRECTION AND DESIGN
JOHN CUNNINGHAM VP – MARKETING **TERRI CUNNINGHAM** VP – EDITORIAL ADMINISTRATION
LARRY GANEM VP – TALENT RELATIONS AND SERVICES **ALISON GILL** SENIOR VP – MANUFACTURING AND OPERATIONS
HANK KANALZ SENIOR VP – VERTIGO AND INTEGRATED PUBLISHING **JAY KOGAN** VP – BUSINESS AND LEGAL AFFAIRS, PUBLISHING
JACK MAHAN VP – BUSINESS AFFAIRS, TALENT **NICK NAPOLITANO** VP – MANUFACTURING ADMINISTRATION
SUE POHJA VP – BOOK SALES **FRED RUIZ** VP – MANUFACTURING OPERATIONS
COURTNEY SIMMONS SENIOR VP – PUBLICITY **BOB WAYNE** SENIOR VP – SALES

BATMAN BLACK AND WHITE
VOLUME FOUR

Published by DC Comics. Copyright © 2014 DC Comics. All Rights Reserved.
Originally published in single magazine form in BATMAN BLACK AND WHITE 1-6 © 2013, 2014 DC Comics. All Rights Reserved.
All characters, their distinctive likenesses and related elements featured in this publication are trademarks of DC Comics.
The stories, characters and incidents featured in this publication are entirely fictional.
DC Comics does not read or accept unsolicited ideas, stories or artwork.

DC Comics, 1700 Broadway, New York, NY 10019
A Warner Bros. Entertainment Company
Printed by RR Donnelley, Owensville, MO, USA. 12/12/14. First Printing.
ISBN: 978-1-4012-5062-1

Library of Congress Cataloging-in-Publication Data

Batman black and white volume 4.
pages cm
ISBN 978-1-4012-5062-1 (pbk.)
1. Graphic novels.
PN6728.B36B37775 2014
741.5'973—dc23

2014010284

CONTENTS

CONTENTS

CONTENTS

DON'T KNOW WHERE,

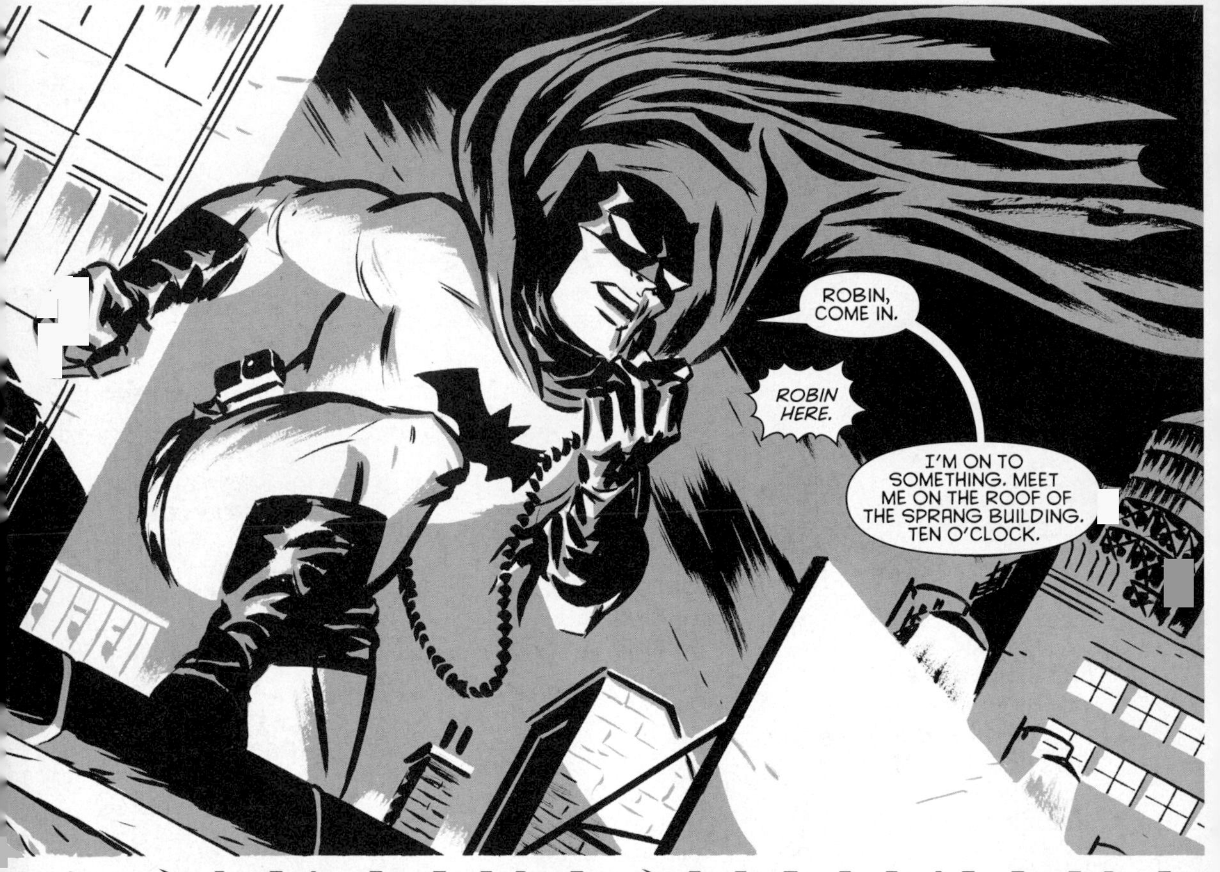
ROBIN, COME IN.
ROBIN HERE.
I'M ON TO SOMETHING. MEET ME ON THE ROOF OF THE SPRANG BUILDING. TEN O'CLOCK.

DON'T KNOW WHEN,

STORY BY CHIP KIDD ART BY MICHAEL CHO LETTERED BY DEZI SIENTY

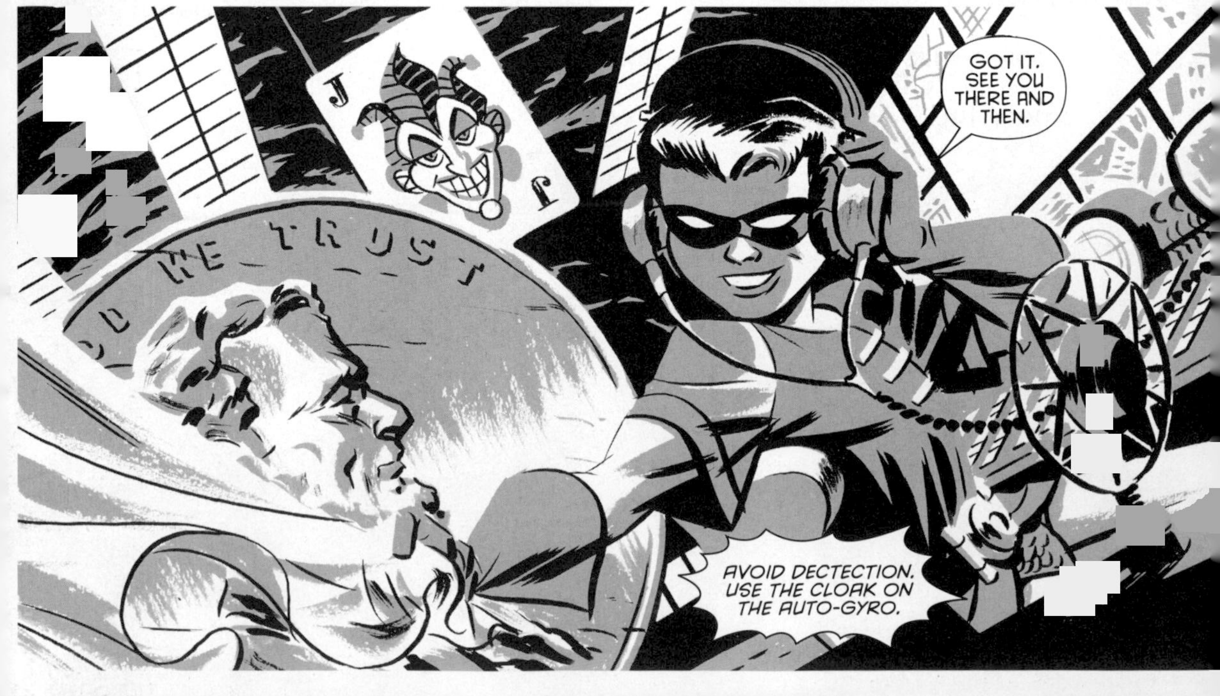
GOT IT. SEE YOU THERE AND THEN.
AVOID DECTECTION. USE THE CLOAK ON THE AUTO-GYRO.

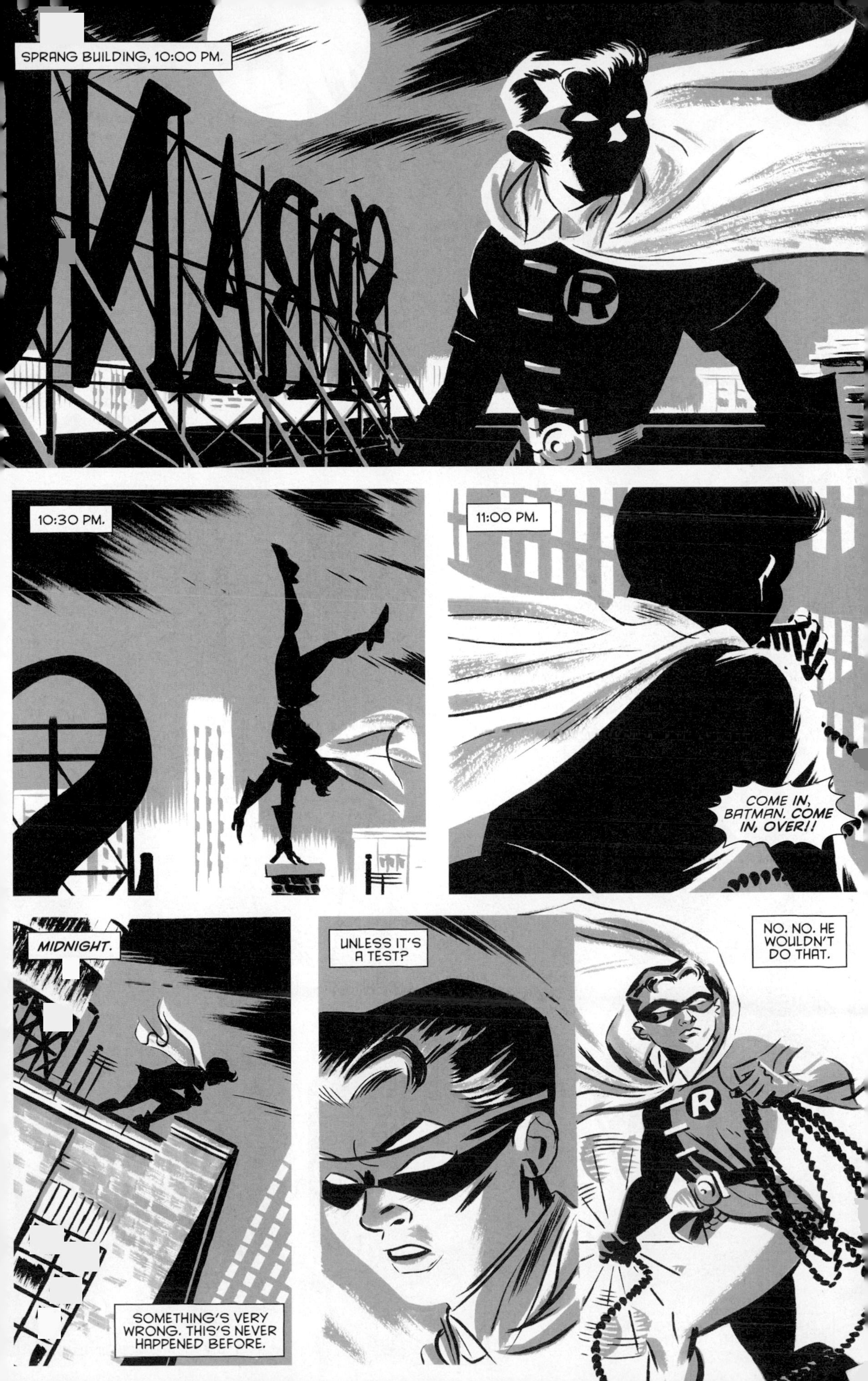
SPRANG BUILDING, 10:00 PM.
10:30 PM.
11:00 PM.
COME IN, BATMAN. COME IN, OVER!!
MIDNIGHT.
SOMETHING'S VERY WRONG. THIS'S NEVER HAPPENED BEFORE.
UNLESS IT'S A TEST?
NO. NO. HE WOULDN'T DO THAT.

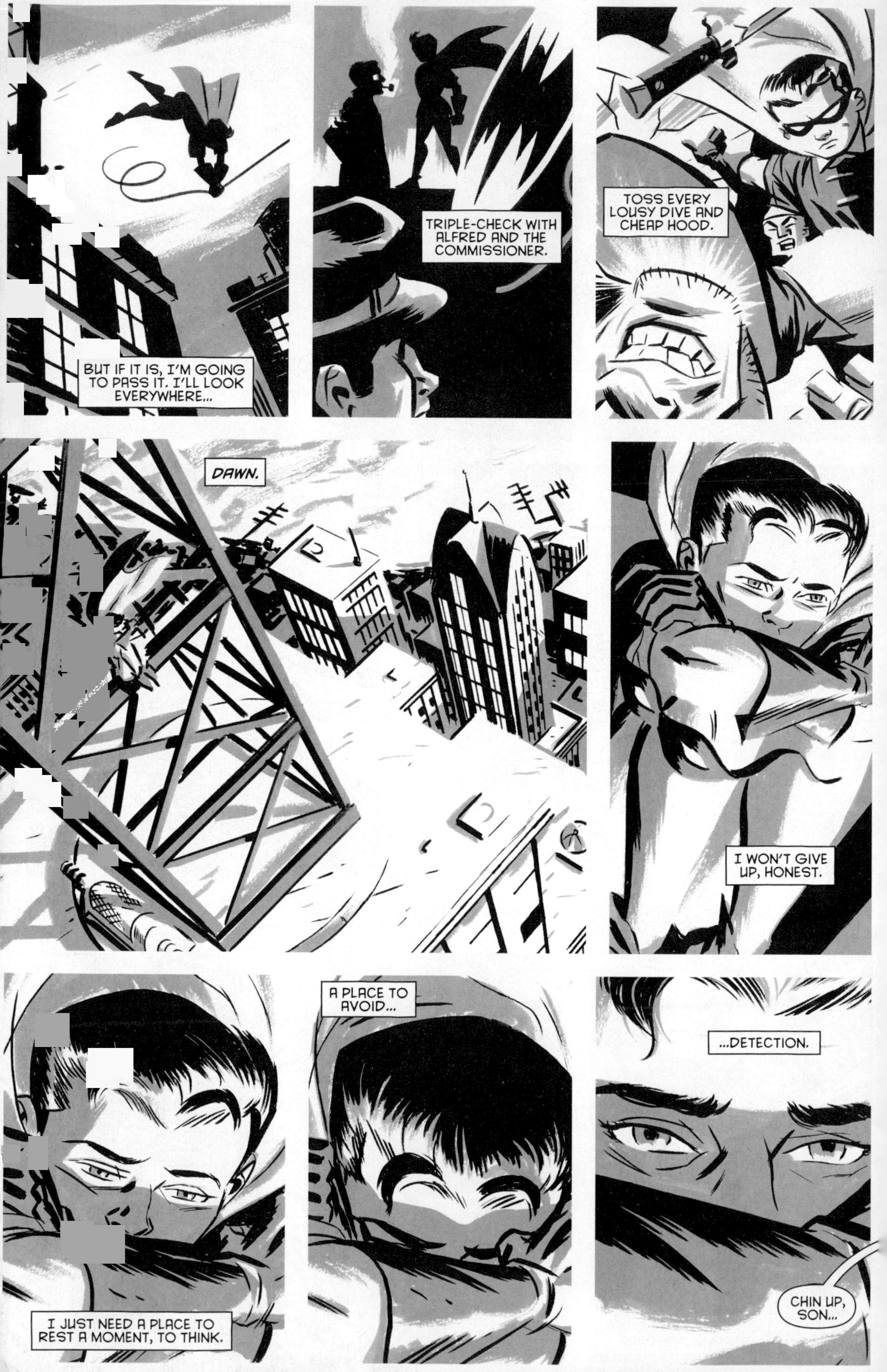

BUT IF IT IS, I'M GOING TO PASS IT. I'LL LOOK EVERYWHERE...
TRIPLE-CHECK WITH ALFRED AND THE COMMISSIONER.
TOSS EVERY LOUSY DIVE AND CHEAP HOOD.
DAWN.
I WON'T GIVE UP, HONEST.
I JUST NEED A PLACE TO REST A MOMENT, TO THINK.
A PLACE TO AVOID...
...DETECTION.
CHIN UP, SON...

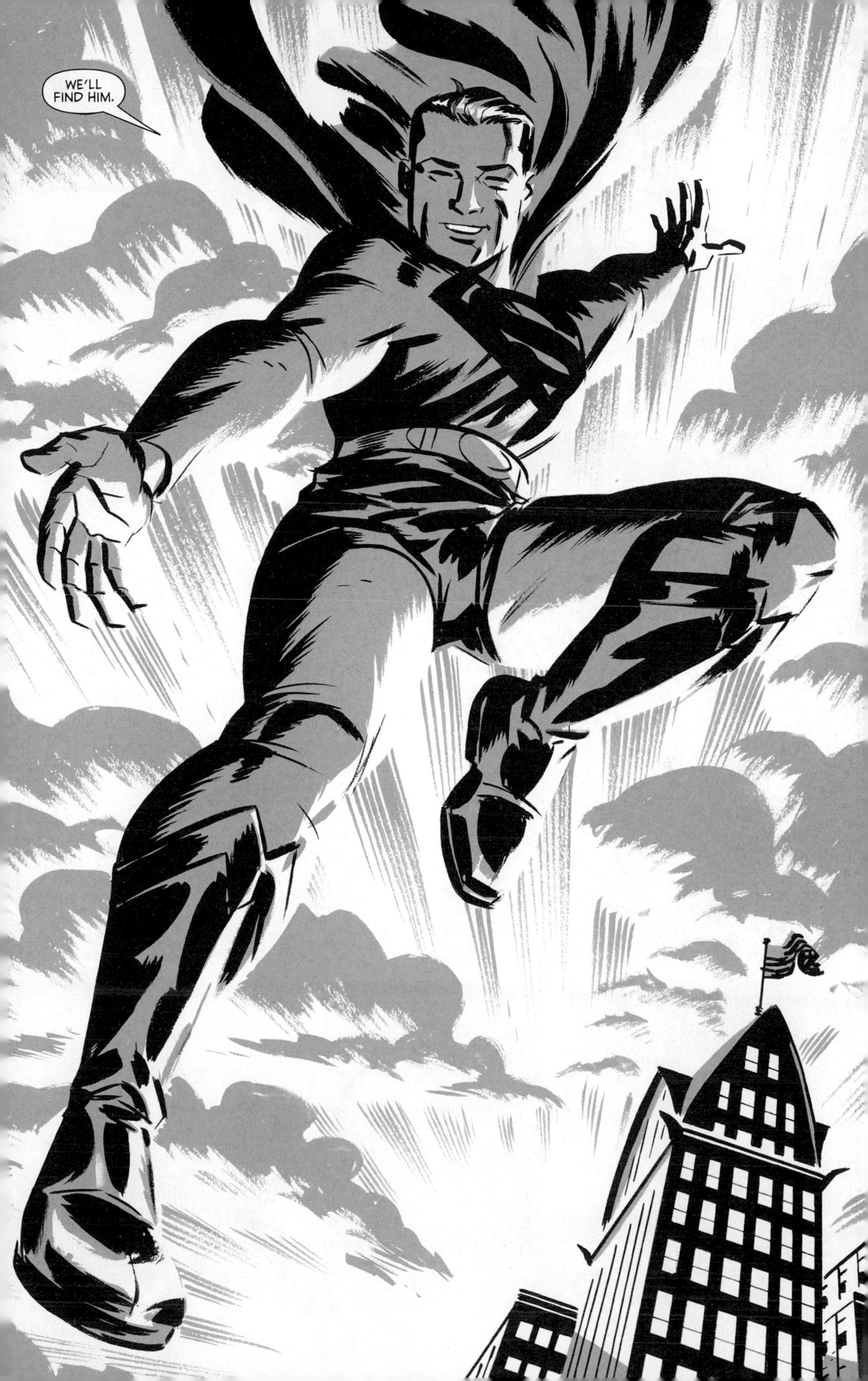
WE'LL FIND HIM.

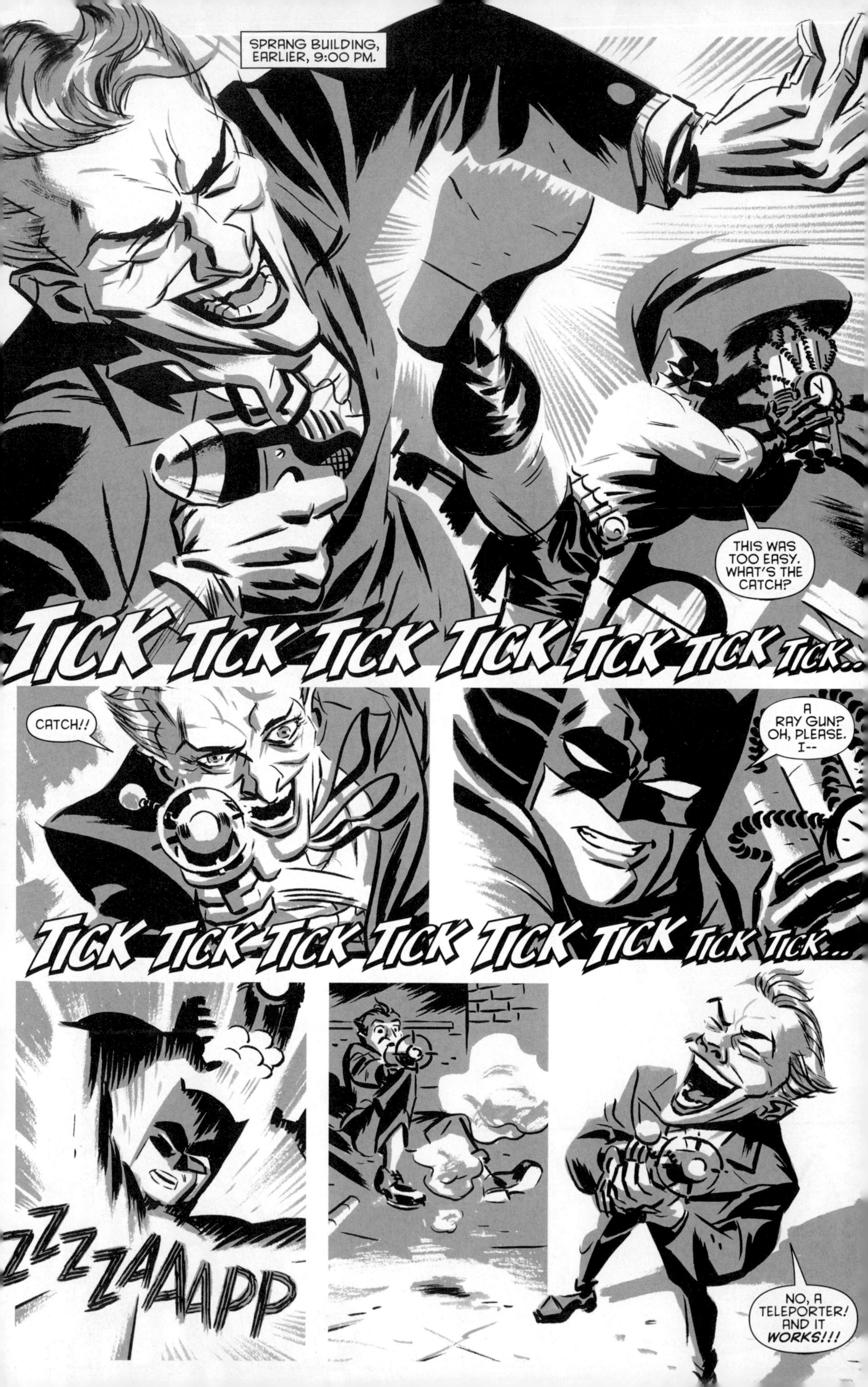
SPRANG BUILDING, EARLIER, 9:00 PM.
THIS WAS TOO EASY. WHAT'S THE CATCH?
TICK TICK TICK TICK TICK TICK TICK..
CATCH!!
A RAY GUN? OH, PLEASE. I--
TICK TICK TICK TICK TICK TICK TICK TICK...
ZZZZAAAPP
NO, A TELEPORTER! AND IT WORKS!!!

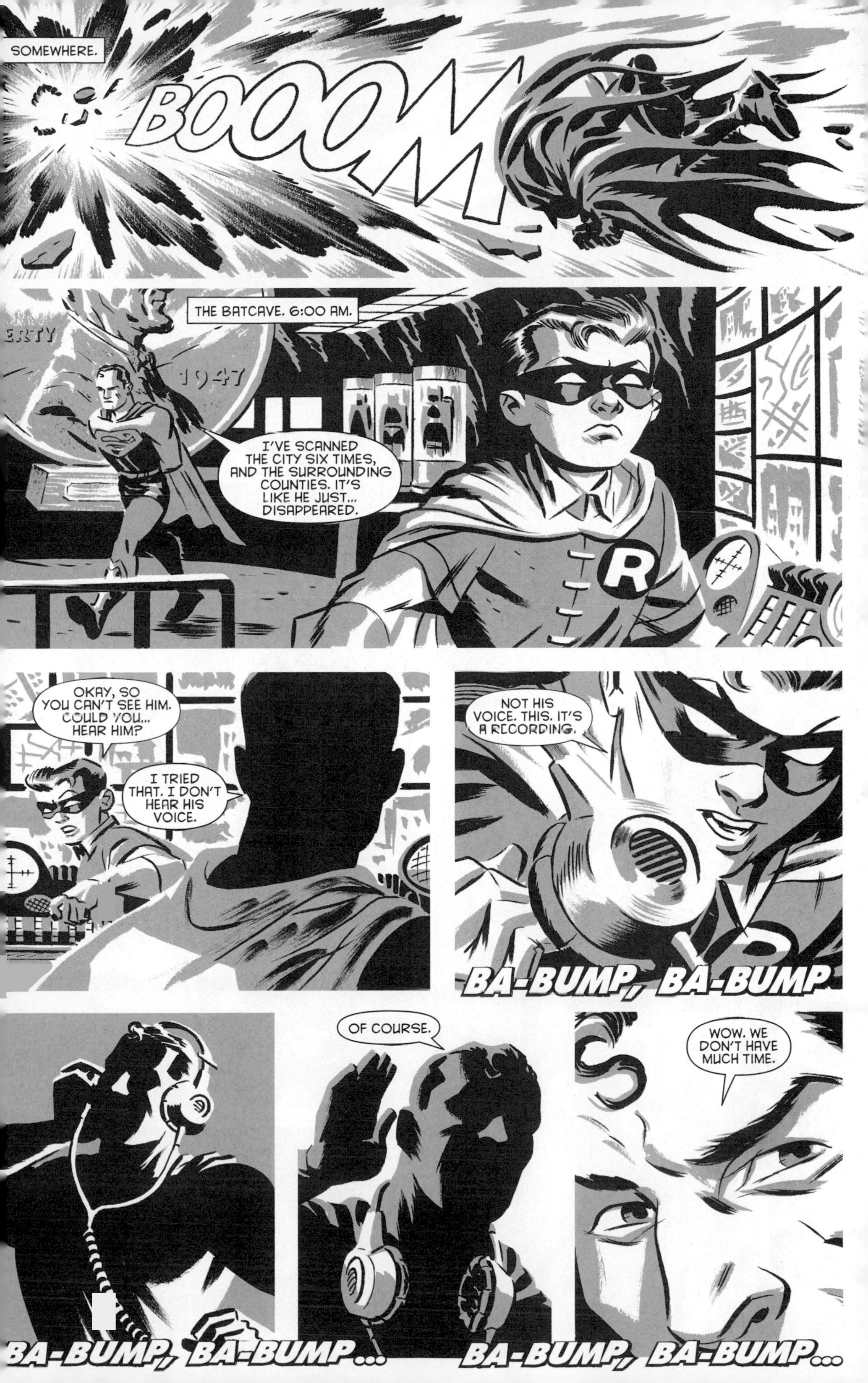
SOMEWHERE.
BOOOOM
THE BATCAVE. 6:00 AM.
ERTY
1947
I'VE SCANNED THE CITY SIX TIMES, AND THE SURROUNDING COUNTIES. IT'S LIKE HE JUST... DISAPPEARED.
R
OKAY, SO YOU CAN'T SEE HIM. COULD YOU... HEAR HIM?
I TRIED THAT. I DON'T HEAR HIS VOICE.
NOT HIS VOICE. THIS. IT'S A RECORDING.
BA-BUMP, BA-BUMP
OF COURSE.
WOW. WE DON'T HAVE MUCH TIME.
BA-BUMP, BA-BUMP...
BA-BUMP, BA-BUMP...

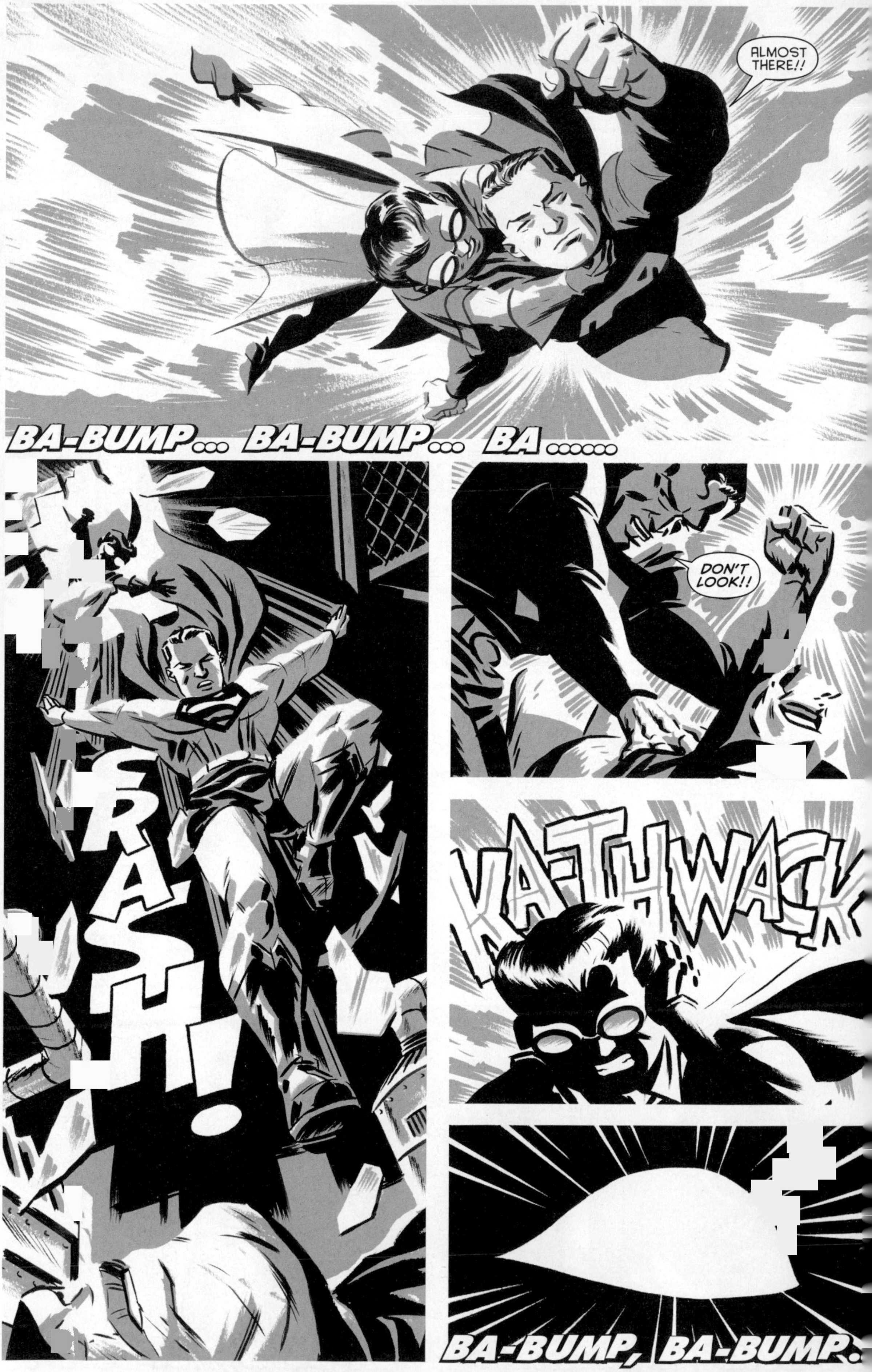
ALMOST THERE!!
BA-BUMP... BA-BUMP... BA......
CRASH!
DON'T LOOK!!
KA-THWACK
BA-BUMP, BA-BUMP.

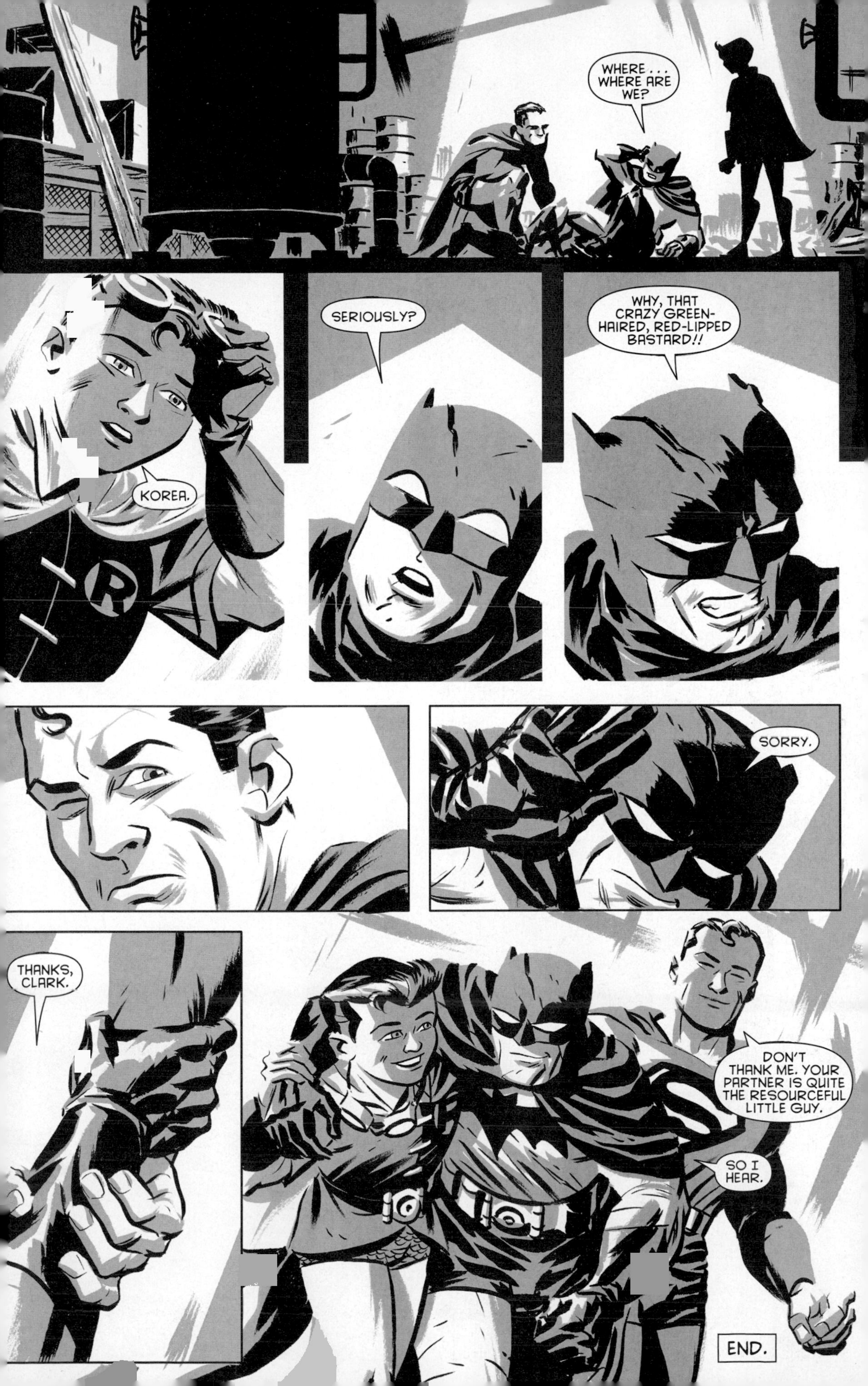
WHERE . . . WHERE ARE WE?
KOREA.
SERIOUSLY?
WHY, THAT CRAZY GREEN-HAIRED, RED-LIPPED BASTARD!!
SORRY.
THANKS, CLARK.
DON'T THANK ME. YOUR PARTNER IS QUITE THE RESOURCEFUL LITTLE GUY.
SO I HEAR.
END.

CHIP KIDD

If the Church of Batman existed, Chip Kidd would be the Pope. One of the world's most respected and celebrated graphic designers, Chip is also one of the leading authorities on all things Batman. A compelling writer who pushes the limits of imagination and story structure, Chip's BATMAN: DEATH BY DESIGN was a 2012 *New York Times* Bestseller.

This four-time Eisner Award winner has changed the landscape of book design by creating what is widely referred to as the "Chip Kidd Look." He is the designer of many, many striking book covers, including Michael Crichton's *Jurassic Park* and Bret Easton Ellis's *American Psycho*.

MICHAEL CHO

Canadian cartoonist, painter and illustrator Michael Cho is an artist whose work evokes the grandeur and flourish of classic Golden and Silver Age comic books. His art has been published in, among others, *The New York Times Book Review*, *The Boston Globe*, *The Village Voice*, *The Washington Post*, and *Scientific American*.

A master of "lost line" illustration, Cho has also created and self-published several independent and web comics, including the innovative and consistently breathtaking *Papercut*.

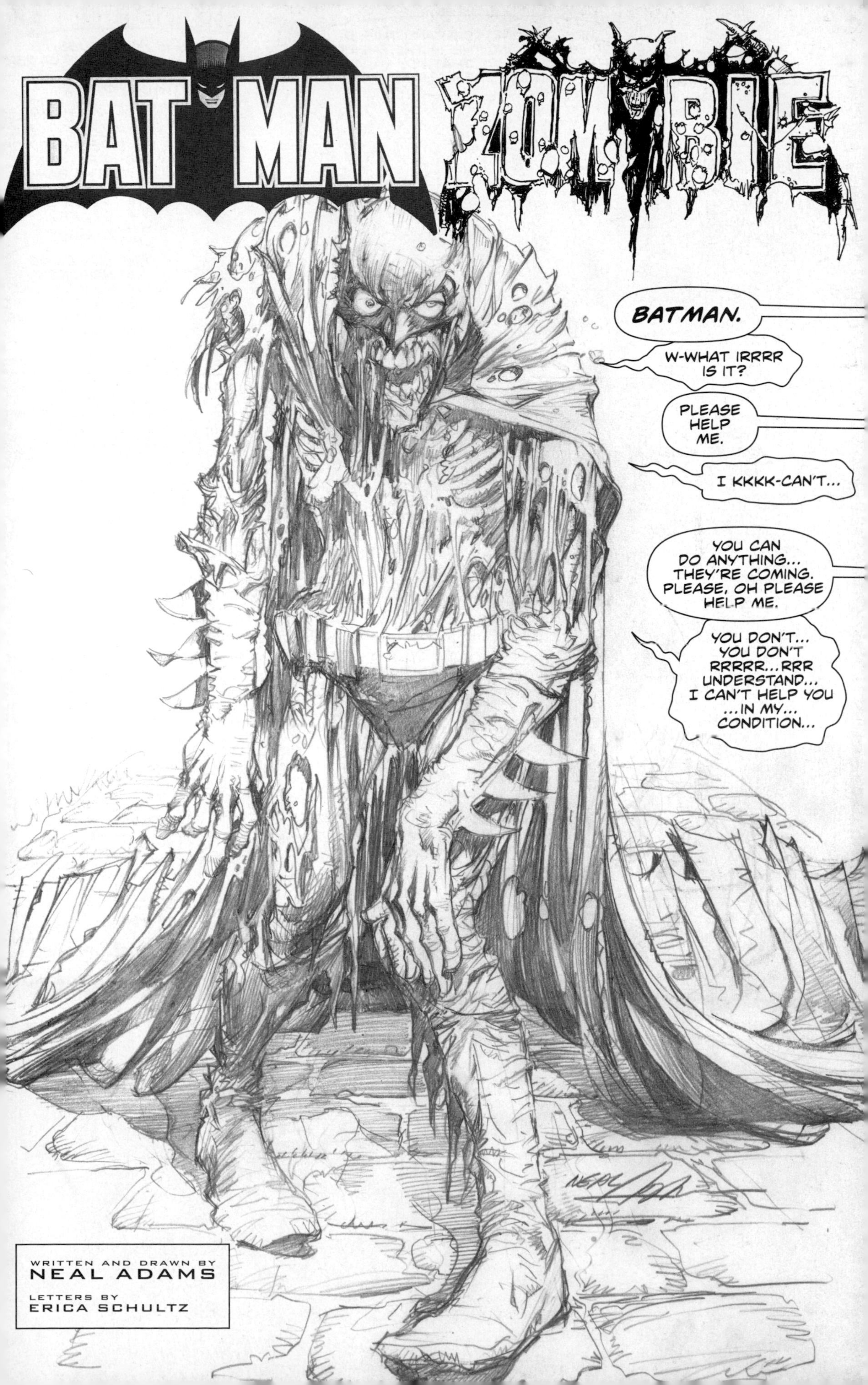
BATMAN ZOMBIE
BATMAN.
W-WHAT IRRRR IS IT?
PLEASE HELP ME.
I KKKK-CAN'T...
YOU CAN DO ANYTHING... THEY'RE COMING. PLEASE, OH PLEASE HELP ME.
YOU DON'T... YOU DON'T RRRRR...RRR UNDERSTAND... I CAN'T HELP YOU ...IN MY... CONDITION...
WRITTEN AND DRAWN BY NEAL ADAMS
LETTERS BY ERICA SCHULTZ

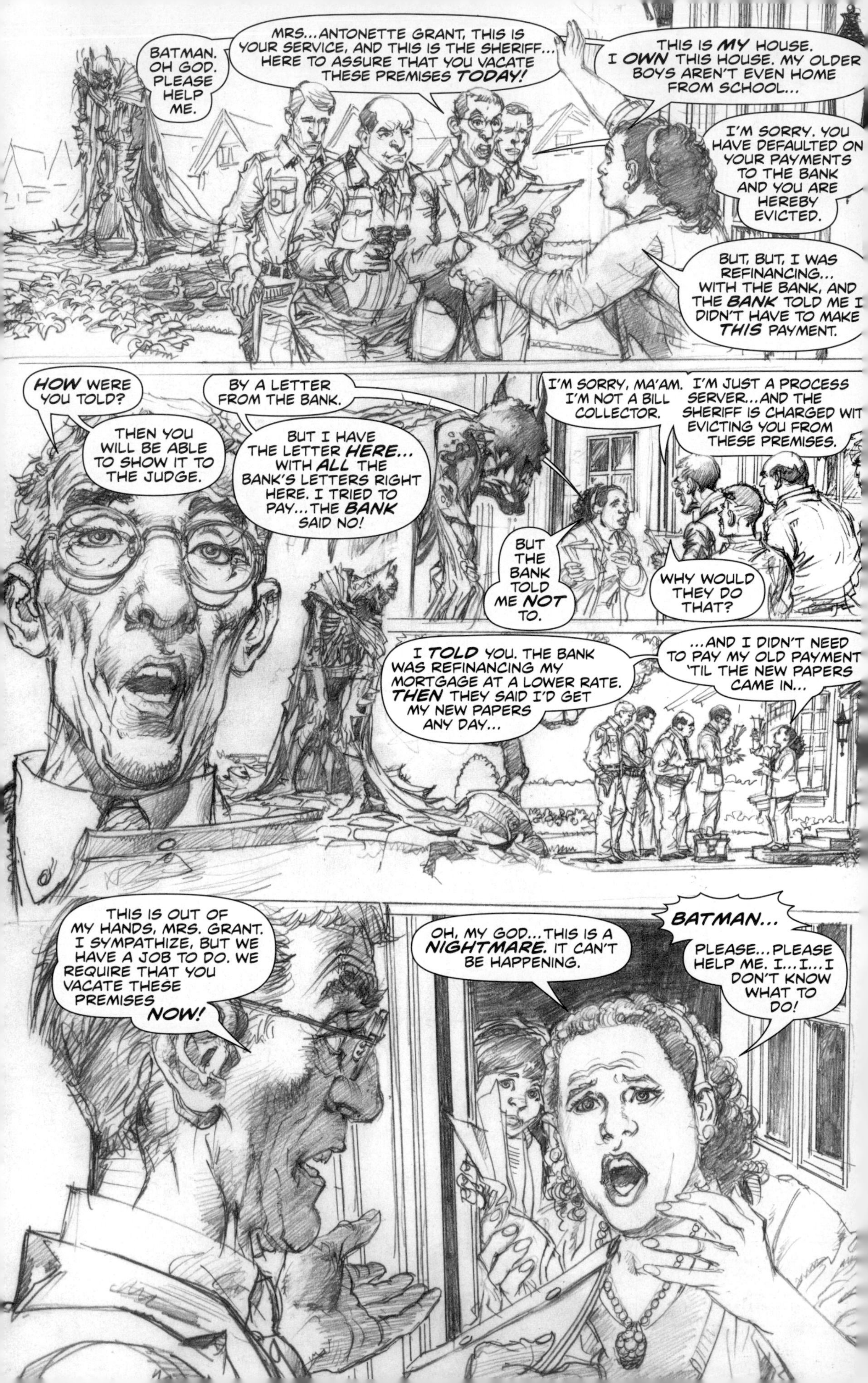
BATMAN. OH GOD. PLEASE HELP ME.
MRS... ANTONETTE GRANT, THIS IS YOUR SERVICE, AND THIS IS THE SHERIFF... HERE TO ASSURE THAT YOU VACATE THESE PREMISES TODAY!
THIS IS MY HOUSE. I OWN THIS HOUSE. MY OLDER BOYS AREN'T EVEN HOME FROM SCHOOL...
I'M SORRY. YOU HAVE DEFAULTED ON YOUR PAYMENTS TO THE BANK AND YOU ARE HEREBY EVICTED.
BUT, BUT, I WAS REFINANCING... WITH THE BANK, AND THE BANK TOLD ME I DIDN'T HAVE TO MAKE THIS PAYMENT.
HOW WERE YOU TOLD?
BY A LETTER FROM THE BANK.
THEN YOU WILL BE ABLE TO SHOW IT TO THE JUDGE.
BUT I HAVE THE LETTER HERE... WITH ALL THE BANK'S LETTERS RIGHT HERE. I TRIED TO PAY... THE BANK SAID NO!
I'M SORRY, MA'AM. I'M NOT A BILL COLLECTOR.
I'M JUST A PROCESS SERVER... AND THE SHERIFF IS CHARGED WIT EVICTING YOU FROM THESE PREMISES.
BUT THE BANK TOLD ME NOT TO.
WHY WOULD THEY DO THAT?
I TOLD YOU. THE BANK WAS REFINANCING MY MORTGAGE AT A LOWER RATE. THEN THEY SAID I'D GET MY NEW PAPERS ANY DAY...
...AND I DIDN'T NEED TO PAY MY OLD PAYMENT 'TIL THE NEW PAPERS CAME IN...
THIS IS OUT OF MY HANDS, MRS. GRANT. I SYMPATHIZE, BUT WE HAVE A JOB TO DO. WE REQUIRE THAT YOU VACATE THESE PREMISES NOW!
OH, MY GOD... THIS IS A NIGHTMARE. IT CAN'T BE HAPPENING.
BATMAN...
PLEASE... PLEASE HELP ME. I... I... I DON'T KNOW WHAT TO DO!

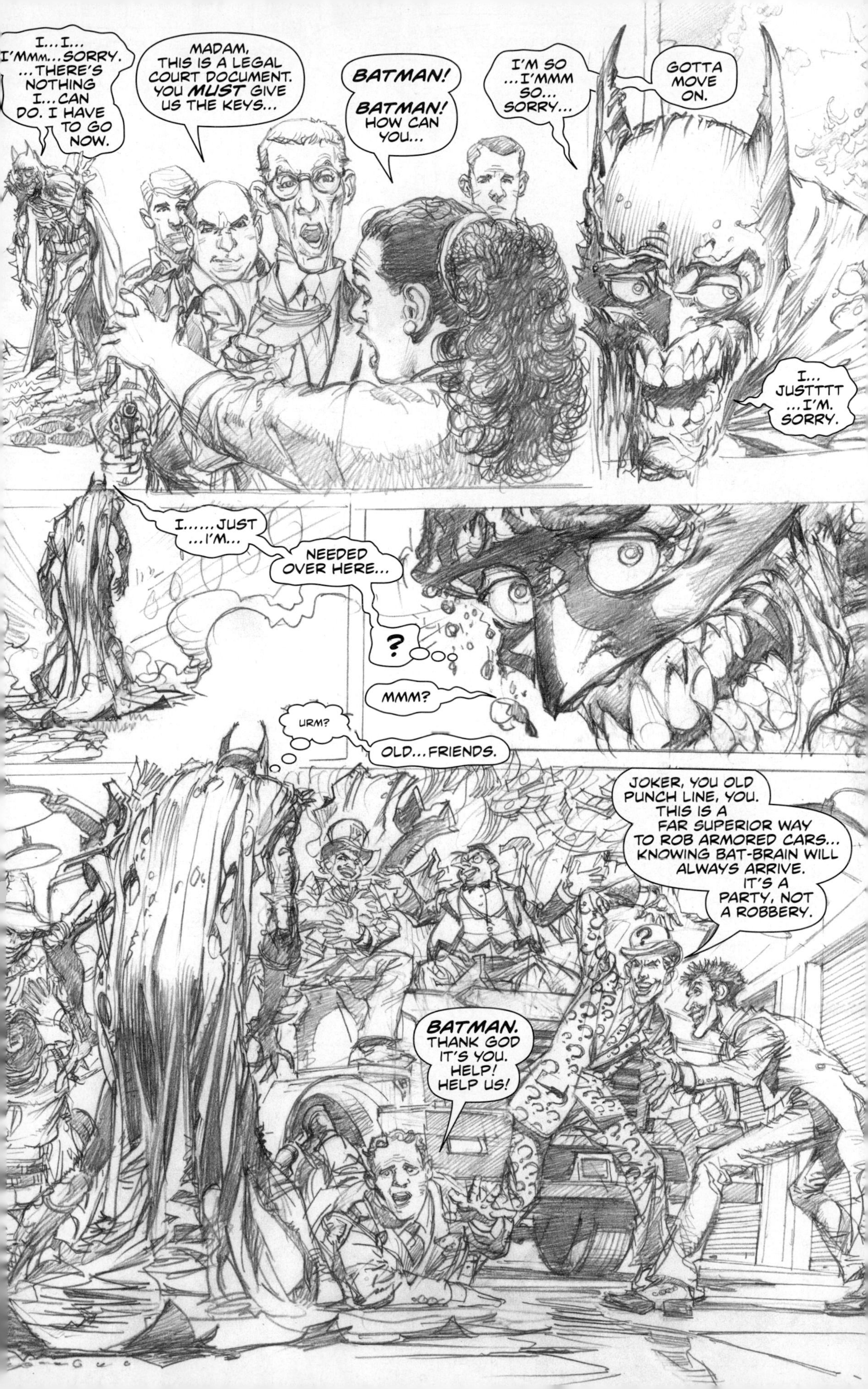
I... I... I'MMM... SORRY. ...THERE'S NOTHING I... CAN DO. I HAVE TO GO NOW.
MADAM, THIS IS A LEGAL COURT DOCUMENT. YOU MUST GIVE US THE KEYS...
BATMAN! BATMAN! HOW CAN YOU...
I'M SO ...I'MMM SO... SORRY...
GOTTA MOVE ON.
I... JUSTTTT ...I'M. SORRY.
I...... JUST ...I'M...
NEEDED OVER HERE...
?
MMM?
URM?
OLD... FRIENDS.
JOKER, YOU OLD PUNCH LINE, YOU. THIS IS A FAR SUPERIOR WAY TO ROB ARMORED CARS... KNOWING BAT-BRAIN WILL ALWAYS ARRIVE. IT'S A PARTY, NOT A ROBBERY.
BATMAN. THANK GOD IT'S YOU. HELP! HELP US!

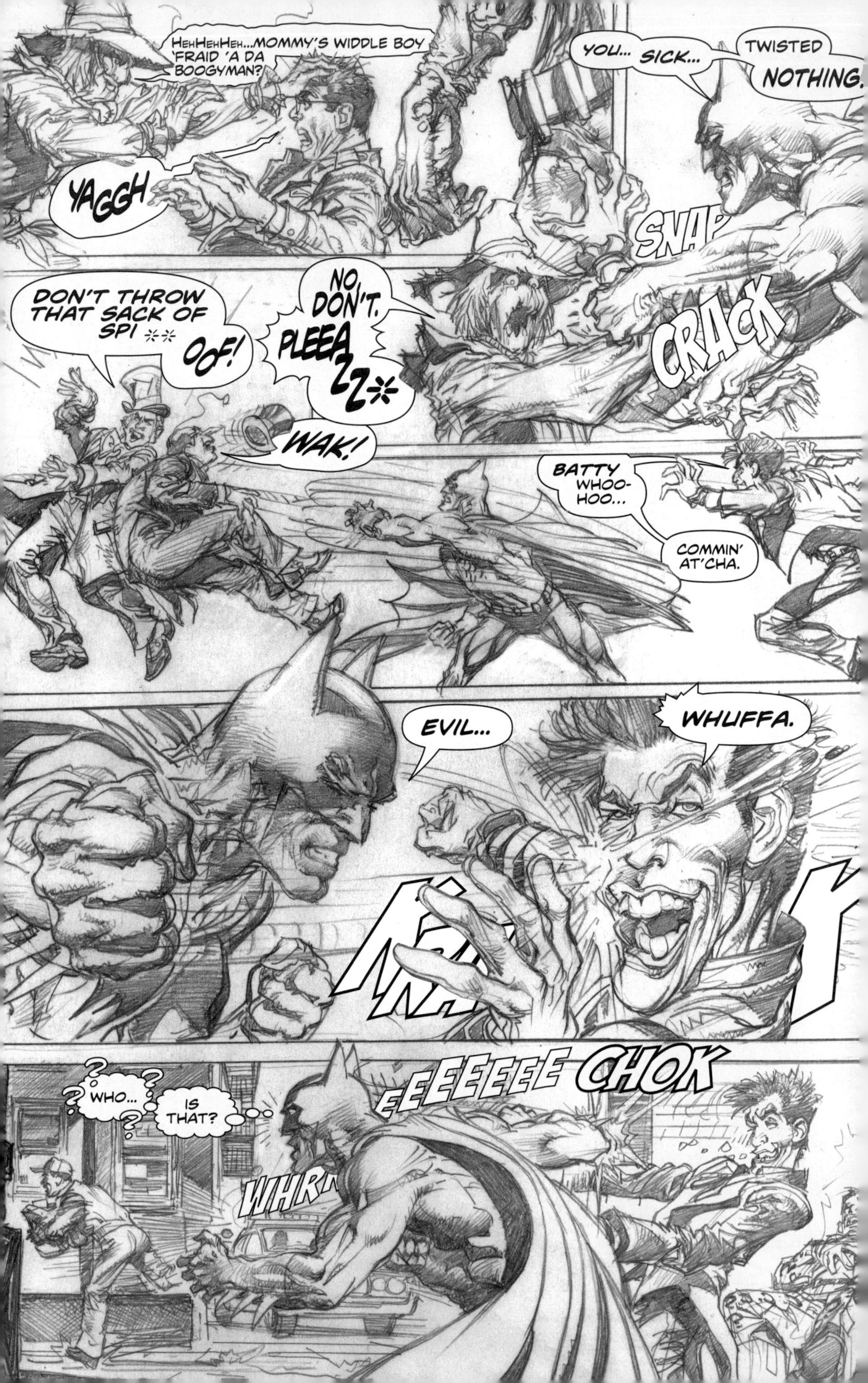
HEHHEHHEH...MOMMY'S WIDDLE BOY 'FRAID 'A DA BOOGYMAN?
YAGGH
YOU... SICK...
TWISTED
NOTHING.
SNAP
DON'T THROW THAT SACK OF SPI ⁂
OOF!
NO, DON'T.
PLEEAZZ*
CRACK
WAK!
BATTY WHOO-HOO...
COMMIN' AT'CHA.
EVIL...
WHUFFA.
WHO...
IS THAT?
EEEEEEE CHOK
WHRR

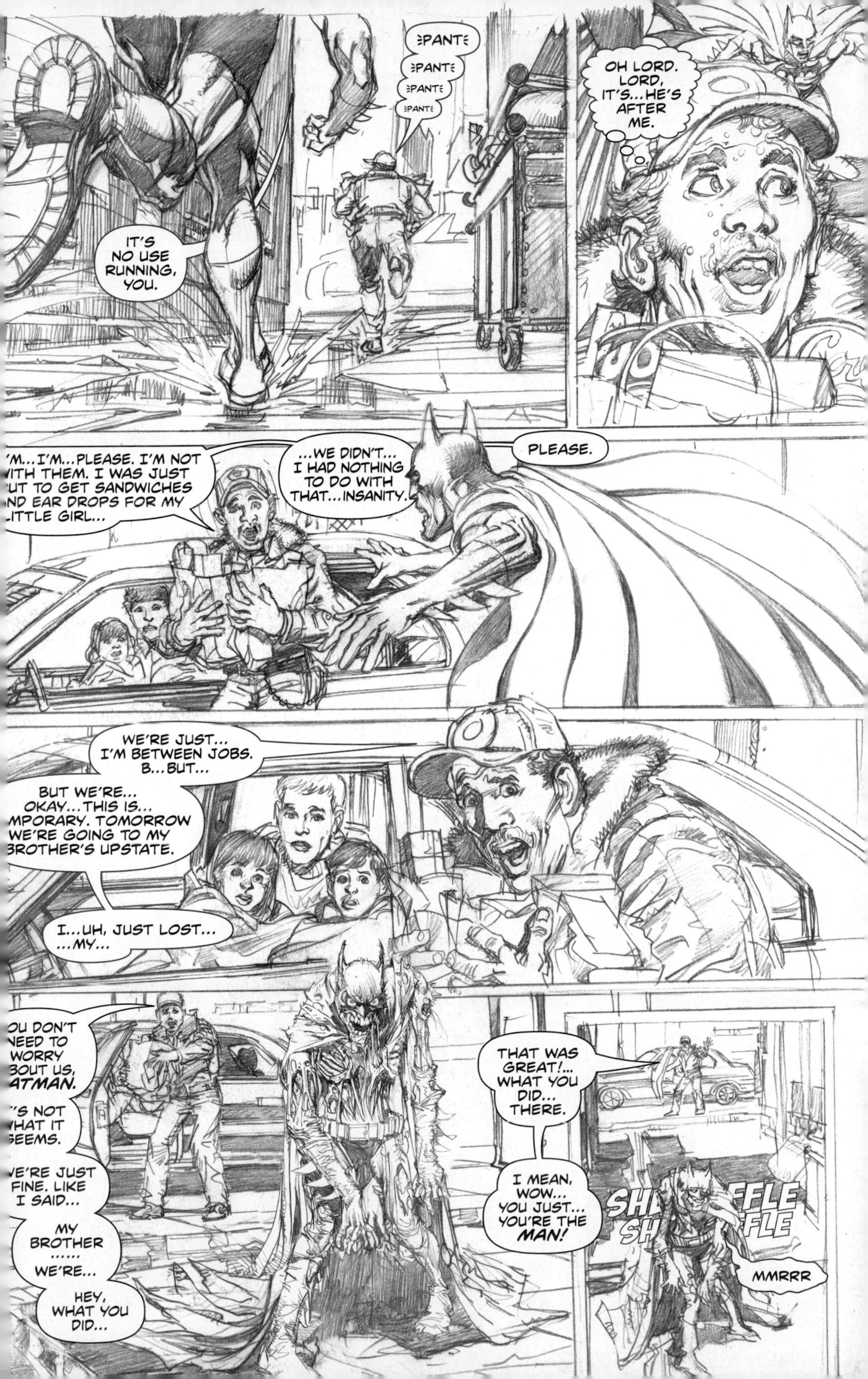
PANT
PANT
PANT
PANT
IT'S NO USE RUNNING, YOU.
OH LORD. LORD, IT'S... HE'S AFTER ME.
'M... I'M... PLEASE. I'M NOT WITH THEM. I WAS JUST UT TO GET SANDWICHES ND EAR DROPS FOR MY LITTLE GIRL...
...WE DIDN'T... I HAD NOTHING TO DO WITH THAT... INSANITY.
PLEASE.
WE'RE JUST... I'M BETWEEN JOBS. B... BUT...
BUT WE'RE... OKAY... THIS IS... MPORARY. TOMORROW WE'RE GOING TO MY BROTHER'S UPSTATE.
I... UH, JUST LOST... ...MY...
OU DON'T NEED TO WORRY BOUT US, ATMAN.
'S NOT WHAT IT SEEMS.
E'RE JUST FINE. LIKE I SAID...
MY BROTHER ...... WE'RE...
HEY, WHAT YOU DID...
THAT WAS GREAT!... WHAT YOU DID... THERE.
I MEAN, WOW... YOU JUST... YOU'RE THE MAN!
MMRRR

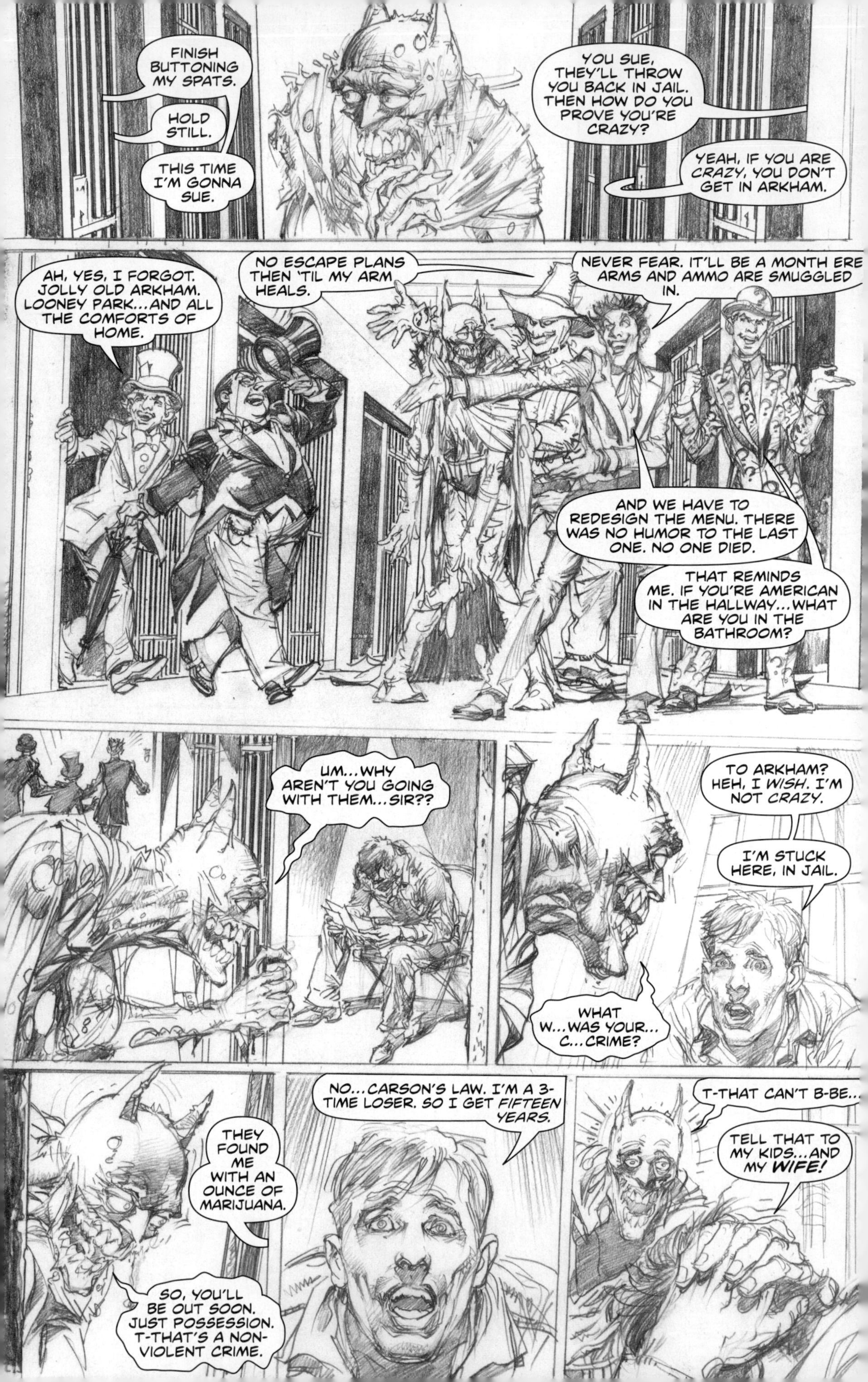
FINISH BUTTONING MY SPATS.
HOLD STILL.
THIS TIME I'M GONNA SUE.
YOU SUE, THEY'LL THROW YOU BACK IN JAIL. THEN HOW DO YOU PROVE YOU'RE CRAZY?
YEAH, IF YOU ARE CRAZY, YOU DON'T GET IN ARKHAM.
AH, YES, I FORGOT. JOLLY OLD ARKHAM. LOONEY PARK...AND ALL THE COMFORTS OF HOME.
NO ESCAPE PLANS THEN 'TIL MY ARM HEALS.
NEVER FEAR. IT'LL BE A MONTH ERE ARMS AND AMMO ARE SMUGGLED IN.
AND WE HAVE TO REDESIGN THE MENU. THERE WAS NO HUMOR TO THE LAST ONE. NO ONE DIED.
THAT REMINDS ME. IF YOU'RE AMERICAN IN THE HALLWAY...WHAT ARE YOU IN THE BATHROOM?
UM...WHY AREN'T YOU GOING WITH THEM...SIR??
TO ARKHAM? HEH, I WISH. I'M NOT CRAZY.
I'M STUCK HERE, IN JAIL.
WHAT W...WAS YOUR... C...CRIME?
THEY FOUND ME WITH AN OUNCE OF MARIJUANA.
SO, YOU'LL BE OUT SOON. JUST POSSESSION. T-THAT'S A NON-VIOLENT CRIME.
NO...CARSON'S LAW. I'M A 3-TIME LOSER. SO I GET FIFTEEN YEARS.
T-THAT CAN'T B-BE...
TELL THAT TO MY KIDS...AND MY WIFE!

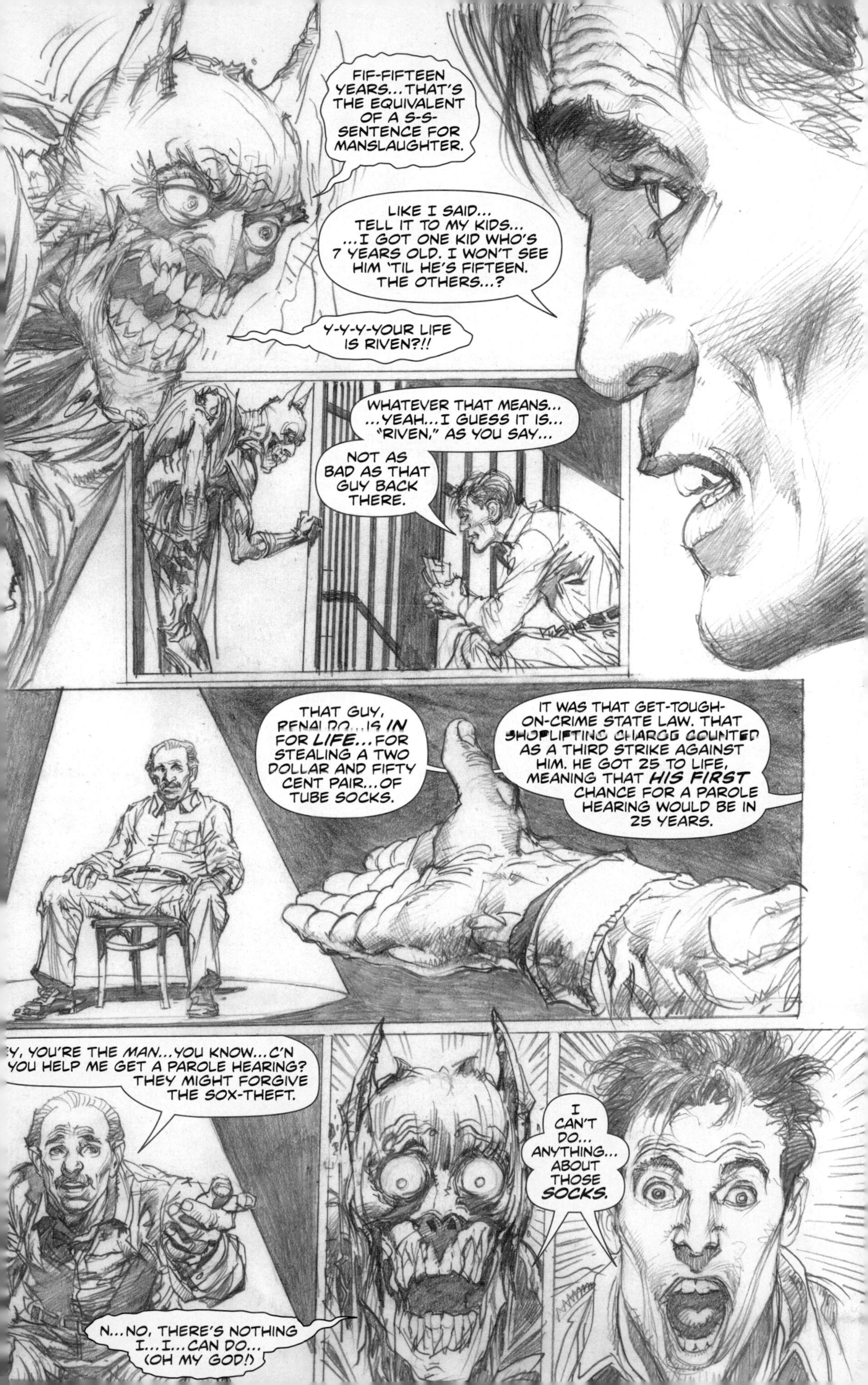
FIF-FIFTEEN YEARS...THAT'S THE EQUIVALENT OF A S-S-SENTENCE FOR MANSLAUGHTER.
LIKE I SAID... TELL IT TO MY KIDS... ...I GOT ONE KID WHO'S 7 YEARS OLD. I WON'T SEE HIM 'TIL HE'S FIFTEEN. THE OTHERS...?
Y-Y-Y-YOUR LIFE IS RIVEN?!!
WHATEVER THAT MEANS... ...YEAH...I GUESS IT IS... "RIVEN," AS YOU SAY...
NOT AS BAD AS THAT GUY BACK THERE.
THAT GUY, RENALDO...IS IN FOR LIFE...FOR STEALING A TWO DOLLAR AND FIFTY CENT PAIR...OF TUBE SOCKS.
IT WAS THAT GET-TOUGH-ON-CRIME STATE LAW. THAT SHOPLIFTING CHARGE COUNTED AS A THIRD STRIKE AGAINST HIM. HE GOT 25 TO LIFE, MEANING THAT HIS FIRST CHANCE FOR A PAROLE HEARING WOULD BE IN 25 YEARS.
Y, YOU'RE THE MAN...YOU KNOW...C'N YOU HELP ME GET A PAROLE HEARING? THEY MIGHT FORGIVE THE SOX-THEFT.
I CAN'T DO... ANYTHING... ABOUT THOSE SOCKS.
N...NO, THERE'S NOTHING I...I...CAN DO... (OH MY GOD!)

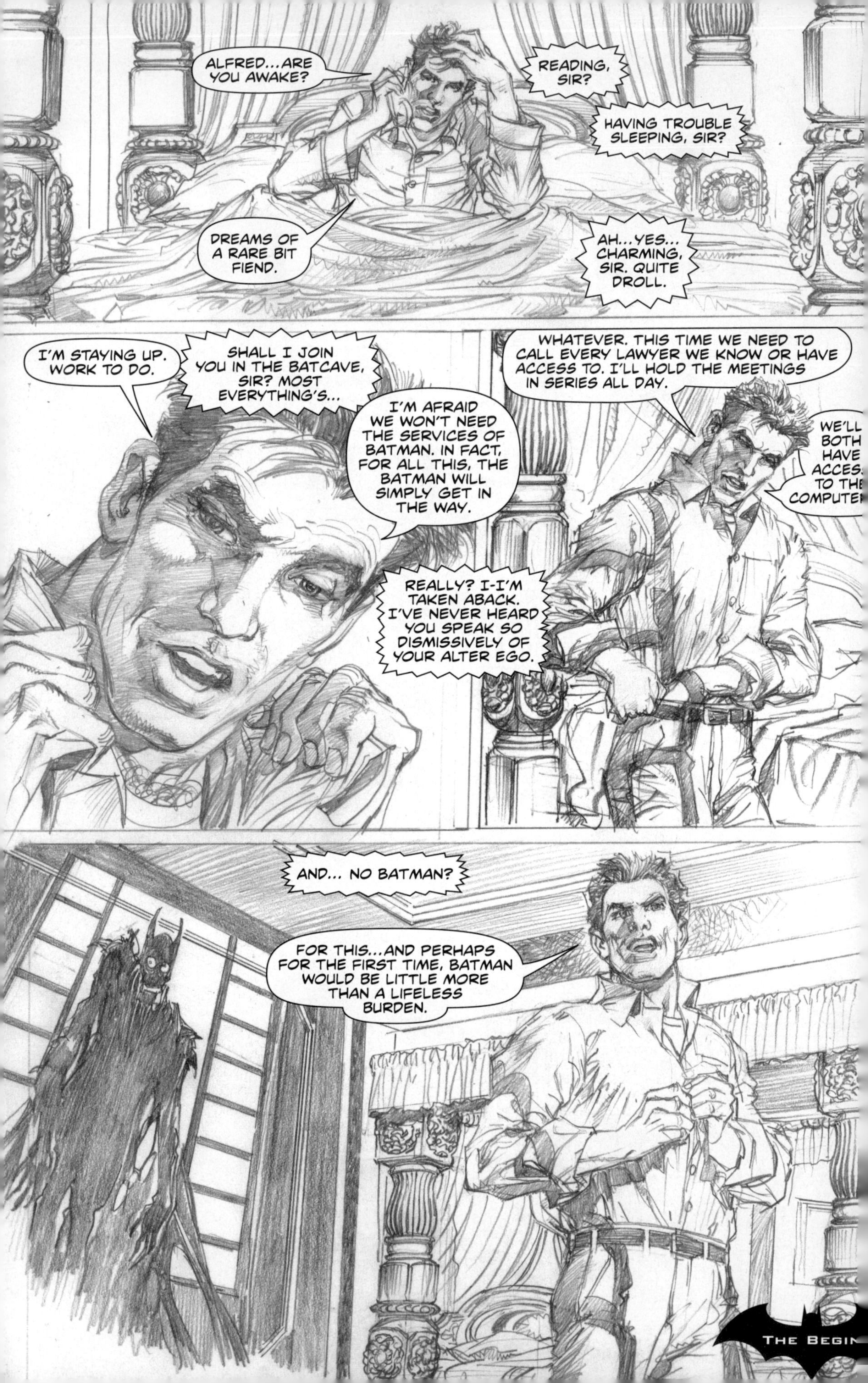
ALFRED...ARE YOU AWAKE?
READING, SIR?
HAVING TROUBLE SLEEPING, SIR?
DREAMS OF A RARE BIT FIEND.
AH...YES... CHARMING, SIR. QUITE DROLL.
I'M STAYING UP. WORK TO DO.
SHALL I JOIN YOU IN THE BATCAVE, SIR? MOST EVERYTHING'S...
I'M AFRAID WE WON'T NEED THE SERVICES OF BATMAN. IN FACT, FOR ALL THIS, THE BATMAN WILL SIMPLY GET IN THE WAY.
REALLY? I-I'M TAKEN ABACK. I'VE NEVER HEARD YOU SPEAK SO DISMISSIVELY OF YOUR ALTER EGO.
WHATEVER. THIS TIME WE NEED TO CALL EVERY LAWYER WE KNOW OR HAVE ACCESS TO. I'LL HOLD THE MEETINGS IN SERIES ALL DAY.
WE'LL BOTH HAVE ACCES TO THE COMPUTE
AND... NO BATMAN?
FOR THIS...AND PERHAPS FOR THE FIRST TIME, BATMAN WOULD BE LITTLE MORE THAN A LIFELESS BURDEN.
THE BEGIN

NEAL ADAMS

One of the most profoundly
influential comic book artists of all time, Neal
Adams was the first artist to integrate
the approach and style of modern
illustration into the comic book medium.
His mature take on many top characters,
including Batman, Superman, and the X-Men
elevated comic books from a children's
medium to an all-ages artform.

Adams's socially relevant work with writer
Dennis O'Neil on Green Arrow in the 1970s
has stood the test of time as one of the true
high-water marks in comics history.

Artist, writer, art director, publisher,
creator's rights activist, Neal Adams
is quite simply a living legend.

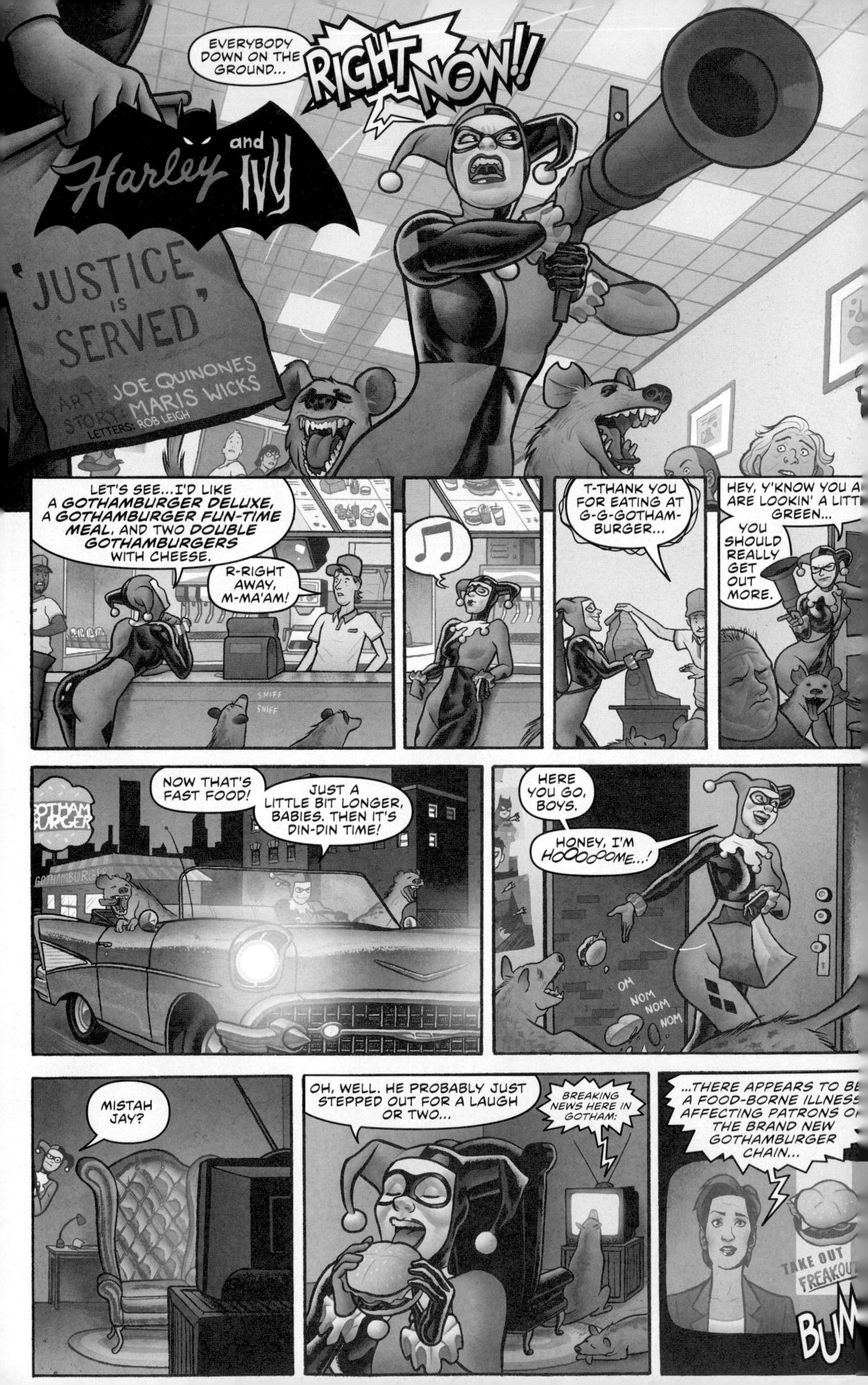
EVERYBODY DOWN ON THE GROUND...
RIGHT NOW!!
Harley and Ivy
'JUSTICE IS SERVED'
ART: JOE QUINONES
STORY: MARIS WICKS
LETTERS: ROB LEIGH
LET'S SEE...I'D LIKE A GOTHAMBURGER DELUXE, A GOTHAMBURGER FUN-TIME MEAL, AND TWO DOUBLE GOTHAMBURGERS WITH CHEESE.
R-RIGHT AWAY, M-MA'AM!
SNIFF
SNIFF
♫
T-THANK YOU FOR EATING AT G-G-GOTHAM-BURGER...
HEY, Y'KNOW YOU A ARE LOOKIN' A LITT GREEN...
YOU SHOULD REALLY GET OUT MORE.
GOTHAM BURGER
GOTHAMBURGER
NOW THAT'S FAST FOOD!
JUST A LITTLE BIT LONGER, BABIES. THEN IT'S DIN-DIN TIME!
HERE YOU GO, BOYS.
HONEY, I'M HOOOOOOME...!
OM NOM NOM NOM
MISTAH JAY?
OH, WELL. HE PROBABLY JUST STEPPED OUT FOR A LAUGH OR TWO...
BREAKING NEWS HERE IN GOTHAM:
...THERE APPEARS TO BE A FOOD-BORNE ILLNESS AFFECTING PATRONS OF THE BRAND NEW GOTHAMBURGER CHAIN...
TAKE OUT FREAKOUT
BUM

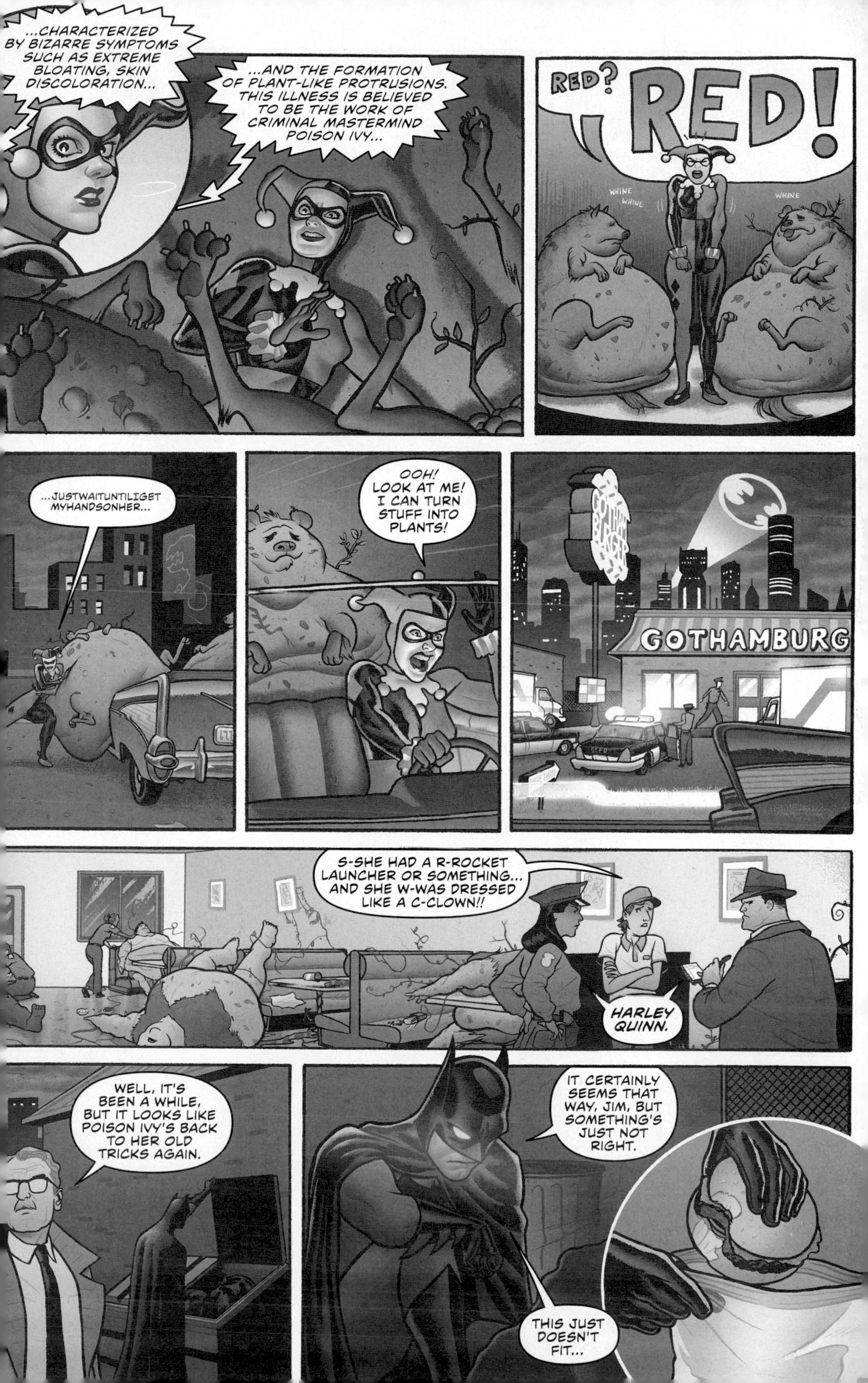
...CHARACTERIZED BY BIZARRE SYMPTOMS SUCH AS EXTREME BLOATING, SKIN DISCOLORATION...
...AND THE FORMATION OF PLANT-LIKE PROTRUSIONS. THIS ILLNESS IS BELIEVED TO BE THE WORK OF CRIMINAL MASTERMIND POISON IVY...
RED? RED!
WHINE WHINE
WHINE
...JUSTWAITUNTILIGET MYHANDSONHER...
OOH! LOOK AT ME! I CAN TURN STUFF INTO PLANTS!
GOTHAM BURGER
GOTHAMBURG
S-SHE HAD A R-ROCKET LAUNCHER OR SOMETHING... AND SHE W-WAS DRESSED LIKE A C-CLOWN!!
HARLEY QUINN.
WELL, IT'S BEEN A WHILE, BUT IT LOOKS LIKE POISON IVY'S BACK TO HER OLD TRICKS AGAIN.
IT CERTAINLY SEEMS THAT WAY, JIM, BUT SOMETHING'S JUST NOT RIGHT.
THIS JUST DOESN'T FIT...

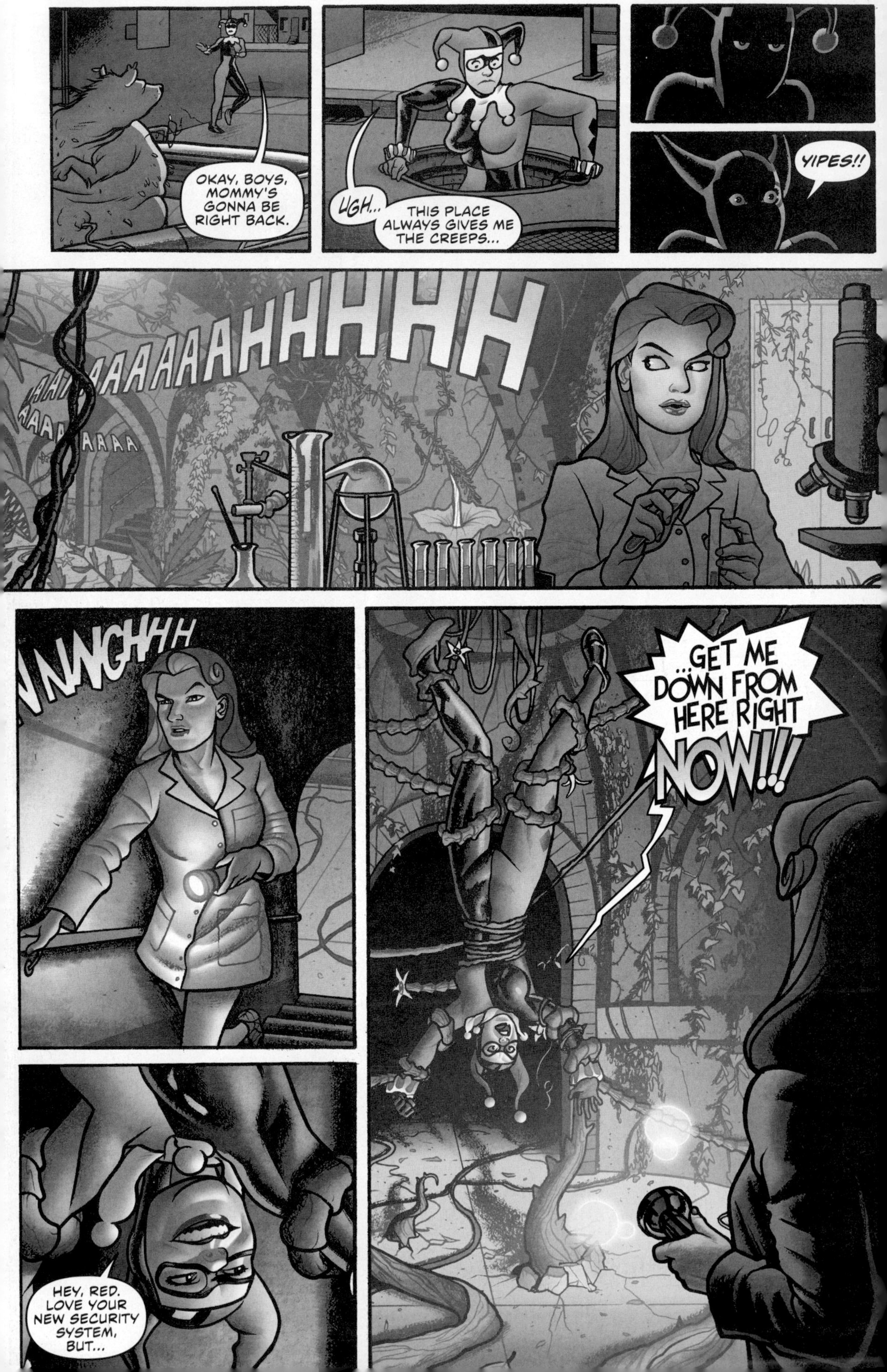
OKAY, BOYS, MOMMY'S GONNA BE RIGHT BACK.
UGH...
THIS PLACE ALWAYS GIVES ME THE CREEPS...
YIPES!!
AAAAAAAAAHHHHHH
AAAAAAAA
NNNGHHHH
HEY, RED. LOVE YOUR NEW SECURITY SYSTEM, BUT...
...GET ME DOWN FROM HERE RIGHT NOW!!!

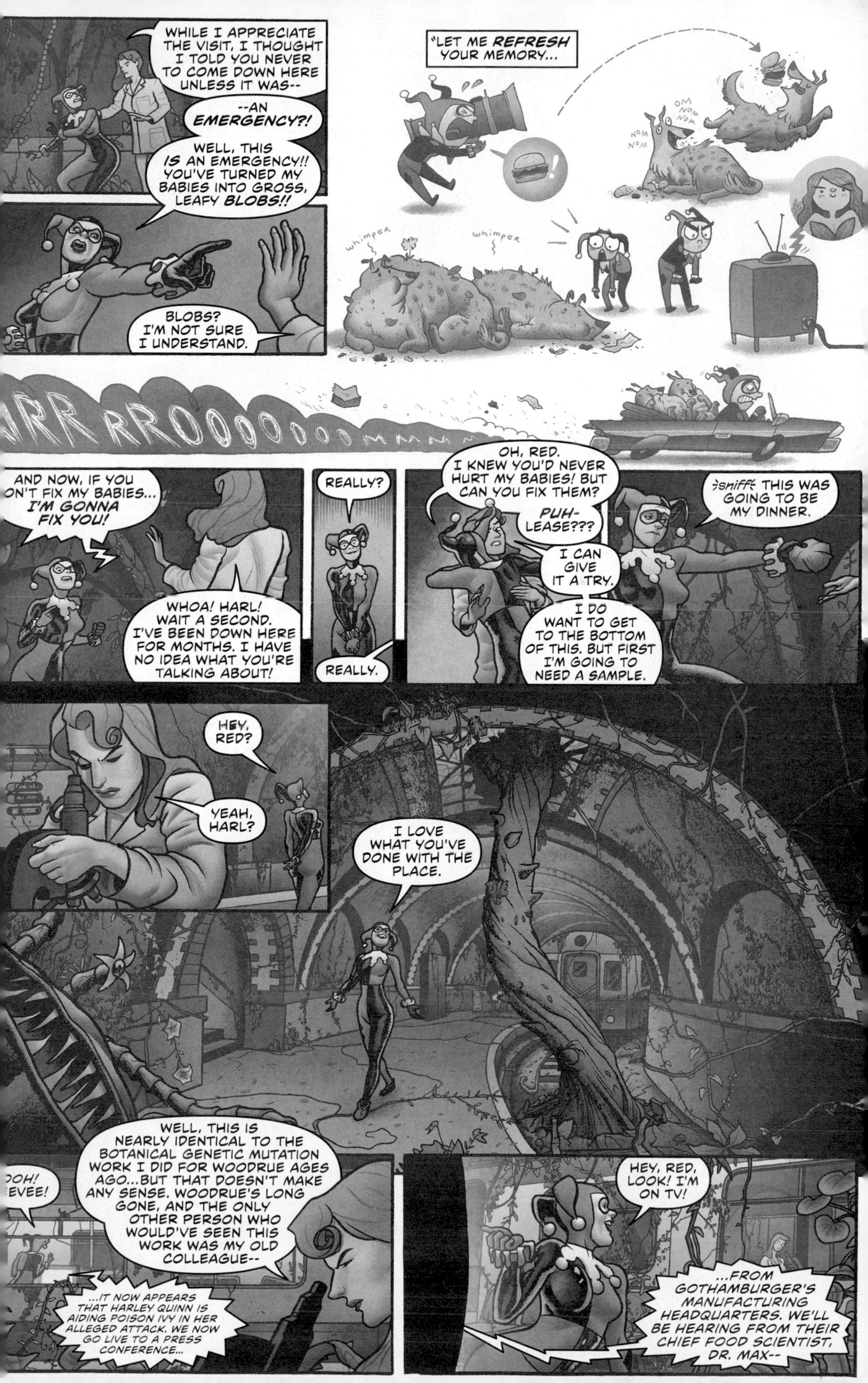
WHILE I APPRECIATE THE VISIT, I THOUGHT I TOLD YOU NEVER TO COME DOWN HERE UNLESS IT WAS--
--AN EMERGENCY?!
WELL, THIS IS AN EMERGENCY!! YOU'VE TURNED MY BABIES INTO GROSS, LEAFY BLOBS!!
BLOBS? I'M NOT SURE I UNDERSTAND.
"LET ME REFRESH YOUR MEMORY...
OM NOM NOM
NOM NOM
whimper
whimper
RRRRROOOOOOOMMMMM
AND NOW, IF YOU DON'T FIX MY BABIES... I'M GONNA FIX YOU!
WHOA! HARL! WAIT A SECOND. I'VE BEEN DOWN HERE FOR MONTHS. I HAVE NO IDEA WHAT YOU'RE TALKING ABOUT!
REALLY?
REALLY.
OH, RED. I KNEW YOU'D NEVER HURT MY BABIES! BUT CAN YOU FIX THEM?
PUH-LEASE???
I CAN GIVE IT A TRY.
I DO WANT TO GET TO THE BOTTOM OF THIS. BUT FIRST I'M GOING TO NEED A SAMPLE.
sniff THIS WAS GOING TO BE MY DINNER.
HEY, RED?
YEAH, HARL?
I LOVE WHAT YOU'VE DONE WITH THE PLACE.
WELL, THIS IS NEARLY IDENTICAL TO THE BOTANICAL GENETIC MUTATION WORK I DID FOR WOODRUE AGES AGO...BUT THAT DOESN'T MAKE ANY SENSE. WOODRUE'S LONG GONE, AND THE ONLY OTHER PERSON WHO WOULD'VE SEEN THIS WORK WAS MY OLD COLLEAGUE--
OOH! EEVEE!
...IT NOW APPEARS THAT HARLEY QUINN IS AIDING POISON IVY IN HER ALLEGED ATTACK. WE NOW GO LIVE TO A PRESS CONFERENCE...
HEY, RED, LOOK! I'M ON TV!
...FROM GOTHAMBURGER'S MANUFACTURING HEADQUARTERS. WE'LL BE HEARING FROM THEIR CHIEF FOOD SCIENTIST, DR. MAX--

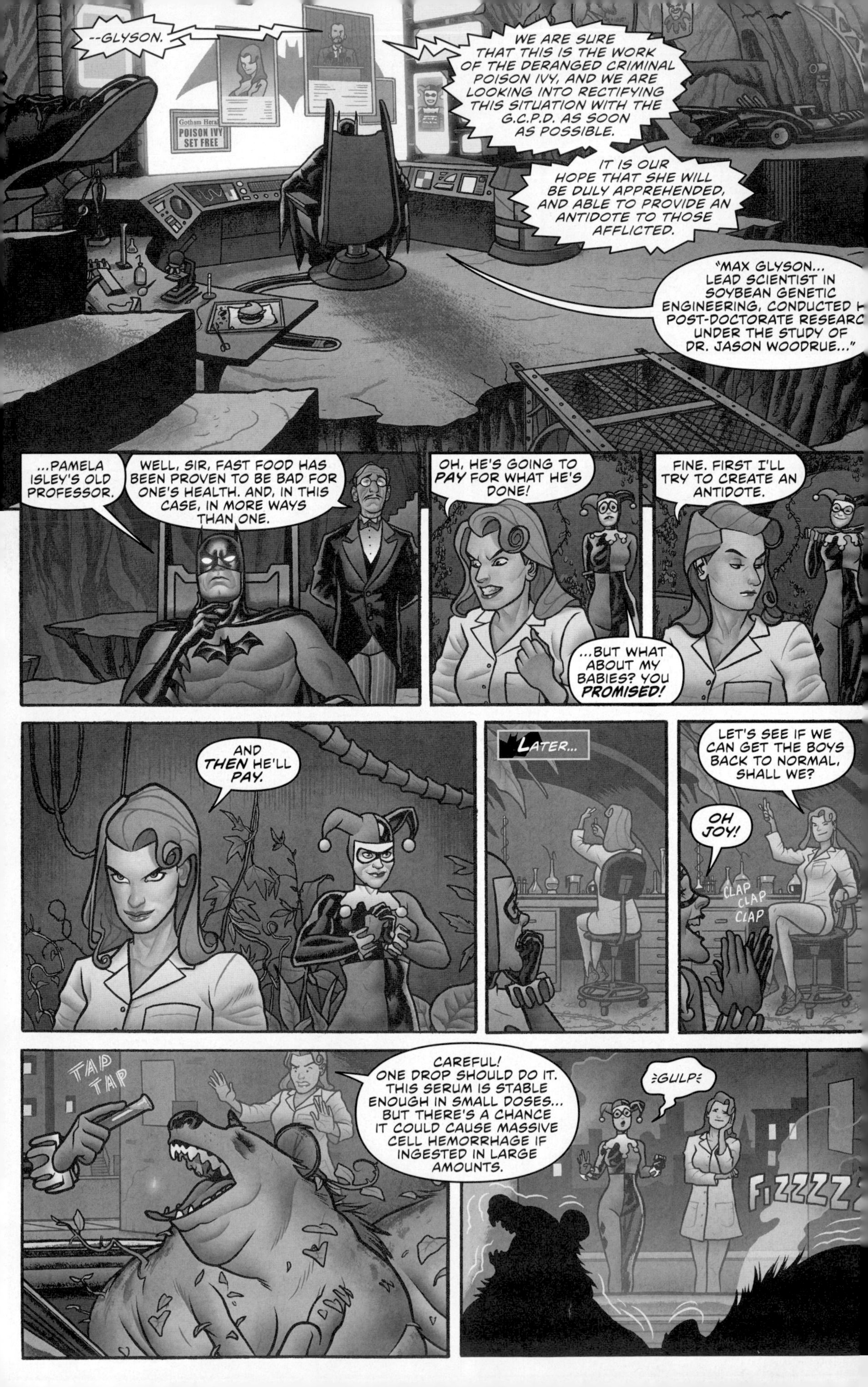
--GLYSON.
WE ARE SURE THAT THIS IS THE WORK OF THE DERANGED CRIMINAL POISON IVY, AND WE ARE LOOKING INTO RECTIFYING THIS SITUATION WITH THE G.C.P.D. AS SOON AS POSSIBLE.
IT IS OUR HOPE THAT SHE WILL BE DULY APPREHENDED, AND ABLE TO PROVIDE AN ANTIDOTE TO THOSE AFFLICTED.
Gotham Hera
POISON IVY SET FREE
"MAX GLYSON... LEAD SCIENTIST IN SOYBEAN GENETIC ENGINEERING, CONDUCTED H POST-DOCTORATE RESEARC UNDER THE STUDY OF DR. JASON WOODRUE..."
...PAMELA ISLEY'S OLD PROFESSOR."
WELL, SIR, FAST FOOD HAS BEEN PROVEN TO BE BAD FOR ONE'S HEALTH. AND, IN THIS CASE, IN MORE WAYS THAN ONE.
OH, HE'S GOING TO PAY FOR WHAT HE'S DONE!
...BUT WHAT ABOUT MY BABIES? YOU PROMISED!
FINE. FIRST I'LL TRY TO CREATE AN ANTIDOTE.
AND THEN HE'LL PAY.
LATER...
LET'S SEE IF WE CAN GET THE BOYS BACK TO NORMAL, SHALL WE?
OH JOY!
CLAP CLAP CLAP
TAP TAP
CAREFUL! ONE DROP SHOULD DO IT. THIS SERUM IS STABLE ENOUGH IN SMALL DOSES... BUT THERE'S A CHANCE IT COULD CAUSE MASSIVE CELL HEMORRHAGE IF INGESTED IN LARGE AMOUNTS.
GULP
FIZZZZZ

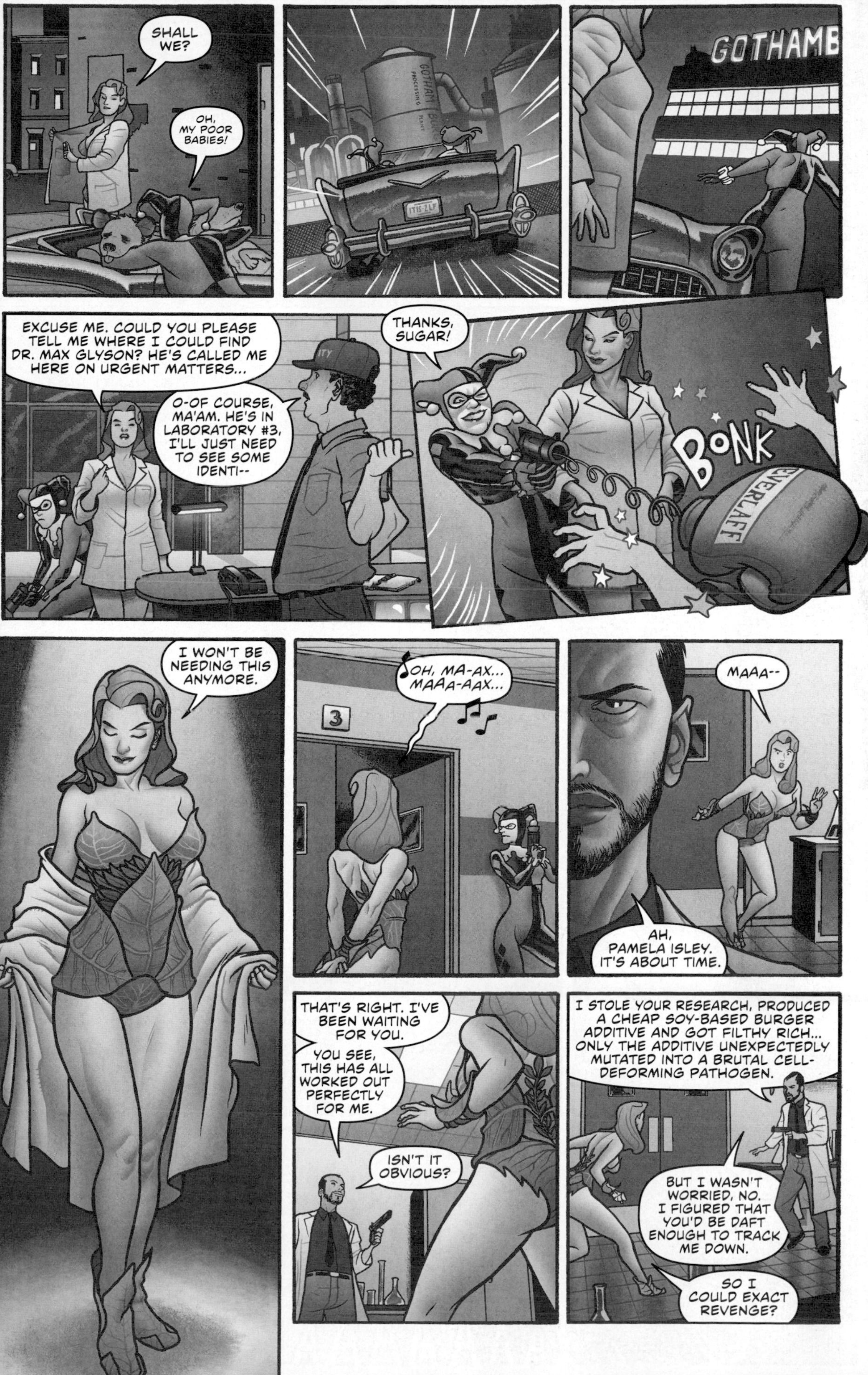
SHALL WE?
OH, MY POOR BABIES!
GOTHAMB
EXCUSE ME. COULD YOU PLEASE TELL ME WHERE I COULD FIND DR. MAX GLYSON? HE'S CALLED ME HERE ON URGENT MATTERS...
O-OF COURSE, MA'AM. HE'S IN LABORATORY #3, I'LL JUST NEED TO SEE SOME IDENTI--
THANKS, SUGAR!
BONK
EVERLAFF
I WON'T BE NEEDING THIS ANYMORE.
OH, MA-AX... MAAA-AAX...
3
MAAA--
AH, PAMELA ISLEY. IT'S ABOUT TIME.
THAT'S RIGHT. I'VE BEEN WAITING FOR YOU.
YOU SEE, THIS HAS ALL WORKED OUT PERFECTLY FOR ME.
ISN'T IT OBVIOUS?
I STOLE YOUR RESEARCH, PRODUCED A CHEAP SOY-BASED BURGER ADDITIVE AND GOT FILTHY RICH... ONLY THE ADDITIVE UNEXPECTEDLY MUTATED INTO A BRUTAL CELL-DEFORMING PATHOGEN.
BUT I WASN'T WORRIED, NO. I FIGURED THAT YOU'D BE DAFT ENOUGH TO TRACK ME DOWN.
SO I COULD EXACT REVENGE?

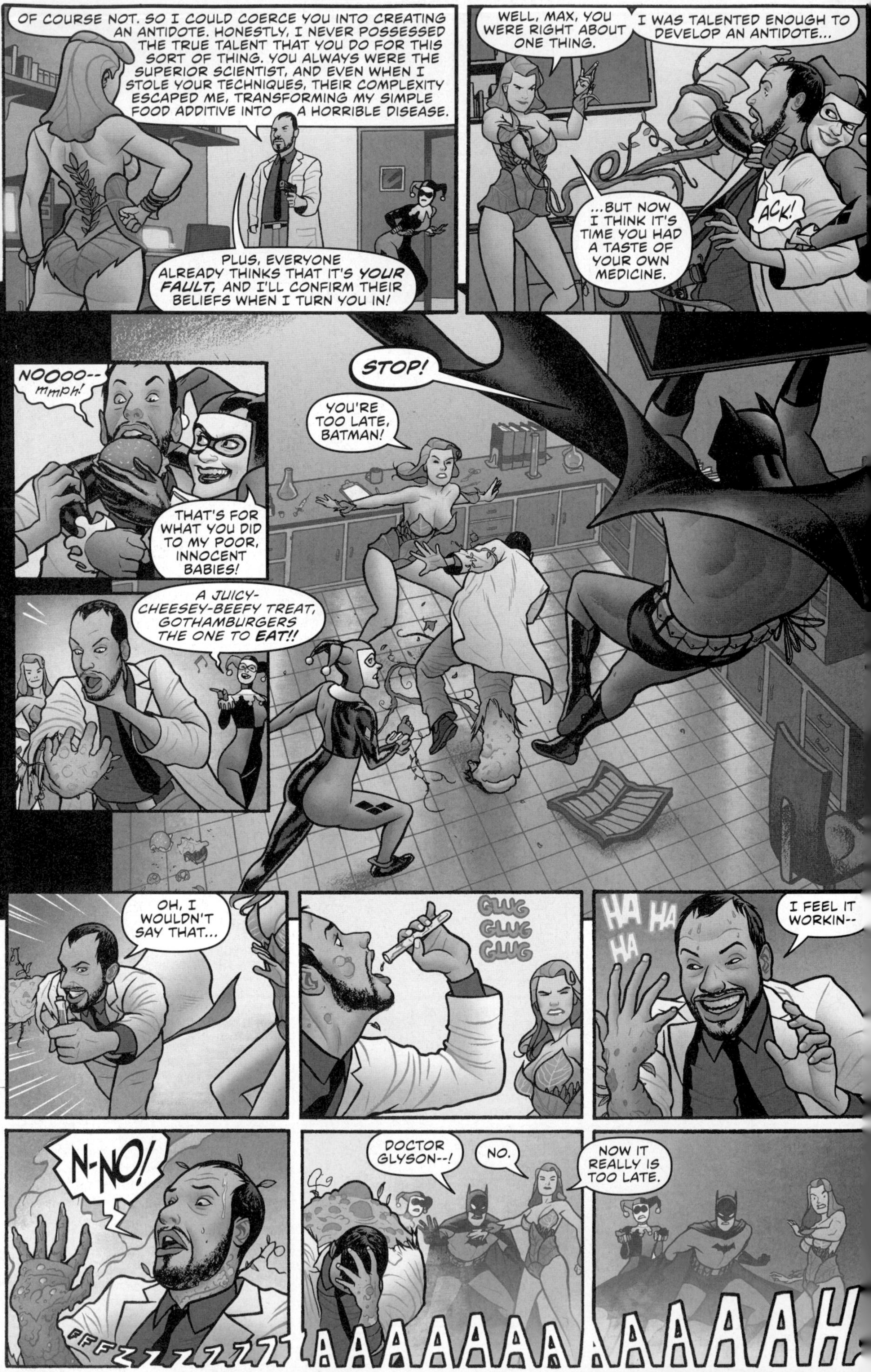
OF COURSE NOT. SO I COULD COERCE YOU INTO CREATING AN ANTIDOTE. HONESTLY, I NEVER POSSESSED THE TRUE TALENT THAT YOU DO FOR THIS SORT OF THING. YOU ALWAYS WERE THE SUPERIOR SCIENTIST, AND EVEN WHEN I STOLE YOUR TECHNIQUES, THEIR COMPLEXITY ESCAPED ME, TRANSFORMING MY SIMPLE FOOD ADDITIVE INTO A HORRIBLE DISEASE.
PLUS, EVERYONE ALREADY THINKS THAT IT'S YOUR FAULT, AND I'LL CONFIRM THEIR BELIEFS WHEN I TURN YOU IN!
WELL, MAX, YOU WERE RIGHT ABOUT ONE THING.
I WAS TALENTED ENOUGH TO DEVELOP AN ANTIDOTE...
...BUT NOW I THINK IT'S TIME YOU HAD A TASTE OF YOUR OWN MEDICINE.
ACK!
NOOOO--mmph!
THAT'S FOR WHAT YOU DID TO MY POOR, INNOCENT BABIES!
STOP!
YOU'RE TOO LATE, BATMAN!
A JUICY-CHEESEY-BEEFY TREAT, GOTHAMBURGERS THE ONE TO EAT!!
OH, I WOULDN'T SAY THAT...
GLUG GLUG GLUG
HA HA HA
I FEEL IT WORKIN--
N-NO!
DOCTOR GLYSON--!
NO.
NOW IT REALLY IS TOO LATE.
FFFZZZZZZZAAAAAAAAAAAAAH

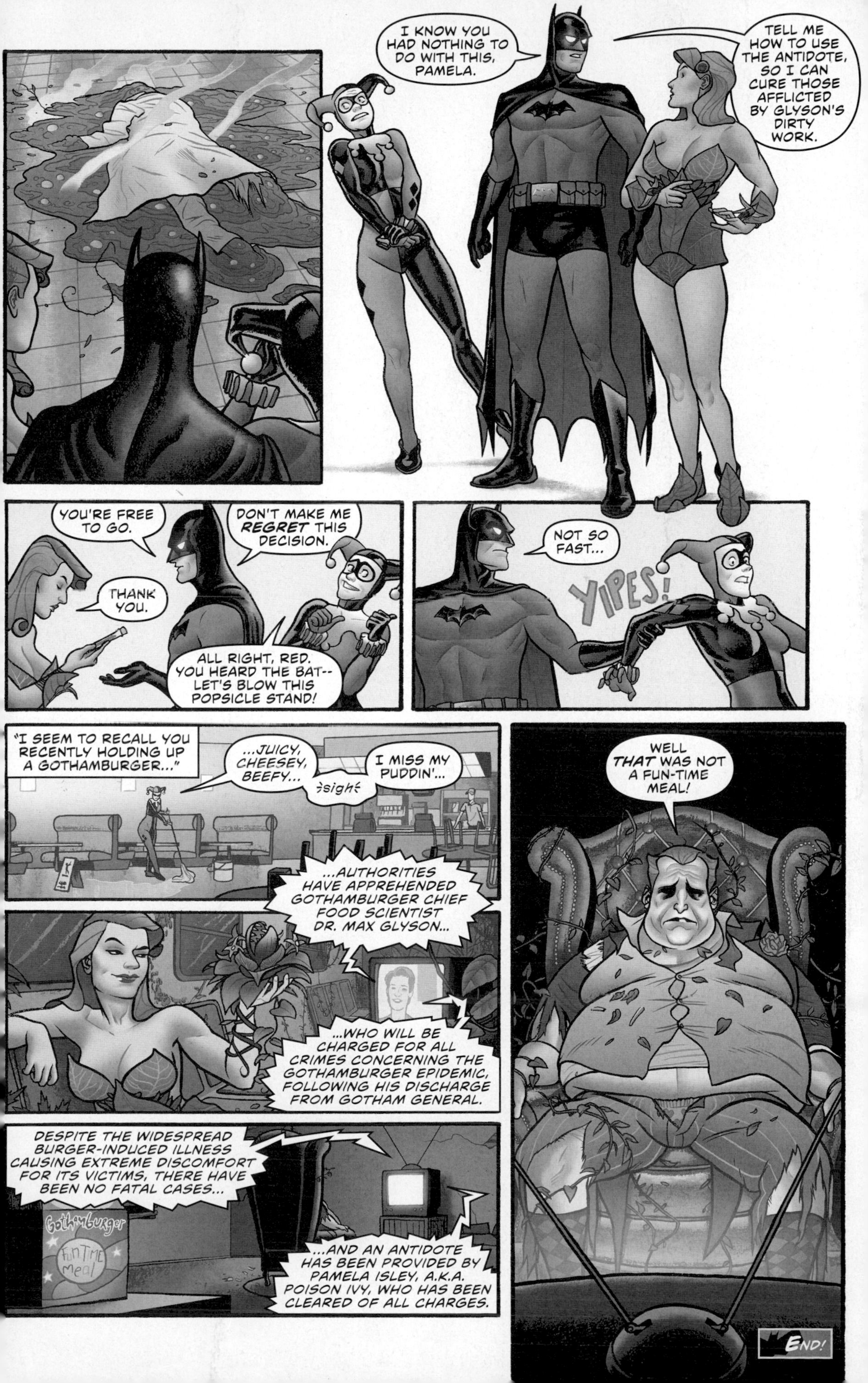
I KNOW YOU HAD NOTHING TO DO WITH THIS, PAMELA.
TELL ME HOW TO USE THE ANTIDOTE, SO I CAN CURE THOSE AFFLICTED BY GLYSON'S DIRTY WORK.
YOU'RE FREE TO GO.
DON'T MAKE ME REGRET THIS DECISION.
THANK YOU.
ALL RIGHT, RED. YOU HEARD THE BAT--LET'S BLOW THIS POPSICLE STAND!
NOT SO FAST...
YIPES!
"I SEEM TO RECALL YOU RECENTLY HOLDING UP A GOTHAMBURGER..."
...JUICY, CHEESEY, BEEFY...
I MISS MY PUDDIN'...
sigh
...AUTHORITIES HAVE APPREHENDED GOTHAMBURGER CHIEF FOOD SCIENTIST DR. MAX GLYSON...
...WHO WILL BE CHARGED FOR ALL CRIMES CONCERNING THE GOTHAMBURGER EPIDEMIC, FOLLOWING HIS DISCHARGE FROM GOTHAM GENERAL.
DESPITE THE WIDESPREAD BURGER-INDUCED ILLNESS CAUSING EXTREME DISCOMFORT FOR ITS VICTIMS, THERE HAVE BEEN NO FATAL CASES...
Gothamburger
Fun Time meal
...AND AN ANTIDOTE HAS BEEN PROVIDED BY PAMELA ISLEY, A.K.A. POISON IVY, WHO HAS BEEN CLEARED OF ALL CHARGES.
WELL THAT WAS NOT A FUN-TIME MEAL!
END!

MARIS WICKS

An artist, writer, and force of nature, Maris Wicks has drawn for Adhouse Books, Tugboat Press, and Spongebob Comics. Her illustration background and passion for science made her the perfect choice for *New York Times* bestseller *Primates: The Fearless Science of Jane Goodall, Dian Fossey, and Biruté Galdikas,* and the children's book *Yes, Let's.*

An infectious wit, kooky sensibility, and knack for dialogue are all a constant thread in Maris's written work, as witnessed here in her first published work for DC.

JOE QUINONES

Joe Quinones honed his skills as an illustration graduate of the Rhode Island School of Design, but it was his unique vision that set him apart. His captivating style is a breath of fresh air in the dark, gritty world of modern American comics. His gift for facial expressions and body language makes him an impeccable storyteller.

With fan favorite projects such as TEEN TITANS GO! and WEDNESDAY COMICS under his belt, Joe's next major project, BLACK CANARY/ZATANNA: BLOODSPELL is guaranteed to be a comics event!

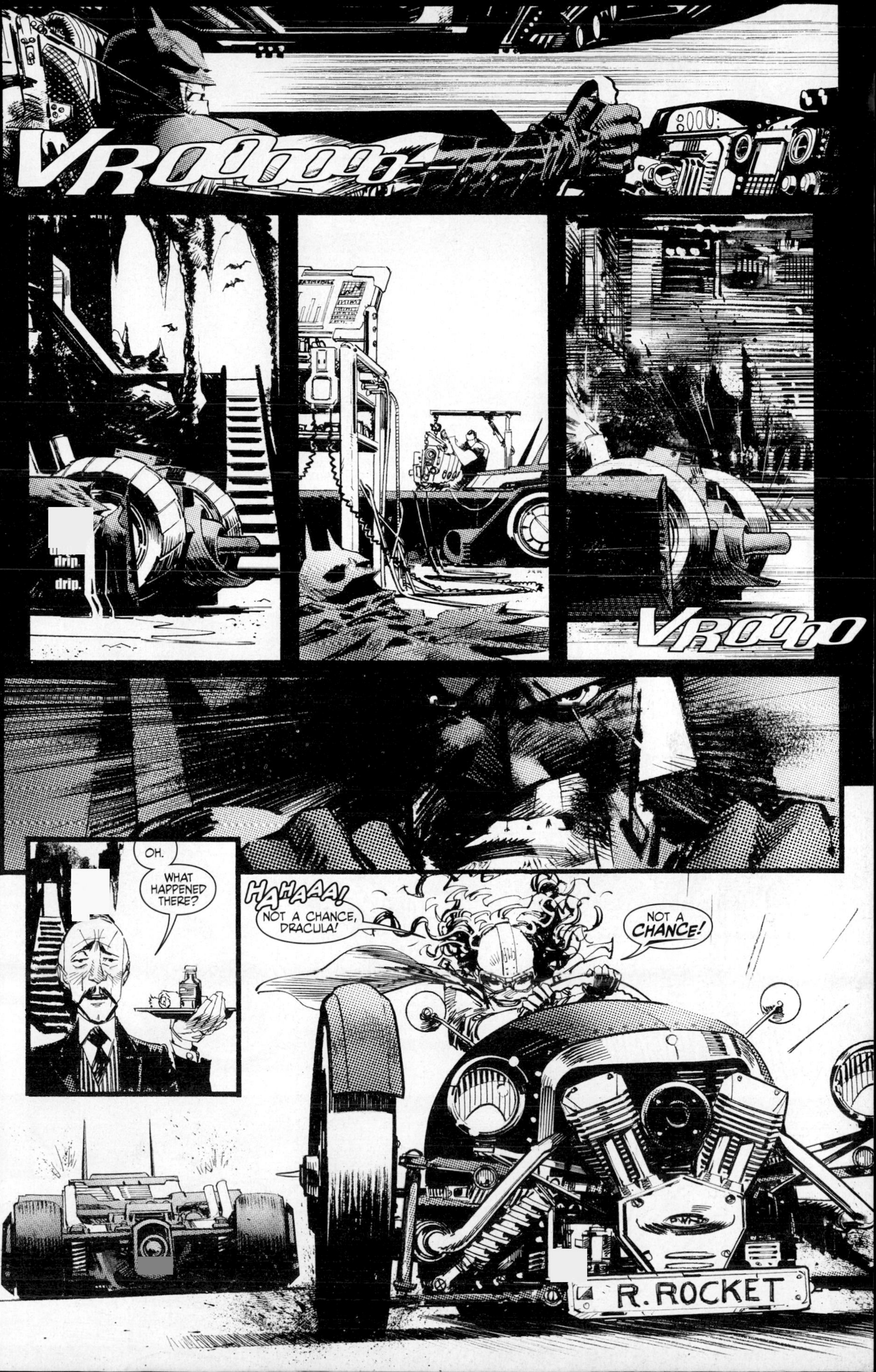
VROOOOOO
drip.
drip.
VROOOO
OH.
WHAT HAPPENED THERE?
HAHAAA!
NOT A CHANCE, DRACULA!
NOT A CHANCE!
R. ROCKET

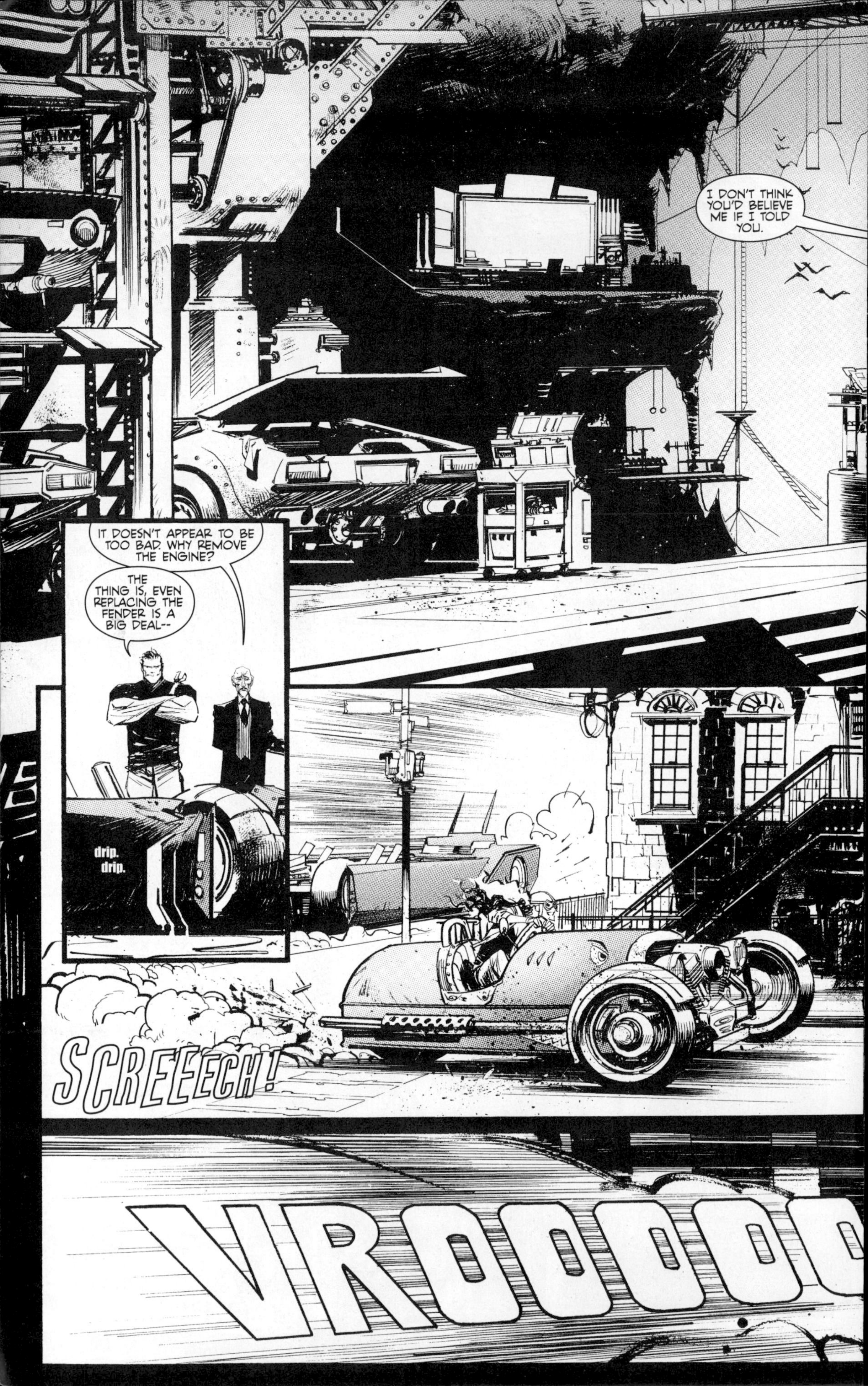
I DON'T THINK YOU'D BELIEVE ME IF I TOLD YOU.
IT DOESN'T APPEAR TO BE TOO BAD. WHY REMOVE THE ENGINE?
THE THING IS, EVEN REPLACING THE FENDER IS A BIG DEAL--
drip. drip.
SCREEECH!
VROOOOO

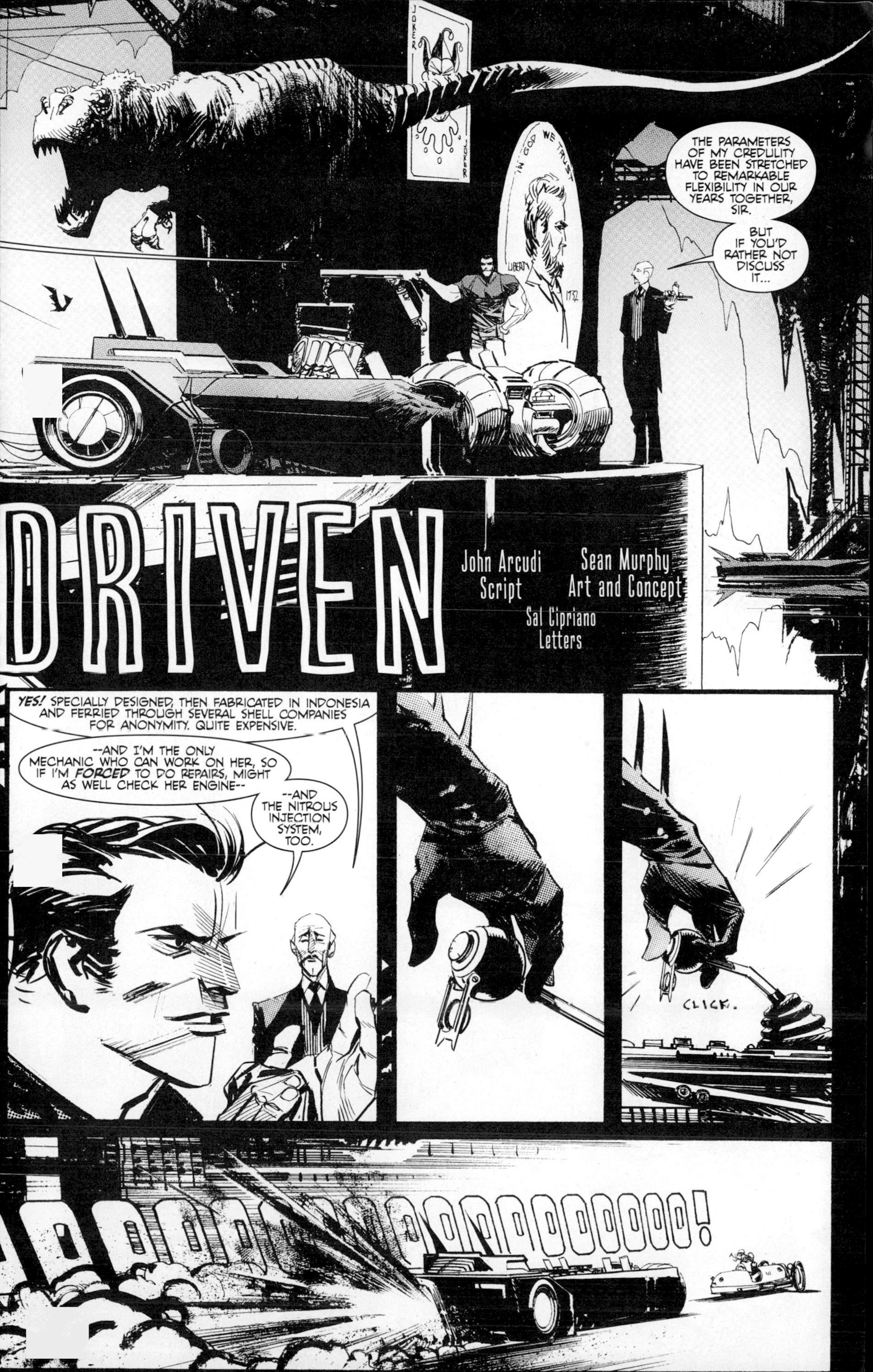
JOKER
IN GOD WE TRUST
LIBERTY
1932
THE PARAMETERS OF MY CREDULITY HAVE BEEN STRETCHED TO REMARKABLE FLEXIBILITY IN OUR YEARS TOGETHER, SIR.
BUT IF YOU'D RATHER NOT DISCUSS IT...
DRIVEN
John Arcudi Script
Sean Murphy Art and Concept
Sal Cipriano Letters
YES! SPECIALLY DESIGNED, THEN FABRICATED IN INDONESIA AND FERRIED THROUGH SEVERAL SHELL COMPANIES FOR ANONYMITY. QUITE EXPENSIVE.
--AND I'M THE ONLY MECHANIC WHO CAN WORK ON HER, SO IF I'M FORCED TO DO REPAIRS, MIGHT AS WELL CHECK HER ENGINE--
--AND THE NITROUS INJECTION SYSTEM, TOO.
CLICK.
OOOOOOOOOOOOOOOOOOOO!

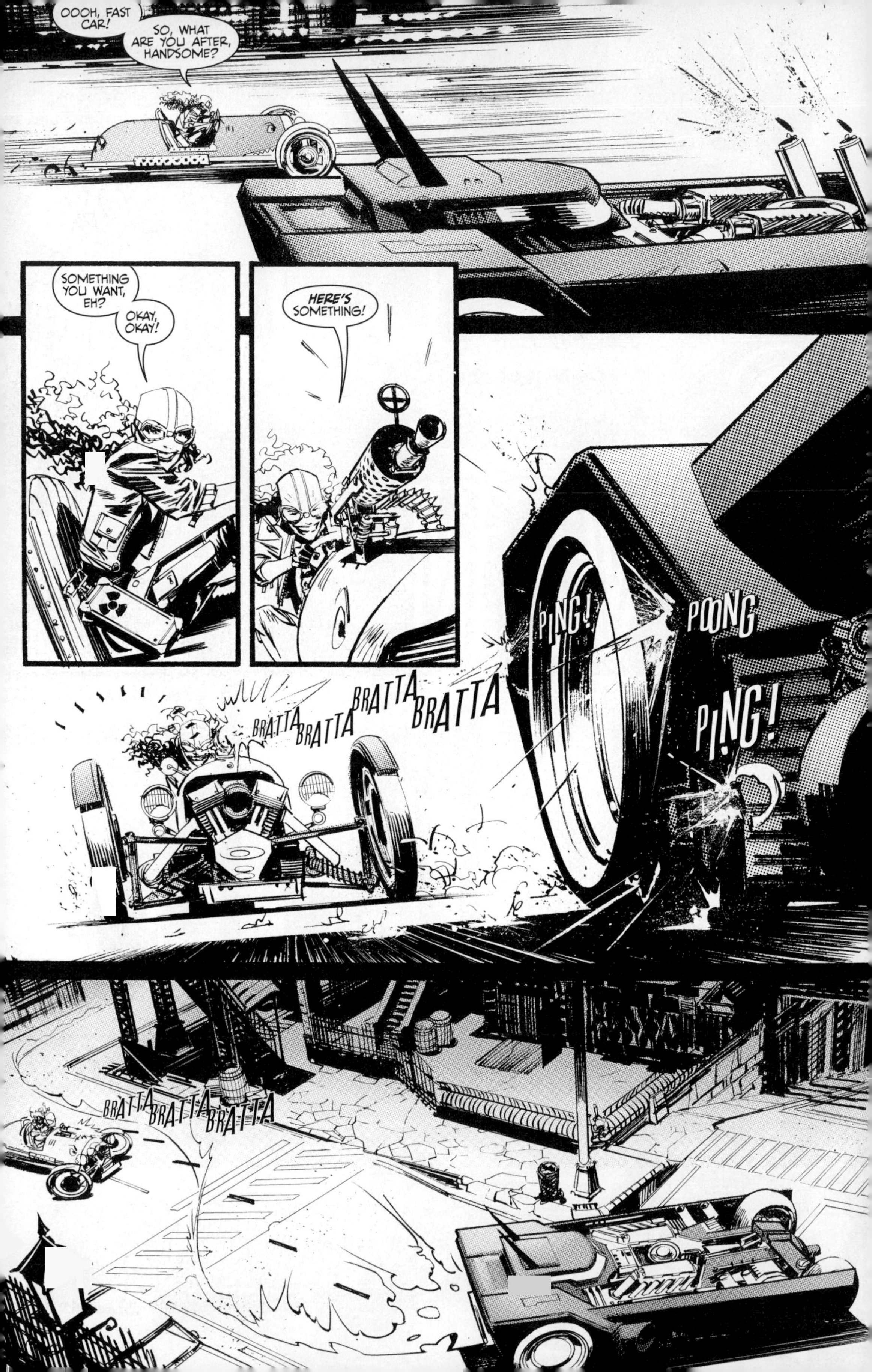
OOOH, FAST CAR!
SO, WHAT ARE YOU AFTER, HANDSOME?
SOMETHING YOU WANT, EH?
OKAY, OKAY!
HERE'S SOMETHING!
PING!
POONG
PING!
BRATTA BRATTA BRATTA BRATTA
BRATTA BRATTA BRATTA

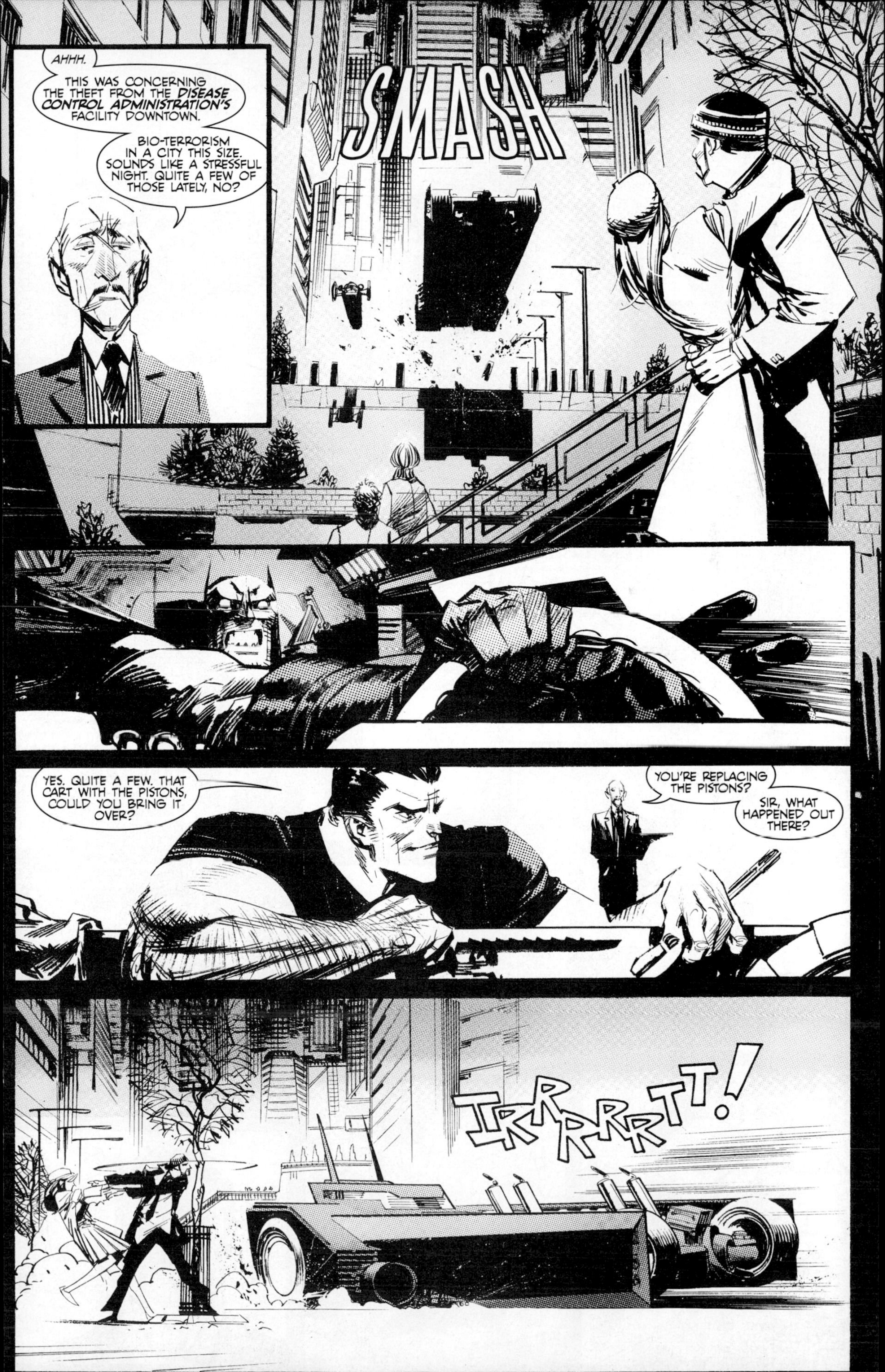
AHHH.
THIS WAS CONCERNING THE THEFT FROM THE DISEASE CONTROL ADMINISTRATION'S FACILITY DOWNTOWN.
BIO-TERRORISM IN A CITY THIS SIZE. SOUNDS LIKE A STRESSFUL NIGHT. QUITE A FEW OF THOSE LATELY, NO?
SMASH
YES. QUITE A FEW. THAT CART WITH THE PISTONS, COULD YOU BRING IT OVER?
YOU'RE REPLACING THE PISTONS?
SIR, WHAT HAPPENED OUT THERE?
IRRRRRTT!

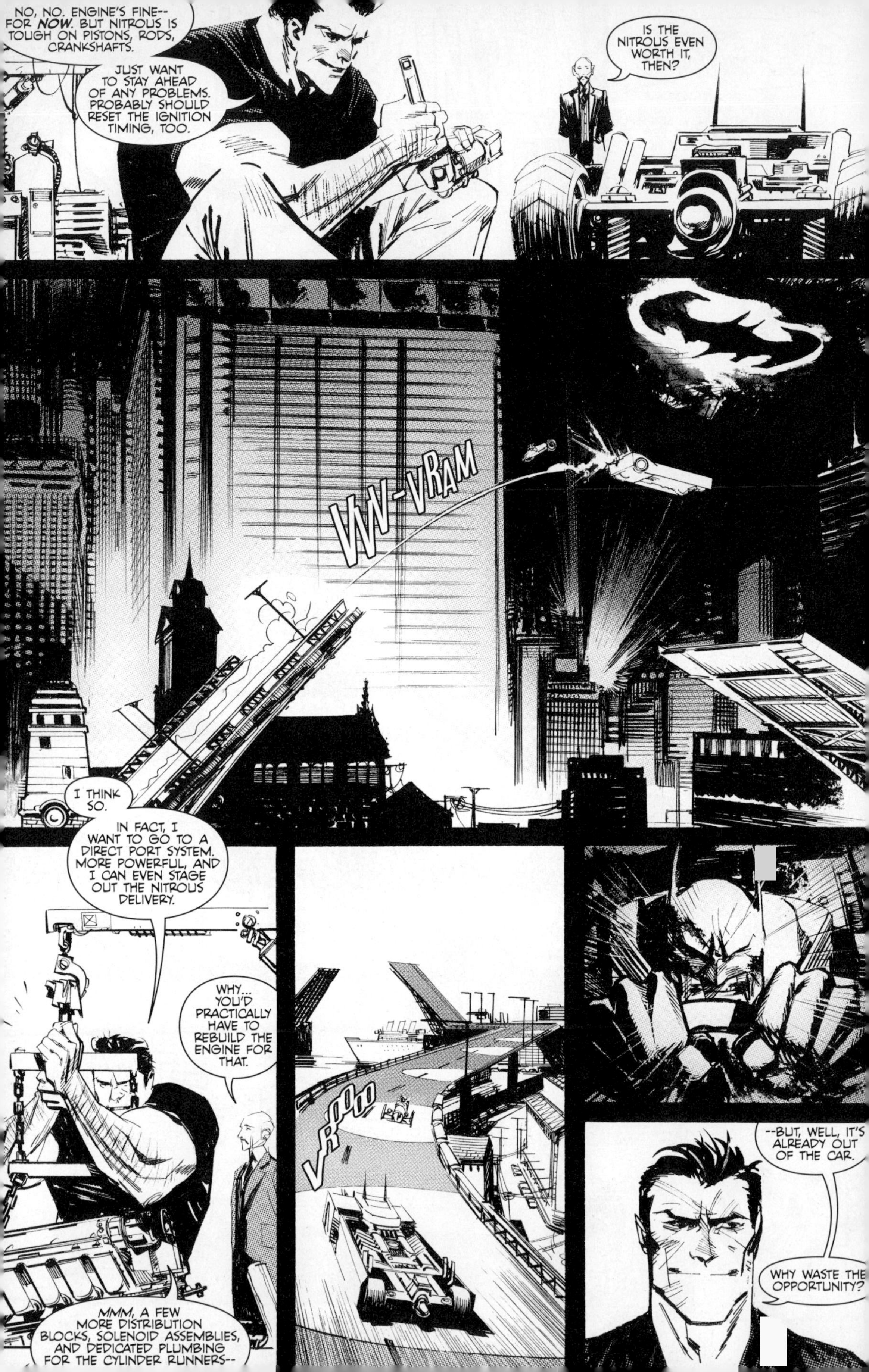
NO, NO. ENGINE'S FINE-- FOR **NOW**. BUT NITROUS IS TOUGH ON PISTONS, RODS, CRANKSHAFTS.
JUST WANT TO STAY AHEAD OF ANY PROBLEMS. PROBABLY SHOULD RESET THE IGNITION TIMING, TOO.
IS THE NITROUS EVEN WORTH IT, THEN?
VVV-VRAM
I THINK SO.
IN FACT, I WANT TO GO TO A DIRECT PORT SYSTEM. MORE POWERFUL, AND I CAN EVEN STAGE OUT THE NITROUS DELIVERY.
WHY... YOU'D PRACTICALLY HAVE TO REBUILD THE ENGINE FOR THAT.
MMM, A FEW MORE DISTRIBUTION BLOCKS, SOLENOID ASSEMBLIES, AND DEDICATED PLUMBING FOR THE CYLINDER RUNNERS--
VROOOO
--BUT, WELL, IT'S ALREADY OUT OF THE CAR.
WHY WASTE THE OPPORTUNITY?

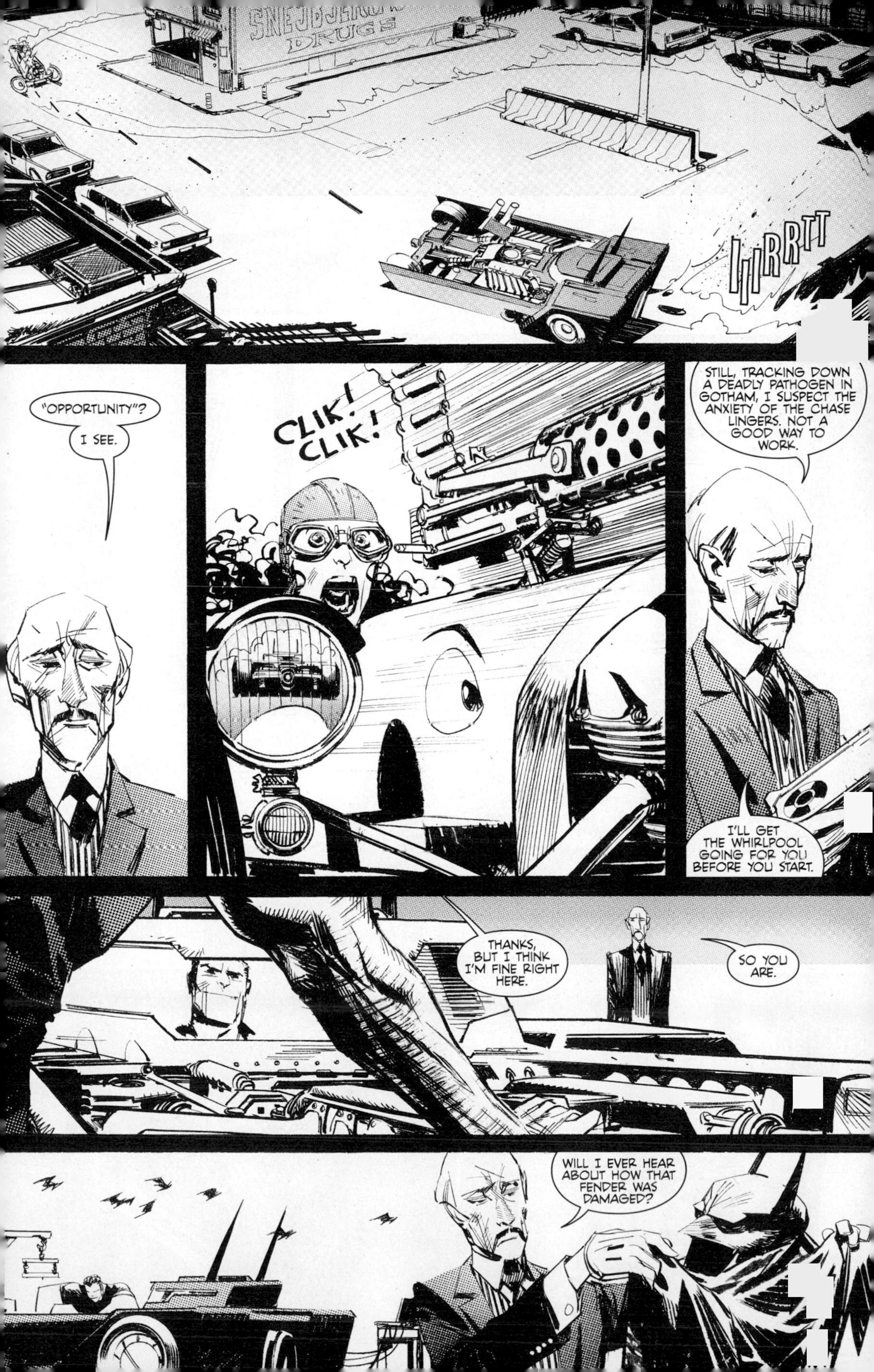

SNEJDJAR DRUGS
IIIRRRTT
"OPPORTUNITY"?
I SEE.
CLIK! CLIK!
STILL, TRACKING DOWN A DEADLY PATHOGEN IN GOTHAM, I SUSPECT THE ANXIETY OF THE CHASE LINGERS. NOT A GOOD WAY TO WORK.
I'LL GET THE WHIRLPOOL GOING FOR YOU BEFORE YOU START.
THANKS, BUT I THINK I'M FINE RIGHT HERE.
SO YOU ARE.
WILL I EVER HEAR ABOUT HOW THAT FENDER WAS DAMAGED?

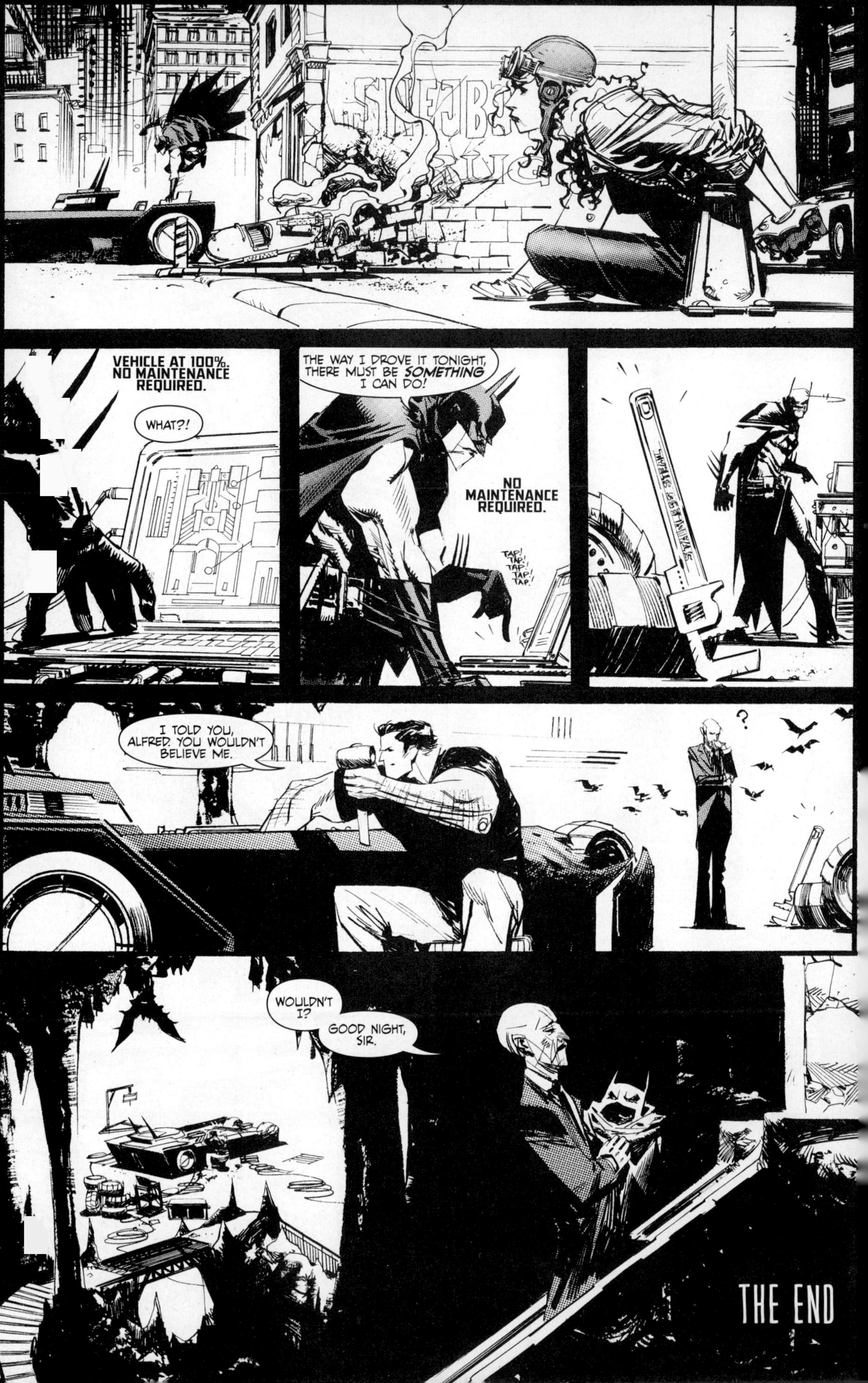
VEHICLE AT 100%. NO MAINTENANCE REQUIRED.
WHAT?!
THE WAY I DROVE IT TONIGHT, THERE MUST BE SOMETHING I CAN DO!
NO MAINTENANCE REQUIRED.
TAP! TAP! TAP! TAP! TAP!
I TOLD YOU, ALFRED. YOU WOULDN'T BELIEVE ME.
?
WOULDN'T I?
GOOD NIGHT, SIR.
THE END

JOHN ARCUDI

John Arcudi is a master of socially
conscious and philosophically charged stories.
Working on such titles as MAJOR BUMMER,
The Mask, GEN13, DOOM PATROL, *B.P.R.D.*, and
WEDNESDAY COMICS, Arcudi has truly
impressed his readers with his insight on
immortality, power, and the human condition.
His provocative narratives often
examine the collision of humor, violence, and
religion, all at the same time, as seen in his
profound 2010 graphic novel
A GOD SOMEWHERE.

SEAN MURPHY

The industry's newest rock star, Sean Murphy
has taken the comic book world by storm.
An incredible draftsman, Murphy's innovative
style synthesizes everything from Manga to
European comics, to mainstream American
illustration. As the artist of JOE THE BARBARIAN,
THE WAKE, and creator of PUNK ROCK JESUS, he
has demonstrated a knack for depicting
action, horror, and fantasy, with a little religion
and politics thrown in.

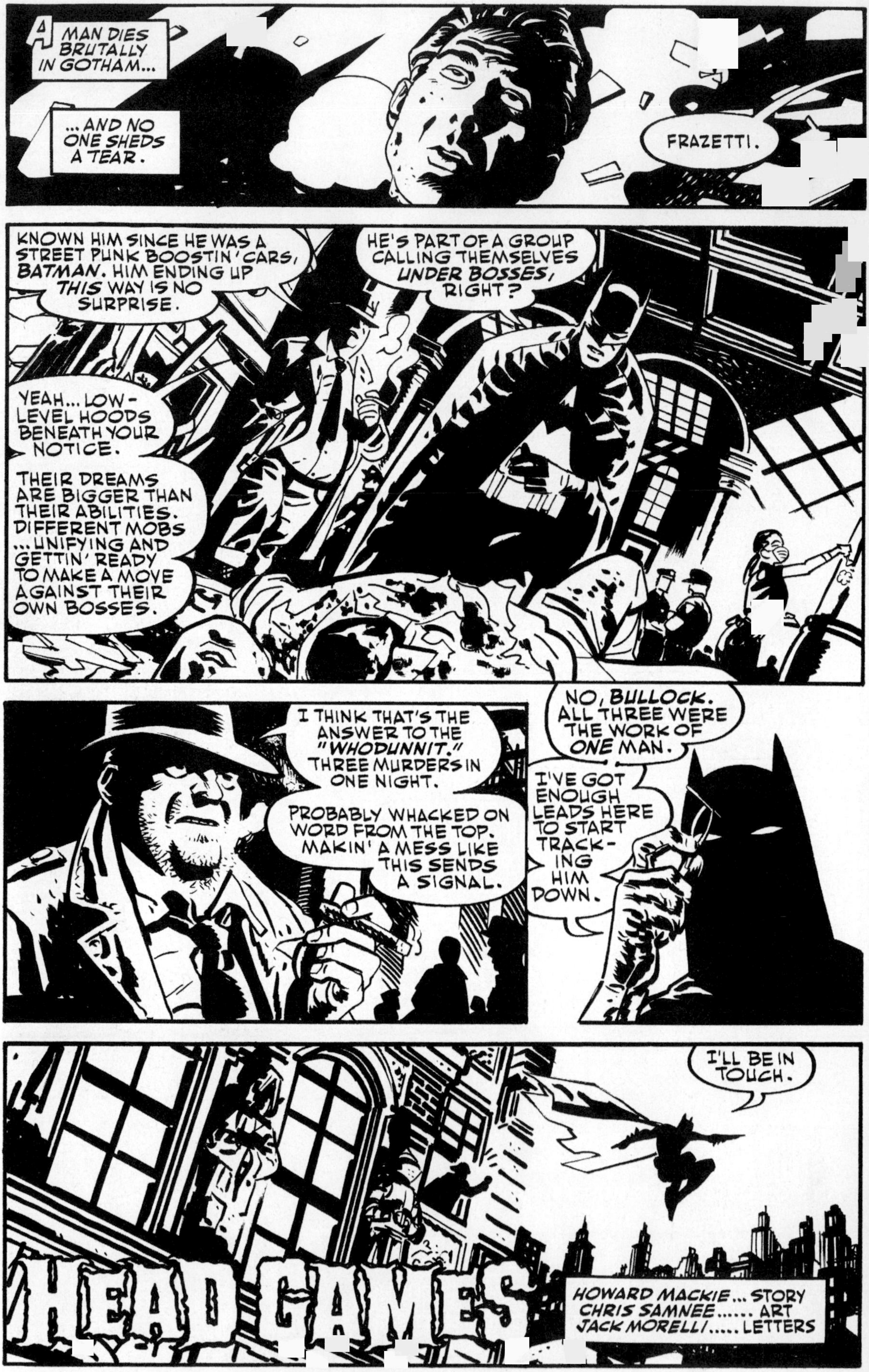
A MAN DIES BRUTALLY IN GOTHAM...
...AND NO ONE SHEDS A TEAR.
FRAZETTI.
KNOWN HIM SINCE HE WAS A STREET PUNK BOOSTIN' CARS, BATMAN. HIM ENDING UP THIS WAY IS NO SURPRISE.
HE'S PART OF A GROUP CALLING THEMSELVES UNDER BOSSES, RIGHT?
YEAH... LOW-LEVEL HOODS BENEATH YOUR NOTICE.
THEIR DREAMS ARE BIGGER THAN THEIR ABILITIES. DIFFERENT MOBS ...UNIFYING AND GETTIN' READY TO MAKE A MOVE AGAINST THEIR OWN BOSSES.
I THINK THAT'S THE ANSWER TO THE "WHODUNNIT." THREE MURDERS IN ONE NIGHT.
PROBABLY WHACKED ON WORD FROM THE TOP. MAKIN' A MESS LIKE THIS SENDS A SIGNAL.
NO, BULLOCK. ALL THREE WERE THE WORK OF ONE MAN.
I'VE GOT ENOUGH LEADS HERE TO START TRACKING HIM DOWN.
I'LL BE IN TOUCH.
HEAD GAMES
HOWARD MACKIE... STORY
CHRIS SAMNEE...... ART
JACK MORELLI..... LETTERS

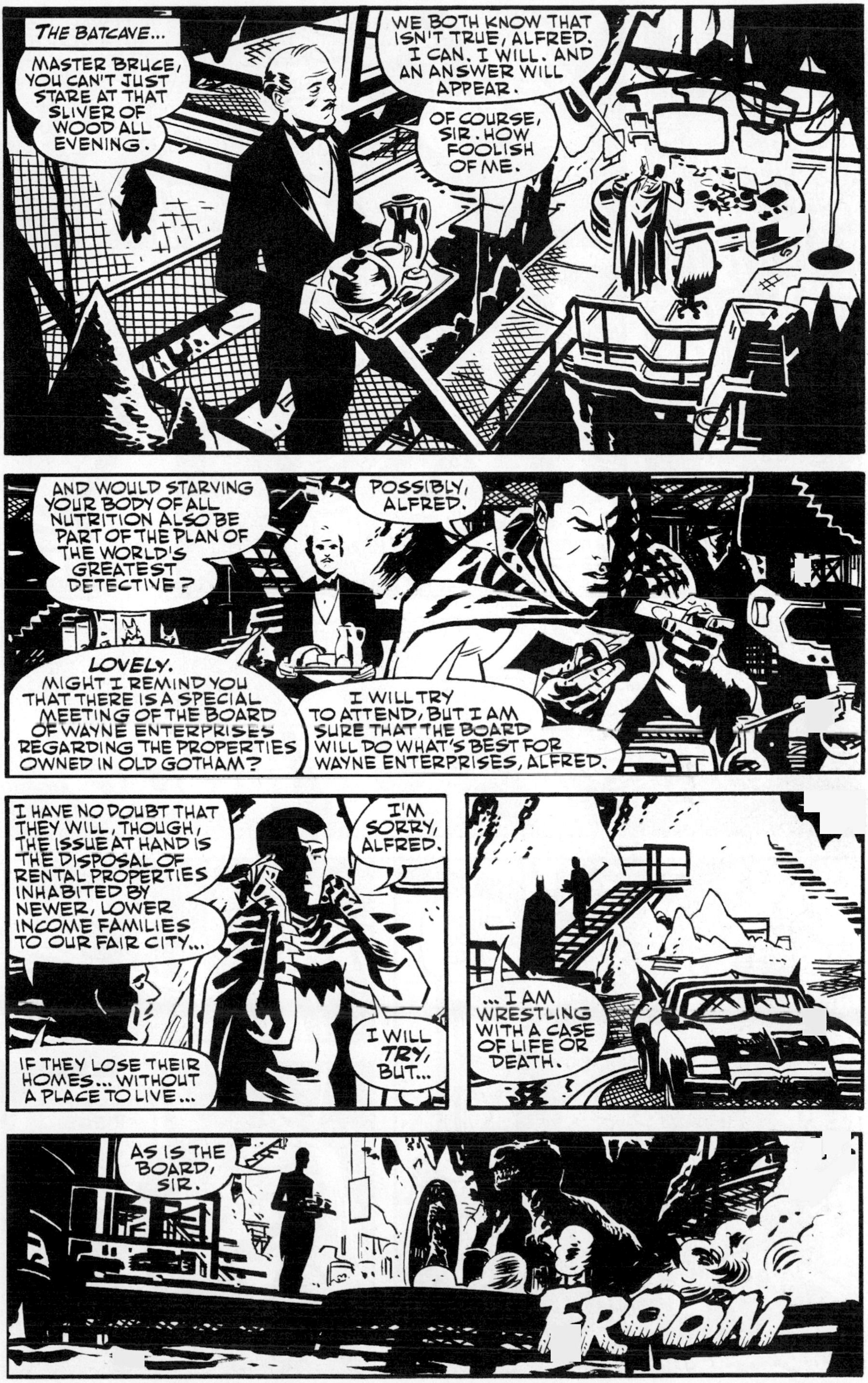
THE BATCAVE...
MASTER BRUCE, YOU CAN'T JUST STARE AT THAT SLIVER OF WOOD ALL EVENING.
WE BOTH KNOW THAT ISN'T TRUE, ALFRED. I CAN. I WILL. AND AN ANSWER WILL APPEAR.
OF COURSE, SIR. HOW FOOLISH OF ME.
AND WOULD STARVING YOUR BODY OF ALL NUTRITION ALSO BE PART OF THE PLAN OF THE WORLD'S GREATEST DETECTIVE?
POSSIBLY, ALFRED.
LOVELY. MIGHT I REMIND YOU THAT THERE IS A SPECIAL MEETING OF THE BOARD OF WAYNE ENTERPRISES REGARDING THE PROPERTIES OWNED IN OLD GOTHAM?
I WILL TRY TO ATTEND, BUT I AM SURE THAT THE BOARD WILL DO WHAT'S BEST FOR WAYNE ENTERPRISES, ALFRED.
I HAVE NO DOUBT THAT THEY WILL, THOUGH, THE ISSUE AT HAND IS THE DISPOSAL OF RENTAL PROPERTIES INHABITED BY NEWER, LOWER INCOME FAMILIES TO OUR FAIR CITY...
I'M SORRY, ALFRED.
IF THEY LOSE THEIR HOMES... WITHOUT A PLACE TO LIVE...
I WILL TRY, BUT...
...I AM WRESTLING WITH A CASE OF LIFE OR DEATH.
AS IS THE BOARD, SIR.
FROOM

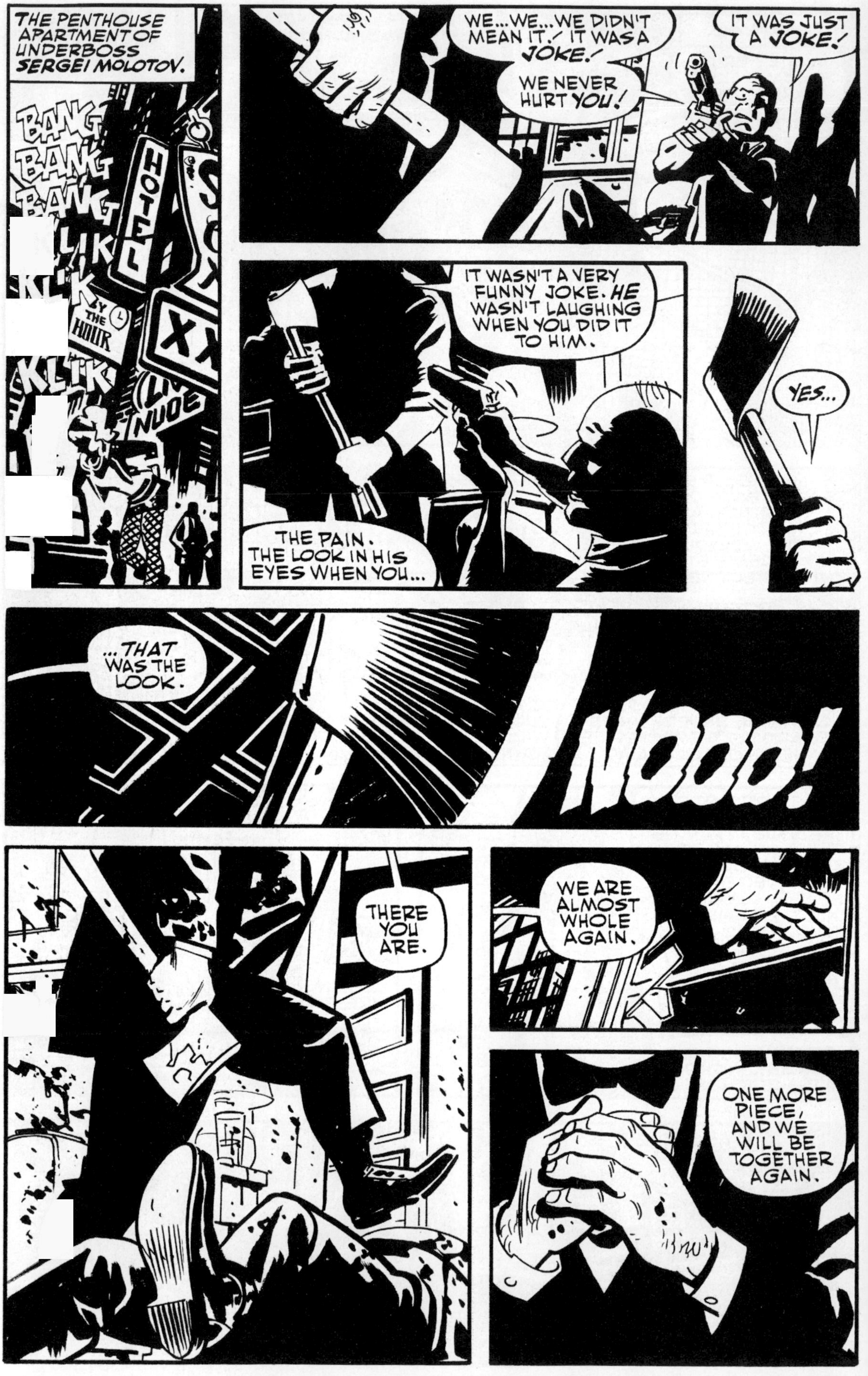
THE PENTHOUSE APARTMENT OF UNDERBOSS SERGEI MOLOTOV.
BANG BANG BANG
HOTEL
BY THE HOUR
NUDE
WE...WE...WE DIDN'T MEAN IT! IT WAS A JOKE!
WE NEVER HURT YOU!
IT WAS JUST A JOKE!
IT WASN'T A VERY FUNNY JOKE. HE WASN'T LAUGHING WHEN YOU DID IT TO HIM.
THE PAIN. THE LOOK IN HIS EYES WHEN YOU...
YES...
...THAT WAS THE LOOK.
NOOO!
THERE YOU ARE.
WE ARE ALMOST WHOLE AGAIN.
ONE MORE PIECE, AND WE WILL BE TOGETHER AGAIN.

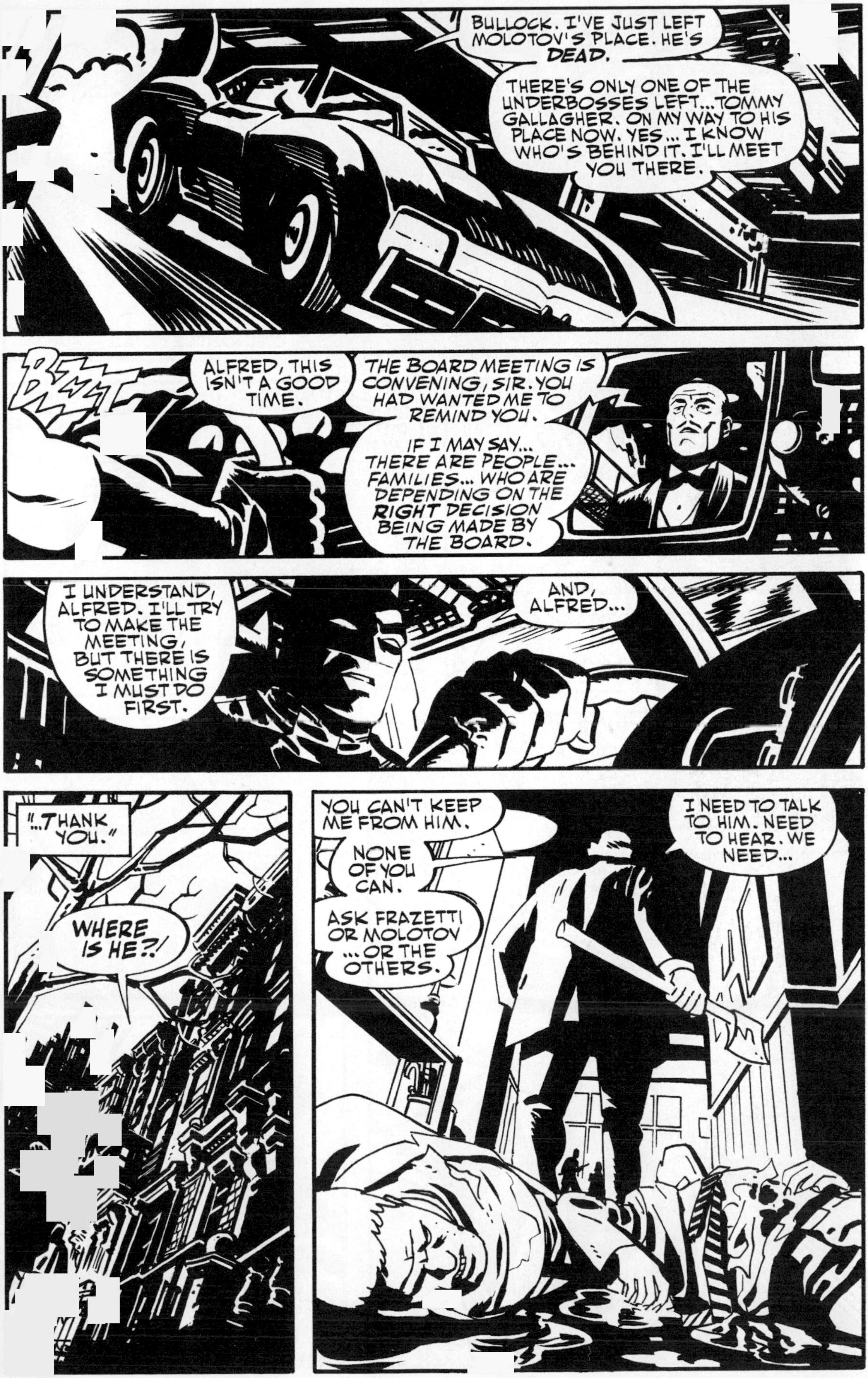
BULLOCK. I'VE JUST LEFT MOLOTOV'S PLACE. HE'S DEAD.
THERE'S ONLY ONE OF THE UNDERBOSSES LEFT... TOMMY GALLAGHER. ON MY WAY TO HIS PLACE NOW. YES... I KNOW WHO'S BEHIND IT. I'LL MEET YOU THERE.
BZZT
ALFRED, THIS ISN'T A GOOD TIME.
THE BOARD MEETING IS CONVENING, SIR. YOU HAD WANTED ME TO REMIND YOU.
IF I MAY SAY... THERE ARE PEOPLE... FAMILIES... WHO ARE DEPENDING ON THE RIGHT DECISION BEING MADE BY THE BOARD.
I UNDERSTAND, ALFRED. I'LL TRY TO MAKE THE MEETING, BUT THERE IS SOMETHING I MUST DO FIRST.
AND, ALFRED...
"...THANK YOU."
WHERE IS HE?!
YOU CAN'T KEEP ME FROM HIM.
NONE OF YOU CAN.
ASK FRAZETTI OR MOLOTOV ...OR THE OTHERS.
I NEED TO TALK TO HIM. NEED TO HEAR. WE NEED...

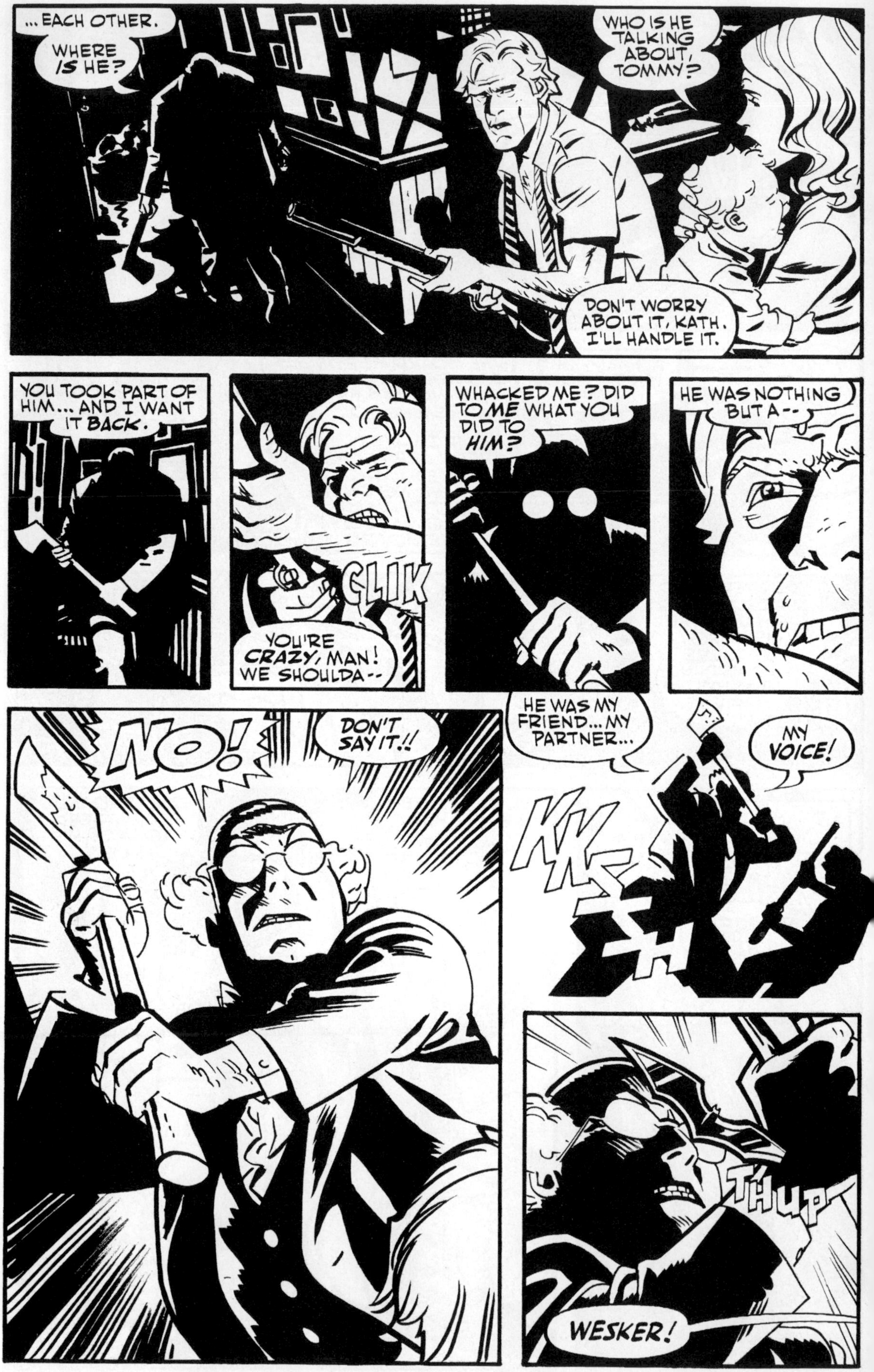

...EACH OTHER.
WHERE IS HE?
WHO IS HE TALKING ABOUT, TOMMY?
DON'T WORRY ABOUT IT, KATH. I'LL HANDLE IT.
YOU TOOK PART OF HIM... AND I WANT IT BACK.
CLIK
YOU'RE CRAZY, MAN! WE SHOULDA--
WHACKED ME? DID TO ME WHAT YOU DID TO HIM?
HE WAS NOTHING BUT A--
NO!
DON'T SAY IT!!
HE WAS MY FRIEND... MY PARTNER...
MY VOICE!
KKKSSHH
THUP
WESKER!

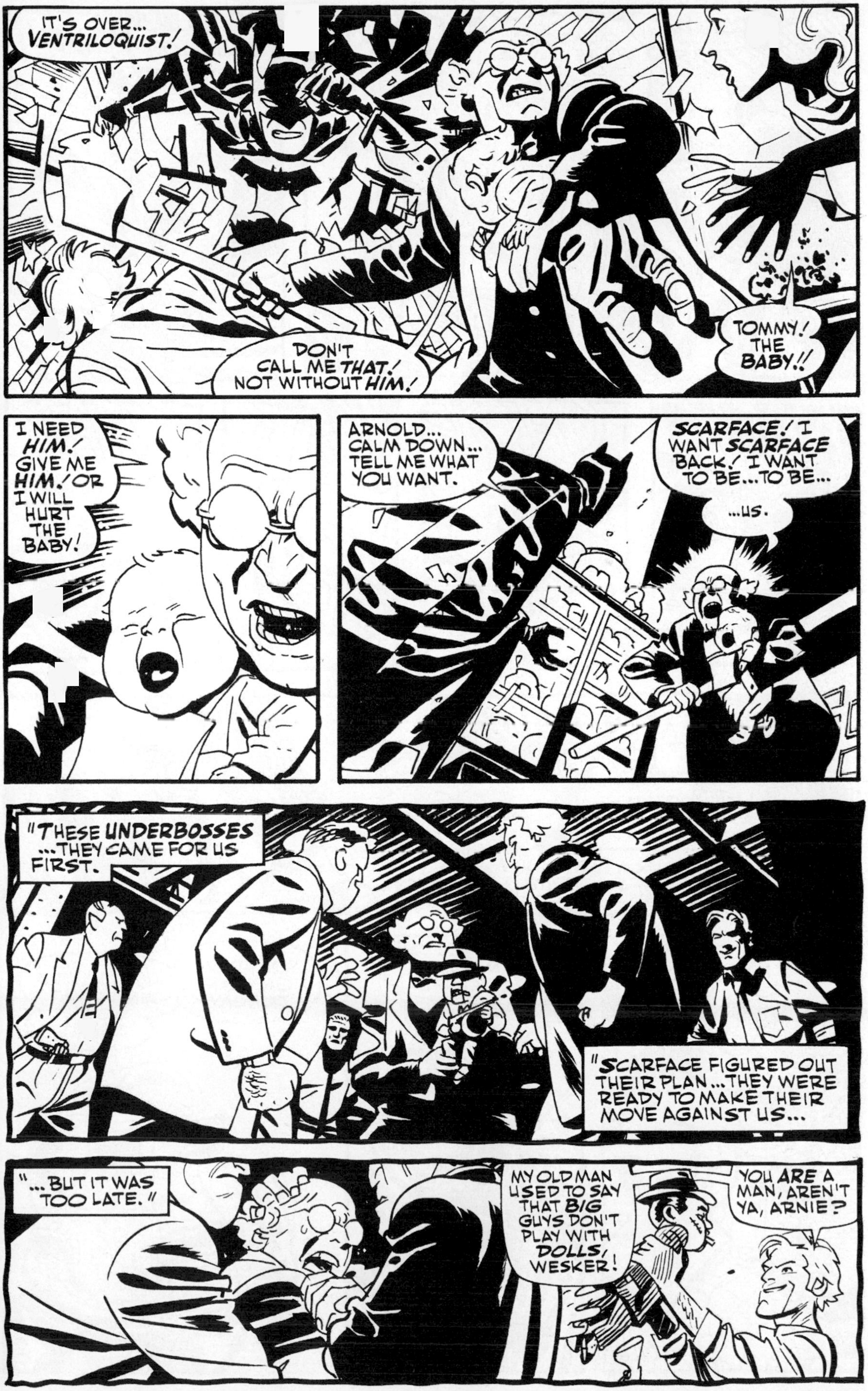
IT'S OVER... VENTRILOQUIST!
DON'T CALL ME THAT! NOT WITHOUT HIM!
TOMMY! THE BABY!!
I NEED HIM! GIVE ME HIM! OR I WILL HURT THE BABY!
ARNOLD... CALM DOWN... TELL ME WHAT YOU WANT.
SCARFACE! I WANT SCARFACE BACK! I WANT TO BE... TO BE...
...US.
"THESE UNDERBOSSES ...THEY CAME FOR US FIRST.
"SCARFACE FIGURED OUT THEIR PLAN... THEY WERE READY TO MAKE THEIR MOVE AGAINST US...
"... BUT IT WAS TOO LATE."
MY OLD MAN USED TO SAY THAT BIG GUYS DON'T PLAY WITH DOLLS, WESKER!
YOU ARE A MAN, AREN'T YA, ARNIE?

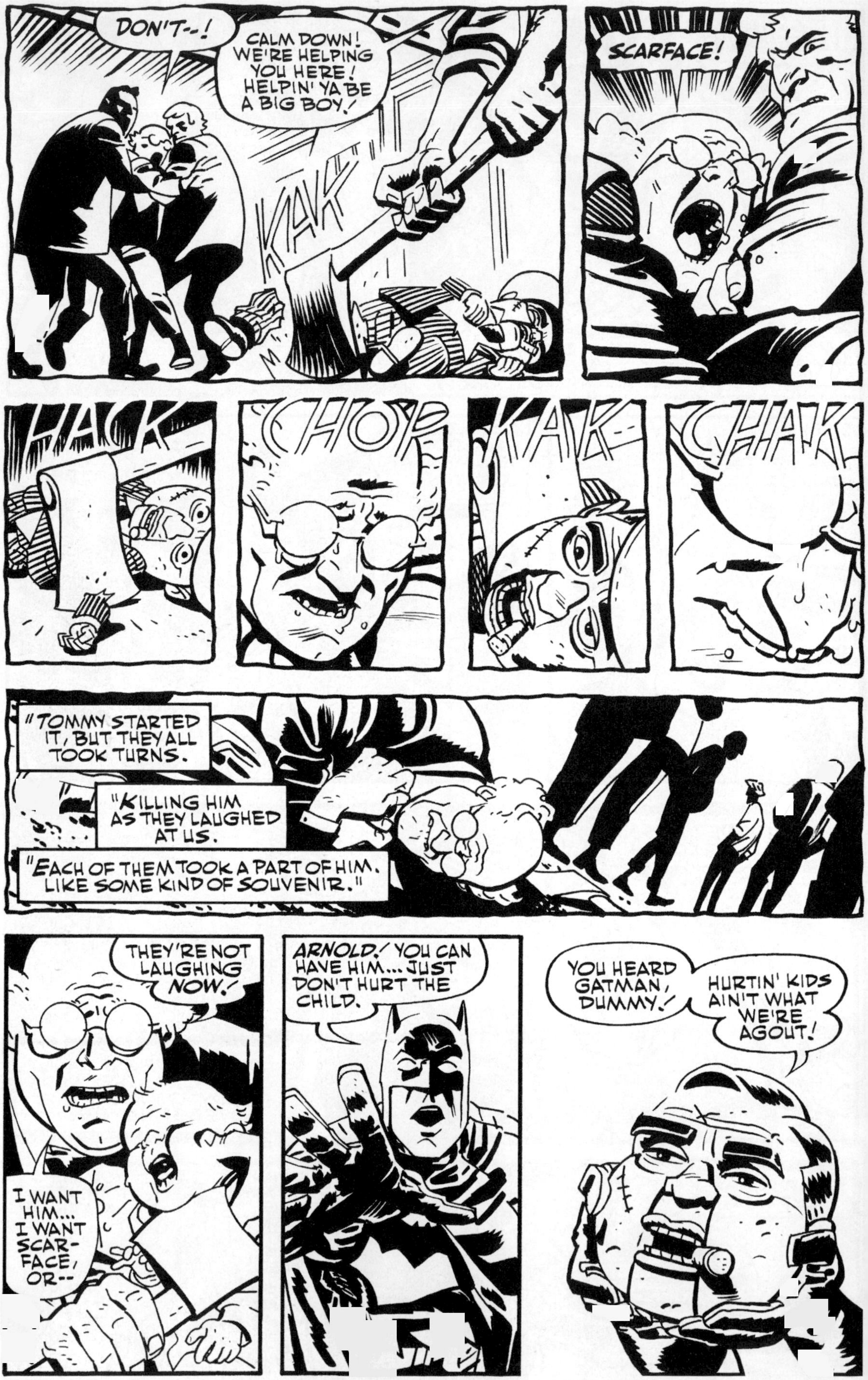
DON'T--!
CALM DOWN! WE'RE HELPING YOU HERE! HELPIN' YA BE A BIG BOY!
KAK
SCARFACE!
HACK
CHOP
KAK
CHAK
"TOMMY STARTED IT, BUT THEY ALL TOOK TURNS.
"KILLING HIM AS THEY LAUGHED AT US.
"EACH OF THEM TOOK A PART OF HIM. LIKE SOME KIND OF SOUVENIR."
THEY'RE NOT LAUGHING NOW!
I WANT HIM... I WANT SCARFACE, OR--
ARNOLD! YOU CAN HAVE HIM... JUST DON'T HURT THE CHILD.
YOU HEARD GATMAN, DUMMY!
HURTIN' KIDS AIN'T WHAT WE'RE AGOUT!

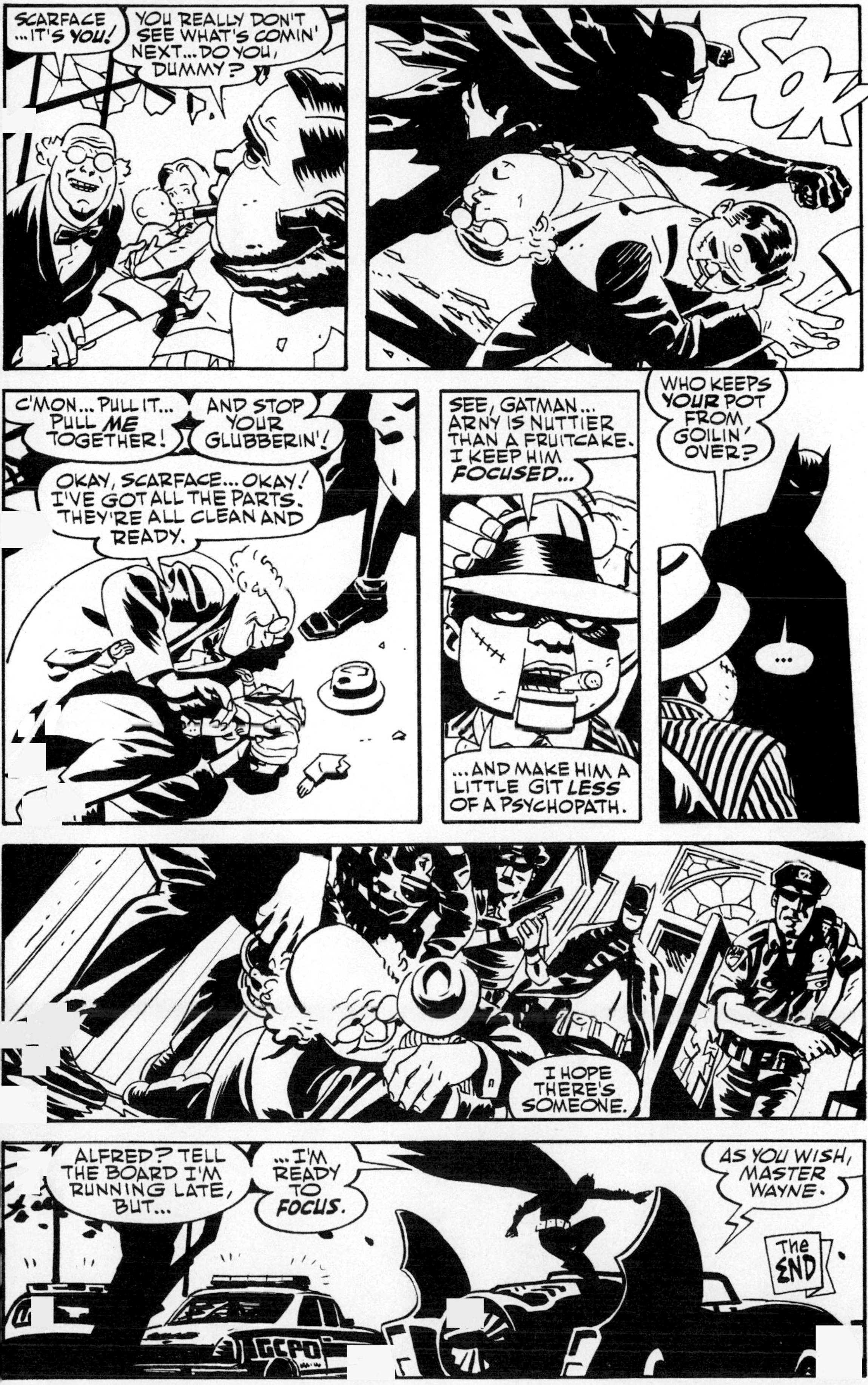
SCARFACE ...IT'S YOU!
YOU REALLY DON'T SEE WHAT'S COMIN' NEXT...DO YOU, DUMMY?
SOK
C'MON... PULL IT... PULL ME TOGETHER!
AND STOP YOUR GLUBBERIN'!
OKAY, SCARFACE...OKAY! I'VE GOT ALL THE PARTS. THEY'RE ALL CLEAN AND READY.
SEE, GATMAN... ARNY IS NUTTIER THAN A FRUITCAKE. I KEEP HIM FOCUSED...
...AND MAKE HIM A LITTLE GIT LESS OF A PSYCHOPATH.
WHO KEEPS YOUR POT FROM GOILIN' OVER?
...
I HOPE THERE'S SOMEONE.
ALFRED? TELL THE BOARD I'M RUNNING LATE, BUT...
...I'M READY TO FOCUS.
AS YOU WISH, MASTER WAYNE.
GCPD
The END

HOWARD MACKIE

As the writer who deconstructed and
re-envisioned Marvel's Ghost Rider character,
Howard Mackie brought a real-world sensibility
to the action-packed world of super heroes.

A former editor at Marvel, Mackie went on to
become one of comics' most popular and
respected writers. His long runs on many of
Marvel's top titles, including *Spider-Man* and
X-Factor, remain fan favorites.

CHRIS SAMNEE

Chris Samnee's work is a throwback to the
great strip artists of the past, like Milton Caniff
and Frank Robbins, yet it somehow always feels
hip, modern, and fresh. His takes on classic
characters, such as the Rocketeer, Daredevil,
and the Shadow showcase Samnee's
high-contrast approach to art.

From the moment Chris first read a Batman
comic book at age six, he hoped he would
some day draw a Batman story. Here, for the
first time, the inky black world of Chris Samnee
meets the shadowy world of the Dark Knight.

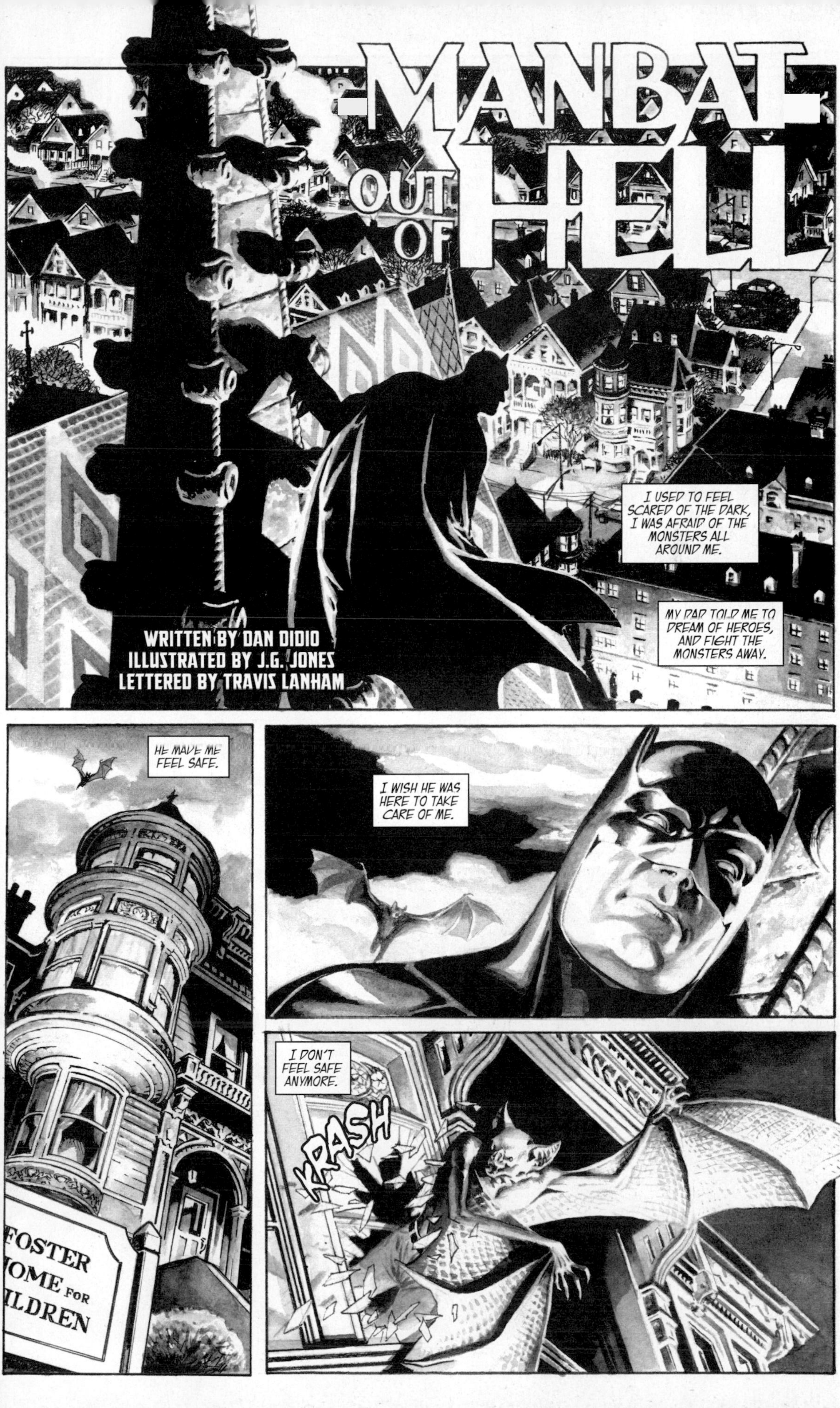
MANBAT OUT OF HELL
WRITTEN BY DAN DIDIO
ILLUSTRATED BY J.G. JONES
LETTERED BY TRAVIS LANHAM
I USED TO FEEL SCARED OF THE DARK, I WAS AFRAID OF THE MONSTERS ALL AROUND ME.
MY DAD TOLD ME TO DREAM OF HEROES, AND FIGHT THE MONSTERS AWAY.
HE MADE ME FEEL SAFE.
FOSTER
OME FOR
ILDREN
I WISH HE WAS HERE TO TAKE CARE OF ME.
I DON'T FEEL SAFE ANYMORE.
KRASH

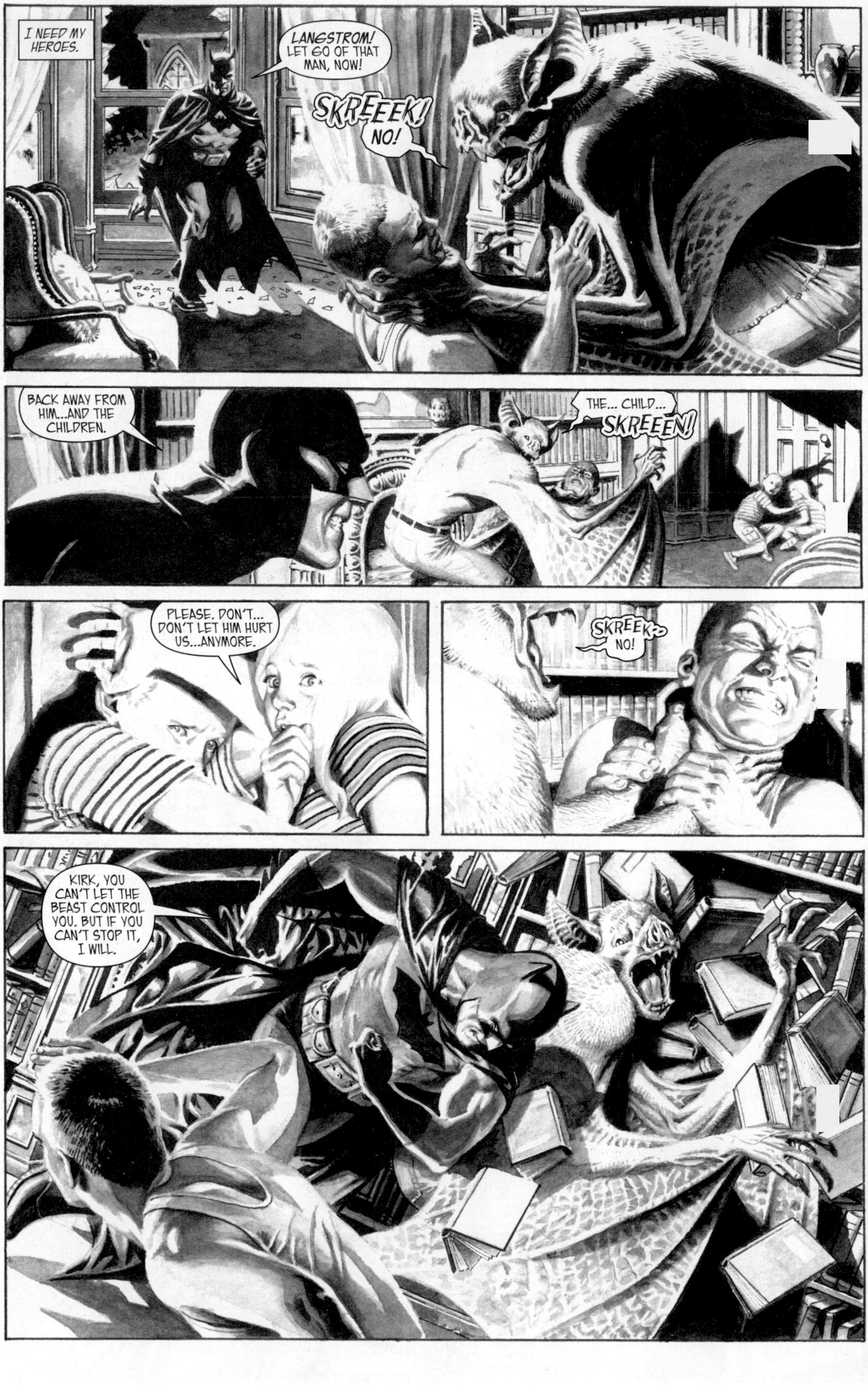

I NEED MY HEROES.
LANGSTROM! LET GO OF THAT MAN, NOW!
SKREEEK! NO!
BACK AWAY FROM HIM...AND THE CHILDREN.
THE... CHILD... SKREEEN!
PLEASE. DON'T... DON'T LET HIM HURT US...ANYMORE.
SKREEK NO!
KIRK, YOU CAN'T LET THE BEAST CONTROL YOU. BUT IF YOU CAN'T STOP IT, I WILL.

SKREEEEEEEEEEEE!
YOU'VE BEEN SIGHTED IN THIS AREA FOR WEEKS. IT WAS JUST A MATTER OF TIME BEFORE I FOUND YOU.
I DON'T KNOW WHY YOU'RE HERE.
BUT I CAN'T LET THIS GO ON.
PAPH!
AFTER DADDY WAS CHANGED, AFTER WE WERE TAKEN AWAY...

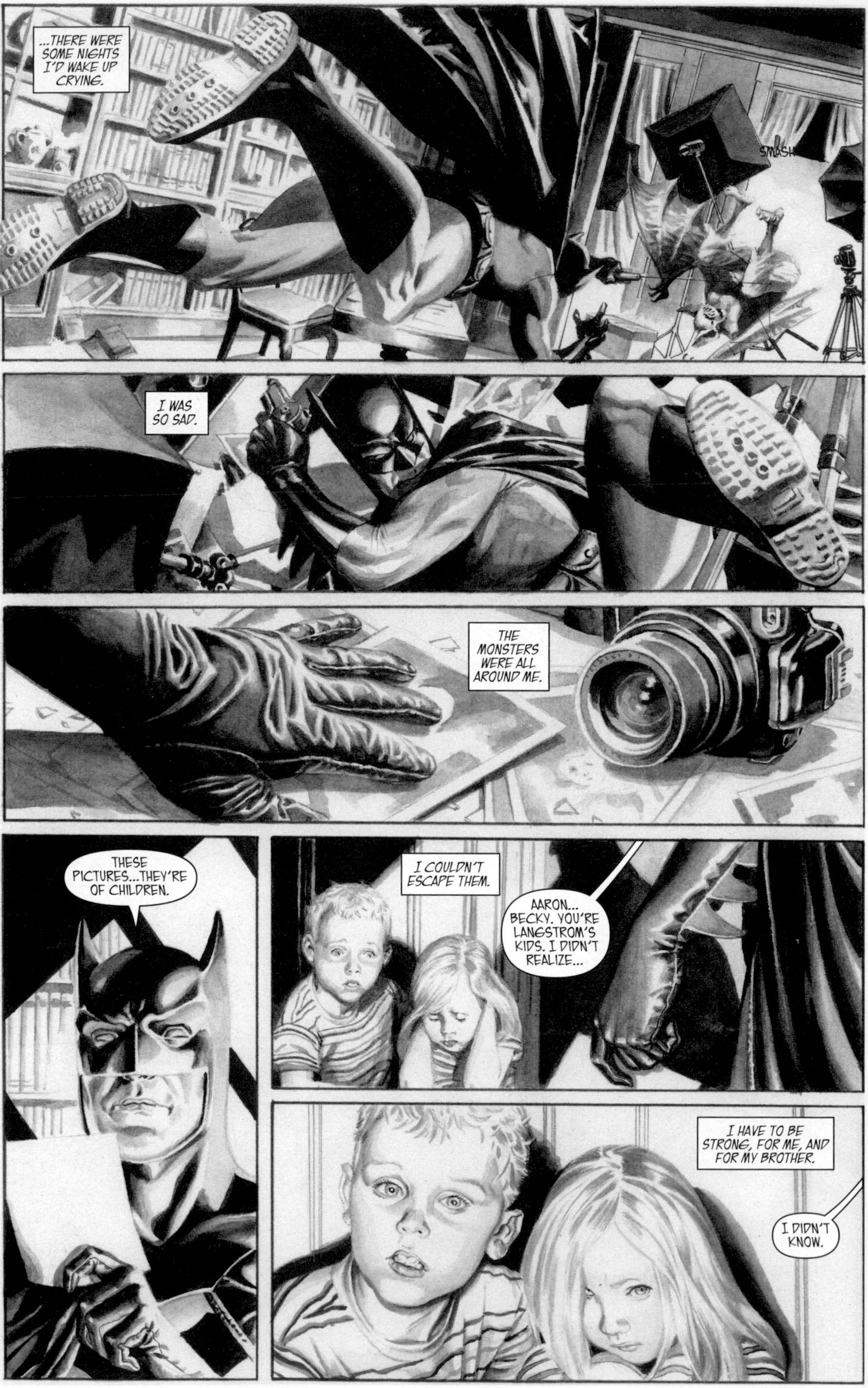
...THERE WERE SOME NIGHTS I'D WAKE UP CRYING.
SMASH
I WAS SO SAD.
THE MONSTERS WERE ALL AROUND ME.
THESE PICTURES...THEY'RE OF CHILDREN.
I COULDN'T ESCAPE THEM.
AARON... BECKY. YOU'RE LANGSTROM'S KIDS. I DIDN'T REALIZE...
I HAVE TO BE STRONG, FOR ME, AND FOR MY BROTHER.
I DIDN'T KNOW.

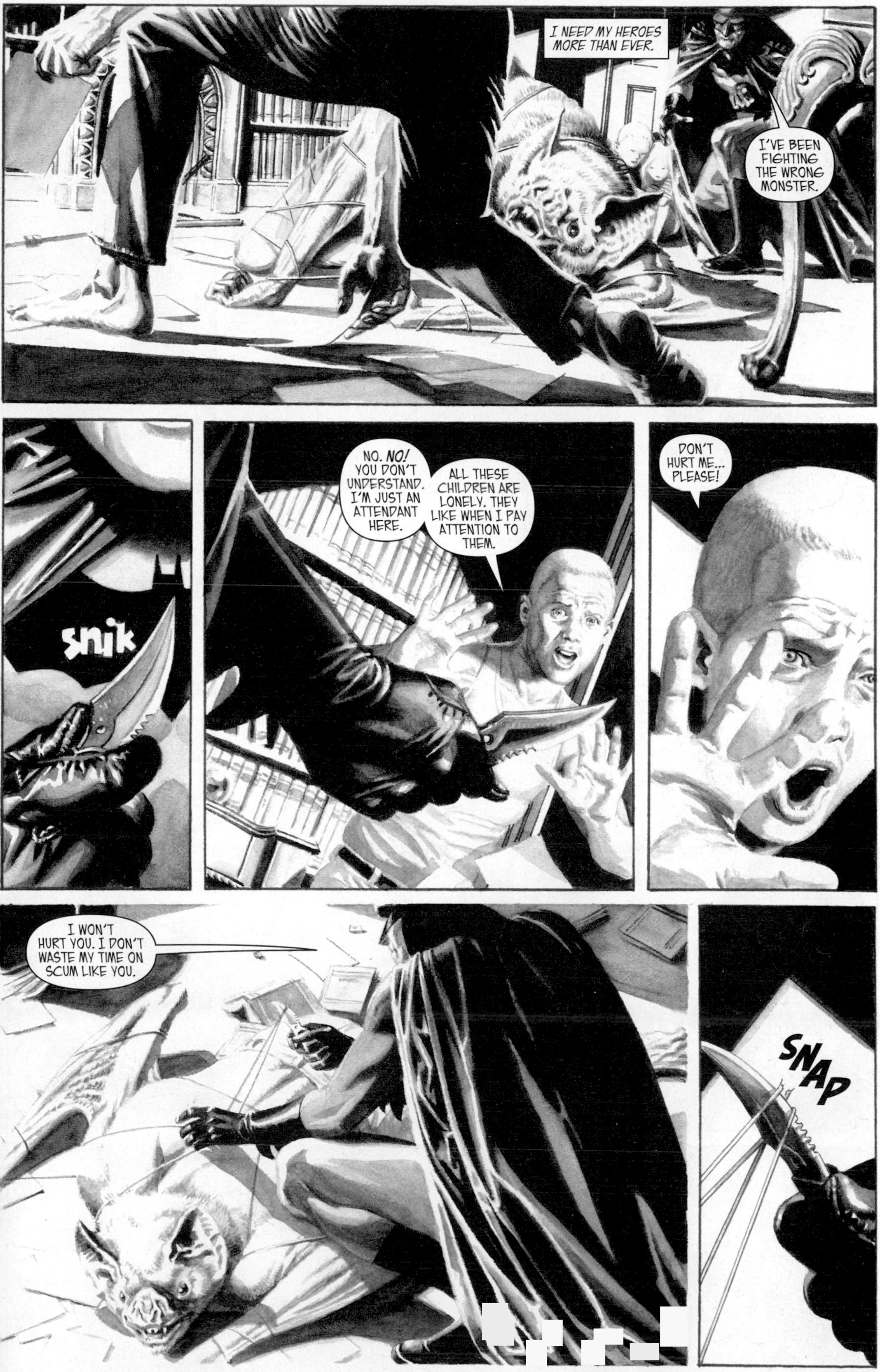
I NEED MY HEROES MORE THAN EVER.
I'VE BEEN FIGHTING THE WRONG MONSTER.
snik
NO. NO! YOU DON'T UNDERSTAND. I'M JUST AN ATTENDANT HERE.
ALL THESE CHILDREN ARE LONELY. THEY LIKE WHEN I PAY ATTENTION TO THEM.
DON'T HURT ME... PLEASE!
I WON'T HURT YOU. I DON'T WASTE MY TIME ON SCUM LIKE YOU.
SNAP

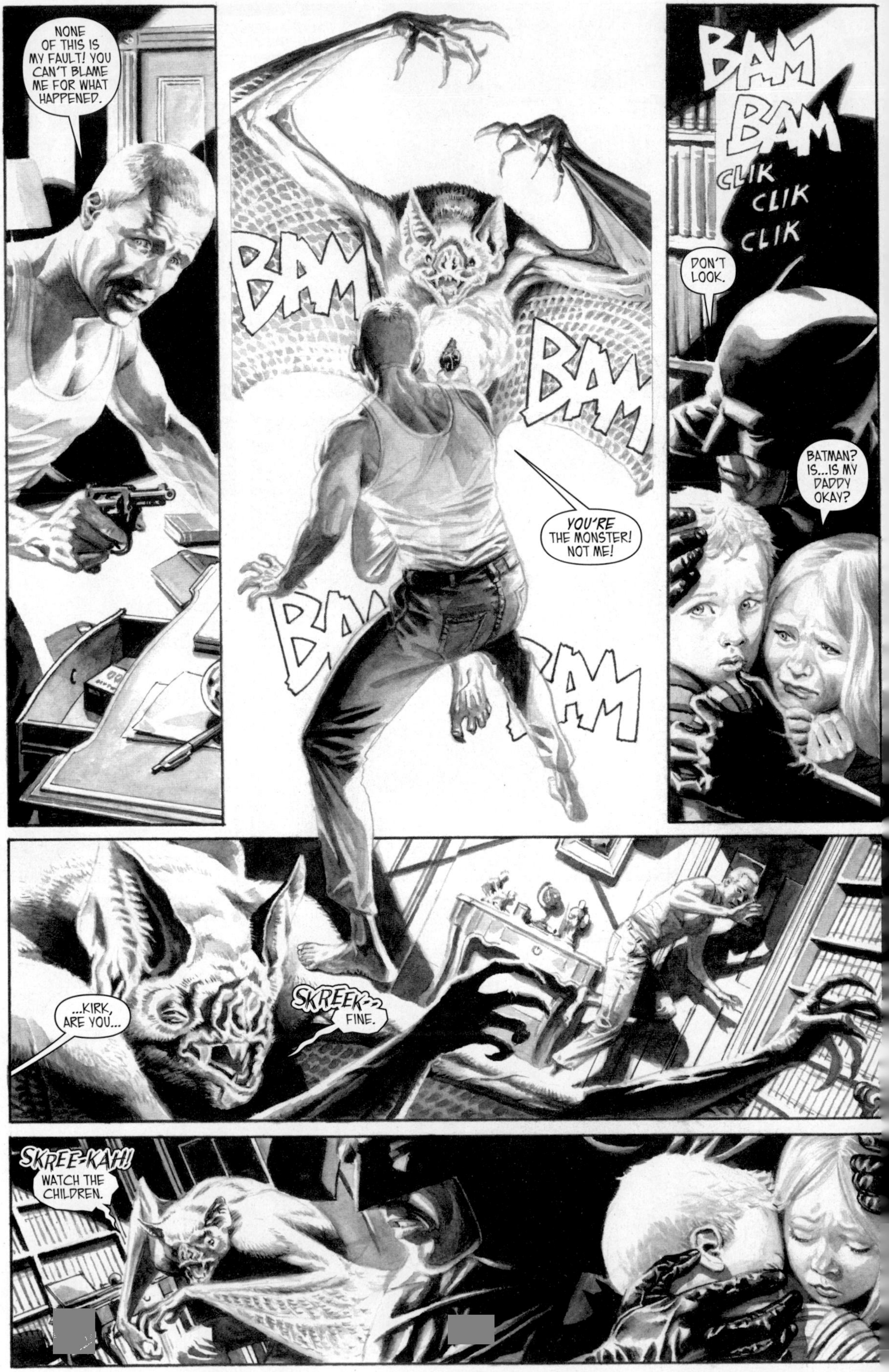
NONE OF THIS IS MY FAULT! YOU CAN'T BLAME ME FOR WHAT HAPPENED.
BAM
BAM
YOU'RE THE MONSTER! NOT ME!
BAM
BAM
CLIK
CLIK
CLIK
DON'T LOOK.
BATMAN? IS...IS MY DADDY OKAY?
...KIRK, ARE YOU...
SKREEK--
FINE.
SKREE-KAH!
WATCH THE CHILDREN.

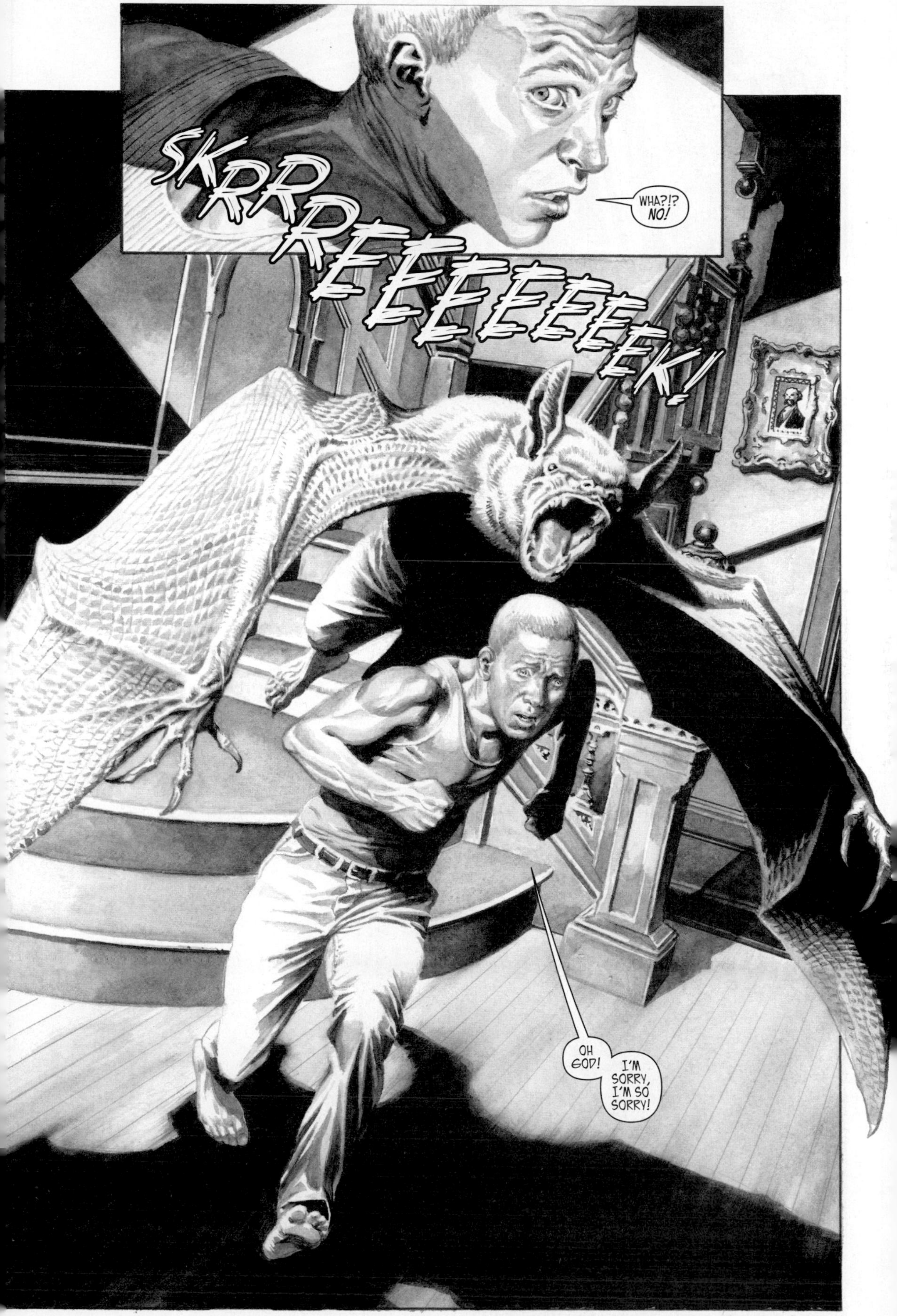
SKRRREEEEEEEEK!
WHA?!? NO!
OH GOD!
I'M SORRY, I'M SO SORRY!

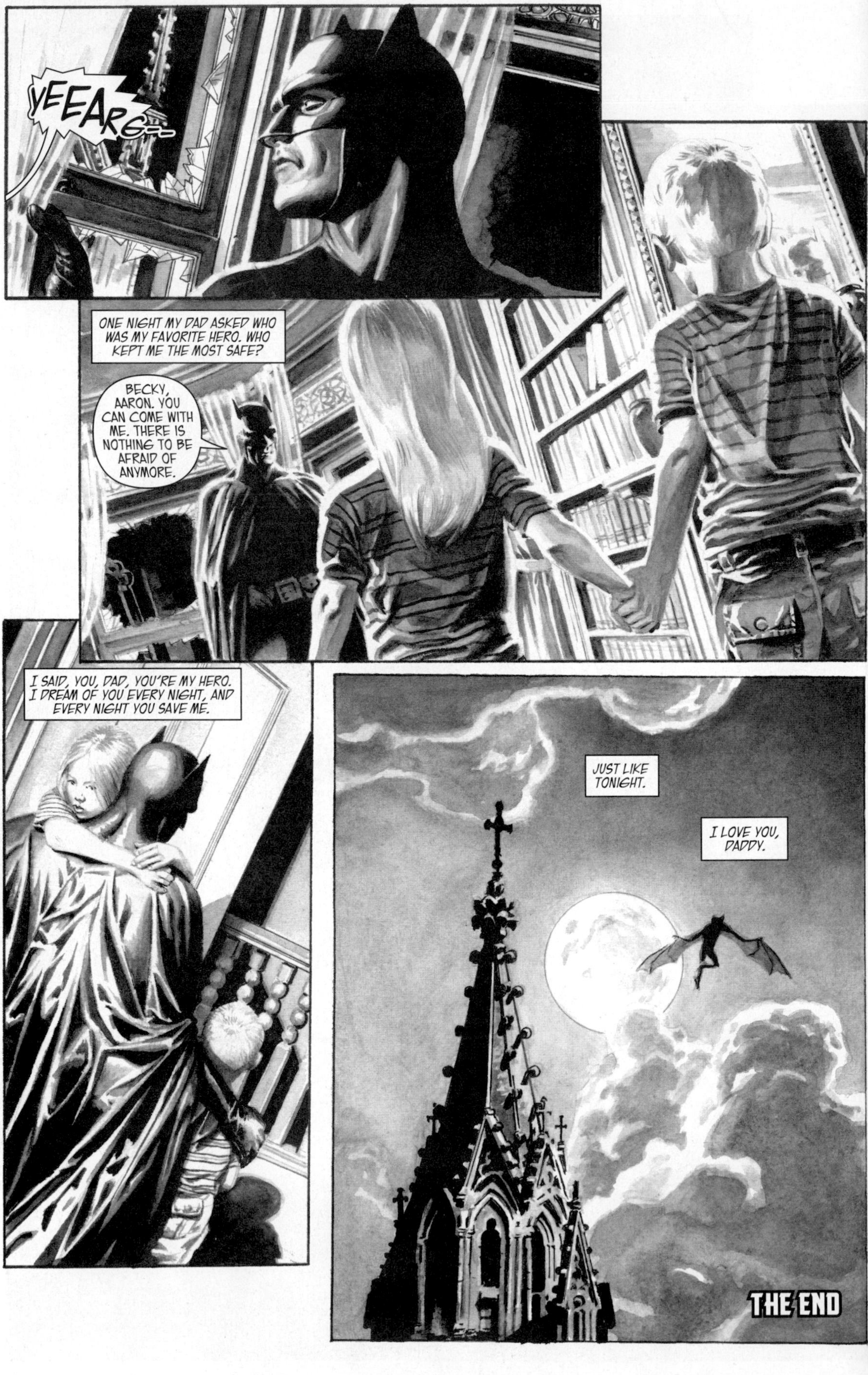
YEEARG--
ONE NIGHT MY DAD ASKED WHO WAS MY FAVORITE HERO. WHO KEPT ME THE MOST SAFE?
BECKY, AARON. YOU CAN COME WITH ME. THERE IS NOTHING TO BE AFRAID OF ANYMORE.
I SAID, YOU, DAD, YOU'RE MY HERO. I DREAM OF YOU EVERY NIGHT, AND EVERY NIGHT YOU SAVE ME.
JUST LIKE TONIGHT.
I LOVE YOU, DADDY.
THE END

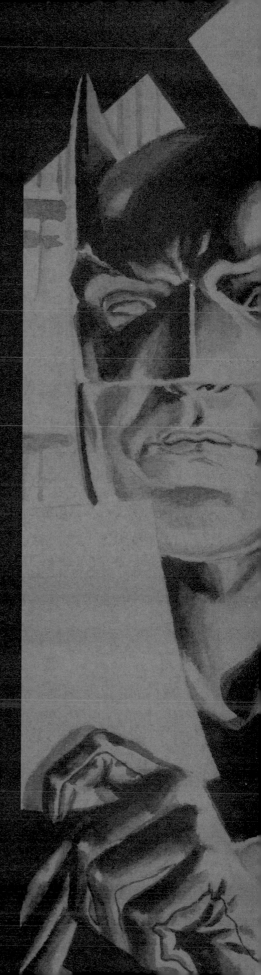

DAN DIDIO

A veteran TV writer and editor, Dan DiDio is
currently Co-Publisher at DC Comics. While
juggling his executive responsibilities, DiDio has
somehow found the time to write the adventures
of such fan favorite DC characters as OMAC,
Phantom Stranger, and the Metal Men in
WEDNESDAY COMICS. Dan is, at his core,
a lifelong comics fan.

J.G. JONES

J.G. Jones bridges the gap from comics to
fine art to mainstream illustration all in the same
brushstroke. His work conjures up visions of
Frank Frazetta, N.C. Wyeth, and John Buscema,
but always with its own personality. Co-creator
of the infamous *Wanted* series, Jones is one of
the most ubiquitous artists in the comic book
world. His classic storytelling can be seen on
WONDER WOMAN: HIKETEIA, FINAL CRISIS and
BEFORE WATCHMEN: COMEDIAN. As one of
the most sought after cover artists, J.G. has
illustrated iconic images for Y: THE LAST MAN,
WONDER WOMAN, 52, and VILLAINS UNITED.

I've been thinking about circles.

A circle is the result of a pattern equation.

It symbolizes the beginning and the end, the opposites united, a man's inner psyche.

And inside the circle there's a bat.

The circle can be a pearl.

The rim of a bullet.

Or a drop of blood. Elements that can also form an equation if joined together.

An equation of trauma.

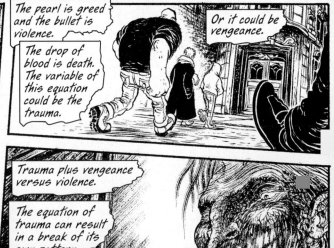

The pearl is greed and the bullet is violence.

The drop of blood is death. The variable of this equation could be the trauma.

Or it could be vengeance.

Trauma plus vengeance versus violence.

The equation of trauma can result in a break of its own pattern.

It can backfire.

written & illustrated by **Rafael Grampá**

lettered by **Steve Wands**

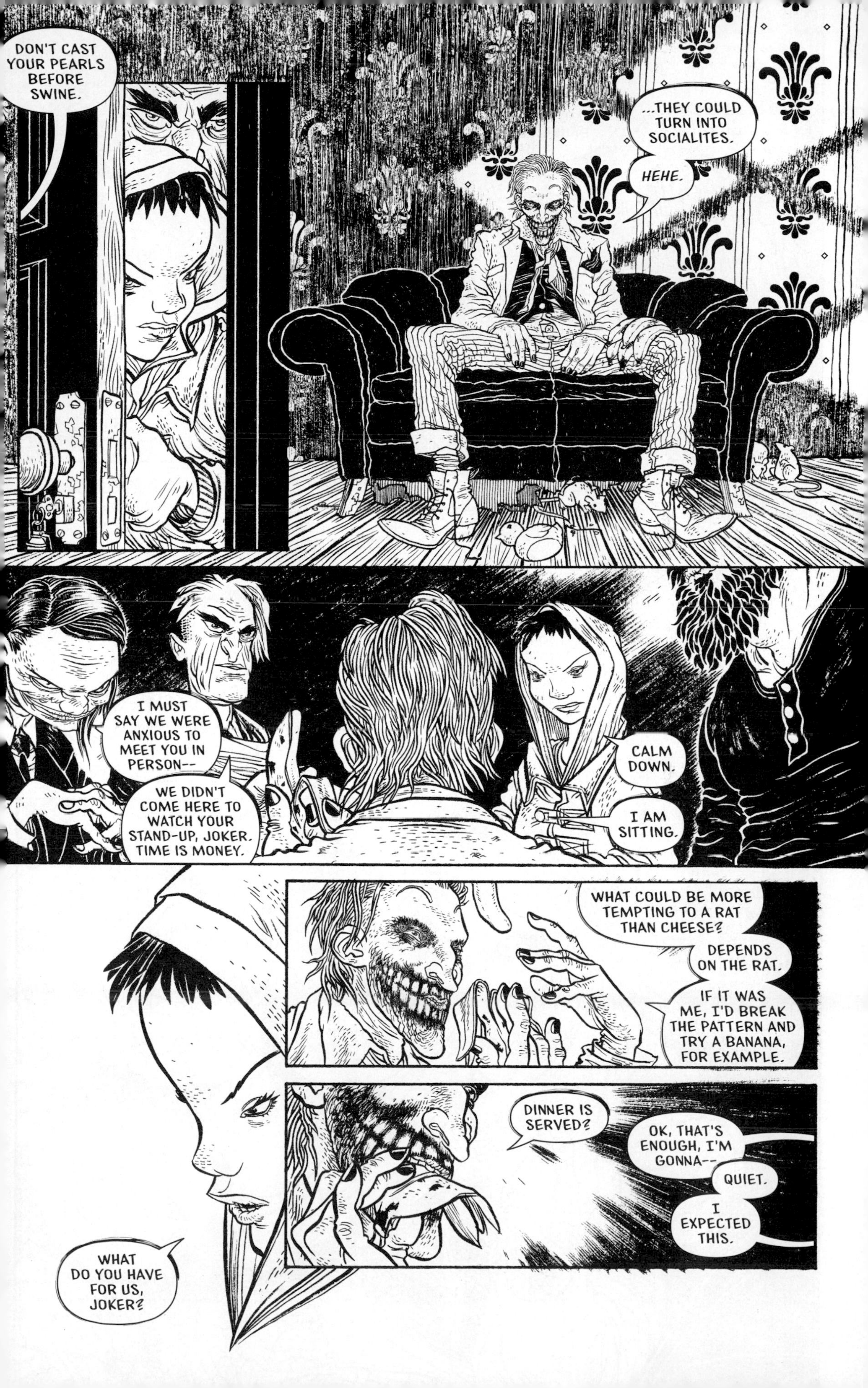
DON'T CAST YOUR PEARLS BEFORE SWINE.
...THEY COULD TURN INTO SOCIALITES.
HEHE.
I MUST SAY WE WERE ANXIOUS TO MEET YOU IN PERSON--
WE DIDN'T COME HERE TO WATCH YOUR STAND-UP, JOKER. TIME IS MONEY.
CALM DOWN.
I AM SITTING.
WHAT COULD BE MORE TEMPTING TO A RAT THAN CHEESE?
DEPENDS ON THE RAT.
IF IT WAS ME, I'D BREAK THE PATTERN AND TRY A BANANA, FOR EXAMPLE.
DINNER IS SERVED?
OK, THAT'S ENOUGH, I'M GONNA--
QUIET.
I EXPECTED THIS.
WHAT DO YOU HAVE FOR US, JOKER?

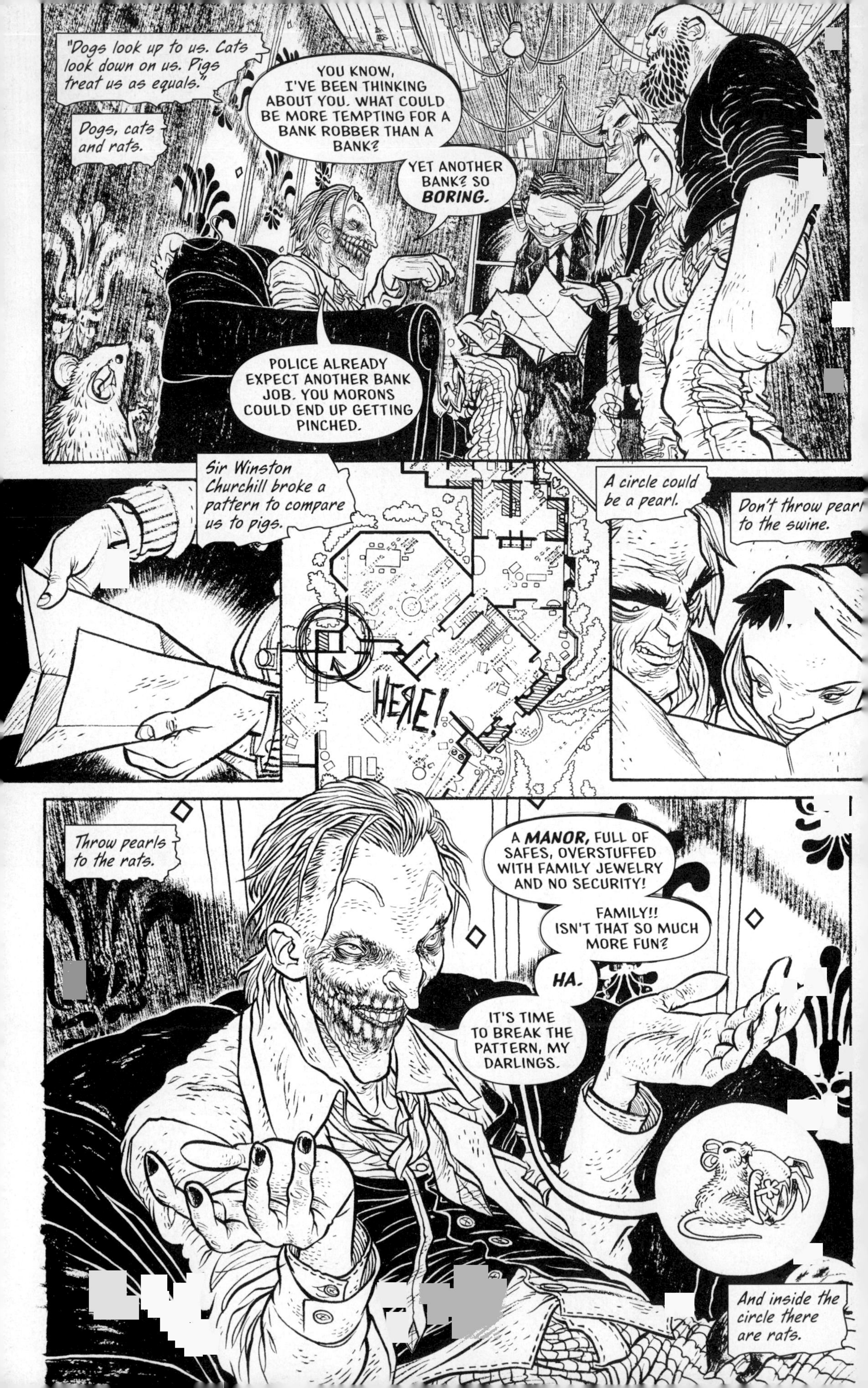
"Dogs look up to us. Cats look down on us. Pigs treat us as equals."
Dogs, cats and rats.
YOU KNOW, I'VE BEEN THINKING ABOUT YOU. WHAT COULD BE MORE TEMPTING FOR A BANK ROBBER THAN A BANK?
YET ANOTHER BANK? SO BORING.
POLICE ALREADY EXPECT ANOTHER BANK JOB. YOU MORONS COULD END UP GETTING PINCHED.
Sir Winston Churchill broke a pattern to compare us to pigs.
HERE!
A circle could be a pearl.
Don't throw pearl
to the swine.
Throw pearls to the rats.
A MANOR, FULL OF SAFES, OVERSTUFFED WITH FAMILY JEWELRY AND NO SECURITY!
FAMILY!! ISN'T THAT SO MUCH MORE FUN?
HA.
IT'S TIME TO BREAK THE PATTERN, MY DARLINGS.
And inside the circle there are rats.

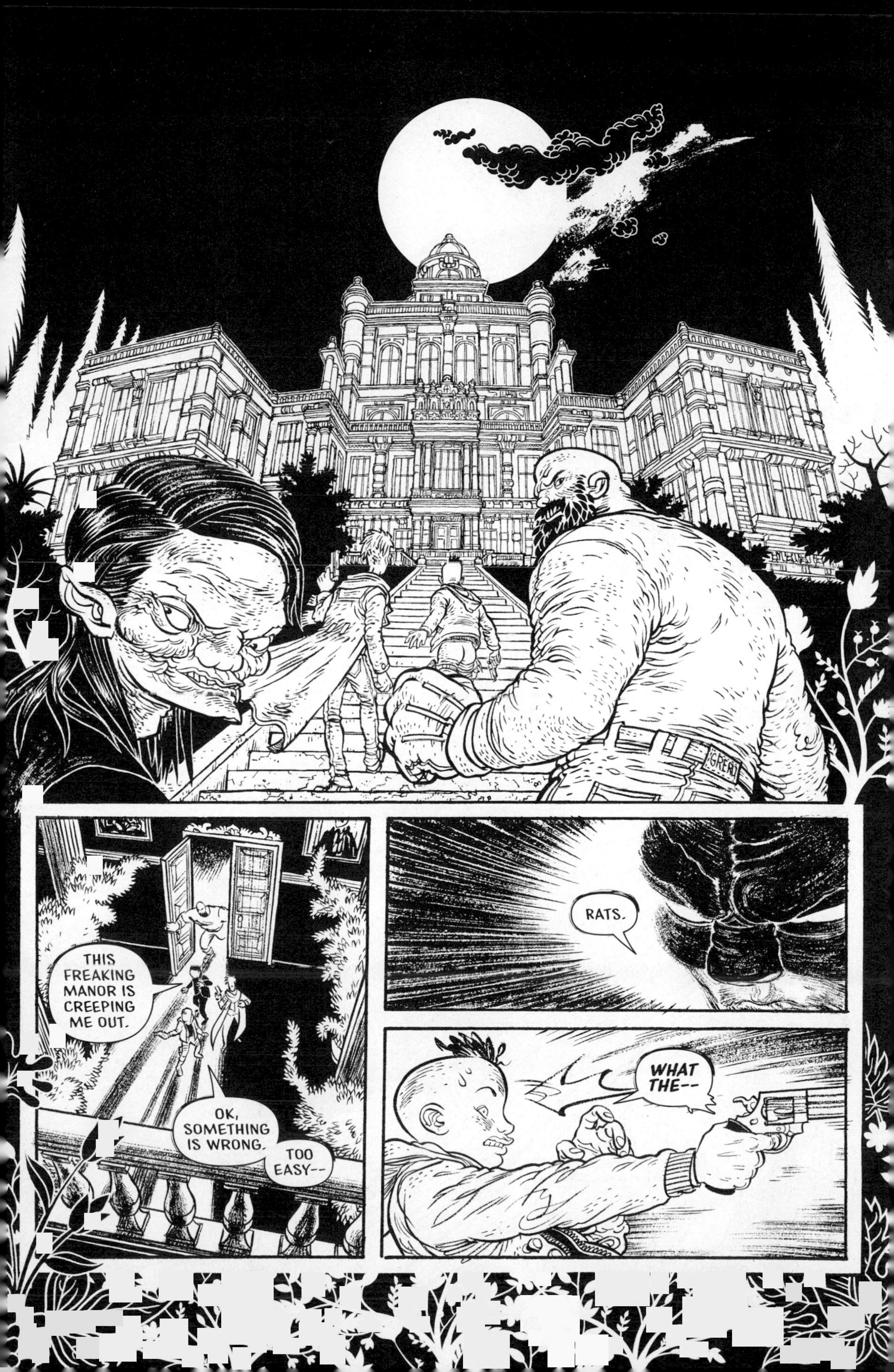
GREAU
THIS FREAKING MANOR IS CREEPING ME OUT.
OK, SOMETHING IS WRONG.
TOO EASY--
RATS.
WHAT THE--

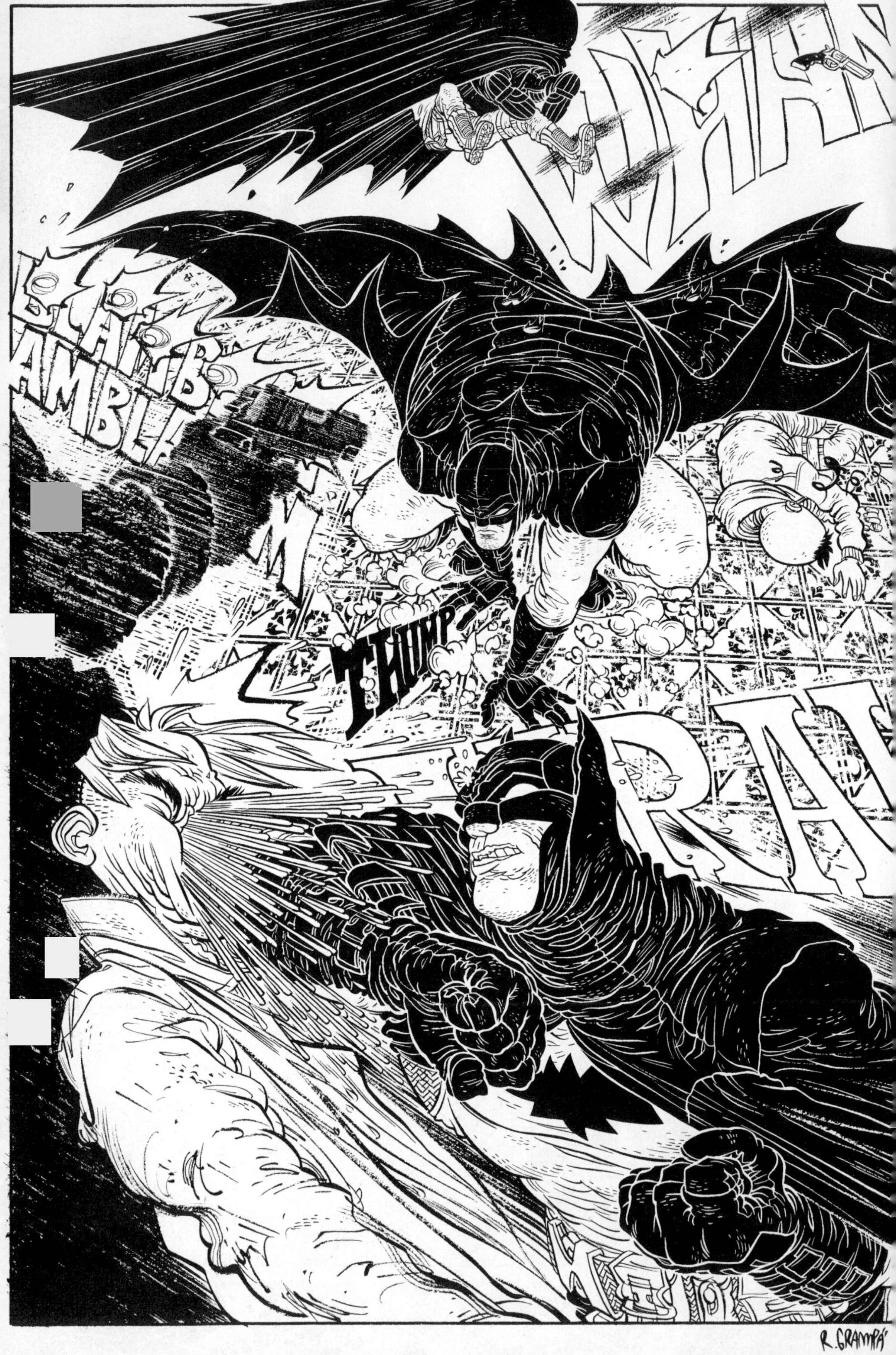
THUMP

R. GRAMPÁ

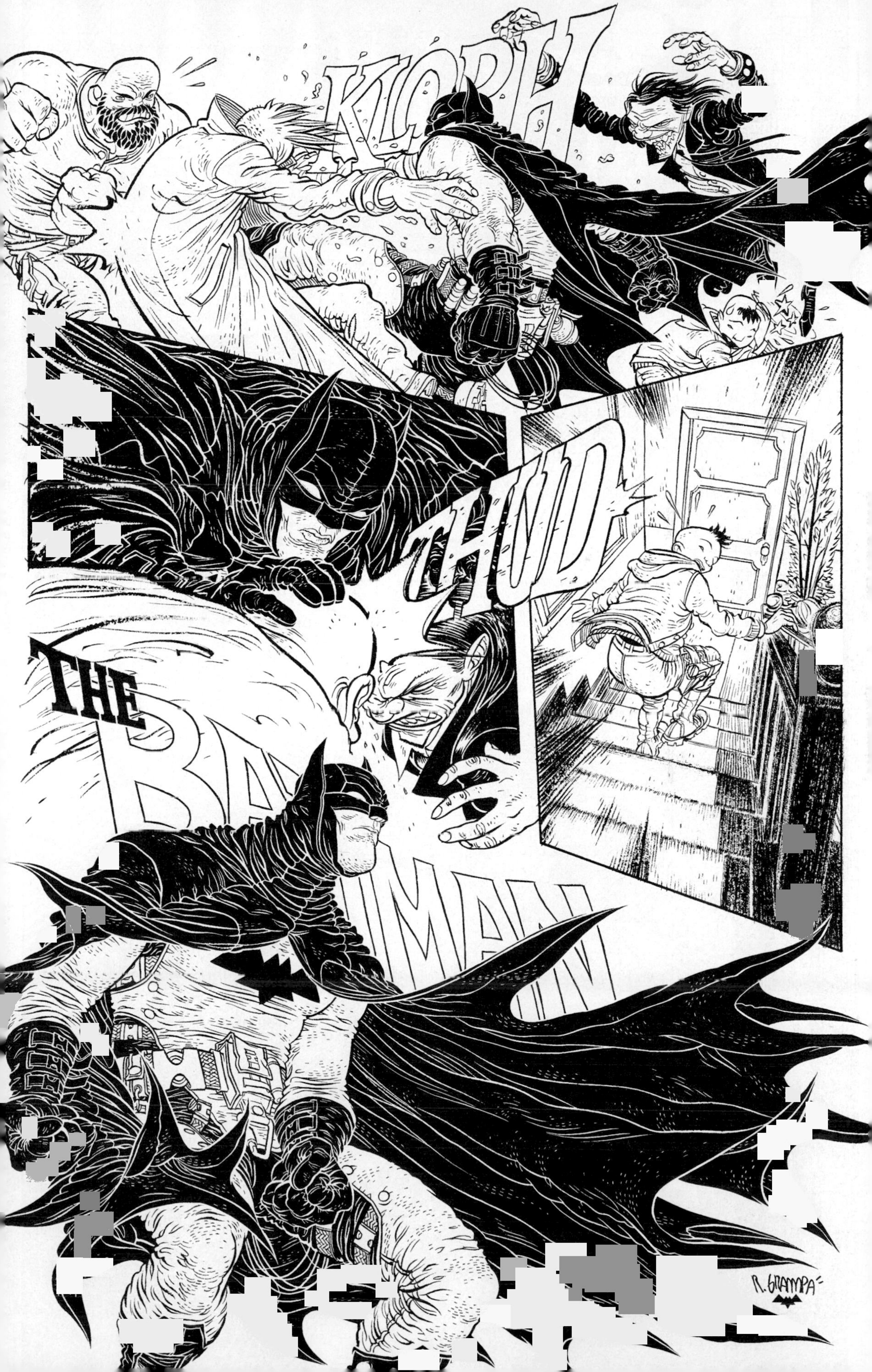
KLORH
THUD
THE BATMAN
R. GRAMPA

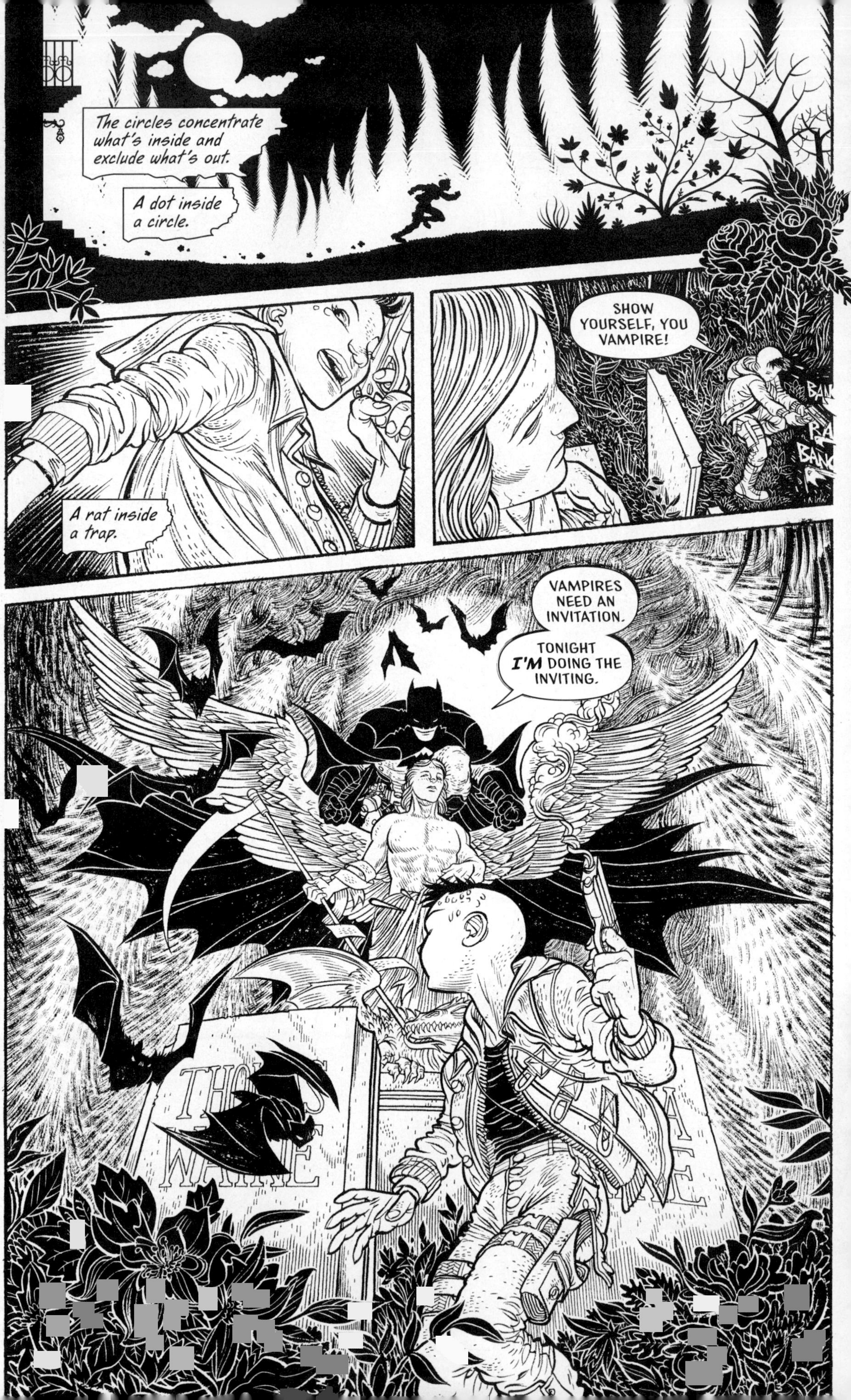
The circles concentrate what's inside and exclude what's out.
A dot inside a circle.
A rat inside a trap.
SHOW YOURSELF, YOU VAMPIRE!
VAMPIRES NEED AN INVITATION.
TONIGHT *I'M* DOING THE INVITING.

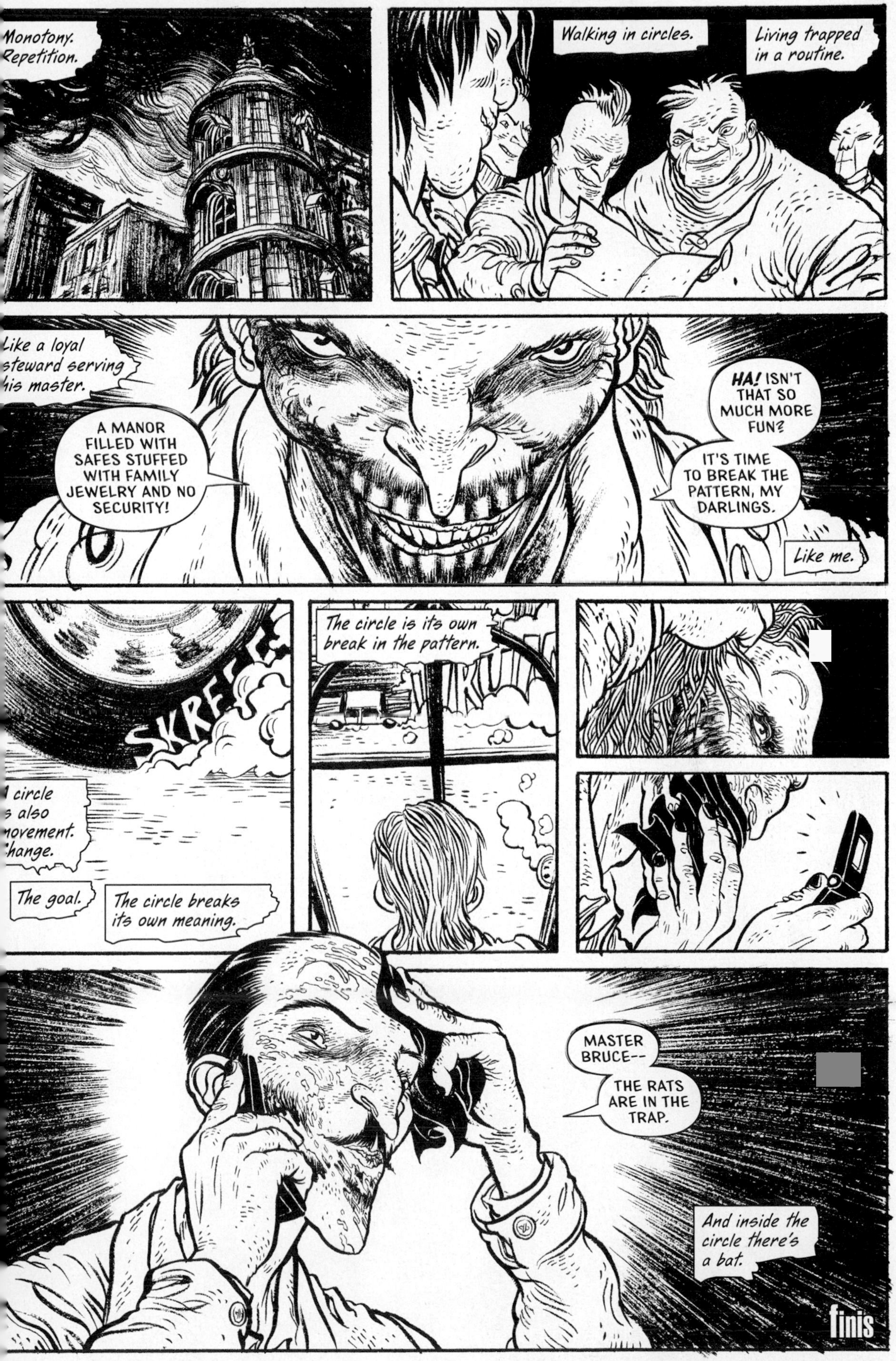
Monotony. Repetition.
Walking in circles.
Living trapped in a routine.
Like a loyal steward serving his master.
A MANOR FILLED WITH SAFES STUFFED WITH FAMILY JEWELRY AND NO SECURITY!
HA! ISN'T THAT SO MUCH MORE FUN?
IT'S TIME TO BREAK THE PATTERN, MY DARLINGS.
Like me.
SKREE
circle s also novement. hange.
The goal.
The circle breaks its own meaning.
The circle is its own break in the pattern.
MASTER BRUCE--
THE RATS ARE IN THE TRAP.
And inside the circle there's a bat.
finis

RAFAEL GRAMPÁ

Brazilian artist and graphic
designer Rafael Grampá is currently taking the
American comics world by storm. As creator of
the graphic novel *Mesmo Delivery*, Grampá
announced his presence as an artist/writer to
keep an eye on. Rafael's work—considered
among the "hippest" in comics—has
been published by DC, Marvel, and
Dark Horse Comics.

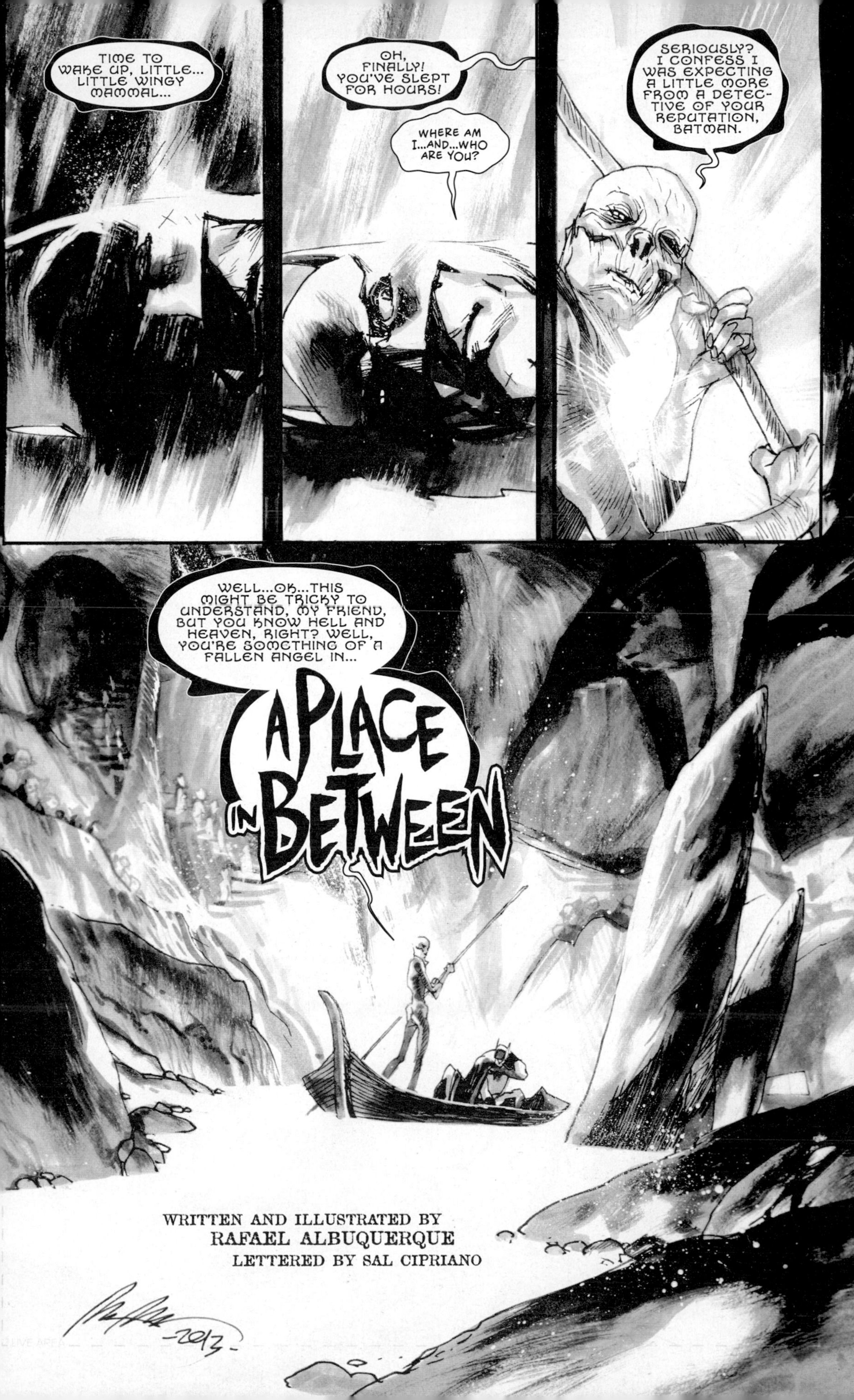
TIME TO WAKE UP, LITTLE... LITTLE WINGY MAMMAL...
OH, FINALLY! YOU'VE SLEPT FOR HOURS!
WHERE AM I...AND...WHO ARE YOU?
SERIOUSLY? I CONFESS I WAS EXPECTING A LITTLE MORE FROM A DETECTIVE OF YOUR REPUTATION, BATMAN.
WELL...OK...THIS MIGHT BE TRICKY TO UNDERSTAND, MY FRIEND, BUT YOU KNOW HELL AND HEAVEN, RIGHT? WELL, YOU'RE SOMETHING OF A FALLEN ANGEL IN...
A PLACE IN BETWEEN
WRITTEN AND ILLUSTRATED BY
RAFAEL ALBUQUERQUE
LETTERED BY SAL CIPRIANO
-2013-

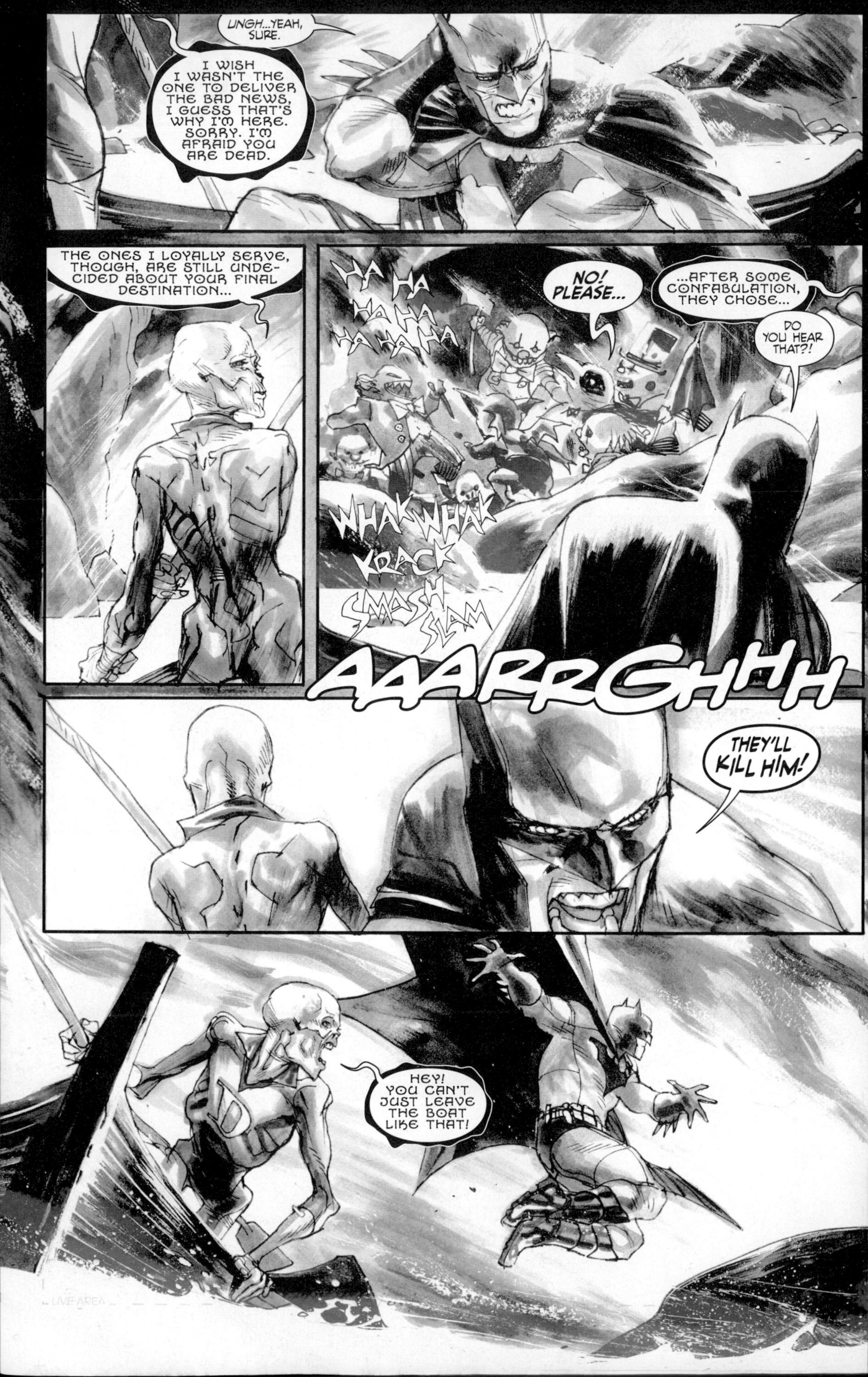
UNGH...YEAH, SURE.
I WISH I WASN'T THE ONE TO DELIVER THE BAD NEWS, I GUESS THAT'S WHY I'M HERE. SORRY. I'M AFRAID YOU ARE DEAD.
THE ONES I LOYALLY SERVE, THOUGH, ARE STILL UNDECIDED ABOUT YOUR FINAL DESTINATION...
HA HA HA HA HA HA HA
NO! PLEASE...
...AFTER SOME CONFABULATION, THEY CHOSE...
DO YOU HEAR THAT?!
WHAK WHAK KRACK SMASH SLAM
AAARRGHHH
THEY'LL KILL HIM!
HEY! YOU CAN'T JUST LEAVE THE BOAT LIKE THAT!

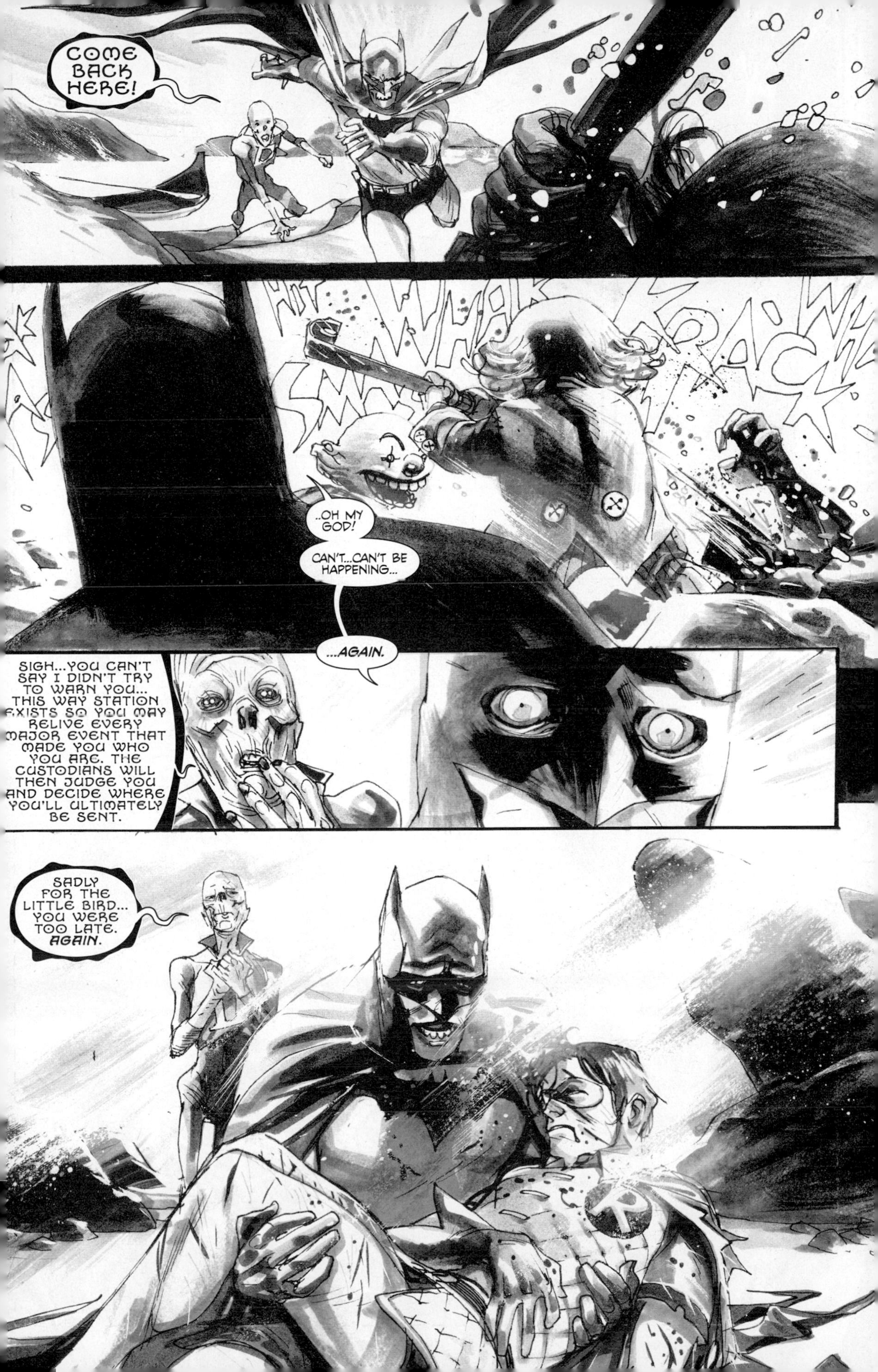
COME BACK HERE!
WHAK
KRACK
..OH MY GOD!
CAN'T...CAN'T BE HAPPENING...
...AGAIN.
SIGH...YOU CAN'T SAY I DIDN'T TRY TO WARN YOU... THIS WAY STATION EXISTS SO YOU MAY RELIVE EVERY MAJOR EVENT THAT MADE YOU WHO YOU ARE. THE CUSTODIANS WILL THEN JUDGE YOU AND DECIDE WHERE YOU'LL ULTIMATELY BE SENT.
SADLY FOR THE LITTLE BIRD... YOU WERE TOO LATE. AGAIN.

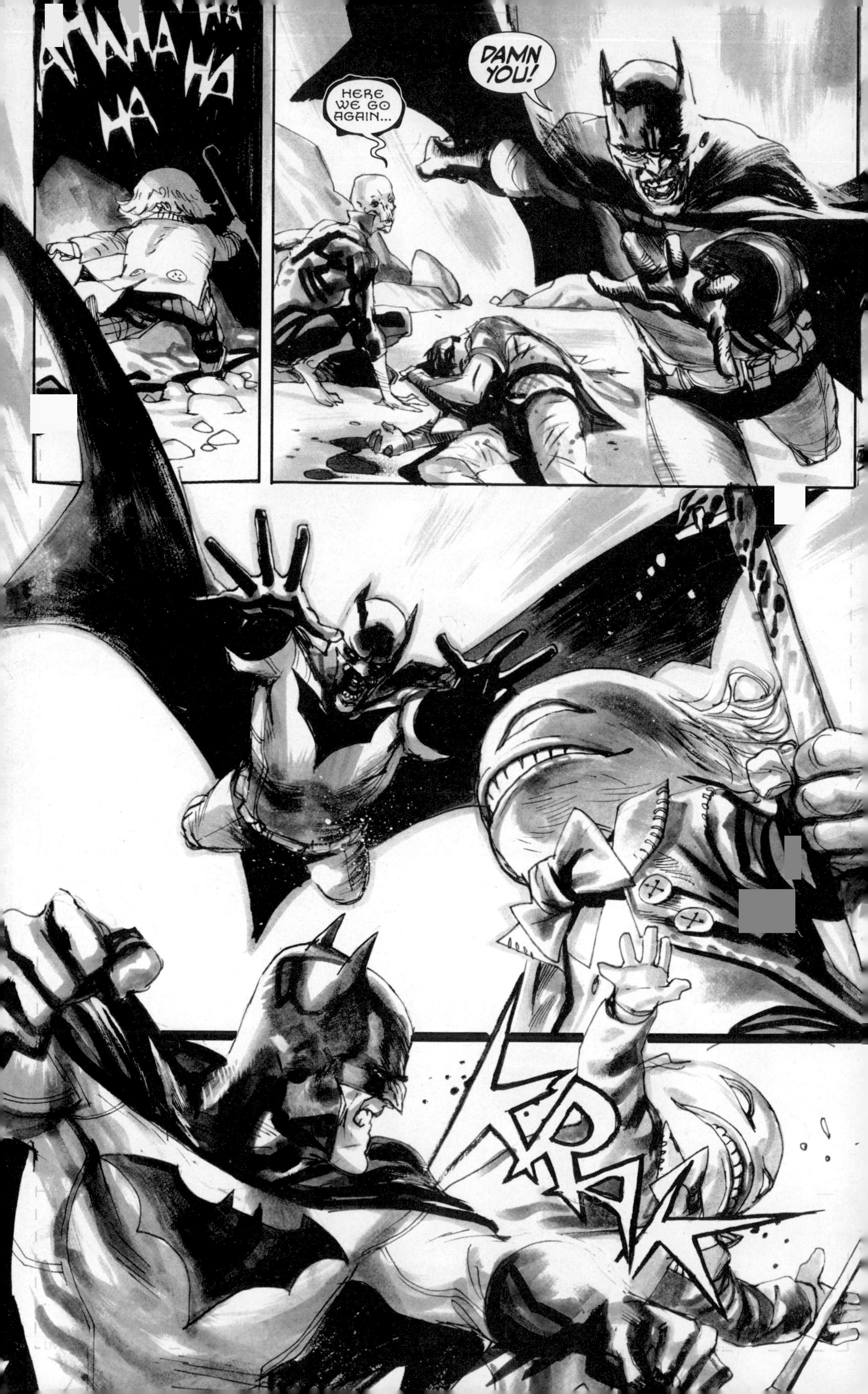
AHAHAHA
HA HA
HERE WE GO AGAIN...
DAMN YOU!
KRAK

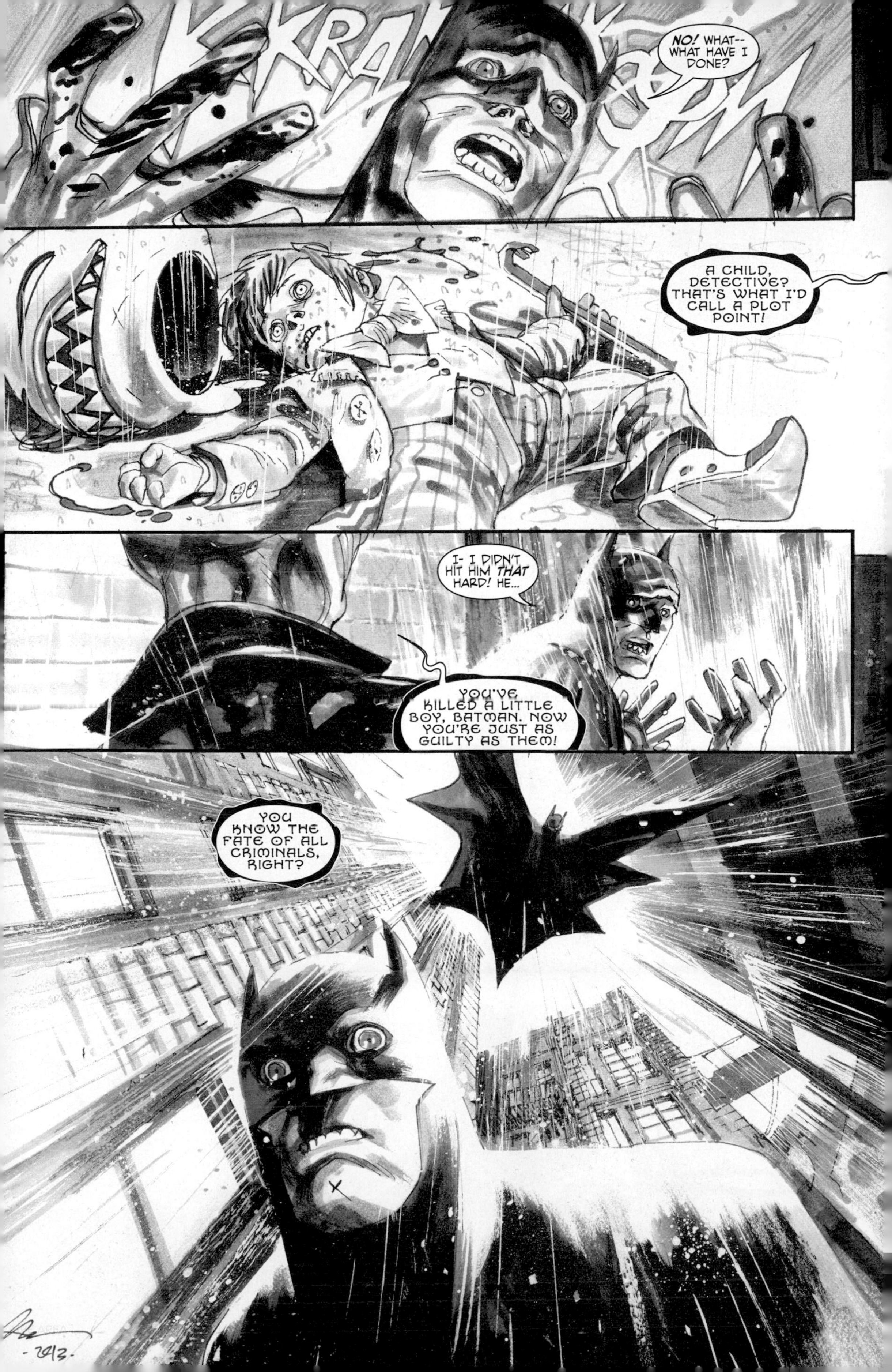
NO! WHAT-- WHAT HAVE I DONE?
A CHILD, DETECTIVE? THAT'S WHAT I'D CALL A PLOT POINT!
I- I DIDN'T HIT HIM THAT HARD! HE...
YOU'VE KILLED A LITTLE BOY, BATMAN. NOW YOU'RE JUST AS GUILTY AS THEM!
YOU KNOW THE FATE OF ALL CRIMINALS, RIGHT?

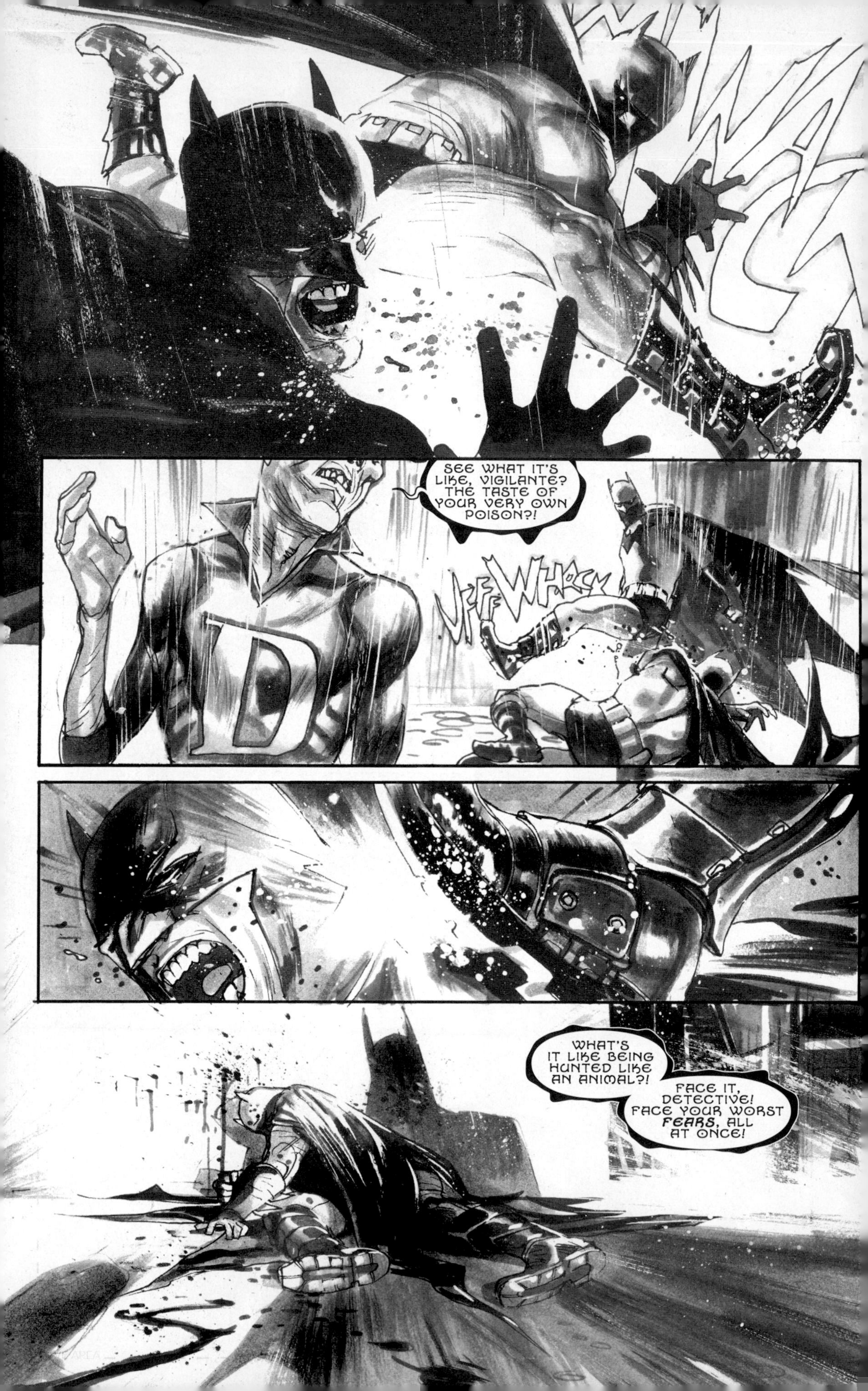
SEE WHAT IT'S LIKE, VIGILANTE? THE TASTE OF YOUR VERY OWN POISON?!
UFF WHACK
WHAT'S IT LIKE BEING HUNTED LIKE AN ANIMAL?!
FACE IT, DETECTIVE! FACE YOUR WORST FEARS, ALL AT ONCE!

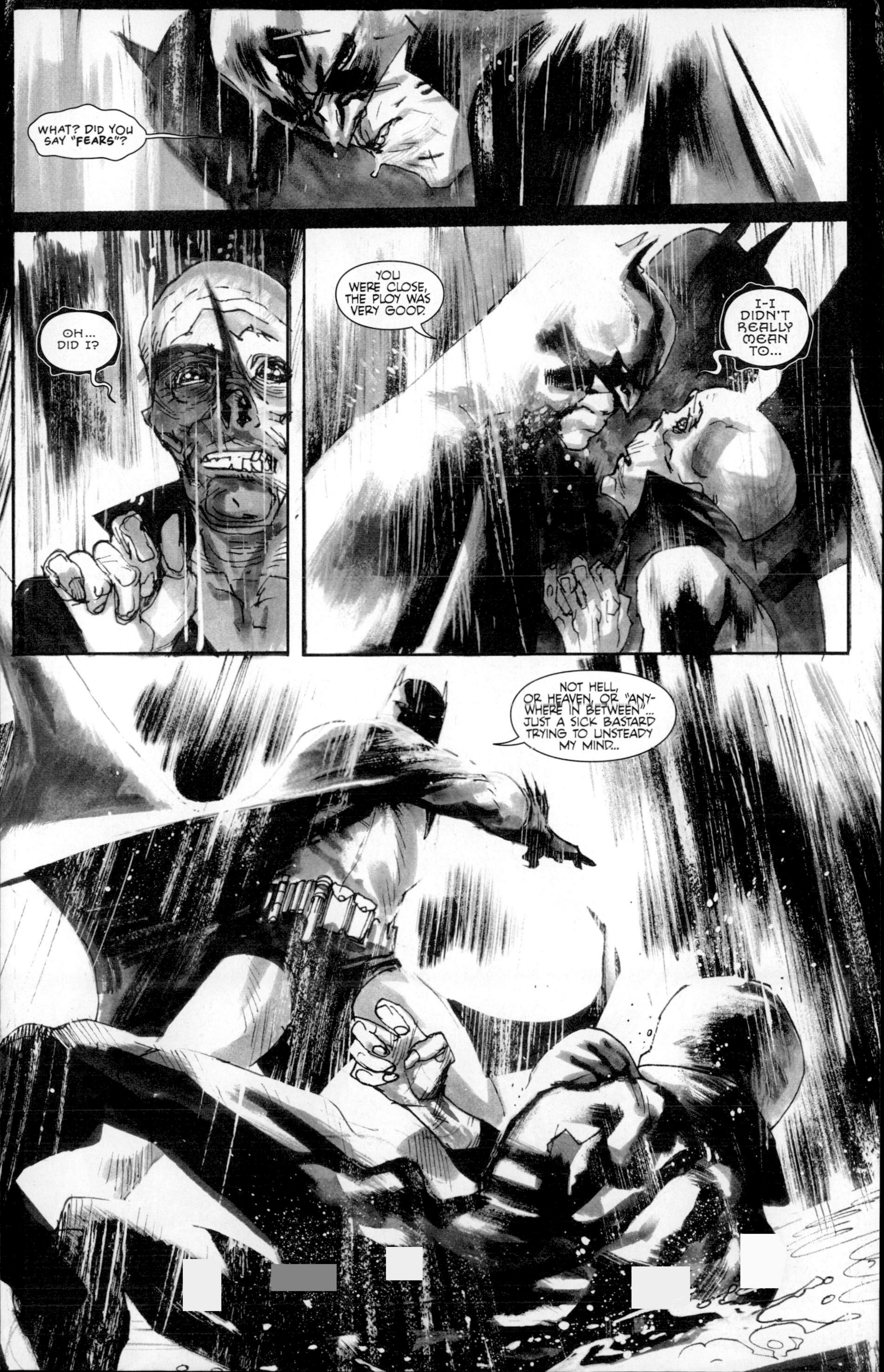
WHAT? DID YOU SAY "FEARS"?
OH... DID I?
YOU WERE CLOSE, THE PLOY WAS VERY GOOD.
I-I DIDN'T REALLY MEAN TO...
NOT HELL, OR HEAVEN, OR "ANY-WHERE IN BETWEEN"... JUST A SICK BASTARD TRYING TO UNSTEADY MY MIND...

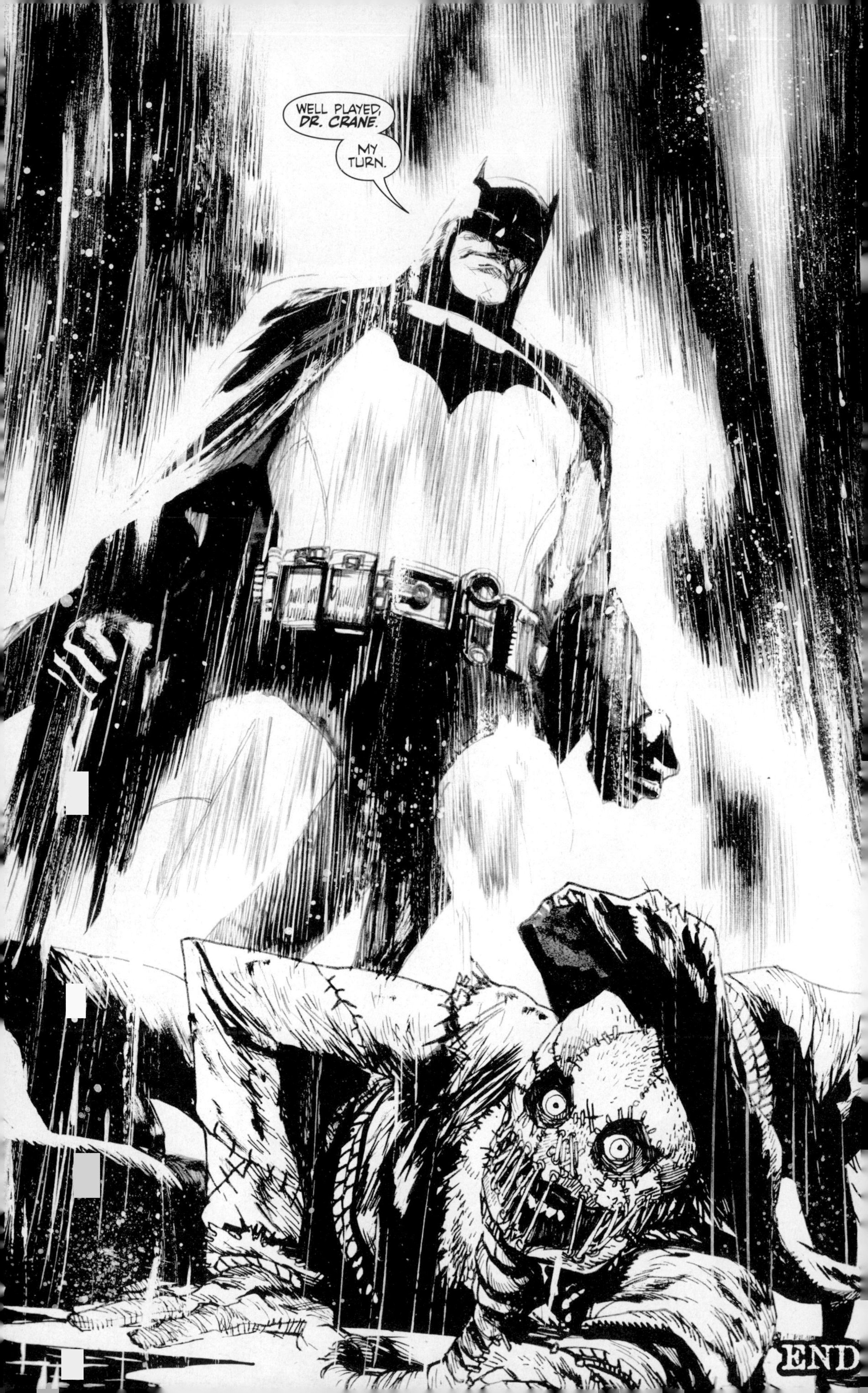
WELL PLAYED, DR. CRANE.
MY TURN.
END

RAFAEL ALBUQUERQUE

As the Eisner and Harvey Award-
winning co-creator of Vertigo's hit series
AMERICAN VAMPIRE, Rafael Albuquerque
has brought a bold new look to comic art.
A storyteller of compelling ability and range,
Albuquerque is at home drawing super heroes,
horror, romance, and crime stories.

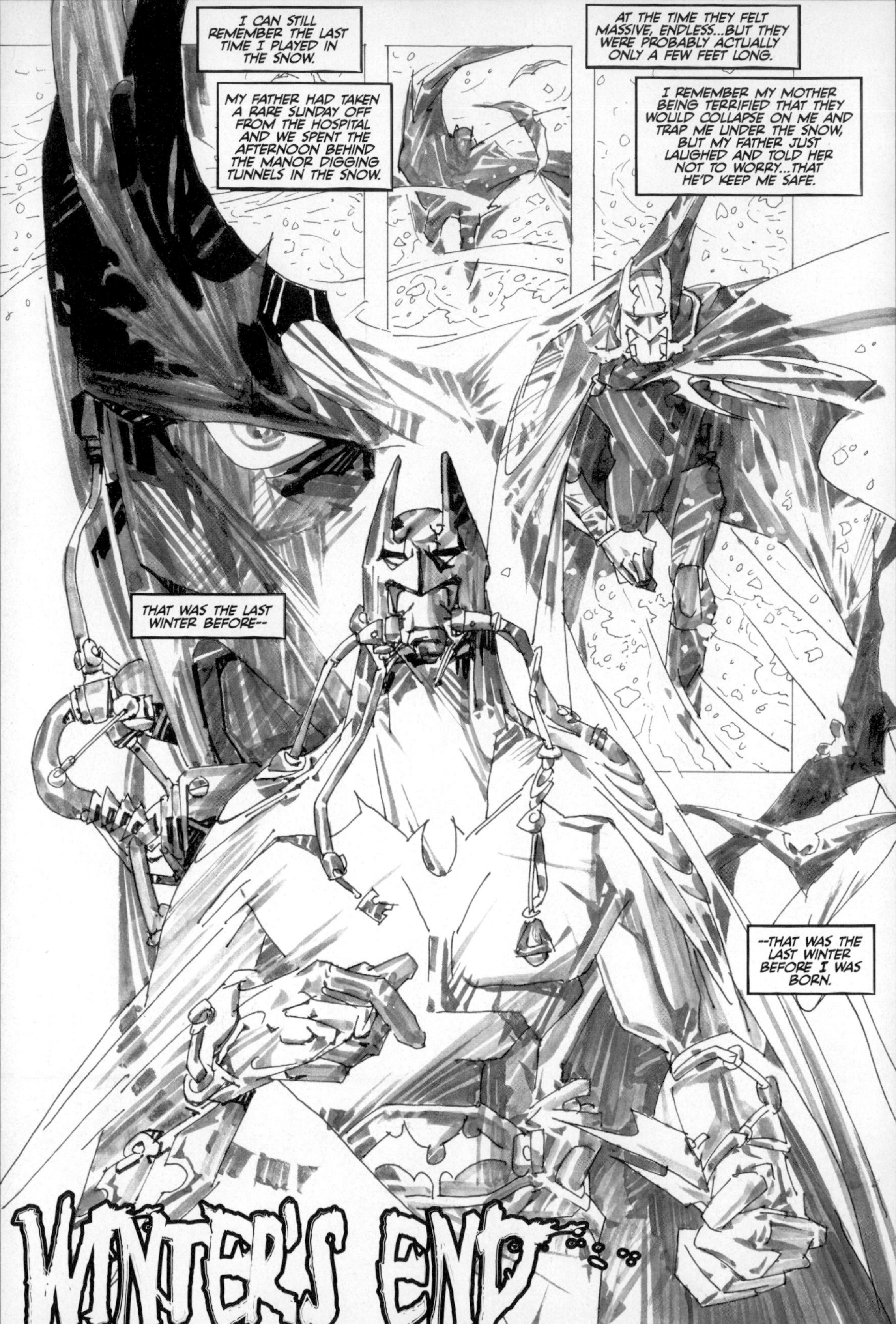

I CAN STILL REMEMBER THE LAST TIME I PLAYED IN THE SNOW.
MY FATHER HAD TAKEN A RARE SUNDAY OFF FROM THE HOSPITAL AND WE SPENT THE AFTERNOON BEHIND THE MANOR DIGGING TUNNELS IN THE SNOW.
AT THE TIME THEY FELT MASSIVE, ENDLESS...BUT THEY WERE PROBABLY ACTUALLY ONLY A FEW FEET LONG.
I REMEMBER MY MOTHER BEING TERRIFIED THAT THEY WOULD COLLAPSE ON ME AND TRAP ME UNDER THE SNOW, BUT MY FATHER JUST LAUGHED AND TOLD HER NOT TO WORRY...THAT HE'D KEEP ME SAFE.
THAT WAS THE LAST WINTER BEFORE--
--THAT WAS THE LAST WINTER BEFORE I WAS BORN.
WINTER'S END

Written by JEFF LEMIRE Illustrated by ALEX NINO Lettered by DEZI SIENTY

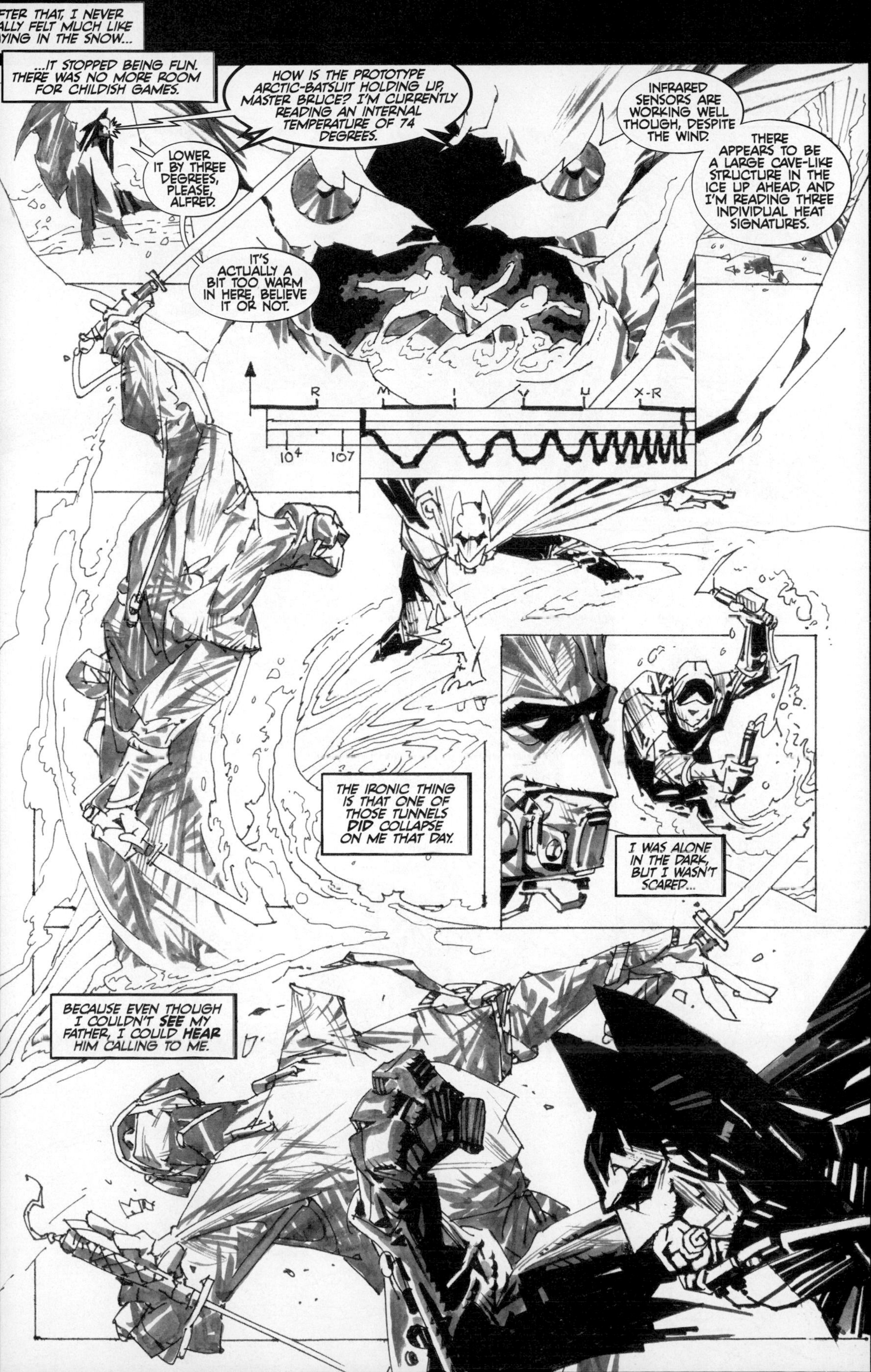
FTER THAT, I NEVER
ALLY FELT MUCH LIKE
YING IN THE SNOW...
...IT STOPPED BEING FUN. THERE WAS NO MORE ROOM FOR CHILDISH GAMES.
HOW IS THE PROTOTYPE ARCTIC-BATSUIT HOLDING UP, MASTER BRUCE? I'M CURRENTLY READING AN INTERNAL TEMPERATURE OF 74 DEGREES.
LOWER IT BY THREE DEGREES, PLEASE, ALFRED.
IT'S ACTUALLY A BIT TOO WARM IN HERE, BELIEVE IT OR NOT.
INFRARED SENSORS ARE WORKING WELL THOUGH, DESPITE THE WIND.
THERE APPEARS TO BE A LARGE CAVE-LIKE STRUCTURE IN THE ICE UP AHEAD, AND I'M READING THREE INDIVIDUAL HEAT SIGNATURES.
R M I Y U X-R
104 107
THE IRONIC THING IS THAT ONE OF THOSE TUNNELS DID COLLAPSE ON ME THAT DAY.
I WAS ALONE IN THE DARK, BUT I WASN'T SCARED...
BECAUSE EVEN THOUGH I COULDN'T SEE MY FATHER, I COULD HEAR HIM CALLING TO ME.

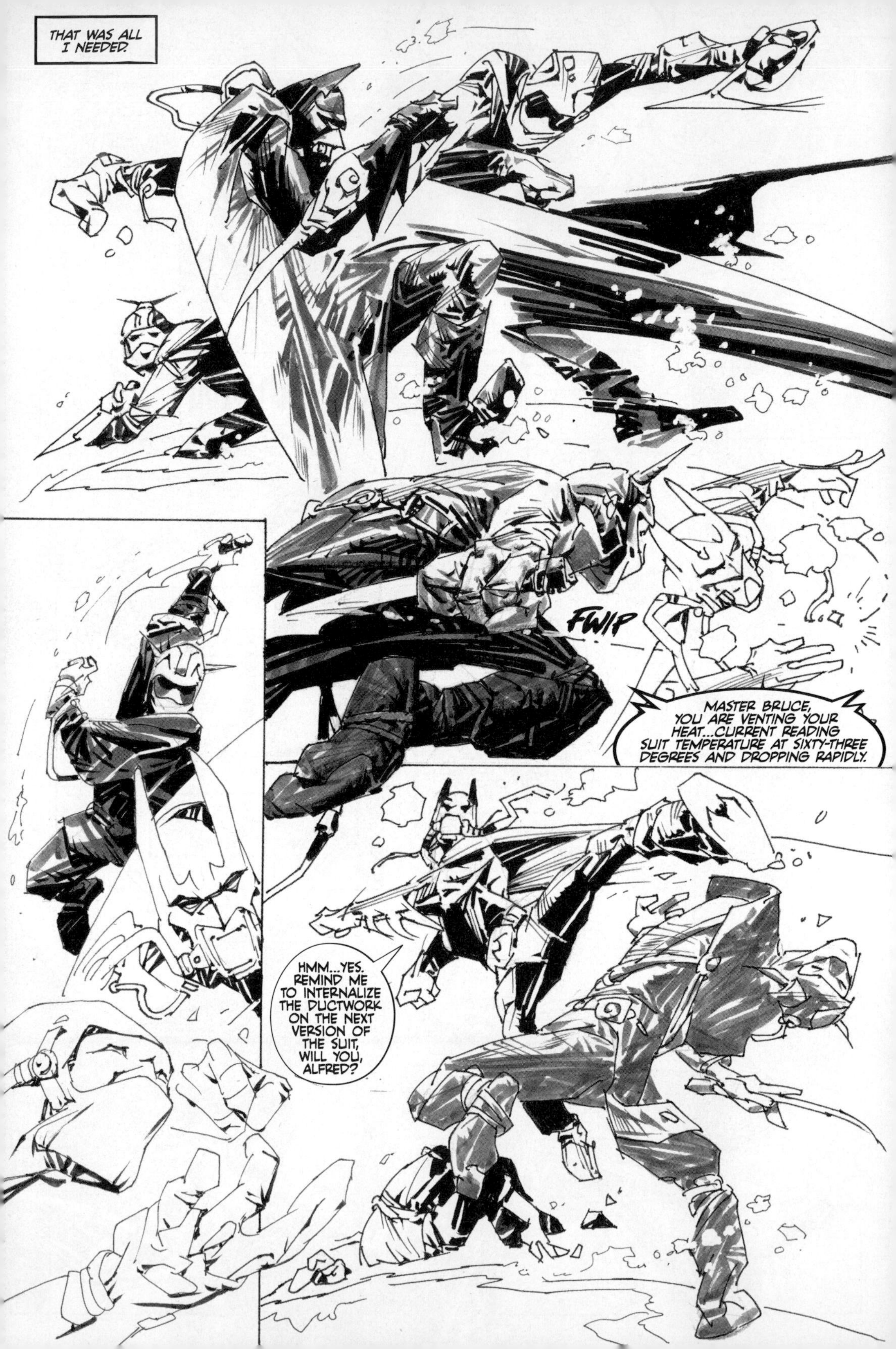
THAT WAS ALL I NEEDED.
FWIP
MASTER BRUCE, YOU ARE VENTING YOUR HEAT...CURRENT READING SUIT TEMPERATURE AT SIXTY-THREE DEGREES AND DROPPING RAPIDLY.
HMM...YES. REMIND ME TO INTERNALIZE THE DUCTWORK ON THE NEXT VERSION OF THE SUIT, WILL YOU, ALFRED?

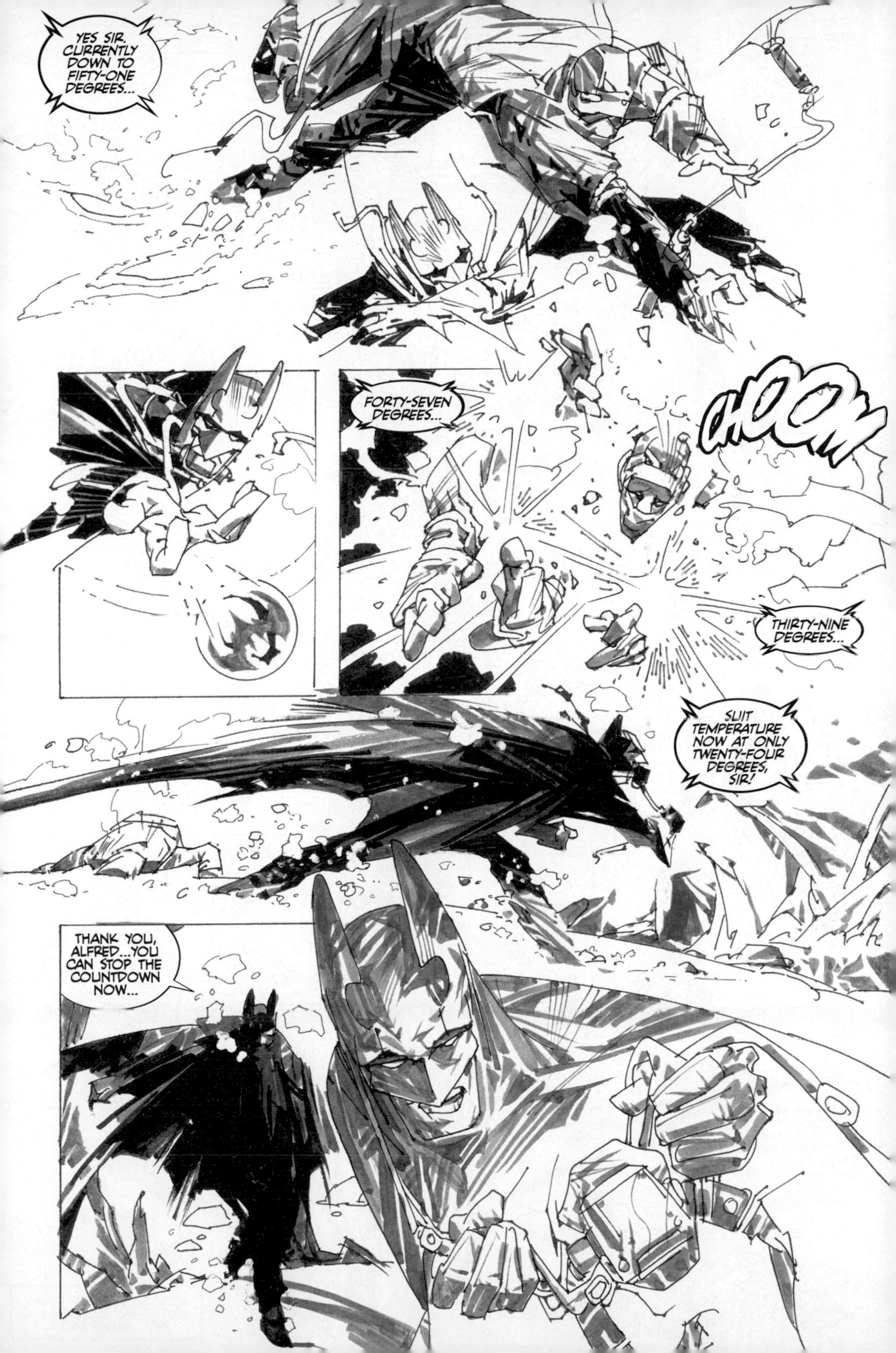
YES SIR. CURRENTLY DOWN TO FIFTY-ONE DEGREES...
FORTY-SEVEN DEGREES...
CHOOM
THIRTY-NINE DEGREES...
SUIT TEMPERATURE NOW AT ONLY TWENTY-FOUR DEGREES, SIR!
THANK YOU, ALFRED...YOU CAN STOP THE COUNTDOWN NOW...

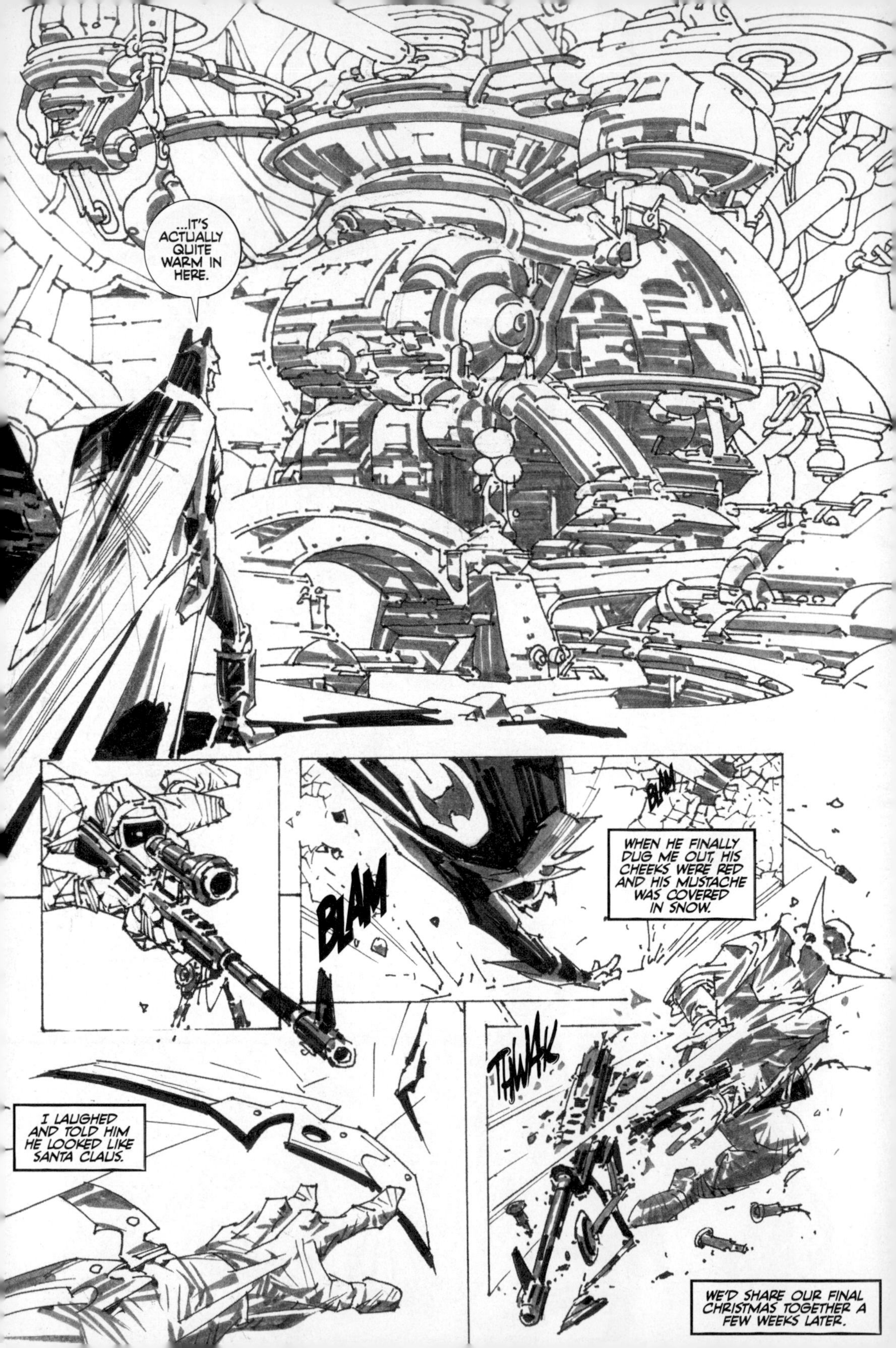
...IT'S ACTUALLY QUITE WARM IN HERE.
BLAM
WHEN HE FINALLY DUG ME OUT, HIS CHEEKS WERE RED AND HIS MUSTACHE WAS COVERED IN SNOW.
BLAM
I LAUGHED AND TOLD HIM HE LOOKED LIKE SANTA CLAUS.
THWAK
WE'D SHARE OUR FINAL CHRISTMAS TOGETHER A FEW WEEKS LATER.

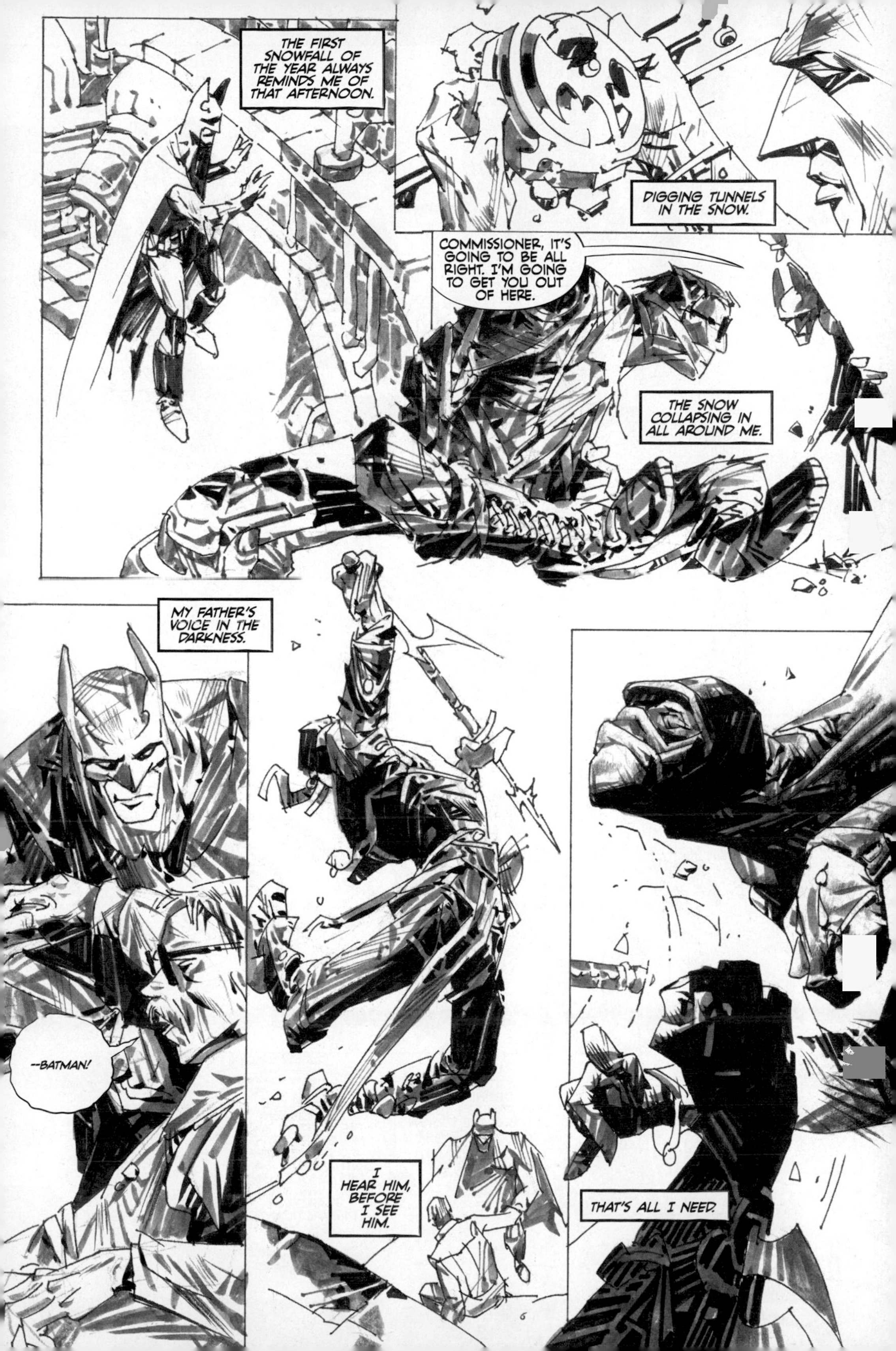
THE FIRST SNOWFALL OF THE YEAR ALWAYS REMINDS ME OF THAT AFTERNOON.
DIGGING TUNNELS IN THE SNOW.
COMMISSIONER, IT'S GOING TO BE ALL RIGHT. I'M GOING TO GET YOU OUT OF HERE.
THE SNOW COLLAPSING IN ALL AROUND ME.
MY FATHER'S VOICE IN THE DARKNESS.
--BATMAN!
I HEAR HIM, BEFORE I SEE HIM.
THAT'S ALL I NEED.

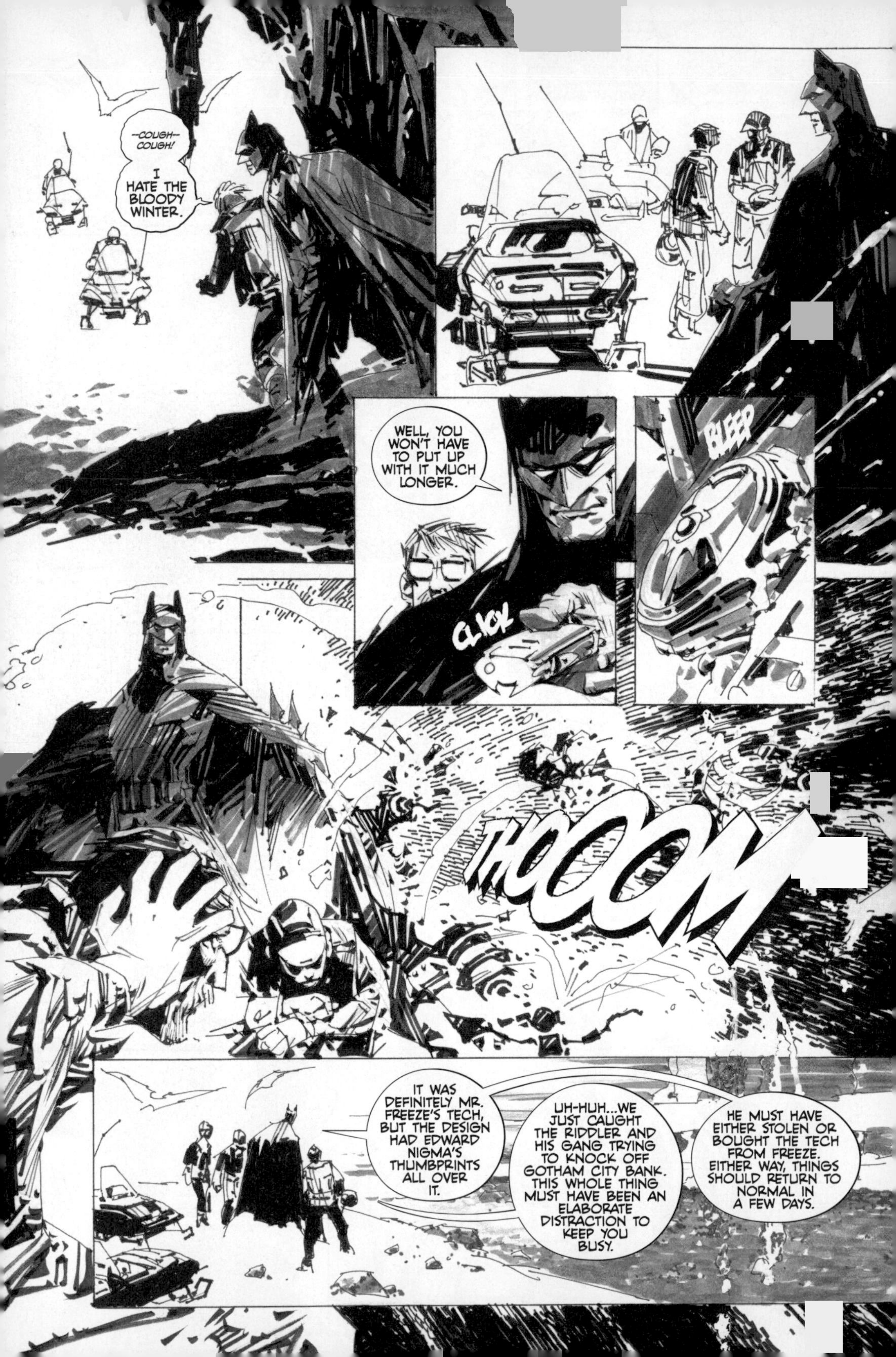

—COUGH— COUGH!
I HATE THE BLOODY WINTER.
WELL, YOU WON'T HAVE TO PUT UP WITH IT MUCH LONGER.
CLICK
BLEEP
THOOOM
IT WAS DEFINITELY MR. FREEZE'S TECH, BUT THE DESIGN HAD EDWARD NIGMA'S THUMBPRINTS ALL OVER IT.
UH-HUH...WE JUST CAUGHT THE RIDDLER AND HIS GANG TRYING TO KNOCK OFF GOTHAM CITY BANK. THIS WHOLE THING MUST HAVE BEEN AN ELABORATE DISTRACTION TO KEEP YOU BUSY.
HE MUST HAVE EITHER STOLEN OR BOUGHT THE TECH FROM FREEZE. EITHER WAY, THINGS SHOULD RETURN TO NORMAL IN A FEW DAYS.

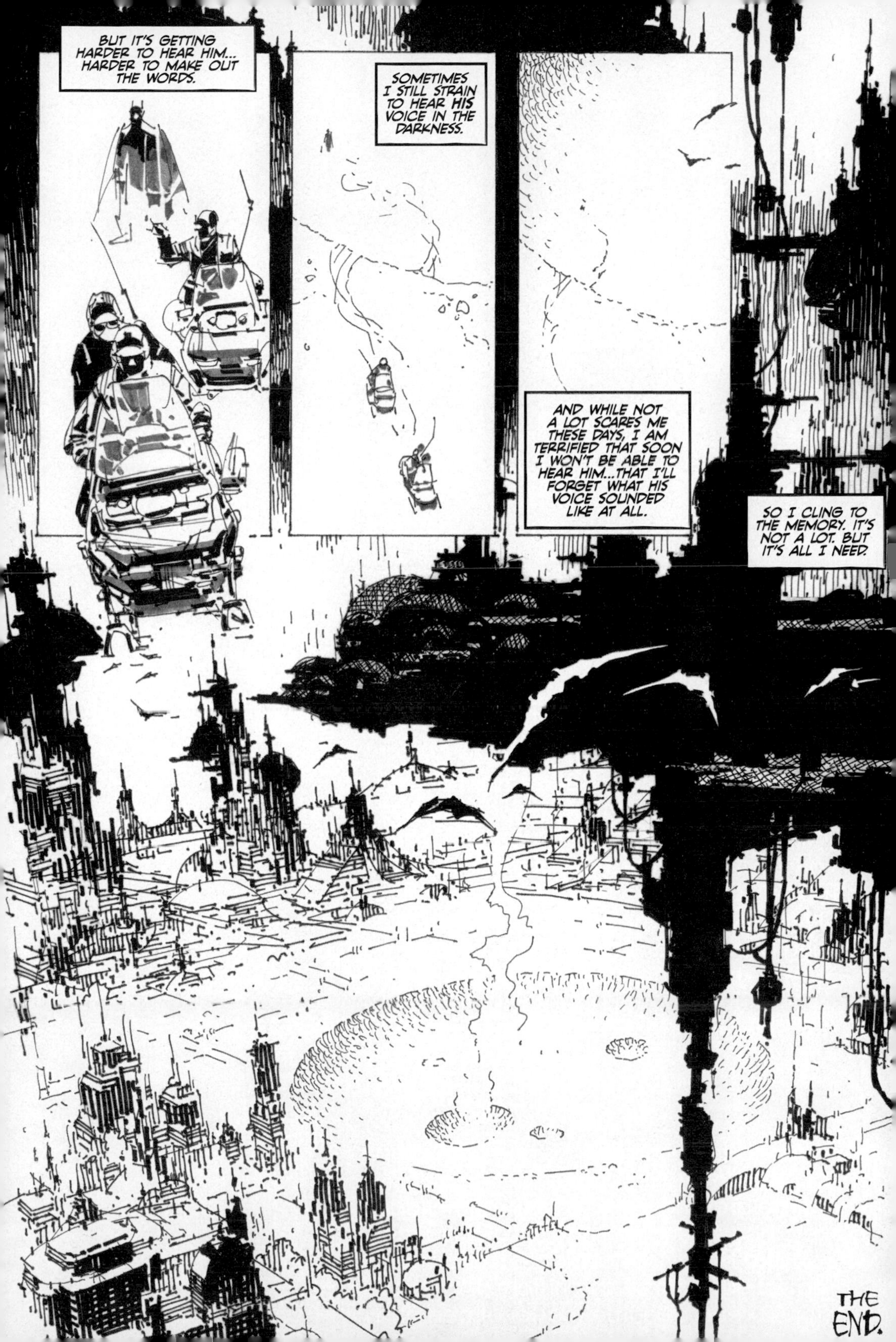
BUT IT'S GETTING HARDER TO HEAR HIM... HARDER TO MAKE OUT THE WORDS.
SOMETIMES I STILL STRAIN TO HEAR HIS VOICE IN THE DARKNESS.
AND WHILE NOT A LOT SCARES ME THESE DAYS, I AM TERRIFIED THAT SOON I WON'T BE ABLE TO HEAR HIM...THAT I'LL FORGET WHAT HIS VOICE SOUNDED LIKE AT ALL.
SO I CLING TO THE MEMORY. IT'S NOT A LOT. BUT IT'S ALL I NEED.
THE END.

JEFF LEMIRE

Canadian-born writer/artist Jeff Lemire brings a
startlingly fresh perspective to American comics.
His haunting *Essex County* trilogy garnered rave
reviews and led to the creation of SWEET TOOTH
and THE NOBODY for Vertigo Comics. Lemire's
ability to create brooding atmosphere while
maintaining a worldly and very human narrative
has cemented him as one of the
top creators in the field.

ALEX NINO

Alex Nino started his career as one of the top
comics artists in the Philippines, but he quickly
moved on to drawing comics for the American
market. His astounding work for DC, Warren,
Marvel, and Heavy Metal places him among
the greatest illustrators in the history of comics.
After 50 years as a true master of pen and
brush, Alex Nino remains one of the most
influential designers, stylists, and
storytellers in comics.

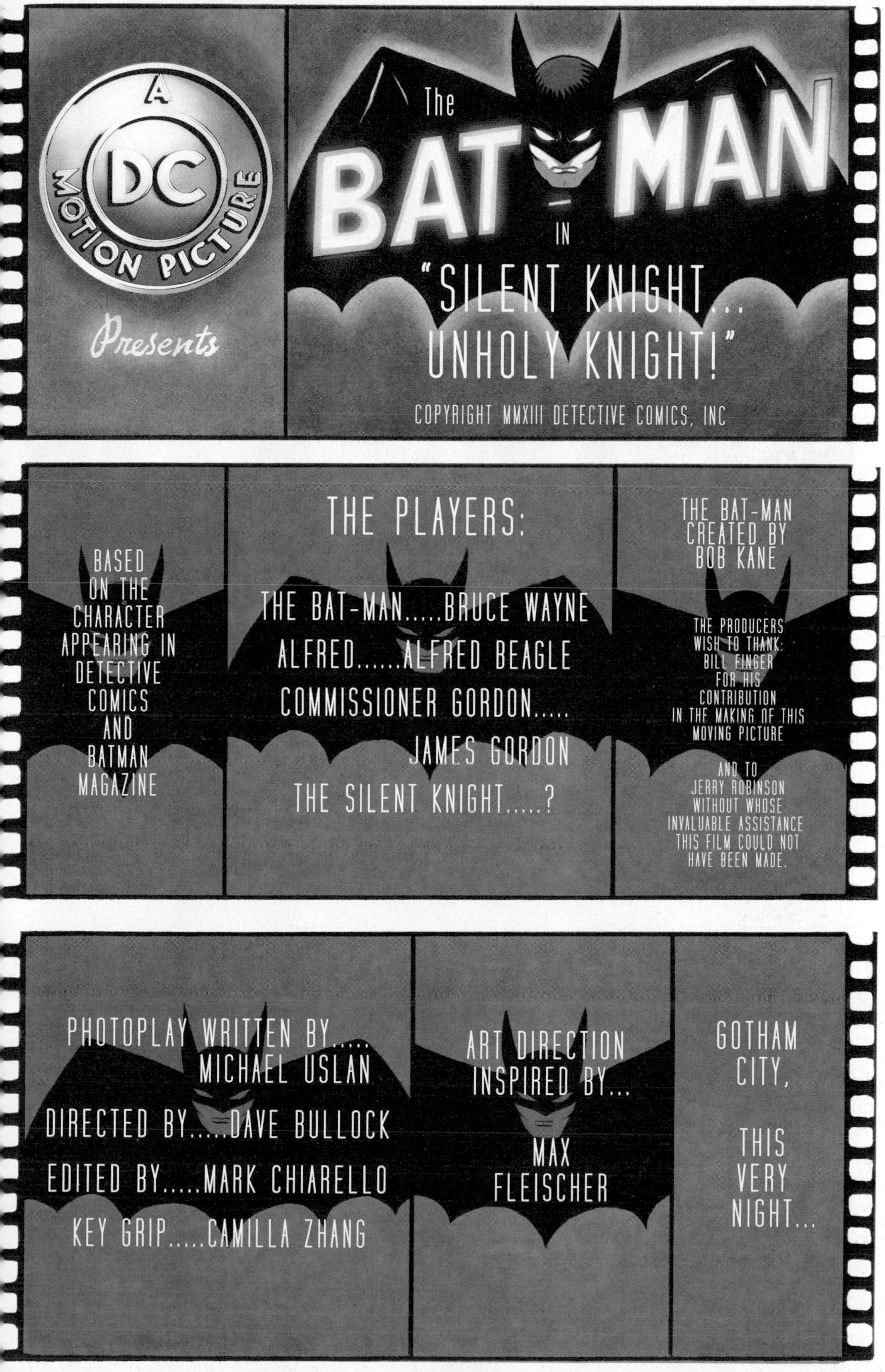
A DC MOTION PICTURE
Presents
The BAT-MAN
IN
"SILENT KNIGHT... UNHOLY KNIGHT!"
COPYRIGHT MMXIII DETECTIVE COMICS, INC
BASED ON THE CHARACTER APPEARING IN DETECTIVE COMICS AND BATMAN MAGAZINE
THE PLAYERS:
THE BAT-MAN.....BRUCE WAYNE
ALFRED......ALFRED BEAGLE
COMMISSIONER GORDON..... JAMES GORDON
THE SILENT KNIGHT.....?
THE BAT-MAN CREATED BY BOB KANE
THE PRODUCERS WISH TO THANK: BILL FINGER FOR HIS CONTRIBUTION IN THE MAKING OF THIS MOVING PICTURE
AND TO JERRY ROBINSON WITHOUT WHOSE INVALUABLE ASSISTANCE THIS FILM COULD NOT HAVE BEEN MADE.
PHOTOPLAY WRITTEN BY..... MICHAEL USLAN
DIRECTED BY.....DAVE BULLOCK
EDITED BY.....MARK CHIARELLO
KEY GRIP.....CAMILLA ZHANG
ART DIRECTION INSPIRED BY... MAX FLEISCHER
GOTHAM CITY,
THIS VERY NIGHT...

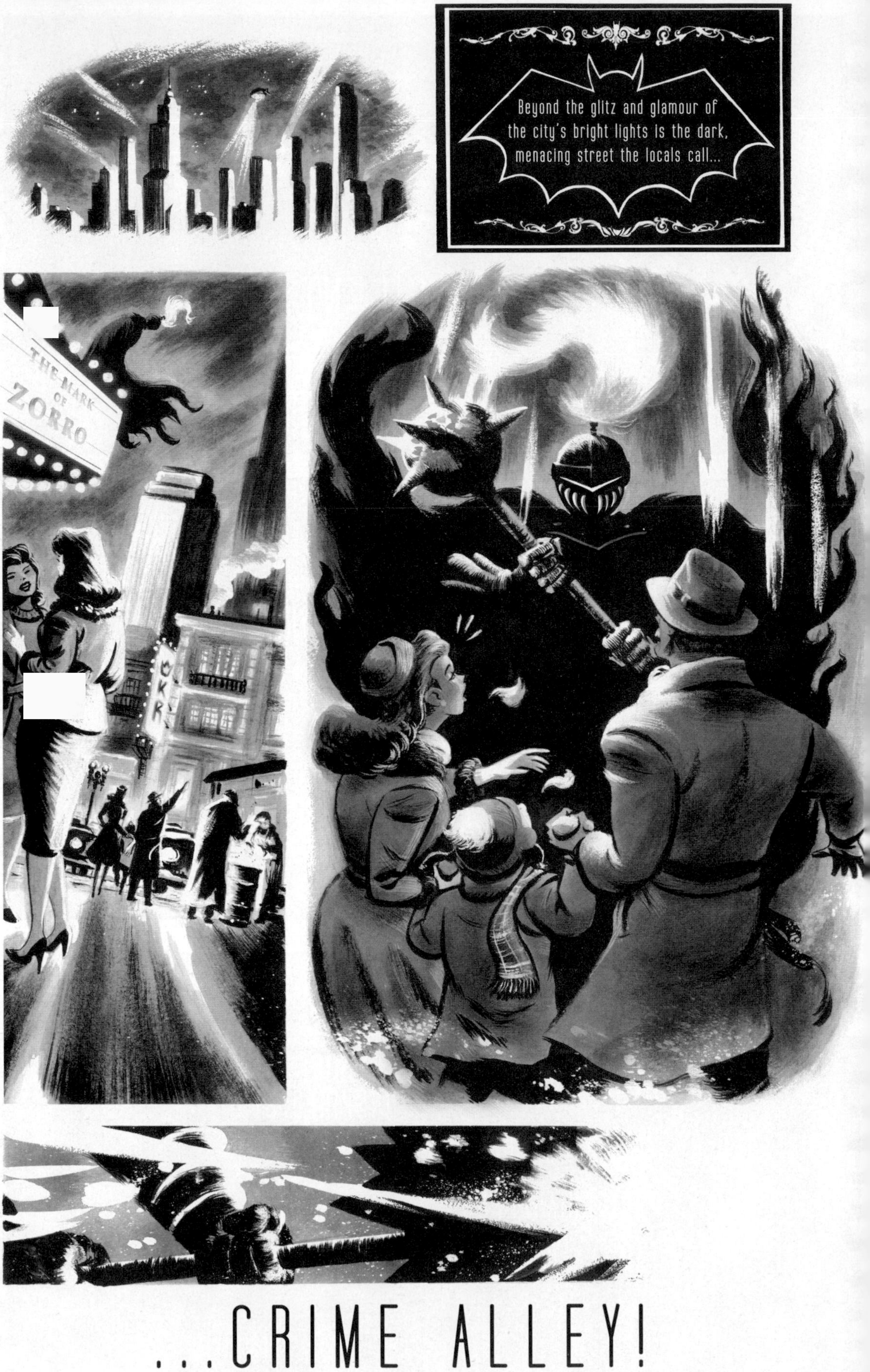
Beyond the glitz and glamour of the city's bright lights is the dark, menacing street the locals call...
THE MARK OF ZORRO
...CRIME ALLEY!

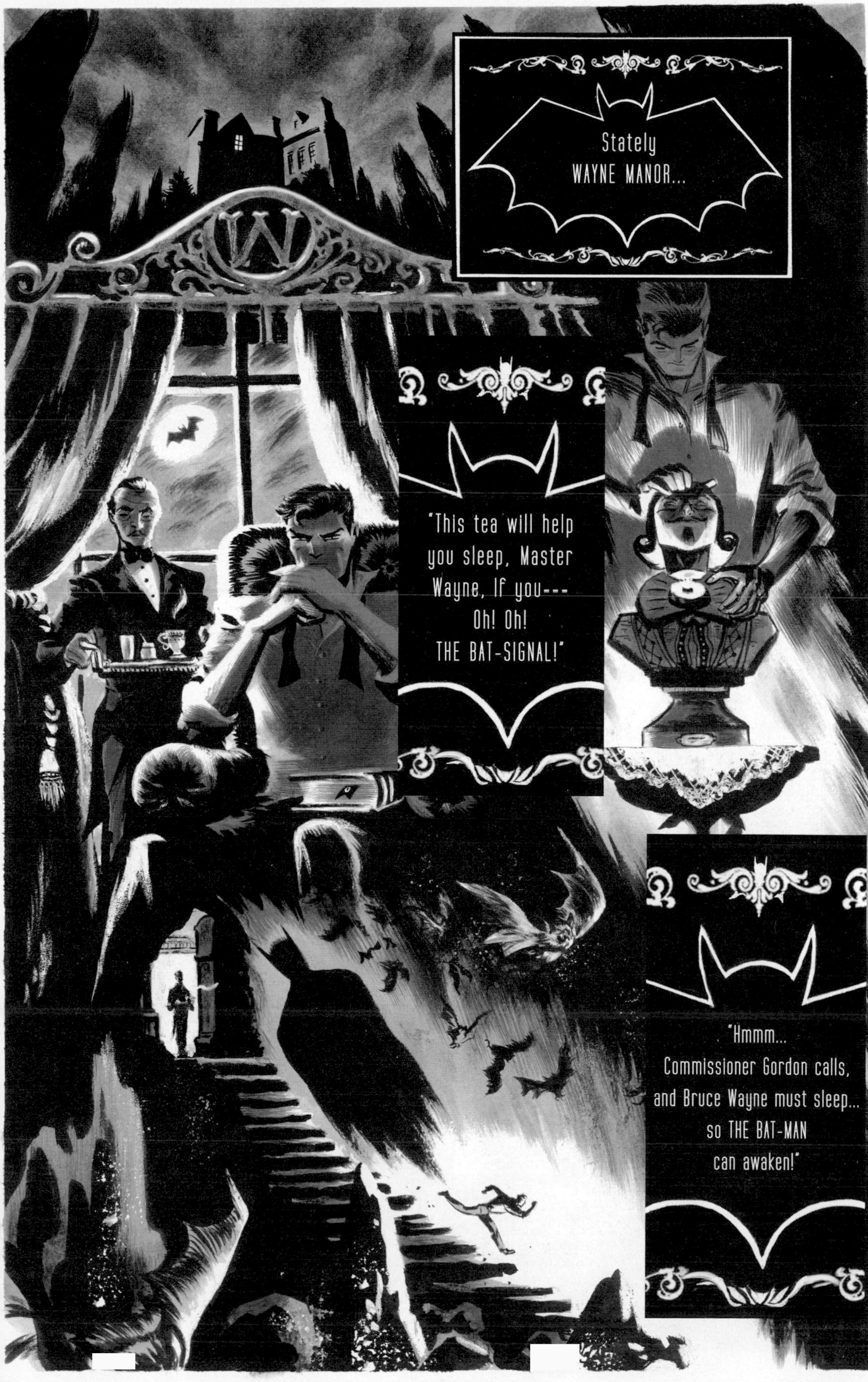
Stately WAYNE MANOR...
"This tea will help you sleep, Master Wayne, If you--- Oh! Oh! THE BAT-SIGNAL!"
"Hmmm... Commissioner Gordon calls, and Bruce Wayne must sleep... so THE BAT-MAN can awaken!"

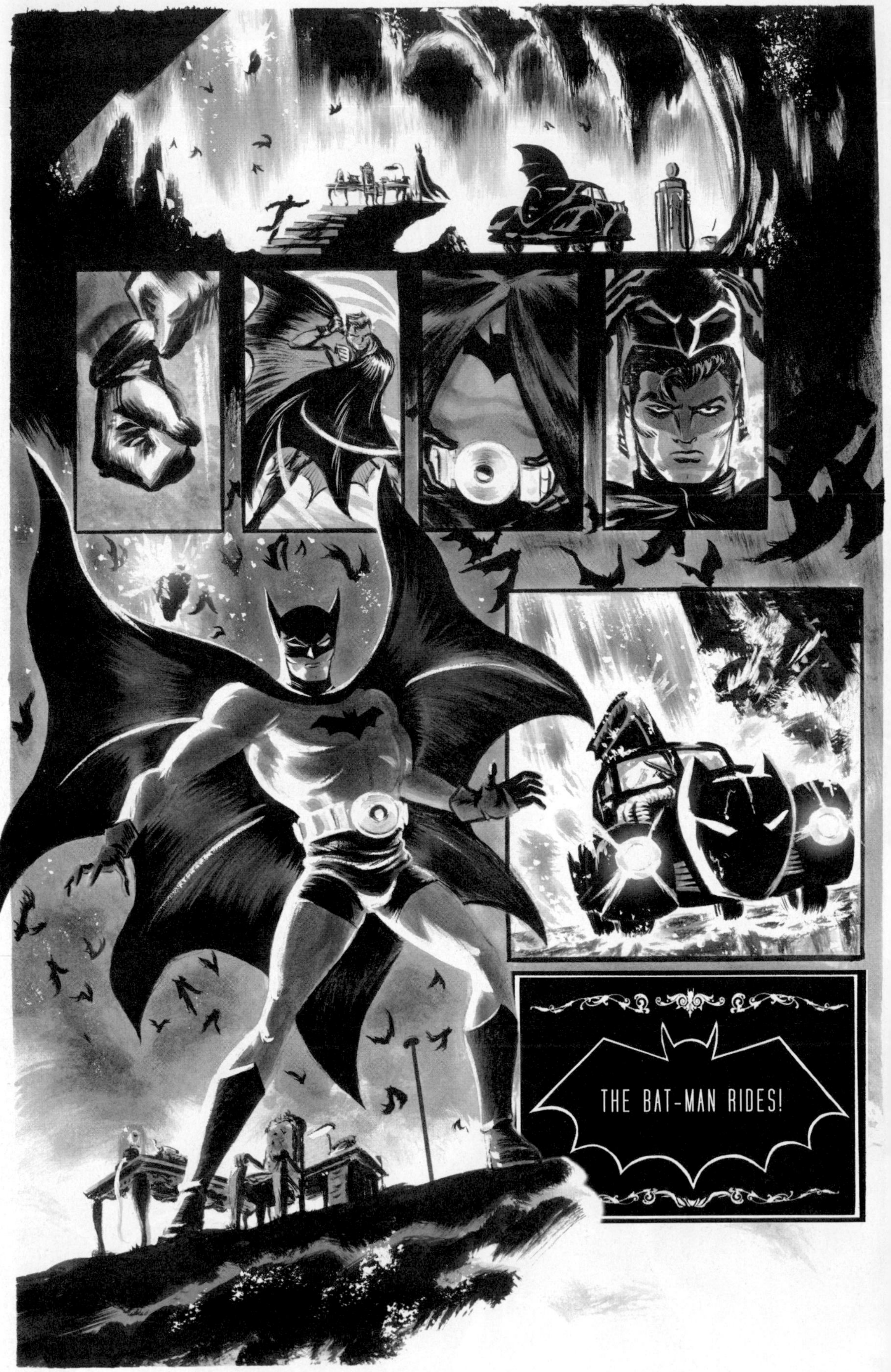
THE BAT-MAN RIDES!

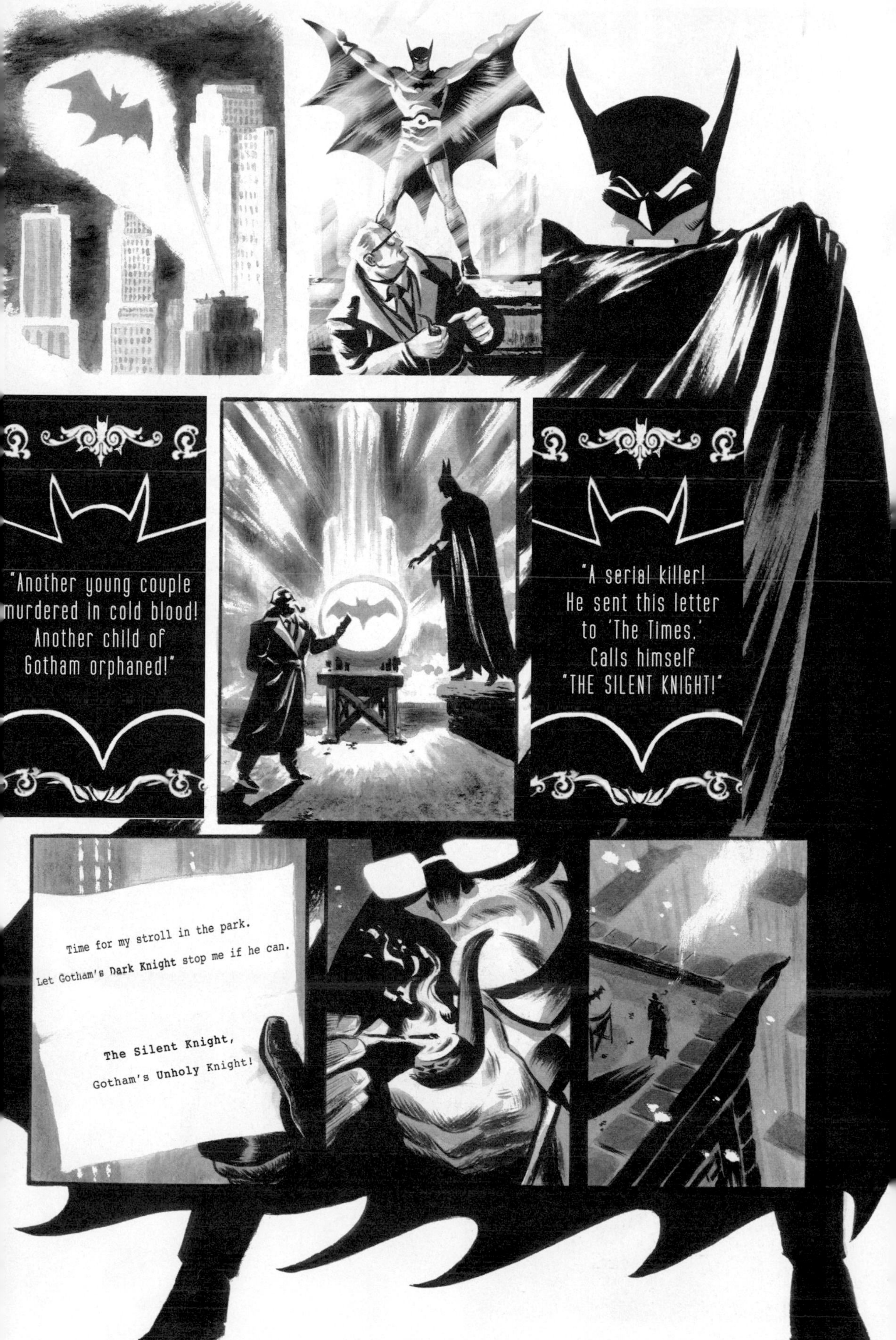
"Another young couple murdered in cold blood! Another child of Gotham orphaned!"
"A serial killer! He sent this letter to 'The Times.' Calls himself "THE SILENT KNIGHT!"
Time for my stroll in the park.
Let Gotham's Dark Knight stop me if he can.
The Silent Knight,
Gotham's Unholy Knight!

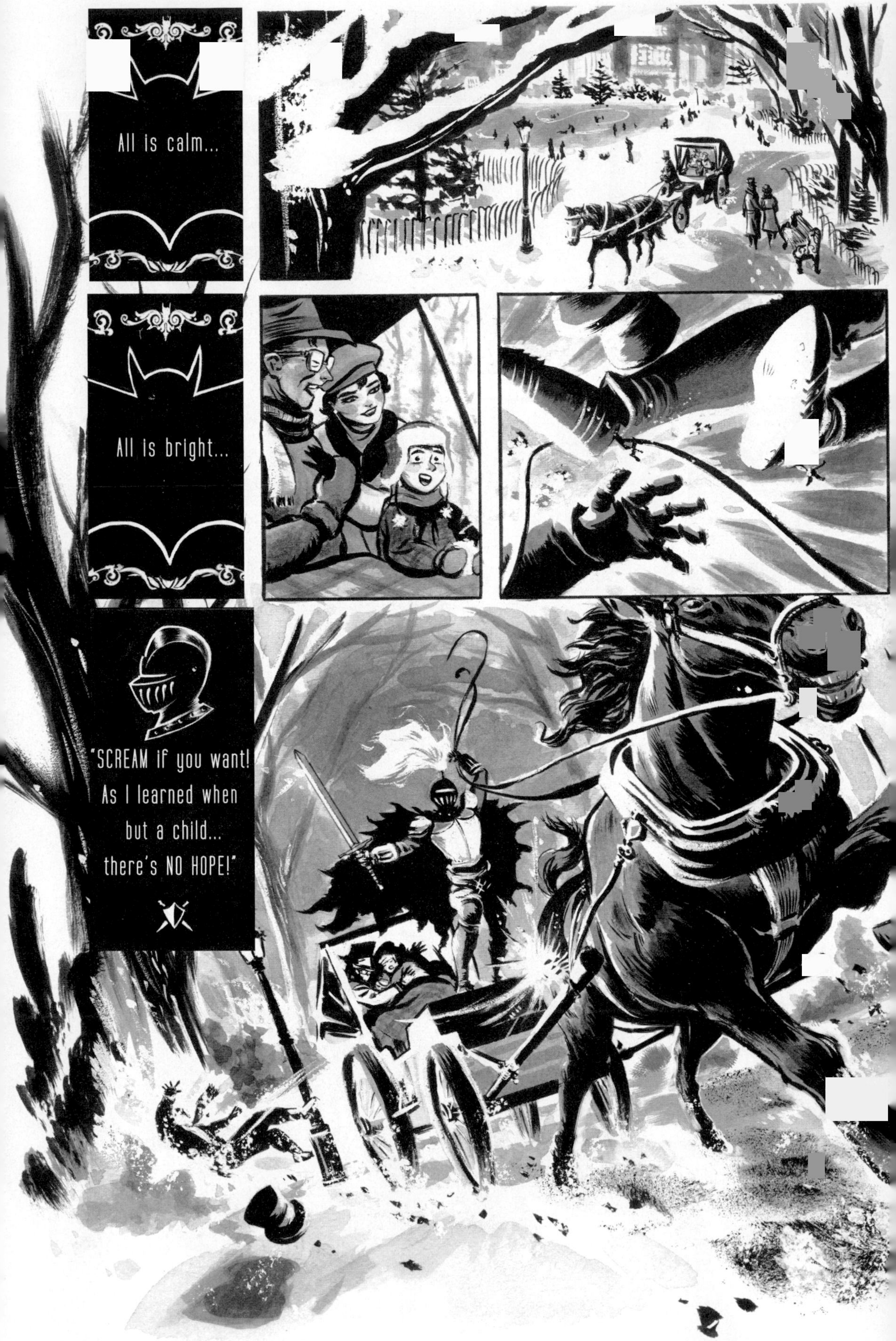
All is calm...
All is bright...
"SCREAM if you want! As I learned when but a child... there's NO HOPE!"

"There's ALWAYS hope!"

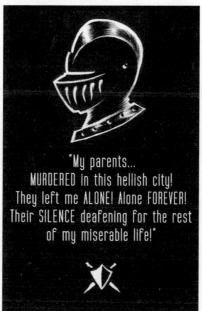

"My parents...
MURDERED in this hellish city!
They left me ALONE! Alone FOREVER!
Their SILENCE deafening for the rest
of my miserable life!"

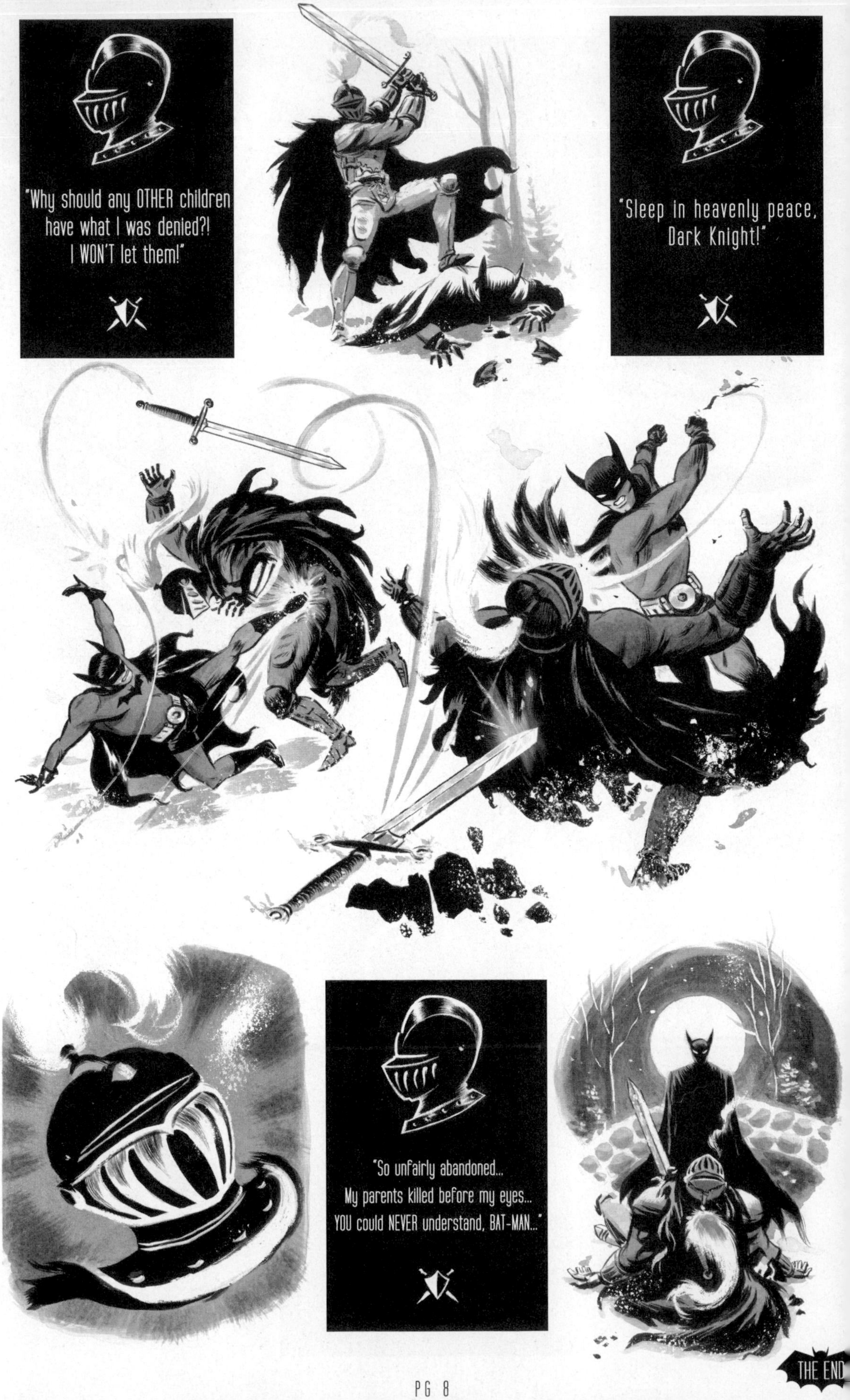
"Why should any OTHER children have what I was denied?! I WON'T let them!"
"Sleep in heavenly peace, Dark Knight!"
"So unfairly abandoned... My parents killed before my eyes... YOU could NEVER understand, BAT-MAN..."
THE END

MICHAEL USLAN

Emmy Award-winning Michael Uslan has devoted most of his life to Batman and has played an integral role in making the character as iconic as it is today. The author of *The Boy Who Loved Batman*, Uslan was, in 1971, the very first instructor to teach an accredited course on comic book folklore at any university. Historian, writer, Hollywood producer (he is a producer of all of the modern Batman movies), Michael Uslan is the ultimate fanboy who made good.

DAVE BULLOCK

Dave Bullock brings his extensive training and experience in the animation field to the world of comics. He has served as director and/or story artist on many animated TV shows and movies, including *Batman Beyond*, *Kim Possible*, *Teen Titans*, and *Star Wars: The Clone Wars*. Bullock's awesome comics work can be seen in WEDNESDAY COMICS (Deadman), SUPERMAN, BLOODSHOT, and his own creation, *King Ronok*.

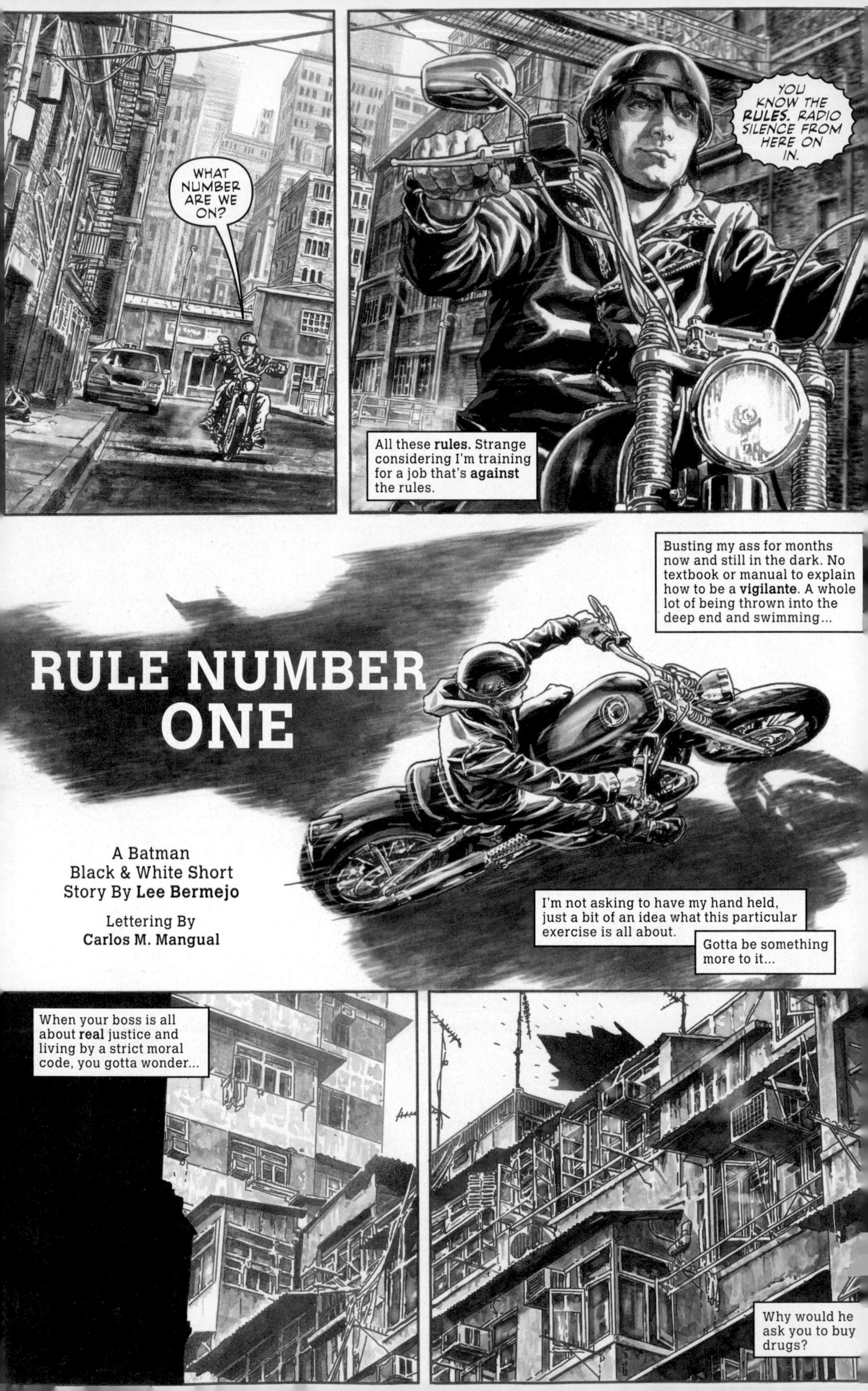
WHAT NUMBER ARE WE ON?
YOU KNOW THE RULES. RADIO SILENCE FROM HERE ON IN.
All these rules. Strange considering I'm training for a job that's against the rules.
Busting my ass for months now and still in the dark. No textbook or manual to explain how to be a vigilante. A whole lot of being thrown into the deep end and swimming...
RULE NUMBER ONE
A Batman Black & White Short Story By Lee Bermejo
Lettering By Carlos M. Mangual
I'm not asking to have my hand held, just a bit of an idea what this particular exercise is all about.
Gotta be something more to it...
When your boss is all about real justice and living by a strict moral code, you gotta wonder...
Why would he ask you to buy drugs?

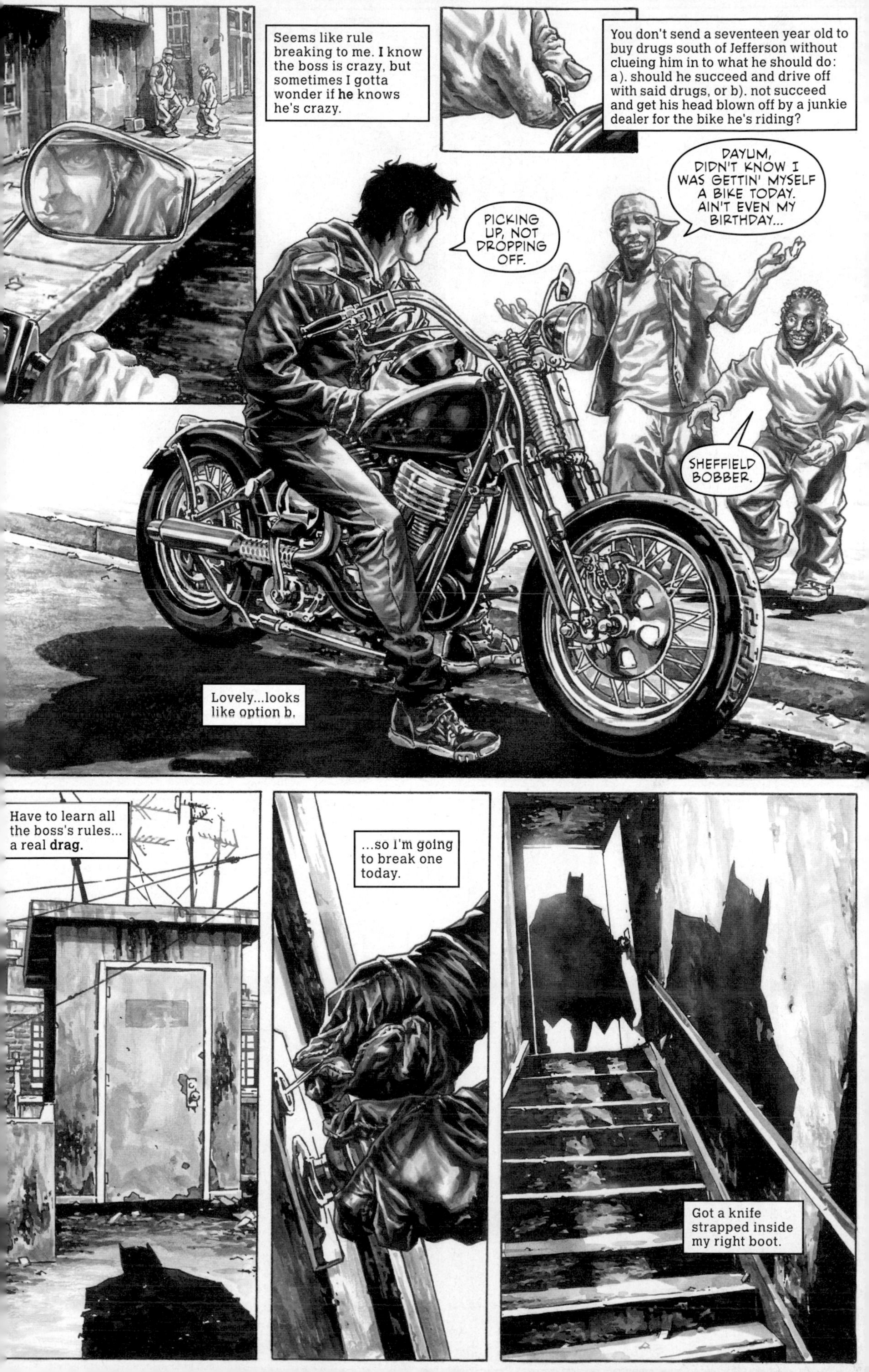
Seems like rule breaking to me. I know the boss is crazy, but sometimes I gotta wonder if **he** knows he's crazy.
You don't send a seventeen year old to buy drugs south of Jefferson without clueing him in to what he should do: a). should he succeed and drive off with said drugs, or b). not succeed and get his head blown off by a junkie dealer for the bike he's riding?
DAYUM, DIDN'T KNOW I WAS GETTIN' MYSELF A BIKE TODAY. AIN'T EVEN MY BIRTHDAY...
PICKING UP, NOT DROPPING OFF.
SHEFFIELD BOBBER.
Lovely...looks like option b.
Have to learn all the boss's rules... a real **drag.**
...so I'm going to break one today.
Got a knife strapped inside my right boot.

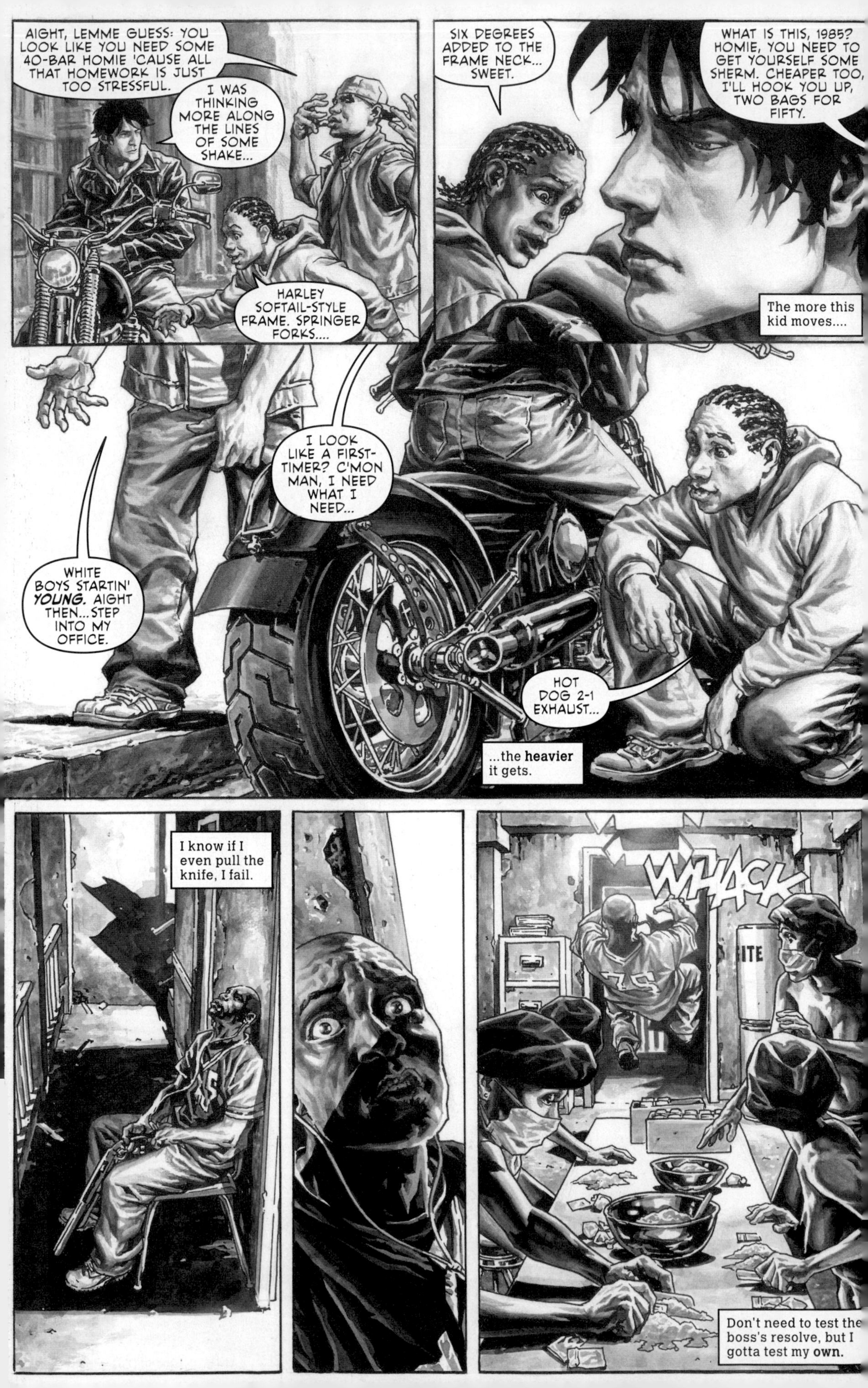
AIGHT, LEMME GUESS: YOU LOOK LIKE YOU NEED SOME 40-BAR HOMIE 'CAUSE ALL THAT HOMEWORK IS JUST TOO STRESSFUL.
I WAS THINKING MORE ALONG THE LINES OF SOME SHAKE...
HARLEY SOFTAIL-STYLE FRAME. SPRINGER FORKS....
SIX DEGREES ADDED TO THE FRAME NECK... SWEET.
WHAT IS THIS, 1985? HOMIE, YOU NEED TO GET YOURSELF SOME SHERM. CHEAPER TOO, I'LL HOOK YOU UP, TWO BAGS FOR FIFTY.
The more this kid moves....
I LOOK LIKE A FIRST-TIMER? C'MON MAN, I NEED WHAT I NEED...
WHITE BOYS STARTIN' YOUNG. AIGHT THEN...STEP INTO MY OFFICE.
HOT DOG 2-1 EXHAUST...
...the heavier it gets.
I know if I even pull the knife, I fail.
WHACK
Don't need to test the boss's resolve, but I gotta test my own.

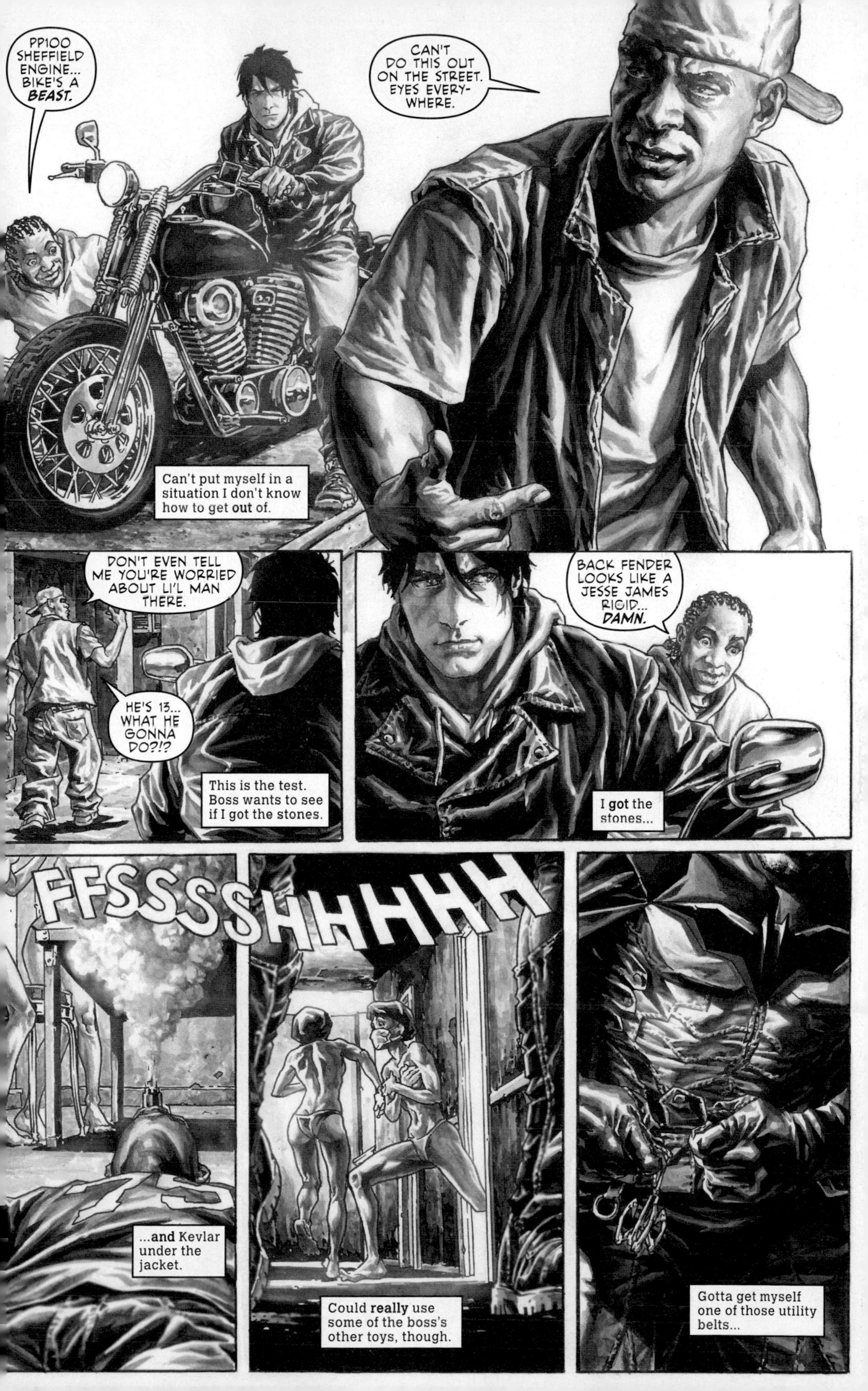
PP100 SHEFFIELD ENGINE... BIKE'S A BEAST.
CAN'T DO THIS OUT ON THE STREET. EYES EVERY-WHERE.
Can't put myself in a situation I don't know how to get out of.
DON'T EVEN TELL ME YOU'RE WORRIED ABOUT LI'L MAN THERE.
HE'S 13... WHAT HE GONNA DO?!?
This is the test. Boss wants to see if I got the stones.
BACK FENDER LOOKS LIKE A JESSE JAMES RIGID... DAMN.
I got the stones...
FFSSSSHHHHH
...and Kevlar under the jacket.
Could really use some of the boss's other toys, though.
Gotta get myself one of those utility belts...

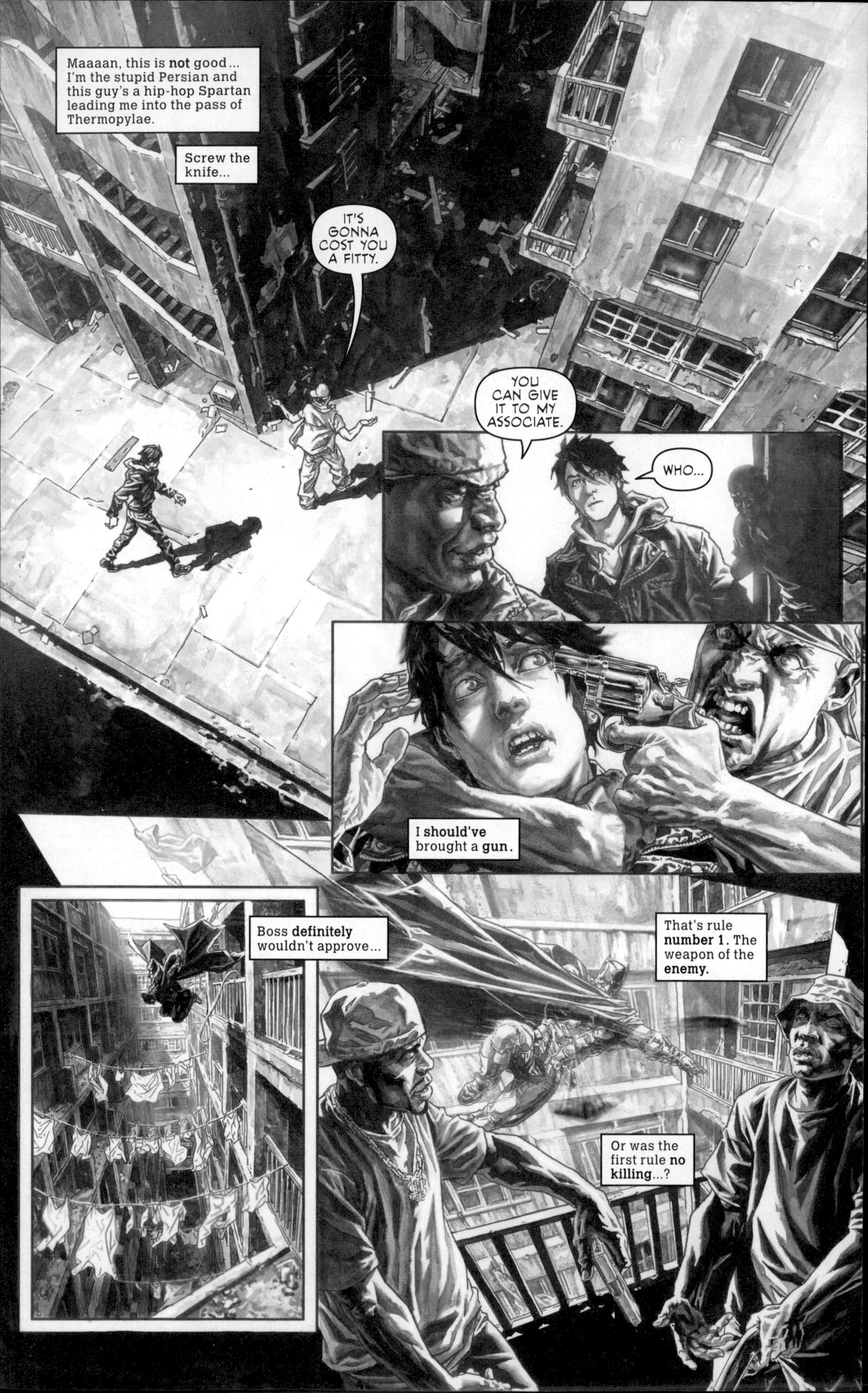
Maaaan, this is **not** good... I'm the stupid Persian and this guy's a hip-hop Spartan leading me into the pass of Thermopylae.
Screw the knife...
IT'S GONNA COST YOU A FITTY.
YOU CAN GIVE IT TO MY ASSOCIATE.
WHO...
I **should've** brought a **gun**.
Boss **definitely** wouldn't approve...
That's rule **number 1**. The weapon of the **enemy.**
Or was the first rule **no killing**...?

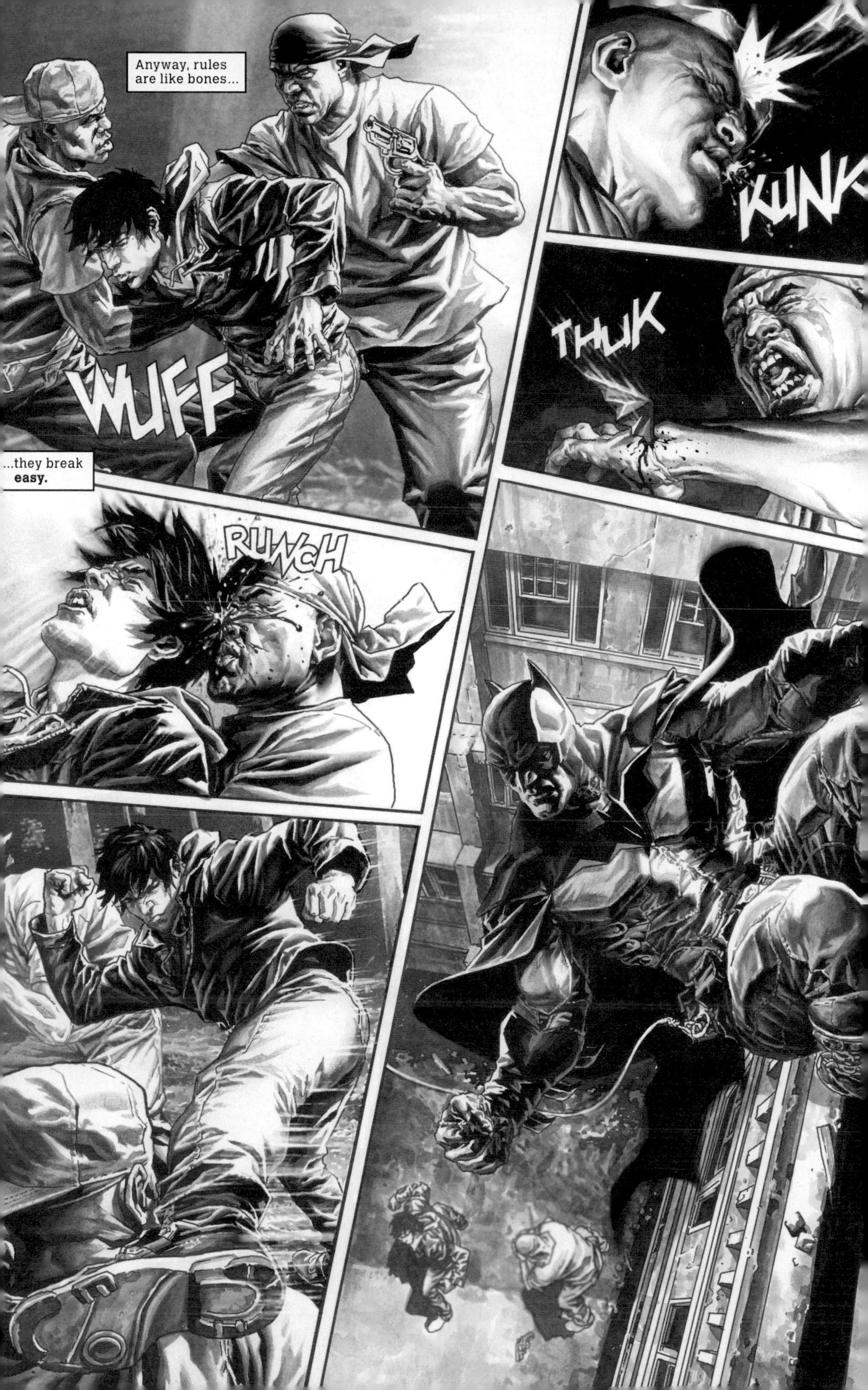
Anyway, rules are like bones...
WUFF
...they break **easy.**
KUNK
THUK
RUNCH

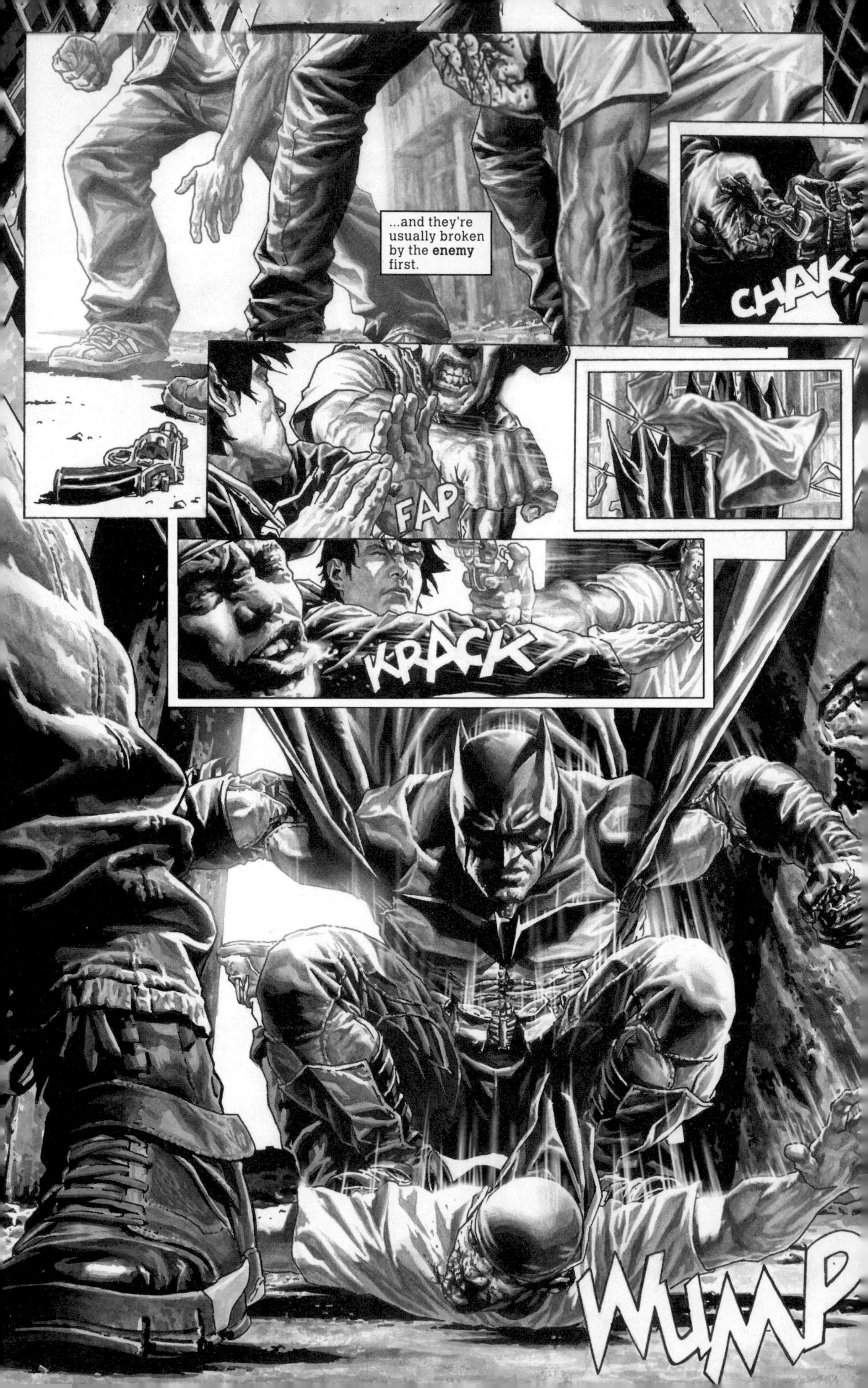

...and they're usually broken by the **enemy** first.
CHAK
FAP
KRACK
WUMP

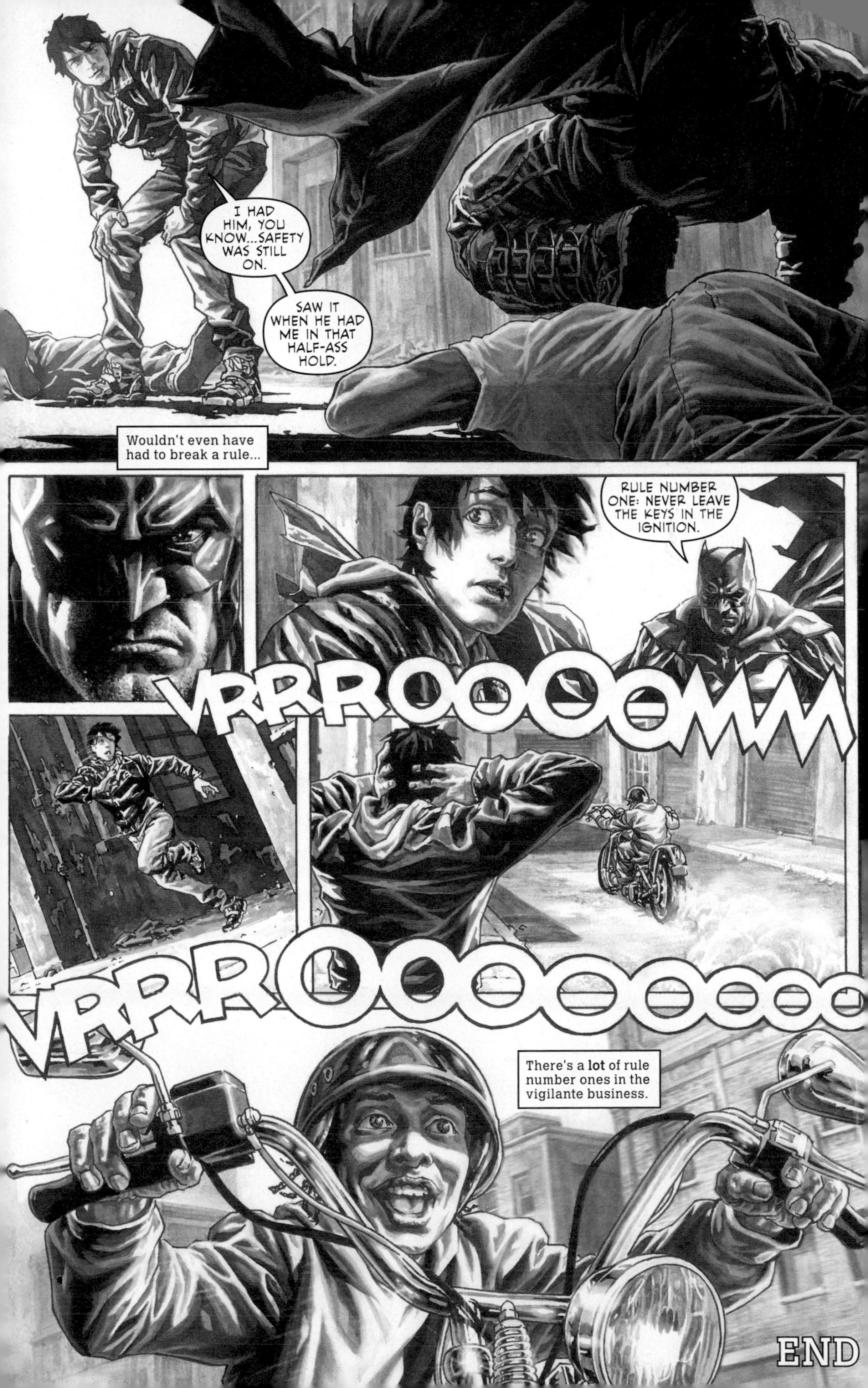
I HAD HIM, YOU KNOW...SAFETY WAS STILL ON.
SAW IT WHEN HE HAD ME IN THAT HALF-ASS HOLD.
Wouldn't even have had to break a rule...
RULE NUMBER ONE: NEVER LEAVE THE KEYS IN THE IGNITION.
VRRROOOOOMMM
VRRROOOOOOOOO
There's a **lot** of rule number ones in the vigilante business.
END

LEE BERMEJO

The artist of JOKER, LUTHOR, BATMAN/DEATHBLOW, and BEFORE WATCHMEN: RORSCHACH (with writer Brian Azzarello), Lee Bermejo stands at the top of the comics world. His gritty, expressionistic style is considered by many to be the next step in the evolution of comic book art. In 2011 Bermejo wrote and drew his first graphic novel, BATMAN: NOËL. He is currently writing and drawing the upcoming Vertigo title THE SUICIDERS. Lee lives in a small town in Italy with his wife Sara and illustrates portraits of dead rock stars in his spare time.

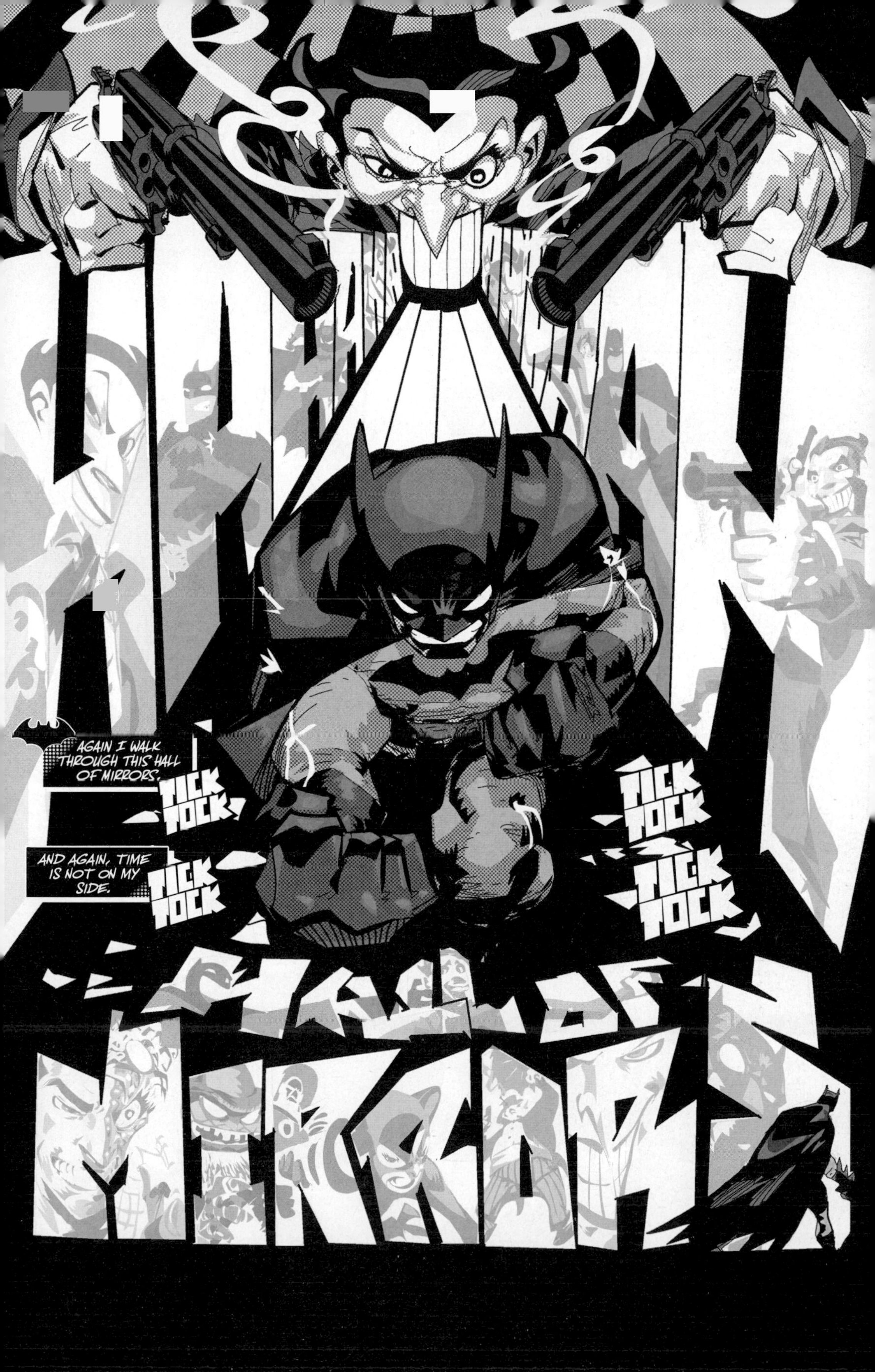
AGAIN I WALK THROUGH THIS HALL OF MIRRORS.
TICK TOCK
AND AGAIN, TIME IS NOT ON MY SIDE.
TICK TOCK
TICK TOCK
TICK TOCK
HALL OF MIRRORS

WRITTEN AND DRAWN BY DAMION SCOTT LETTERED BY DEZI SIENTY

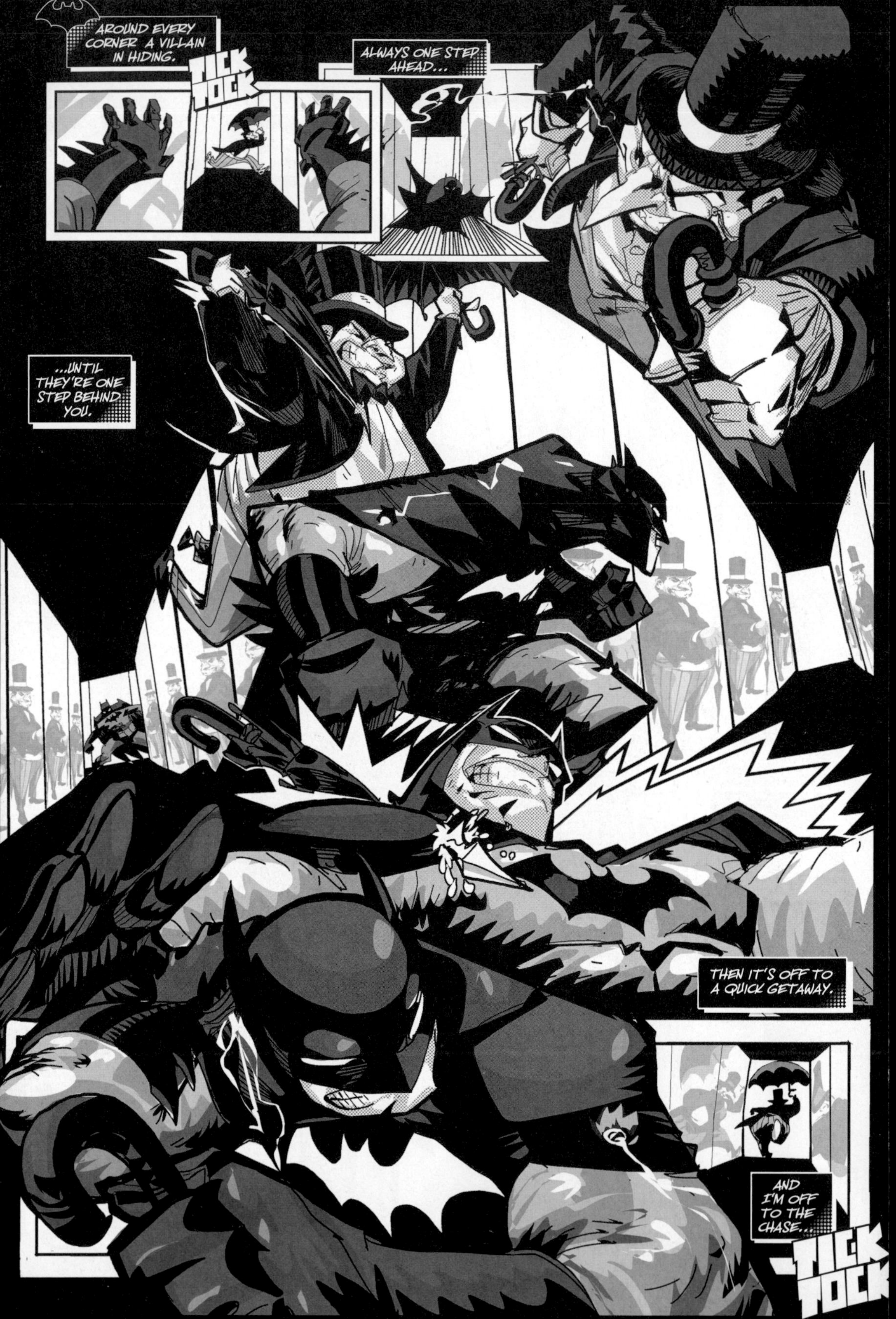

AROUND EVERY CORNER A VILLAIN IN HIDING.
TICK TOCK
ALWAYS ONE STEP AHEAD...
...UNTIL THEY'RE ONE STEP BEHIND YOU.
THEN IT'S OFF TO A QUICK GETAWAY.
AND I'M OFF TO THE CHASE...
TICK TOCK

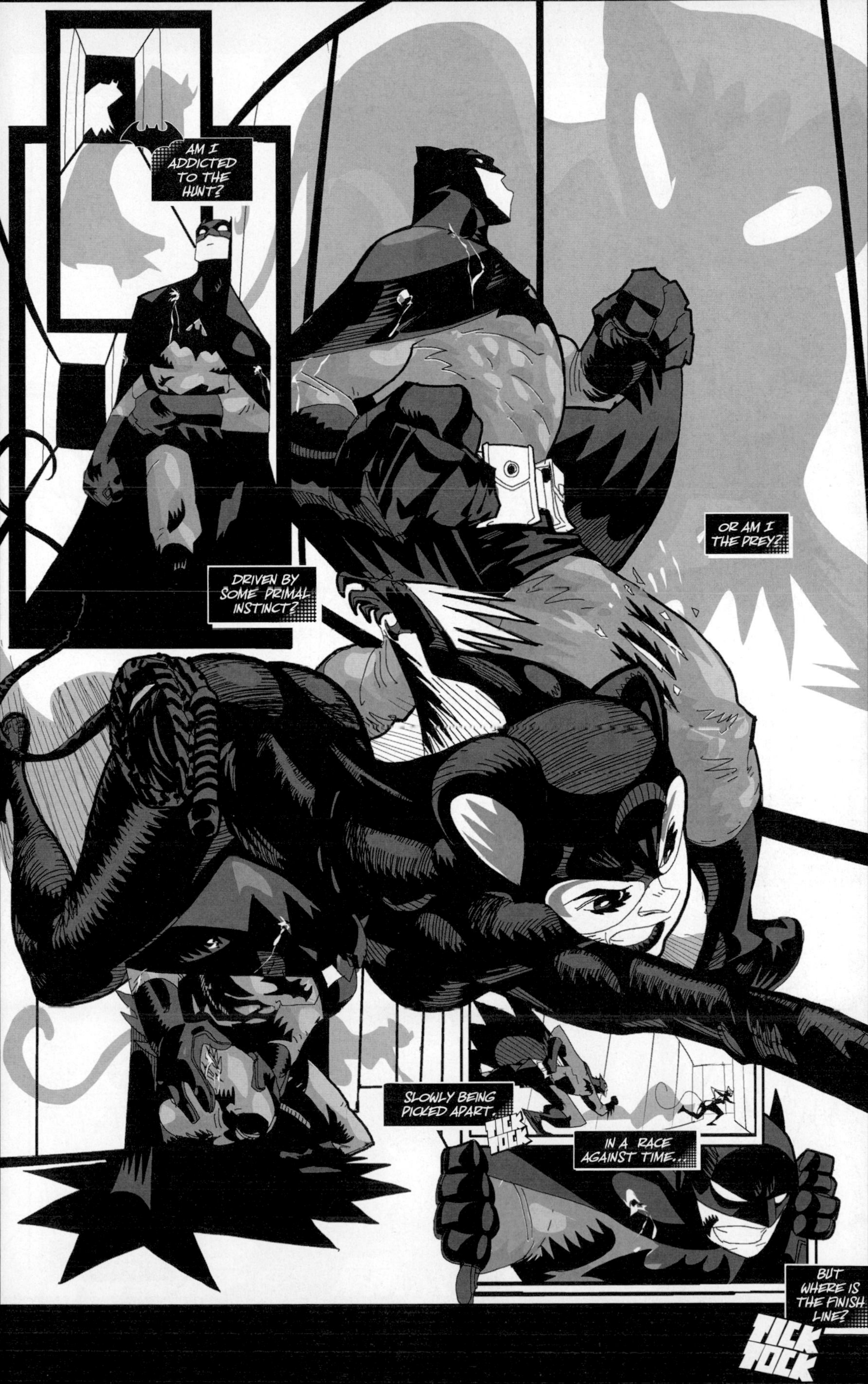
AM I ADDICTED TO THE HUNT?
DRIVEN BY SOME PRIMAL INSTINCT?
OR AM I THE PREY?
SLOWLY BEING PICKED APART.
TICK TOCK
IN A RACE AGAINST TIME...
BUT WHERE IS THE FINISH LINE?
TICK TOCK

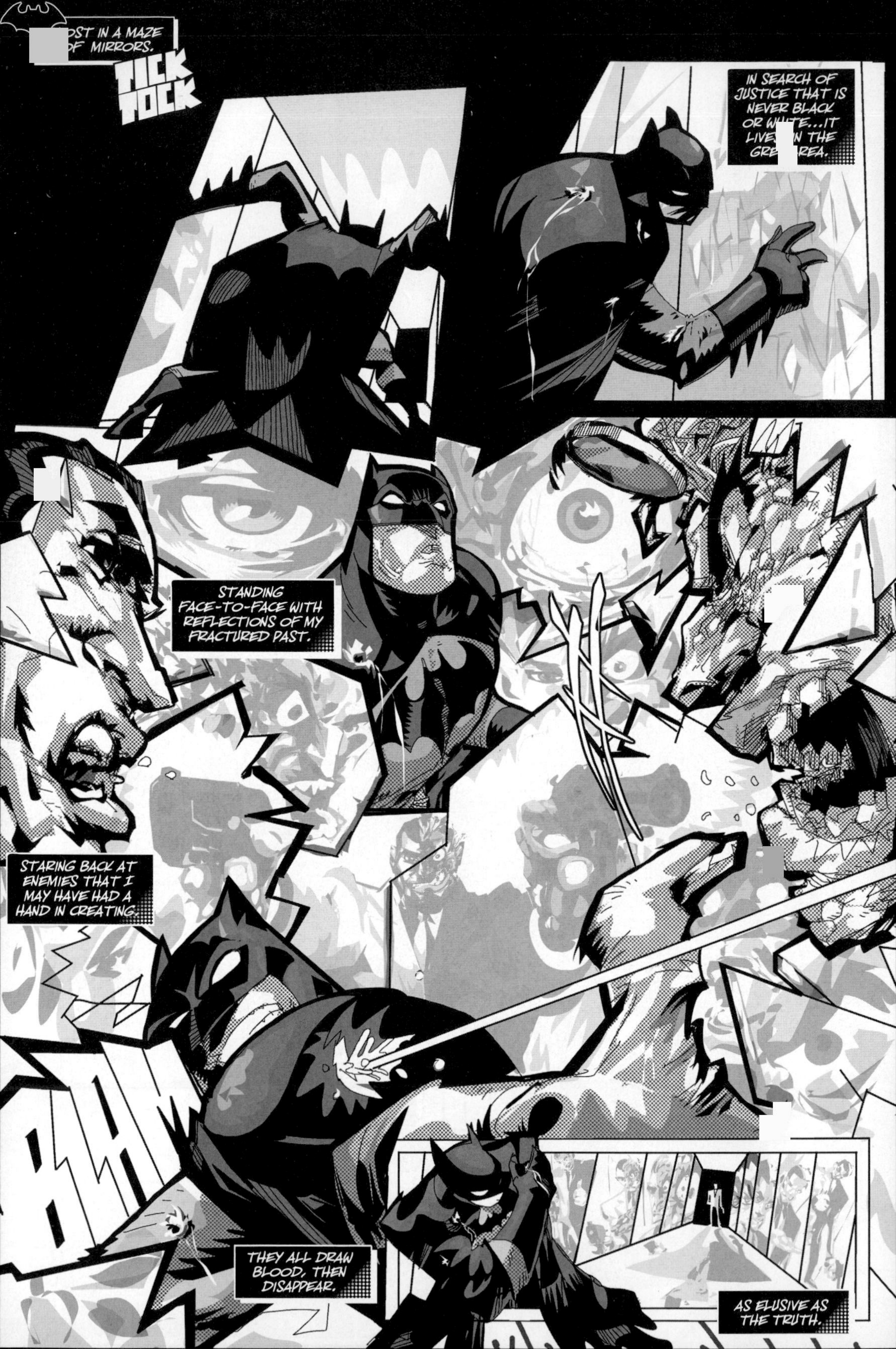
OST IN A MAZE OF MIRRORS.
TICK TOCK
IN SEARCH OF JUSTICE THAT IS NEVER BLACK OR WHITE...IT LIVE N THE GRE REA.
STANDING FACE-TO-FACE WITH REFLECTIONS OF MY FRACTURED PAST.
STARING BACK AT ENEMIES THAT I MAY HAVE HAD A HAND IN CREATING.
THEY ALL DRAW BLOOD, THEN DISAPPEAR.
AS ELUSIVE AS THE TRUTH.

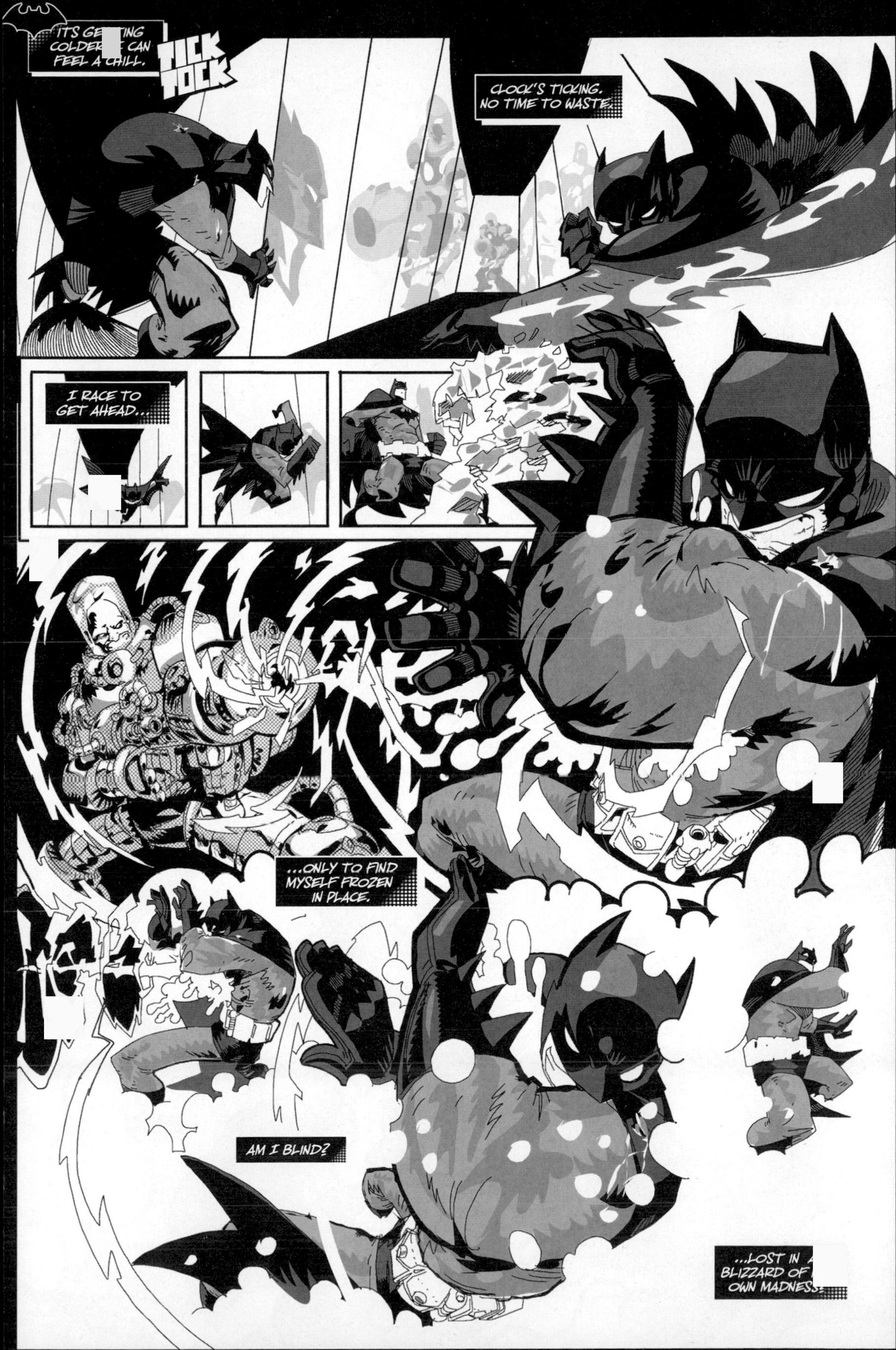

IT'S GE TING COLDER CAN FEEL A CHILL.
TICK TOCK
CLOCK'S TICKING. NO TIME TO WASTE.
I RACE TO GET AHEAD...
...ONLY TO FIND MYSELF FROZEN IN PLACE.
AM I BLIND?
...LOST IN A BLIZZARD OF OWN MADNESS

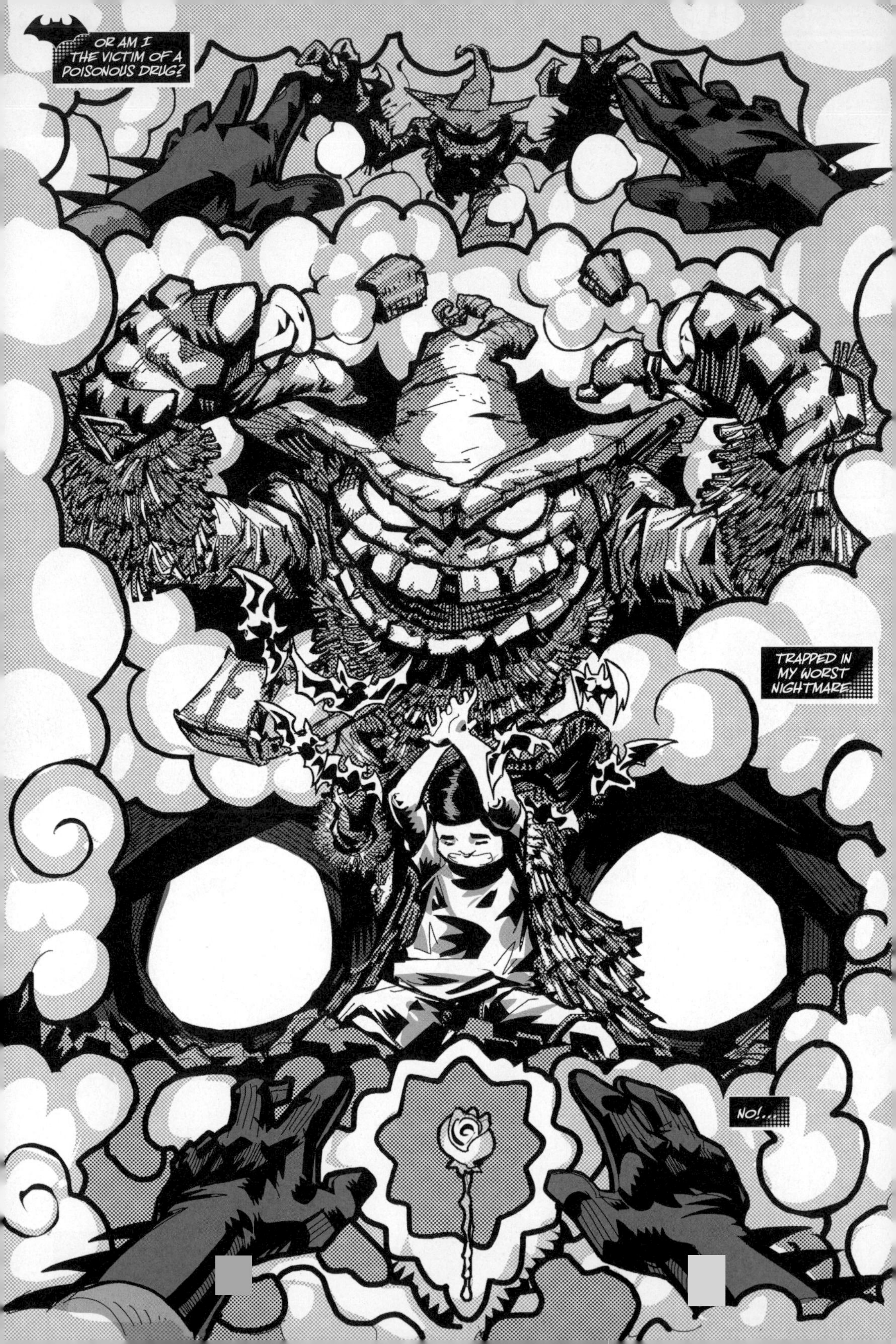
OR AM I THE VICTIM OF A POISONOUS DRUG?
TRAPPED IN MY WORST NIGHTMARE.
NO!..

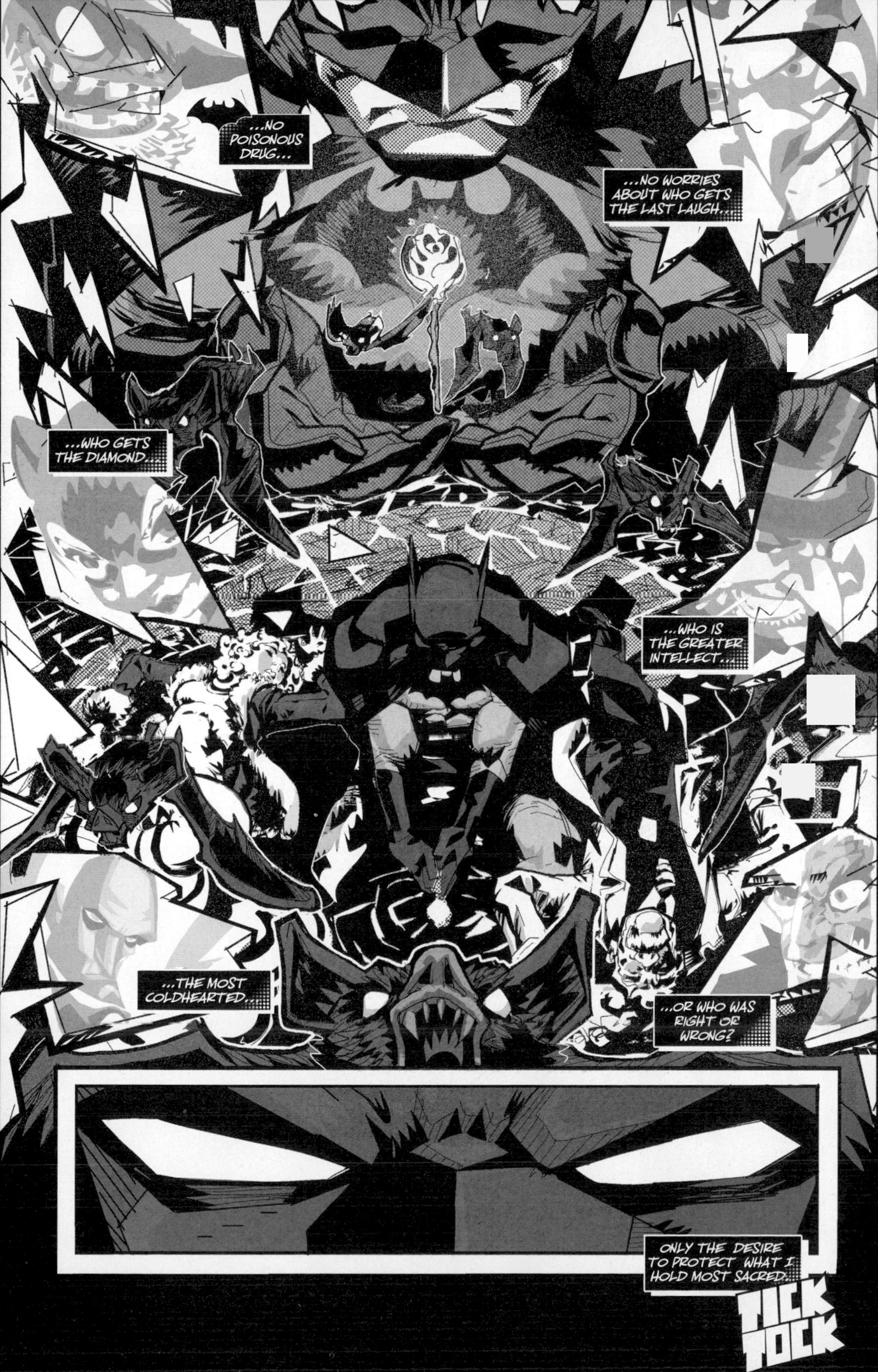
...NO POISONOUS DRUG...
...NO WORRIES ABOUT WHO GETS THE LAST LAUGH...
...WHO GETS THE DIAMOND...
...WHO IS THE GREATER INTELLECT...
...THE MOST COLDHEARTED...
...OR WHO WAS RIGHT OR WRONG?
ONLY THE DESIRE TO PROTECT WHAT I HOLD MOST SACRED.
TICK TOCK

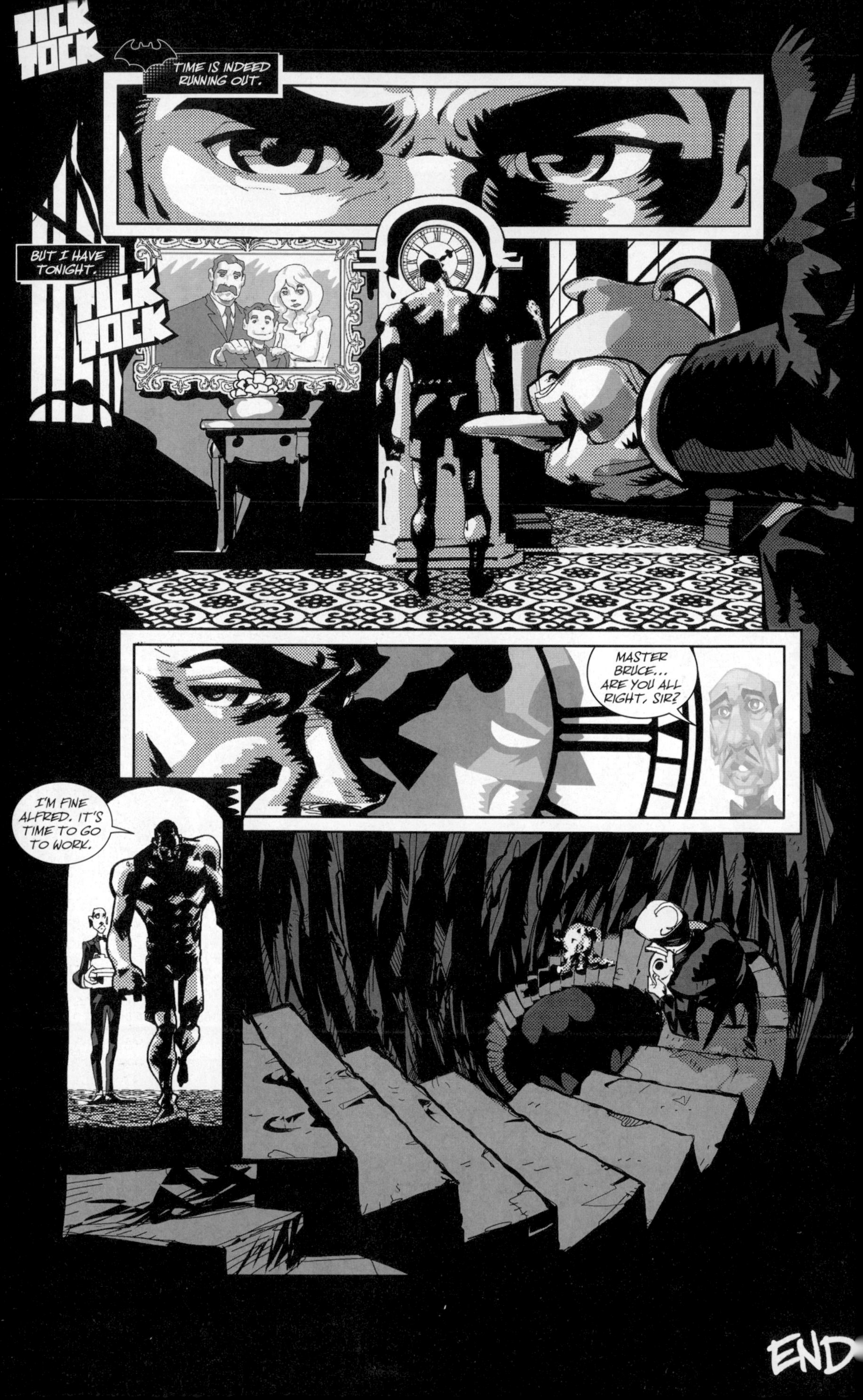
TICK TOCK
TIME IS INDEED RUNNING OUT.
BUT I HAVE TONIGHT.
TICK TOCK
MASTER BRUCE... ARE YOU ALL RIGHT, SIR?
I'M FINE ALFRED. IT'S TIME TO GO TO WORK.
END

DAMION SCOTT

Damion Scott is a Hip Hop phenomenon.
A graduate of the Joe Kubert School, Scott is
internationally known for his electrifying melding
of graffiti, super heroes, and hip hop graphics.
Scott's most popular work was seen in the
pages of BATMAN, ROBIN, and especially
BATGIRL, which caused a sensation among his
fans. Born in Jamaica and raised in Brooklyn,
Scott now lives and works in Japan.

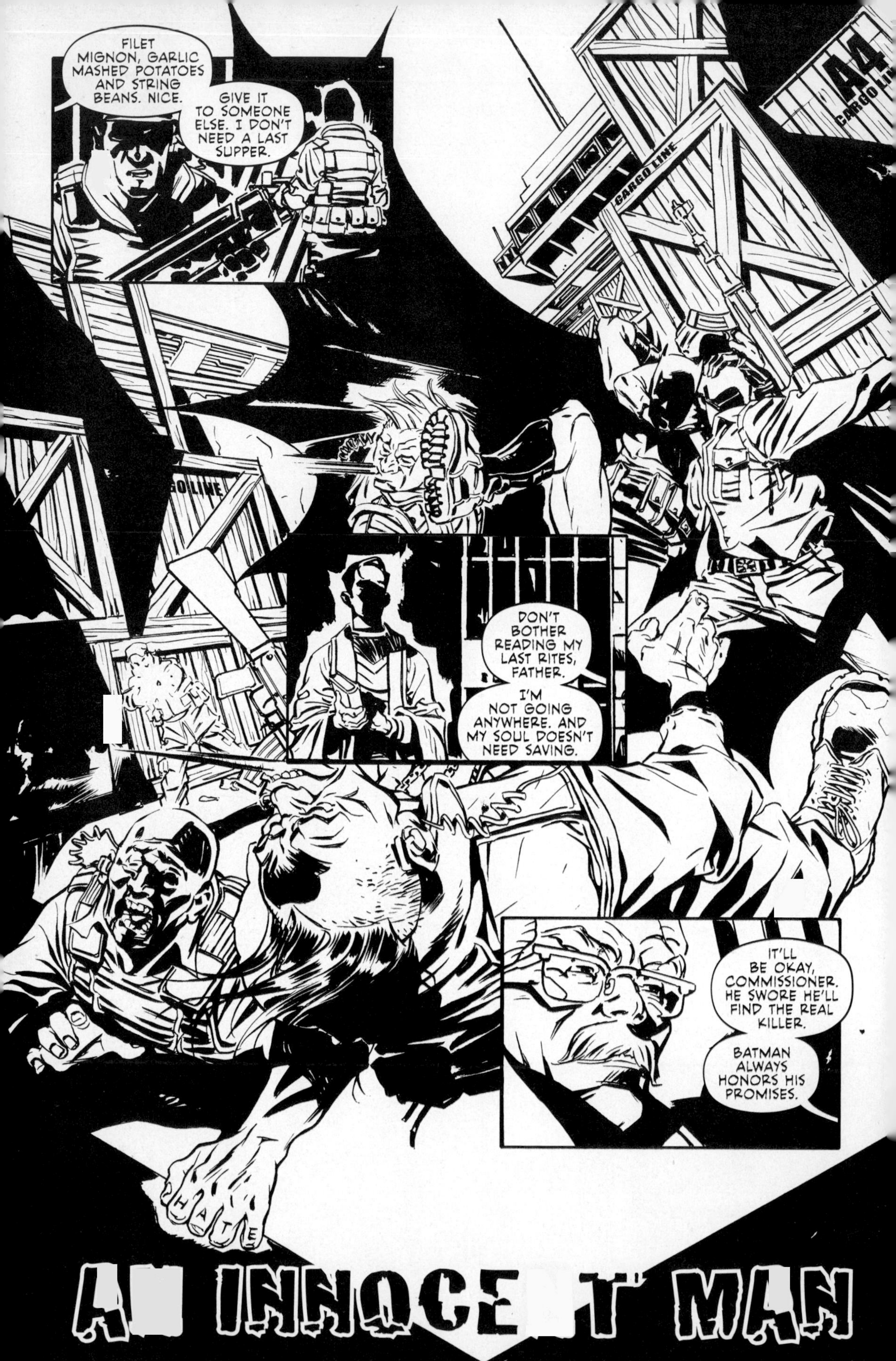
FILET MIGNON, GARLIC MASHED POTATOES AND STRING BEANS. NICE.
GIVE IT TO SOMEONE ELSE. I DON'T NEED A LAST SUPPER.
CARGO LINE
A4
DON'T BOTHER READING MY LAST RITES, FATHER.
I'M NOT GOING ANYWHERE. AND MY SOUL DOESN'T NEED SAVING.
IT'LL BE OKAY, COMMISSIONER. HE SWORE HE'LL FIND THE REAL KILLER.
BATMAN ALWAYS HONORS HIS PROMISES.
HATE

MARV WOLFMAN writer RICCARDO BURCHIELLI artist TAYLOR ESPOSITO letterer and thank you, C.D.

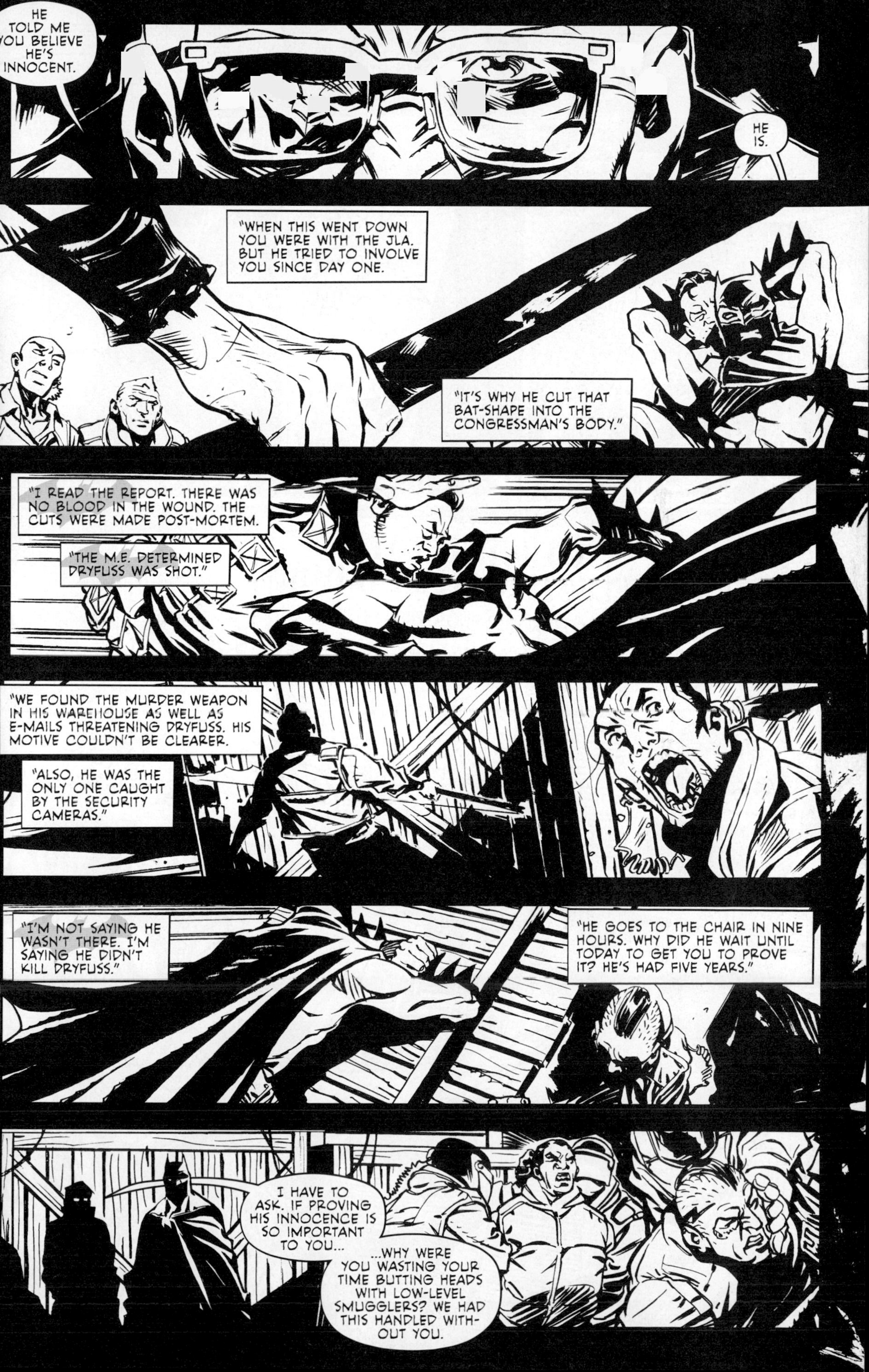
HE TOLD ME YOU BELIEVE HE'S INNOCENT.
HE IS.
"WHEN THIS WENT DOWN YOU WERE WITH THE JLA. BUT HE TRIED TO INVOLVE YOU SINCE DAY ONE.
"IT'S WHY HE CUT THAT BAT-SHAPE INTO THE CONGRESSMAN'S BODY."
"I READ THE REPORT. THERE WAS NO BLOOD IN THE WOUND. THE CUTS WERE MADE POST-MORTEM.
"THE M.E. DETERMINED DRYFUSS WAS SHOT."
"WE FOUND THE MURDER WEAPON IN HIS WAREHOUSE AS WELL AS E-MAILS THREATENING DRYFUSS. HIS MOTIVE COULDN'T BE CLEARER.
"ALSO, HE WAS THE ONLY ONE CAUGHT BY THE SECURITY CAMERAS."
"I'M NOT SAYING HE WASN'T THERE. I'M SAYING HE DIDN'T KILL DRYFUSS."
"HE GOES TO THE CHAIR IN NINE HOURS. WHY DID HE WAIT UNTIL TODAY TO GET YOU TO PROVE IT? HE'S HAD FIVE YEARS."
I HAVE TO ASK. IF PROVING HIS INNOCENCE IS SO IMPORTANT TO YOU...
...WHY WERE YOU WASTING YOUR TIME BUTTING HEADS WITH LOW-LEVEL SMUGGLERS? WE HAD THIS HANDLED WITH-OUT YOU.

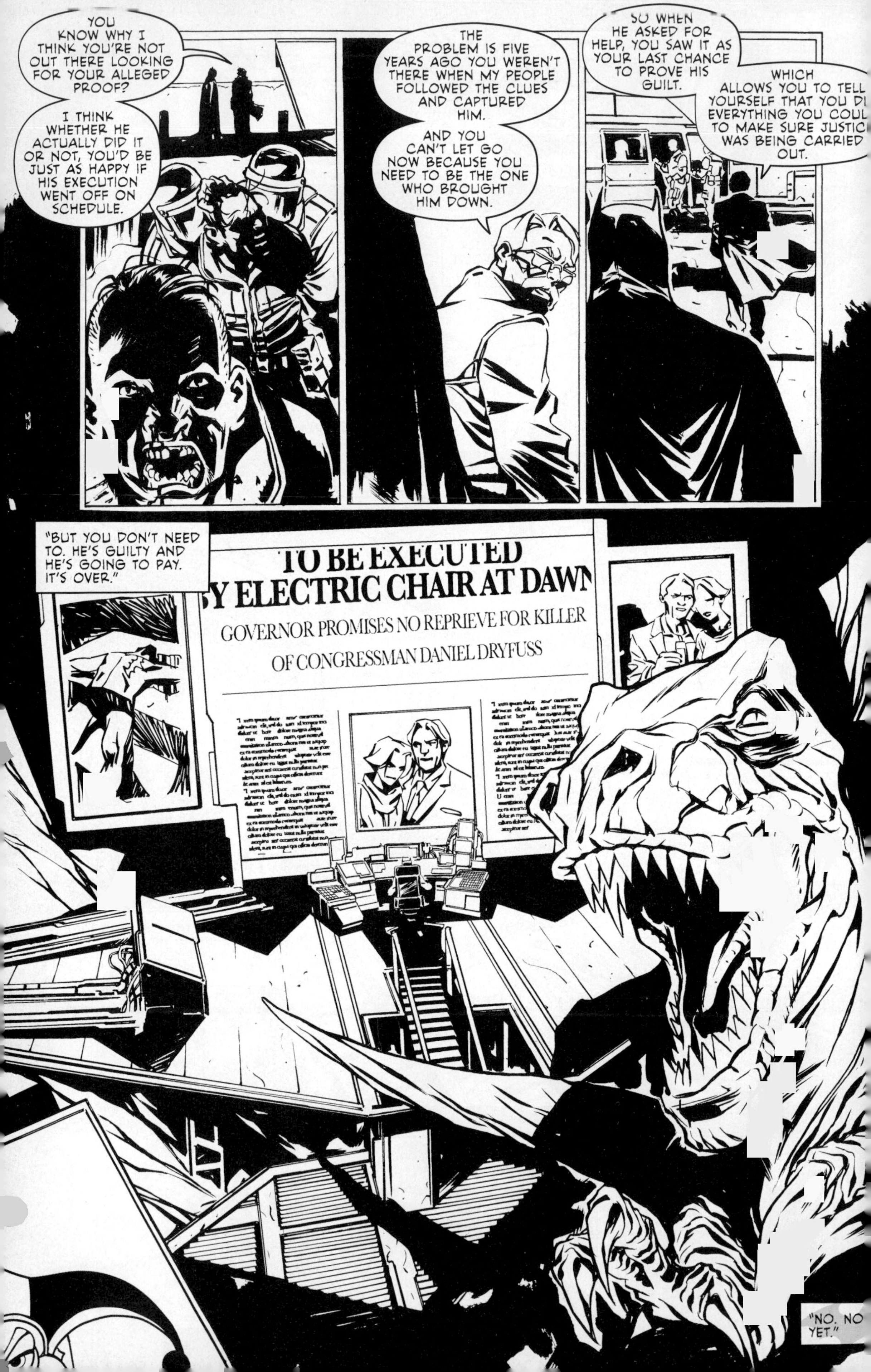
YOU KNOW WHY I THINK YOU'RE NOT OUT THERE LOOKING FOR YOUR ALLEGED PROOF?
I THINK WHETHER HE ACTUALLY DID IT OR NOT, YOU'D BE JUST AS HAPPY IF HIS EXECUTION WENT OFF ON SCHEDULE.
THE PROBLEM IS FIVE YEARS AGO YOU WEREN'T THERE WHEN MY PEOPLE FOLLOWED THE CLUES AND CAPTURED HIM.
AND YOU CAN'T LET GO NOW BECAUSE YOU NEED TO BE THE ONE WHO BROUGHT HIM DOWN.
SO WHEN HE ASKED FOR HELP, YOU SAW IT AS YOUR LAST CHANCE TO PROVE HIS GUILT.
WHICH ALLOWS YOU TO TELL YOURSELF THAT YOU DI EVERYTHING YOU COUL TO MAKE SURE JUSTIC WAS BEING CARRIED OUT.
"BUT YOU DON'T NEED TO. HE'S GUILTY AND HE'S GOING TO PAY. IT'S OVER."
TO BE EXECUTED
Y ELECTRIC CHAIR AT DAWN
GOVERNOR PROMISES NO REPRIEVE FOR KILLER OF CONGRESSMAN DANIEL DRYFUSS
"NO. NO YET."

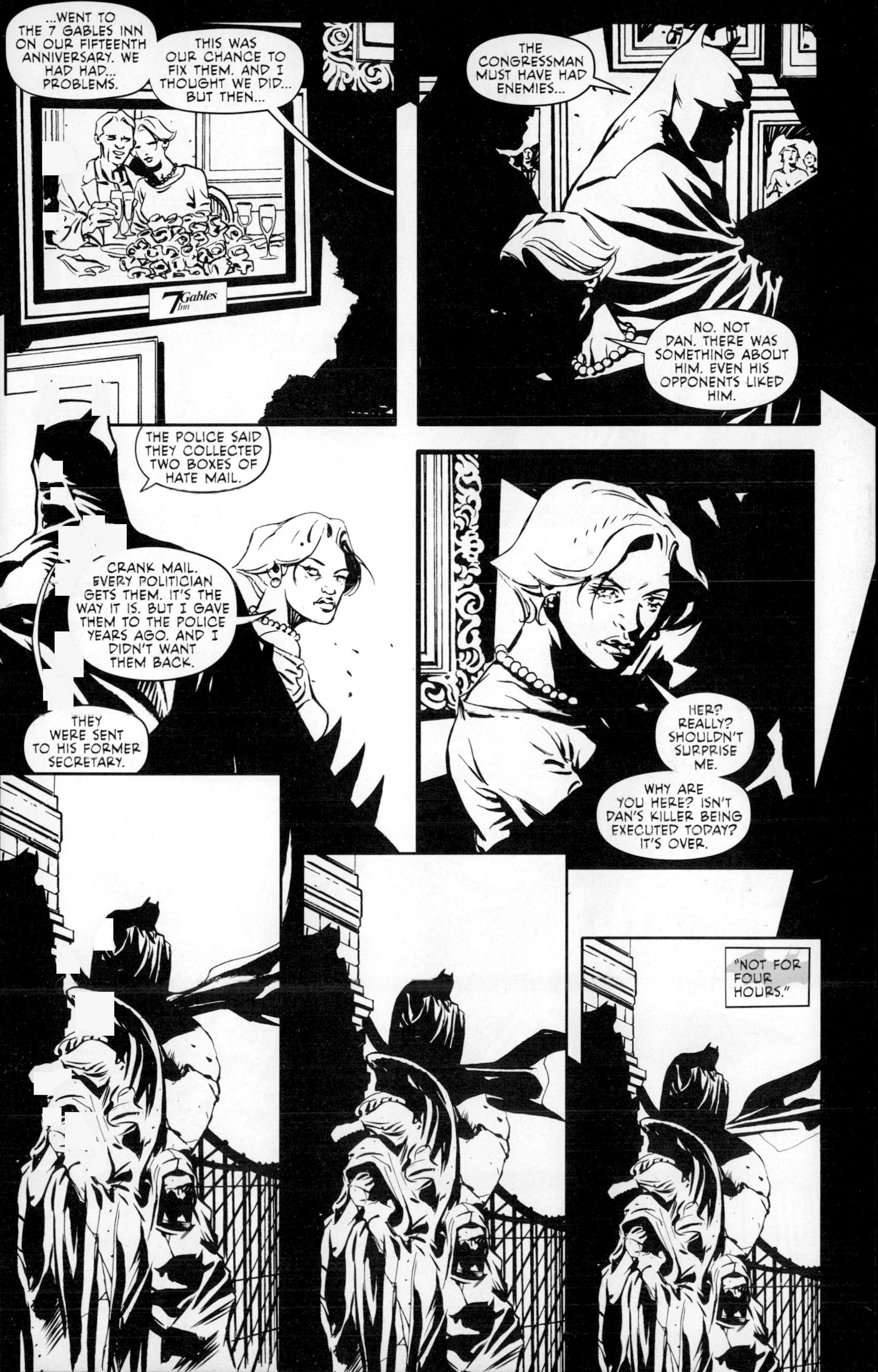
...WENT TO THE 7 GABLES INN ON OUR FIFTEENTH ANNIVERSARY. WE HAD HAD... PROBLEMS.
THIS WAS OUR CHANCE TO FIX THEM. AND I THOUGHT WE DID... BUT THEN...
7 Gables Inn
THE CONGRESSMAN MUST HAVE HAD ENEMIES...
NO. NOT DAN. THERE WAS SOMETHING ABOUT HIM. EVEN HIS OPPONENTS LIKED HIM.
THE POLICE SAID THEY COLLECTED TWO BOXES OF HATE MAIL.
CRANK MAIL. EVERY POLITICIAN GETS THEM. IT'S THE WAY IT IS. BUT I GAVE THEM TO THE POLICE YEARS AGO. AND I DIDN'T WANT THEM BACK.
THEY WERE SENT TO HIS FORMER SECRETARY.
HER? REALLY? SHOULDN'T SURPRISE ME.
WHY ARE YOU HERE? ISN'T DAN'S KILLER BEING EXECUTED TODAY? IT'S OVER.
"NOT FOR FOUR HOURS."

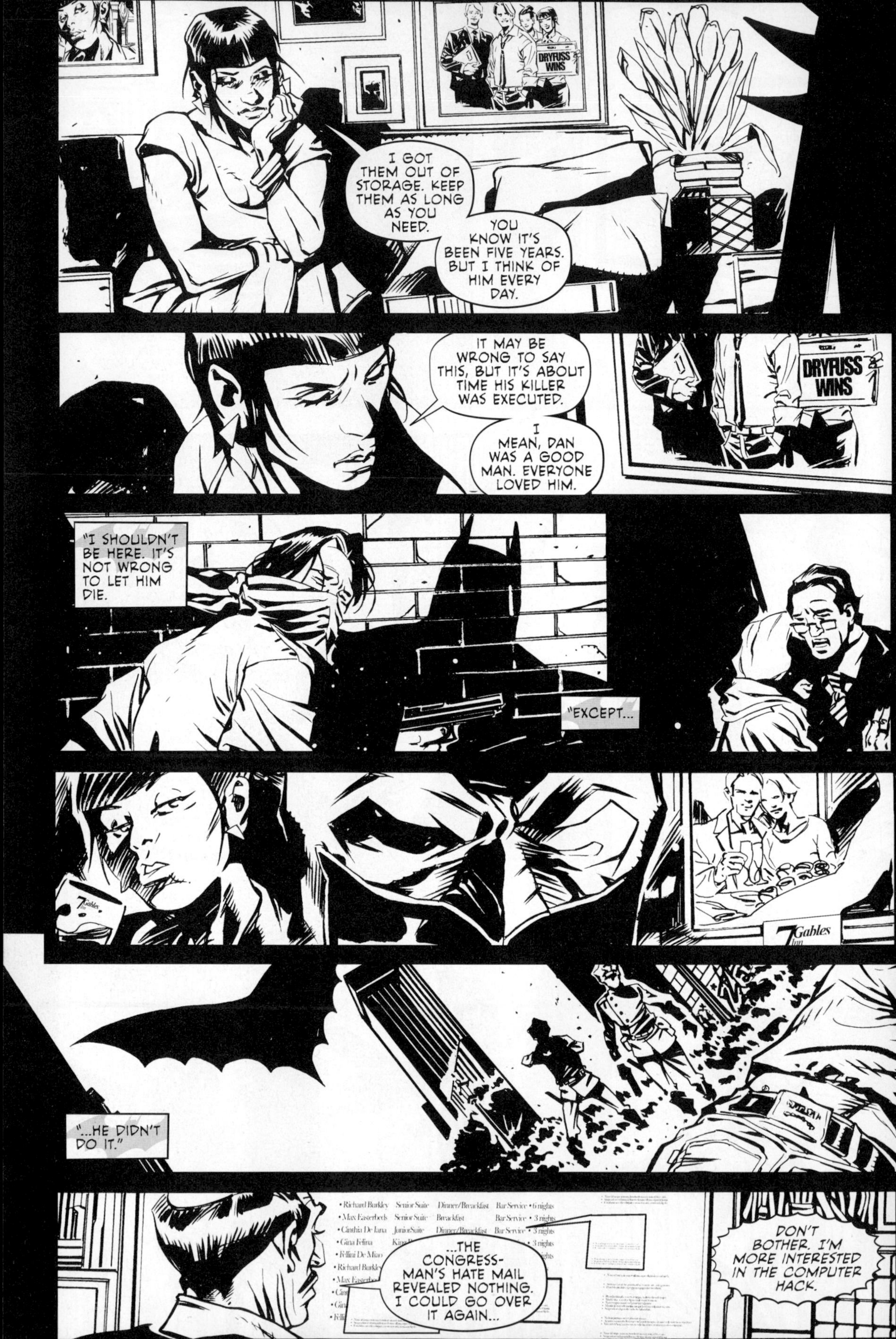

DRYFUSS WINS
I GOT THEM OUT OF STORAGE. KEEP THEM AS LONG AS YOU NEED.
YOU KNOW IT'S BEEN FIVE YEARS. BUT I THINK OF HIM EVERY DAY.
IT MAY BE WRONG TO SAY THIS, BUT IT'S ABOUT TIME HIS KILLER WAS EXECUTED.
I MEAN, DAN WAS A GOOD MAN. EVERYONE LOVED HIM.
DRYFUSS WINS
"I SHOULDN'T BE HERE. IT'S NOT WRONG TO LET HIM DIE.
"EXCEPT...
7 Gables
7 Gables Inn
"...HE DIDN'T DO IT."
...THE CONGRESS-MAN'S HATE MAIL REVEALED NOTHING. I COULD GO OVER IT AGAIN...
DON'T BOTHER. I'M MORE INTERESTED IN THE COMPUTER HACK.

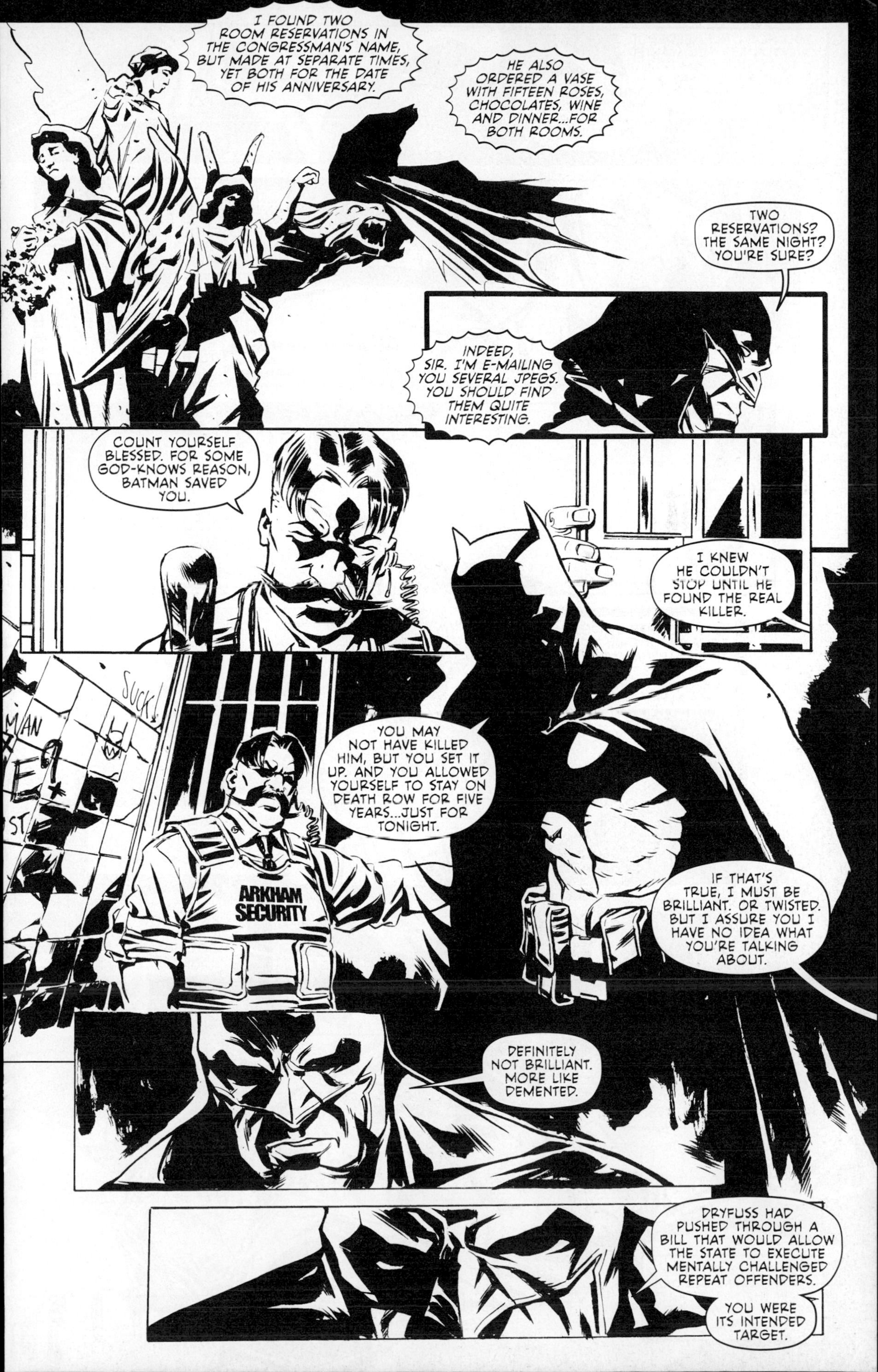

I FOUND TWO ROOM RESERVATIONS IN THE CONGRESSMAN'S NAME, BUT MADE AT SEPARATE TIMES, YET BOTH FOR THE DATE OF HIS ANNIVERSARY.
HE ALSO ORDERED A VASE WITH FIFTEEN ROSES, CHOCOLATES, WINE AND DINNER...FOR BOTH ROOMS.
TWO RESERVATIONS? THE SAME NIGHT? YOU'RE SURE?
INDEED, SIR. I'M E-MAILING YOU SEVERAL JPEGS. YOU SHOULD FIND THEM QUITE INTERESTING.
COUNT YOURSELF BLESSED. FOR SOME GOD-KNOWS REASON, BATMAN SAVED YOU.
I KNEW HE COULDN'T STOP UNTIL HE FOUND THE REAL KILLER.
SUCK!
YOU MAY NOT HAVE KILLED HIM, BUT YOU SET IT UP. AND YOU ALLOWED YOURSELF TO STAY ON DEATH ROW FOR FIVE YEARS...JUST FOR TONIGHT.
ARKHAM SECURITY
IF THAT'S TRUE, I MUST BE BRILLIANT. OR TWISTED. BUT I ASSURE YOU I HAVE NO IDEA WHAT YOU'RE TALKING ABOUT.
DEFINITELY NOT BRILLIANT. MORE LIKE DEMENTED.
DRYFUSS HAD PUSHED THROUGH A BILL THAT WOULD ALLOW THE STATE TO EXECUTE MENTALLY CHALLENGED REPEAT OFFENDERS.
YOU WERE ITS INTENDED TARGET.

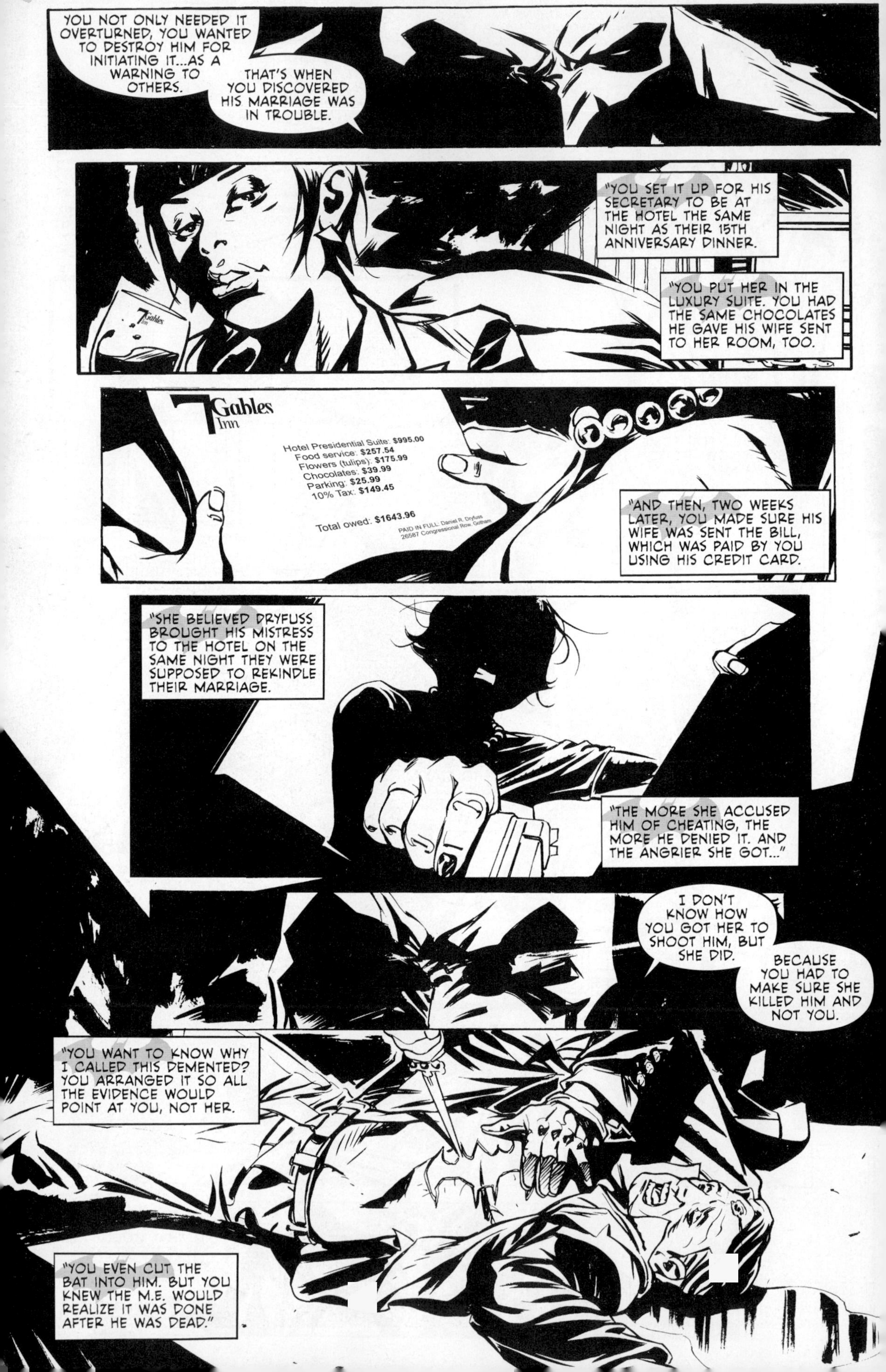
YOU NOT ONLY NEEDED IT OVERTURNED, YOU WANTED TO DESTROY HIM FOR INITIATING IT...AS A WARNING TO OTHERS.
THAT'S WHEN YOU DISCOVERED HIS MARRIAGE WAS IN TROUBLE.
"YOU SET IT UP FOR HIS SECRETARY TO BE AT THE HOTEL THE SAME NIGHT AS THEIR 15TH ANNIVERSARY DINNER.
"YOU PUT HER IN THE LUXURY SUITE. YOU HAD THE SAME CHOCOLATES HE GAVE HIS WIFE SENT TO HER ROOM, TOO.
7 Gables Inn
Hotel Presidential Suite: $995.00
Food service: $257.54
Flowers (tulips): $175.99
Chocolates: $39.99
Parking: $25.99
10% Tax: $149.45
Total owed: $1643.96
PAID IN FULL: Daniel R. Dryfuss
26587 Congressional Row, Gotham
"AND THEN, TWO WEEKS LATER, YOU MADE SURE HIS WIFE WAS SENT THE BILL, WHICH WAS PAID BY YOU USING HIS CREDIT CARD.
"SHE BELIEVED DRYFUSS BROUGHT HIS MISTRESS TO THE HOTEL ON THE SAME NIGHT THEY WERE SUPPOSED TO REKINDLE THEIR MARRIAGE.
"THE MORE SHE ACCUSED HIM OF CHEATING, THE MORE HE DENIED IT. AND THE ANGRIER SHE GOT..."
I DON'T KNOW HOW YOU GOT HER TO SHOOT HIM, BUT SHE DID.
BECAUSE YOU HAD TO MAKE SURE SHE KILLED HIM AND NOT YOU.
"YOU WANT TO KNOW WHY I CALLED THIS DEMENTED? YOU ARRANGED IT SO ALL THE EVIDENCE WOULD POINT AT YOU, NOT HER.
"YOU EVEN CUT THE BAT INTO HIM. BUT YOU KNEW THE M.E. WOULD REALIZE IT WAS DONE AFTER HE WAS DEAD."

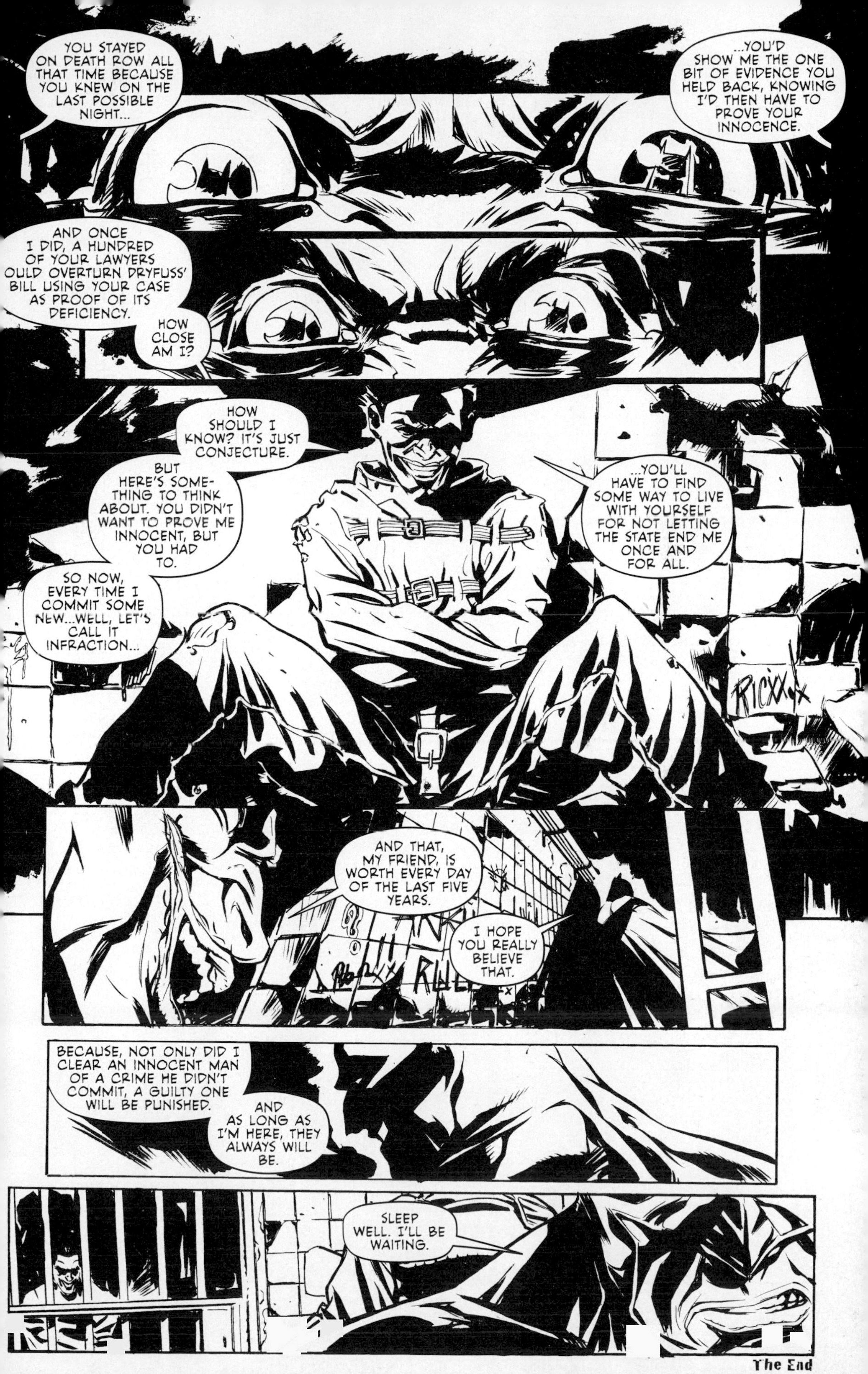
YOU STAYED ON DEATH ROW ALL THAT TIME BECAUSE YOU KNEW ON THE LAST POSSIBLE NIGHT...
...YOU'D SHOW ME THE ONE BIT OF EVIDENCE YOU HELD BACK, KNOWING I'D THEN HAVE TO PROVE YOUR INNOCENCE.
AND ONCE I DID, A HUNDRED OF YOUR LAWYERS OULD OVERTURN DRYFUSS' BILL USING YOUR CASE AS PROOF OF ITS DEFICIENCY.
HOW CLOSE AM I?
HOW SHOULD I KNOW? IT'S JUST CONJECTURE.
BUT HERE'S SOME-THING TO THINK ABOUT. YOU DIDN'T WANT TO PROVE ME INNOCENT, BUT YOU HAD TO.
SO NOW, EVERY TIME I COMMIT SOME NEW...WELL, LET'S CALL IT INFRACTION...
...YOU'LL HAVE TO FIND SOME WAY TO LIVE WITH YOURSELF FOR NOT LETTING THE STATE END ME ONCE AND FOR ALL.
RICXX
AND THAT, MY FRIEND, IS WORTH EVERY DAY OF THE LAST FIVE YEARS.
I HOPE YOU REALLY BELIEVE THAT.
BECAUSE, NOT ONLY DID I CLEAR AN INNOCENT MAN OF A CRIME HE DIDN'T COMMIT, A GUILTY ONE WILL BE PUNISHED.
AND AS LONG AS I'M HERE, THEY ALWAYS WILL BE.
SLEEP WELL. I'LL BE WAITING.

The End

MARV WOLFMAN

Marv Wolfman began his professional writing career in the late 1960s and has since written just about every major character for both DC and Marvel. After long and creative runs on DC's THE NEW TEEN TITANS and Marvel's *Tomb of Dracula,* Marv teamed up with artist George Perez on the groundbreaking CRISIS ON INFINITE EARTHS, which redefined the entire DC Universe. In addition to his comics work, Marv continues to be a writer for TV, animation, video games, and novels.

RICCARDO BURCHIELLI

Italian artist Riccardo Burchielli made his American comics splash with his memorable work on Vertigo's DMZ. Originally an art director in the advertising field, Riccardo became a full-time comics artist in 2003. His blend of immediate, no-nonsense storytelling and bold draftsmanship makes him one of the most sought-after artists in comics today.

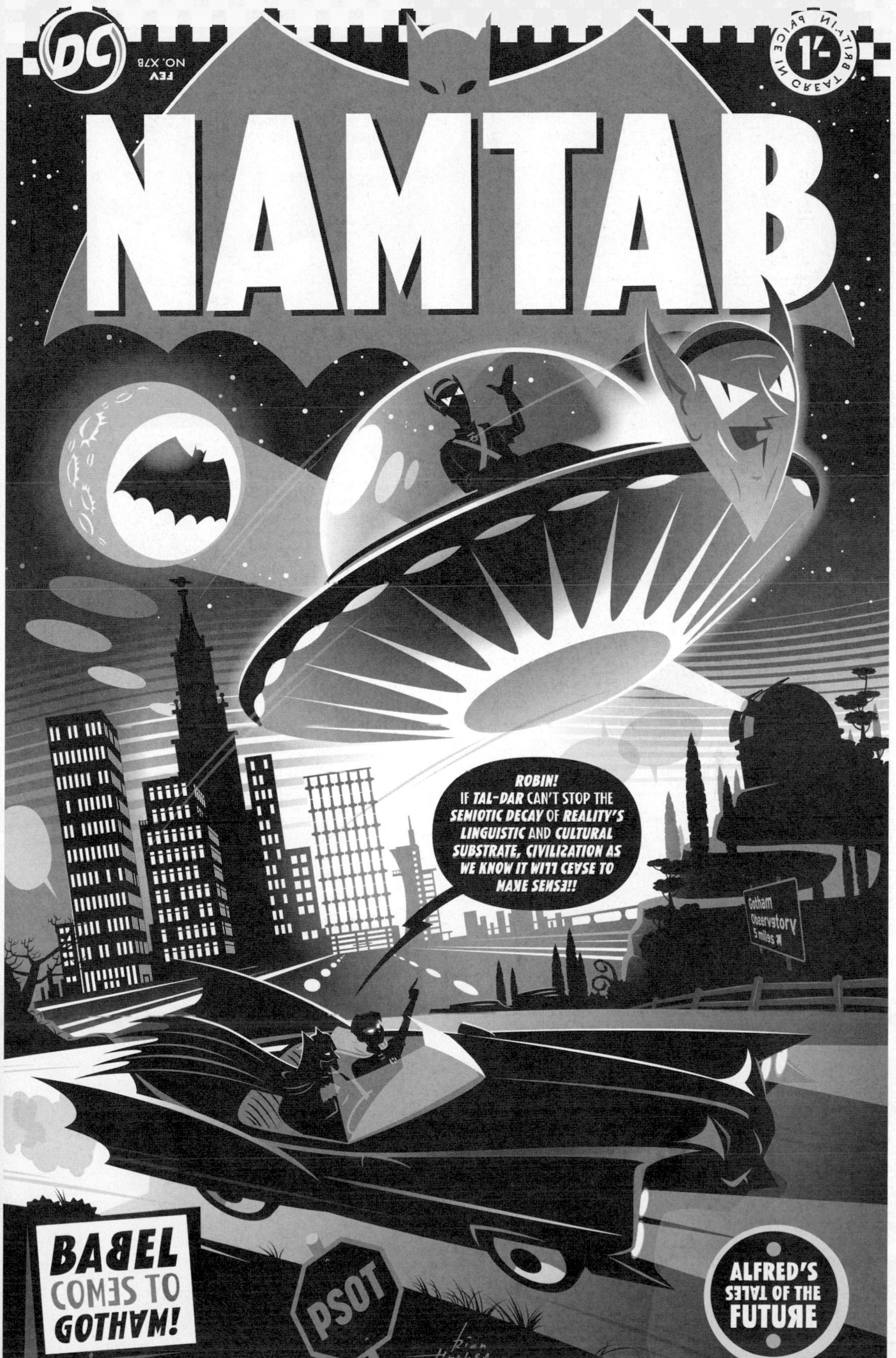
DC
FEV NO. X7B
PRICE IN GREAT BRITAIN 1/-
NAMTAB
ROBIN! IF TAL-DAR CAN'T STOP THE SEMIOTIC DECAY OF REALITY'S LINGUISTIC AND CULTURAL SUBSTRATE, CIVILIZATION AS WE KNOW IT WITT CEVSE TO MAKE SENSE!!
Gotham Observatory 5 miles
BABEL COMES TO GOTHAM!
PSOT
ALFRED'S TALES OF THE FUTURE
Rian Hughes

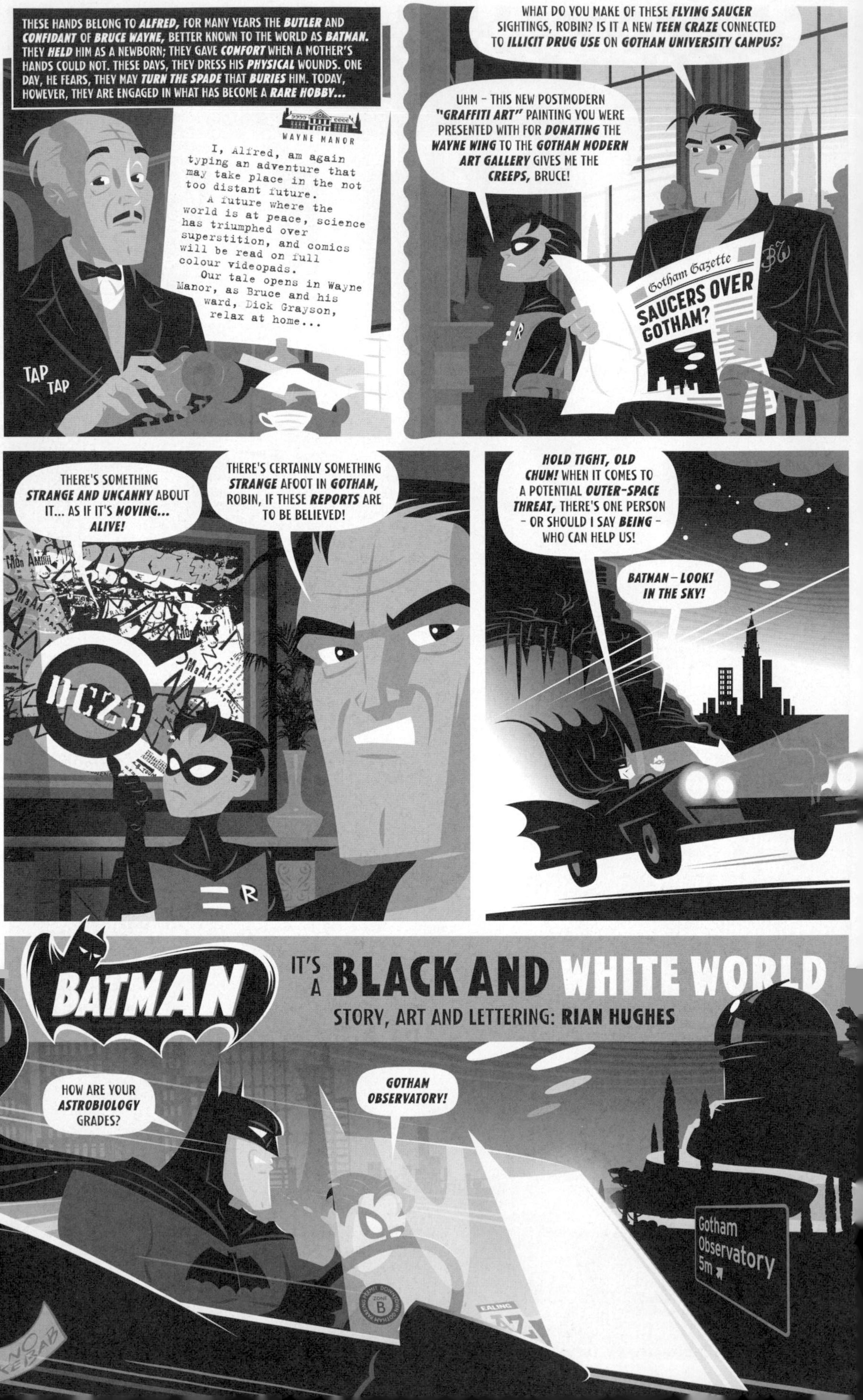
THESE HANDS BELONG TO ALFRED, FOR MANY YEARS THE BUTLER AND CONFIDANT OF BRUCE WAYNE, BETTER KNOWN TO THE WORLD AS BATMAN. THEY HELD HIM AS A NEWBORN; THEY GAVE COMFORT WHEN A MOTHER'S HANDS COULD NOT. THESE DAYS, THEY DRESS HIS PHYSICAL WOUNDS. ONE DAY, HE FEARS, THEY MAY TURN THE SPADE THAT BURIES HIM. TODAY, HOWEVER, THEY ARE ENGAGED IN WHAT HAS BECOME A RARE HOBBY...
WAYNE MANOR
I, Alfred, am again typing an adventure that may take place in the not too distant future. A future where the world is at peace, science has triumphed over superstition, and comics will be read on full colour videopads. Our tale opens in Wayne Manor, as Bruce and his ward, Dick Grayson, relax at home...
TAP TAP
WHAT DO YOU MAKE OF THESE FLYING SAUCER SIGHTINGS, ROBIN? IS IT A NEW TEEN CRAZE CONNECTED TO ILLICIT DRUG USE ON GOTHAM UNIVERSITY CAMPUS?
UHM – THIS NEW POSTMODERN "GRAFFITI ART" PAINTING YOU WERE PRESENTED WITH FOR DONATING THE WAYNE WING TO THE GOTHAM MODERN ART GALLERY GIVES ME THE CREEPS, BRUCE!
Gotham Gazette
SAUCERS OVER GOTHAM?
THERE'S SOMETHING STRANGE AND UNCANNY ABOUT IT... AS IF IT'S MOVING... ALIVE!
THERE'S CERTAINLY SOMETHING STRANGE AFOOT IN GOTHAM, ROBIN, IF THESE REPORTS ARE TO BE BELIEVED!
DCZ3
HOLD TIGHT, OLD CHUM! WHEN IT COMES TO A POTENTIAL OUTER-SPACE THREAT, THERE'S ONE PERSON – OR SHOULD I SAY BEING – WHO CAN HELP US!
BATMAN – LOOK! IN THE SKY!
BATMAN
IT'S A BLACK AND WHITE WORLD
STORY, ART AND LETTERING: RIAN HUGHES
HOW ARE YOUR ASTROBIOLOGY GRADES?
GOTHAM OBSERVATORY!
Gotham Observatory 5m
NO KEBAB

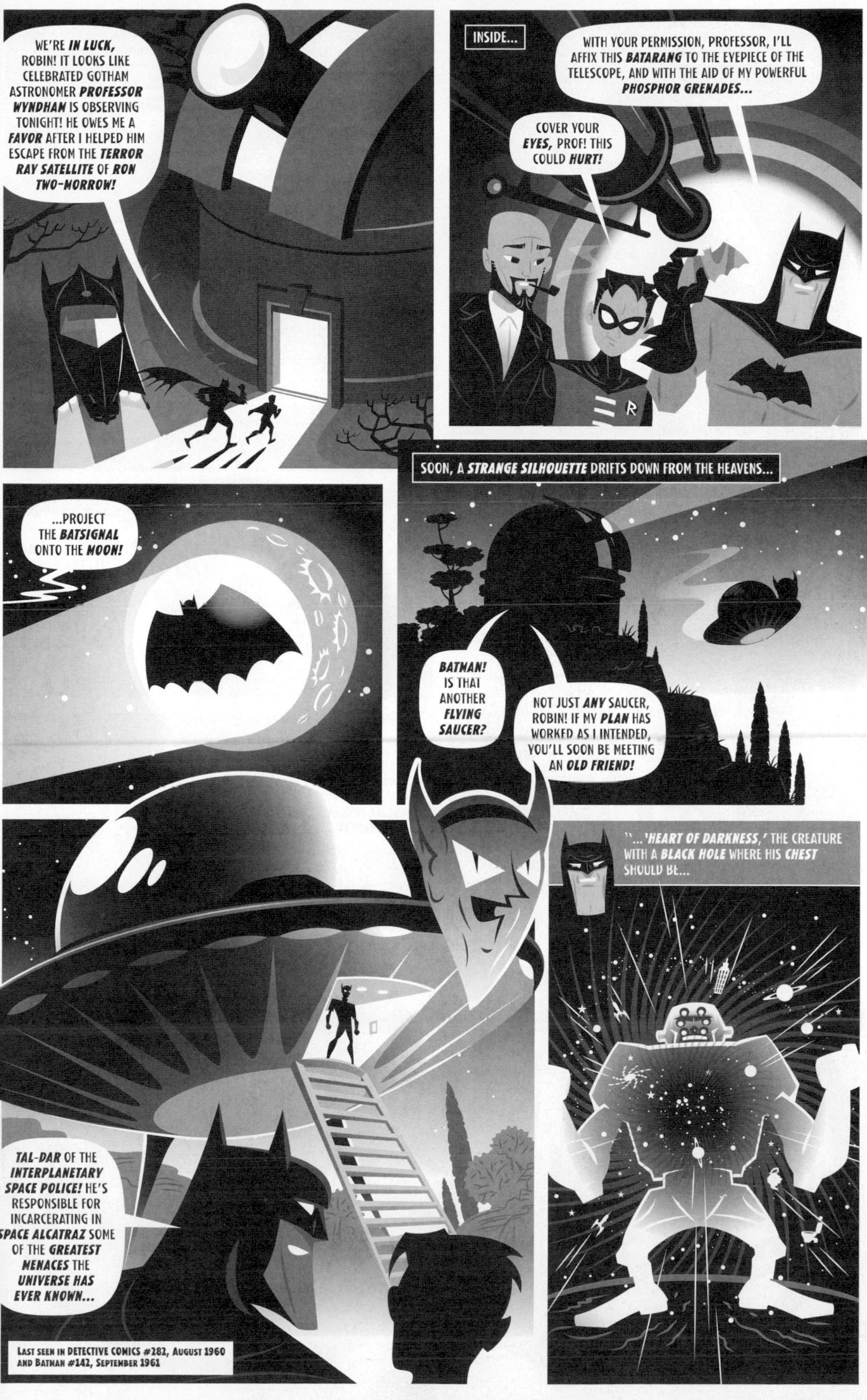

WE'RE IN LUCK, ROBIN! IT LOOKS LIKE CELEBRATED GOTHAM ASTRONOMER PROFESSOR WYNDHAM IS OBSERVING TONIGHT! HE OWES ME A FAVOR AFTER I HELPED HIM ESCAPE FROM THE TERROR RAY SATELLITE OF RON TWO-MORROW!
INSIDE...
WITH YOUR PERMISSION, PROFESSOR, I'LL AFFIX THIS BATARANG TO THE EYEPIECE OF THE TELESCOPE, AND WITH THE AID OF MY POWERFUL PHOSPHOR GRENADES...
COVER YOUR EYES, PROF! THIS COULD HURT!
R
...PROJECT THE BATSIGNAL ONTO THE MOON!
SOON, A STRANGE SILHOUETTE DRIFTS DOWN FROM THE HEAVENS...
BATMAN! IS THAT ANOTHER FLYING SAUCER?
NOT JUST ANY SAUCER, ROBIN! IF MY PLAN HAS WORKED AS I INTENDED, YOU'LL SOON BE MEETING AN OLD FRIEND!
TAL-DAR OF THE INTERPLANETARY SPACE POLICE! HE'S RESPONSIBLE FOR INCARCERATING IN SPACE ALCATRAZ SOME OF THE GREATEST MENACES THE UNIVERSE HAS EVER KNOWN...
LAST SEEN IN DETECTIVE COMICS #282, AUGUST 1960 AND BATMAN #142, SEPTEMBER 1961
"...'HEART OF DARKNESS,' THE CREATURE WITH A BLACK HOLE WHERE HIS CHEST SHOULD BE...

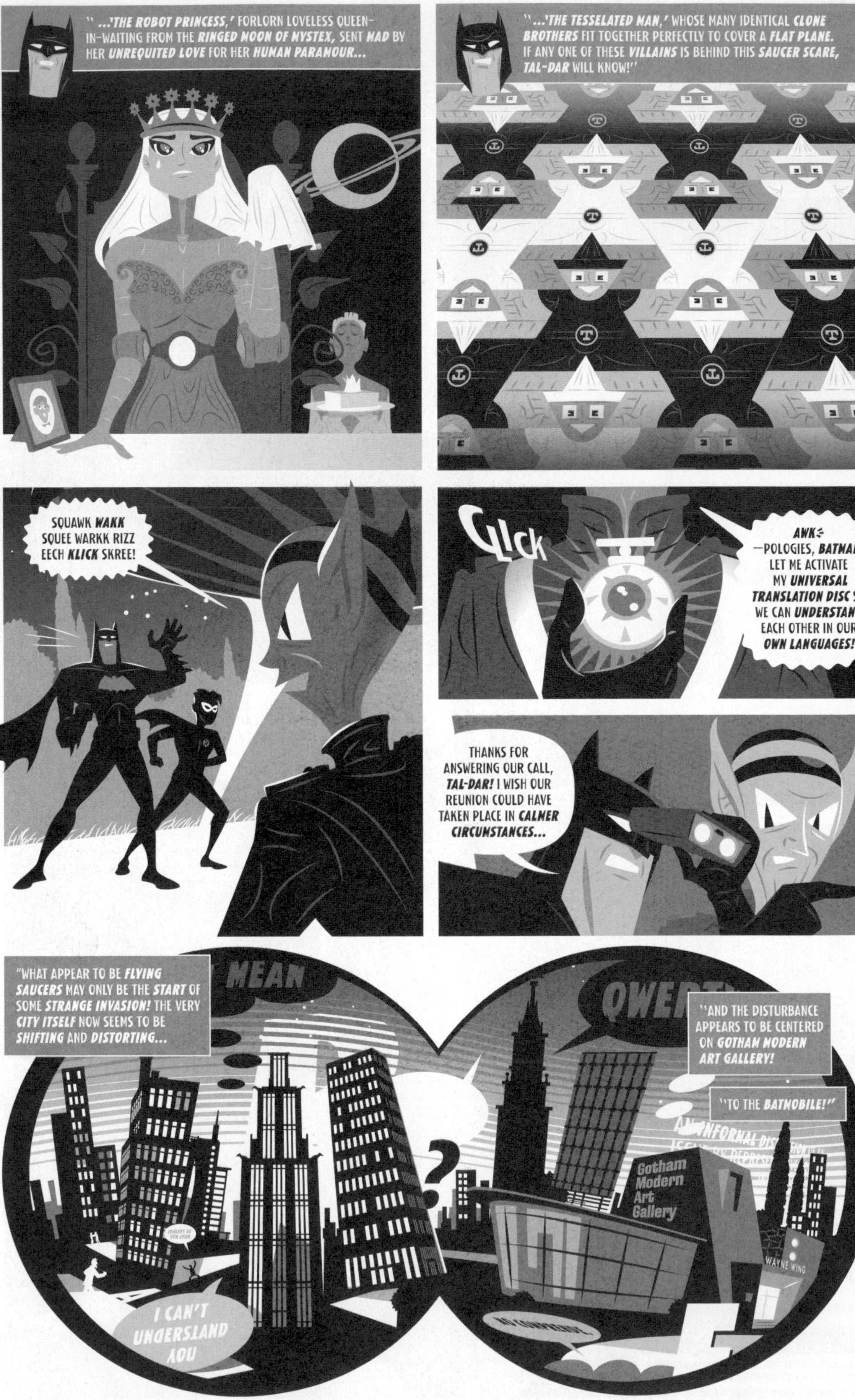
''...'THE ROBOT PRINCESS,' FORLORN LOVELESS QUEEN-IN-WAITING FROM THE RINGED MOON OF MYSTEX, SENT MAD BY HER UNREQUITED LOVE FOR HER HUMAN PARAMOUR...
''...'THE TESSELATED MAN,' WHOSE MANY IDENTICAL CLONE BROTHERS FIT TOGETHER PERFECTLY TO COVER A FLAT PLANE. IF ANY ONE OF THESE VILLAINS IS BEHIND THIS SAUCER SCARE, TAL-DAR WILL KNOW!''
SQUAWK WAKK SQUEE WARKK RIZZ EECH KLICK SKREE!
CLICK
AWK— —POLOGIES, BATMAN! LET ME ACTIVATE MY UNIVERSAL TRANSLATION DISC SO WE CAN UNDERSTAND EACH OTHER IN OUR OWN LANGUAGES!
THANKS FOR ANSWERING OUR CALL, TAL-DAR! I WISH OUR REUNION COULD HAVE TAKEN PLACE IN CALMER CIRCUMSTANCES...
"WHAT APPEAR TO BE FLYING SAUCERS MAY ONLY BE THE START OF SOME STRANGE INVASION! THE VERY CITY ITSELF NOW SEEMS TO BE SHIFTING AND DISTORTING...
''AND THE DISTURBANCE APPEARS TO BE CENTERED ON GOTHAM MODERN ART GALLERY!
''TO THE BATMOBILE!''
?
Gotham Modern Art Gallery
WAYNE WING
I CAN'T UNDERSLAND YOU

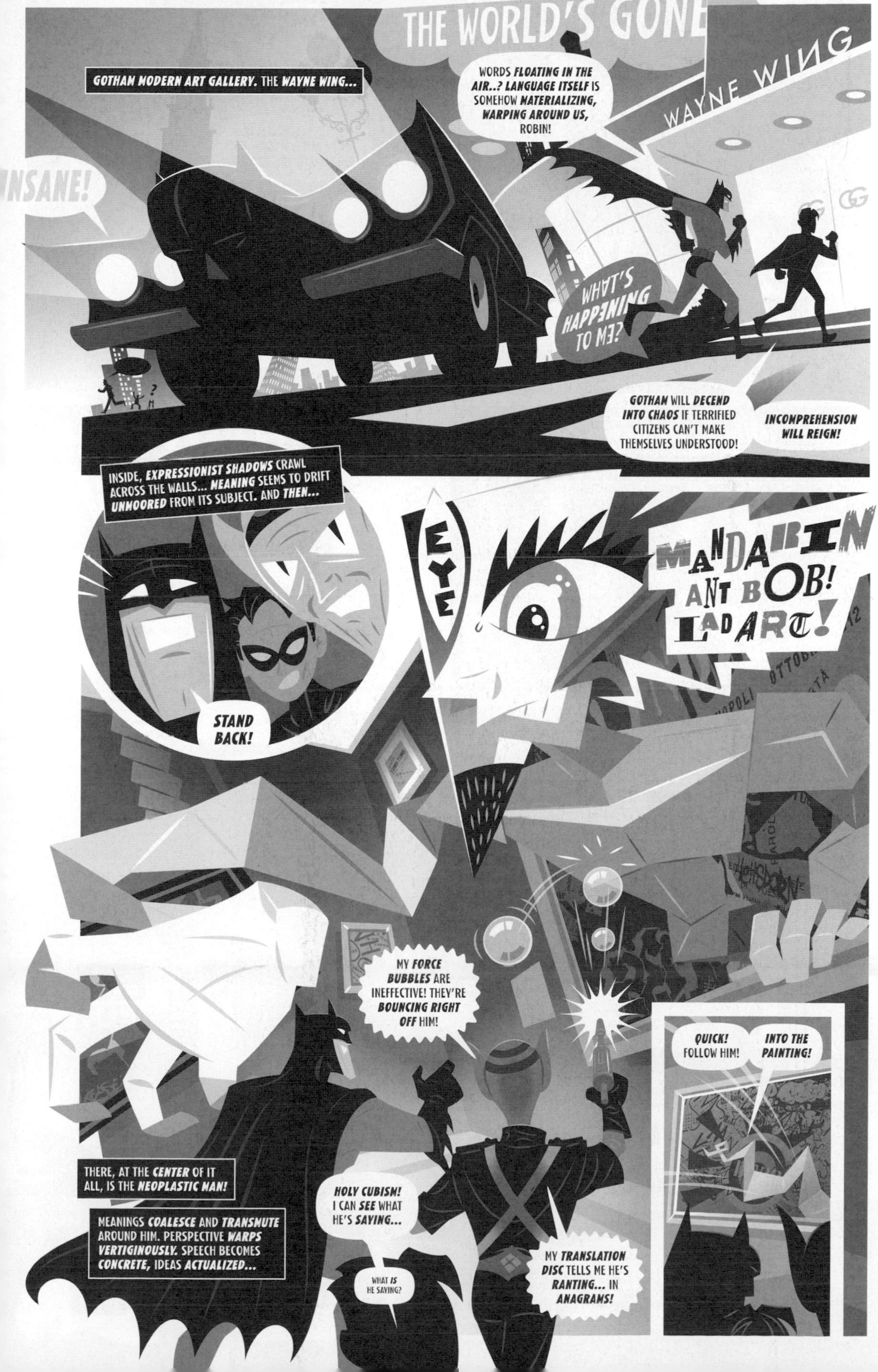
THE WORLD'S GONE
INSANE!
GOTHAM MODERN ART GALLERY. THE WAYNE WING...
WORDS FLOATING IN THE AIR..? LANGUAGE ITSELF IS SOMEHOW MATERIALIZING, WARPING AROUND US, ROBIN!
WAYNE WING
WHAT'S HAPPENING TO ME?
GOTHAM WILL DECEND INTO CHAOS IF TERRIFIED CITIZENS CAN'T MAKE THEMSELVES UNDERSTOOD!
INCOMPREHENSION WILL REIGN!
INSIDE, EXPRESSIONIST SHADOWS CRAWL ACROSS THE WALLS... MEANING SEEMS TO DRIFT UNMOORED FROM ITS SUBJECT. AND THEN...
EYE
MANDABIN ANT BOB! LADART!
STAND BACK!
MY FORCE BUBBLES ARE INEFFECTIVE! THEY'RE BOUNCING RIGHT OFF HIM!
QUICK! FOLLOW HIM!
INTO THE PAINTING!
THERE, AT THE CENTER OF IT ALL, IS THE NEOPLASTIC MAN!
MEANINGS COALESCE AND TRANSMUTE AROUND HIM. PERSPECTIVE WARPS VERTIGINOUSLY. SPEECH BECOMES CONCRETE, IDEAS ACTUALIZED...
HOLY CUBISM! I CAN SEE WHAT HE'S SAYING...
WHAT IS HE SAYING?
MY TRANSLATION DISC TELLS ME HE'S RANTING... IN ANAGRAMS!

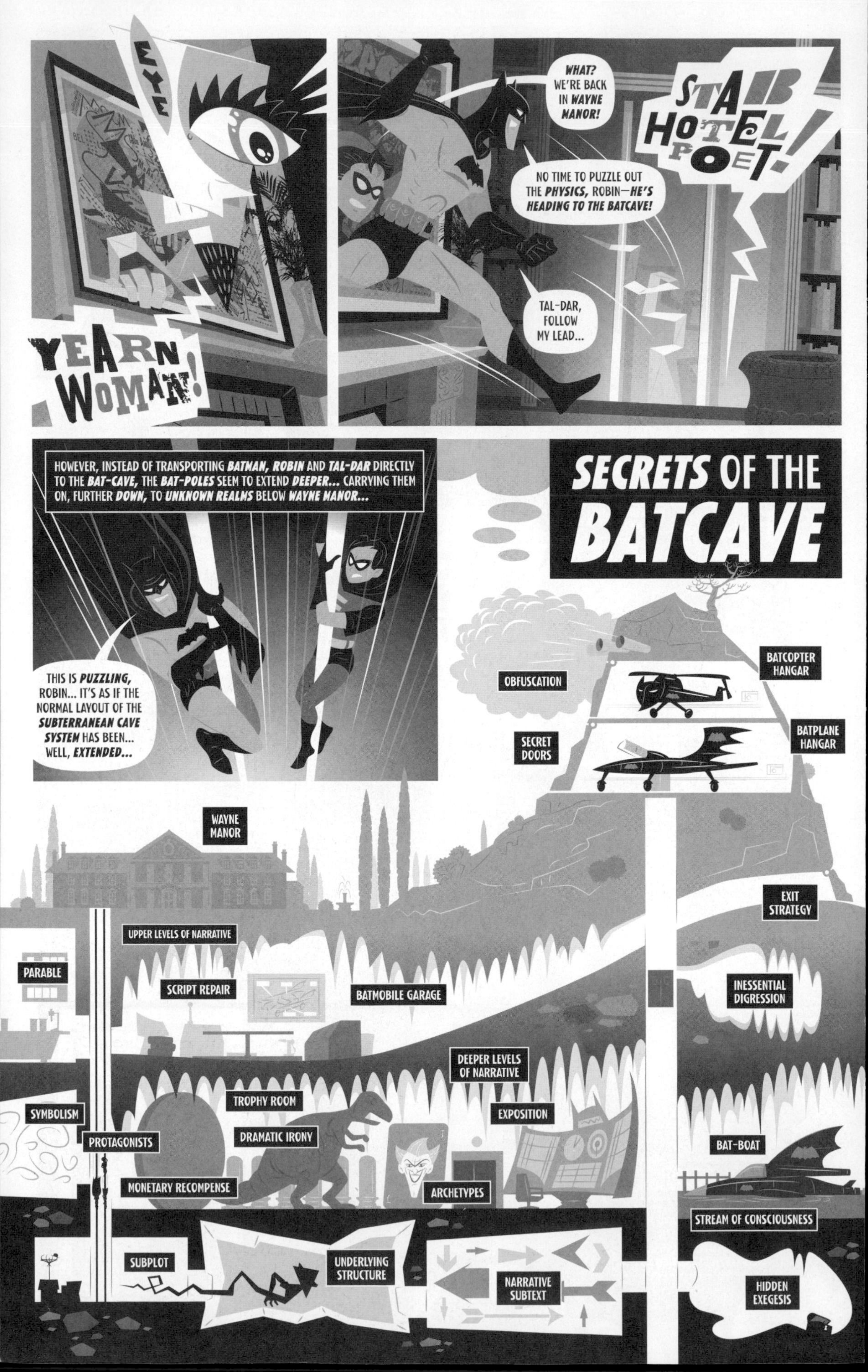
EYE
YEARN WOMAN!
WHAT? WE'RE BACK IN WAYNE MANOR!
STAB HOTEL POET!
NO TIME TO PUZZLE OUT THE PHYSICS, ROBIN—HE'S HEADING TO THE BATCAVE!
TAL-DAR, FOLLOW MY LEAD...
HOWEVER, INSTEAD OF TRANSPORTING BATMAN, ROBIN AND TAL-DAR DIRECTLY TO THE BAT-CAVE, THE BAT-POLES SEEM TO EXTEND DEEPER... CARRYING THEM ON, FURTHER DOWN, TO UNKNOWN REALMS BELOW WAYNE MANOR...
THIS IS PUZZLING, ROBIN... IT'S AS IF THE NORMAL LAYOUT OF THE SUBTERRANEAN CAVE SYSTEM HAS BEEN... WELL, EXTENDED...
SECRETS OF THE BATCAVE
OBFUSCATION
BATCOPTER HANGAR
SECRET DOORS
BATPLANE HANGAR
WAYNE MANOR
EXIT STRATEGY
UPPER LEVELS OF NARRATIVE
PARABLE
SCRIPT REPAIR
BATMOBILE GARAGE
INESSENTIAL DIGRESSION
DEEPER LEVELS OF NARRATIVE
TROPHY ROOM
EXPOSITION
SYMBOLISM
PROTAGONISTS
DRAMATIC IRONY
BAT-BOAT
MONETARY RECOMPENSE
ARCHETYPES
STREAM OF CONSCIOUSNESS
SUBPLOT
UNDERLYING STRUCTURE
NARRATIVE SUBTEXT
HIDDEN EXEGESIS

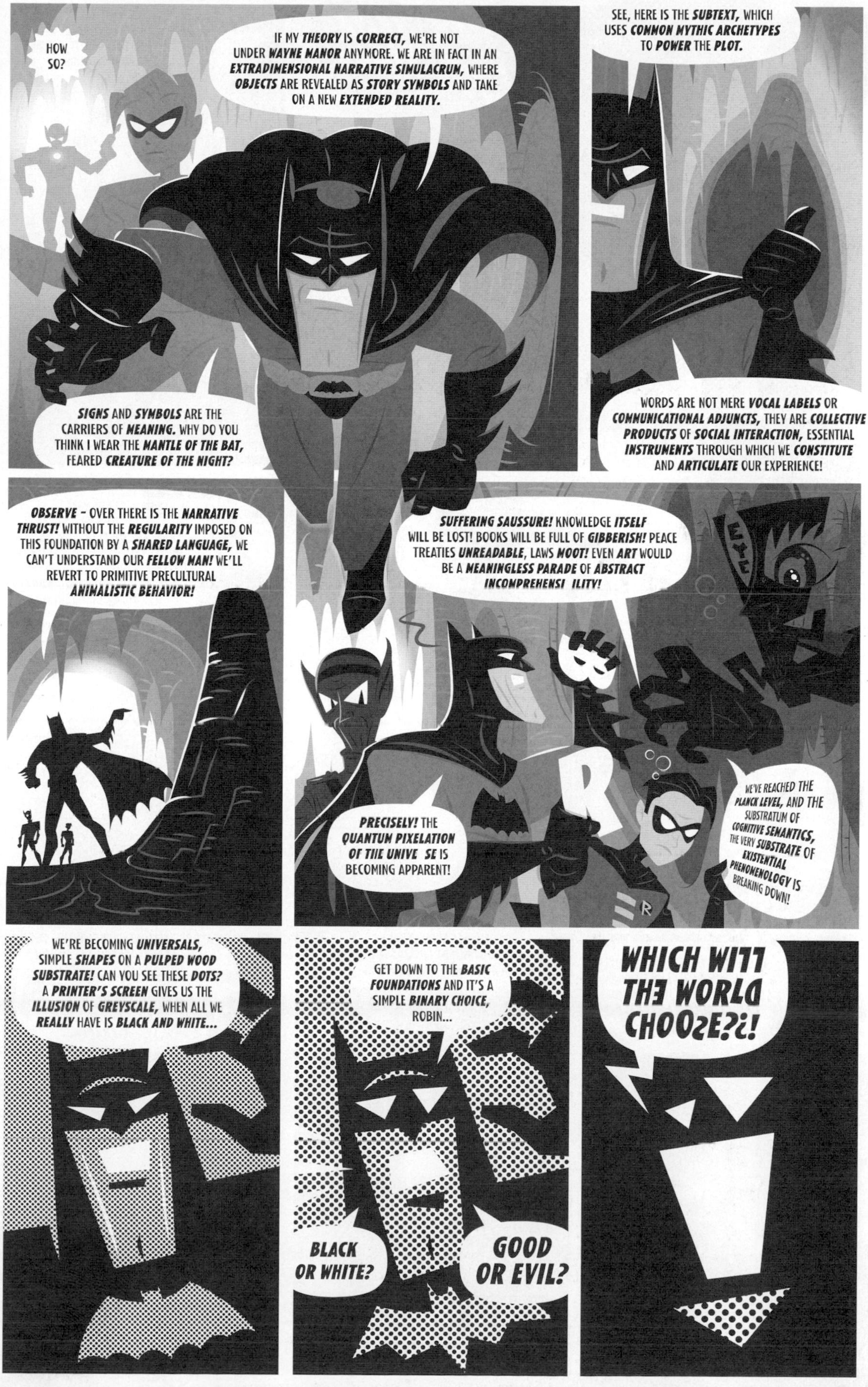
HOW SO?
IF MY THEORY IS CORRECT, WE'RE NOT UNDER WAYNE MANOR ANYMORE. WE ARE IN FACT IN AN EXTRADIMENSIONAL NARRATIVE SIMULACRUM, WHERE OBJECTS ARE REVEALED AS STORY SYMBOLS AND TAKE ON A NEW EXTENDED REALITY.
SIGNS AND SYMBOLS ARE THE CARRIERS OF MEANING. WHY DO YOU THINK I WEAR THE MANTLE OF THE BAT, FEARED CREATURE OF THE NIGHT?
SEE, HERE IS THE SUBTEXT, WHICH USES COMMON MYTHIC ARCHETYPES TO POWER THE PLOT.
WORDS ARE NOT MERE VOCAL LABELS OR COMMUNICATIONAL ADJUNCTS, THEY ARE COLLECTIVE PRODUCTS OF SOCIAL INTERACTION, ESSENTIAL INSTRUMENTS THROUGH WHICH WE CONSTITUTE AND ARTICULATE OUR EXPERIENCE!
OBSERVE - OVER THERE IS THE NARRATIVE THRUST! WITHOUT THE REGULARITY IMPOSED ON THIS FOUNDATION BY A SHARED LANGUAGE, WE CAN'T UNDERSTAND OUR FELLOW MAN! WE'LL REVERT TO PRIMITIVE PRECULTURAL ANIMALISTIC BEHAVIOR!
SUFFERING SAUSSURE! KNOWLEDGE ITSELF WILL BE LOST! BOOKS WILL BE FULL OF GIBBERISH! PEACE TREATIES UNREADABLE, LAWS MOOT! EVEN ART WOULD BE A MEANINGLESS PARADE OF ABSTRACT INCOMPREHENSI ILITY!
PRECISELY! THE QUANTUM PIXELATION OF THE UNIVE SE IS BECOMING APPARENT!
WE'VE REACHED THE PLANCK LEVEL, AND THE SUBSTRATUM OF COGNITIVE SEMANTICS, THE VERY SUBSTRATE OF EXISTENTIAL PHENOMENOLOGY IS BREAKING DOWN!
WE'RE BECOMING UNIVERSALS, SIMPLE SHAPES ON A PULPED WOOD SUBSTRATE! CAN YOU SEE THESE DOTS? A PRINTER'S SCREEN GIVES US THE ILLUSION OF GREYSCALE, WHEN ALL WE REALLY HAVE IS BLACK AND WHITE...
GET DOWN TO THE BASIC FOUNDATIONS AND IT'S A SIMPLE BINARY CHOICE, ROBIN...
BLACK OR WHITE?
GOOD OR EVIL?
WHICH WILL THE WORLD CHOOSE??!

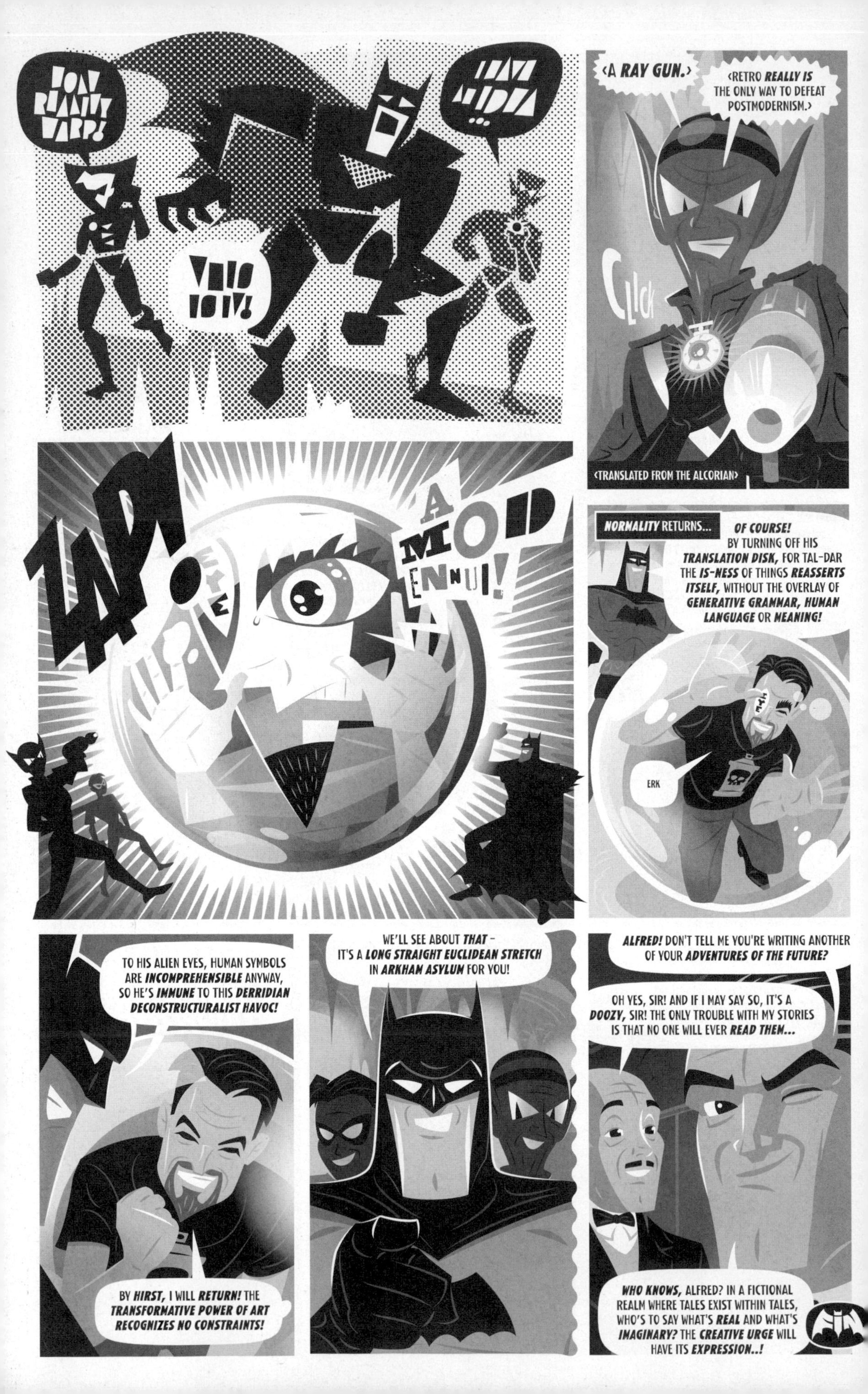
<A RAY GUN.>
<RETRO REALLY IS THE ONLY WAY TO DEFEAT POSTMODERNISM.>
CLICK
<TRANSLATED FROM THE ALCORIAN>
ZAP!
A MOD ENNUI!
NORMALITY RETURNS...
OF COURSE! BY TURNING OFF HIS TRANSLATION DISK, FOR TAL-DAR THE IS-NESS OF THINGS REASSERTS ITSELF, WITHOUT THE OVERLAY OF GENERATIVE GRAMMAR, HUMAN LANGUAGE OR MEANING!
ERK
TO HIS ALIEN EYES, HUMAN SYMBOLS ARE INCOMPREHENSIBLE ANYWAY, SO HE'S IMMUNE TO THIS DERRIDIAN DECONSTRUCTURALIST HAVOC!
BY HIRST, I WILL RETURN! THE TRANSFORMATIVE POWER OF ART RECOGNIZES NO CONSTRAINTS!
WE'LL SEE ABOUT THAT - IT'S A LONG STRAIGHT EUCLIDEAN STRETCH IN ARKHAM ASYLUM FOR YOU!
ALFRED! DON'T TELL ME YOU'RE WRITING ANOTHER OF YOUR ADVENTURES OF THE FUTURE?
OH YES, SIR! AND IF I MAY SAY SO, IT'S A DOOZY, SIR! THE ONLY TROUBLE WITH MY STORIES IS THAT NO ONE WILL EVER READ THEM...
WHO KNOWS, ALFRED? IN A FICTIONAL REALM WHERE TALES EXIST WITHIN TALES, WHO'S TO SAY WHAT'S REAL AND WHAT'S IMAGINARY? THE CREATIVE URGE WILL HAVE ITS EXPRESSION..!
FIN

OR ANY MORE. WE ARE IN FACT IN
L NARRATIVE SIMULACRUM, WI
LED AS *STORY SYMBOLS* AND TA
W *EXTENDED REALITY.*

SUFFERI
WILL BE LOST! B
TREATIES *UNR*
BE A *ME*

RIAN HUGHES

One of Britain's leading
graphic designers, Rian Hughes is also an
accomplished illustrator and comics artist.
Whether designing a magazine cover, creating
a new font, or illustrating the adventures of
our favorite heroes, Rian always leaves his
indelible mark on the publishing world. His
work on *2000AD* and *Dan Dare* featured the
unmistakably hyper-stylized and bold,
graphic approach that have made Rian an
artist and designer of worldwide fame.

ROLE MODELS

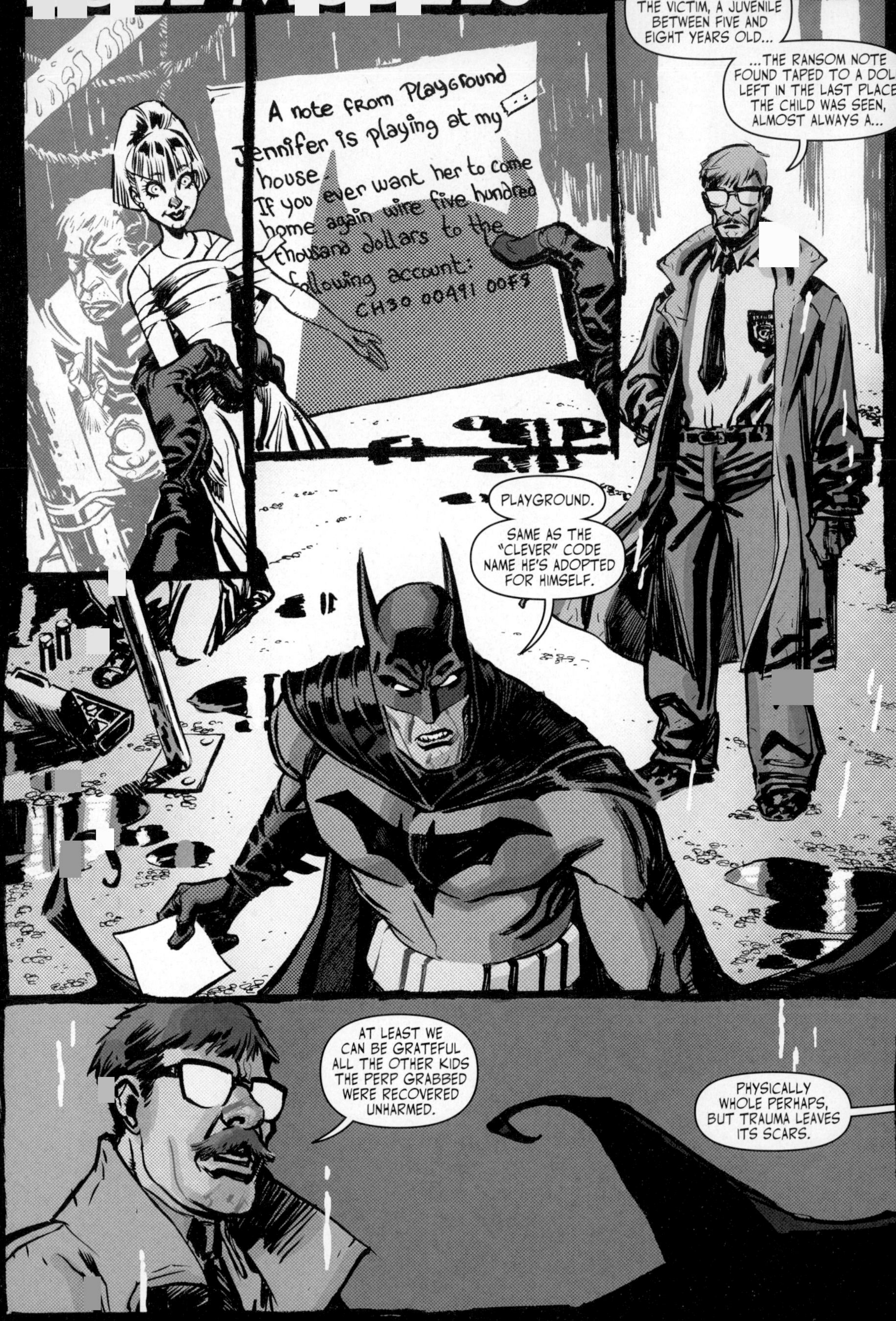
A note from Playground
Jennifer is playing at my house
If you ever want her to come home again wire five hundred thousand dollars to the following account:
CH30 00491 00F8
THE KIDNAPPING FITS THE PATTERN. THE VICTIM, A JUVENILE BETWEEN FIVE AND EIGHT YEARS OLD...
...THE RANSOM NOTE FOUND TAPED TO A DOLL LEFT IN THE LAST PLACE THE CHILD WAS SEEN, ALMOST ALWAYS A...
PLAYGROUND.
SAME AS THE "CLEVER" CODE NAME HE'S ADOPTED FOR HIMSELF.
AT LEAST WE CAN BE GRATEFUL ALL THE OTHER KIDS THE PERP GRABBED WERE RECOVERED UNHARMED.
PHYSICALLY WHOLE PERHAPS, BUT TRAUMA LEAVES ITS SCARS.

PAUL DINI writer STÉPHANE ROUX artist JARED K. FLETCHER letters

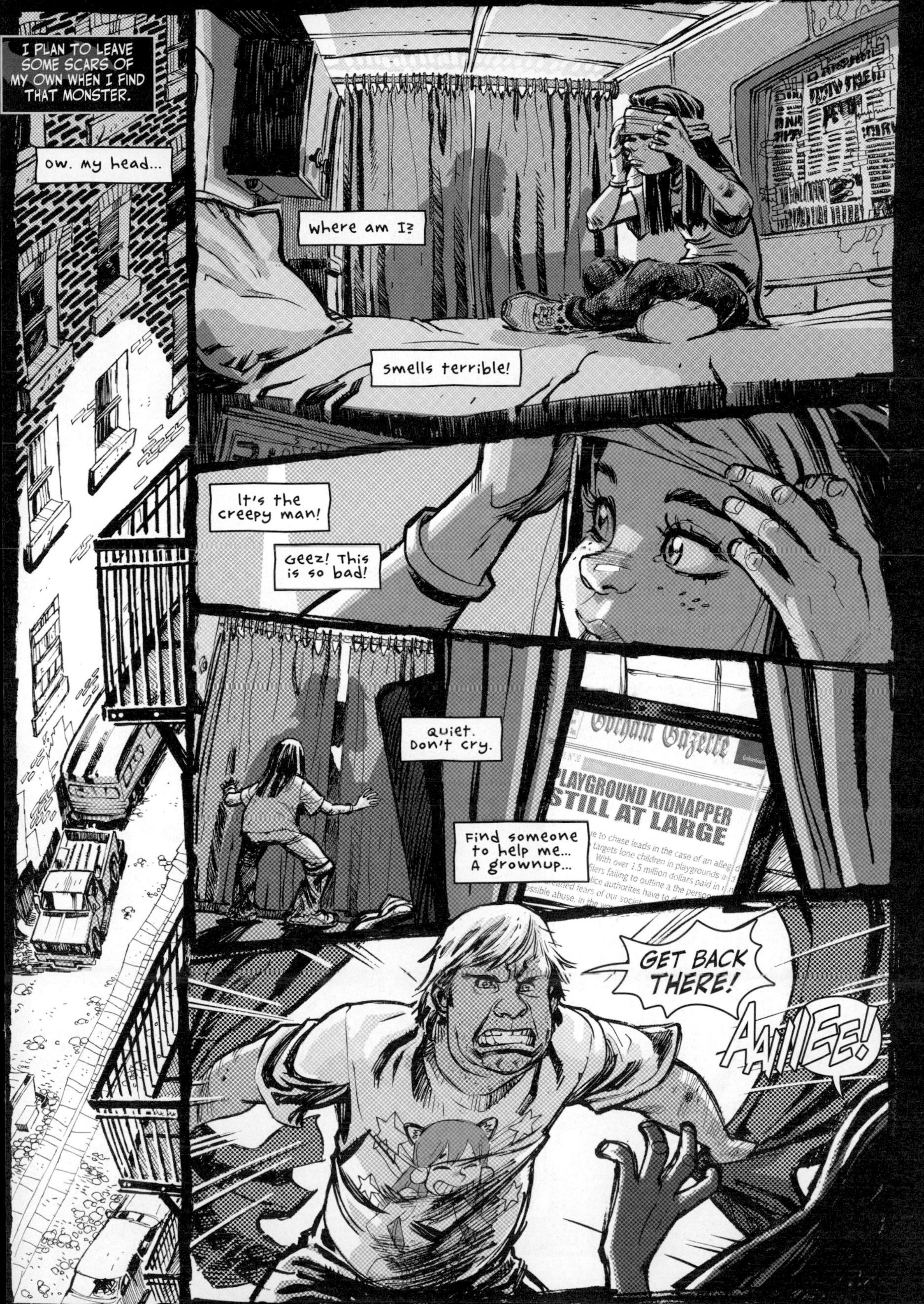
I PLAN TO LEAVE SOME SCARS OF MY OWN WHEN I FIND THAT MONSTER.
ow. my head...
where am I?
smells terrible!
It's the creepy man!
Geez! This is so bad!
quiet. Don't cry.
Gotham Gazette
PLAYGROUND KIDNAPPER STILL AT LARGE
Find someone to help me... A grownup...
GET BACK THERE!
AAIIIEEE!

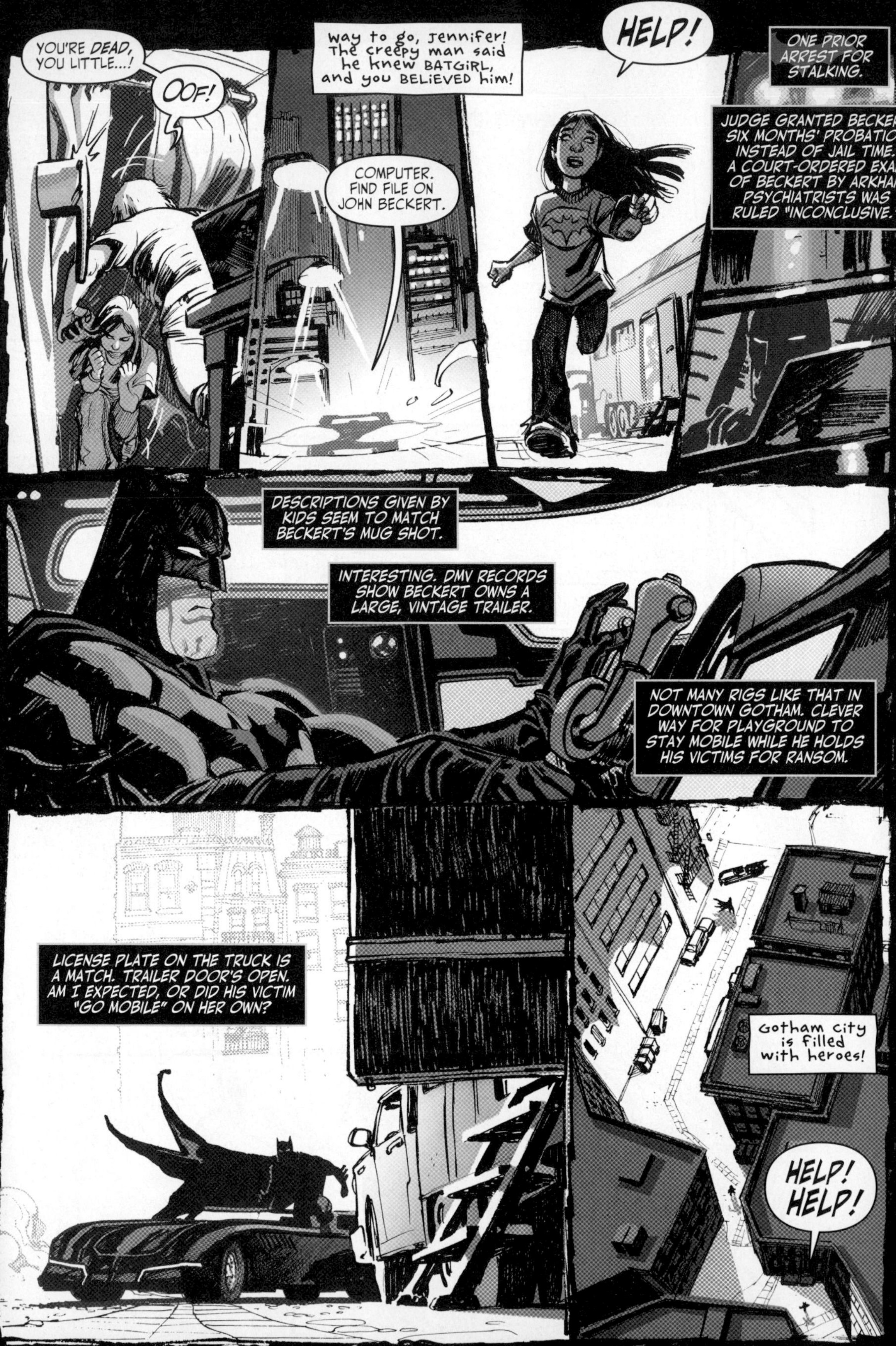
YOU'RE DEAD, YOU LITTLE...!
OOF!
way to go, jennifer! The creepy man said he knew BATGIRL, and you BELIEVED him!
COMPUTER. FIND FILE ON JOHN BECKERT.
HELP!
ONE PRIOR ARREST FOR STALKING.
JUDGE GRANTED BECKER SIX MONTHS' PROBATIO INSTEAD OF JAIL TIME. A COURT-ORDERED EXA OF BECKERT BY ARKHA PSYCHIATRISTS WAS RULED "INCONCLUSIVE.
DESCRIPTIONS GIVEN BY KIDS SEEM TO MATCH BECKERT'S MUG SHOT.
INTERESTING. DMV RECORDS SHOW BECKERT OWNS A LARGE, VINTAGE TRAILER.
NOT MANY RIGS LIKE THAT IN DOWNTOWN GOTHAM. CLEVER WAY FOR PLAYGROUND TO STAY MOBILE WHILE HE HOLDS HIS VICTIMS FOR RANSOM.
LICENSE PLATE ON THE TRUCK IS A MATCH. TRAILER DOOR'S OPEN. AM I EXPECTED, OR DID HIS VICTIM "GO MOBILE" ON HER OWN?
Gotham city is filled with heroes!
HELP! HELP!

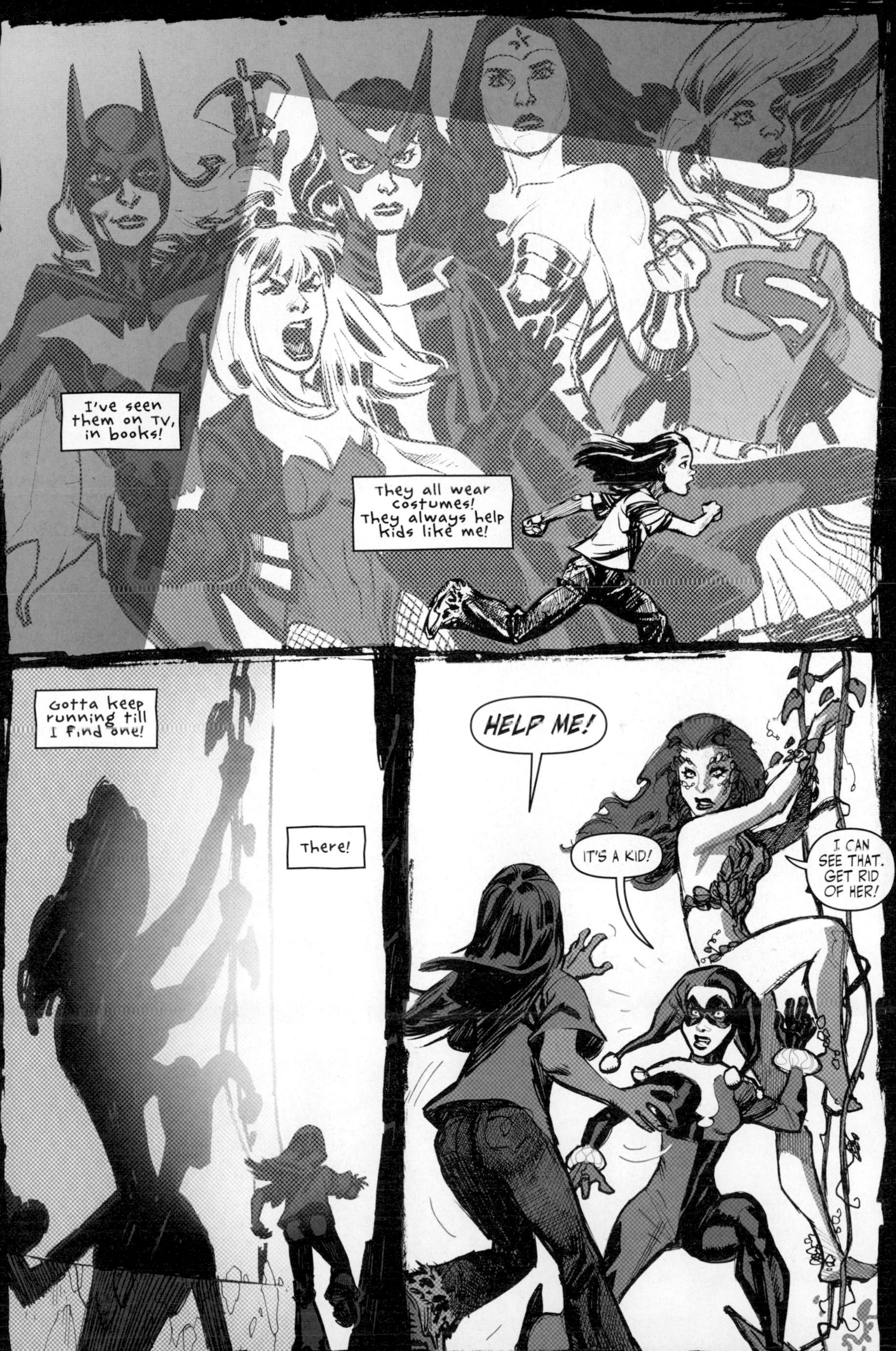

I've seen them on TV, in books!
They all wear costumes! They always help kids like me!
Gotta keep running till I find one!
There!
HELP ME!
IT'S A KID!
I CAN SEE THAT. GET RID OF HER!

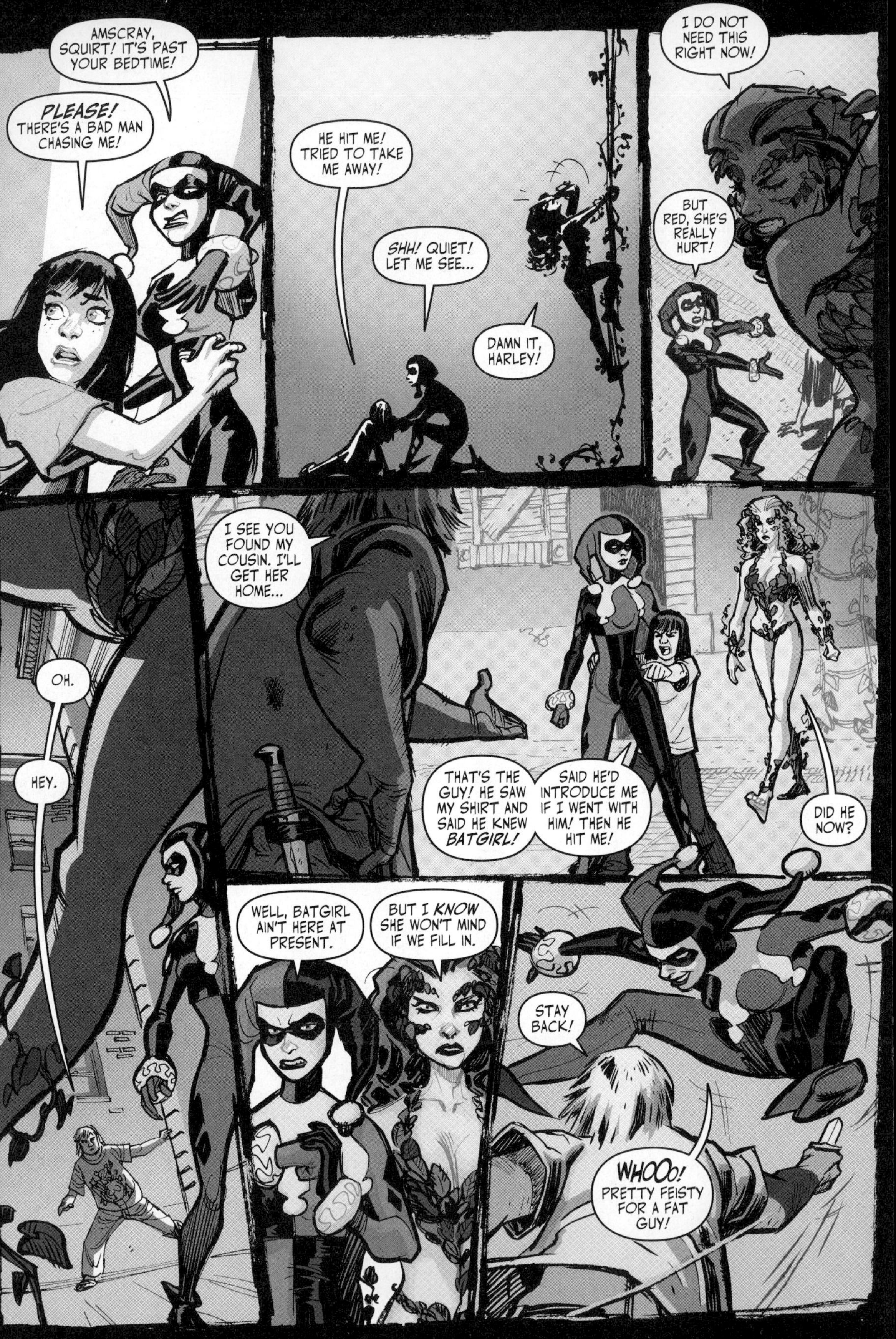
AMSCRAY, SQUIRT! IT'S PAST YOUR BEDTIME!
PLEASE! THERE'S A BAD MAN CHASING ME!
HE HIT ME! TRIED TO TAKE ME AWAY!
SHH! QUIET! LET ME SEE...
DAMN IT, HARLEY!
I DO NOT NEED THIS RIGHT NOW!
BUT RED, SHE'S REALLY HURT!
I SEE YOU FOUND MY COUSIN. I'LL GET HER HOME...
OH.
HEY.
THAT'S THE GUY! HE SAW MY SHIRT AND SAID HE KNEW BATGIRL!
SAID HE'D INTRODUCE ME IF I WENT WITH HIM! THEN HE HIT ME!
DID HE NOW?
WELL, BATGIRL AIN'T HERE AT PRESENT.
BUT I KNOW SHE WON'T MIND IF WE FILL IN.
STAY BACK!
WHOOo! PRETTY FEISTY FOR A FAT GUY!

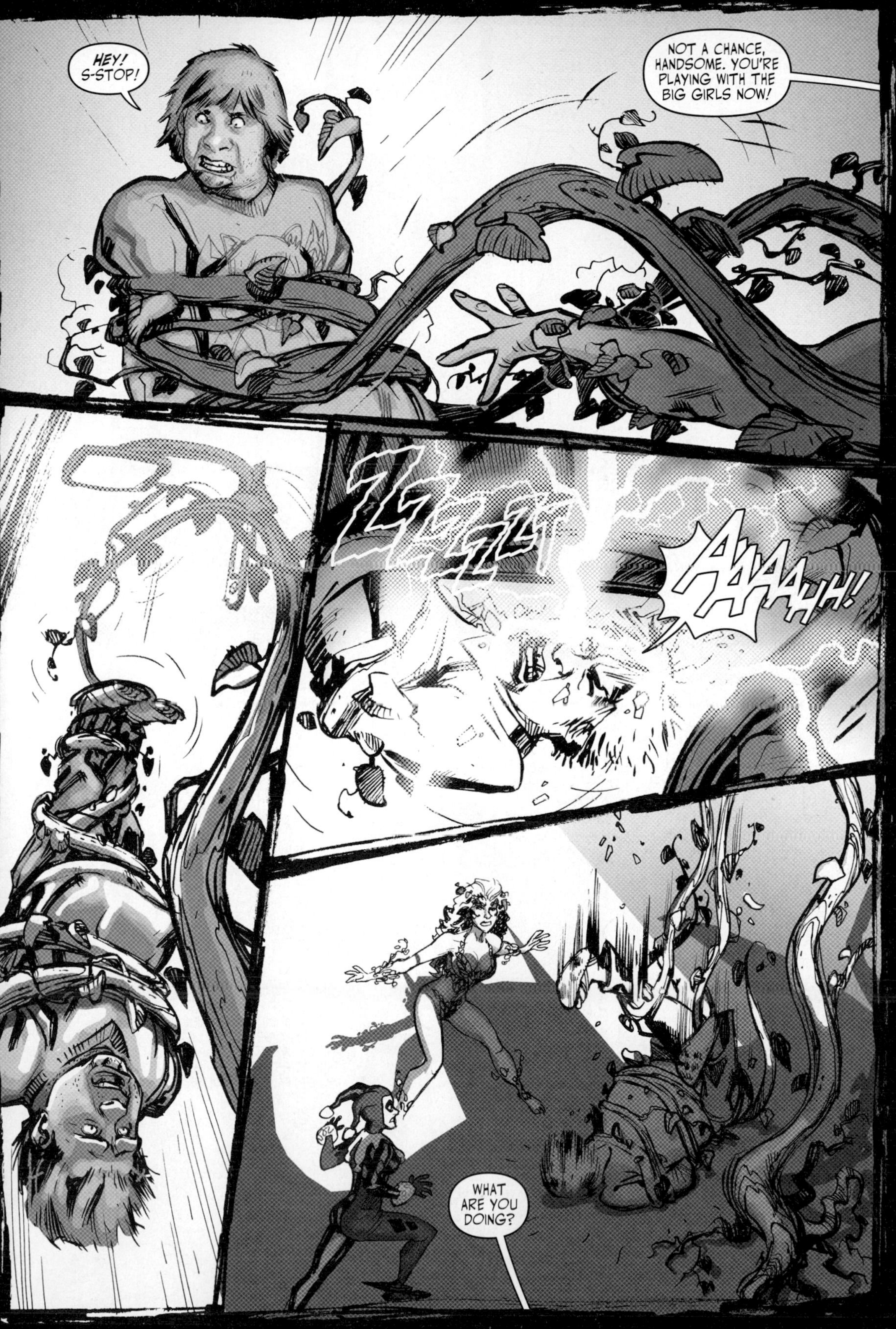

HEY! S-STOP!
NOT A CHANCE, HANDSOME. YOU'RE PLAYING WITH THE BIG GIRLS NOW!
ZZZZT
AAAAAHH!
WHAT ARE YOU DOING?

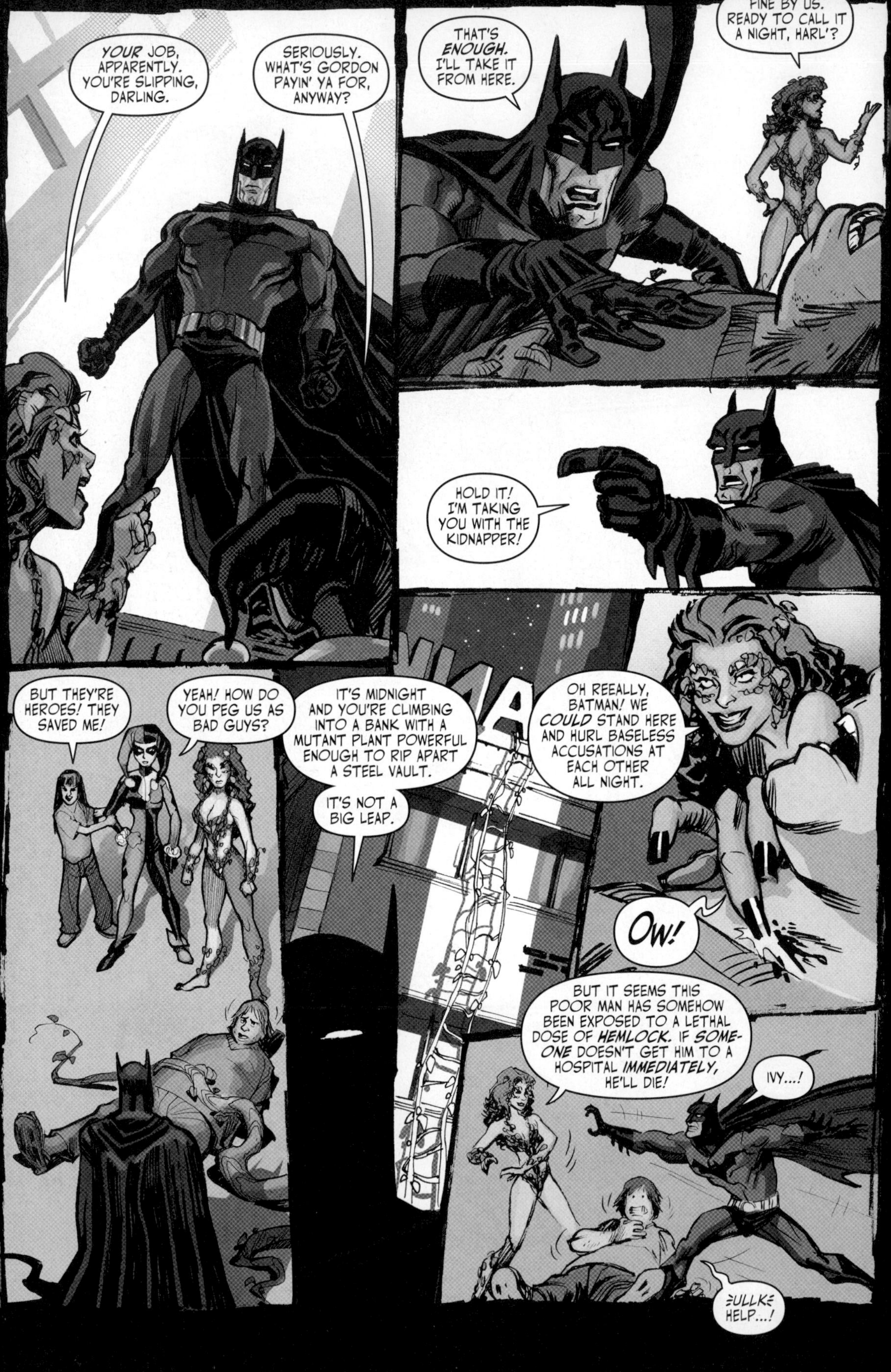
YOUR JOB, APPARENTLY. YOU'RE SLIPPING, DARLING.
SERIOUSLY. WHAT'S GORDON PAYIN' YA FOR, ANYWAY?
THAT'S ENOUGH. I'LL TAKE IT FROM HERE.
FINE BY US. READY TO CALL IT A NIGHT, HARL'?
HOLD IT! I'M TAKING YOU WITH THE KIDNAPPER!
BUT THEY'RE HEROES! THEY SAVED ME!
YEAH! HOW DO YOU PEG US AS BAD GUYS?
IT'S MIDNIGHT AND YOU'RE CLIMBING INTO A BANK WITH A MUTANT PLANT POWERFUL ENOUGH TO RIP APART A STEEL VAULT.
IT'S NOT A BIG LEAP.
OH REEALLY, BATMAN! WE COULD STAND HERE AND HURL BASELESS ACCUSATIONS AT EACH OTHER ALL NIGHT.
OW!
BUT IT SEEMS THIS POOR MAN HAS SOMEHOW BEEN EXPOSED TO A LETHAL DOSE OF HEMLOCK. IF SOMEONE DOESN'T GET HIM TO A HOSPITAL IMMEDIATELY, HE'LL DIE!
IVY...!
ULLK HELP...!

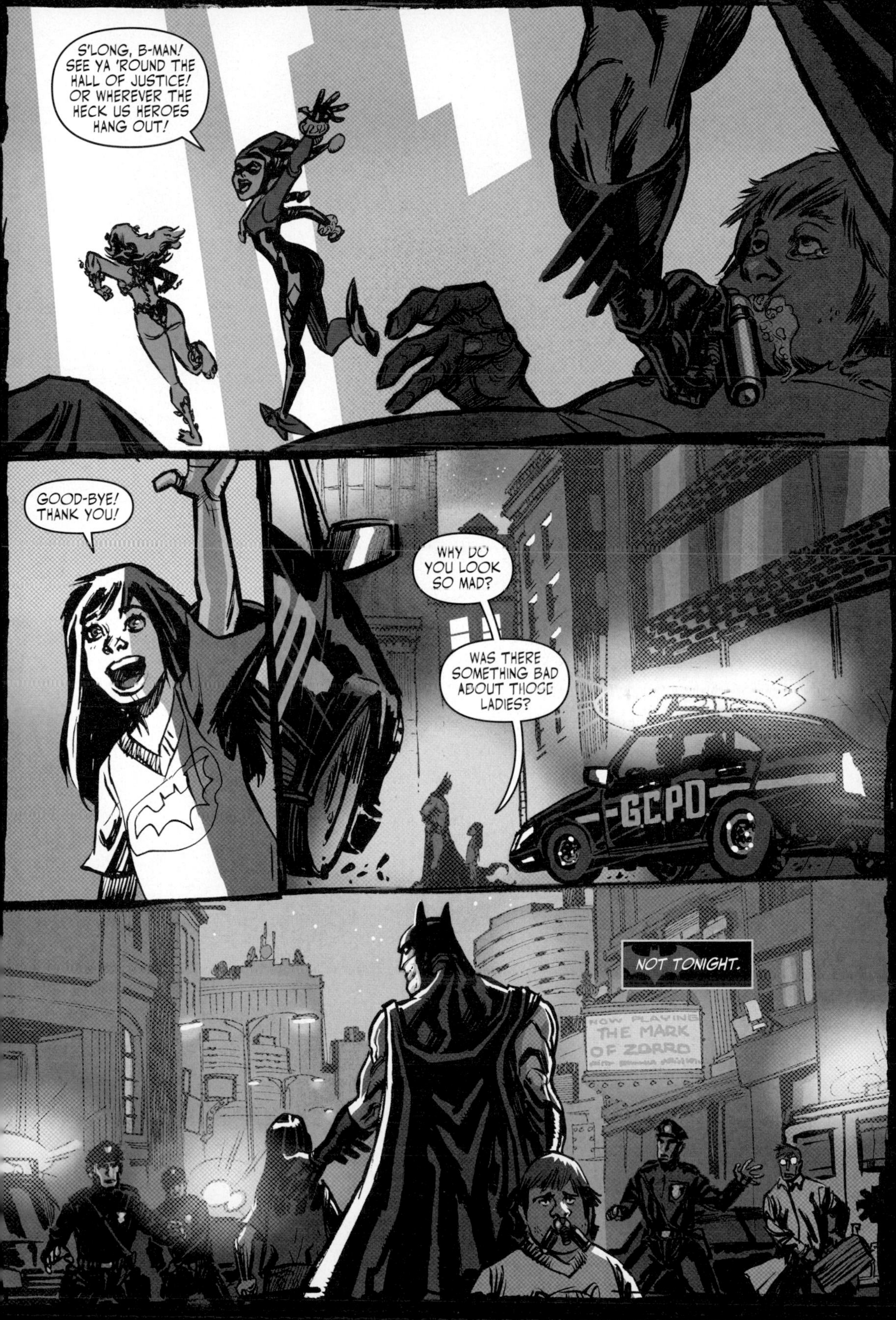
S'LONG, B-MAN! SEE YA 'ROUND THE HALL OF JUSTICE! OR WHEREVER THE HECK US HEROES HANG OUT!
GOOD-BYE! THANK YOU!
WHY DO YOU LOOK SO MAD?
WAS THERE SOMETHING BAD ABOUT THOSE LADIES?
GCPD
NOT TONIGHT.
NOW PLAYING THE MARK OF ZORRO

END

PAUL DINI

A five-time Emmy Award-winner,
Paul Dini splits his time between writing (and
producing) television and being one of the best,
most respected comic book writers around.
After working on the animated series
Tiny Toon Adventures, Dini turned heads with his
iconic depiction of the Dark Knight on the highly
celebrated *Batman: The Animated Series*.
His comics work includes DETECTIVE COMICS,
STREETS OF GOTHAM, GOTHAM CITY SIRENS, and
the graphic novel MAD LOVE, which is hailed
as one of the greatest comics of all time.
Recently, Dini has branched out into the video
game world by penning storylines for the
ridiculously popular *Batman: Arkham Asylum* and
its sequel *Batman: Arkham City*.

STÉPHANE ROUX

Known primarily for his breathtaking covers,
Stéphane Roux is a versatile French artist who
excels at drawing the female form. His work
on BIRDS OF PREY, ZATANNA, *Star Wars* and
The Rocketeer have made a lasting impression
on his fans and the comic book world

THERE'S A CHILL IN THE OCTOBER AIR. A PALPABLE FEAR. IN THE SHOPS, ON THE TRAIN, IN THE POLICE STATION THERE ARE WHISPERS OF A GHOST IN GOTHAM.

A GHOST THAT PROWLS. A GHOST THAT ENTERS HOMES AND LEAVES WITH VALUABLES...

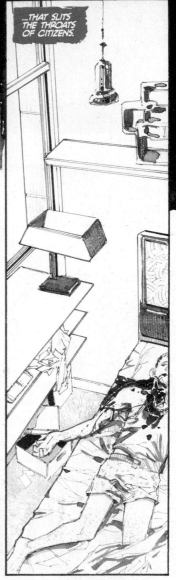

...THAT SLITS THE THROATS OF CITIZENS.

THE RUMORS ARE THAT THE PHANTOM RISES FROM GOTHAM CEMETERY. A SOUL RESTLESS AND DISTURBED.

THE GHOST IS WHY I'M HERE TONIGHT.

NOT BECAUSE I BELIEVE A WRAITH HAS ESCAPED THE SHORES OF THE NETHERWORLD AND IS HUNTING DOWN THE PEOPLE OF GOTHAM...

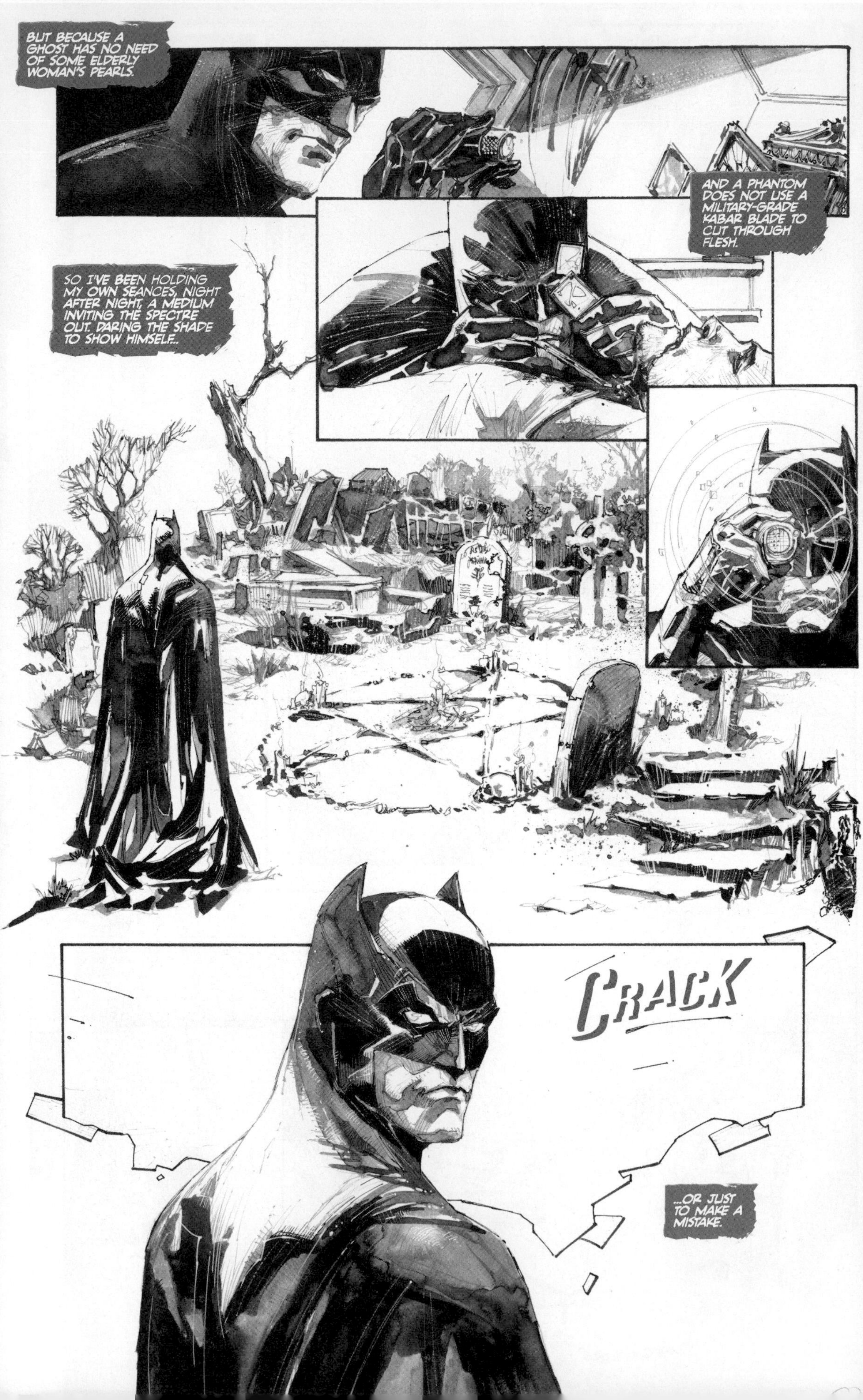
BUT BECAUSE A GHOST HAS NO NEED OF SOME ELDERLY WOMAN'S PEARLS.
AND A PHANTOM DOES NOT USE A MILITARY-GRADE KABAR BLADE TO CUT THROUGH FLESH.
SO I'VE BEEN HOLDING MY OWN SEANCES, NIGHT AFTER NIGHT, A MEDIUM INVITING THE SPECTRE OUT. DARING THE SHADE TO SHOW HIMSELF...
CRACK
...OR JUST TO MAKE A MISTAKE.

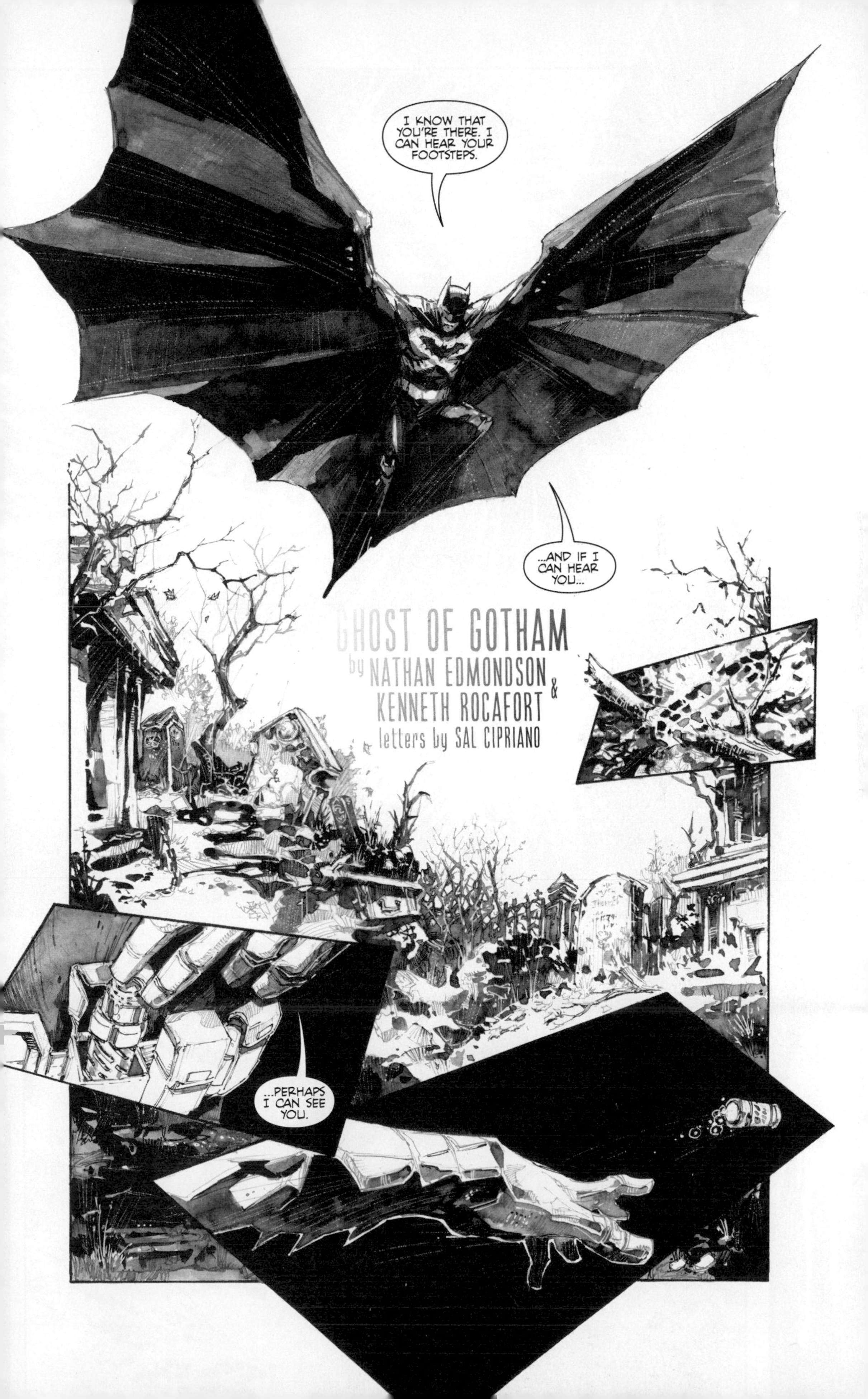

I KNOW THAT YOU'RE THERE. I CAN HEAR YOUR FOOTSTEPS.
...AND IF I CAN HEAR YOU...
GHOST OF GOTHAM
by NATHAN EDMONDSON & KENNETH ROCAFORT
letters by SAL CIPRIANO
...PERHAPS I CAN SEE YOU.

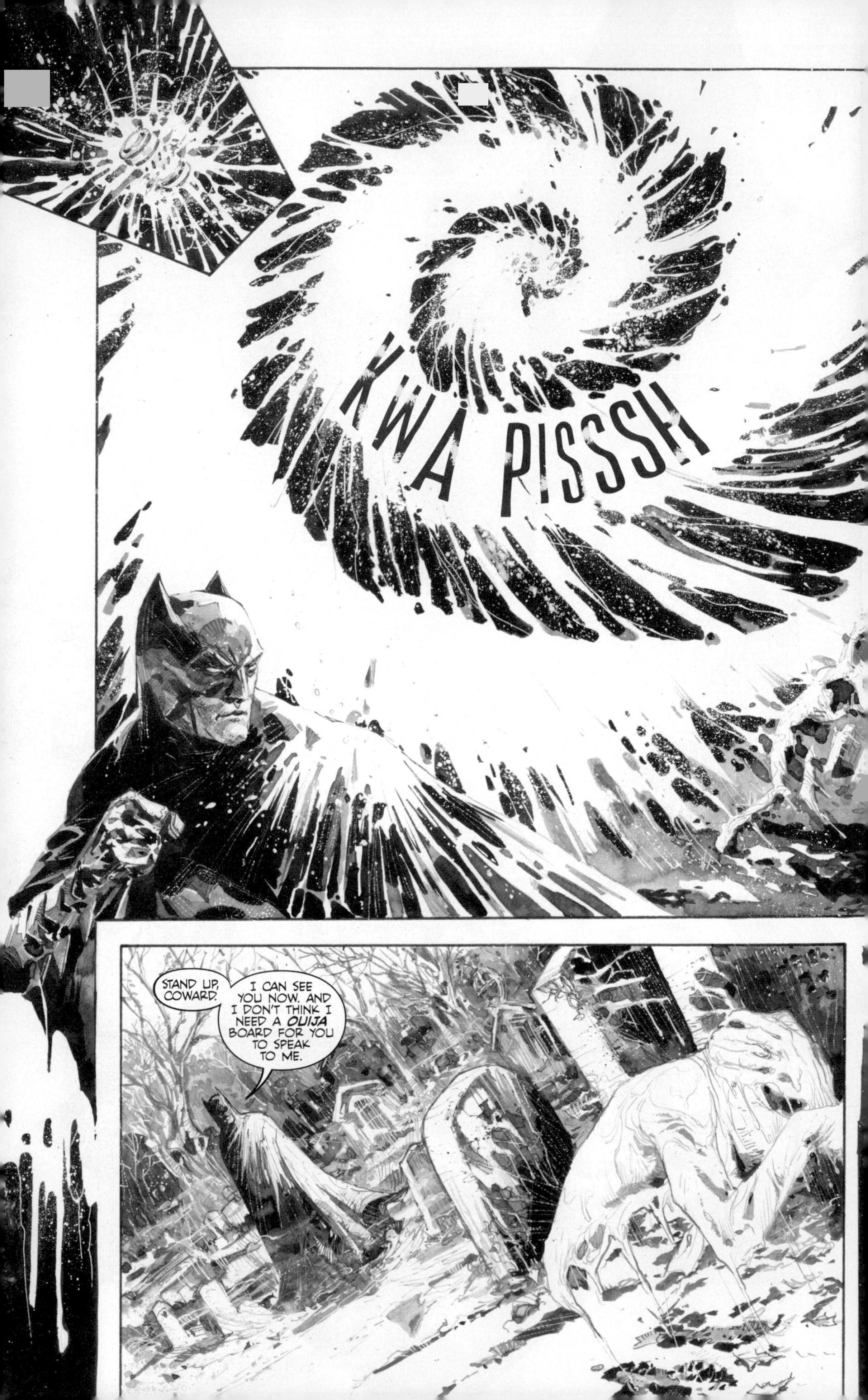
KWA PISSSH
STAND UP, COWARD.
I CAN SEE YOU NOW. AND I DON'T THINK I NEED A OUIJA BOARD FOR YOU TO SPEAK TO ME.

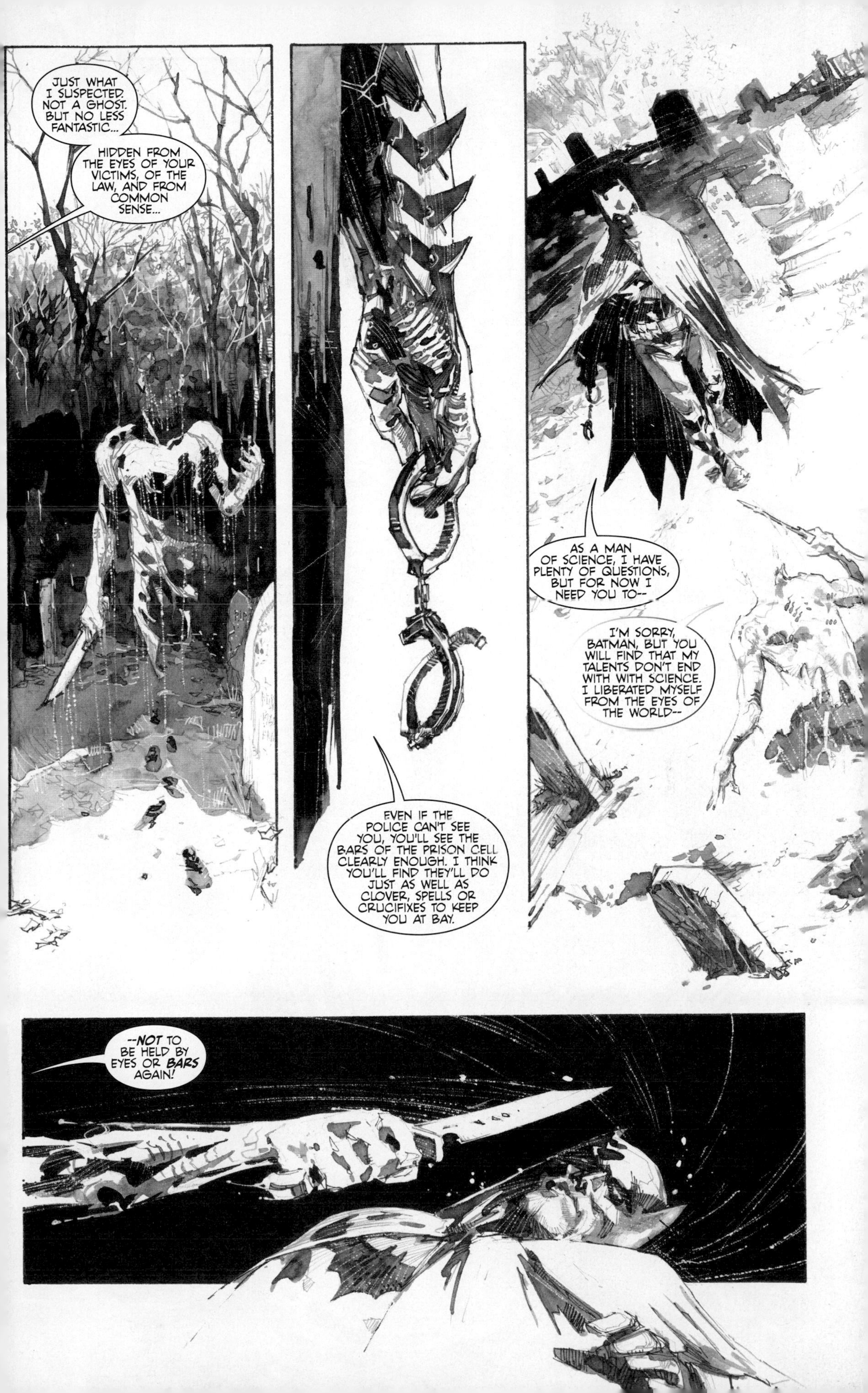
JUST WHAT I SUSPECTED. NOT A GHOST. BUT NO LESS FANTASTIC...
HIDDEN FROM THE EYES OF YOUR VICTIMS, OF THE LAW, AND FROM COMMON SENSE...
EVEN IF THE POLICE CAN'T SEE YOU, YOU'LL SEE THE BARS OF THE PRISON CELL CLEARLY ENOUGH. I THINK YOU'LL FIND THEY'LL DO JUST AS WELL AS CLOVER, SPELLS OR CRUCIFIXES TO KEEP YOU AT BAY.
AS A MAN OF SCIENCE, I HAVE PLENTY OF QUESTIONS, BUT FOR NOW I NEED YOU TO--
I'M SORRY, BATMAN, BUT YOU WILL FIND THAT MY TALENTS DON'T END WITH WITH SCIENCE. I LIBERATED MYSELF FROM THE EYES OF THE WORLD--
--*NOT* TO BE HELD BY EYES OR *BARS* AGAIN!

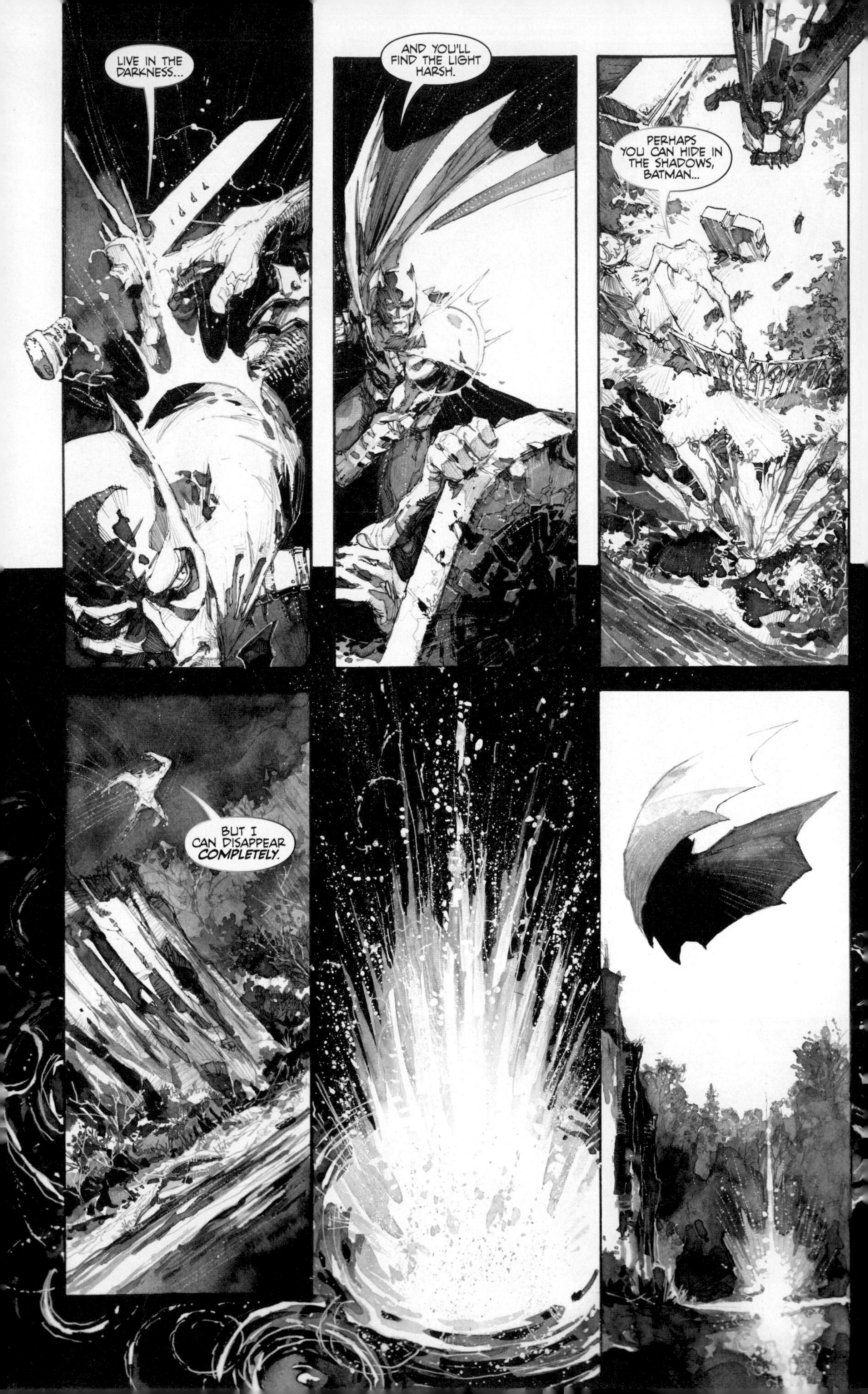
LIVE IN THE DARKNESS...
AND YOU'LL FIND THE LIGHT HARSH.
PERHAPS YOU CAN HIDE IN THE SHADOWS, BATMAN...
BUT I CAN DISAPPEAR *COMPLETELY*.

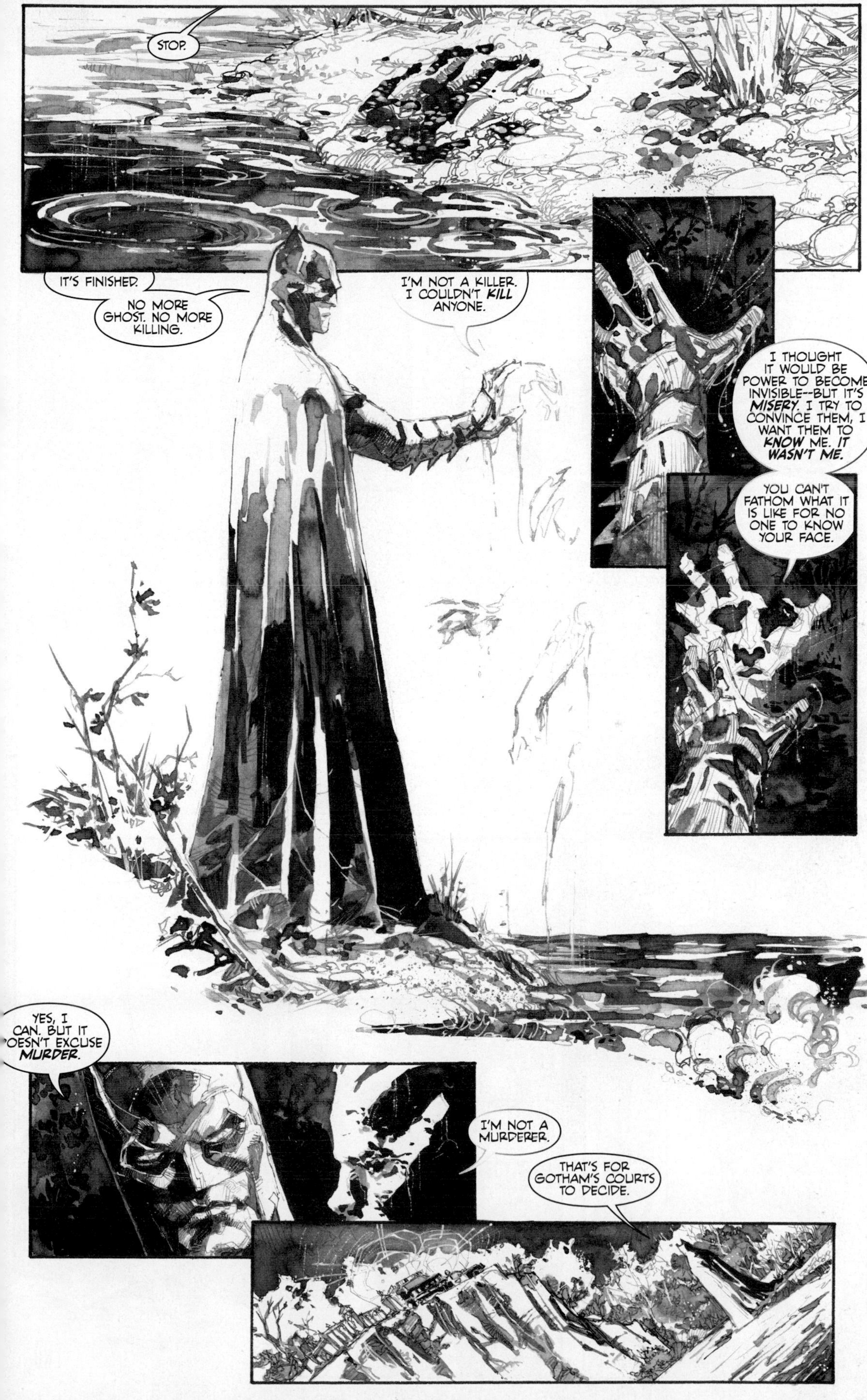
STOP.
IT'S FINISHED.
NO MORE GHOST. NO MORE KILLING.
I'M NOT A KILLER. I COULDN'T KILL ANYONE.
I THOUGHT IT WOULD BE POWER TO BECOME INVISIBLE--BUT IT'S MISERY. I TRY TO CONVINCE THEM, I WANT THEM TO KNOW ME. IT WASN'T ME.
YOU CAN'T FATHOM WHAT IT IS LIKE FOR NO ONE TO KNOW YOUR FACE.
YES, I CAN. BUT IT OESN'T EXCUSE MURDER.
I'M NOT A MURDERER.
THAT'S FOR GOTHAM'S COURTS TO DECIDE.

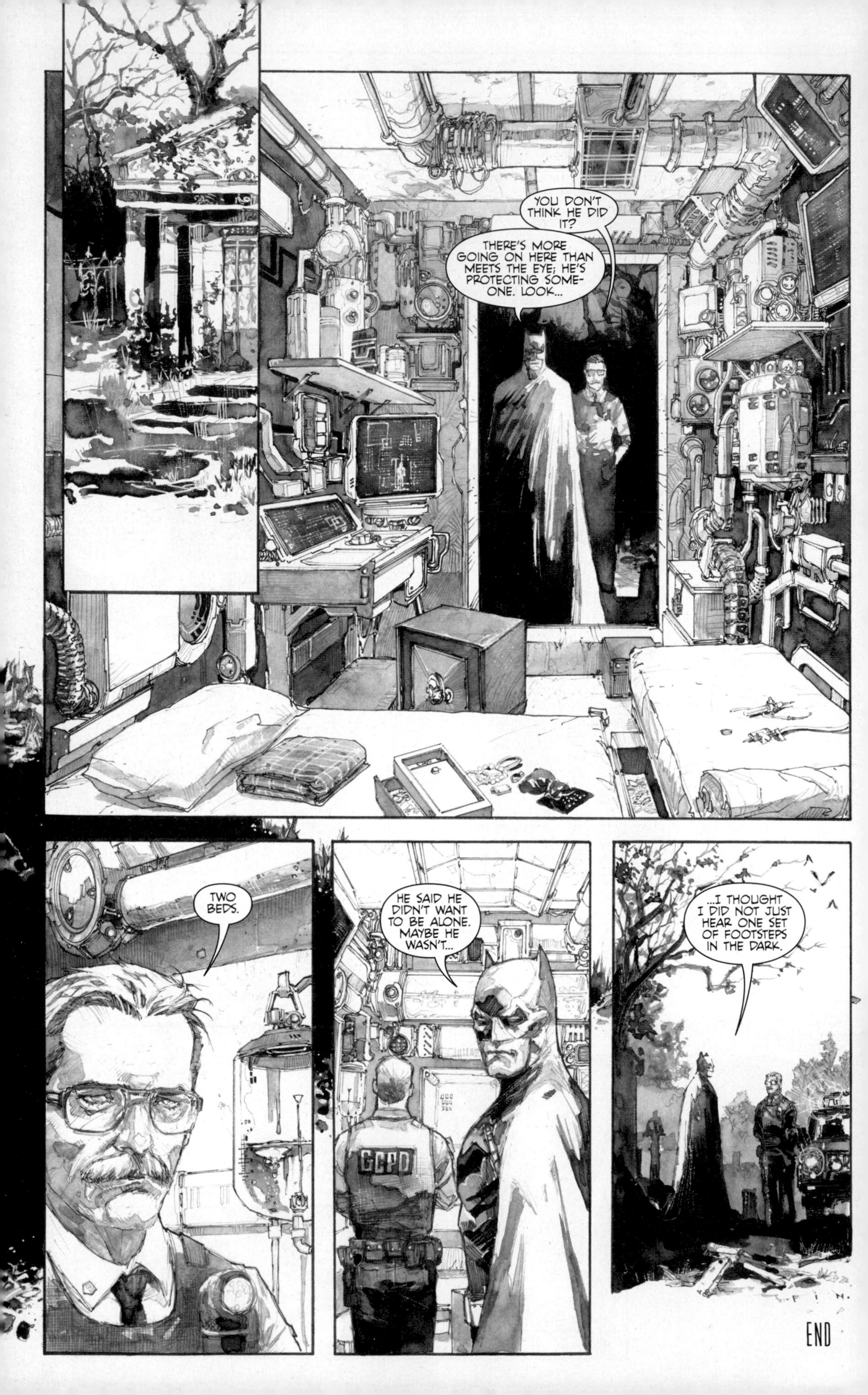
YOU DON'T THINK HE DID IT?
THERE'S MORE GOING ON HERE THAN MEETS THE EYE; HE'S PROTECTING SOME-ONE. LOOK...
TWO BEDS.
HE SAID HE DIDN'T WANT TO BE ALONE. MAYBE HE WASN'T...
...I THOUGHT I DID NOT JUST HEAR ONE SET OF FOOTSTEPS IN THE DARK.
GCPD
FIN.
END

NATHAN EDMONDSON

In 2011, Nathan Edmondson made a
sizable impact on the comics world with his
edgy creator-owned series *Who Is Jake Ellis?*
He immediately followed that up as the
writer of the New 52's GRIFTER for DC and
Ultimate Iron Man for Marvel Comics.
Praised for their tense, action-packed style and
use of psychologically offbeat characters,
Nathan's stories are always unexpected,
always electrifying.

KENNETH ROCAFORT

This young, multi-talented illustrator has
already worked in many areas of art, including
animation, theatre stage design, scientific
illustration and, of course, comic books.
With the launch of the New 52,
Kenneth's depiction of DC's flagship character,
Superman, became a fan favorite overnight.
Featuring a strong modern
drawing style, brilliant colors, and inspired page
esign, Rocafort's art is as absorbing as it is cool.

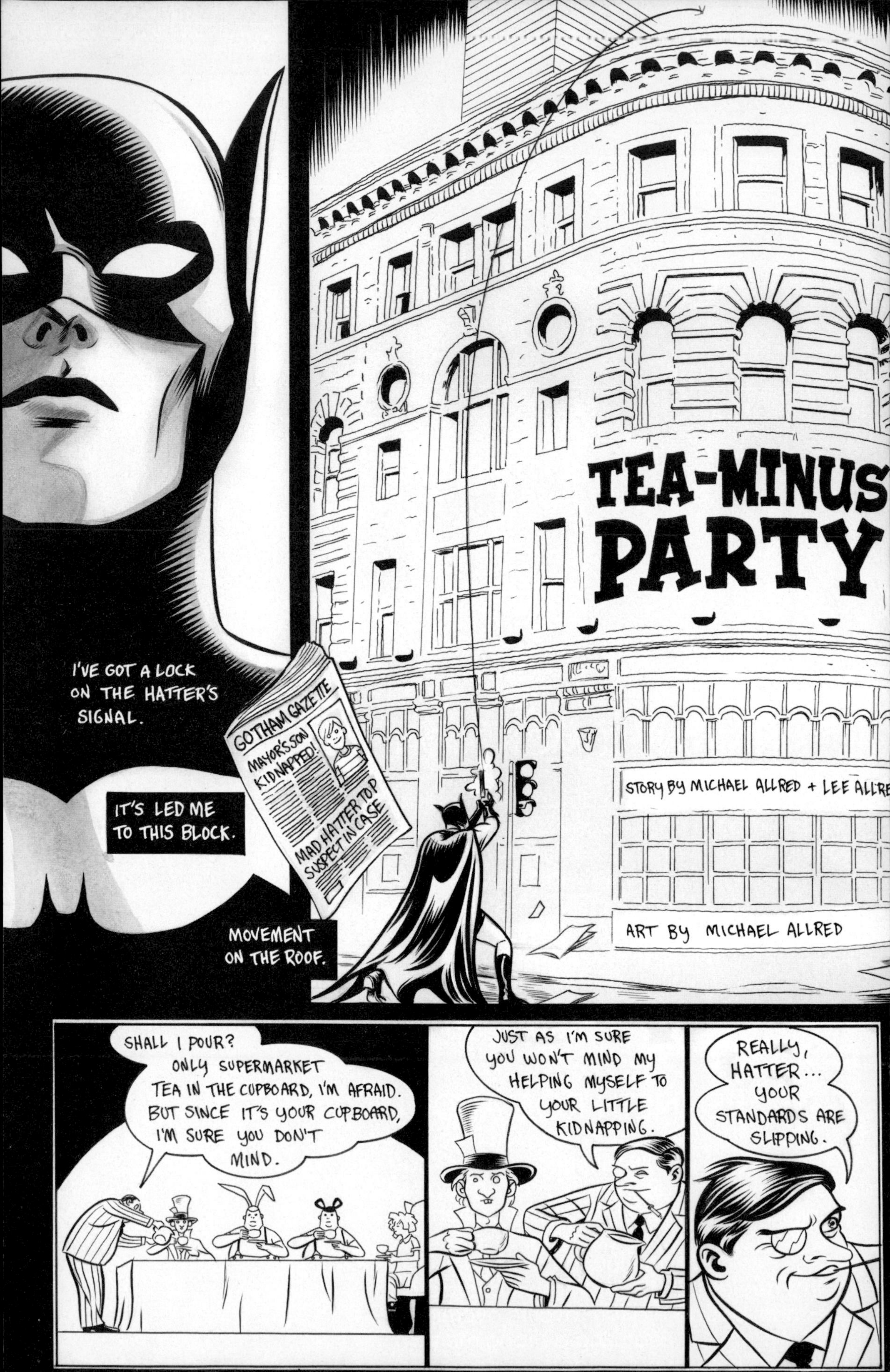

TEA-MINUS
PARTY
I'VE GOT A LOCK ON THE HATTER'S SIGNAL.
IT'S LED ME TO THIS BLOCK.
GOTHAM GAZETTE
MAYOR'S SON KIDNAPPED!
MAD HATTER TOP SUSPECT IN CASE
MOVEMENT ON THE ROOF.
STORY BY MICHAEL ALLRED + LEE ALLRE
ART BY MICHAEL ALLRED
SHALL I POUR? ONLY SUPERMARKET TEA IN THE CUPBOARD, I'M AFRAID. BUT SINCE IT'S YOUR CUPBOARD, I'M SURE YOU DON'T MIND.
JUST AS I'M SURE YOU WON'T MIND MY HELPING MYSELF TO YOUR LITTLE KIDNAPPING.
REALLY, HATTER... YOUR STANDARDS ARE SLIPPING.

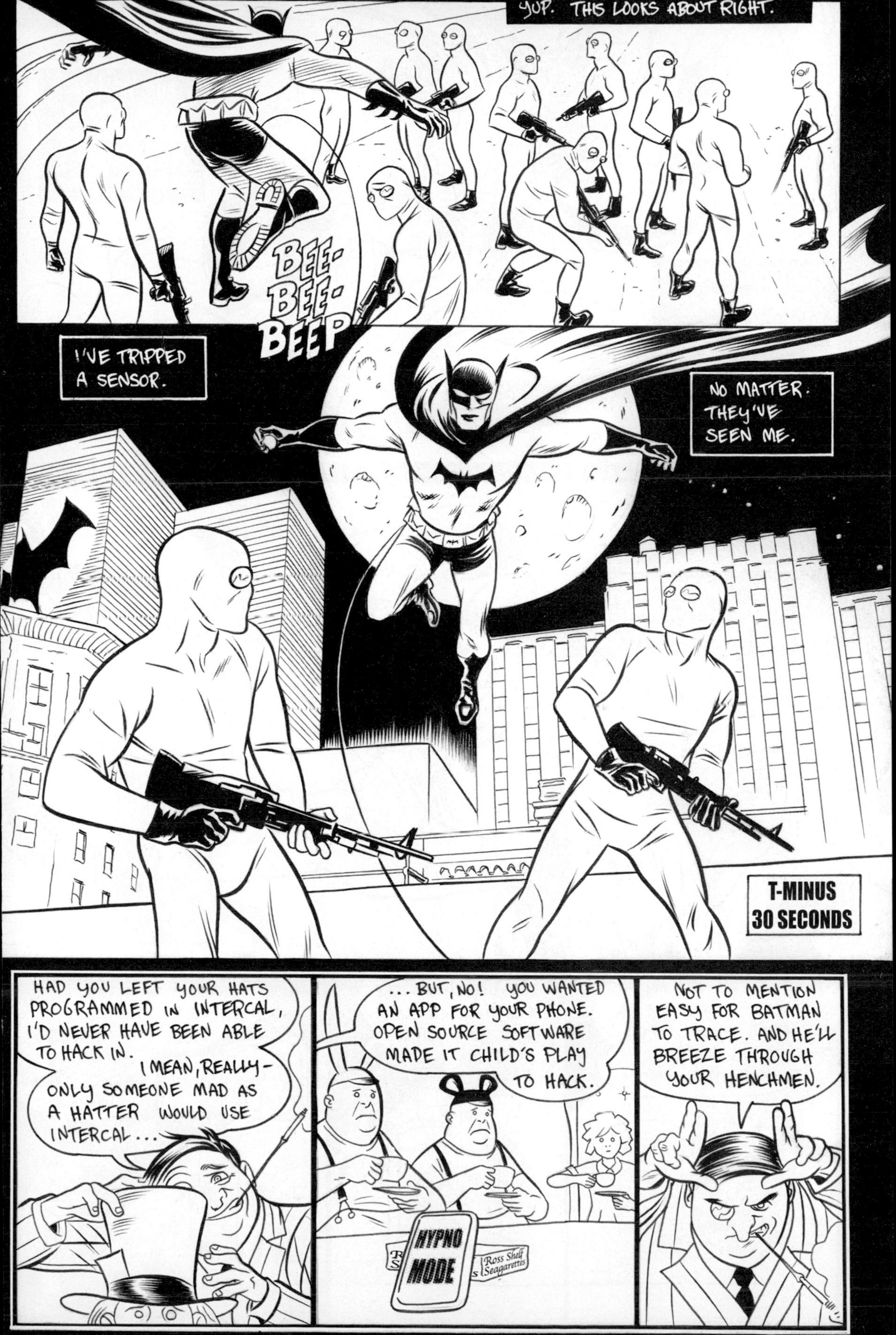
YUP. THIS LOOKS ABOUT RIGHT.
BEE-BEE-BEEP
I'VE TRIPPED A SENSOR.
NO MATTER. THEY'VE SEEN ME.
T-MINUS 30 SECONDS
HAD YOU LEFT YOUR HATS PROGRAMMED IN INTERCAL, I'D NEVER HAVE BEEN ABLE TO HACK IN.
I MEAN, REALLY- ONLY SOMEONE MAD AS A HATTER WOULD USE INTERCAL...
...BUT, NO! YOU WANTED AN APP FOR YOUR PHONE. OPEN SOURCE SOFTWARE MADE IT CHILD'S PLAY TO HACK.
HYPNO MODE
Ross Shelf Seagarettes
NOT TO MENTION EASY FOR BATMAN TO TRACE. AND HE'LL BREEZE THROUGH YOUR HENCHMEN.

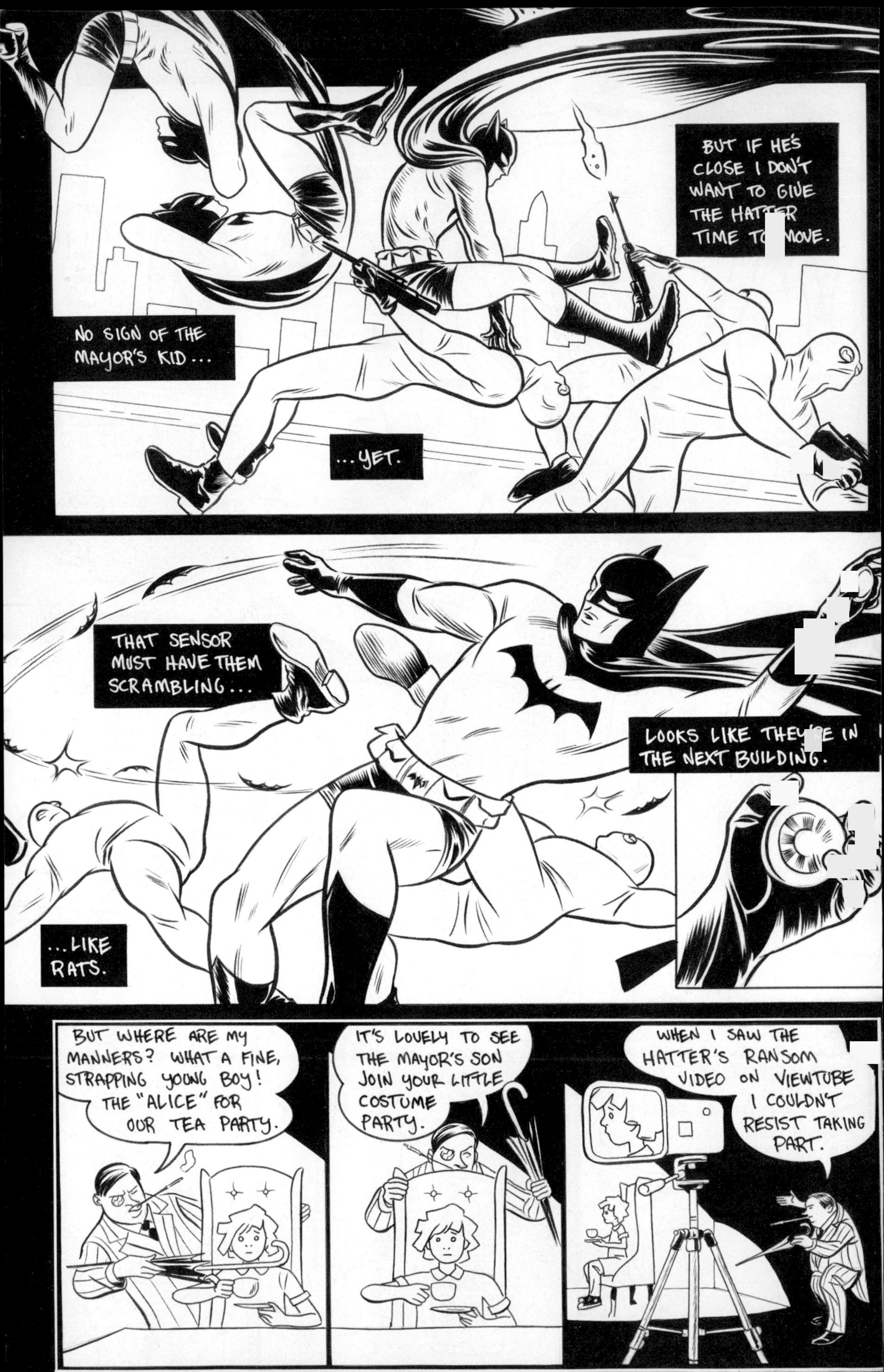
BUT IF HE'S CLOSE I DON'T WANT TO GIVE THE HATTER TIME TO MOVE.
NO SIGN OF THE MAYOR'S KID...
...YET.
THAT SENSOR MUST HAVE THEM SCRAMBLING...
...LIKE RATS.
LOOKS LIKE THEY'RE IN THE NEXT BUILDING.
BUT WHERE ARE MY MANNERS? WHAT A FINE, STRAPPING YOUNG BOY! THE "ALICE" FOR OUR TEA PARTY.
IT'S LOVELY TO SEE THE MAYOR'S SON JOIN YOUR LITTLE COSTUME PARTY.
WHEN I SAW THE HATTER'S RANSOM VIDEO ON VIEWTUBE I COULDN'T RESIST TAKING PART.

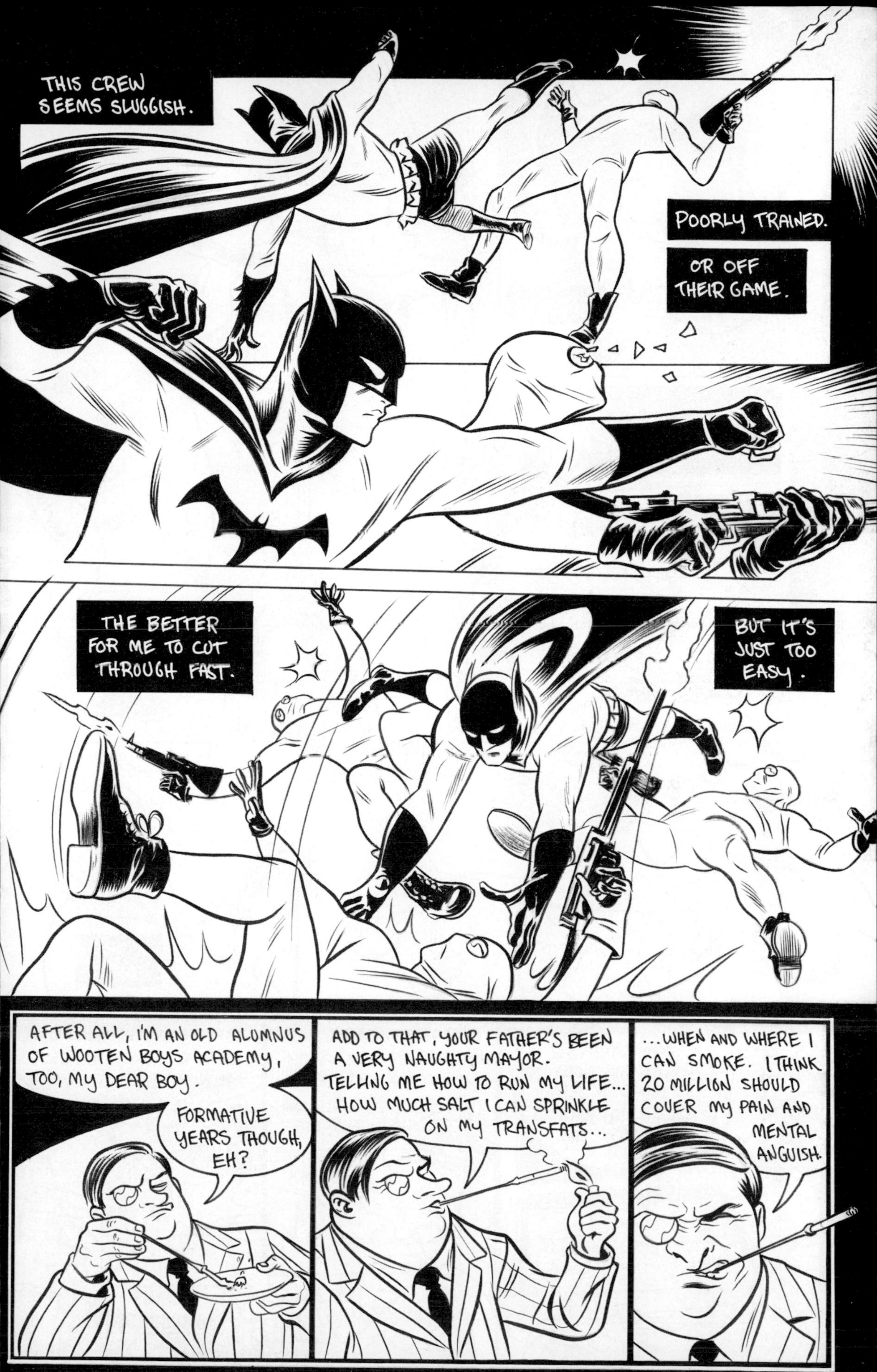
THIS CREW SEEMS SLUGGISH.
POORLY TRAINED.
OR OFF THEIR GAME.
THE BETTER FOR ME TO CUT THROUGH FAST.
BUT IT'S JUST TOO EASY.
AFTER ALL, I'M AN OLD ALUMNUS OF WOOTEN BOYS ACADEMY, TOO, MY DEAR BOY.
FORMATIVE YEARS THOUGH, EH?
ADD TO THAT, YOUR FATHER'S BEEN A VERY NAUGHTY MAYOR. TELLING ME HOW TO RUN MY LIFE... HOW MUCH SALT I CAN SPRINKLE ON MY TRANSFATS...
...WHEN AND WHERE I CAN SMOKE. I THINK 20 MILLION SHOULD COVER MY PAIN AND MENTAL ANGUISH.

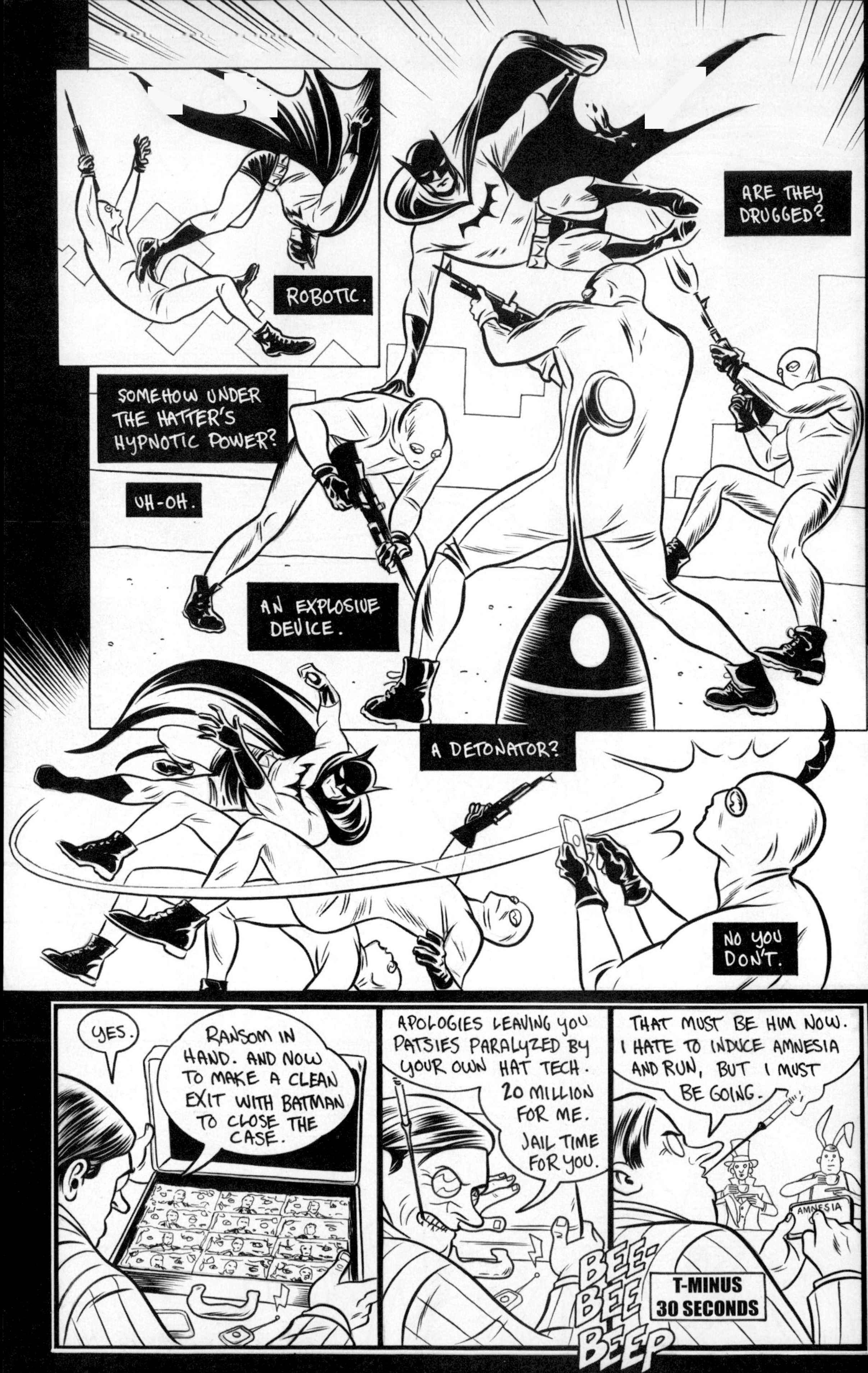
ROBOTIC.
ARE THEY DRUGGED?
SOMEHOW UNDER THE HATTER'S HYPNOTIC POWER?
UH-OH.
AN EXPLOSIVE DEVICE.
A DETONATOR?
NO YOU DON'T.
YES.
RANSOM IN HAND. AND NOW TO MAKE A CLEAN EXIT WITH BATMAN TO CLOSE THE CASE.
APOLOGIES LEAVING YOU PATSIES PARALYZED BY YOUR OWN HAT TECH.
20 MILLION FOR ME.
JAIL TIME FOR YOU.
BEE-BEE-BEEP
THAT MUST BE HIM NOW. I HATE TO INDUCE AMNESIA AND RUN, BUT I MUST BE GOING.
AMNESIA
T-MINUS 30 SECONDS

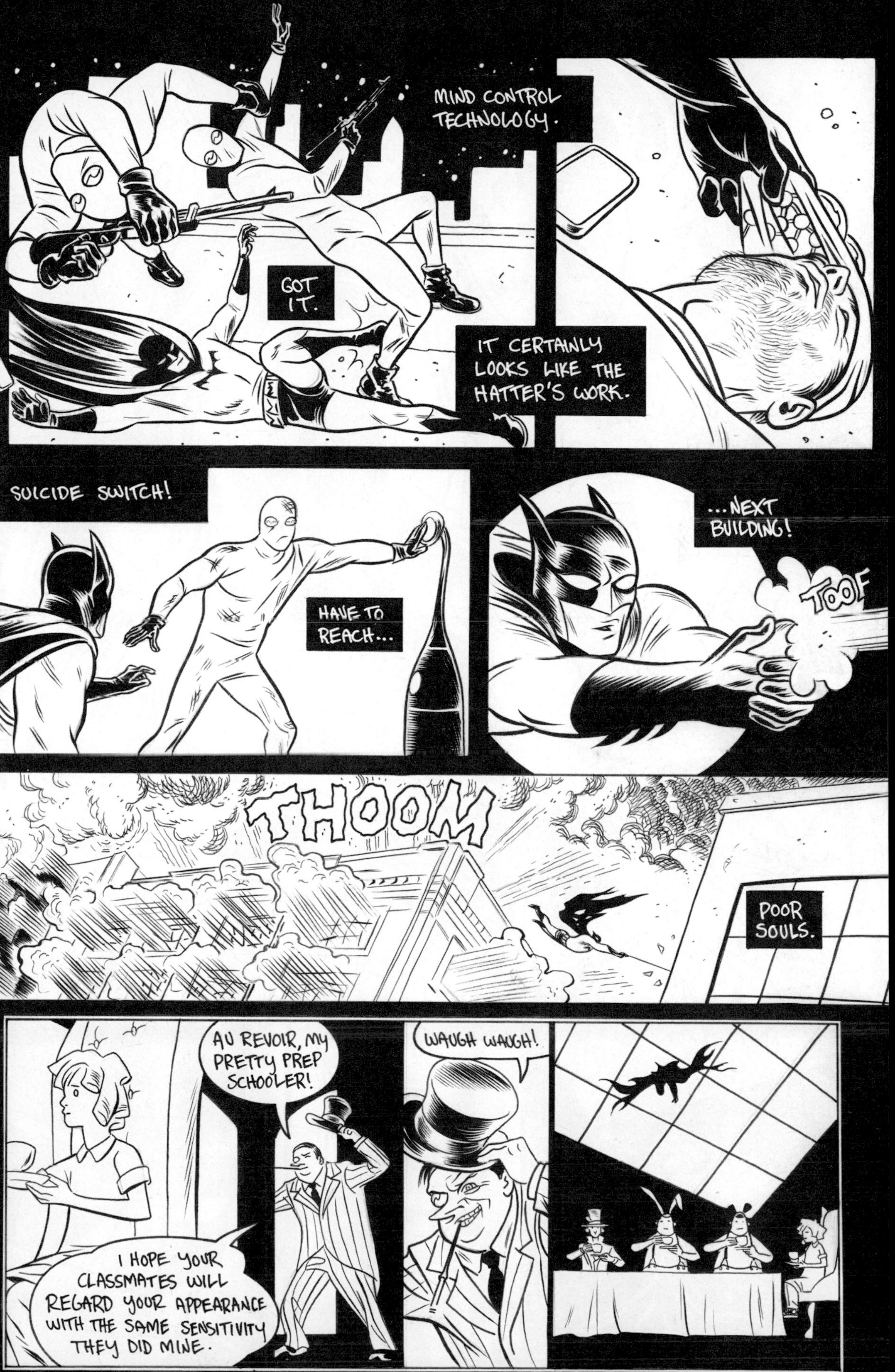
MIND CONTROL TECHNOLOGY.
GOT IT.
IT CERTAINLY LOOKS LIKE THE HATTER'S WORK.
SUICIDE SWITCH!
HAVE TO REACH...
...NEXT BUILDING!
TOOF
THOOM
POOR SOULS.
AU REVOIR, MY PRETTY PREP SCHOOLER!
I HOPE YOUR CLASSMATES WILL REGARD YOUR APPEARANCE WITH THE SAME SENSITIVITY THEY DID MINE.
WAUGH WAUGH!

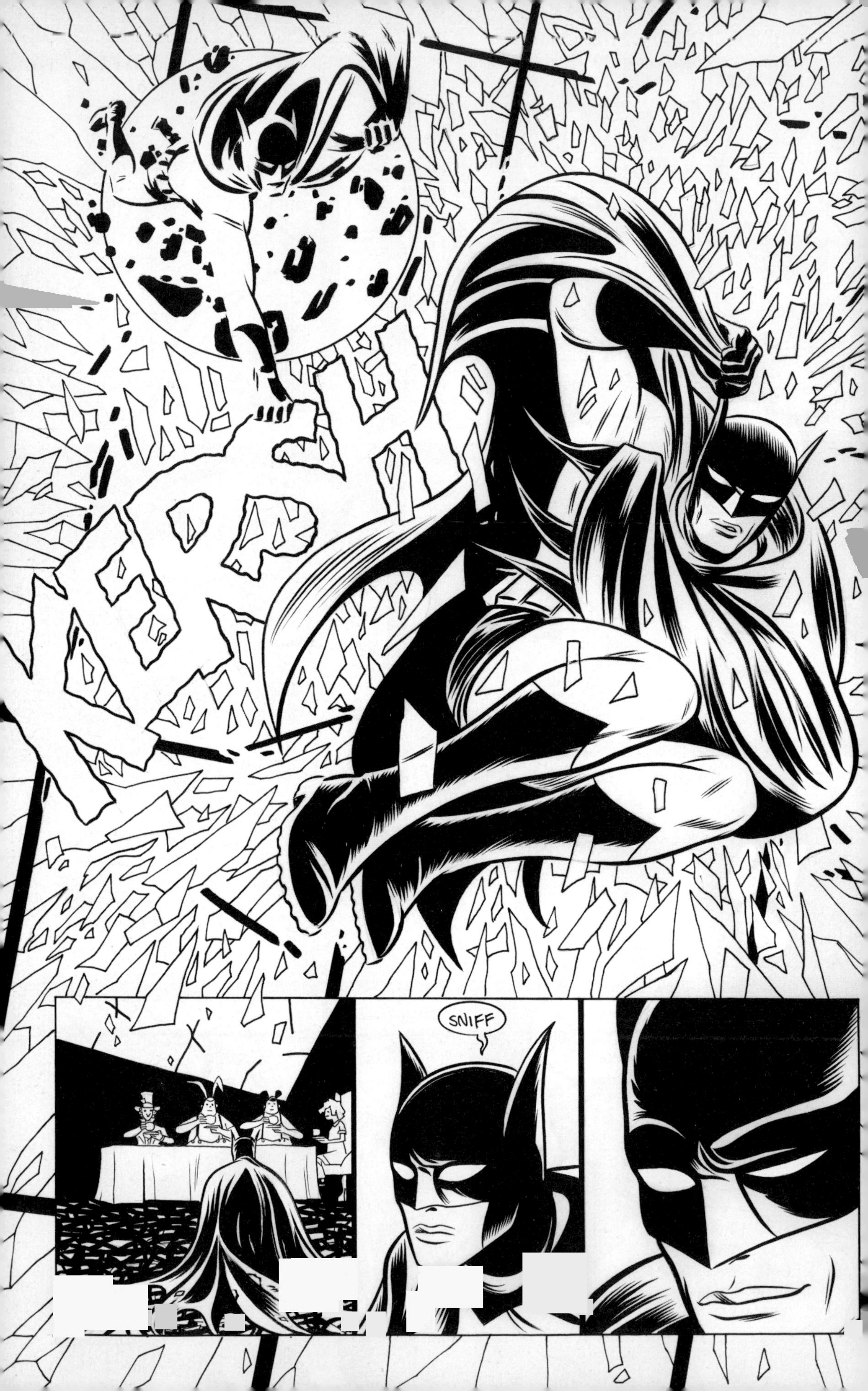
SNIFF

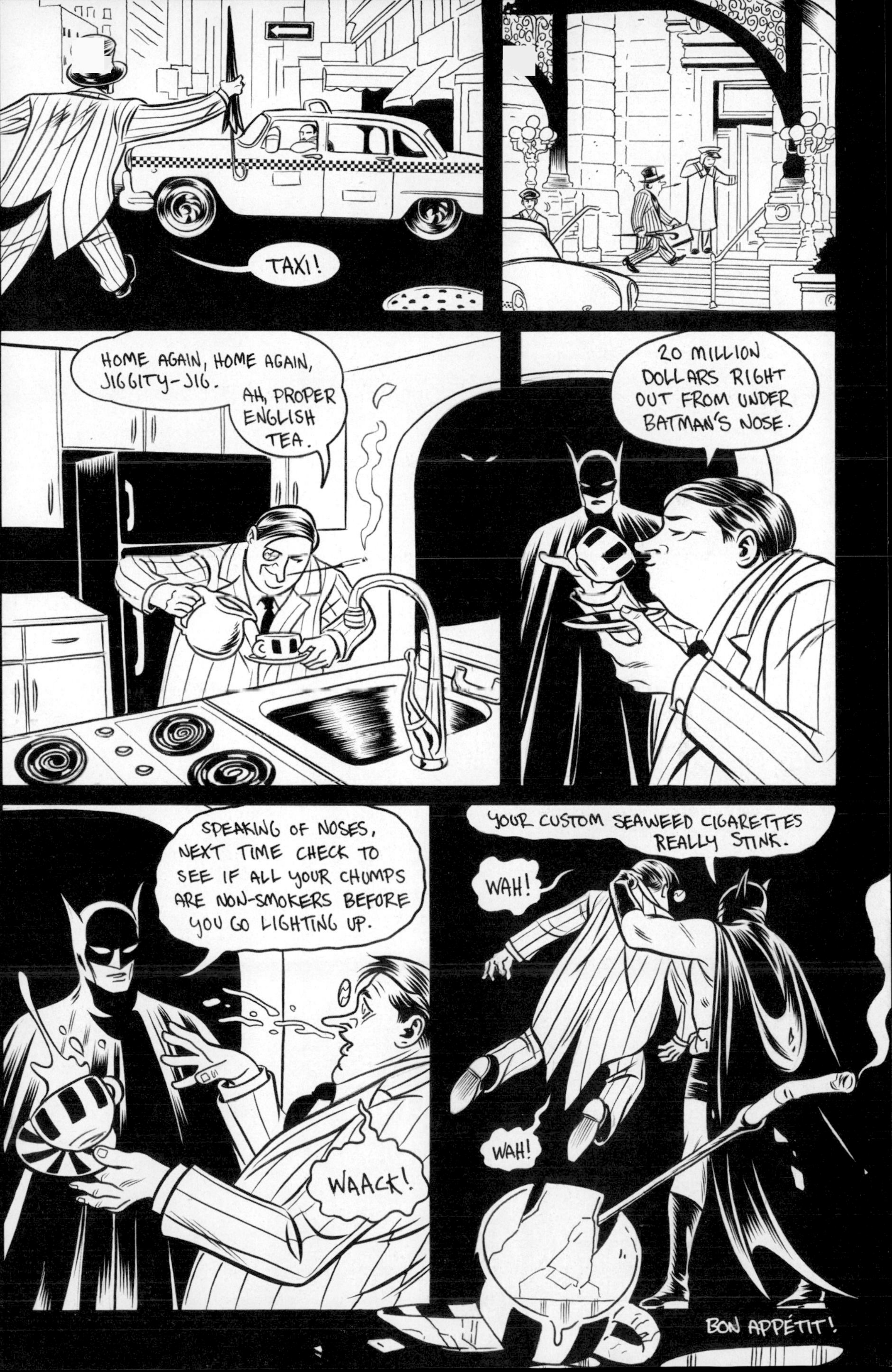
TAXI!
HOME AGAIN, HOME AGAIN, JIGGITY-JIG.
AH, PROPER ENGLISH TEA.
20 MILLION DOLLARS RIGHT OUT FROM UNDER BATMAN'S NOSE.
SPEAKING OF NOSES, NEXT TIME CHECK TO SEE IF ALL YOUR CHUMPS ARE NON-SMOKERS BEFORE YOU GO LIGHTING UP.
WAACK!
YOUR CUSTOM SEAWEED CIGARETTES REALLY STINK.
WAH!
WAH!
BON APPÉTIT!

MICHAEL ALLRED

Creator of the wildly hip and popular
character Madman, Michael Allred is
himself a pop phenomenon.
Artist, writer, and all-around good guy, Allred
began his career as a TV reporter in Europe.
He somehow became a comic book artist and
went on to have a stellar career, drawing,
among others, *Madman*, *Red Rocket 7*, *X-Force*,
iZOMBIE, *FF,* SOLO, and WEDNESDAY COMICS.
Allred's art is a crazed mix of many,
many sources and influences, including 1960s
pop culture (the Beatles and James Bond),
European illustrators (Moebius and Daniel Torres),
and good old American comic book art
(Jack Kirby, Alex Toth, and los Bros Hernandez).

LEE ALLRED

The co-writer of Marvel's *FF*, Lee Allred is a
comics, sci-fi, and alternate history prose author.
His outrageous stories for DC's SOLO included the
awesomely wacky BATMAN A-GO-GO, which
was illustrated by his brother, Michael Allred.
A former Master Sergeant in the USAF,
Lee is at heart a storyteller of the
fantastic and extraordinary.

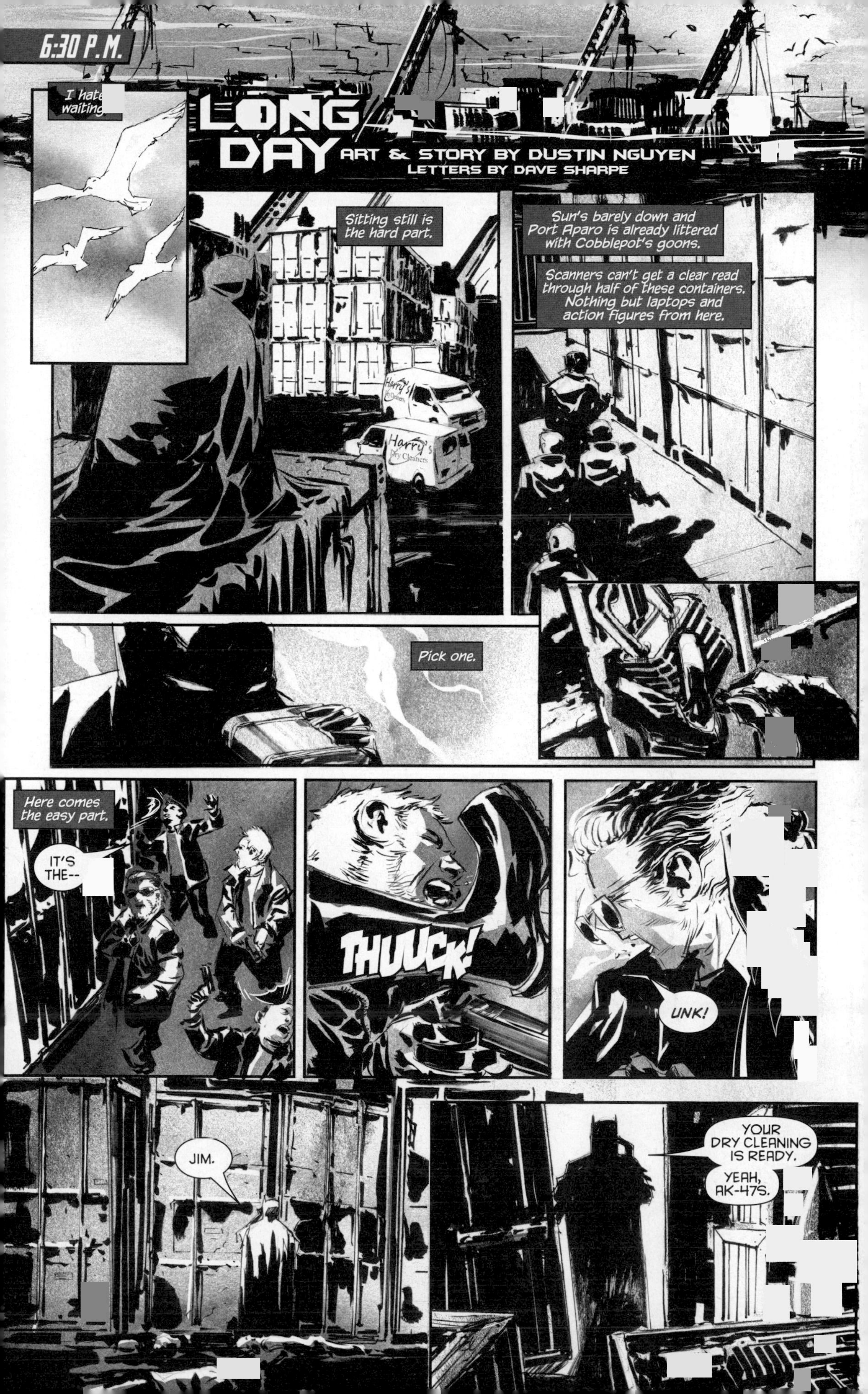
6:30 P.M.
I hate waiting
LONG DAY
ART & STORY BY DUSTIN NGUYEN
LETTERS BY DAVE SHARPE
Sitting still is the hard part.
Harry's Dry Cleaners
Sun's barely down and Port Aparo is already littered with Cobblepot's goons.
Scanners can't get a clear read through half of these containers. Nothing but laptops and action figures from here.
Pick one.
Here comes the easy part.
IT'S THE--
THUUCK!
UNK!
JIM.
YOUR DRY CLEANING IS READY.
YEAH, AK-47S.

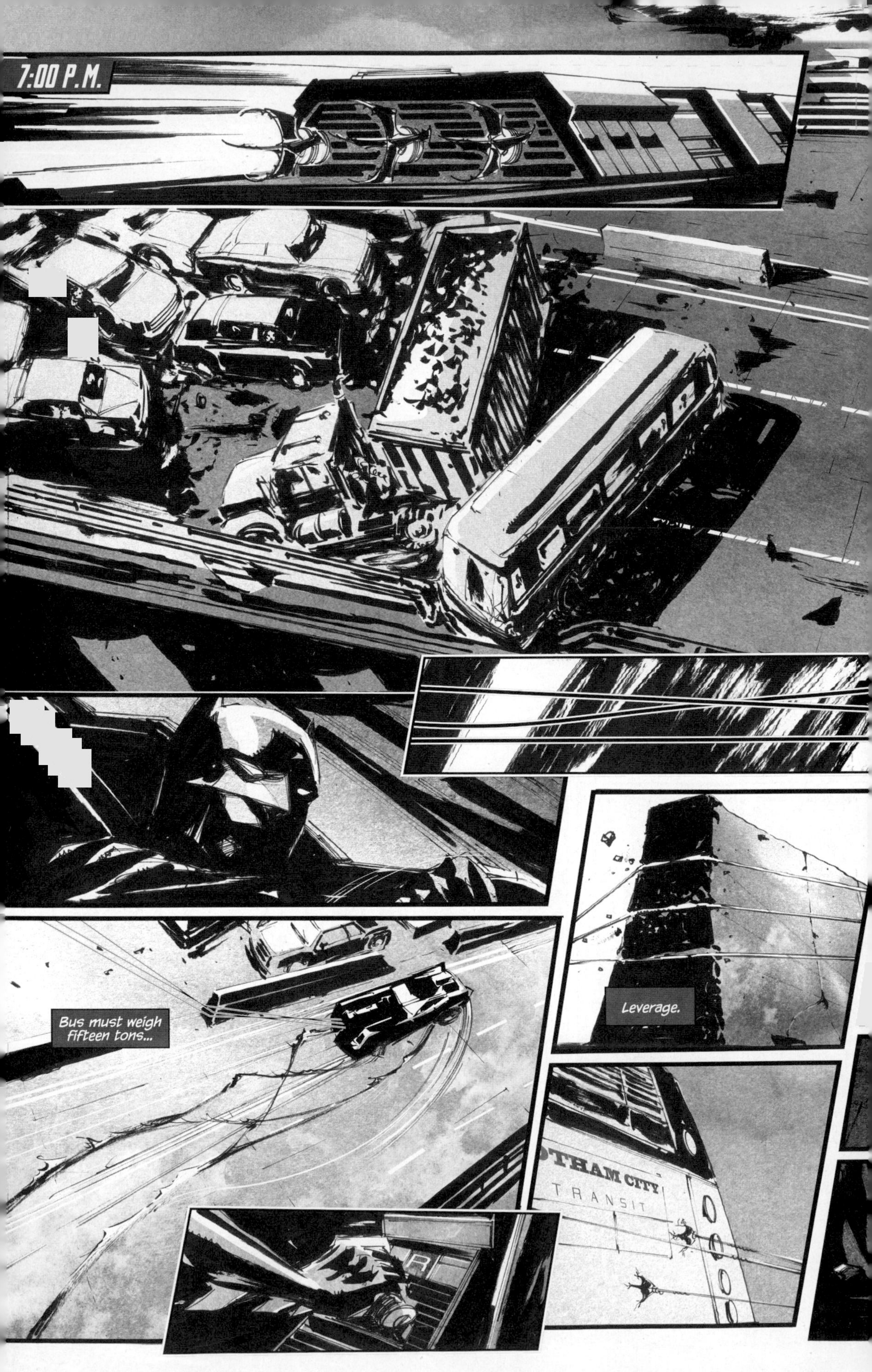
7:00 P.M.
Bus must weigh fifteen tons...
Leverage.
OTHAM CITY
TRANSIT

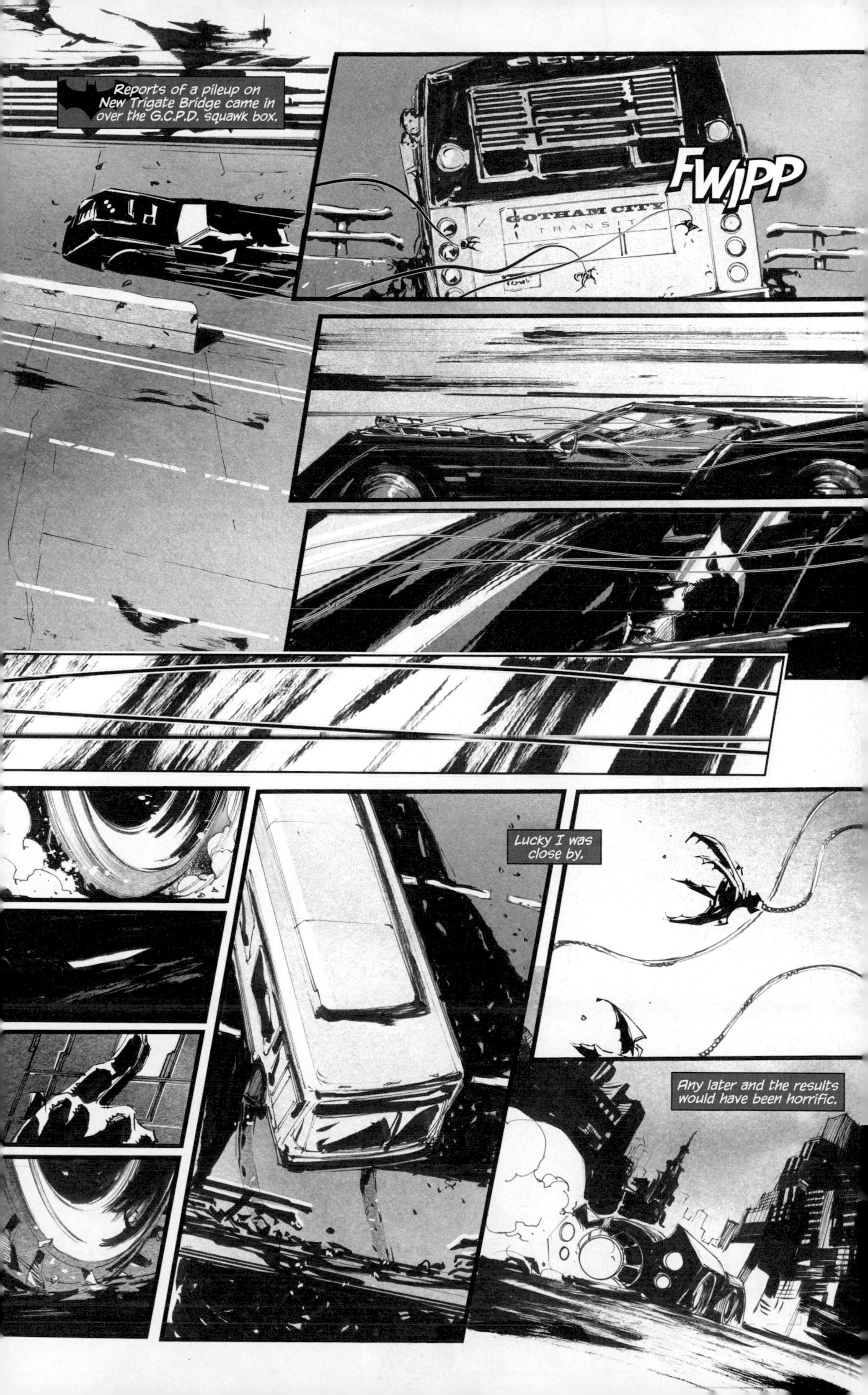
Reports of a pileup on New Trigate Bridge came in over the G.C.P.D. squawk box.
FWIPP
GOTHAM CITY TRANSIT
Lucky I was close by.
Any later and the results would have been horrific.

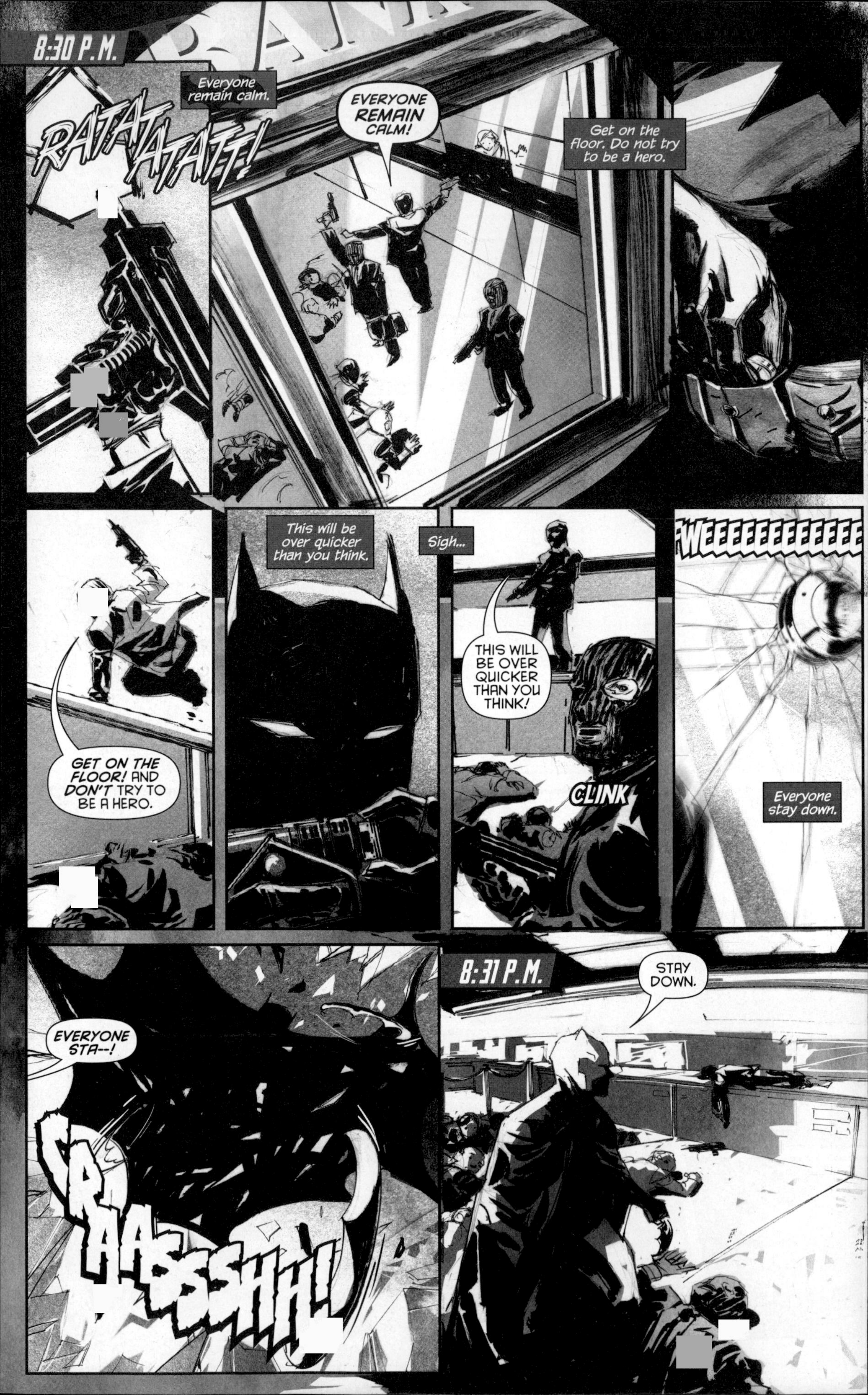
8:30 P.M.
RATATATATATT!
Everyone remain calm.
EVERYONE REMAIN CALM!
Get on the floor. Do not try to be a hero.
GET ON THE FLOOR! AND DON'T TRY TO BE A HERO.
This will be over quicker than you think.
Sigh...
THIS WILL BE OVER QUICKER THAN YOU THINK!
CLINK
FWEEEEEEEEEEEE
Everyone stay down.
EVERYONE STA--!
CRAASSHH!
8:31 P.M.
STAY DOWN.

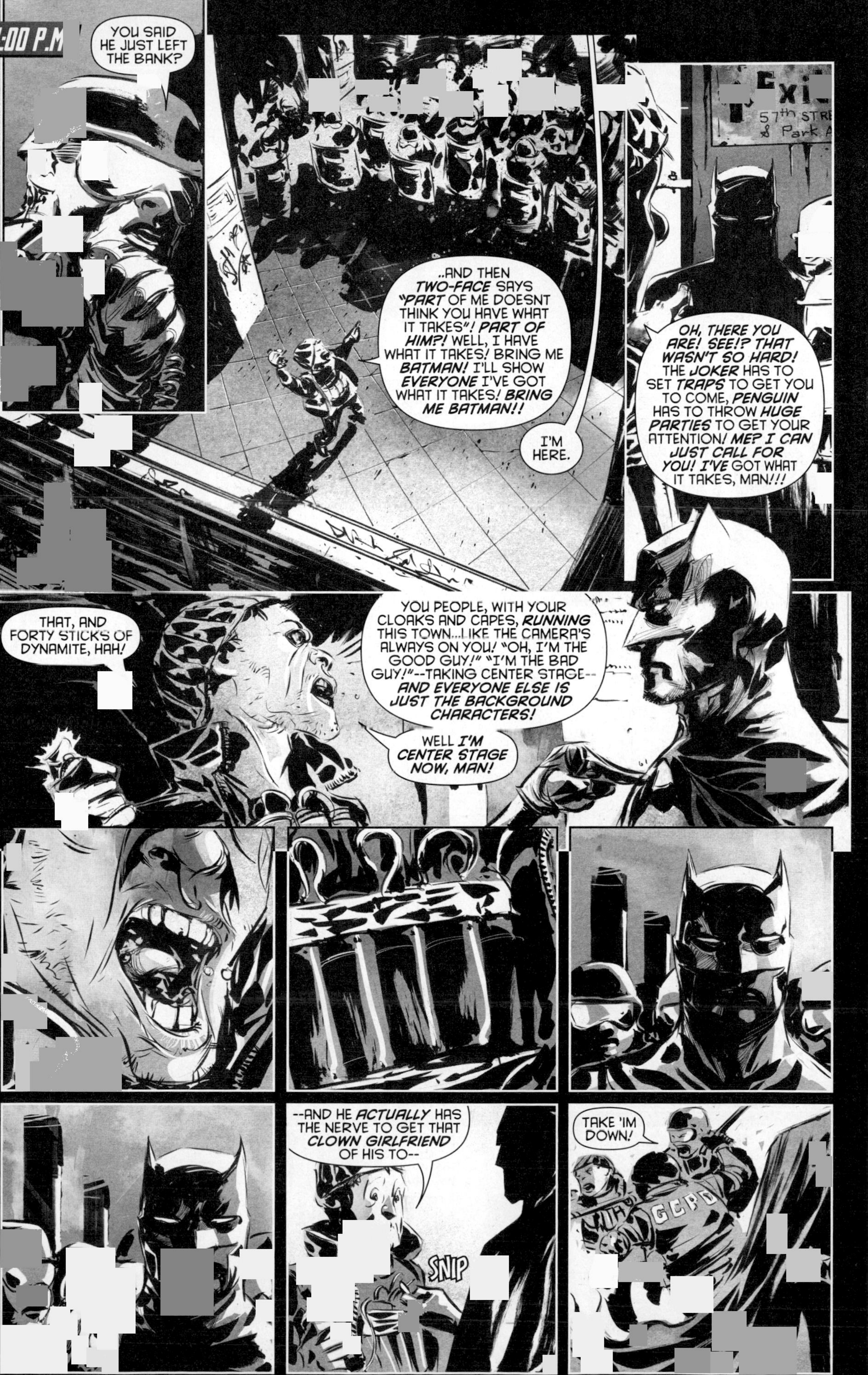

YOU SAID HE JUST LEFT THE BANK?
..AND THEN TWO-FACE SAYS "PART OF ME DOESNT THINK YOU HAVE WHAT IT TAKES"! PART OF HIM?! WELL, I HAVE WHAT IT TAKES! BRING ME BATMAN! I'LL SHOW EVERYONE I'VE GOT WHAT IT TAKES! BRING ME BATMAN!!
I'M HERE.
OH, THERE YOU ARE! SEE!? THAT WASN'T SO HARD! THE JOKER HAS TO SET TRAPS TO GET YOU TO COME, PENGUIN HAS TO THROW HUGE PARTIES TO GET YOUR ATTENTION! ME? I CAN JUST CALL FOR YOU! I'VE GOT WHAT IT TAKES, MAN!!!
THAT, AND FORTY STICKS OF DYNAMITE, HAH!
YOU PEOPLE, WITH YOUR CLOAKS AND CAPES, RUNNING THIS TOWN...LIKE THE CAMERA'S ALWAYS ON YOU! "OH, I'M THE GOOD GUY!" "I'M THE BAD GUY!"--TAKING CENTER STAGE--AND EVERYONE ELSE IS JUST THE BACKGROUND CHARACTERS!
WELL I'M CENTER STAGE NOW, MAN!
--AND HE ACTUALLY HAS THE NERVE TO GET THAT CLOWN GIRLFRIEND OF HIS TO--
SNIP
TAKE 'IM DOWN!
GCPD

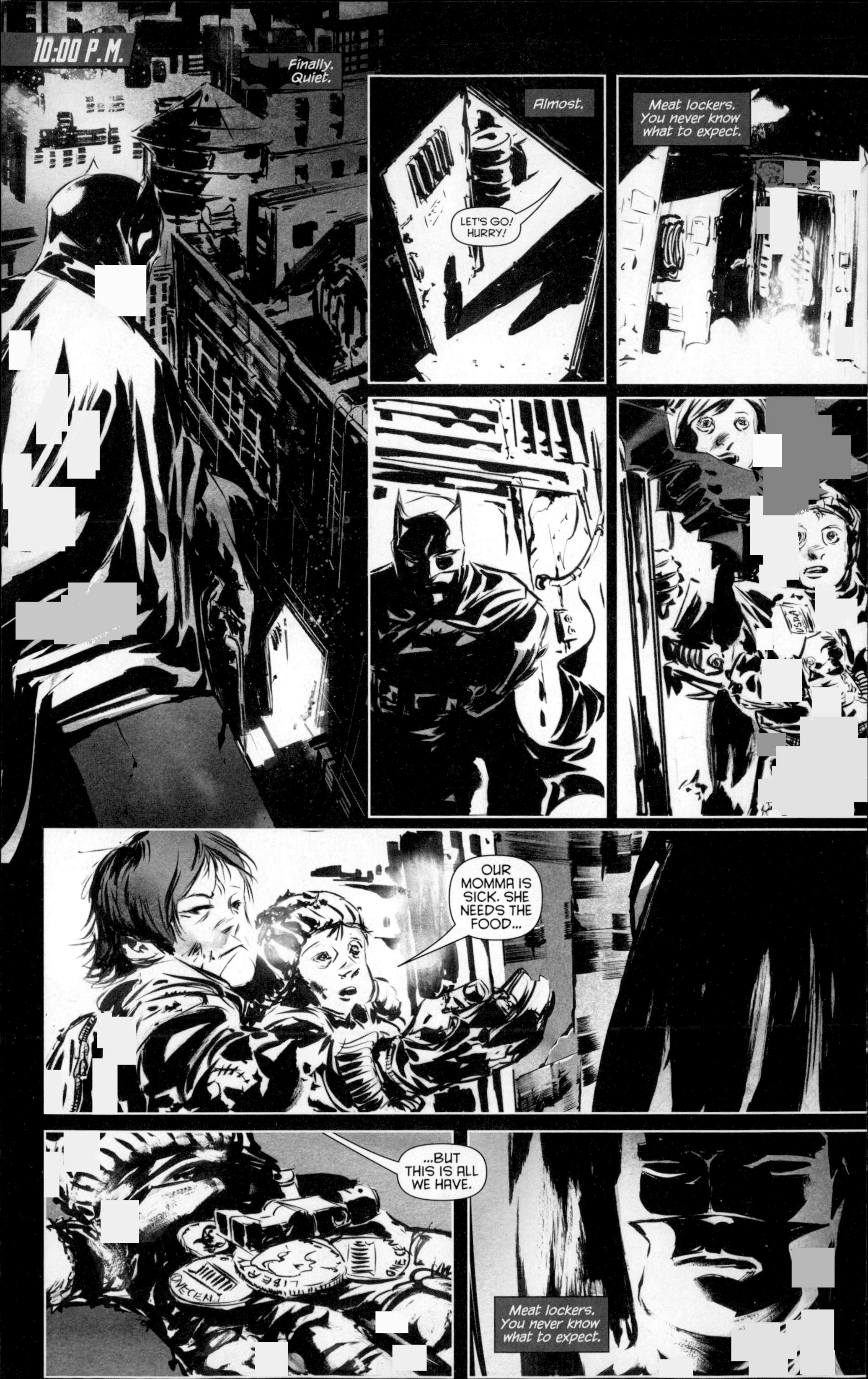
10:00 P.M.
Finally. Quiet.
Almost.
LET'S GO! HURRY!
Meat lockers. You never know what to expect.
OUR MOMMA IS SICK. SHE NEEDS THE FOOD...
...BUT THIS IS ALL WE HAVE.
Meat lockers. You never know what to expect.

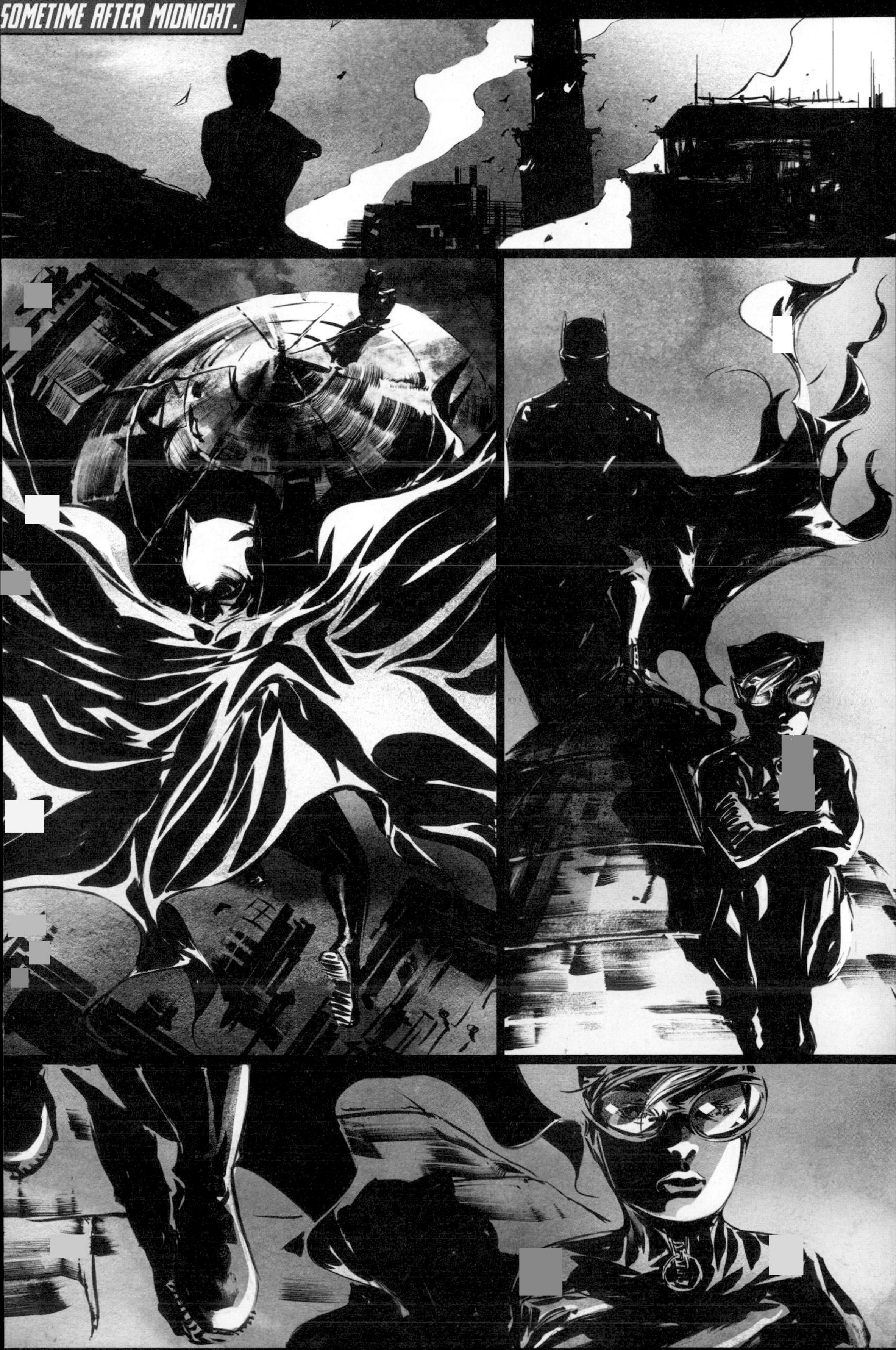
SOMETIME AFTER MIDNIGHT.

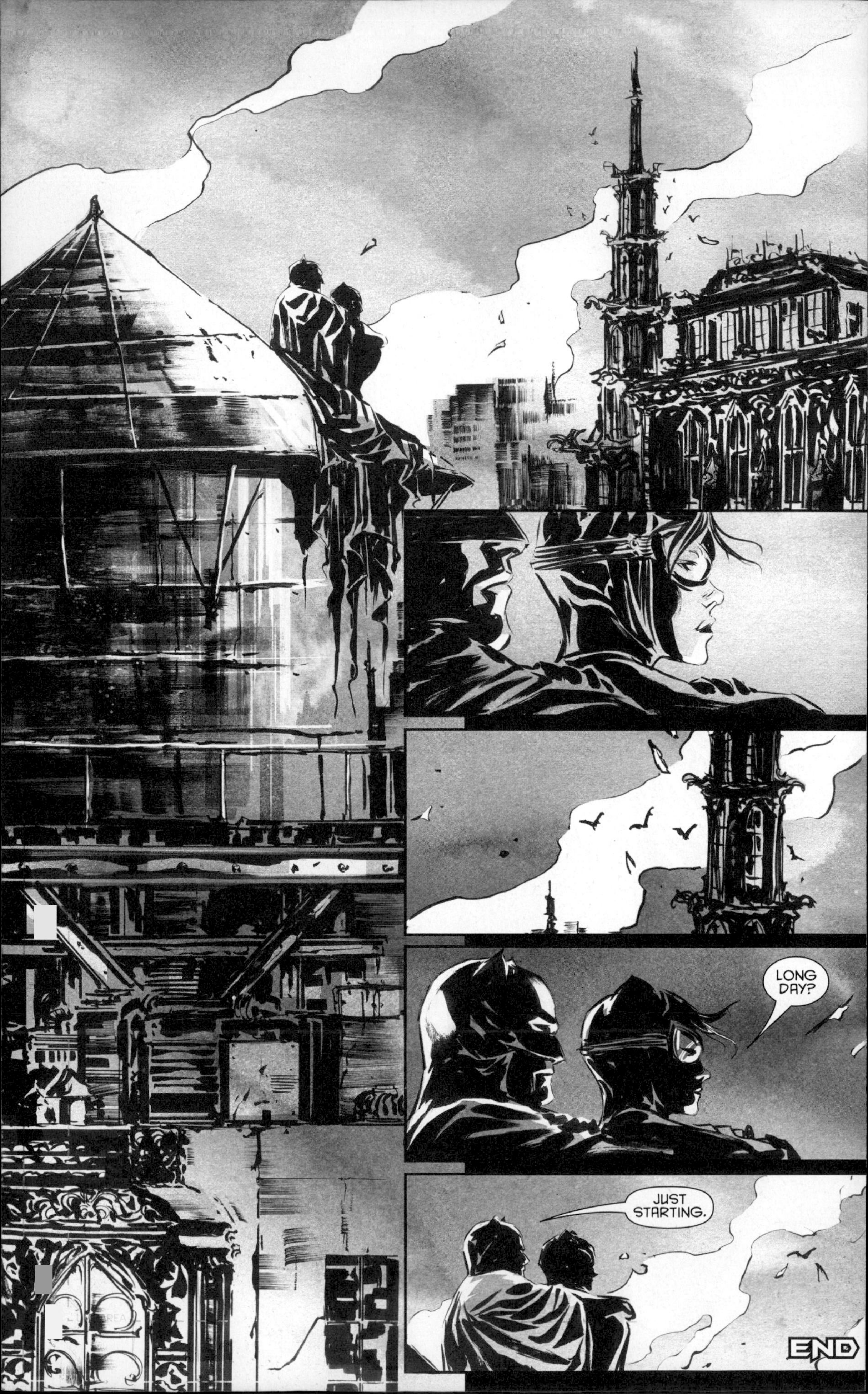
LONG DAY?
JUST STARTING.
END

DUSTIN NGUYEN

One of the most fun and exciting stylists in
comics today, Dustin Nguyen is a breath of
fresh air in the gritty world of super-hero comics.
After long and popular runs on
DETECTIVE COMICS and STREETS OF GOTHAM,
Dustin went on to write and draw Li'L GOTHAM,
which immediately became a fan favorite.
Taking its cue from TV cartoons,
classic comics, and children's book illustration,
Nguyen's art synthesizes the sheer joy of
comic books and the extraordinary.

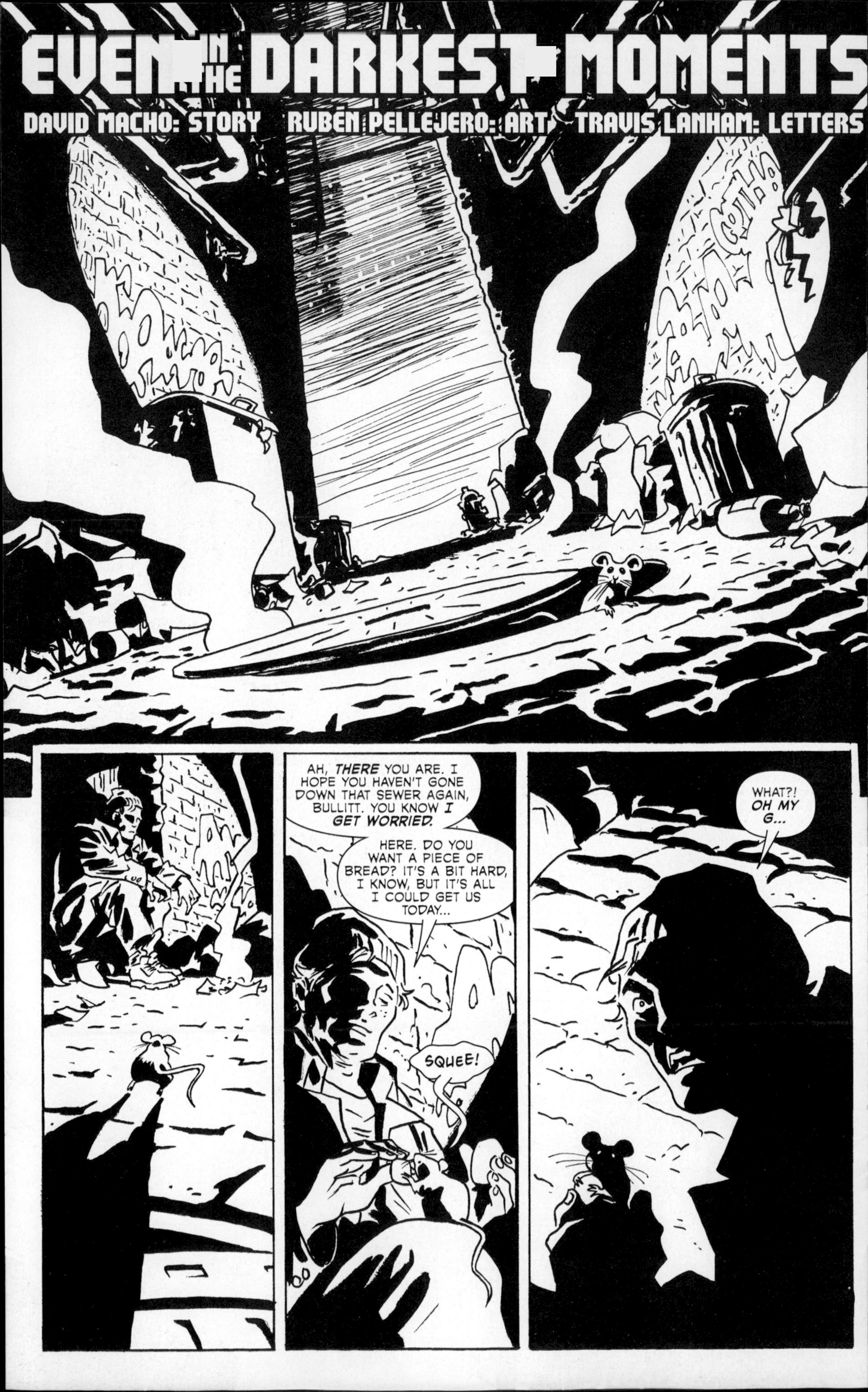
EVEN IN THE DARKEST MOMENTS
DAVID MACHO: STORY RUBEN PELLEJERO: ART TRAVIS LANHAM: LETTERS
AH, *THERE* YOU ARE. I HOPE YOU HAVEN'T GONE DOWN THAT SEWER AGAIN, BULLITT. YOU KNOW *I GET WORRIED.*
HERE. DO YOU WANT A PIECE OF BREAD? IT'S A BIT HARD, I KNOW, BUT IT'S ALL I COULD GET US TODAY...
SQUEE!
WHAT?! *OH MY G...*

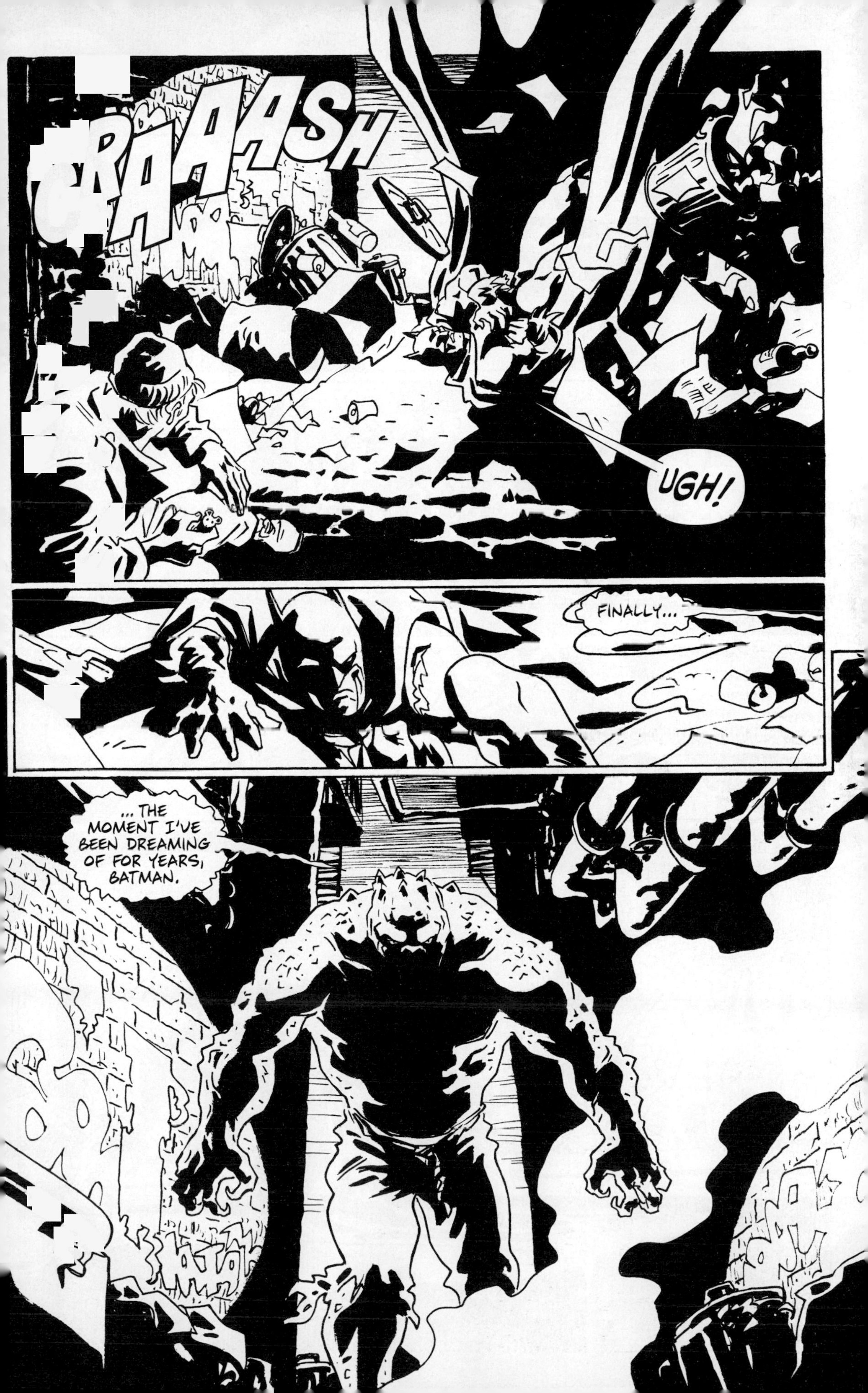
CRAAASH
UGH!
FINALLY...
...THE MOMENT I'VE BEEN DREAMING OF FOR YEARS, BATMAN.

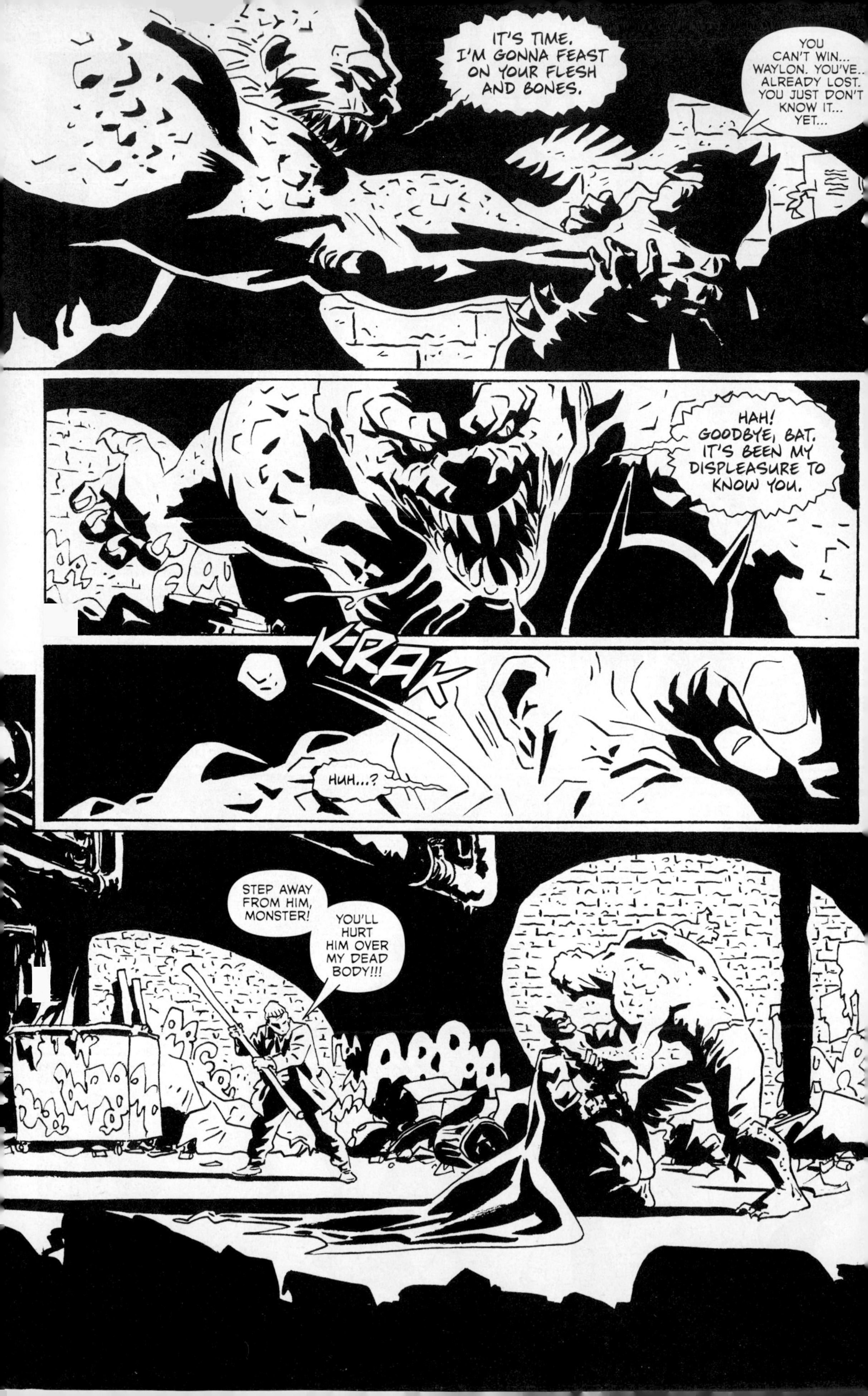
IT'S TIME. I'M GONNA FEAST ON YOUR FLESH AND BONES.
YOU CAN'T WIN... WAYLON. YOU'VE... ALREADY LOST. YOU JUST DON'T KNOW IT... YET...
HAH! GOODBYE, BAT. IT'S BEEN MY DISPLEASURE TO KNOW YOU.
KRAK
HUH...?
STEP AWAY FROM HIM, MONSTER!
YOU'LL HURT HIM OVER MY DEAD BODY!!!

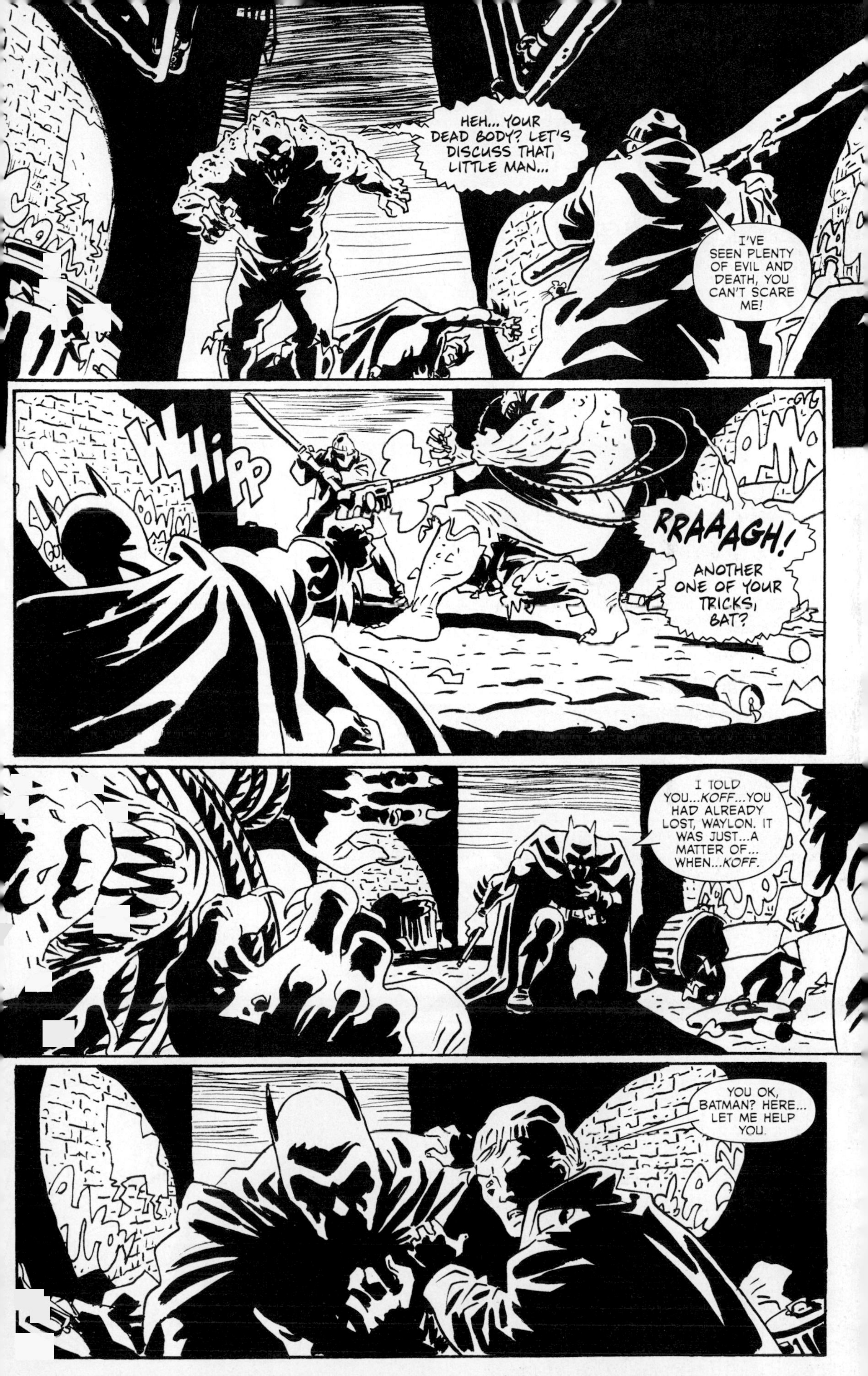
HEH... YOUR DEAD BODY? LET'S DISCUSS THAT, LITTLE MAN...
I'VE SEEN PLENTY OF EVIL AND DEATH, YOU CAN'T SCARE ME!
WHIPP
RRAAAGH!
ANOTHER ONE OF YOUR TRICKS, BAT?
I TOLD YOU...*KOFF*...YOU HAD ALREADY LOST, WAYLON. IT WAS JUST...A MATTER OF... WHEN...*KOFF.*
YOU OK, BATMAN? HERE... LET ME HELP YOU.

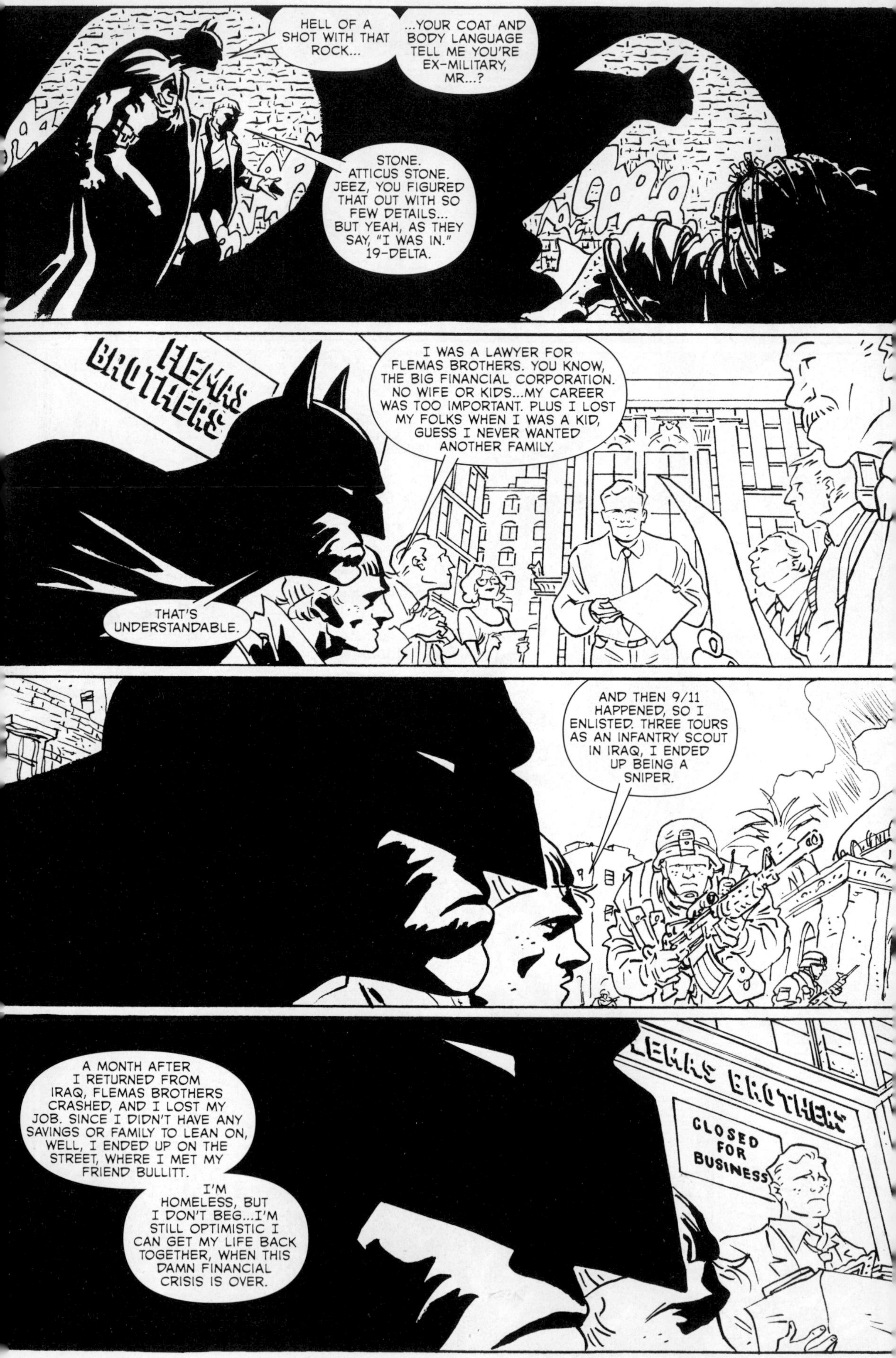
HELL OF A SHOT WITH THAT ROCK...
...YOUR COAT AND BODY LANGUAGE TELL ME YOU'RE EX-MILITARY, MR...?
STONE. ATTICUS STONE. JEEZ, YOU FIGURED THAT OUT WITH SO FEW DETAILS... BUT YEAH, AS THEY SAY, "I WAS IN." 19-DELTA.
FLEMAS BROTHERS
I WAS A LAWYER FOR FLEMAS BROTHERS. YOU KNOW, THE BIG FINANCIAL CORPORATION. NO WIFE OR KIDS...MY CAREER WAS TOO IMPORTANT. PLUS I LOST MY FOLKS WHEN I WAS A KID, GUESS I NEVER WANTED ANOTHER FAMILY.
THAT'S UNDERSTANDABLE.
AND THEN 9/11 HAPPENED, SO I ENLISTED. THREE TOURS AS AN INFANTRY SCOUT IN IRAQ, I ENDED UP BEING A SNIPER.
A MONTH AFTER I RETURNED FROM IRAQ, FLEMAS BROTHERS CRASHED, AND I LOST MY JOB. SINCE I DIDN'T HAVE ANY SAVINGS OR FAMILY TO LEAN ON, WELL, I ENDED UP ON THE STREET, WHERE I MET MY FRIEND BULLITT.
I'M HOMELESS, BUT I DON'T BEG...I'M STILL OPTIMISTIC I CAN GET MY LIFE BACK TOGETHER, WHEN THIS DAMN FINANCIAL CRISIS IS OVER.
CLOSED FOR BUSINESS

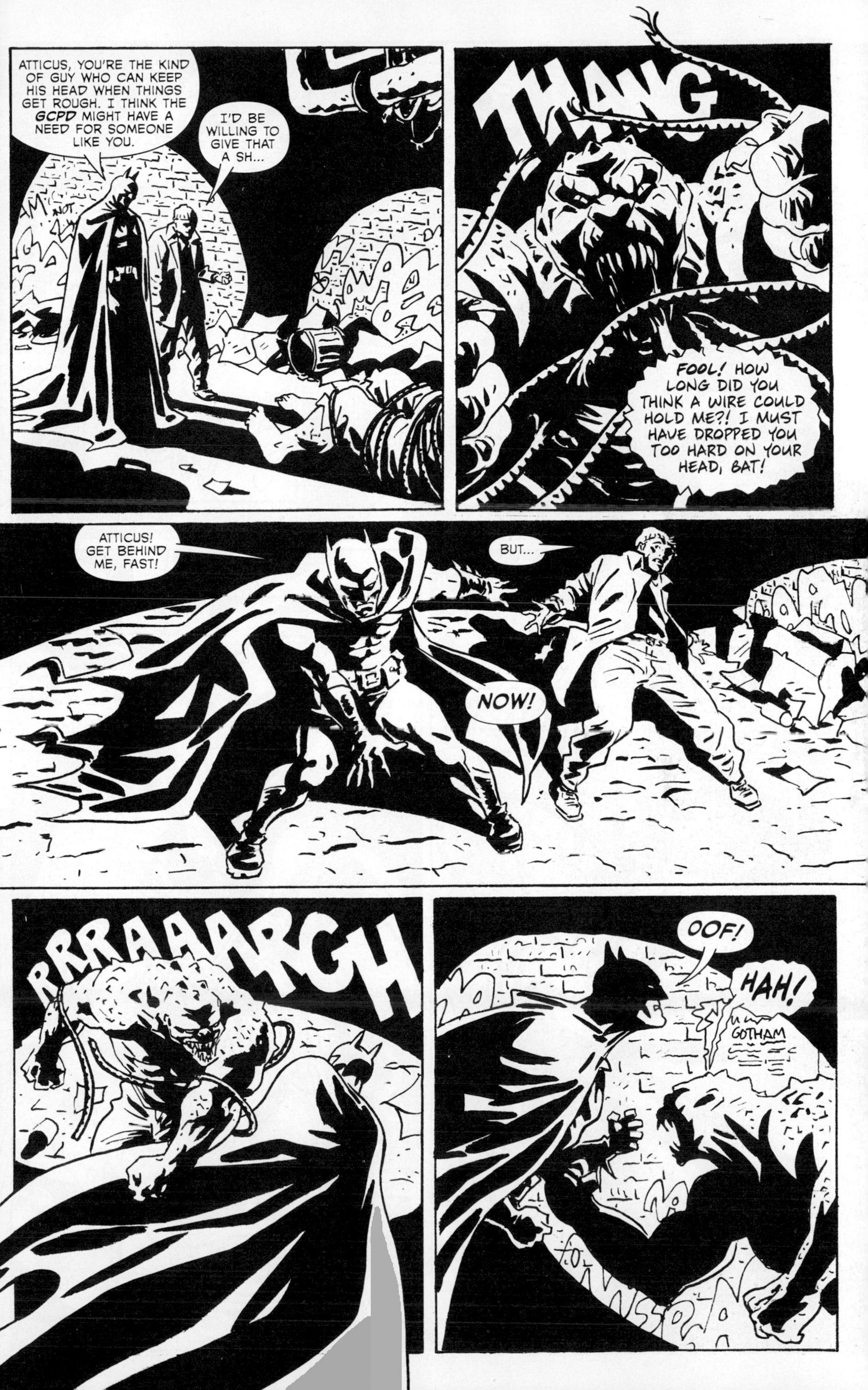
ATTICUS, YOU'RE THE KIND OF GUY WHO CAN KEEP HIS HEAD WHEN THINGS GET ROUGH. I THINK THE GCPD MIGHT HAVE A NEED FOR SOMEONE LIKE YOU.
I'D BE WILLING TO GIVE THAT A SH...
THANG
FOOL! HOW LONG DID YOU THINK A WIRE COULD HOLD ME?! I MUST HAVE DROPPED YOU TOO HARD ON YOUR HEAD, BAT!
ATTICUS! GET BEHIND ME, FAST!
BUT...
NOW!
RRRAAAARGH
OOF!
HAH!
GOTHAM

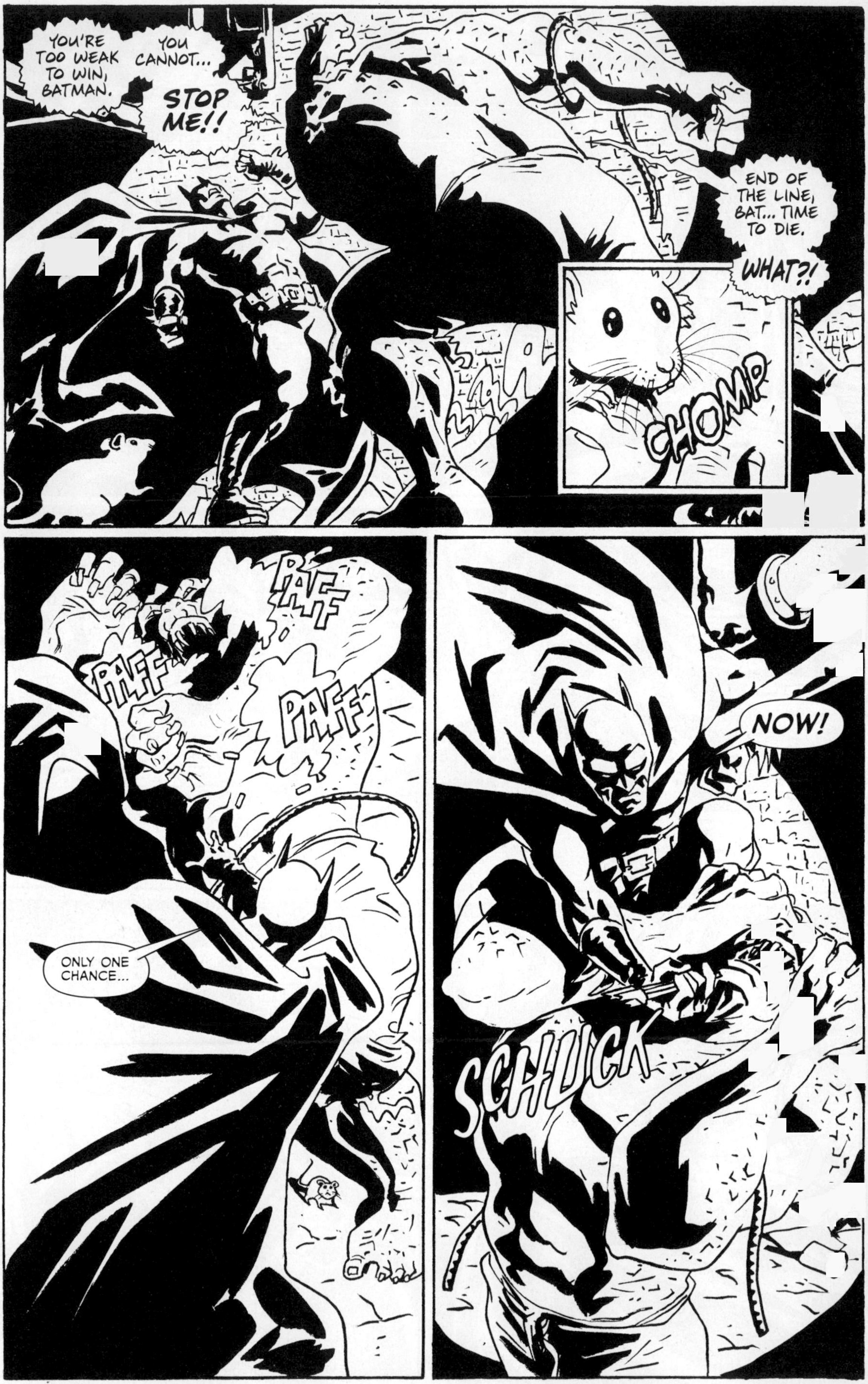
YOU'RE TOO WEAK TO WIN, BATMAN.
YOU CANNOT...
STOP ME!!
END OF THE LINE, BAT... TIME TO DIE.
WHAT?!
CHOMP
PAFF
PAFF
PAFF
ONLY ONE CHANCE...
NOW!
SCHUCK

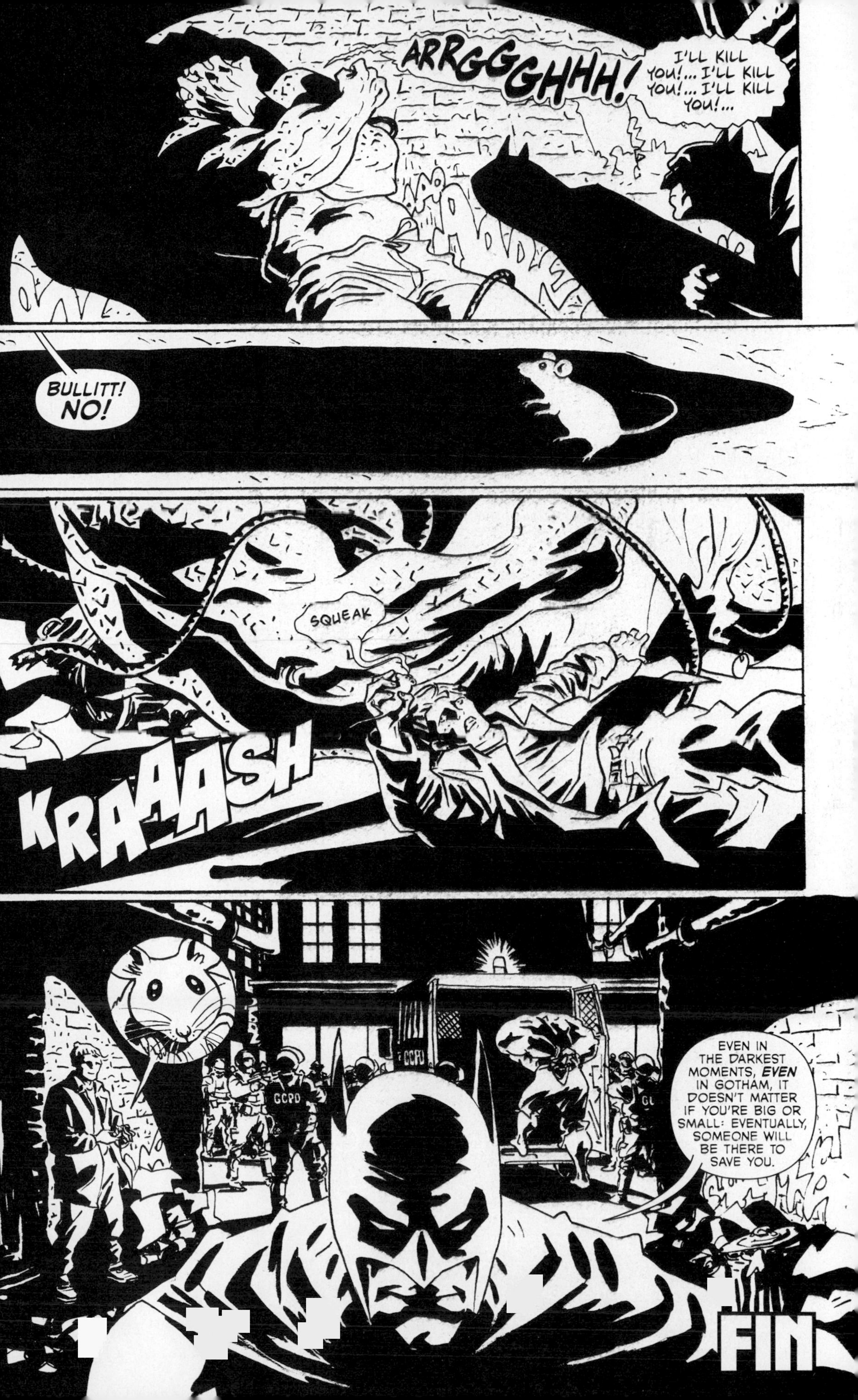
ARRGGGHHH!
I'LL KILL YOU!... I'LL KILL YOU!... I'LL KILL YOU!...
BULLITT! NO!
SQUEAK
KRAAASH
EVEN IN THE DARKEST MOMENTS, EVEN IN GOTHAM, IT DOESN'T MATTER IF YOU'RE BIG OR SMALL: EVENTUALLY, SOMEONE WILL BE THERE TO SAVE YOU.
FIN

DAVID MACHO

Spanish author, artist representative,
comics translator, and convention organizer,
David Macho is a singular personality in
the international comics world.
Although he's previously written the exploits of
the Justice League, this marks Macho's
first time writing a Batman tale.

RUBÉN PELLEJERO

Born in Badalona, Spain in 1952,
Rubén Pellejero is a grand master of comic book art.
Together with Argentinian writer Jorge Zentner,
Pellejero created the famous antihero
and world traveller Dieter Lumpen.
One of the great graphic novelists and
storytellers in comics history, Pellejero
has published his work all over the globe.

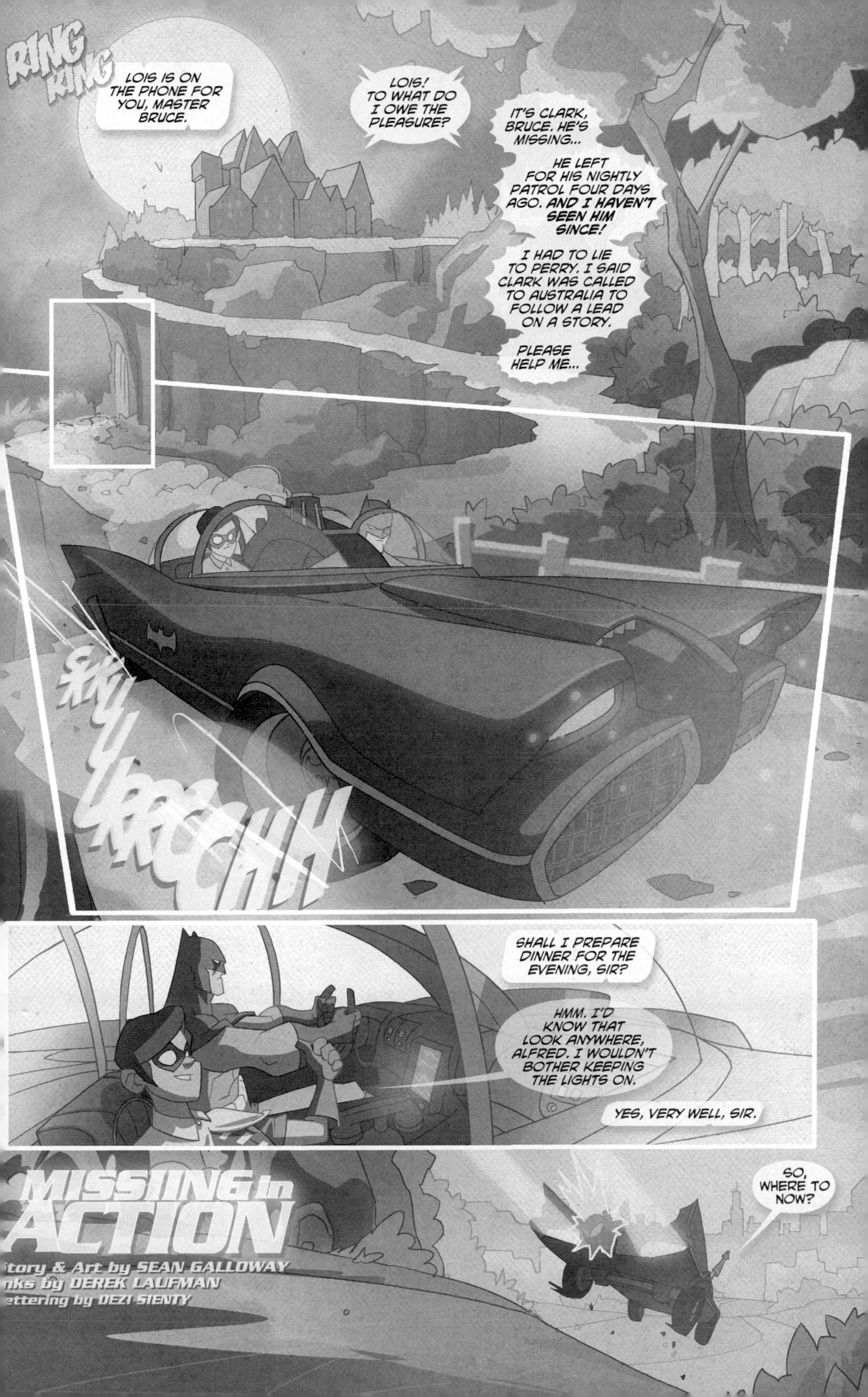

RING RING
LOIS IS ON THE PHONE FOR YOU, MASTER BRUCE.
LOIS! TO WHAT DO I OWE THE PLEASURE?
IT'S CLARK, BRUCE. HE'S MISSING...
HE LEFT FOR HIS NIGHTLY PATROL FOUR DAYS AGO. AND I HAVEN'T SEEN HIM SINCE!
I HAD TO LIE TO PERRY. I SAID CLARK WAS CALLED TO AUSTRALIA TO FOLLOW A LEAD ON A STORY.
PLEASE HELP ME...
SKYURRRCHH
SHALL I PREPARE DINNER FOR THE EVENING, SIR?
HMM. I'D KNOW THAT LOOK ANYWHERE, ALFRED. I WOULDN'T BOTHER KEEPING THE LIGHTS ON.
YES, VERY WELL, SIR.
MISSING in ACTION
Story & Art by SEAN GALLOWAY
Inks by DEREK LAUFMAN
Lettering by DEZI SIENTY
SO, WHERE TO NOW?

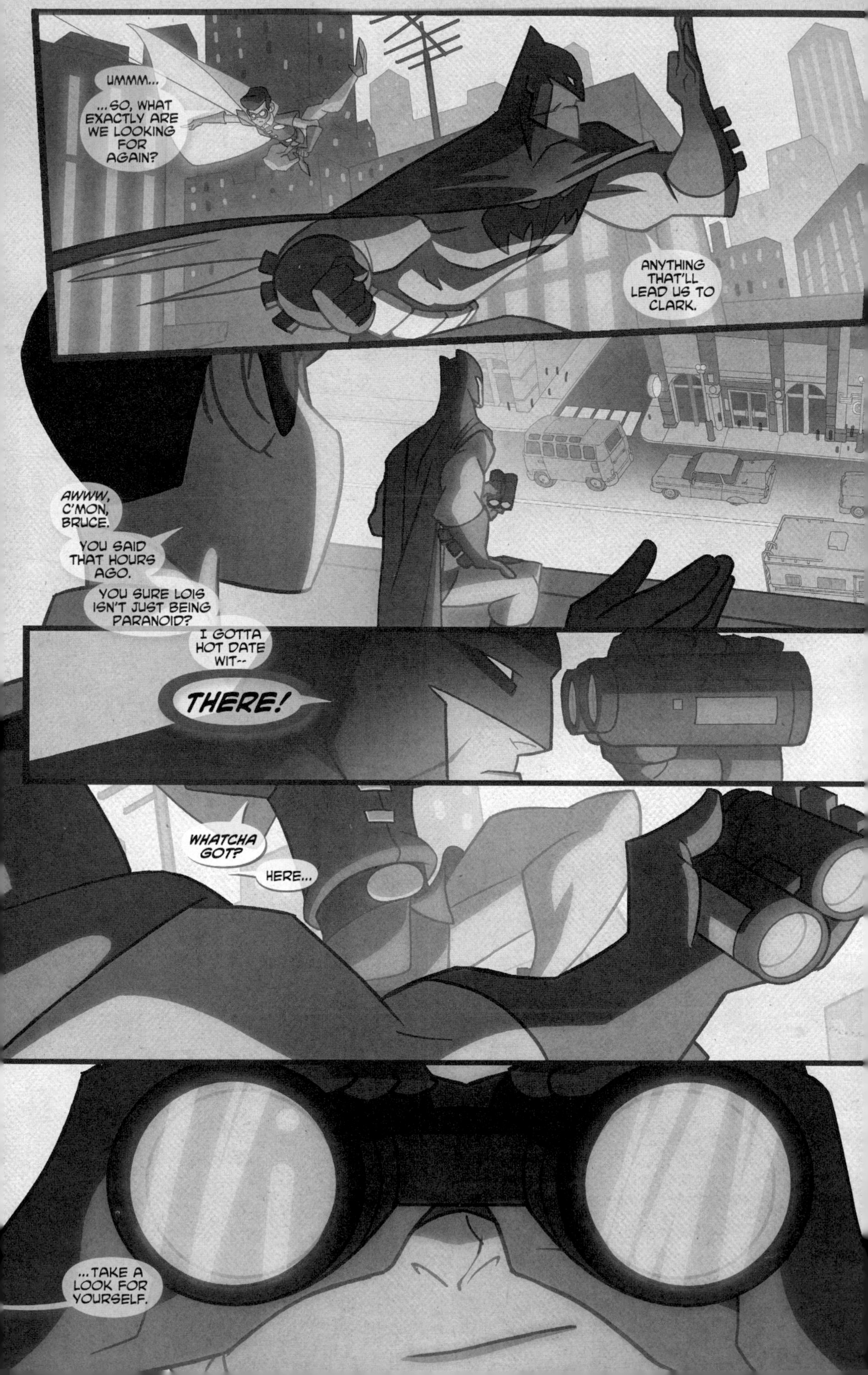
UMMM...
...SO, WHAT EXACTLY ARE WE LOOKING FOR AGAIN?
ANYTHING THAT'LL LEAD US TO CLARK.
AWWW, C'MON, BRUCE.
YOU SAID THAT HOURS AGO.
YOU SURE LOIS ISN'T JUST BEING PARANOID?
I GOTTA HOT DATE WIT--
THERE!
WHATCHA GOT?
HERE...
...TAKE A LOOK FOR YOURSELF.

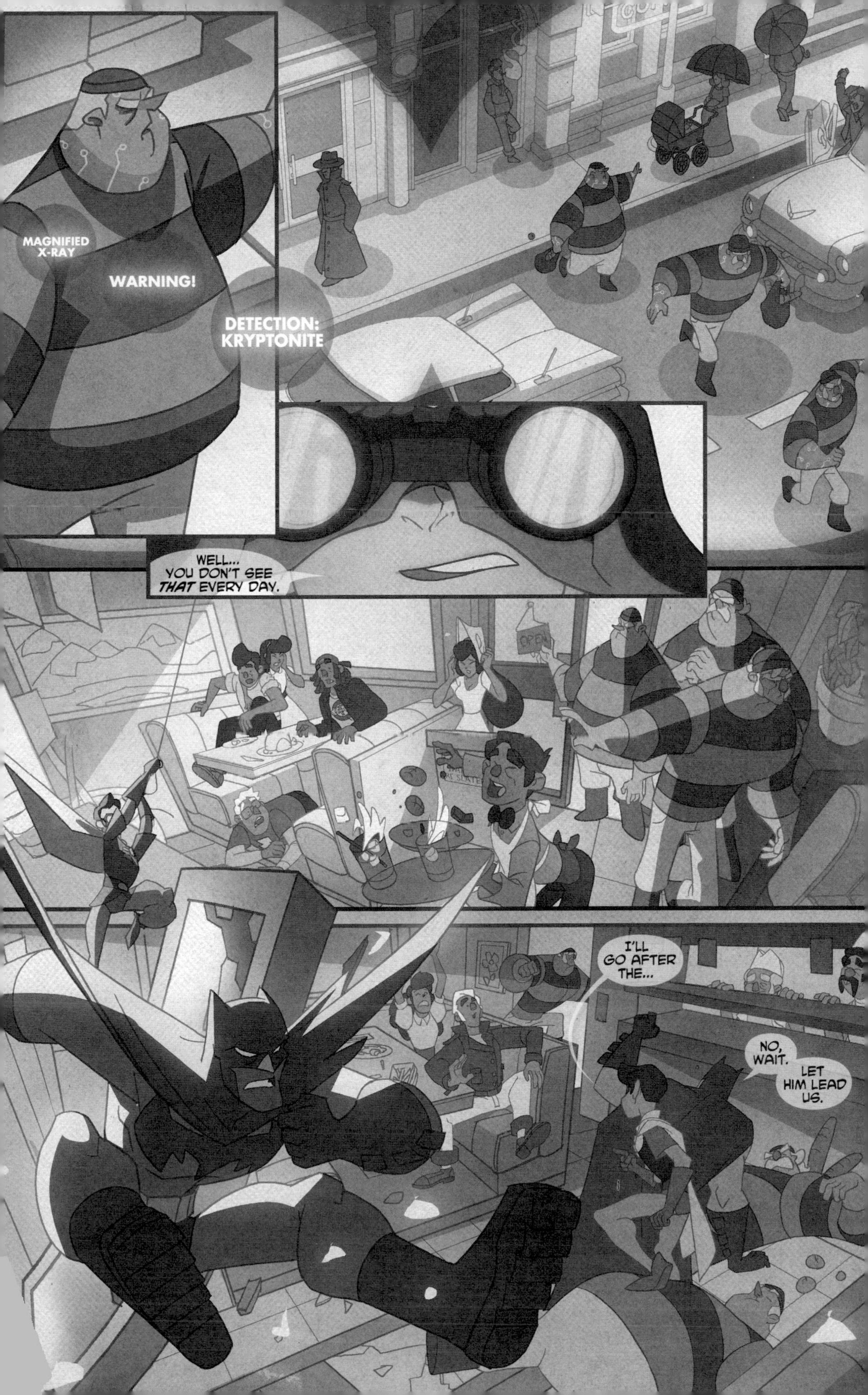

MAGNIFIED X-RAY
WARNING!
DETECTION: KRYPTONITE
WELL... YOU DON'T SEE *THAT* EVERY DAY.
I'LL GO AFTER THE...
NO, WAIT.
LET HIM LEAD US.

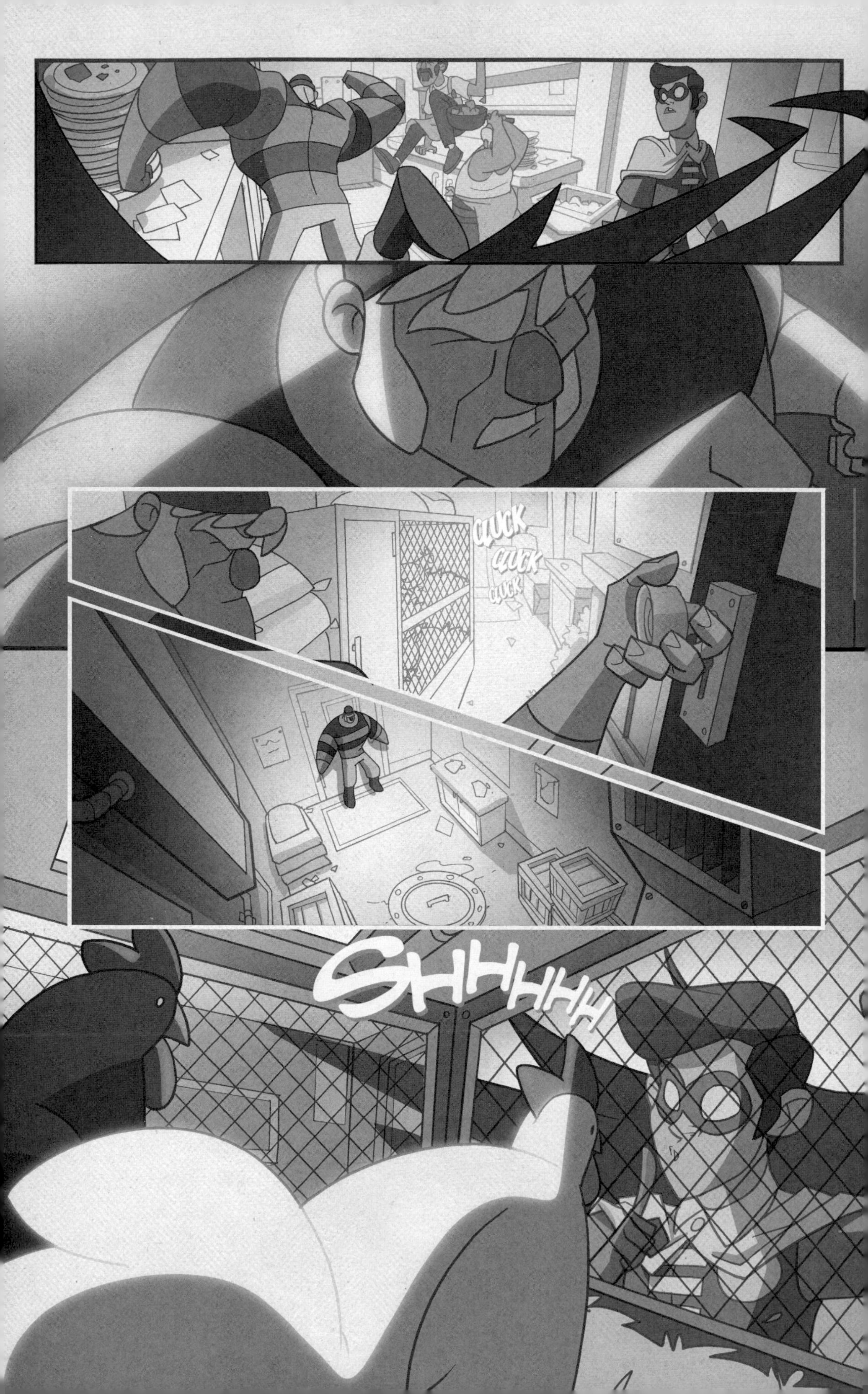
CLUCK
CLUCK
CLUCK
SHHHHH

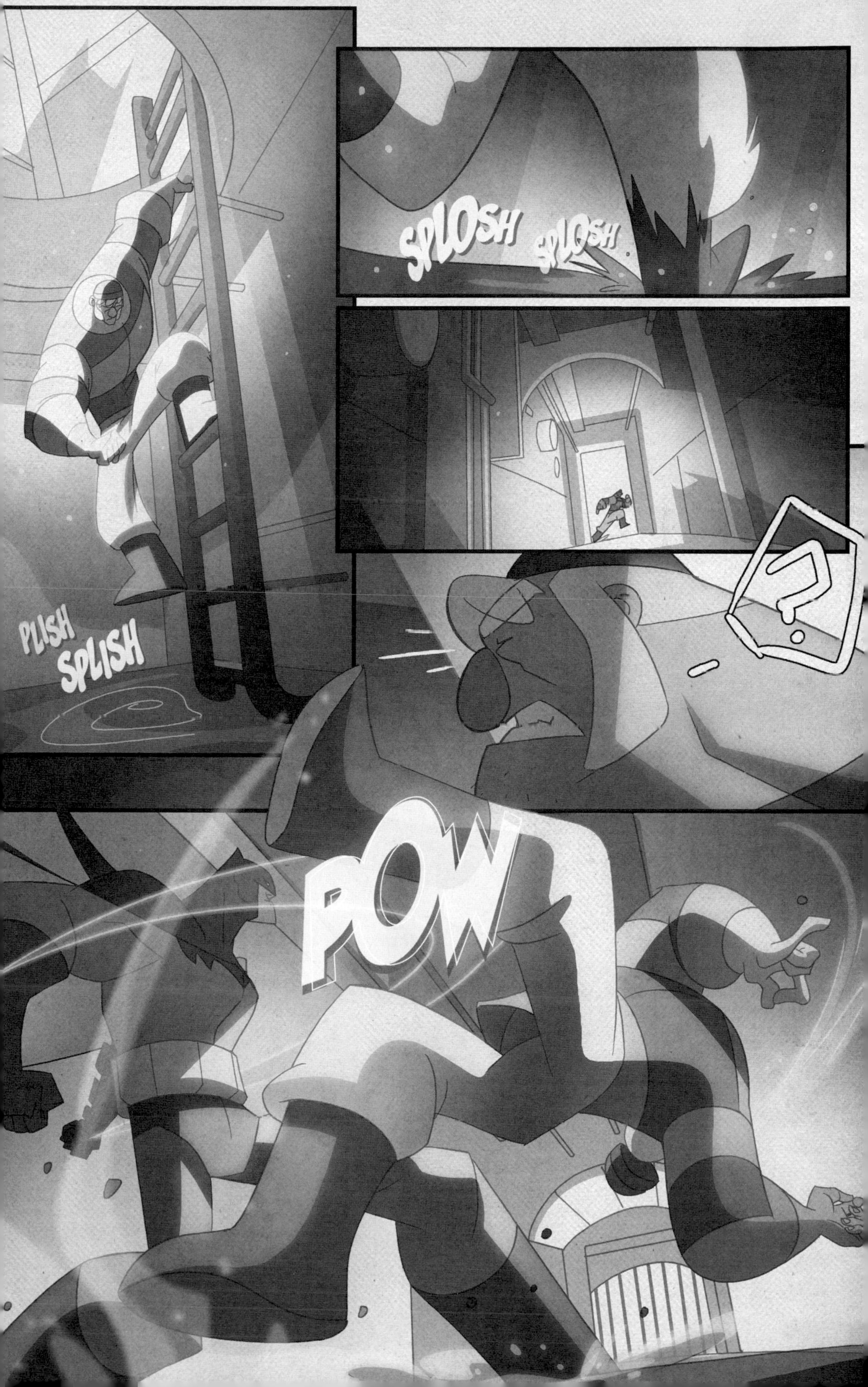
SPLOSH SPLOSH
PLISH
SPLISH
?
POW

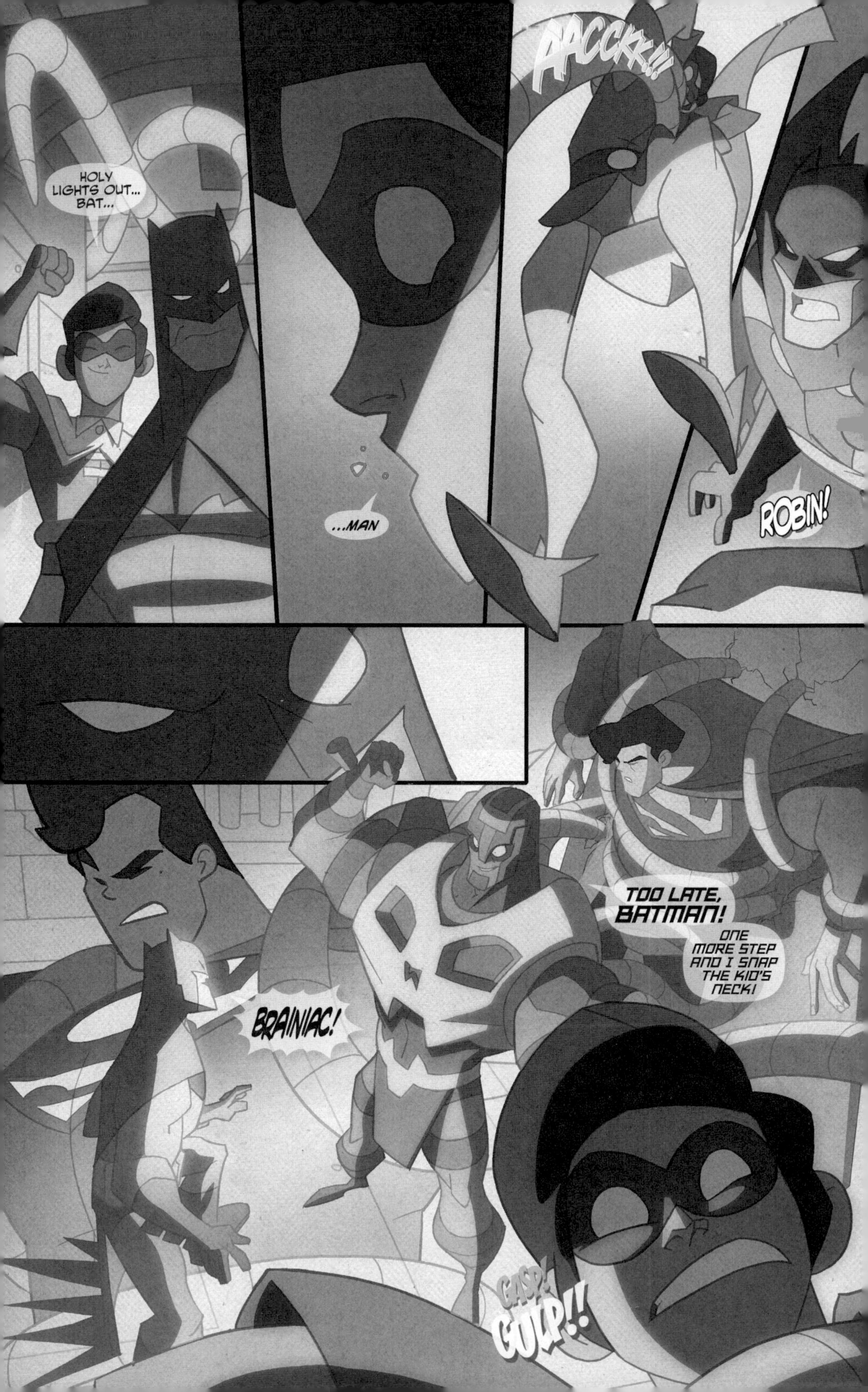
HOLY LIGHTS OUT... BAT...
...MAN
AACCKK!!!
ROBIN!
BRAINIAC!
TOO LATE, BATMAN!
ONE MORE STEP AND I SNAP THE KID'S NECK!
GASP! GULP!!

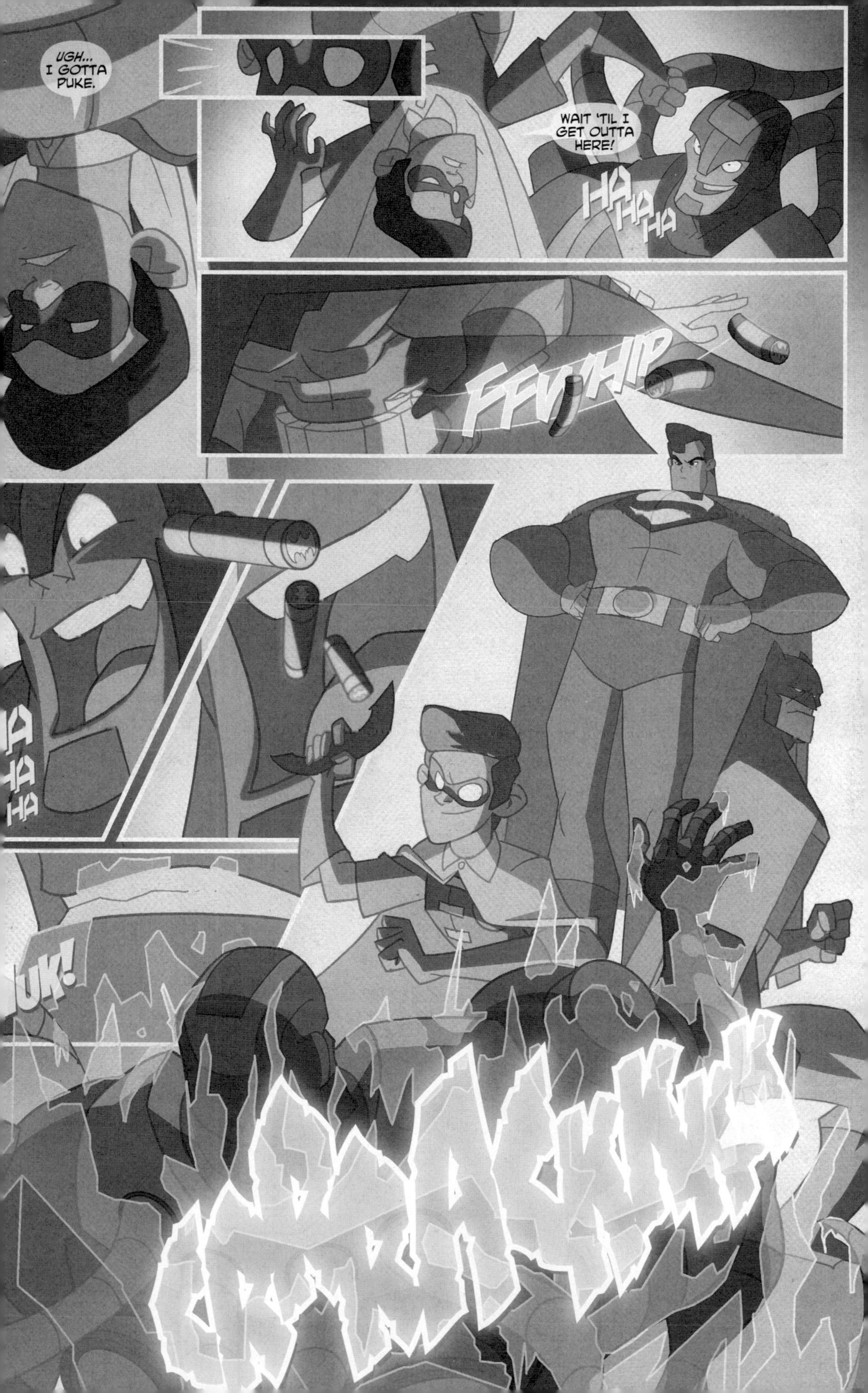

UGH... I GOTTA PUKE.
WAIT 'TIL I GET OUTTA HERE!
HA HA HA
FFWHIP
HA HA HA
UK!

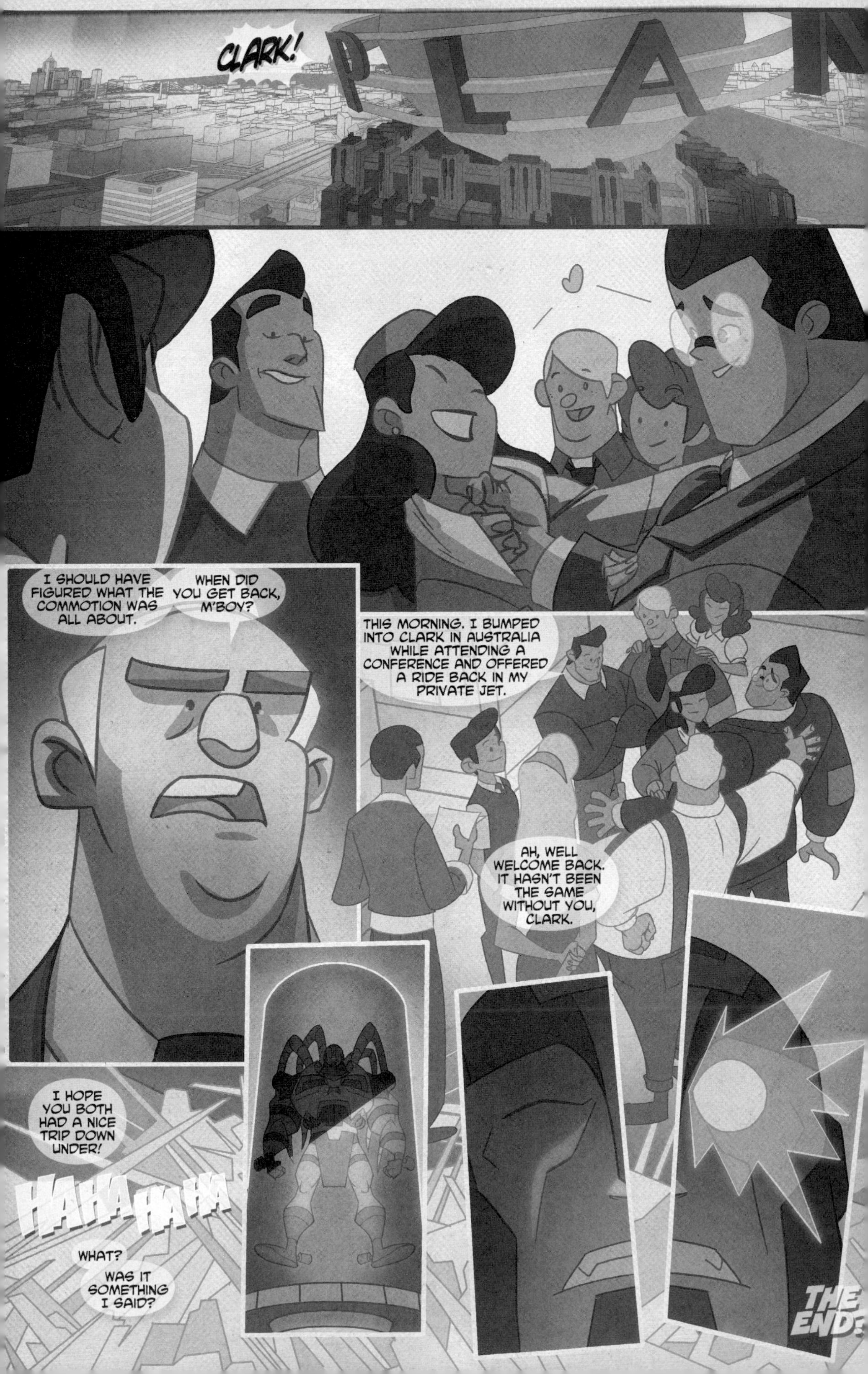
CLARK!
I SHOULD HAVE FIGURED WHAT THE COMMOTION WAS ALL ABOUT.
WHEN DID YOU GET BACK, M'BOY?
THIS MORNING. I BUMPED INTO CLARK IN AUSTRALIA WHILE ATTENDING A CONFERENCE AND OFFERED A RIDE BACK IN MY PRIVATE JET.
AH, WELL WELCOME BACK. IT HASN'T BEEN THE SAME WITHOUT YOU, CLARK.
I HOPE YOU BOTH HAD A NICE TRIP DOWN UNDER!
HAHAHAHA
WHAT?
WAS IT SOMETHING I SAID?
THE END!

SEAN GALLOWAY

Sean 'Cheeks' Galloway's vibrant and imaginative art ranges from comics, to animation, to video game and toy design. He's probably best known for his character design work on the animated shows: *Spectacular Spider-Man*, *Hellboy*, and *Transformers Animated*. His comics work includes WEDNESDAY COMICS, WORLD OF WARCRAFT: PEARL OF PANDARIA, and covers for TEEN TITANS GO! Recently, 'Cheeks' has been devoting a good portion of his drawing time to his creator-owned and Kickstarter projects *Bastion's 7: Gumshoes 4 Hire*, and *Little Big Heads*.

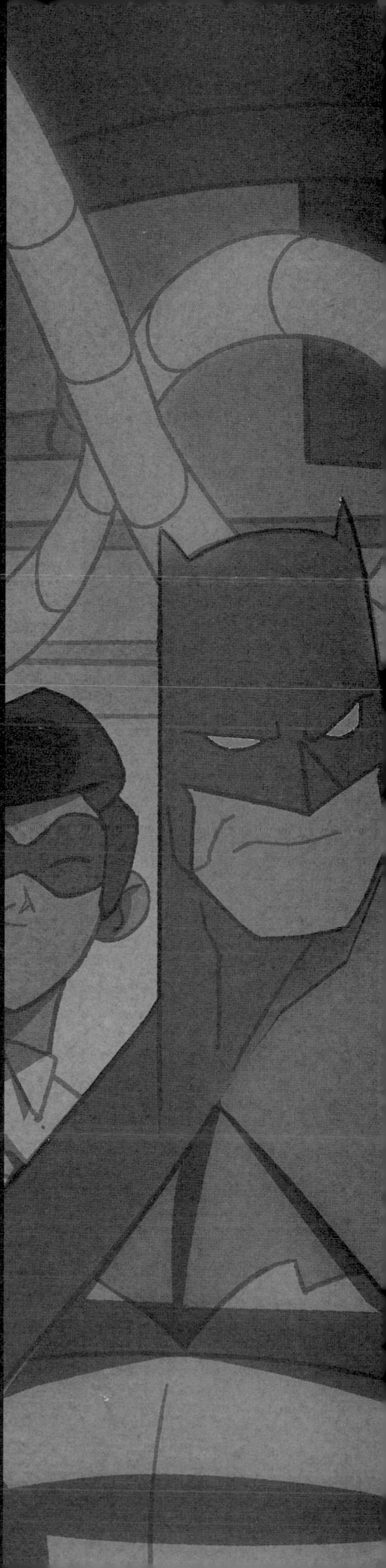

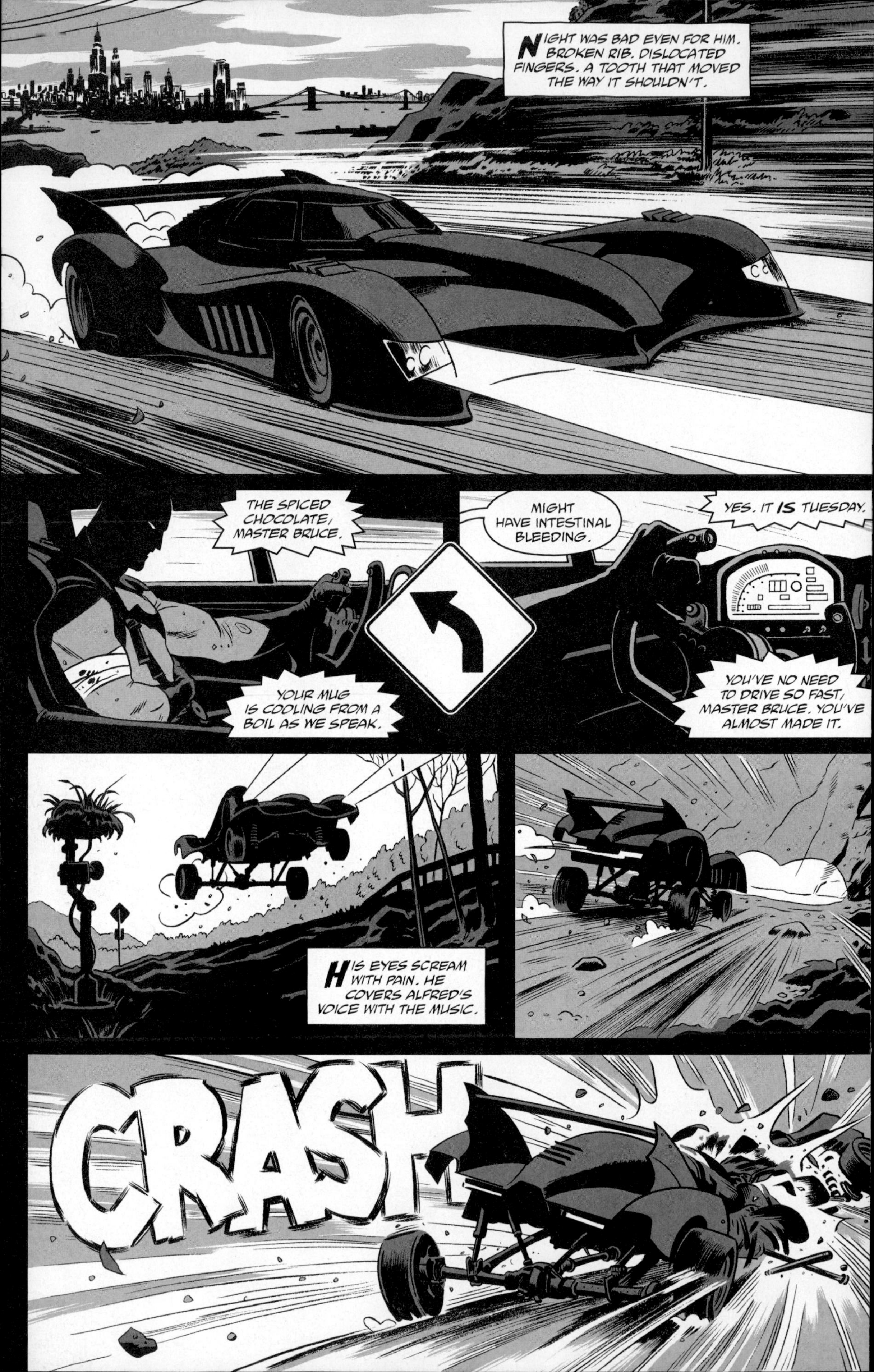
NIGHT WAS BAD EVEN FOR HIM. BROKEN RIB. DISLOCATED FINGERS. A TOOTH THAT MOVED THE WAY IT SHOULDN'T.
THE SPICED CHOCOLATE, MASTER BRUCE.
YOUR MUG IS COOLING FROM A BOIL AS WE SPEAK.
MIGHT HAVE INTESTINAL BLEEDING.
YES. IT IS TUESDAY.
YOU'VE NO NEED TO DRIVE SO FAST, MASTER BRUCE. YOU'VE ALMOST MADE IT.
HIS EYES SCREAM WITH PAIN. HE COVERS ALFRED'S VOICE WITH THE MUSIC.
CRASH

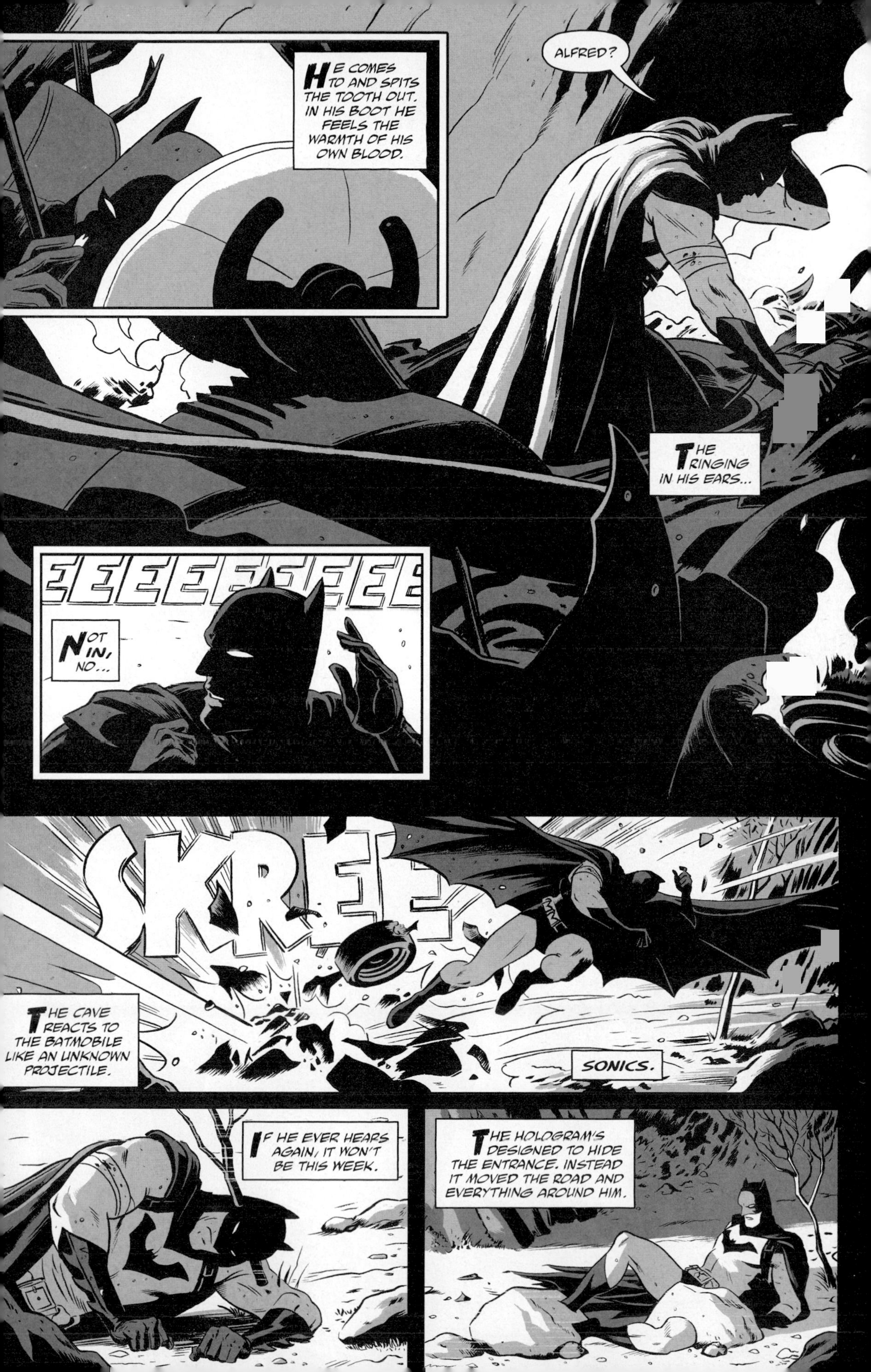
HE COMES TO AND SPITS THE TOOTH OUT. IN HIS BOOT HE FEELS THE WARMTH OF HIS OWN BLOOD.
ALFRED?
THE RINGING IN HIS EARS...
EEEEEEEEE
NOT IN, NO...
SKREE
THE CAVE REACTS TO THE BATMOBILE LIKE AN UNKNOWN PROJECTILE.
SONICS.
IF HE EVER HEARS AGAIN, IT WON'T BE THIS WEEK.
THE HOLOGRAM'S DESIGNED TO HIDE THE ENTRANCE. INSTEAD IT MOVED THE ROAD AND EVERYTHING AROUND HIM.

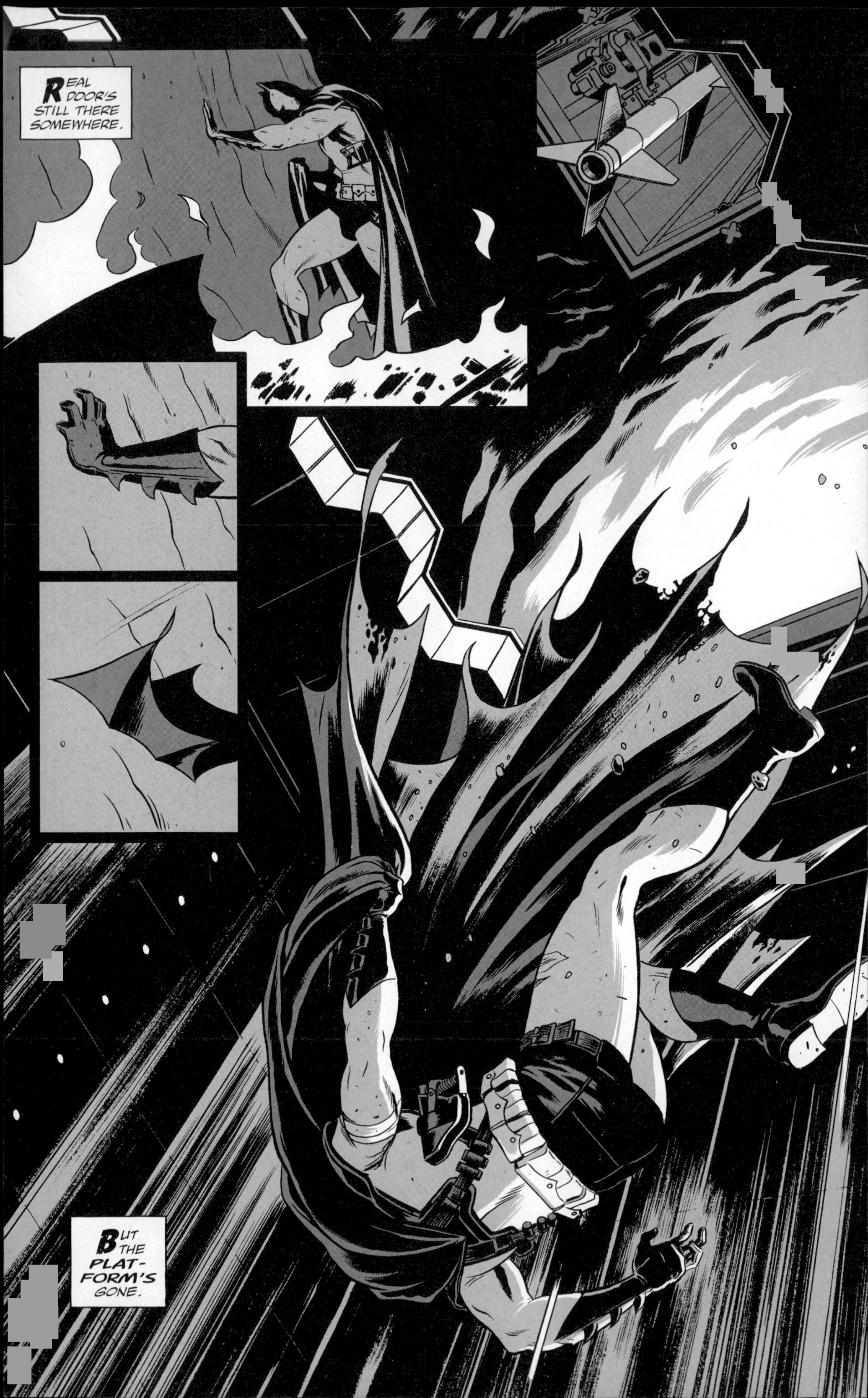
REAL DOOR'S STILL THERE SOMEWHERE.
BUT THE PLAT-FORM'S GONE.

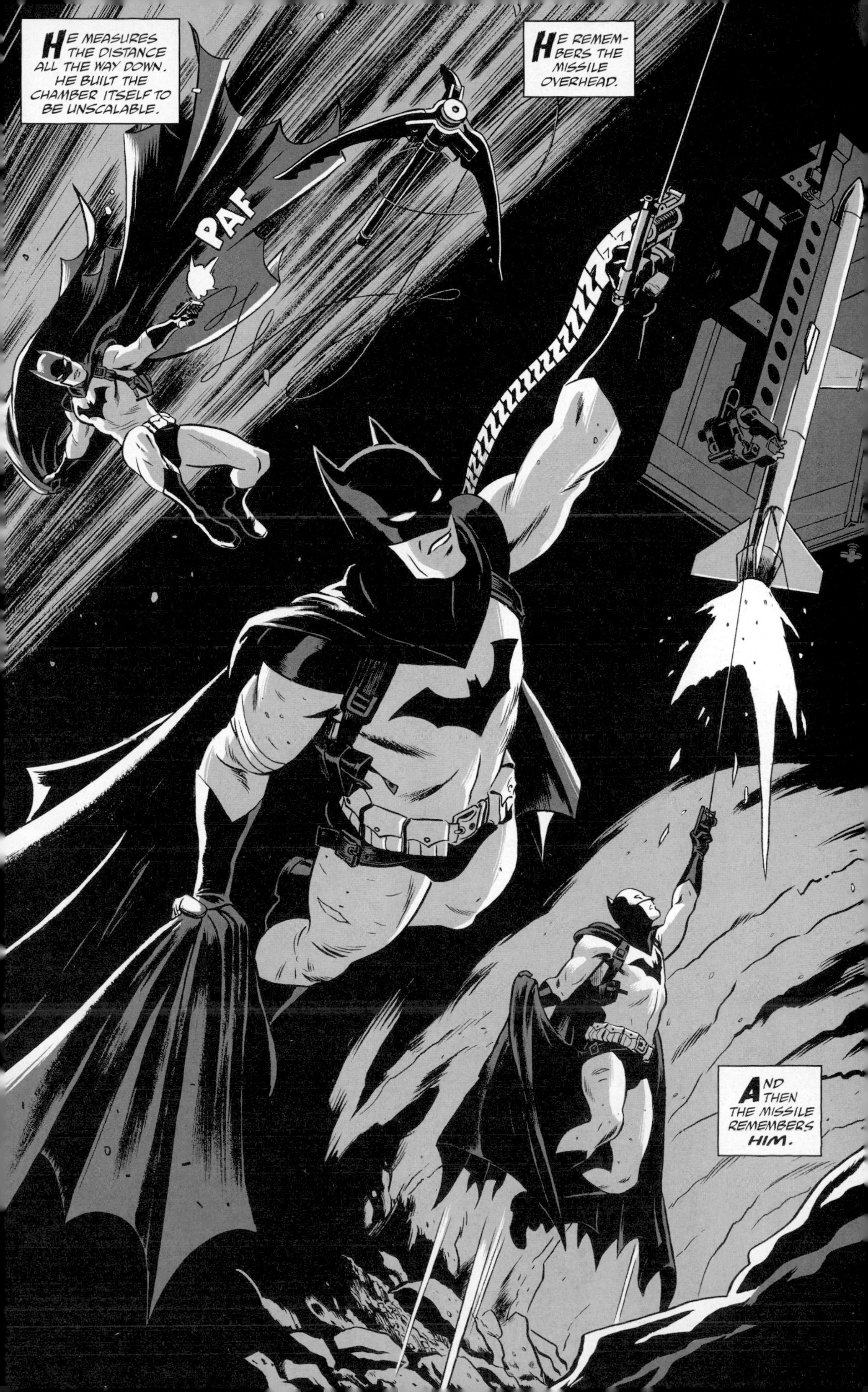
HE MEASURES THE DISTANCE ALL THE WAY DOWN. HE BUILT THE CHAMBER ITSELF TO BE UNSCALABLE.
HE REMEMBERS THE MISSILE OVERHEAD.
PAF
AND THEN THE MISSILE REMEMBERS HIM.

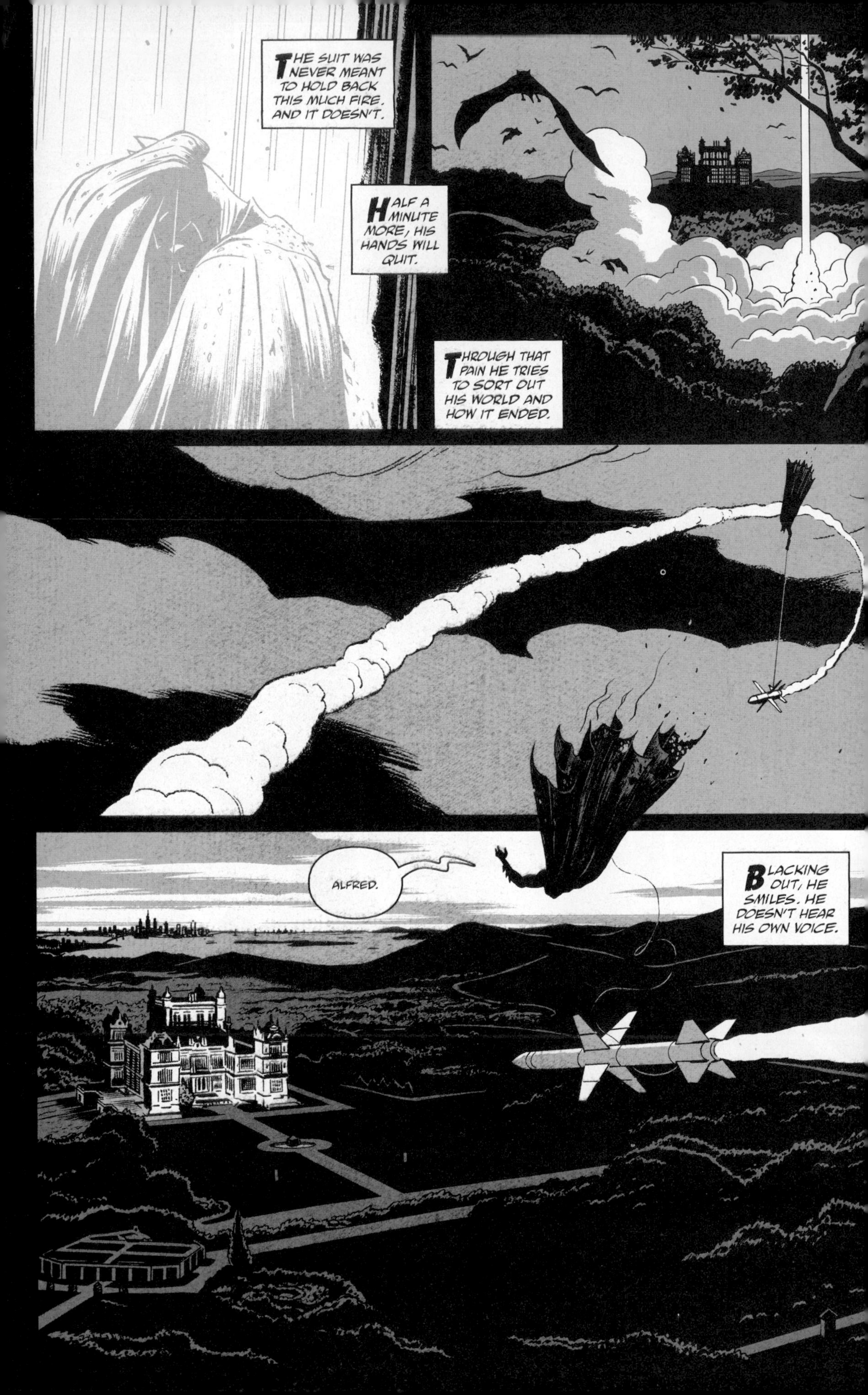
THE SUIT WAS NEVER MEANT TO HOLD BACK THIS MUCH FIRE. AND IT DOESN'T.
HALF A MINUTE MORE, HIS HANDS WILL QUIT.
THROUGH THAT PAIN HE TRIES TO SORT OUT HIS WORLD AND HOW IT ENDED.
ALFRED.
BLACKING OUT, HE SMILES. HE DOESN'T HEAR HIS OWN VOICE.

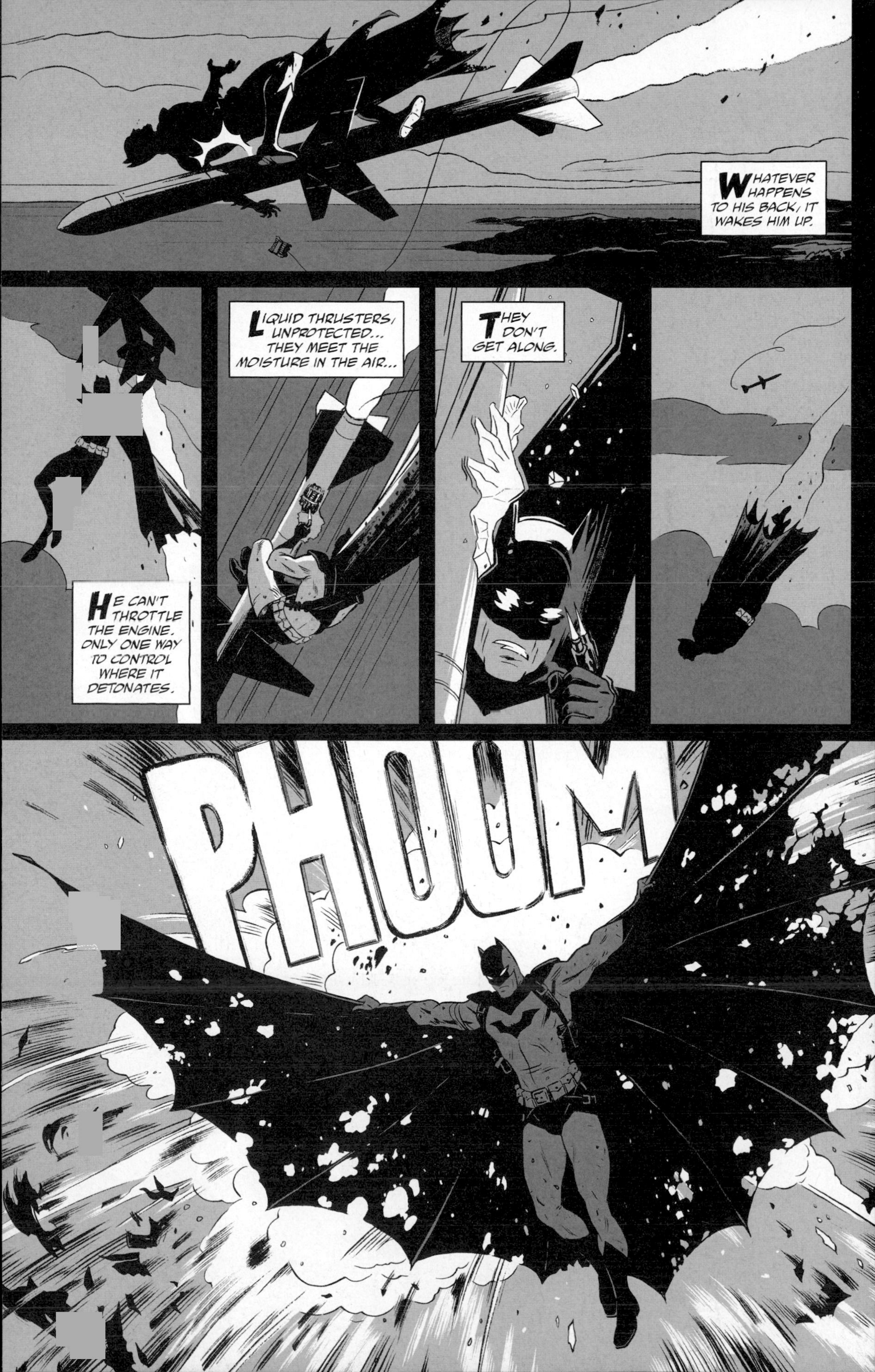
WHATEVER HAPPENS TO HIS BACK, IT WAKES HIM UP.
HE CAN'T THROTTLE THE ENGINE. ONLY ONE WAY TO CONTROL WHERE IT DETONATES.
LIQUID THRUSTERS, UNPROTECTED... THEY MEET THE MOISTURE IN THE AIR...
THEY DON'T GET ALONG.
PHOOM

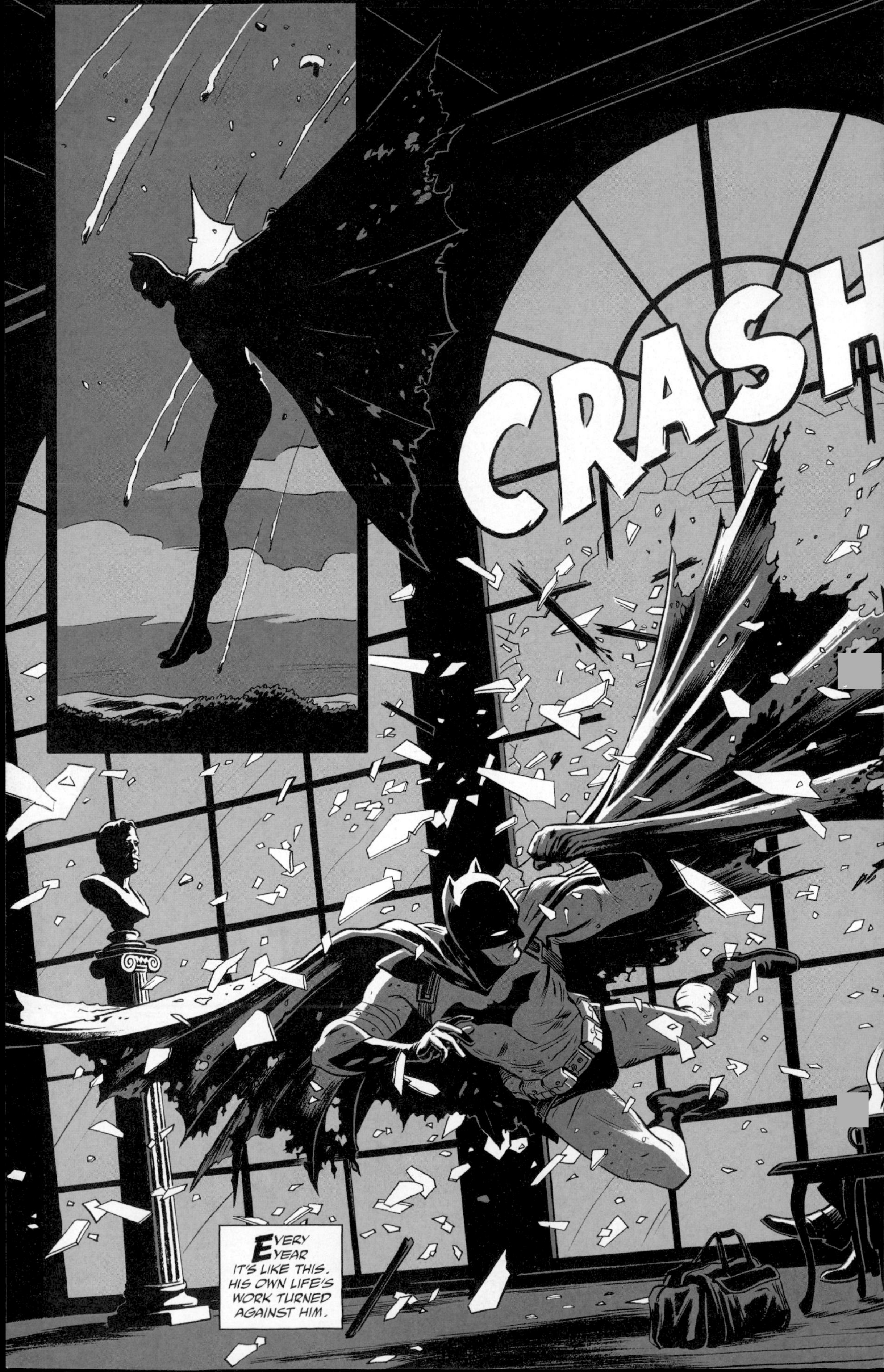
CRASH
EVERY YEAR IT'S LIKE THIS. HIS OWN LIFE'S WORK TURNED AGAINST HIM.

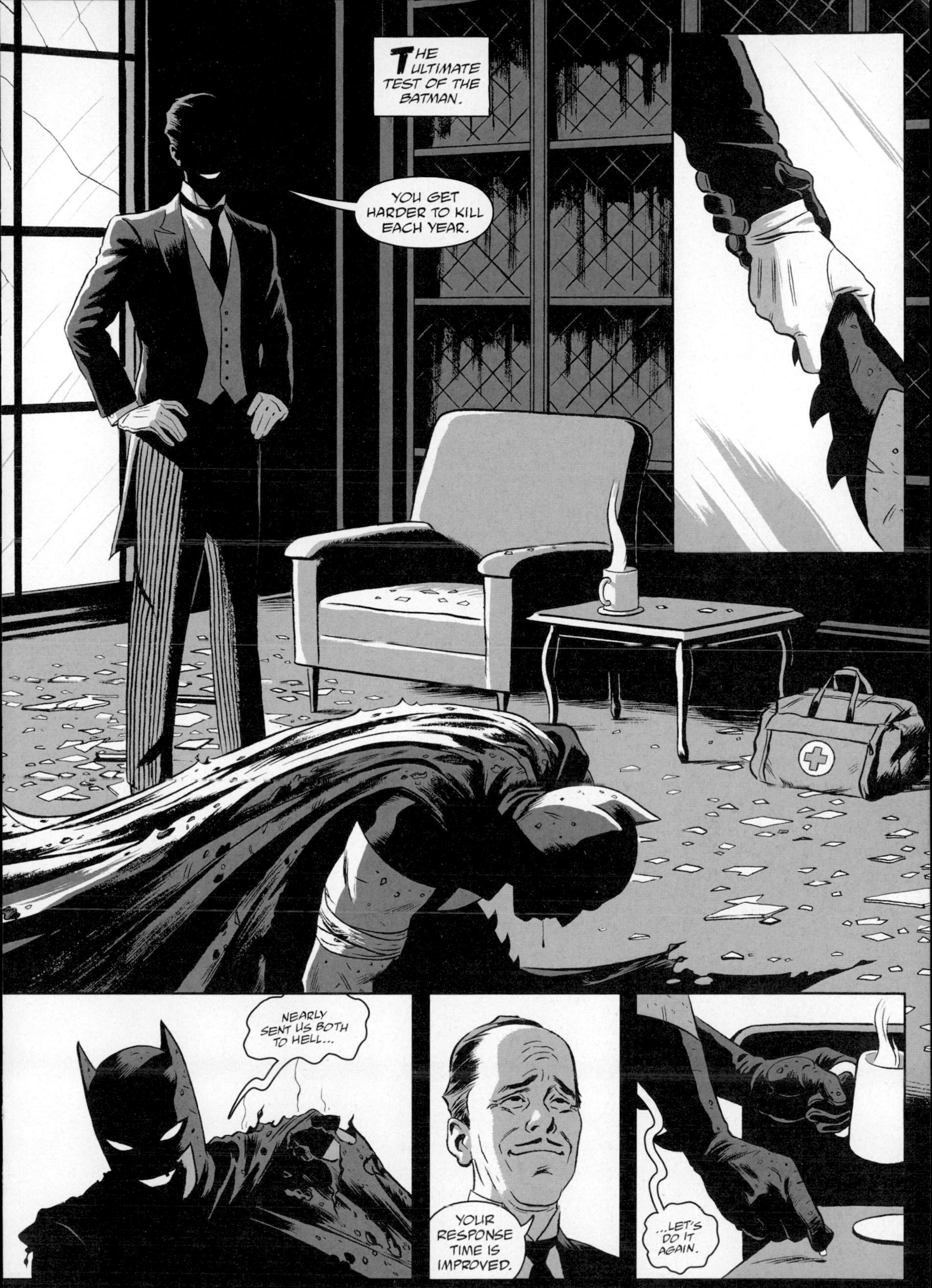
THE ULTIMATE TEST OF THE BATMAN.
YOU GET HARDER TO KILL EACH YEAR.
NEARLY SENT US BOTH TO HELL...
YOUR RESPONSE TIME IS IMPROVED.
...LET'S DO IT AGAIN.

BATMAN: HELL NIGHT

SCRIPT BY **IVAN BRANDON**

ART BY **PAOLO RIVERA**

INKS BY **JOE RIVERA**

LETTERED BY **CLEM ROBINS**

IVAN BRANDON

Creator and producer of the
Eisner-nominated anthology series 24Seven,
Ivan Brandon has also written MEN OF WAR,
Wolverine, Viking, NYC Mech, and
FINAL CRISIS AFTERMATH: ESCAPE.
Brandon's knack for placing the
reader into absurd worlds and situations
has made him one of the medium's most
sought after, cutting-edge writers.

PAOLO RIVERA

Multiple Eisner Award-winner Paolo Rivera
brings a classic, iconic style to everything he
draws. Taking his artistic inspiration from such
master comics artists as Jack Kirby, Milton Caniff,
and Noel Sickles, Rivera has quickly become
one of the industry's class acts.
While he is known primarily for his work with
Marvel Comics (*Daredevil*, *Mythos*, *Spider-Man*),
this issue marks the first time Paolo has lent his
talents to the mythos of the Dark Knight.
Of special note: the considerably talented
Eisner Award-winning inker of this Batman tale,
Joe Rivera, also just happens to be Paolo's Dad.

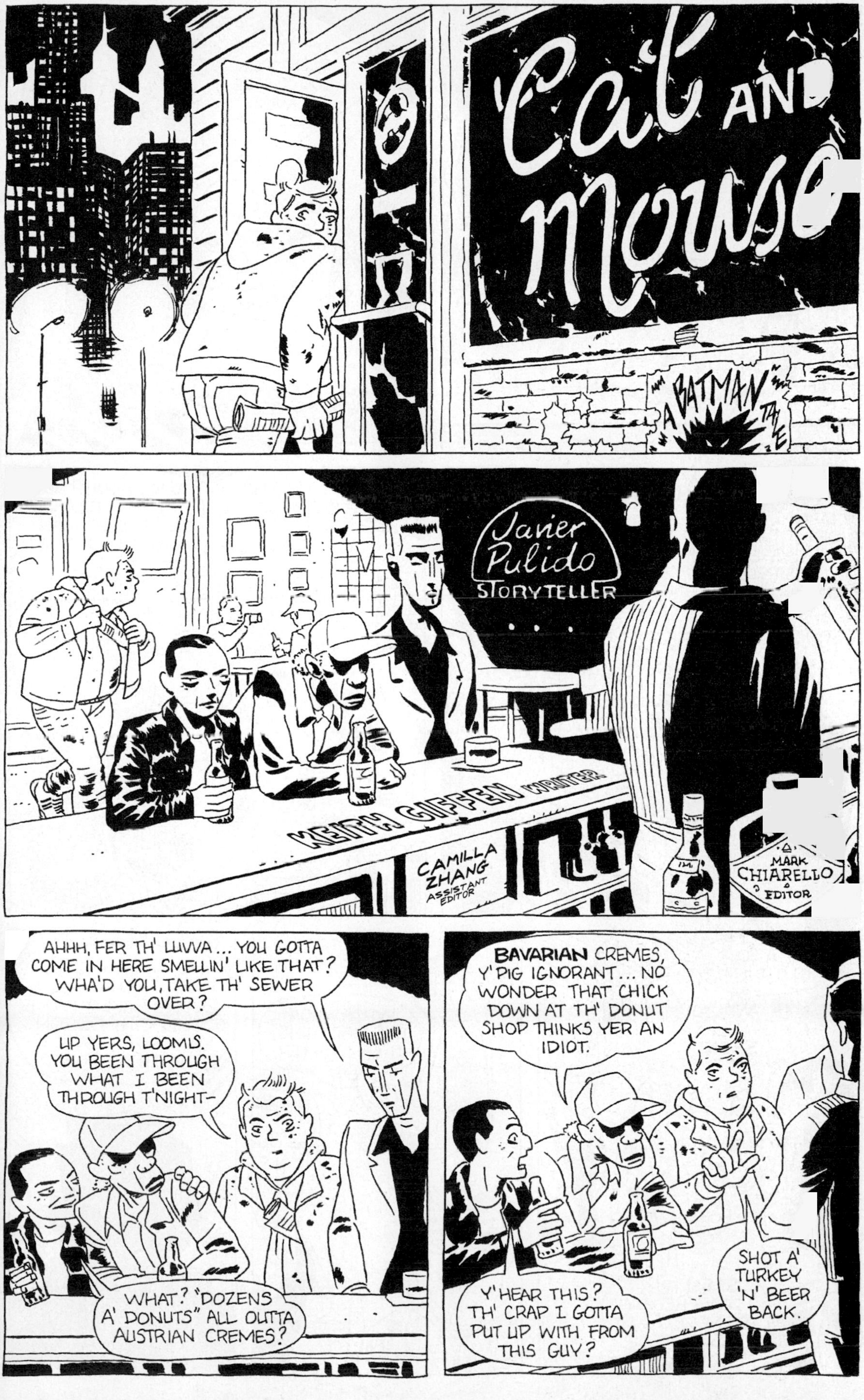
Cat AND Mouse
A BATMAN TALE
Javier Pulido STORYTELLER
KEITH GIFFEN WRITER
CAMILLA ZHANG ASSISTANT EDITOR
MARK CHIARELLO EDITOR
AHHH, FER TH' LUVVA... YOU GOTTA COME IN HERE SMELLIN' LIKE THAT? WHA'D YOU, TAKE TH' SEWER OVER?
UP YERS, LOOMIS. YOU BEEN THROUGH WHAT I BEEN THROUGH T'NIGHT-
WHAT? "DOZENS A' DONUTS" ALL OUTTA AUSTRIAN CREMES?
BAVARIAN CREMES, Y' PIG IGNORANT... NO WONDER THAT CHICK DOWN AT TH' DONUT SHOP THINKS YER AN IDIOT.
Y' HEAR THIS? TH' CRAP I GOTTA PUT UP WITH FROM THIS GUY?
SHOT A' TURKEY 'N' BEER BACK.

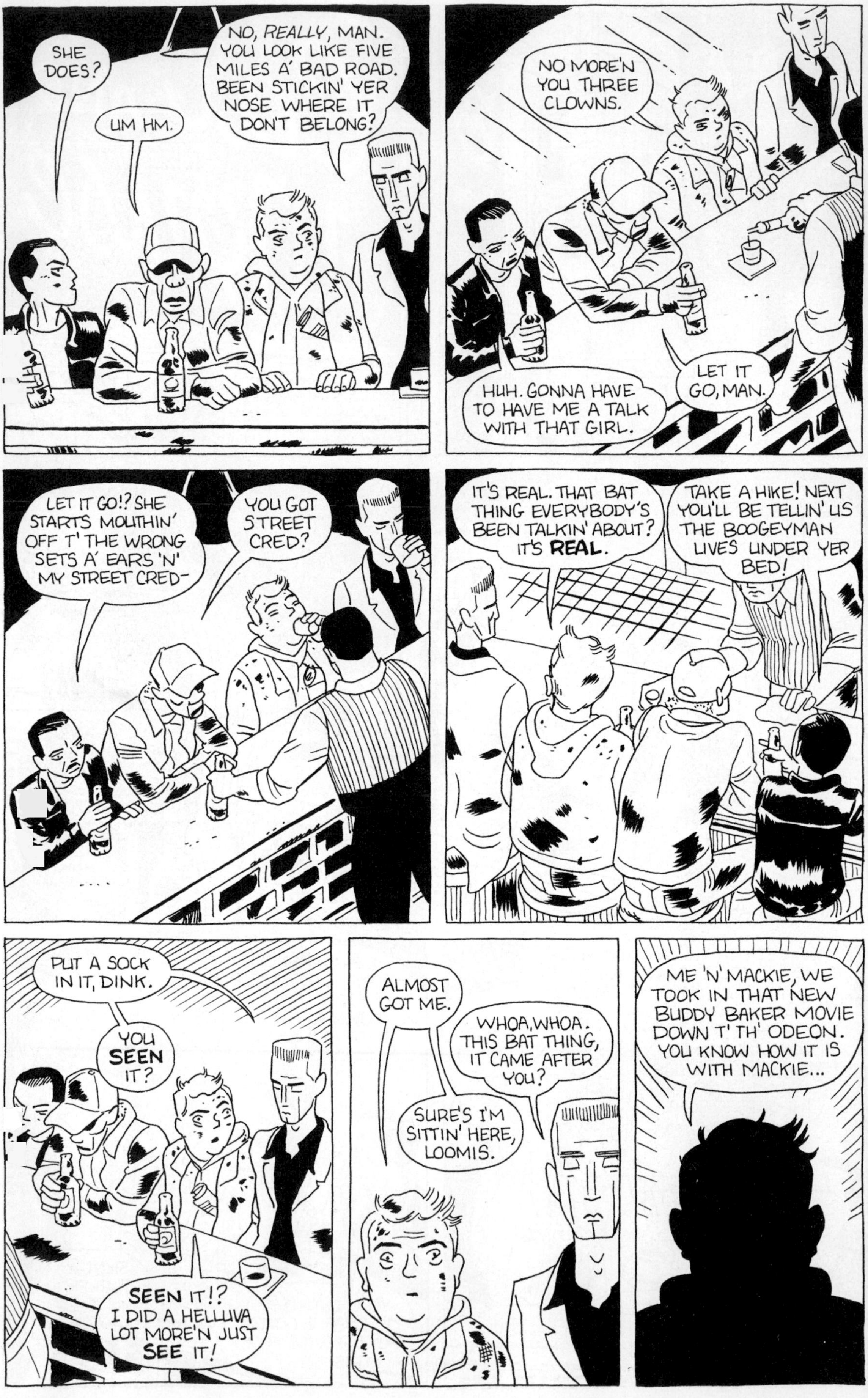
SHE DOES?
NO, REALLY, MAN. YOU LOOK LIKE FIVE MILES A' BAD ROAD. BEEN STICKIN' YER NOSE WHERE IT DON'T BELONG?
UM HM.
NO MORE'N YOU THREE CLOWNS.
HUH. GONNA HAVE TO HAVE ME A TALK WITH THAT GIRL.
LET IT GO, MAN.
LET IT GO!? SHE STARTS MOUTHIN' OFF T' THE WRONG SETS A' EARS 'N' MY STREET CRED-
YOU GOT STREET CRED?
IT'S REAL. THAT BAT THING EVERYBODY'S BEEN TALKIN' ABOUT? IT'S REAL.
TAKE A HIKE! NEXT YOU'LL BE TELLIN' US THE BOOGEYMAN LIVES UNDER YER BED!
PUT A SOCK IN IT, DINK.
YOU SEEN IT?
SEEN IT!? I DID A HELLUVA LOT MORE'N JUST SEE IT!
ALMOST GOT ME.
WHOA, WHOA. THIS BAT THING, IT CAME AFTER YOU?
SURE'S I'M SITTIN' HERE, LOOMIS.
ME 'N' MACKIE, WE TOOK IN THAT NEW BUDDY BAKER MOVIE DOWN T' TH' ODEON. YOU KNOW HOW IT IS WITH MACKIE...

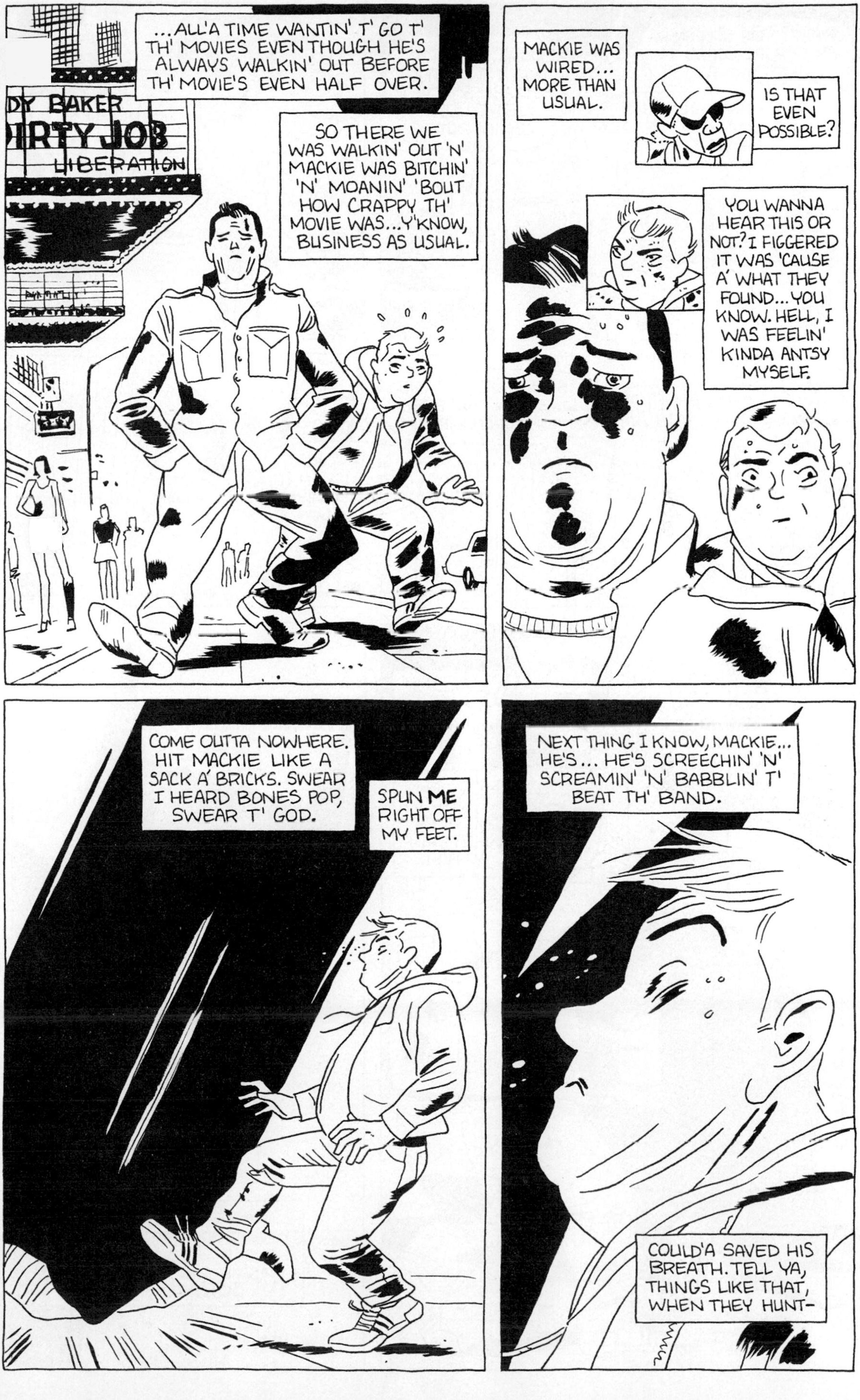

DY BAKER
DIRTY JOB
LIBERATION
...ALL'A TIME WANTIN' T' GO T' TH' MOVIES EVEN THOUGH HE'S ALWAYS WALKIN' OUT BEFORE TH' MOVIE'S EVEN HALF OVER.
SO THERE WE WAS WALKIN' OUT 'N' MACKIE WAS BITCHIN' 'N' MOANIN' 'BOUT HOW CRAPPY TH' MOVIE WAS...Y'KNOW, BUSINESS AS USUAL.
MACKIE WAS WIRED... MORE THAN USUAL.
IS THAT EVEN POSSIBLE?
YOU WANNA HEAR THIS OR NOT? I FIGGERED IT WAS 'CAUSE A' WHAT THEY FOUND... YOU KNOW. HELL, I WAS FEELIN' KINDA ANTSY MYSELF.
COME OUTTA NOWHERE. HIT MACKIE LIKE A SACK A' BRICKS. SWEAR I HEARD BONES POP, SWEAR T' GOD.
SPUN **ME** RIGHT OFF MY FEET.
NEXT THING I KNOW, MACKIE... HE'S... HE'S SCREECHIN' 'N' SCREAMIN' 'N' BABBLIN' T' BEAT TH' BAND.
COULD'A SAVED HIS BREATH. TELL YA, THINGS LIKE THAT, WHEN THEY HUNT-

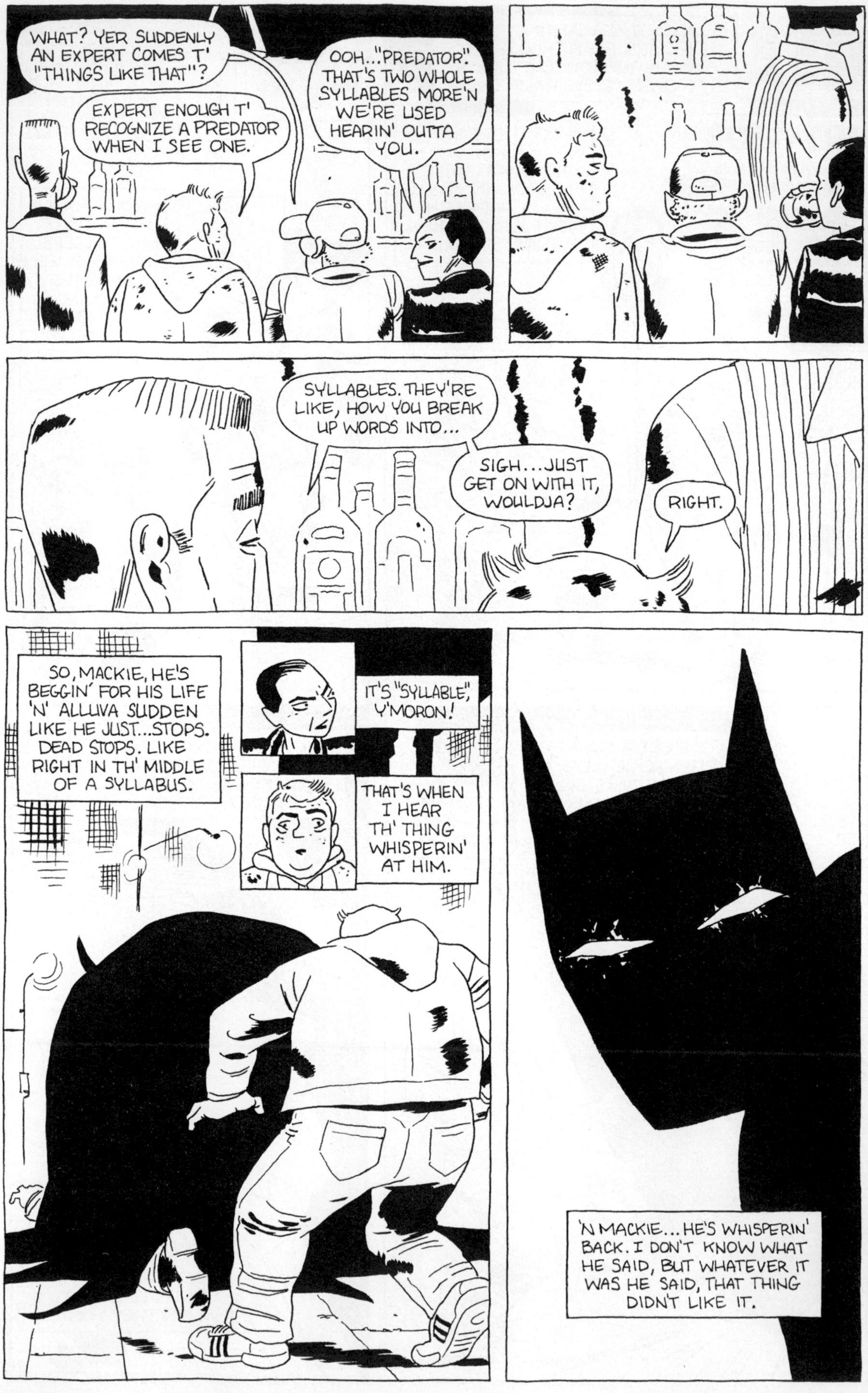
WHAT? YER SUDDENLY AN EXPERT COMES T' "THINGS LIKE THAT"?
EXPERT ENOUGH T' RECOGNIZE A PREDATOR WHEN I SEE ONE.
OOH..."PREDATOR". THAT'S TWO WHOLE SYLLABLES MORE'N WE'RE USED HEARIN' OUTTA YOU.
SYLLABLES. THEY'RE LIKE, HOW YOU BREAK UP WORDS INTO...
SIGH...JUST GET ON WITH IT, WOULDJA?
RIGHT.
SO, MACKIE, HE'S BEGGIN' FOR HIS LIFE 'N' ALLUVA SUDDEN LIKE HE JUST...STOPS. DEAD STOPS. LIKE RIGHT IN TH' MIDDLE OF A SYLLABUS.
IT'S "SYLLABLE", Y'MORON!
THAT'S WHEN I HEAR TH' THING WHISPERIN' AT HIM.
'N MACKIE... HE'S WHISPERIN' BACK. I DON'T KNOW WHAT HE SAID, BUT WHATEVER IT WAS HE SAID, THAT THING DIDN'T LIKE IT.

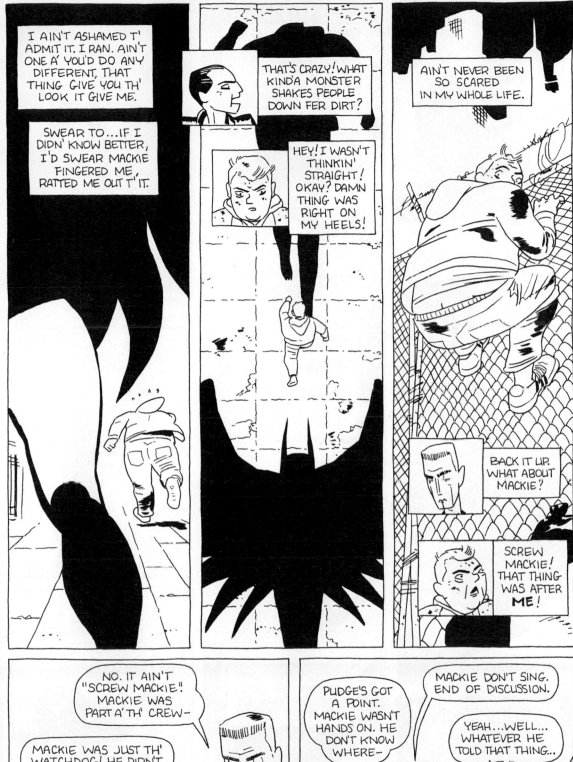

I AIN'T ASHAMED T' ADMIT IT. I RAN. AIN'T ONE A' YOU'D DO ANY DIFFERENT, THAT THING GIVE YOU TH' LOOK IT GIVE ME.

SWEAR TO...IF I DIDN' KNOW BETTER, I'D SWEAR MACKIE FINGERED ME, RATTED ME OUT T' IT.

THAT'S CRAZY! WHAT KIND'A MONSTER SHAKES PEOPLE DOWN FER DIRT?

HEY! I WASN'T THINKIN' STRAIGHT! OKAY? DAMN THING WAS RIGHT ON MY HEELS!

AIN'T NEVER BEEN SO SCARED IN MY WHOLE LIFE.

BACK IT UP. WHAT ABOUT MACKIE?

SCREW MACKIE! THAT THING WAS AFTER ME!

NO. IT AIN'T "SCREW MACKIE"! MACKIE WAS PART A' TH' CREW—

MACKIE WAS JUST TH' WATCHDOG! HE DIDN'T MAKE THE SNATCH!

PUDGE'S GOT A POINT. MACKIE WASN'T HANDS ON. HE DON'T KNOW WHERE—

MACKIE DON'T SING. END OF DISCUSSION.

YEAH...WELL... WHATEVER HE TOLD THAT THING...

...PAINTED A BULL'S-EYE ON ME. NO DOUBT ABOUT IT.

'MEMBER WHEN WE WAS KIDS, HOW WE USED T' BOOST FROM THAT BODEGA PLACE 'N' DODGE OUT WHOEVER TOOK AFTER US?

GOT T' KNOW TH' NEIGHBORHOOD LIKE TH' PALMS OF OUR HANDS. WASN'T A SHORTCUT OR HIDEY-HOLE WE DIDN'T KNOW ABOUT.

FOR ALL TH' GOOD IT DID. THAT THING WAS ON ME LIKE STINK ON A BAG LADY.

AND QUIET? AIN'T NEVER SEEN NOTHIN' THAT BIG MOVE SO QUIET LIKE.

I PUT THAT T' GOOD USE, LEMME TELL YA.

YOU WASN'T THERE. YOU GOT **NO** IDEA.

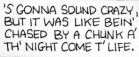

'S GONNA SOUND CRAZY, BUT IT WAS LIKE BEIN' CHASED BY A CHUNK A' TH' NIGHT COME T' LIFE.

BEST BE WIPIN' THAT LOOK OFF YER FACE, DINK, BEFORE I WIPE IT OFF FOR YOU.

I VANT TO SUCK YOUR BLOOD.

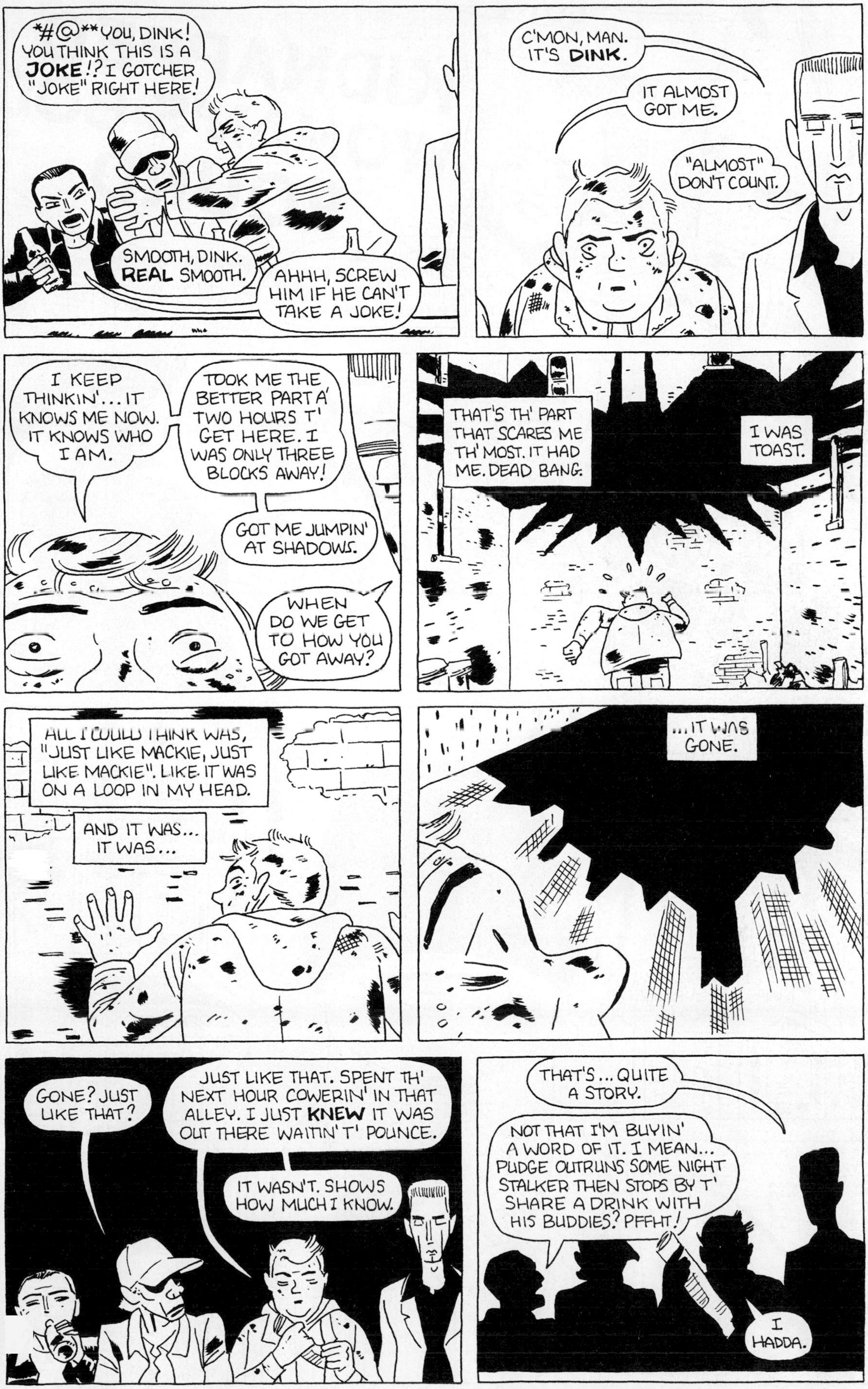
*#@**YOU, DINK! YOU THINK THIS IS A JOKE!? I GOTCHER "JOKE" RIGHT HERE!
SMOOTH, DINK. REAL SMOOTH.
AHHH, SCREW HIM IF HE CAN'T TAKE A JOKE!
C'MON, MAN. IT'S DINK.
IT ALMOST GOT ME.
"ALMOST" DON'T COUNT.
I KEEP THINKIN'... IT KNOWS ME NOW. IT KNOWS WHO I AM.
TOOK ME THE BETTER PART A' TWO HOURS T' GET HERE. I WAS ONLY THREE BLOCKS AWAY!
GOT ME JUMPIN' AT SHADOWS.
WHEN DO WE GET TO HOW YOU GOT AWAY?
THAT'S TH' PART THAT SCARES ME TH' MOST. IT HAD ME. DEAD BANG.
I WAS TOAST.
ALL I COULD THINK WAS, "JUST LIKE MACKIE, JUST LIKE MACKIE". LIKE IT WAS ON A LOOP IN MY HEAD.
AND IT WAS... IT WAS...
...IT WAS GONE.
GONE? JUST LIKE THAT?
JUST LIKE THAT. SPENT TH' NEXT HOUR COWERIN' IN THAT ALLEY. I JUST KNEW IT WAS OUT THERE WAITIN' T' POUNCE.
IT WASN'T. SHOWS HOW MUCH I KNOW.
THAT'S... QUITE A STORY.
NOT THAT I'M BUYIN' A WORD OF IT. I MEAN... PUDGE OUTRUNS SOME NIGHT STALKER THEN STOPS BY T' SHARE A DRINK WITH HIS BUDDIES? PFFHT!
I HADDA.

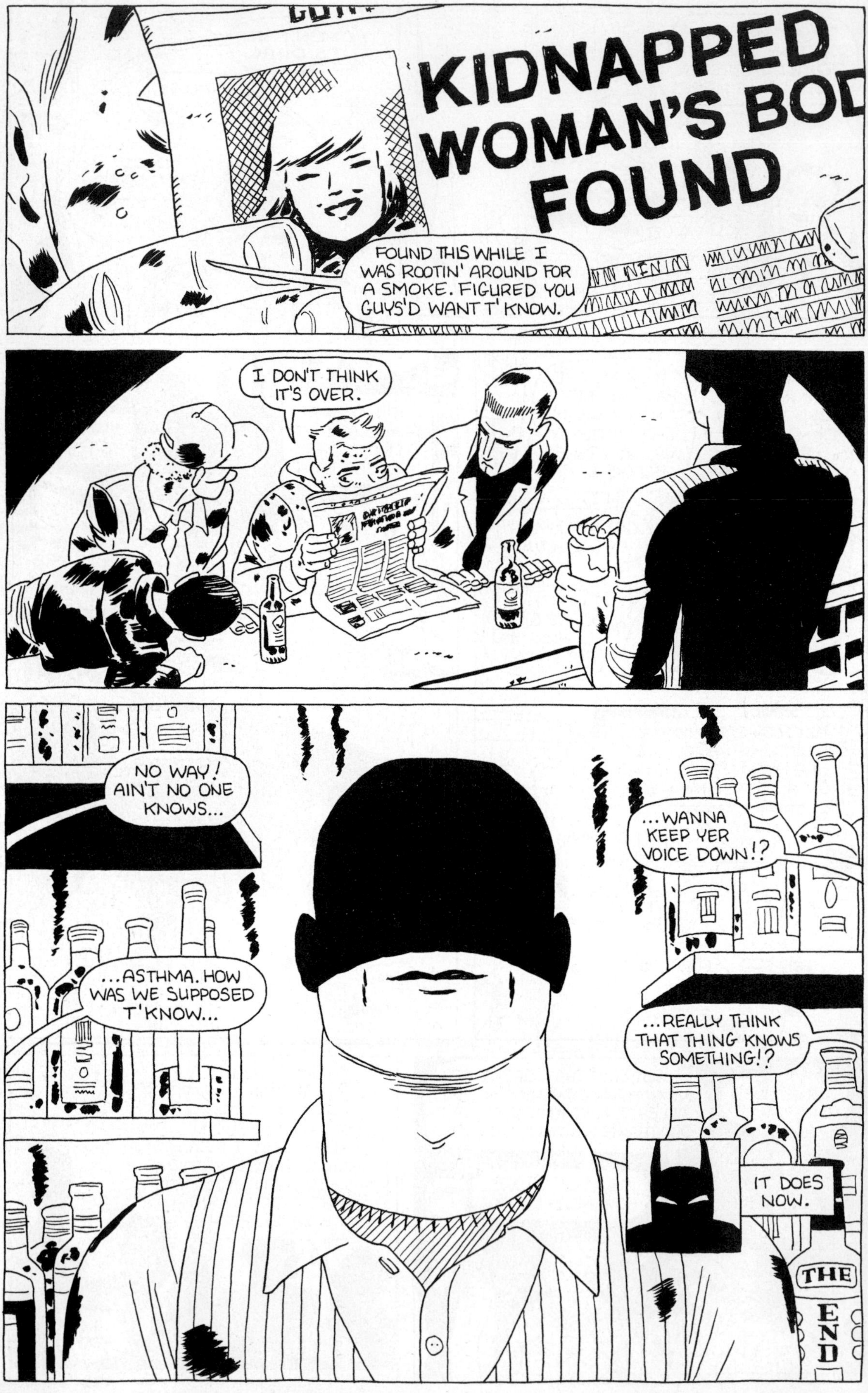
KIDNAPPED
WOMAN'S BOD
FOUND
FOUND THIS WHILE I WAS ROOTIN' AROUND FOR A SMOKE. FIGURED YOU GUYS'D WANT T' KNOW.
I DON'T THINK IT'S OVER.
NO WAY! AIN'T NO ONE KNOWS...
...WANNA KEEP YER VOICE DOWN!?
...ASTHMA. HOW WAS WE SUPPOSED T'KNOW...
...REALLY THINK THAT THING KNOWS SOMETHING!?
IT DOES NOW.
THE END

KEITH GIFFEN

It's quite possible that Keith Giffen was created by the fertile imagination of writer/artist extraordinaire Keith Giffen. One of the most prolific and talented craftsmen in the history of the medium, Giffen has been setting the comics world on its ear for over forty years. Best known for extended runs both writing and drawing the LEGION OF SUPER-HEROES, he has also chronicled the exploits of THE CREEPER, RAGMAN, *The Defenders*, AQUAMAN, and many, many others. Giffen is the co-creator of DC's popular characters Lobo and Ambush Bug.

JAVIER PULIDO

Spanish illustrator Javier Pulido's art is at once unpretentious, immediate, and sophisticated. Although his work is reminiscent of legendary artists Alex Toth and David Mazzucchelli, Javier's style and approach are purely his own. A visionary artist, his work can be seen on HELLBLAZER, THE BATMAN CHRONICLES, CATWOMAN, ROBIN: YEAR ONE, and Vertigo's HUMAN TARGET.

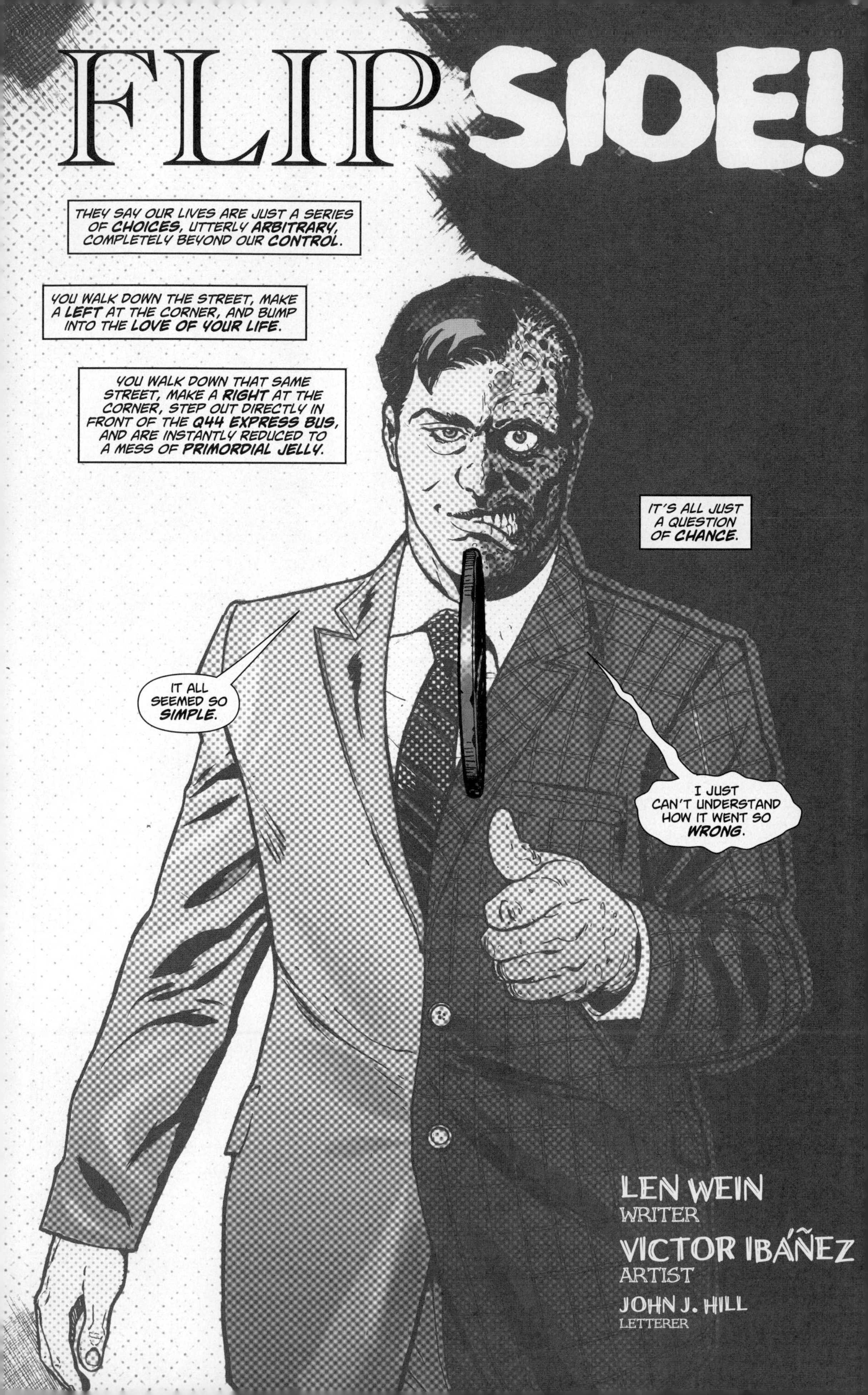
FLIP SIDE!
THEY SAY OUR LIVES ARE JUST A SERIES OF CHOICES, UTTERLY ARBITRARY, COMPLETELY BEYOND OUR CONTROL.
YOU WALK DOWN THE STREET, MAKE A LEFT AT THE CORNER, AND BUMP INTO THE LOVE OF YOUR LIFE.
YOU WALK DOWN THAT SAME STREET, MAKE A RIGHT AT THE CORNER, STEP OUT DIRECTLY IN FRONT OF THE Q44 EXPRESS BUS, AND ARE INSTANTLY REDUCED TO A MESS OF PRIMORDIAL JELLY.
IT'S ALL JUST A QUESTION OF CHANCE.
IT ALL SEEMED SO SIMPLE.
I JUST CAN'T UNDERSTAND HOW IT WENT SO WRONG.
LEN WEIN
WRITER
VICTOR IBÁÑEZ
ARTIST
JOHN J. HILL
LETTERER

IT WAS TUESDAY, THE PERFECT DAY, WHEN MY SECOND-IN-COMMAND BROUGHT ME THE MORNING NEWSPAPER...

HEY, BOSS--TAKE A LOOK AT THIS!

I THINK I JUST FOUND US OUR NEXT CAPER.

REALLY?

LET ME SEE THAT.

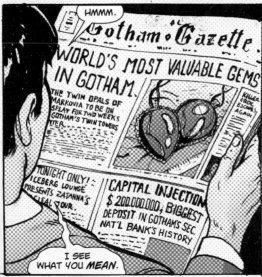

HMMM.

Gotham Gazette

WORLD'S MOST VALUABLE GEMS IN GOTHAM

THE TWIN OPALS OF MARKOVIA TO BE ON DISPLAY FOR TWO WEEKS GOTHAM'S TWIN TOWERS ...TER.

KILLER CROC ESCAPES AGAIN

TONIGHT ONLY! ICEBERG LOUNGE PRESENTS ZATANNA'S FINAL TOUR

CAPITAL INJECTION
$ 200,000,000, BIGGEST DEPOSIT IN GOTHAM'S SEC. NAT'L BANK'S HISTORY

I SEE WHAT YOU MEAN.

AN INTERESTING PROPOSITION.

SHALL WE SEE WHAT THE COIN HAS TO SAY ABOUT THIS?

SO?

WHAT'S THE VERDICT?

WHAT SAY WE TRY FOR THE BEST TWO OUT OF THREE, EH?

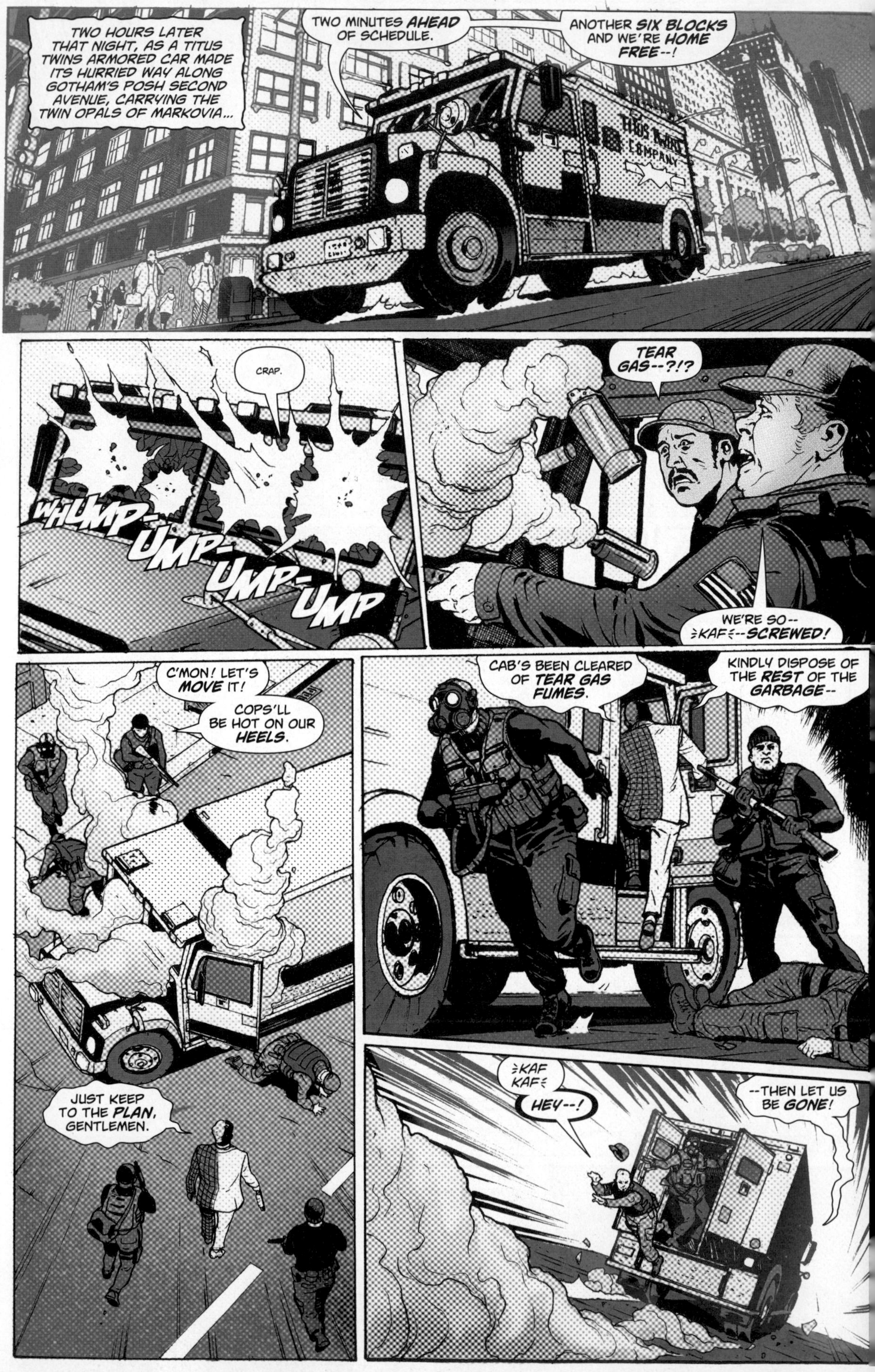
TWO HOURS LATER THAT NIGHT, AS A TITUS TWINS ARMORED CAR MADE ITS HURRIED WAY ALONG GOTHAM'S POSH SECOND AVENUE, CARRYING THE TWIN OPALS OF MARKOVIA...
TWO MINUTES AHEAD OF SCHEDULE.
ANOTHER SIX BLOCKS AND WE'RE HOME FREE--!
TITUS TWINS COMPANY
CRAP.
WHUMP-UMP-UMP-UMP
TEAR GAS--?!?
WE'RE SO-- KAF --SCREWED!
C'MON! LET'S MOVE IT!
COPS'LL BE HOT ON OUR HEELS.
JUST KEEP TO THE PLAN, GENTLEMEN.
CAB'S BEEN CLEARED OF TEAR GAS FUMES.
KINDLY DISPOSE OF THE REST OF THE GARBAGE--
KAF KAF
HEY--!
--THEN LET US BE GONE!

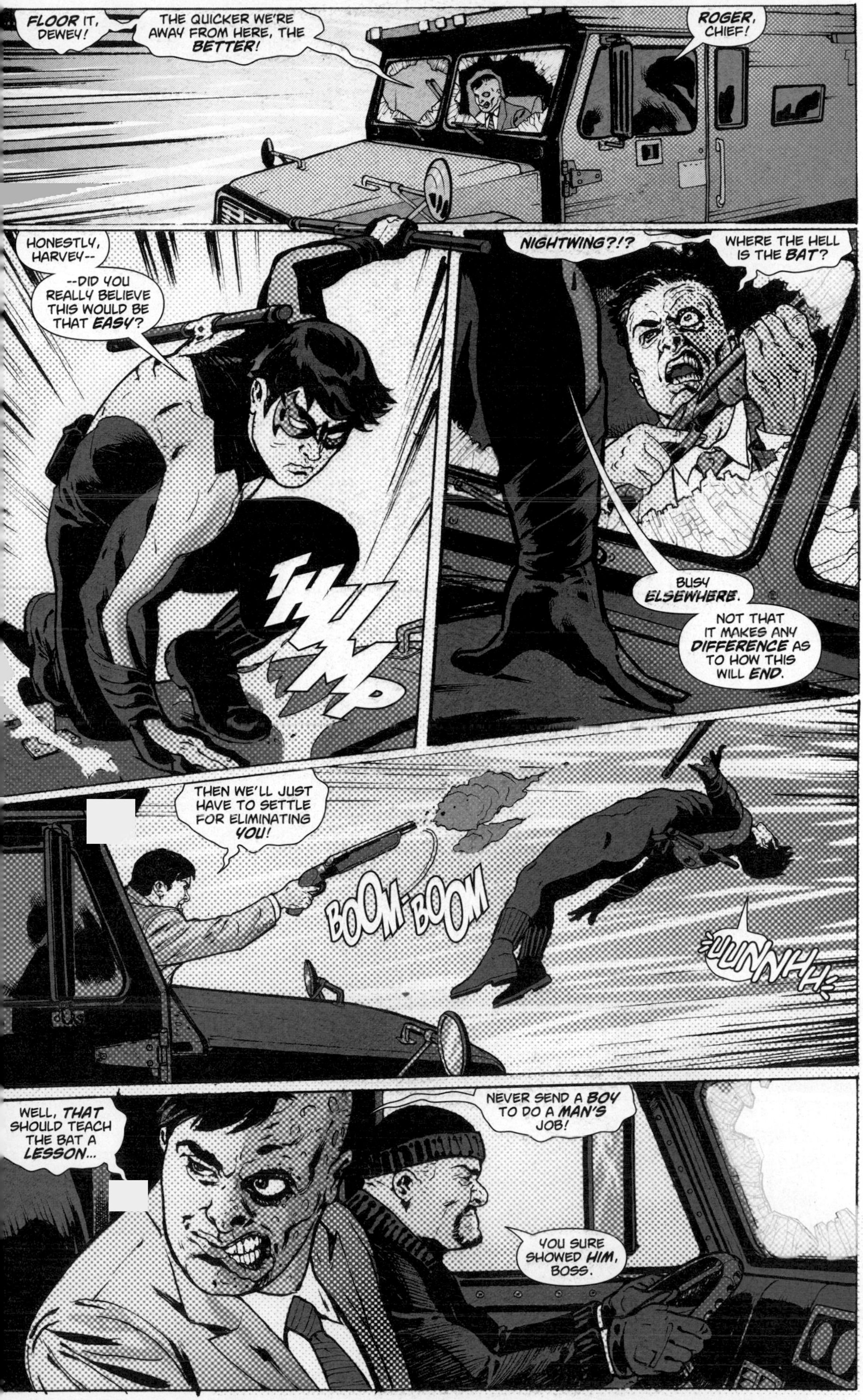
FLOOR IT, DEWEY!
THE QUICKER WE'RE AWAY FROM HERE, THE BETTER!
ROGER, CHIEF!
HONESTLY, HARVEY--
--DID YOU REALLY BELIEVE THIS WOULD BE THAT EASY?
THUMP
NIGHTWING?!?
WHERE THE HELL IS THE BAT?
BUSY ELSEWHERE.
NOT THAT IT MAKES ANY DIFFERENCE AS TO HOW THIS WILL END.
THEN WE'LL JUST HAVE TO SETTLE FOR ELIMINATING YOU!
BOOM-BOOM
UUNNHH
WELL, THAT SHOULD TEACH THE BAT A LESSON...
NEVER SEND A BOY TO DO A MAN'S JOB!
YOU SURE SHOWED HIM, BOSS.

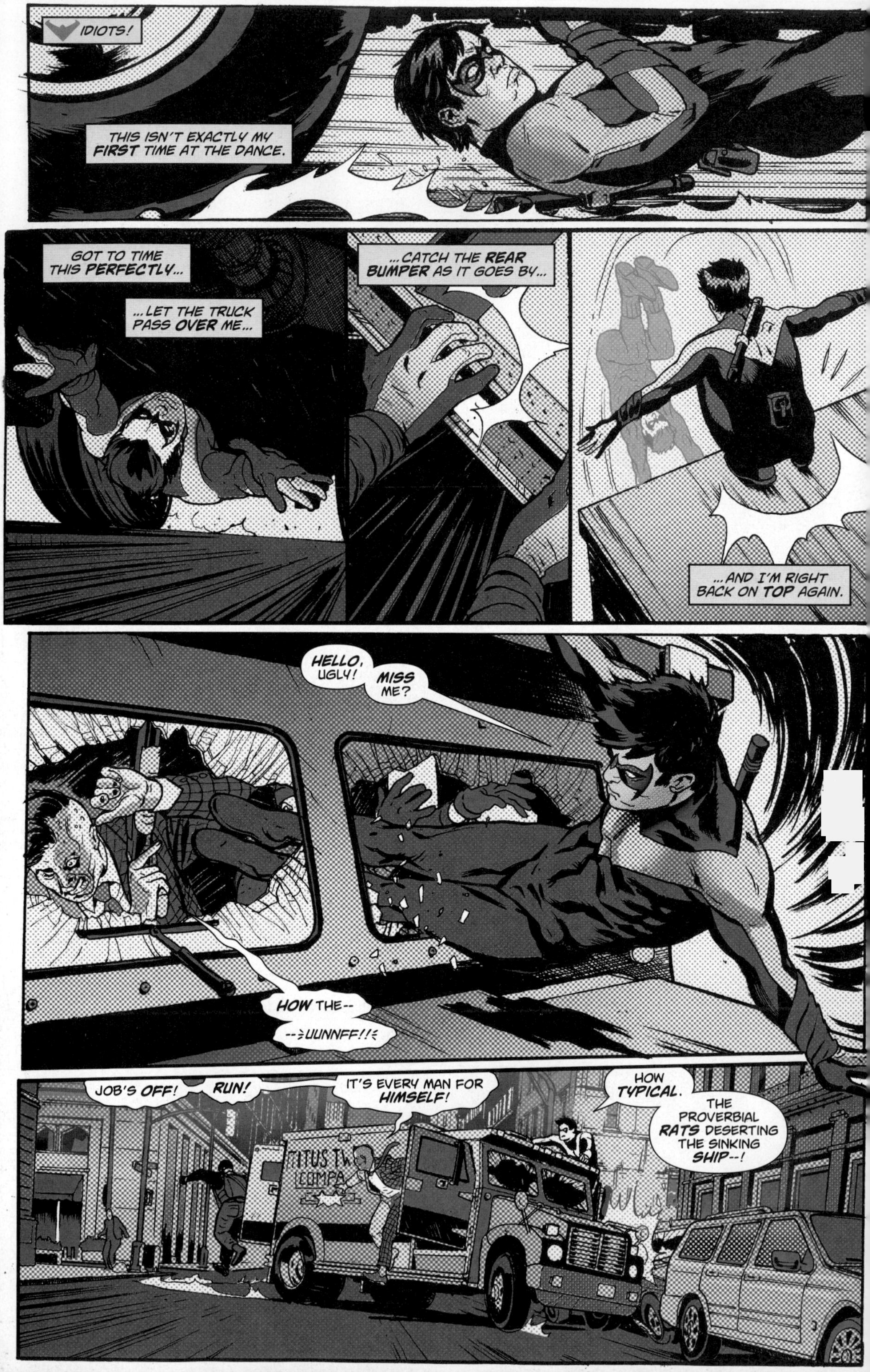
IDIOTS!
THIS ISN'T EXACTLY MY FIRST TIME AT THE DANCE.
GOT TO TIME THIS PERFECTLY...
...LET THE TRUCK PASS OVER ME...
...CATCH THE REAR BUMPER AS IT GOES BY...
...AND I'M RIGHT BACK ON TOP AGAIN.
HELLO, UGLY!
MISS ME?
HOW THE--
--UUNNFF!!
JOB'S OFF!
RUN!
IT'S EVERY MAN FOR HIMSELF!
HOW TYPICAL.
THE PROVERBIAL RATS DESERTING THE SINKING SHIP--!

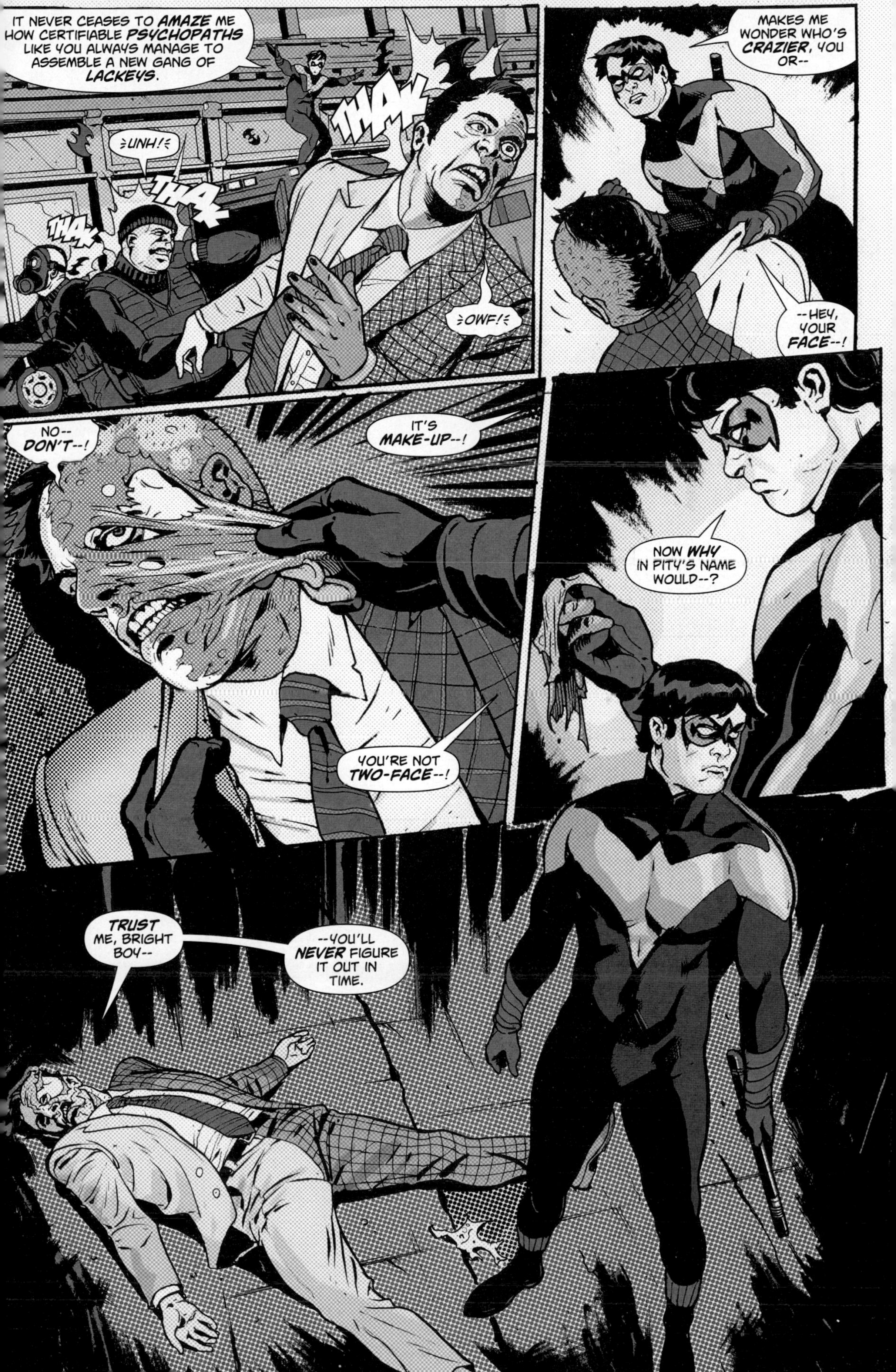
IT NEVER CEASES TO AMAZE ME HOW CERTIFIABLE PSYCHOPATHS LIKE YOU ALWAYS MANAGE TO ASSEMBLE A NEW GANG OF LACKEYS.
THAK
UNH!
THAK
THAK
OWF!
MAKES ME WONDER WHO'S CRAZIER, YOU OR--
--HEY, YOUR FACE--!
NO-- DON'T--!
IT'S MAKE-UP--!
YOU'RE NOT TWO-FACE--!
NOW WHY IN PITY'S NAME WOULD--?
TRUST ME, BRIGHT BOY--
--YOU'LL NEVER FIGURE IT OUT IN TIME.

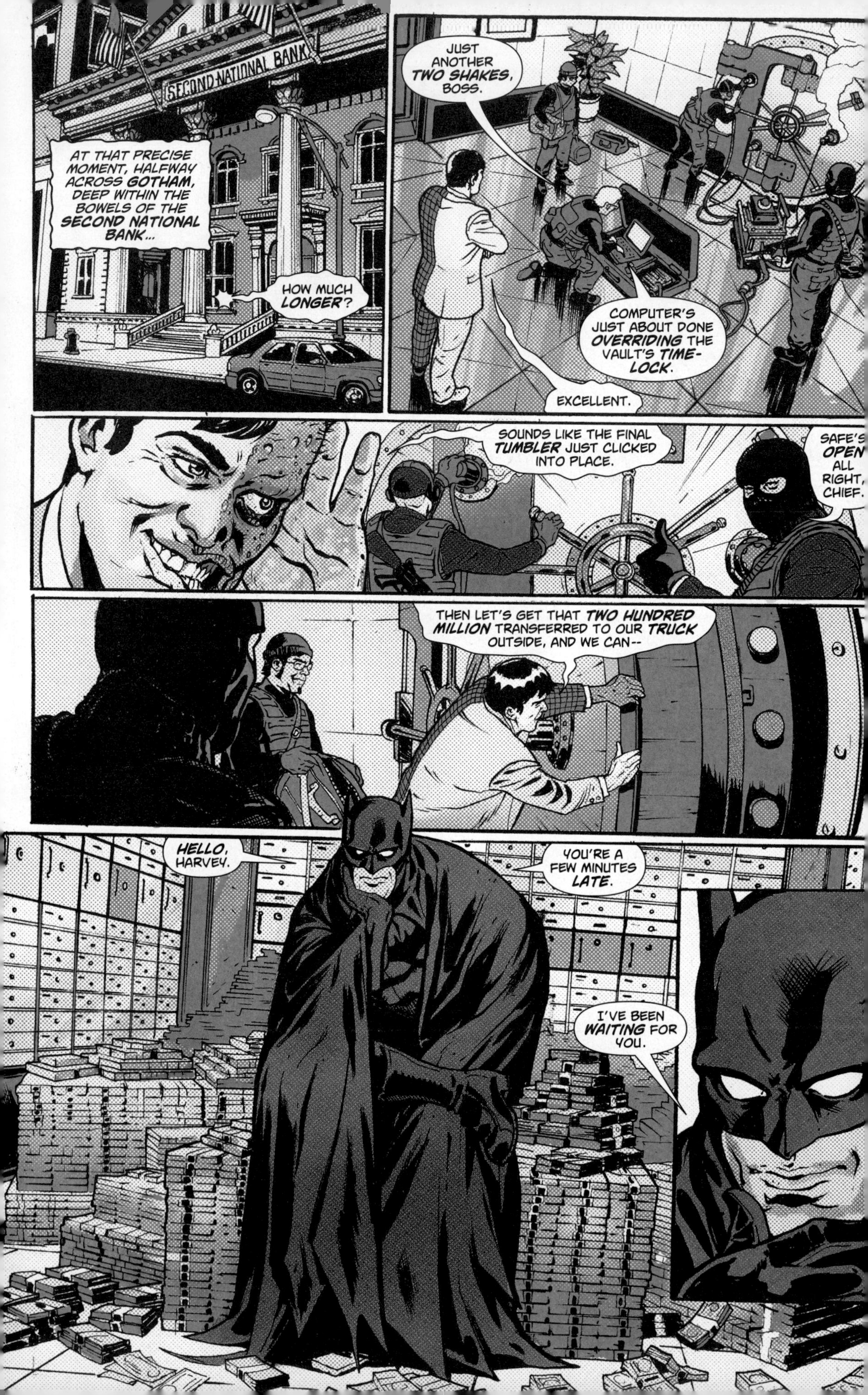
SECOND NATIONAL BANK
AT THAT PRECISE MOMENT, HALFWAY ACROSS GOTHAM, DEEP WITHIN THE BOWELS OF THE SECOND NATIONAL BANK...
HOW MUCH LONGER?
JUST ANOTHER TWO SHAKES, BOSS.
COMPUTER'S JUST ABOUT DONE OVERRIDING THE VAULT'S TIME-LOCK.
EXCELLENT.
SOUNDS LIKE THE FINAL TUMBLER JUST CLICKED INTO PLACE.
SAFE'S OPEN ALL RIGHT, CHIEF.
THEN LET'S GET THAT TWO HUNDRED MILLION TRANSFERRED TO OUR TRUCK OUTSIDE, AND WE CAN--
HELLO, HARVEY.
YOU'RE A FEW MINUTES LATE.
I'VE BEEN WAITING FOR YOU.

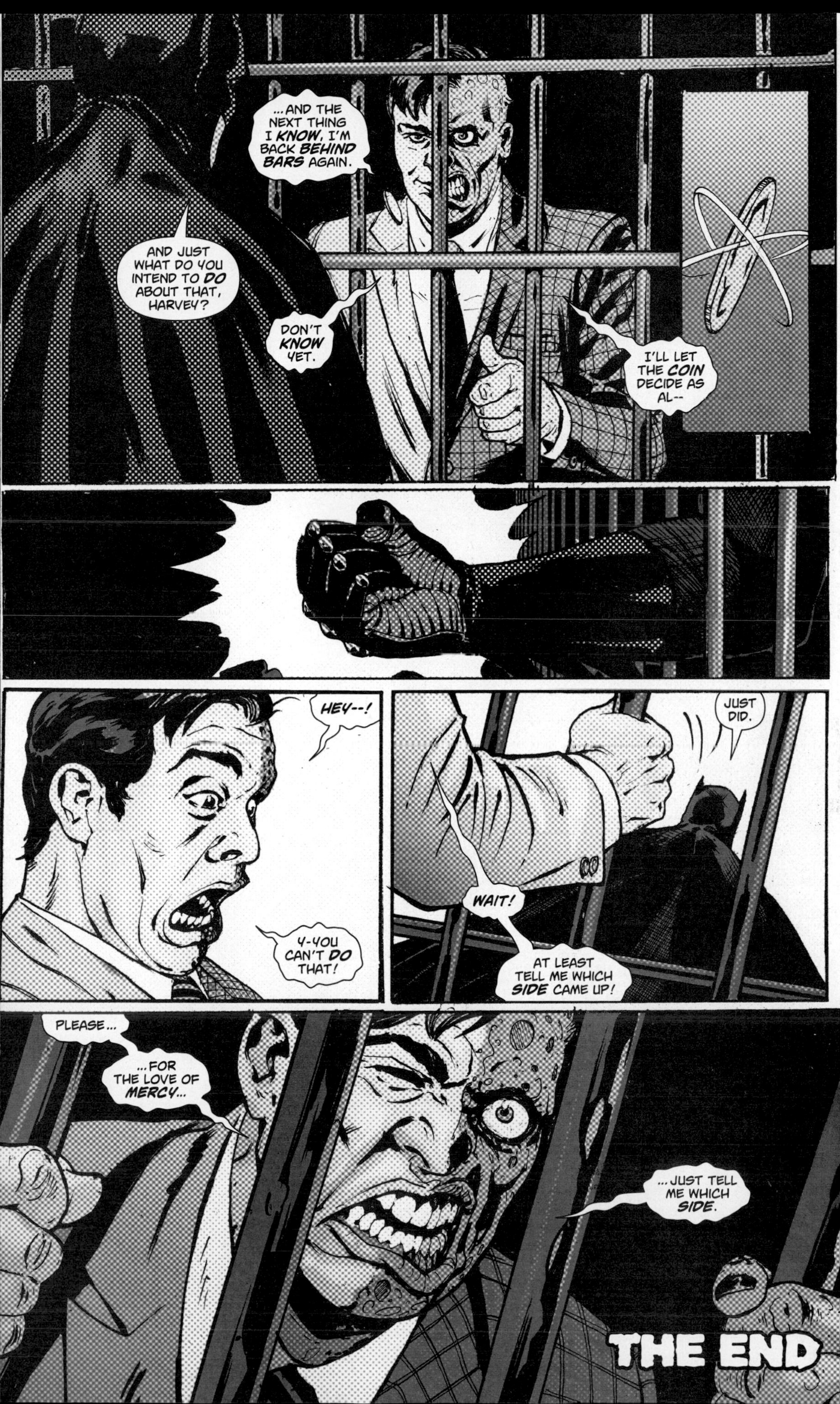
...AND THE NEXT THING I KNOW, I'M BACK BEHIND BARS AGAIN.
AND JUST WHAT DO YOU INTEND TO DO ABOUT THAT, HARVEY?
DON'T KNOW YET.
I'LL LET THE COIN DECIDE AS AL--
HEY--!
Y-YOU CAN'T DO THAT!
JUST DID.
WAIT!
AT LEAST TELL ME WHICH SIDE CAME UP!
PLEASE...
...FOR THE LOVE OF MERCY...
...JUST TELL ME WHICH SIDE.
THE END

LEN WEIN

Comics legend Len Wein has done
everything in comics, including co-creating
many of its most popular characters, including
Swamp Thing, Wolverine, Nightcrawler, Storm,
and Colossus. He's also served as Senior Editor
at DC, and Editor in Chief at both
Marvel and Disney Comics.
Having written just about every major
character in the comic book world, Wein has
also written for television, animation, and film.

VICTOR IBÁÑEZ

Spanish artist Victor Ibáñez grew up
reading American comic books and
eventually attended The Escola Joso de Comic,
Barcelona's only comic art school.
A practitioner of the "clean line," Ibanez has
brought his distinct style to, among
other titles, MEN AT WAR, RAT CATCHER,
ROBIN/SPOILER SPECIAL, and THE SPIRIT.

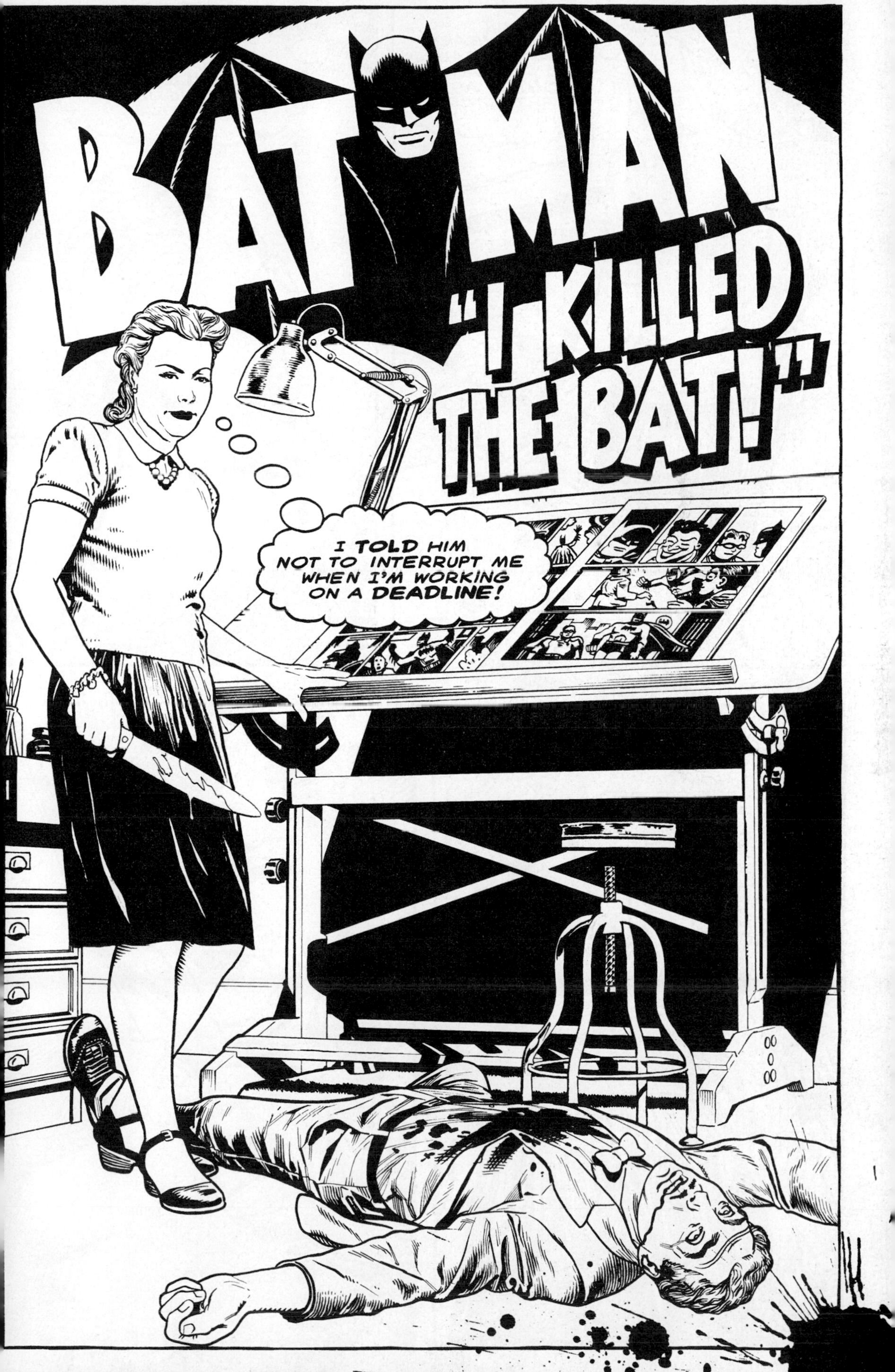
BATMAN
"I KILLED THE BAT!"
I TOLD HIM NOT TO INTERRUPT ME WHEN I'M WORKING ON A DEADLINE!

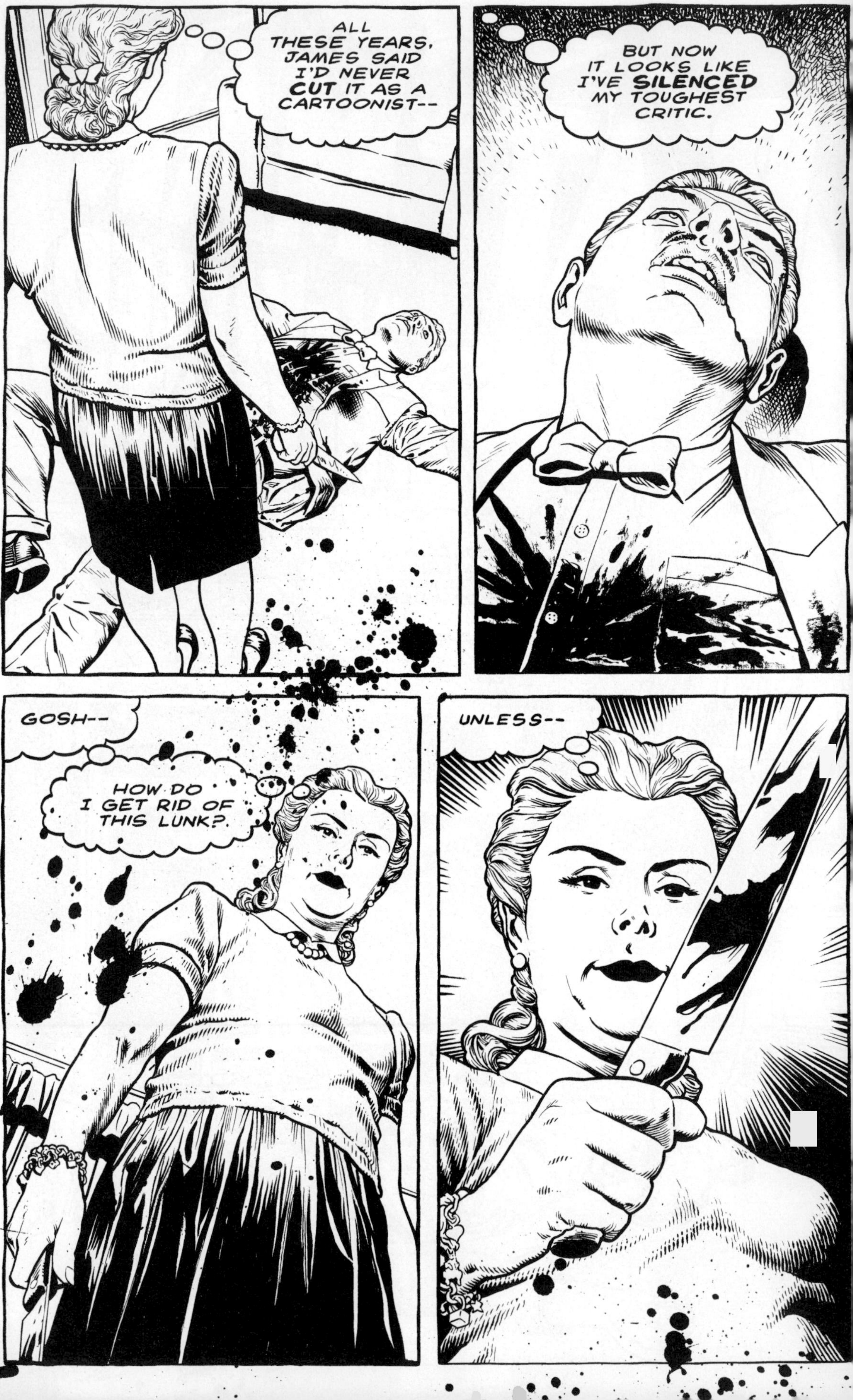
ALL THESE YEARS, JAMES SAID I'D NEVER CUT IT AS A CARTOONIST--
BUT NOW IT LOOKS LIKE I'VE SILENCED MY TOUGHEST CRITIC.
GOSH--
HOW DO I GET RID OF THIS LUNK?
UNLESS--

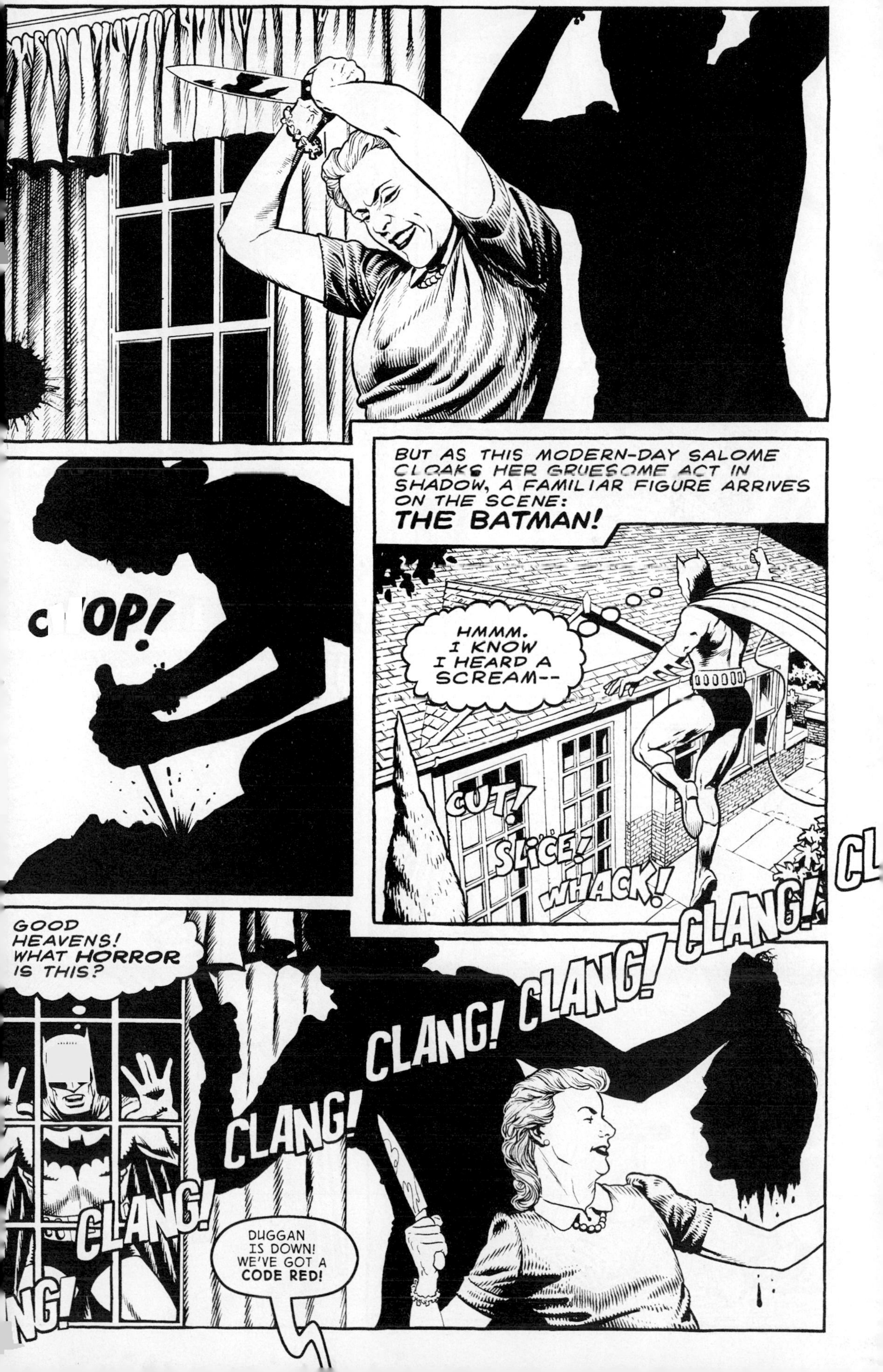
CHOP!
BUT AS THIS MODERN-DAY SALOME CLOAKS HER GRUESOME ACT IN SHADOW, A FAMILIAR FIGURE ARRIVES ON THE SCENE: THE BATMAN!
HMMM. I KNOW I HEARD A SCREAM--
CUT!
SLICE!
WHACK!
GOOD HEAVENS! WHAT HORROR IS THIS?
CLANG! CLANG! CLANG! CLANG! CLANG! CLANG!
DUGGAN IS DOWN! WE'VE GOT A CODE RED!

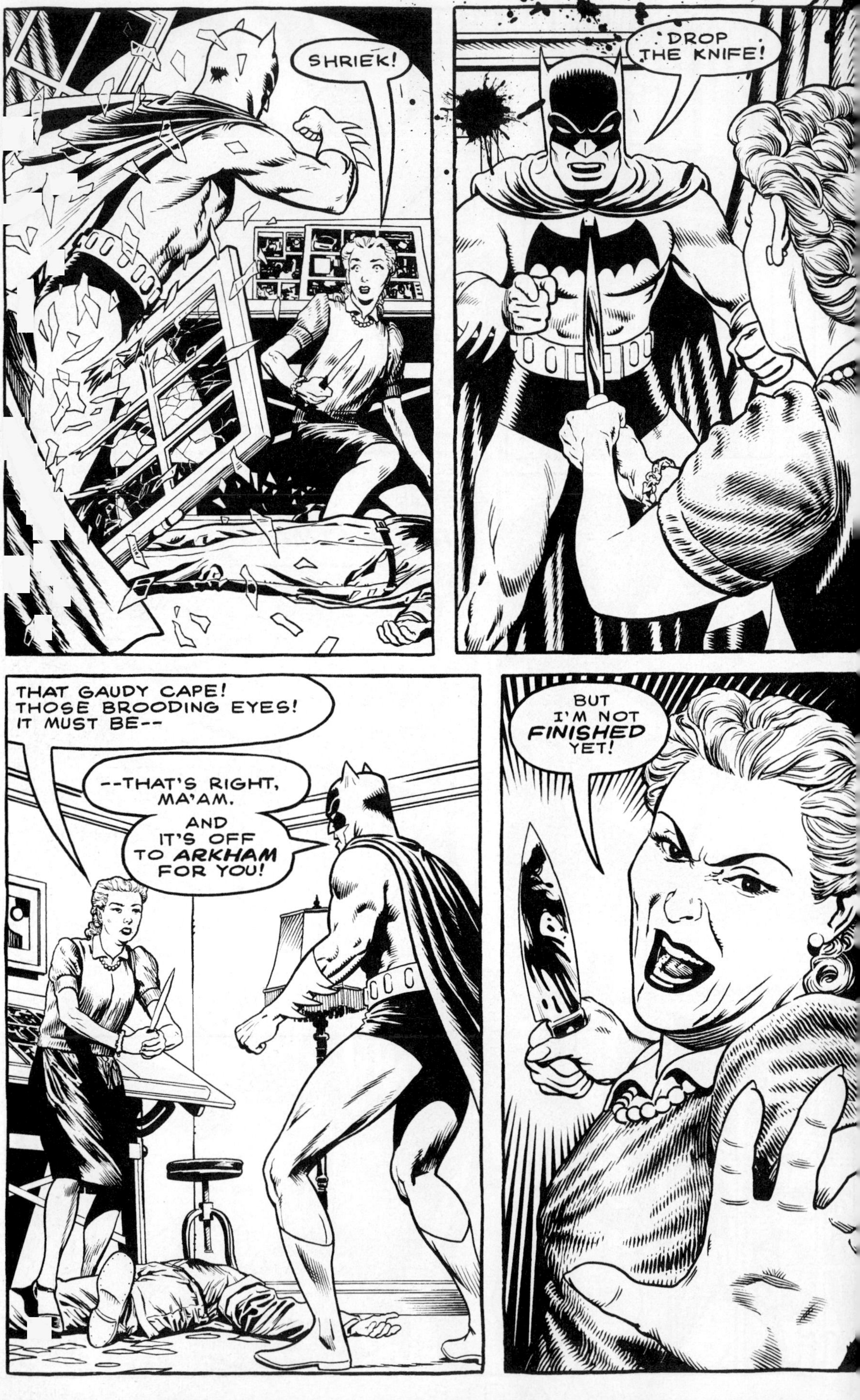
SHRIEK!
DROP THE KNIFE!
THAT GAUDY CAPE! THOSE BROODING EYES! IT MUST BE--
--THAT'S RIGHT, MA'AM.
AND IT'S OFF TO ARKHAM FOR YOU!
BUT I'M NOT FINISHED YET!

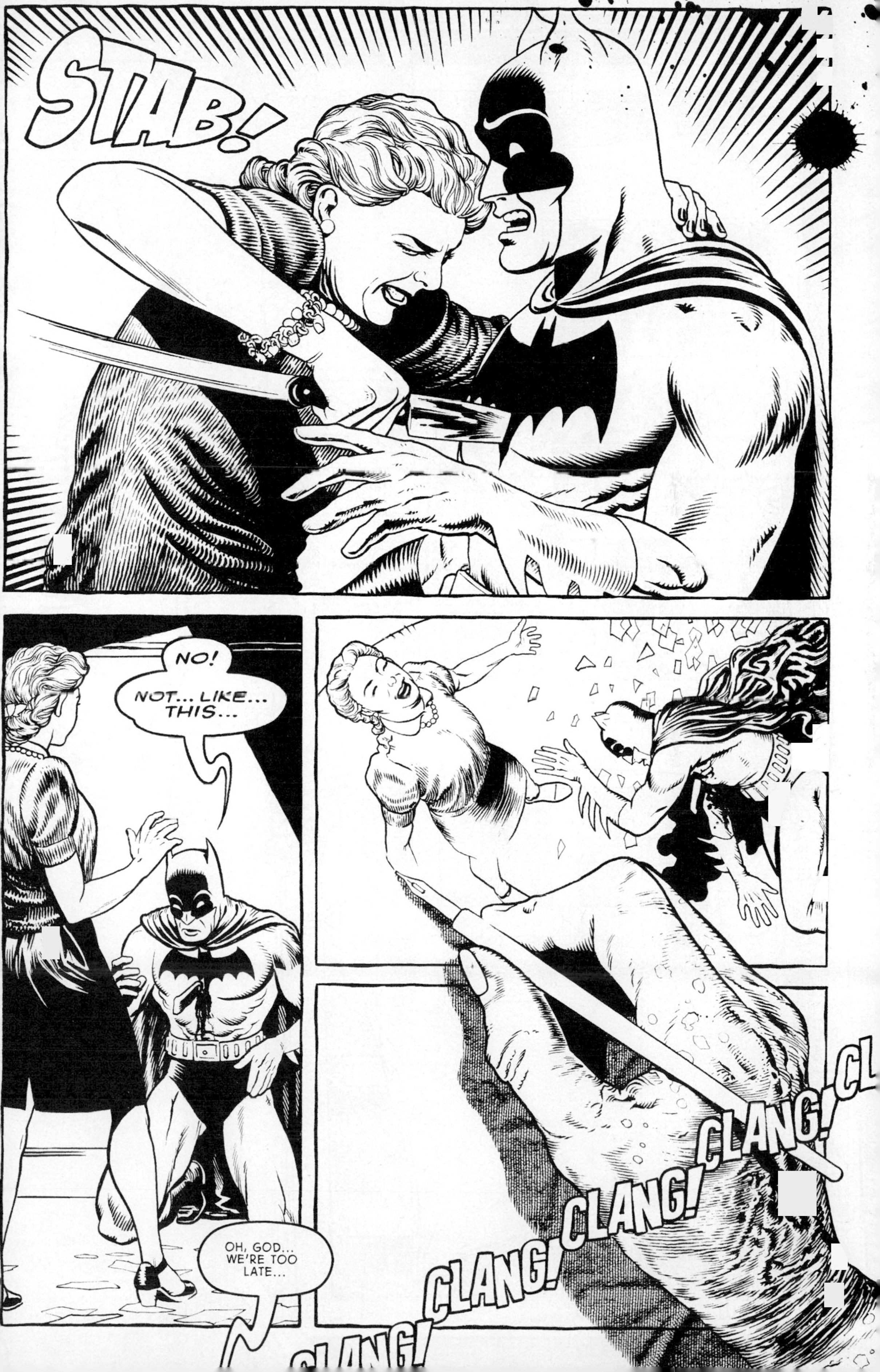
STAB!
NO!
NOT... LIKE... THIS...
OH, GOD... WE'RE TOO LATE...
CLANG!
CLANG!
CLANG!

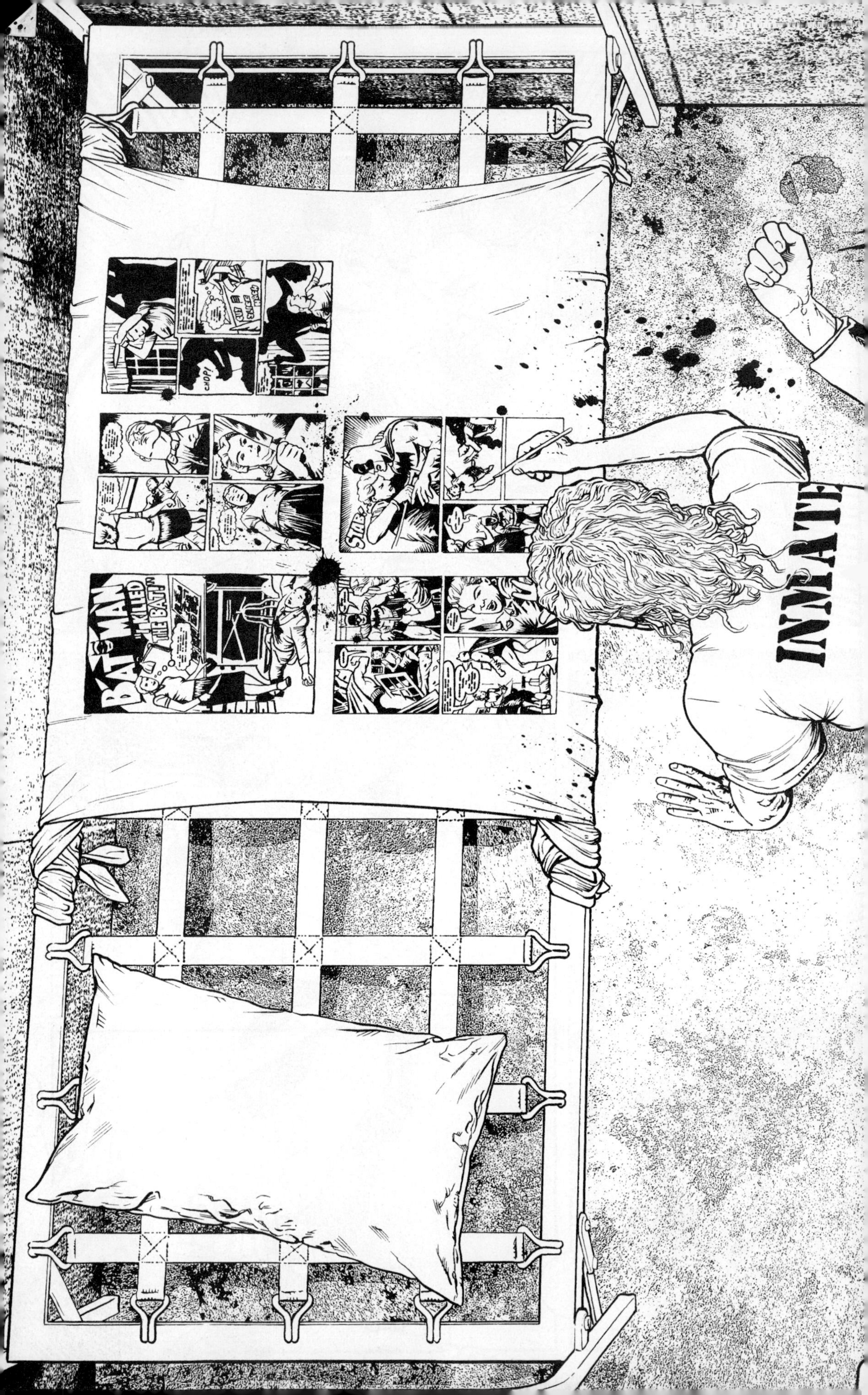
INMATE
BATMAN
"I KILLED THE BAT!"
CHOP!
STAB!

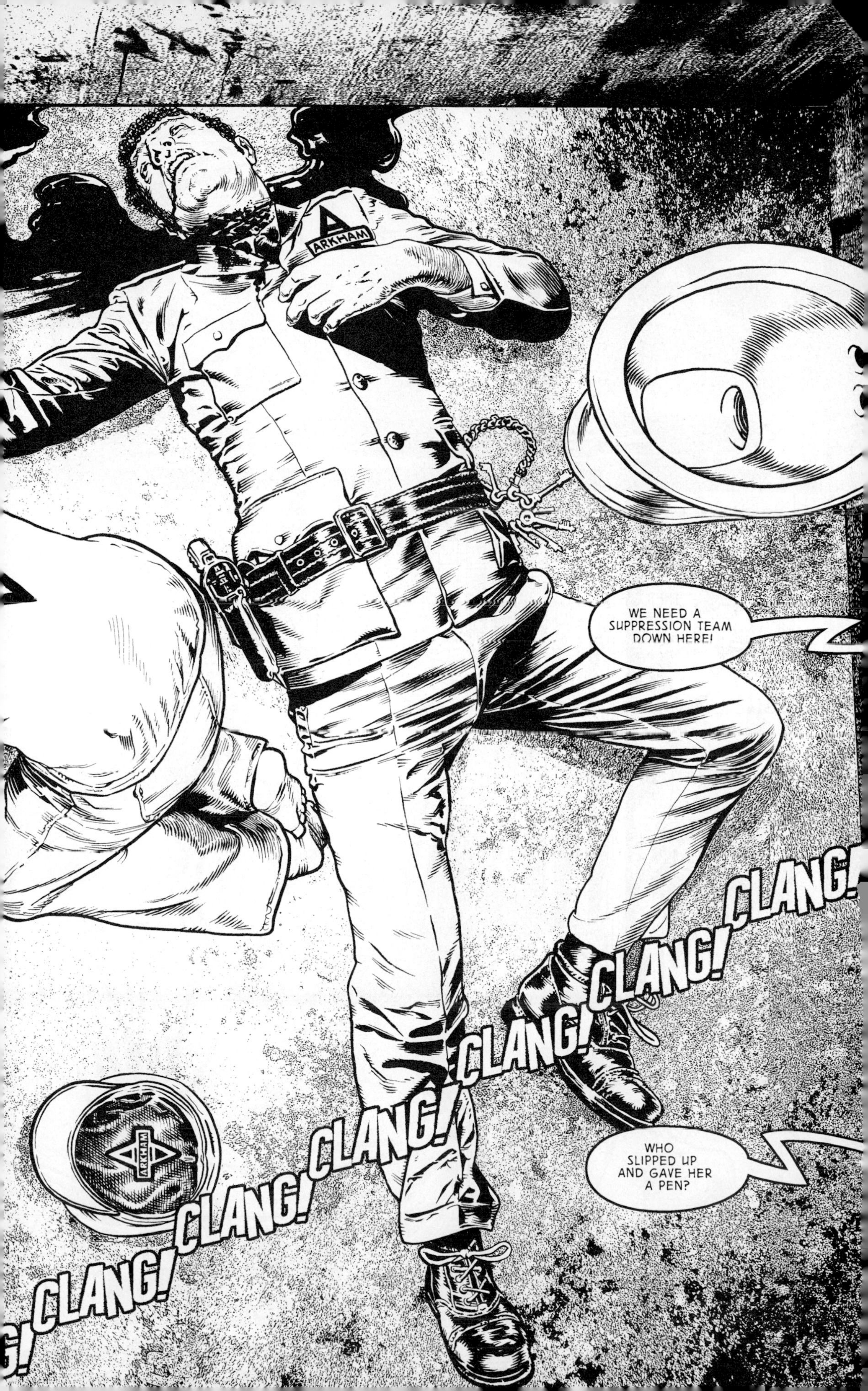
WE NEED A SUPPRESSION TEAM DOWN HERE!
WHO SLIPPED UP AND GAVE HER A PEN?
CLANG! CLANG! CLANG! CLANG! CLANG! CLANG! CLANG! CLANG!

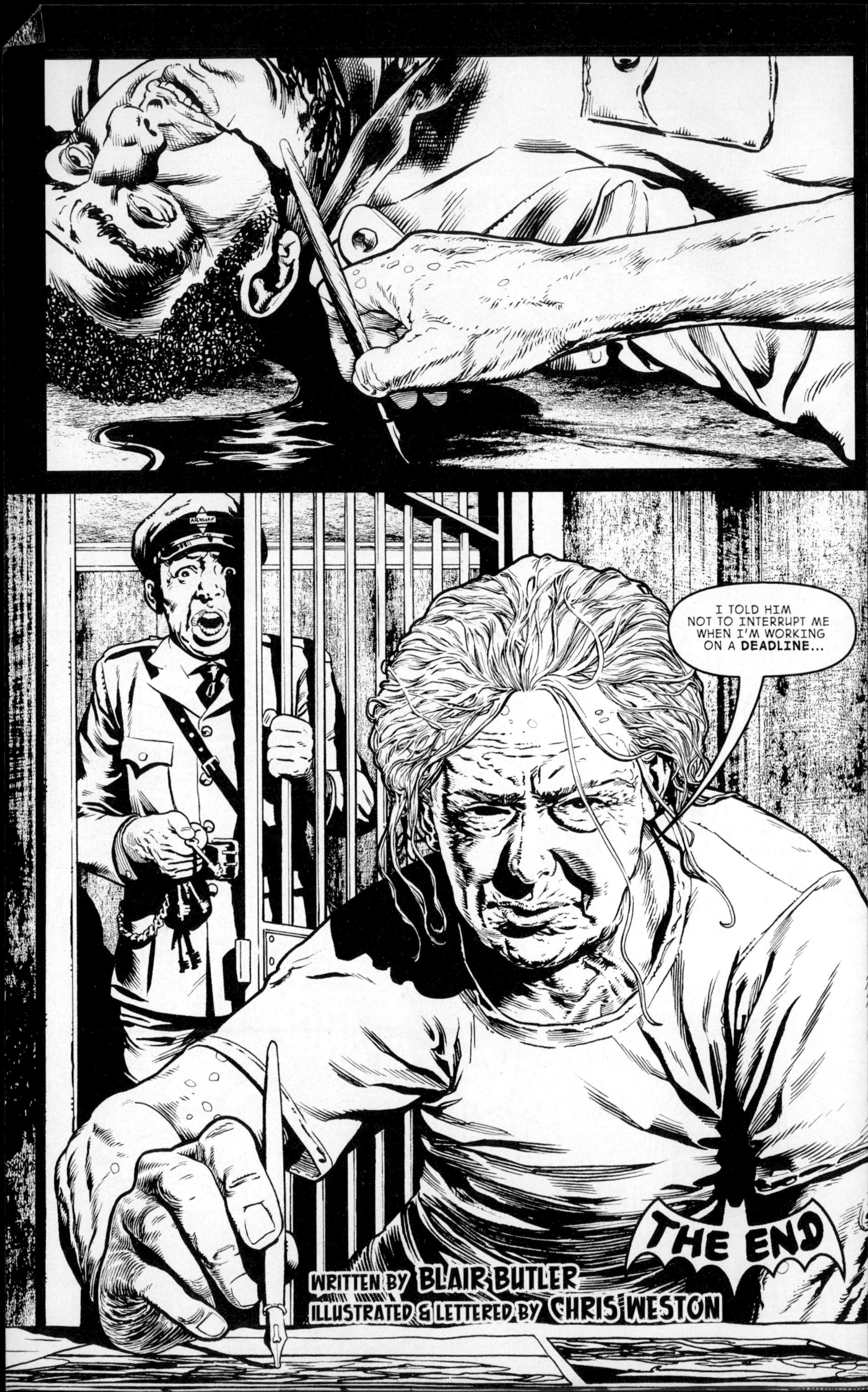
I TOLD HIM NOT TO INTERRUPT ME WHEN I'M WORKING ON A **DEADLINE**...
THE END
WRITTEN BY BLAIR BUTLER
ILLUSTRATED & LETTERED BY CHRIS WESTON

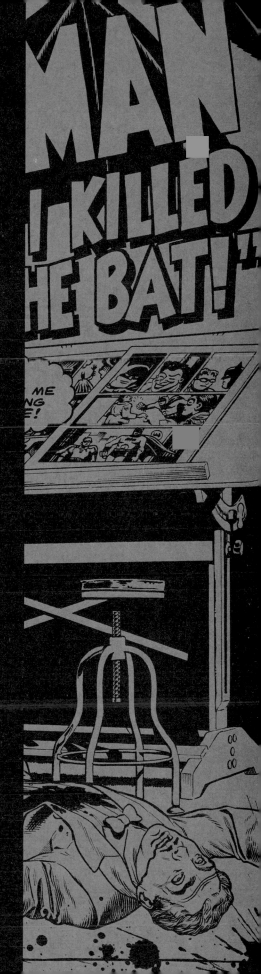

BLAIR BUTLER

Writer, stand-up comic, television personality, comic book critic (and fan!), Blair Butler is also the host of Marvel's "Earth's Mightiest Show." Writer of the miniseries *Heart* from Image Comics, Butler is a familiar face to viewers of the G4 television network. She regularly reviews new comics on her "Fresh Ink" segment on Attack of the Show and has served as head writer of G4's *X-Play*.

CHRIS WESTON

British comic book artist Chris Weston has illustrated the adventures of Batman, Judge Dredd, the Fantastic Four, and the Twelve, but is probably best known for his creator-owned Vertigo Comics series THE FILTH. Also very active as an artist in the film industry, Weston has created conceptual art and storyboards for *The Book of Eli* and the live action adaptation of *Akira*. Impeccable draftsmanship and a crisp, brilliant line make Weston's work fantastically popular on both sides of the Atlantic.

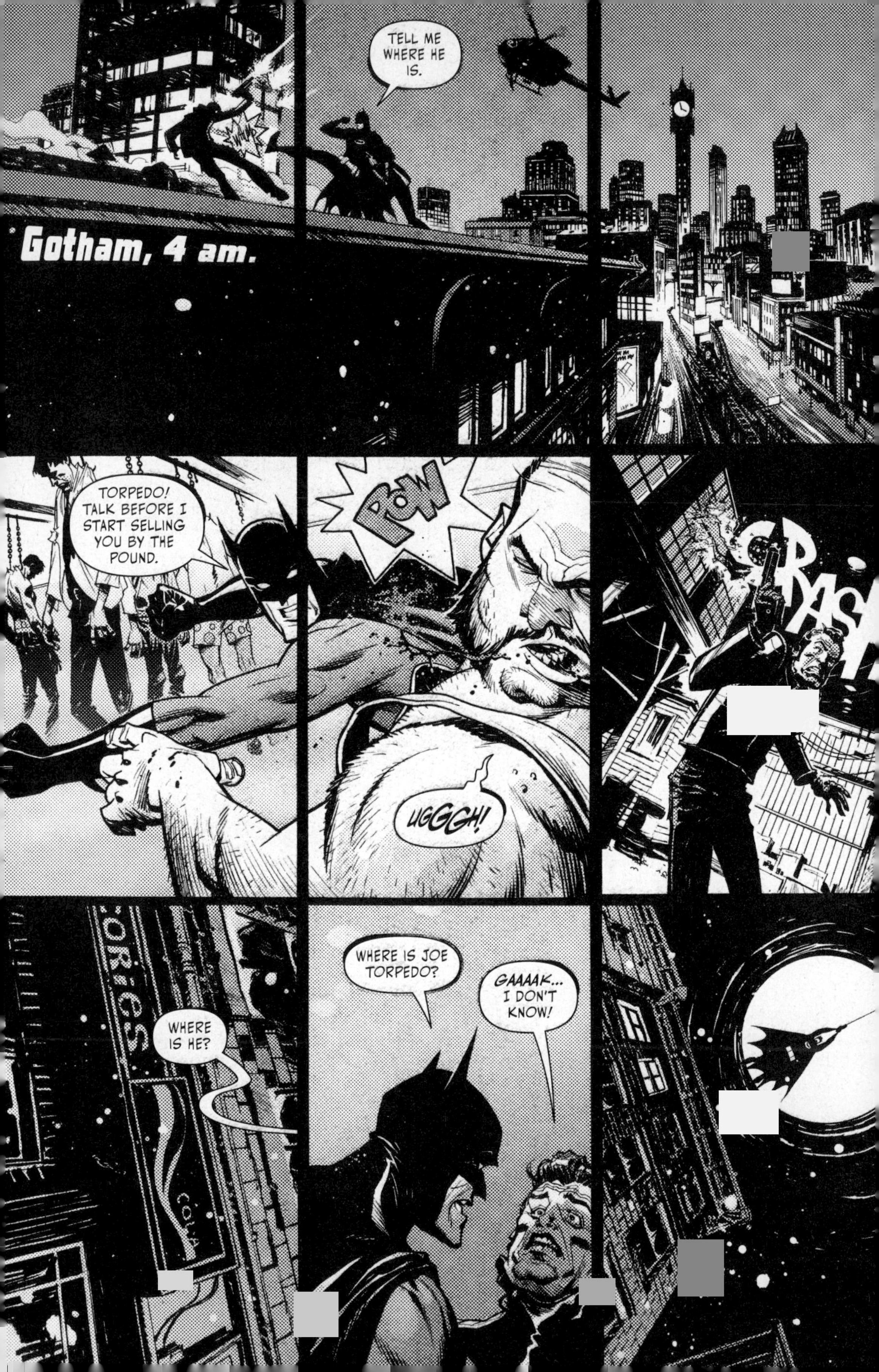
Gotham, 4 am.
TELL ME WHERE HE IS.
TORPEDO! TALK BEFORE I START SELLING YOU BY THE POUND.
POW
UGGGH!
WHERE IS HE?
WHERE IS JOE TORPEDO?
GAAAAK... I DON'T KNOW!

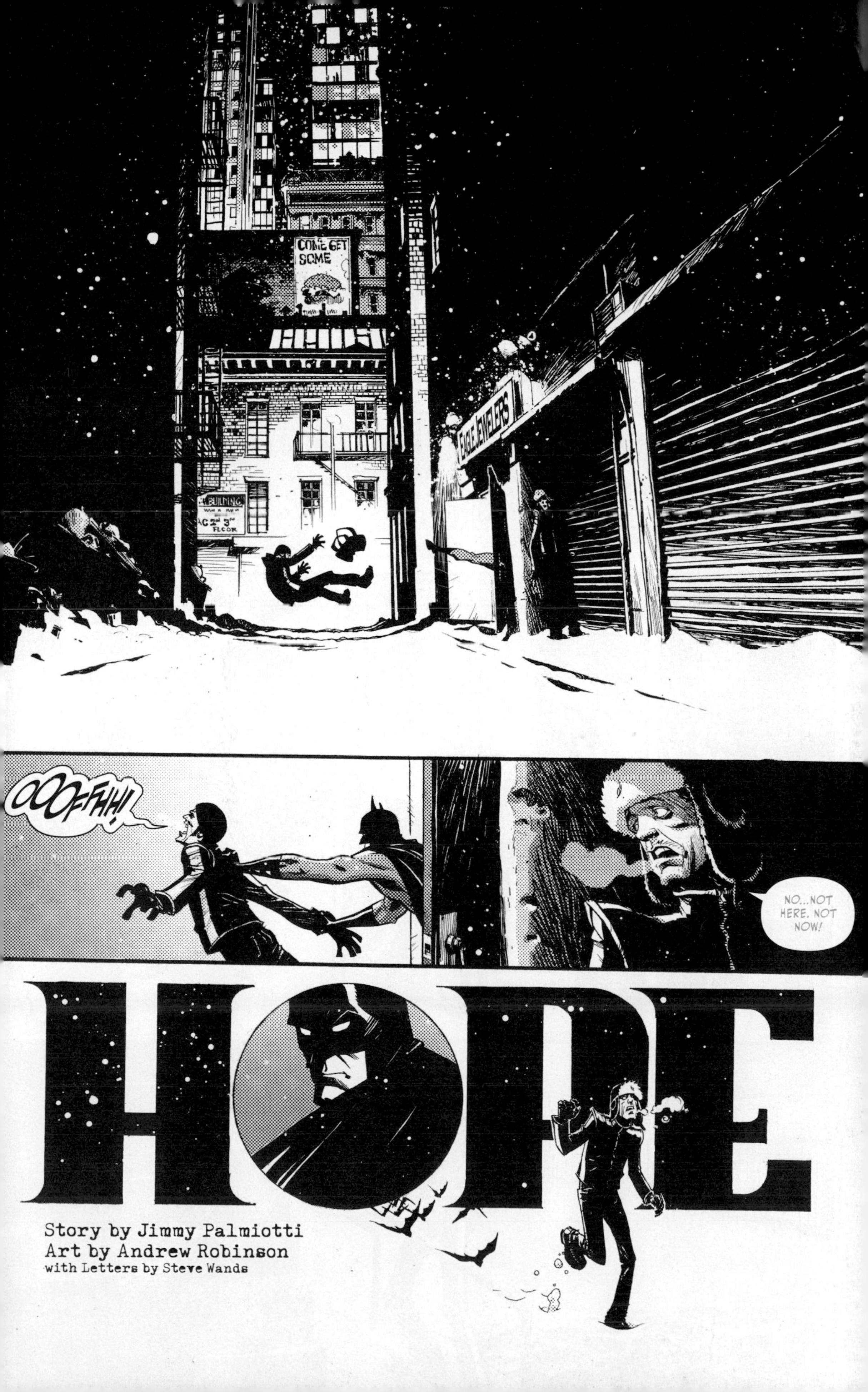
COME GET SOME
BUILDING
AC 2nd 3rd FLOOR
EAGLE JEWELERS
OOOF-FHH!
NO...NOT HERE. NOT NOW!
HOPE

Story by Jimmy Palmiotti
Art by Andrew Robinson
with Letters by Steve Wands

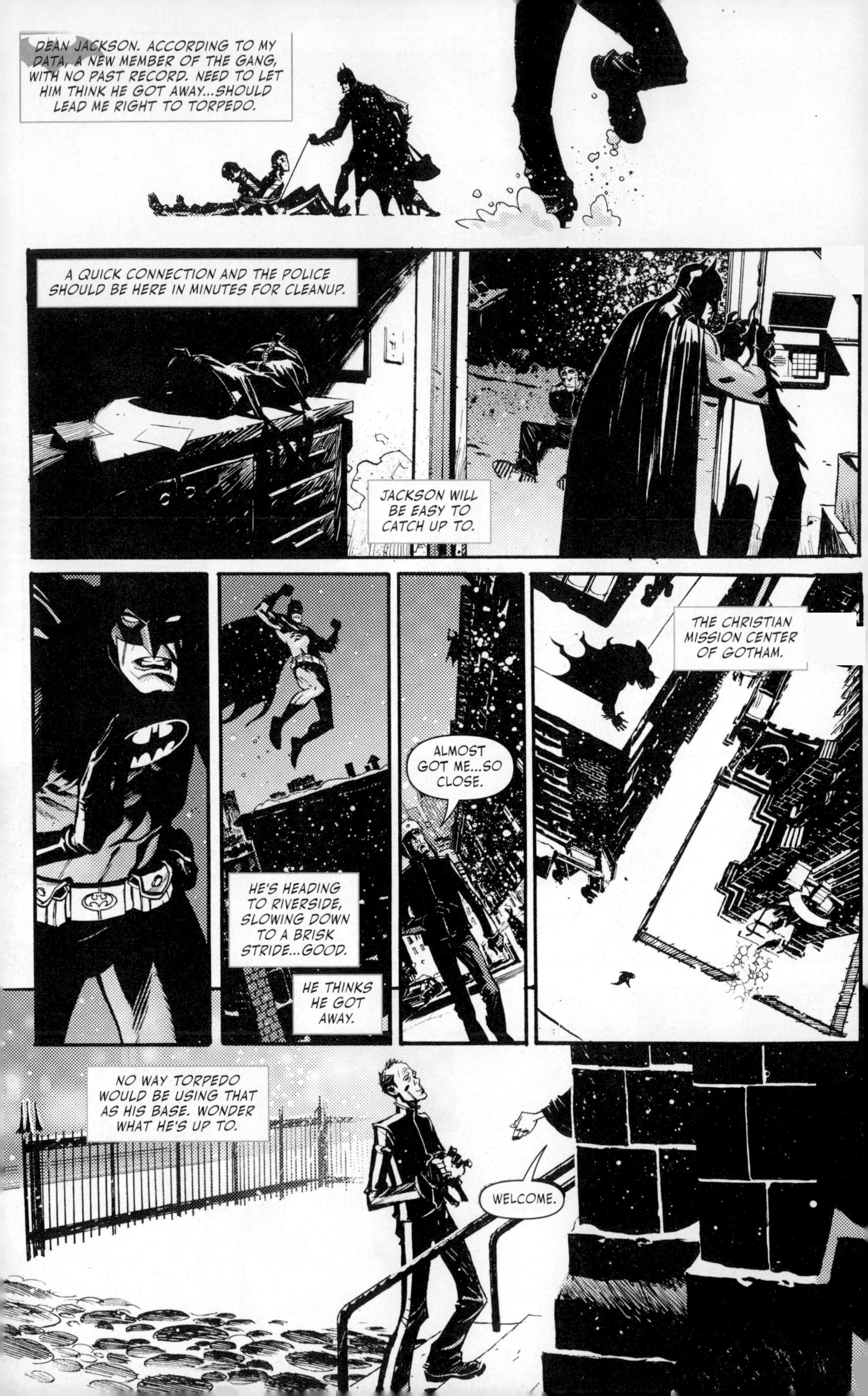
DEAN JACKSON. ACCORDING TO MY DATA, A NEW MEMBER OF THE GANG, WITH NO PAST RECORD. NEED TO LET HIM THINK HE GOT AWAY...SHOULD LEAD ME RIGHT TO TORPEDO.
A QUICK CONNECTION AND THE POLICE SHOULD BE HERE IN MINUTES FOR CLEANUP.
JACKSON WILL BE EASY TO CATCH UP TO.
HE'S HEADING TO RIVERSIDE, SLOWING DOWN TO A BRISK STRIDE...GOOD.
HE THINKS HE GOT AWAY.
ALMOST GOT ME...SO CLOSE.
THE CHRISTIAN MISSION CENTER OF GOTHAM.
NO WAY TORPEDO WOULD BE USING THAT AS HIS BASE. WONDER WHAT HE'S UP TO.
WELCOME.

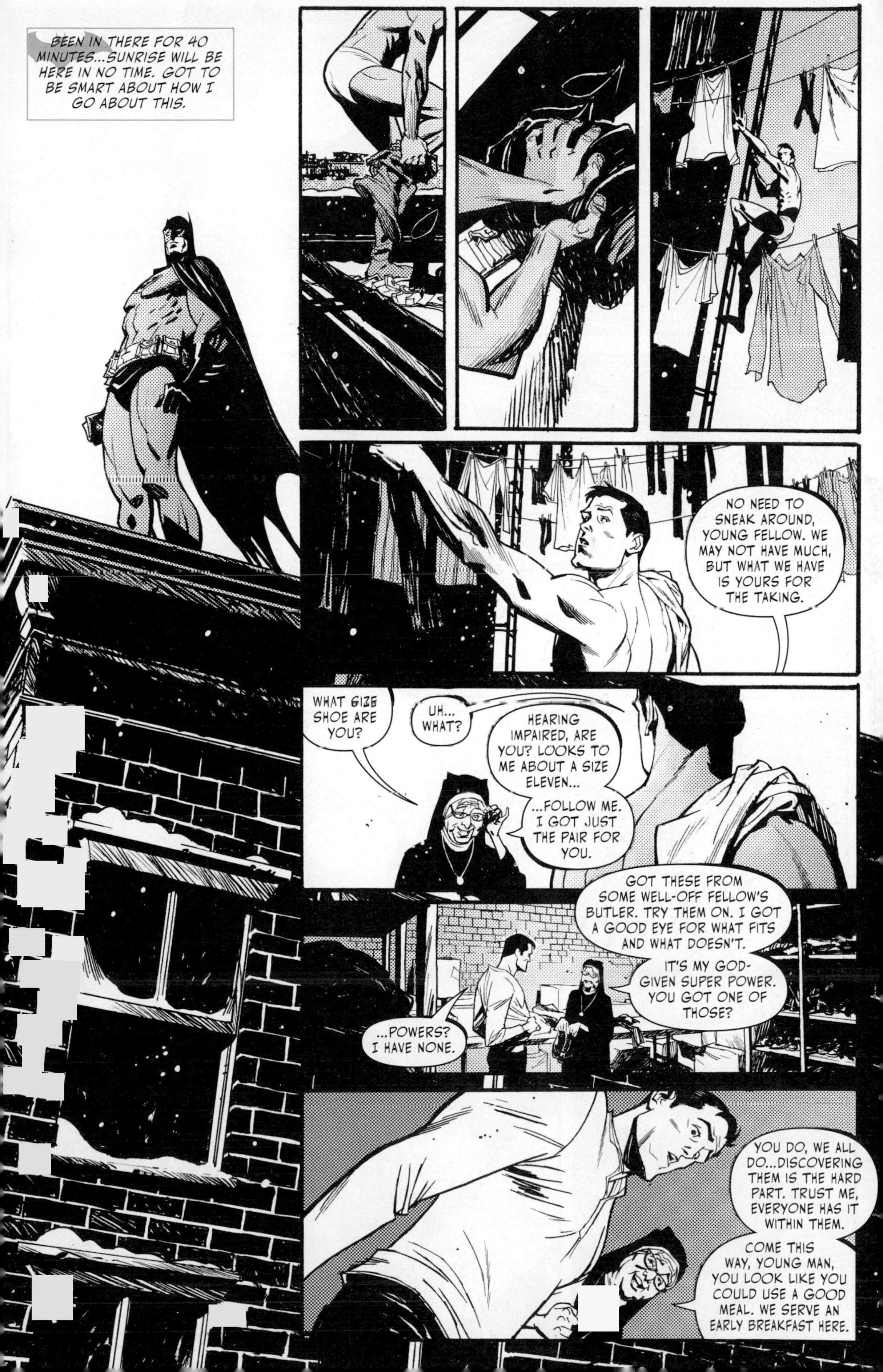

BEEN IN THERE FOR 40 MINUTES...SUNRISE WILL BE HERE IN NO TIME. GOT TO BE SMART ABOUT HOW I GO ABOUT THIS.
NO NEED TO SNEAK AROUND, YOUNG FELLOW. WE MAY NOT HAVE MUCH, BUT WHAT WE HAVE IS YOURS FOR THE TAKING.
WHAT SIZE SHOE ARE YOU?
UH... WHAT?
HEARING IMPAIRED, ARE YOU? LOOKS TO ME ABOUT A SIZE ELEVEN...
...FOLLOW ME. I GOT JUST THE PAIR FOR YOU.
GOT THESE FROM SOME WELL-OFF FELLOW'S BUTLER. TRY THEM ON. I GOT A GOOD EYE FOR WHAT FITS AND WHAT DOESN'T.
IT'S MY GOD-GIVEN SUPER POWER. YOU GOT ONE OF THOSE?
...POWERS? I HAVE NONE.
YOU DO, WE ALL DO...DISCOVERING THEM IS THE HARD PART. TRUST ME, EVERYONE HAS IT WITHIN THEM.
COME THIS WAY, YOUNG MAN, YOU LOOK LIKE YOU COULD USE A GOOD MEAL. WE SERVE AN EARLY BREAKFAST HERE.

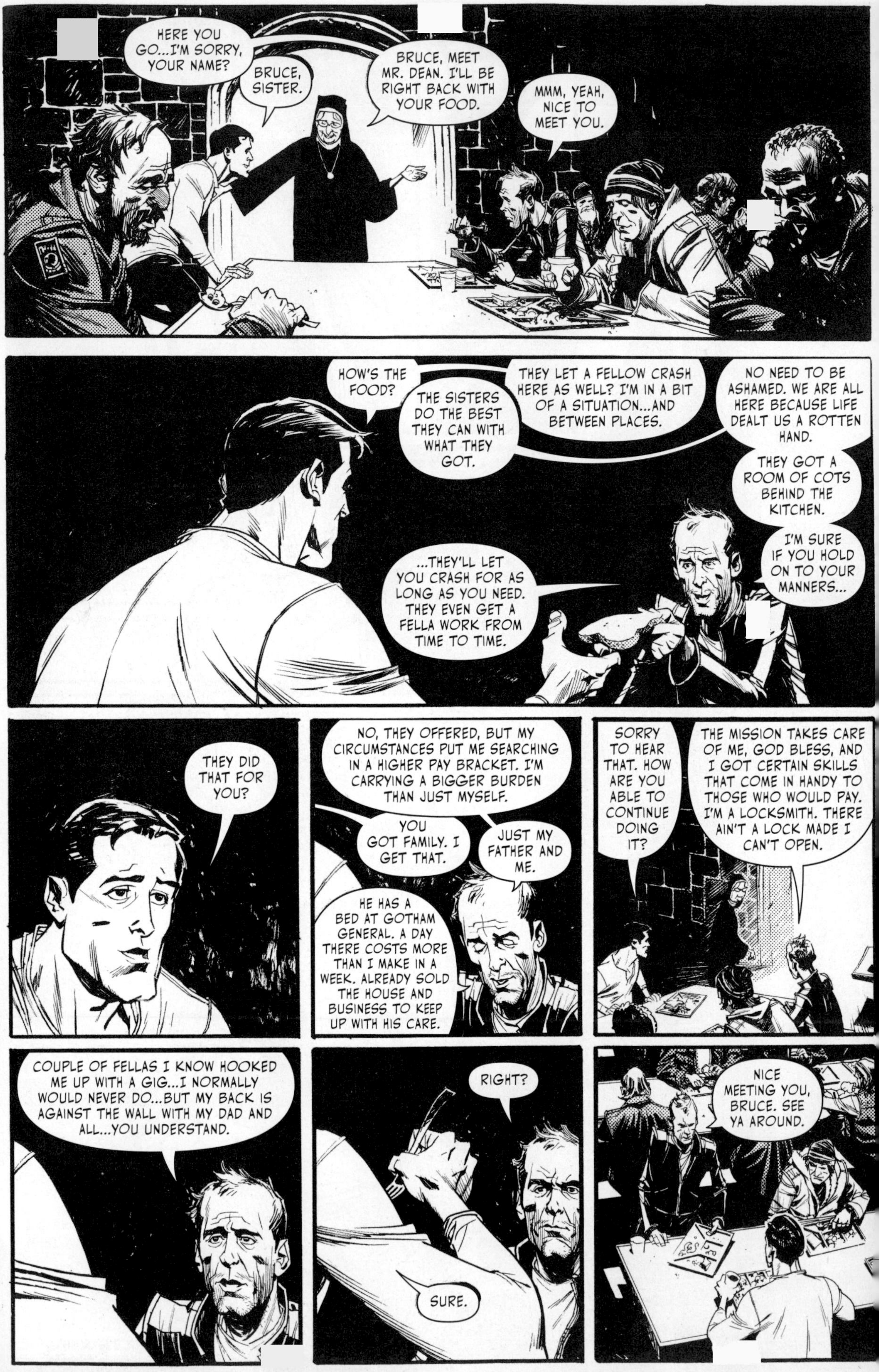
HERE YOU GO...I'M SORRY, YOUR NAME?
BRUCE, SISTER.
BRUCE, MEET MR. DEAN. I'LL BE RIGHT BACK WITH YOUR FOOD.
MMM, YEAH, NICE TO MEET YOU.
HOW'S THE FOOD?
THE SISTERS DO THE BEST THEY CAN WITH WHAT THEY GOT.
THEY LET A FELLOW CRASH HERE AS WELL? I'M IN A BIT OF A SITUATION...AND BETWEEN PLACES.
NO NEED TO BE ASHAMED. WE ARE ALL HERE BECAUSE LIFE DEALT US A ROTTEN HAND.
THEY GOT A ROOM OF COTS BEHIND THE KITCHEN.
I'M SURE IF YOU HOLD ON TO YOUR MANNERS...
...THEY'LL LET YOU CRASH FOR AS LONG AS YOU NEED. THEY EVEN GET A FELLA WORK FROM TIME TO TIME.
THEY DID THAT FOR YOU?
NO, THEY OFFERED, BUT MY CIRCUMSTANCES PUT ME SEARCHING IN A HIGHER PAY BRACKET. I'M CARRYING A BIGGER BURDEN THAN JUST MYSELF.
YOU GOT FAMILY. I GET THAT.
JUST MY FATHER AND ME.
HE HAS A BED AT GOTHAM GENERAL. A DAY THERE COSTS MORE THAN I MAKE IN A WEEK. ALREADY SOLD THE HOUSE AND BUSINESS TO KEEP UP WITH HIS CARE.
SORRY TO HEAR THAT. HOW ARE YOU ABLE TO CONTINUE DOING IT?
THE MISSION TAKES CARE OF ME, GOD BLESS, AND I GOT CERTAIN SKILLS THAT COME IN HANDY TO THOSE WHO WOULD PAY. I'M A LOCKSMITH. THERE AIN'T A LOCK MADE I CAN'T OPEN.
COUPLE OF FELLAS I KNOW HOOKED ME UP WITH A GIG...I NORMALLY WOULD NEVER DO...BUT MY BACK IS AGAINST THE WALL WITH MY DAD AND ALL...YOU UNDERSTAND.
RIGHT?
SURE.
NICE MEETING YOU, BRUCE. SEE YA AROUND.

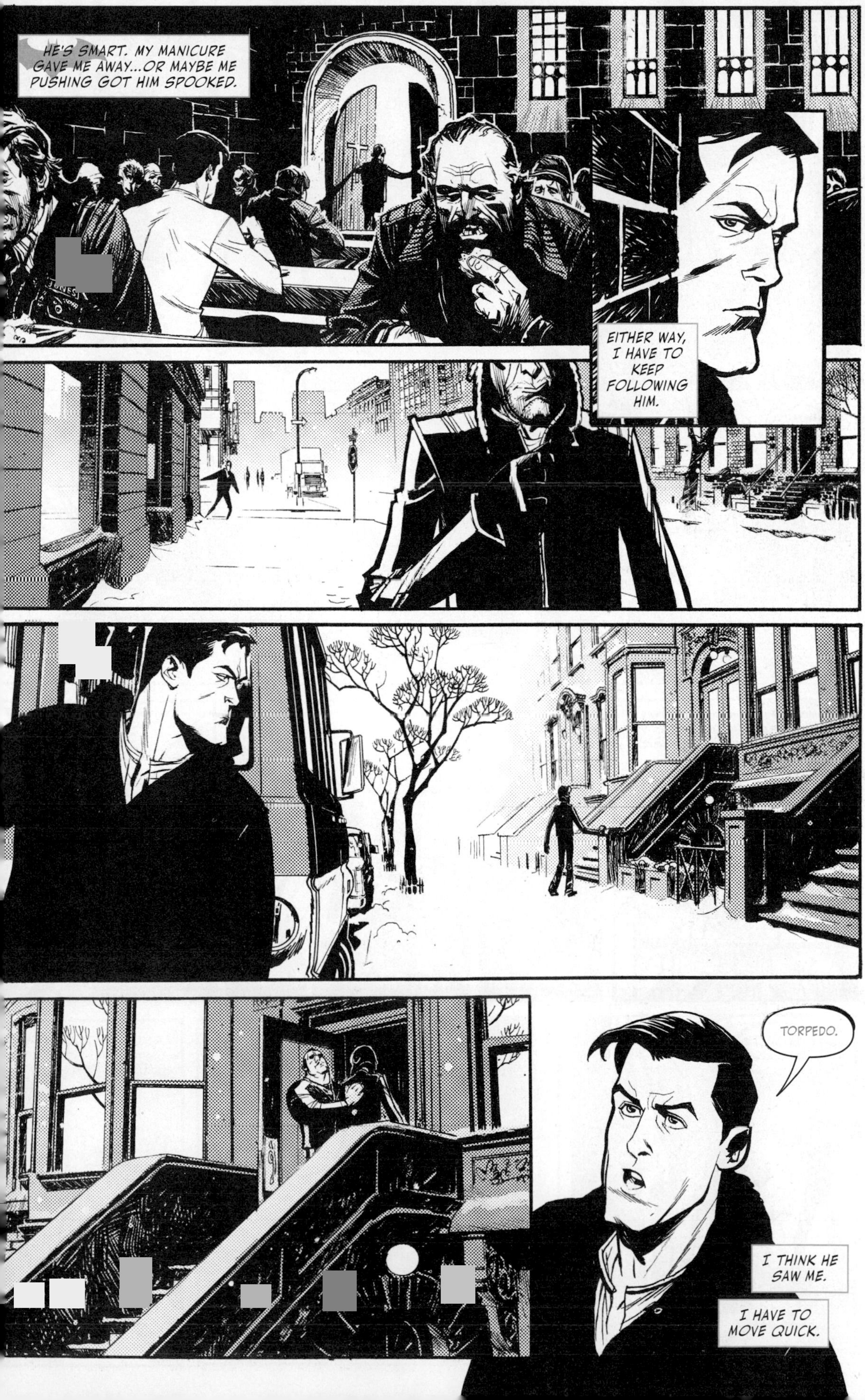
HE'S SMART. MY MANICURE GAVE ME AWAY...OR MAYBE ME PUSHING GOT HIM SPOOKED.
EITHER WAY, I HAVE TO KEEP FOLLOWING HIM.
TORPEDO.
I THINK HE SAW ME.
I HAVE TO MOVE QUICK.

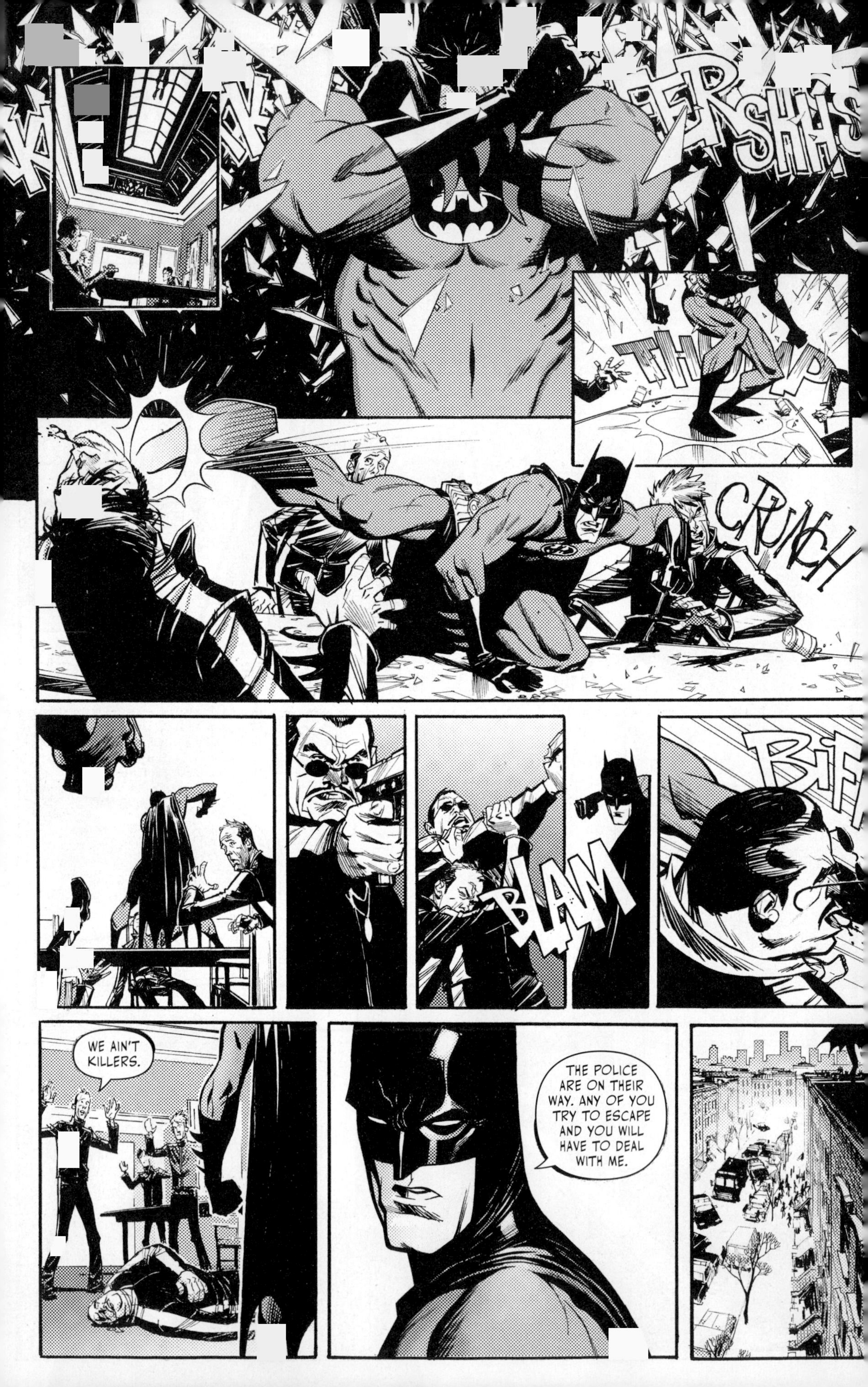
CRUNCH
BLAM
WE AIN'T KILLERS.
THE POLICE ARE ON THEIR WAY. ANY OF YOU TRY TO ESCAPE AND YOU WILL HAVE TO DEAL WITH ME.

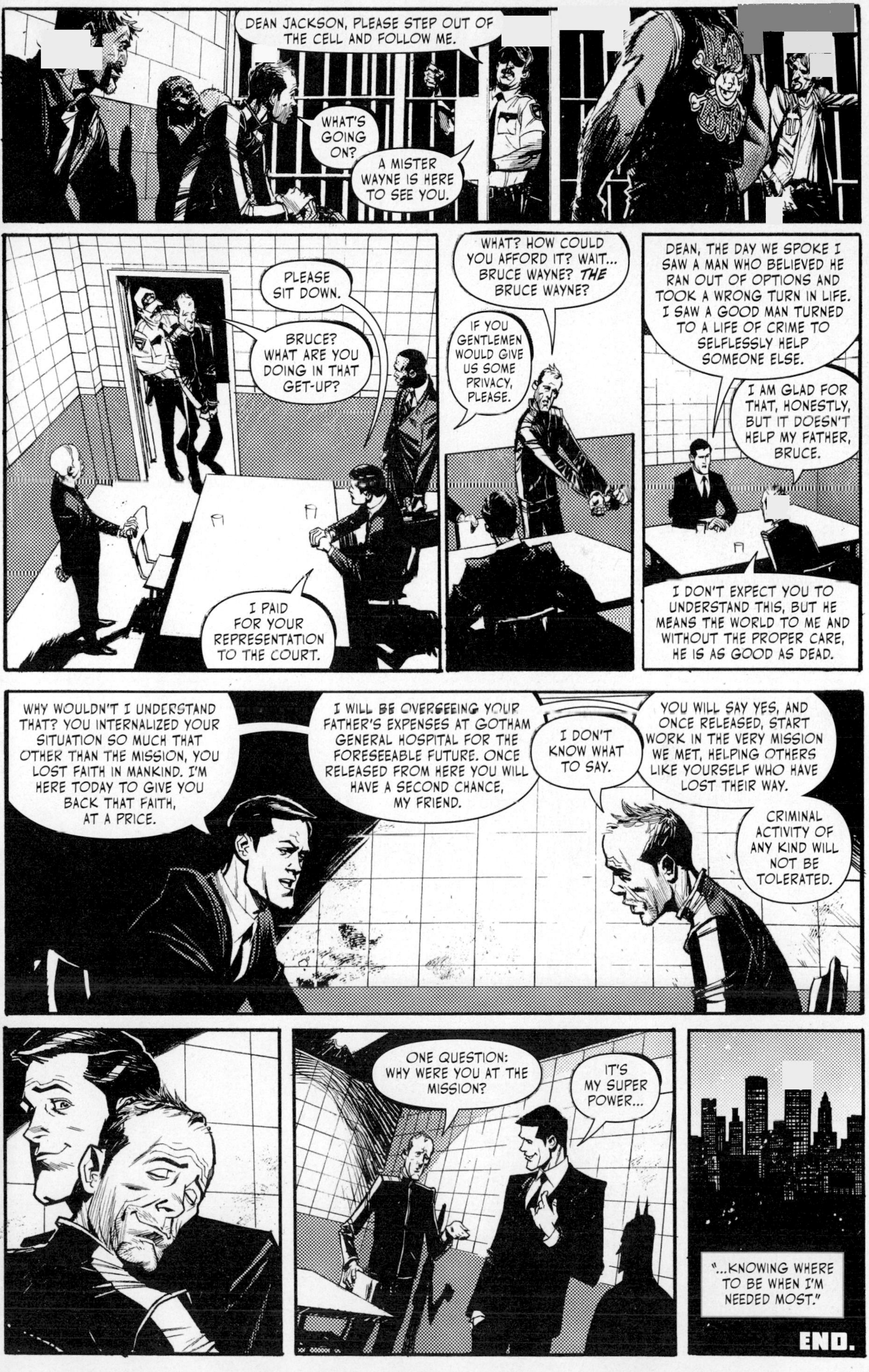

DEAN JACKSON, PLEASE STEP OUT OF THE CELL AND FOLLOW ME.
WHAT'S GOING ON?
A MISTER WAYNE IS HERE TO SEE YOU.
PLEASE SIT DOWN.
BRUCE? WHAT ARE YOU DOING IN THAT GET-UP?
I PAID FOR YOUR REPRESENTATION TO THE COURT.
WHAT? HOW COULD YOU AFFORD IT? WAIT... BRUCE WAYNE? THE BRUCE WAYNE?
IF YOU GENTLEMEN WOULD GIVE US SOME PRIVACY, PLEASE.
DEAN, THE DAY WE SPOKE I SAW A MAN WHO BELIEVED HE RAN OUT OF OPTIONS AND TOOK A WRONG TURN IN LIFE. I SAW A GOOD MAN TURNED TO A LIFE OF CRIME TO SELFLESSLY HELP SOMEONE ELSE.
I AM GLAD FOR THAT, HONESTLY, BUT IT DOESN'T HELP MY FATHER, BRUCE.
I DON'T EXPECT YOU TO UNDERSTAND THIS, BUT HE MEANS THE WORLD TO ME AND WITHOUT THE PROPER CARE, HE IS AS GOOD AS DEAD.
WHY WOULDN'T I UNDERSTAND THAT? YOU INTERNALIZED YOUR SITUATION SO MUCH THAT OTHER THAN THE MISSION, YOU LOST FAITH IN MANKIND. I'M HERE TODAY TO GIVE YOU BACK THAT FAITH, AT A PRICE.
I WILL BE OVERSEEING YOUR FATHER'S EXPENSES AT GOTHAM GENERAL HOSPITAL FOR THE FORESEEABLE FUTURE. ONCE RELEASED FROM HERE YOU WILL HAVE A SECOND CHANCE, MY FRIEND.
I DON'T KNOW WHAT TO SAY.
YOU WILL SAY YES, AND ONCE RELEASED, START WORK IN THE VERY MISSION WE MET, HELPING OTHERS LIKE YOURSELF WHO HAVE LOST THEIR WAY.
CRIMINAL ACTIVITY OF ANY KIND WILL NOT BE TOLERATED.
ONE QUESTION: WHY WERE YOU AT THE MISSION?
IT'S MY SUPER POWER...
"...KNOWING WHERE TO BE WHEN I'M NEEDED MOST."
END.

JIMMY PALMIOTTI

The hardest-working man in comics,
Jimmy Palmiotti has been a writer, artist,
and editor since the early '90s.
Whether he's writing TV, films, games
or comics, Palmiotti always brings a sense
of the "real" to the fantastical worlds he
creates. Jimmy's current wealth of stories
can be seen and enjoyed in the pages
of HARLEY QUINN, ALL-STAR WESTERN,
BATWING, and *Painkiller Jane*.

ANDREW ROBINSON

A graduate of the
Savannah College of Art & Design, Andrew
Robinson has created dazzling art for many
comics and gaming companies.
Although known primarily as a cover artist
(STARMAN, HAWKMAN, BATMAN, *Star Wars*),
Robinson has just completed work on
The Fifth Beatle, a 120-page graphic novel
biography of famed Beatle
manager Brian Epstein.

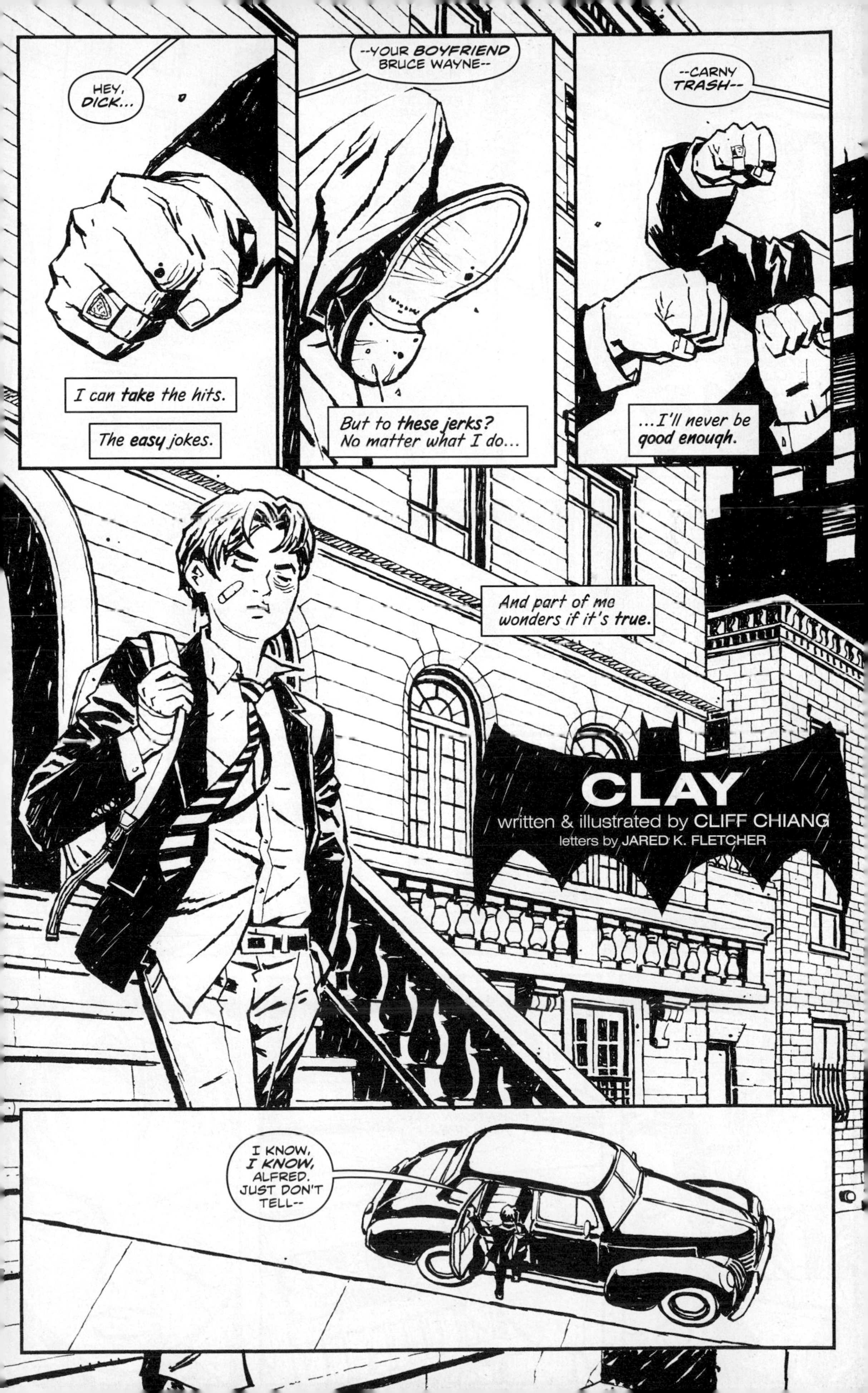
HEY, DICK...
I can take the hits.
The easy jokes.
--YOUR BOYFRIEND BRUCE WAYNE--
But to these jerks? No matter what I do...
--CARNY TRASH--
...I'll never be good enough.
And part of me wonders if it's true.
CLAY
written & illustrated by CLIFF CHIANG
letters by JARED K. FLETCHER
I KNOW, I KNOW, ALFRED. JUST DON'T TELL--

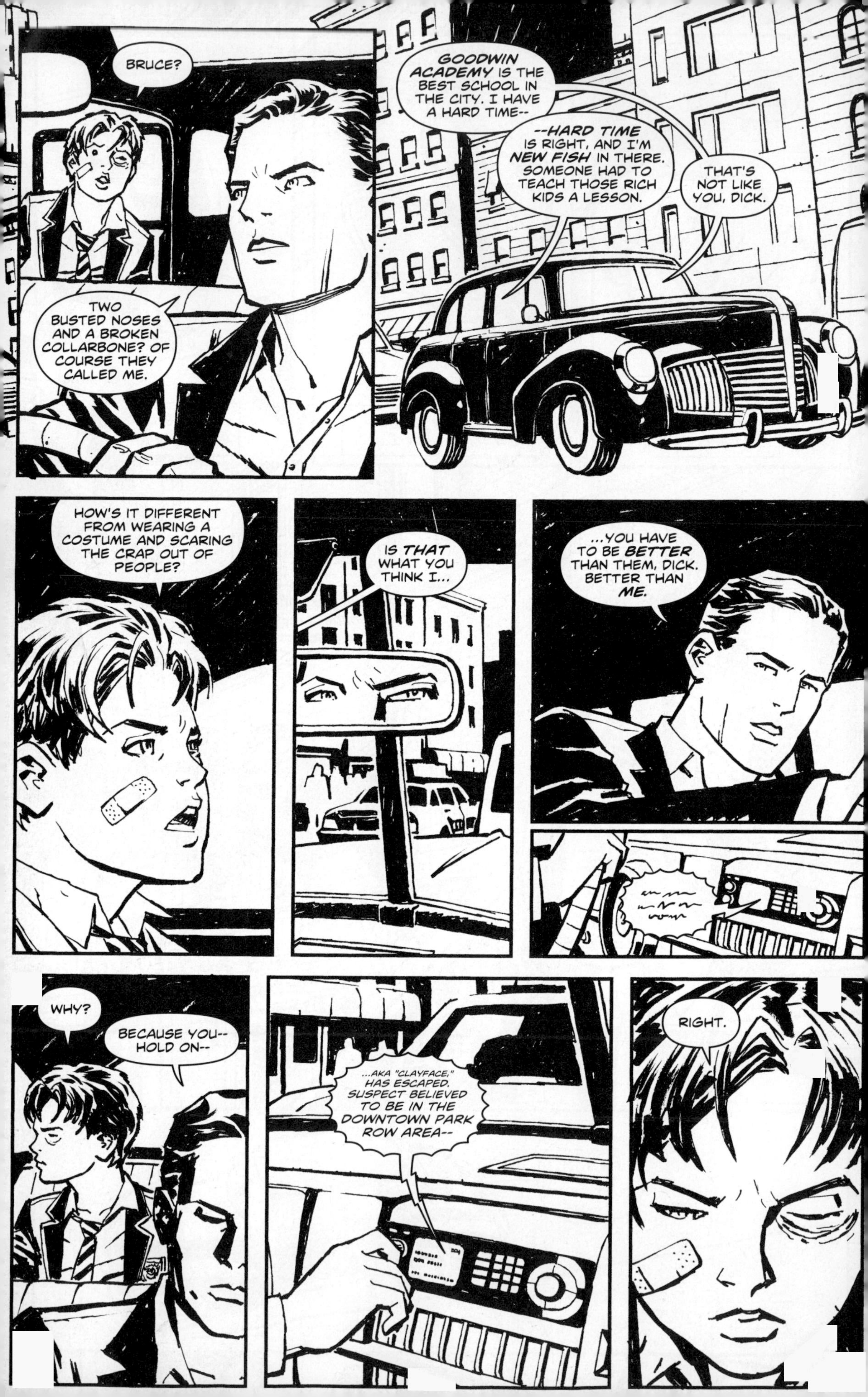
BRUCE?
TWO BUSTED NOSES AND A BROKEN COLLARBONE? OF COURSE THEY CALLED ME.
GOODWIN ACADEMY IS THE BEST SCHOOL IN THE CITY. I HAVE A HARD TIME--
--HARD TIME IS RIGHT, AND I'M NEW FISH IN THERE. SOMEONE HAD TO TEACH THOSE RICH KIDS A LESSON.
THAT'S NOT LIKE YOU, DICK.
HOW'S IT DIFFERENT FROM WEARING A COSTUME AND SCARING THE CRAP OUT OF PEOPLE?
IS THAT WHAT YOU THINK I...
...YOU HAVE TO BE BETTER THAN THEM, DICK. BETTER THAN ME.
WHY?
BECAUSE YOU-- HOLD ON--
...AKA "CLAYFACE," HAS ESCAPED. SUSPECT BELIEVED TO BE IN THE DOWNTOWN PARK ROW AREA--
RIGHT.

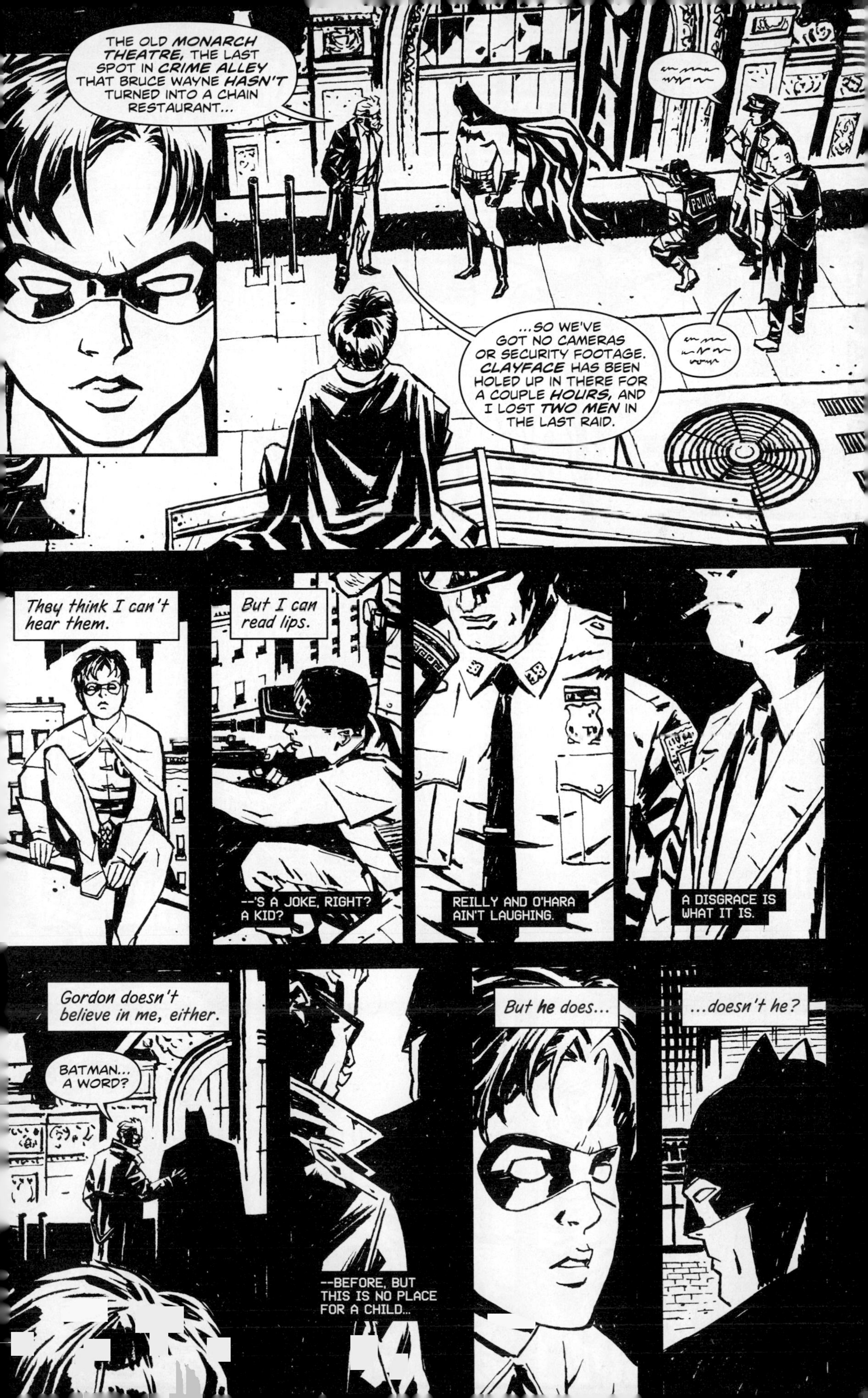
THE OLD MONARCH THEATRE, THE LAST SPOT IN CRIME ALLEY THAT BRUCE WAYNE HASN'T TURNED INTO A CHAIN RESTAURANT...
...SO WE'VE GOT NO CAMERAS OR SECURITY FOOTAGE. CLAYFACE HAS BEEN HOLED UP IN THERE FOR A COUPLE HOURS, AND I LOST TWO MEN IN THE LAST RAID.
They think I can't hear them.
But I can read lips.
--'S A JOKE, RIGHT? A KID?
REILLY AND O'HARA AIN'T LAUGHING.
A DISGRACE IS WHAT IT IS.
Gordon doesn't believe in me, either.
BATMAN... A WORD?
--BEFORE, BUT THIS IS NO PLACE FOR A CHILD...
But he does...
...doesn't he?

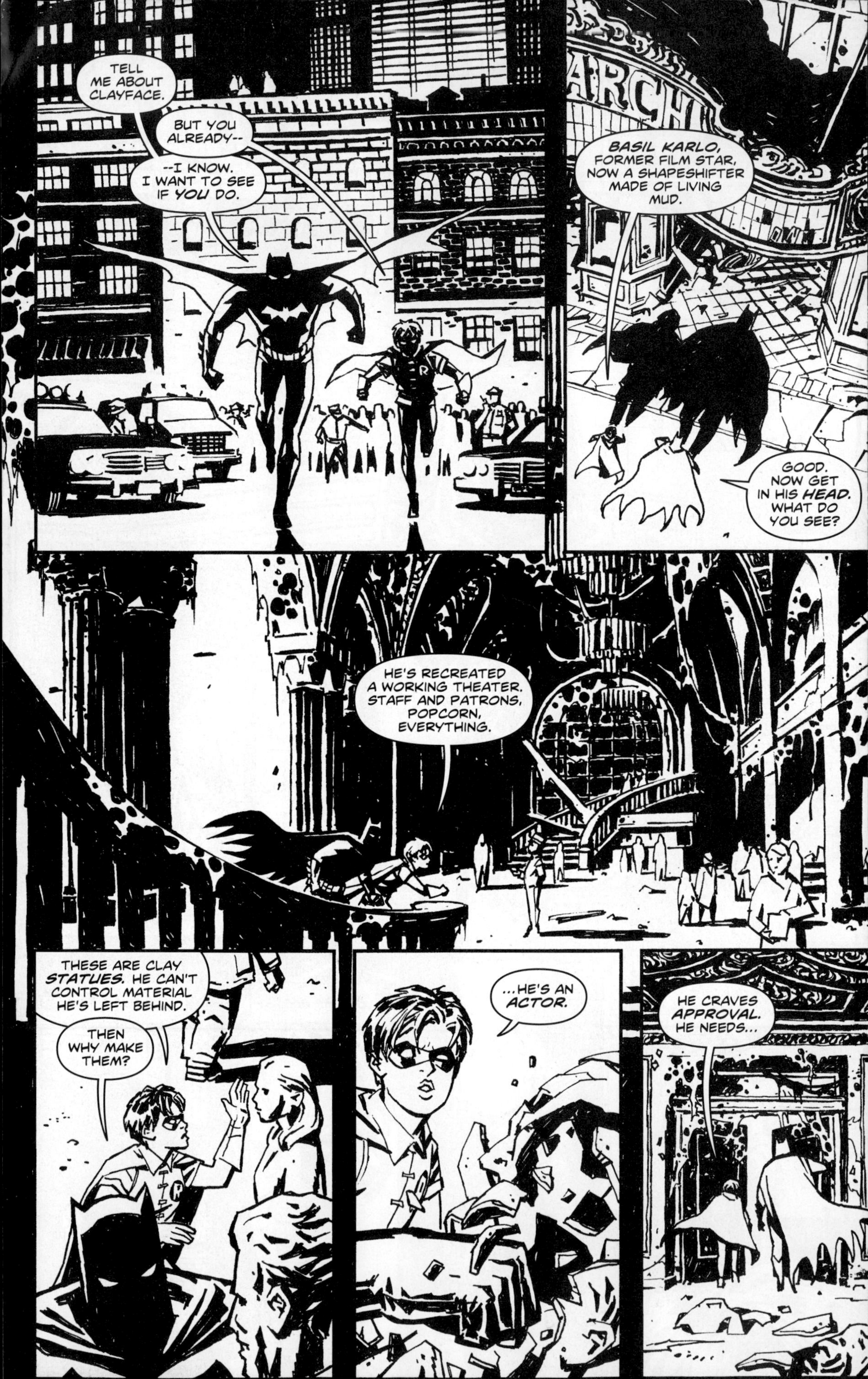
TELL ME ABOUT CLAYFACE.
BUT YOU ALREADY--
--I KNOW. I WANT TO SEE IF YOU DO.
ARCH
BASIL KARLO, FORMER FILM STAR, NOW A SHAPESHIFTER MADE OF LIVING MUD.
GOOD. NOW GET IN HIS HEAD. WHAT DO YOU SEE?
HE'S RECREATED A WORKING THEATER. STAFF AND PATRONS, POPCORN, EVERYTHING.
THESE ARE CLAY STATUES. HE CAN'T CONTROL MATERIAL HE'S LEFT BEHIND.
THEN WHY MAKE THEM?
...HE'S AN ACTOR.
HE CRAVES APPROVAL. HE NEEDS...

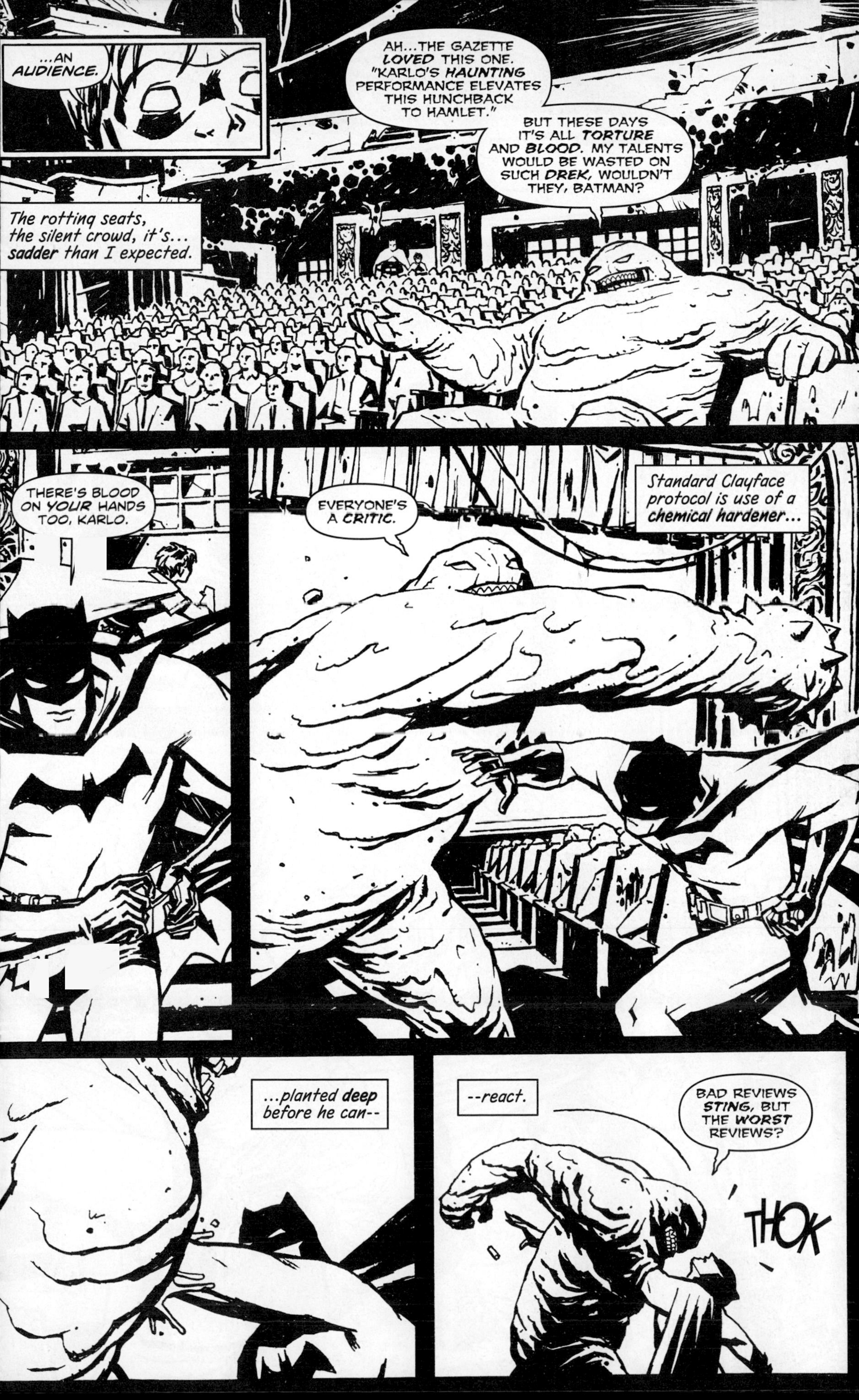
...AN AUDIENCE.
AH...THE GAZETTE LOVED THIS ONE. "KARLO'S HAUNTING PERFORMANCE ELEVATES THIS HUNCHBACK TO HAMLET."
BUT THESE DAYS IT'S ALL TORTURE AND BLOOD. MY TALENTS WOULD BE WASTED ON SUCH DREK, WOULDN'T THEY, BATMAN?
The rotting seats, the silent crowd, it's... sadder than I expected.
THERE'S BLOOD ON YOUR HANDS TOO, KARLO.
EVERYONE'S A CRITIC.
Standard Clayface protocol is use of a chemical hardener...
...planted deep before he can--
--react.
BAD REVIEWS STING, BUT THE WORST REVIEWS?
THOK

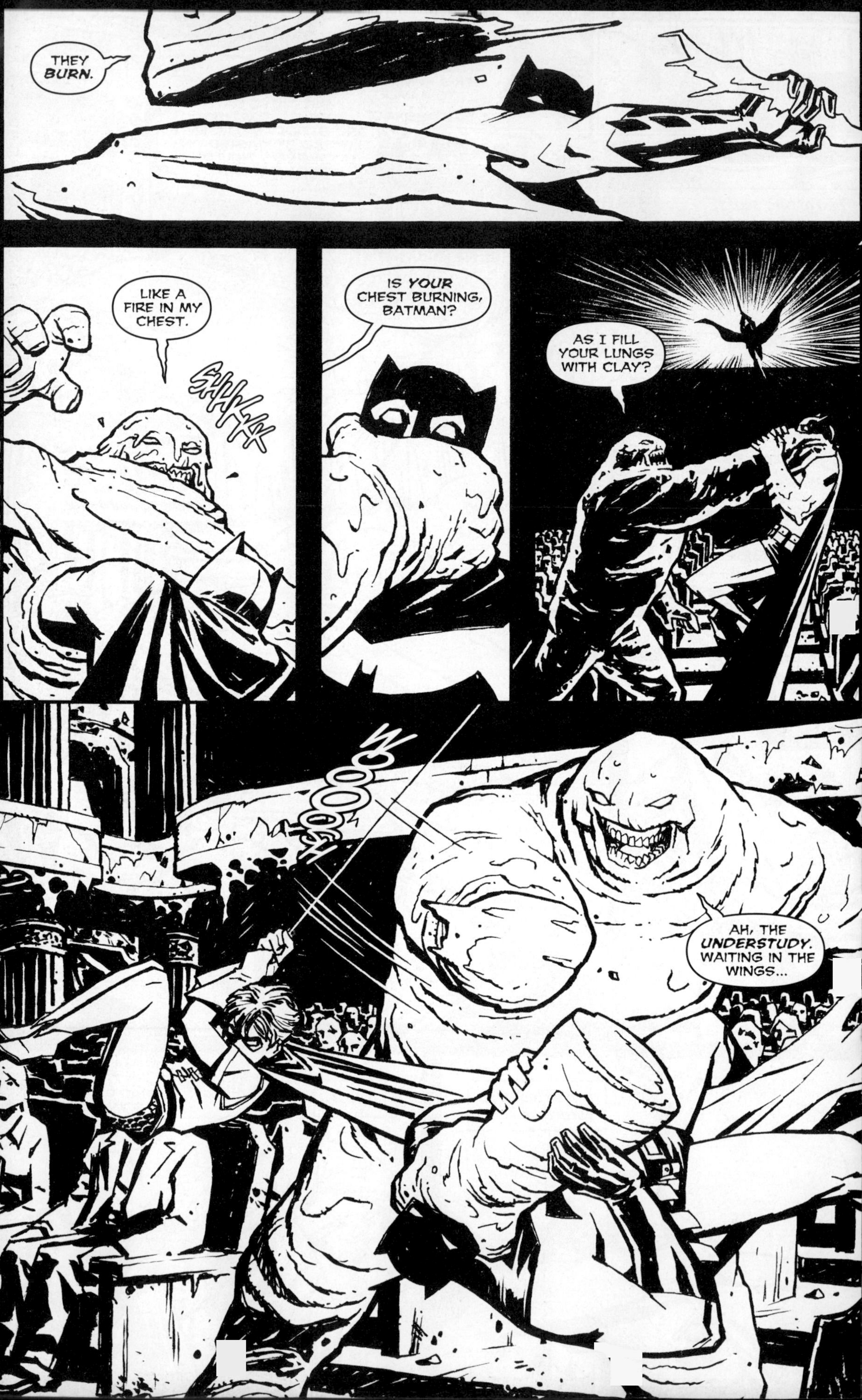
THEY BURN.
LIKE A FIRE IN MY CHEST.
SHHKKKK
IS YOUR CHEST BURNING, BATMAN?
AS I FILL YOUR LUNGS WITH CLAY?
WOOOOSH
AH, THE UNDERSTUDY. WAITING IN THE WINGS...

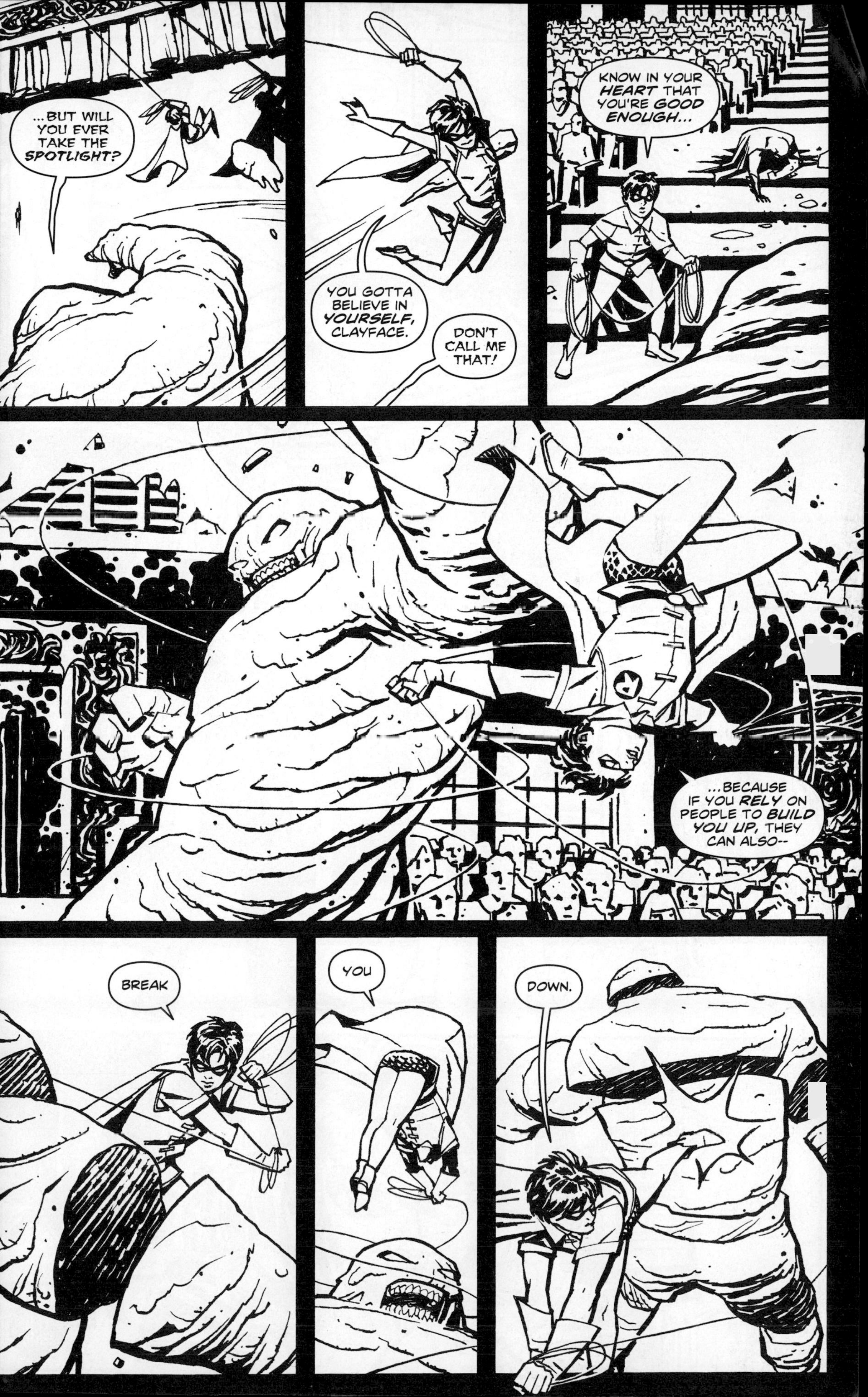

...BUT WILL YOU EVER TAKE THE SPOTLIGHT?
YOU GOTTA BELIEVE IN YOURSELF, CLAYFACE.
DON'T CALL ME THAT!
KNOW IN YOUR HEART THAT YOU'RE GOOD ENOUGH...
...BECAUSE IF YOU RELY ON PEOPLE TO BUILD YOU UP, THEY CAN ALSO--
BREAK
YOU
DOWN.

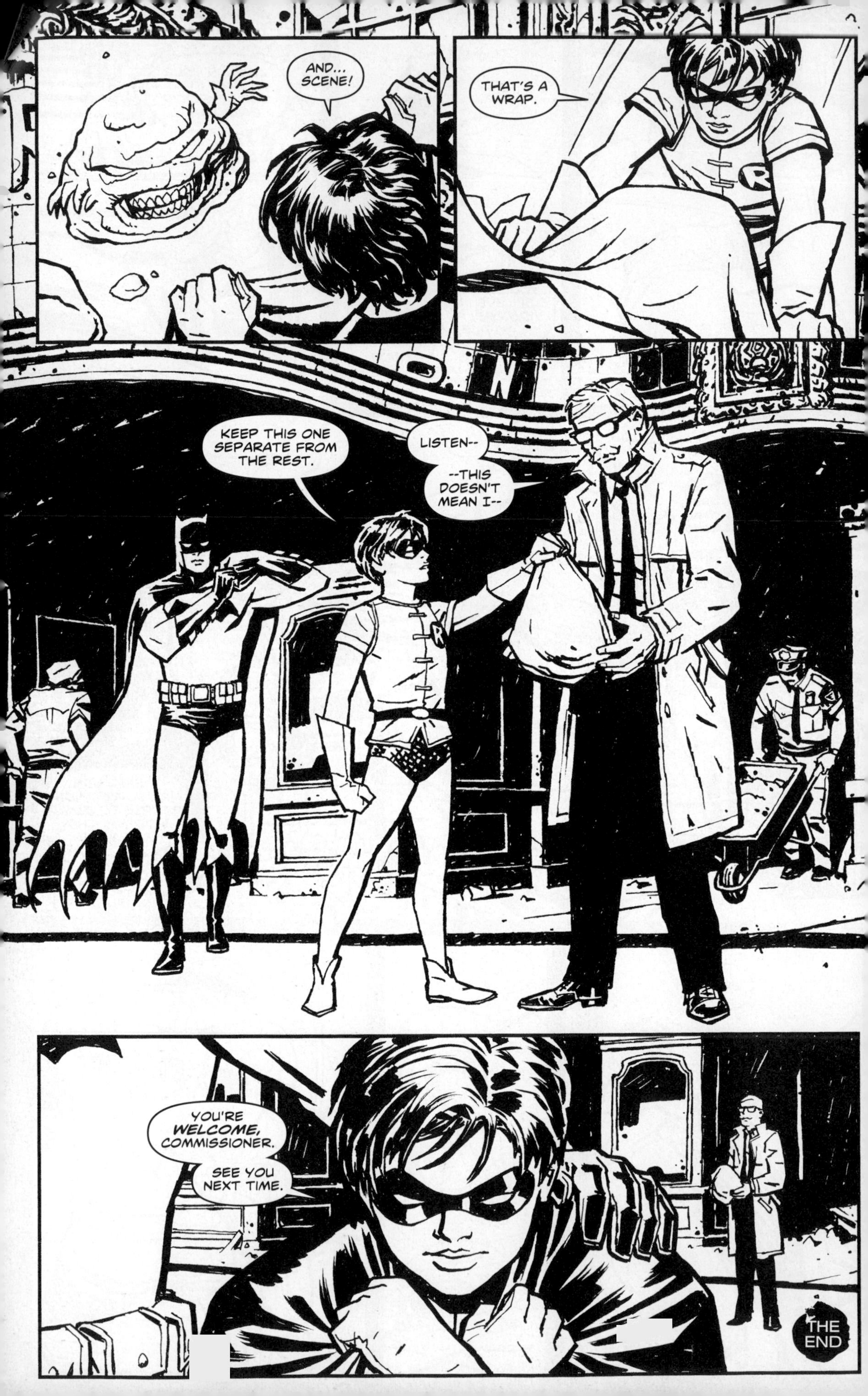
AND... SCENE!
THAT'S A WRAP.
KEEP THIS ONE SEPARATE FROM THE REST.
LISTEN--
--THIS DOESN'T MEAN I--
YOU'RE *WELCOME*, COMMISSIONER.
SEE YOU NEXT TIME.
THE END

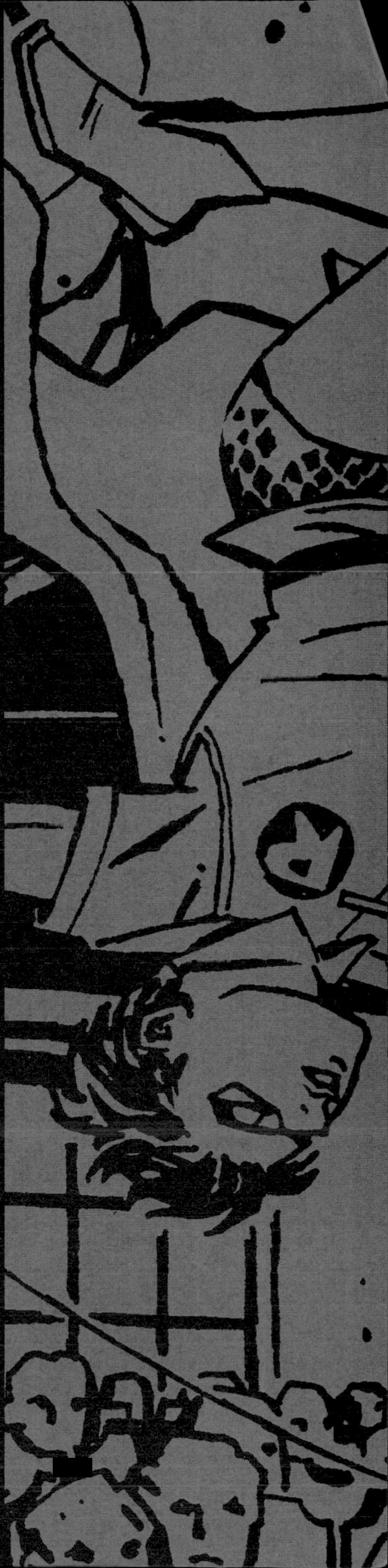

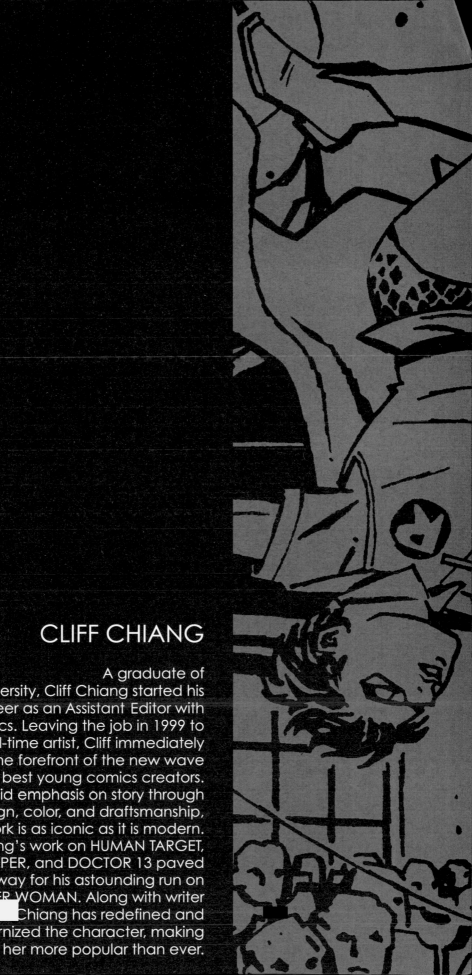

CLIFF CHIANG

A graduate of Harvard University, Cliff Chiang started his comics career as an Assistant Editor with Vertigo Comics. Leaving the job in 1999 to become a full-time artist, Cliff immediately stepped to the forefront of the new wave of the very best young comics creators. With a rock-solid emphasis on story through classic design, color, and draftsmanship, Cliff's work is as iconic as it is modern. Chiang's work on HUMAN TARGET, EWARE THE CREEPER, and DOCTOR 13 paved the way for his astounding run on WONDER WOMAN. Along with writer Brian Azzarel [redacted] Chiang has redefined and modernized the character, making her more popular than ever.

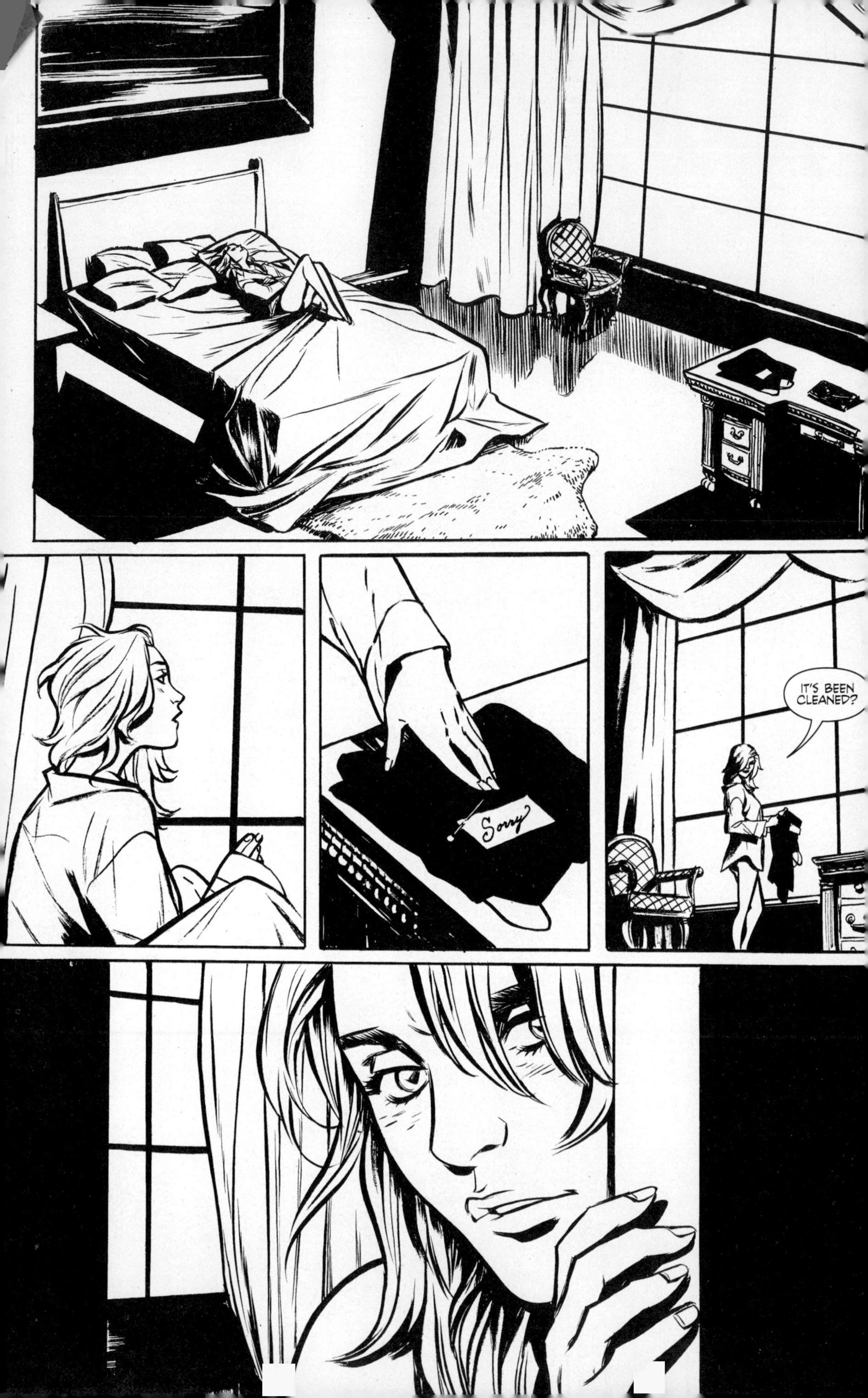
Sorry
IT'S BEEN CLEANED?

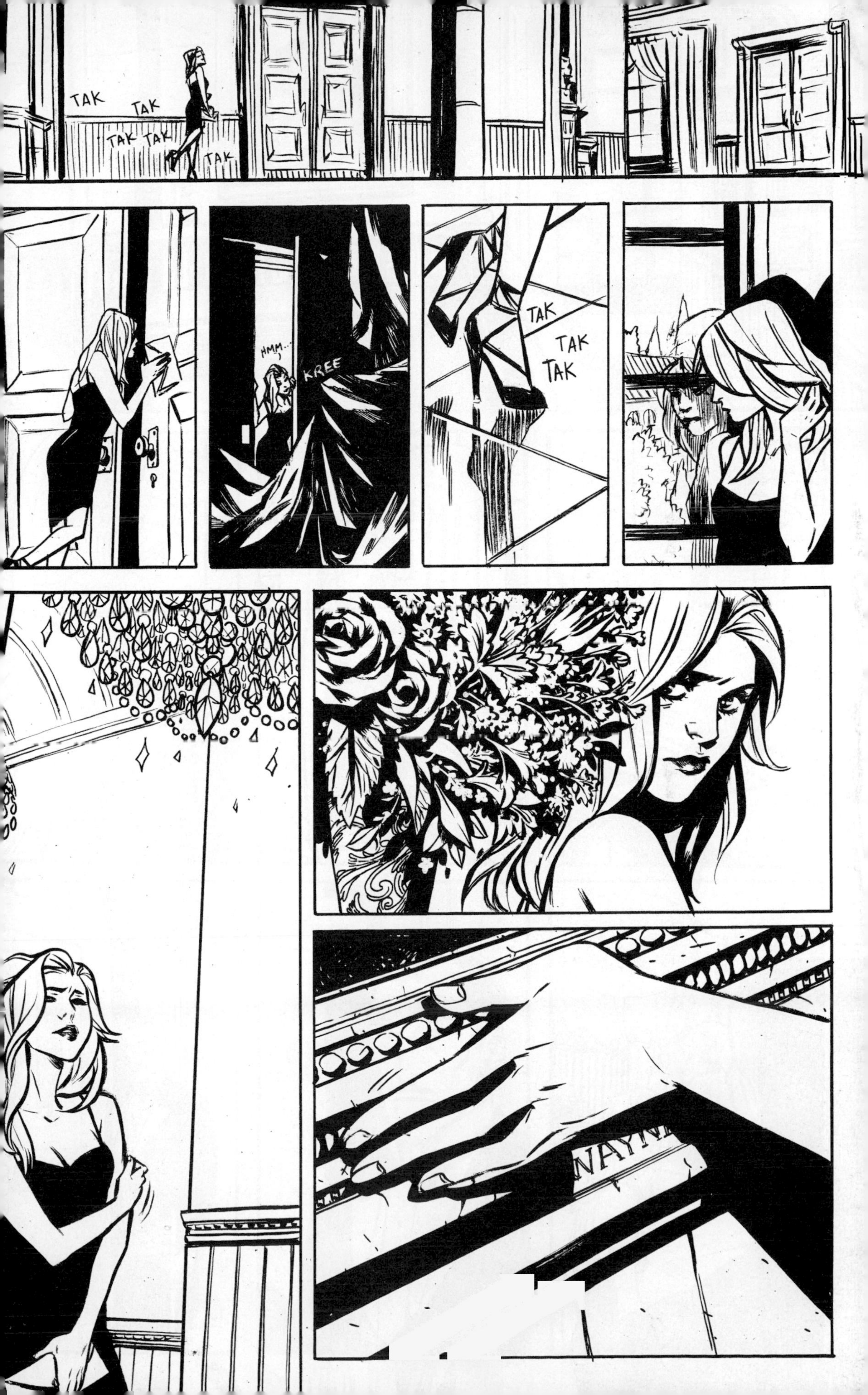
TAK
TAK
TAK TAK
TAK
HMM...
KREE
TAK
TAK
TAK
NAYN

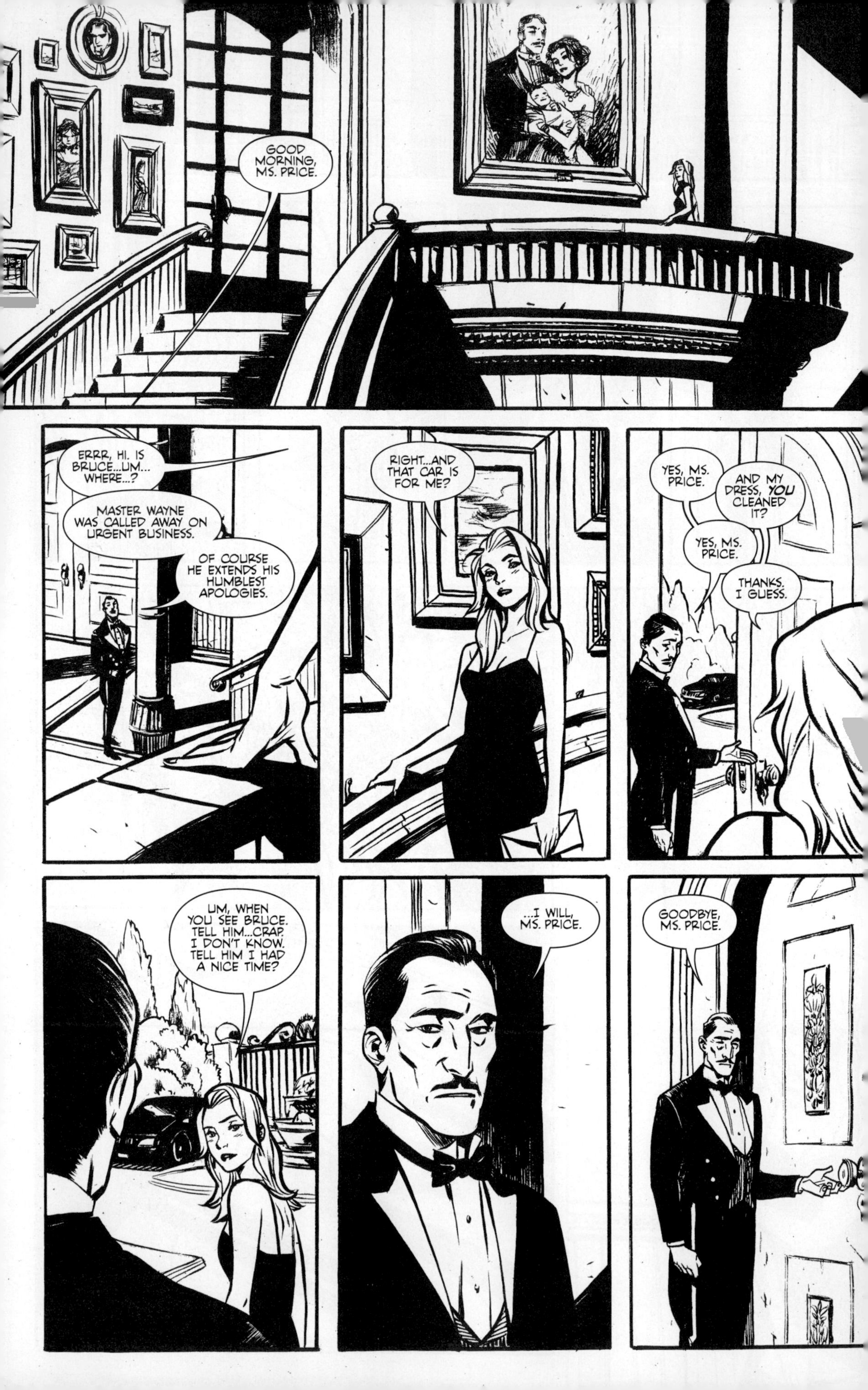
GOOD MORNING, MS. PRICE.
ERRR, HI. IS BRUCE...UM... WHERE...?
MASTER WAYNE WAS CALLED AWAY ON URGENT BUSINESS.
OF COURSE HE EXTENDS HIS HUMBLEST APOLOGIES.
RIGHT...AND THAT CAR IS FOR ME?
YES, MS. PRICE.
AND MY DRESS, YOU CLEANED IT?
YES, MS. PRICE.
THANKS. I GUESS.
UM, WHEN YOU SEE BRUCE. TELL HIM...CRAP. I DON'T KNOW. TELL HIM I HAD A NICE TIME?
...I WILL, MS. PRICE.
GOODBYE, MS. PRICE.

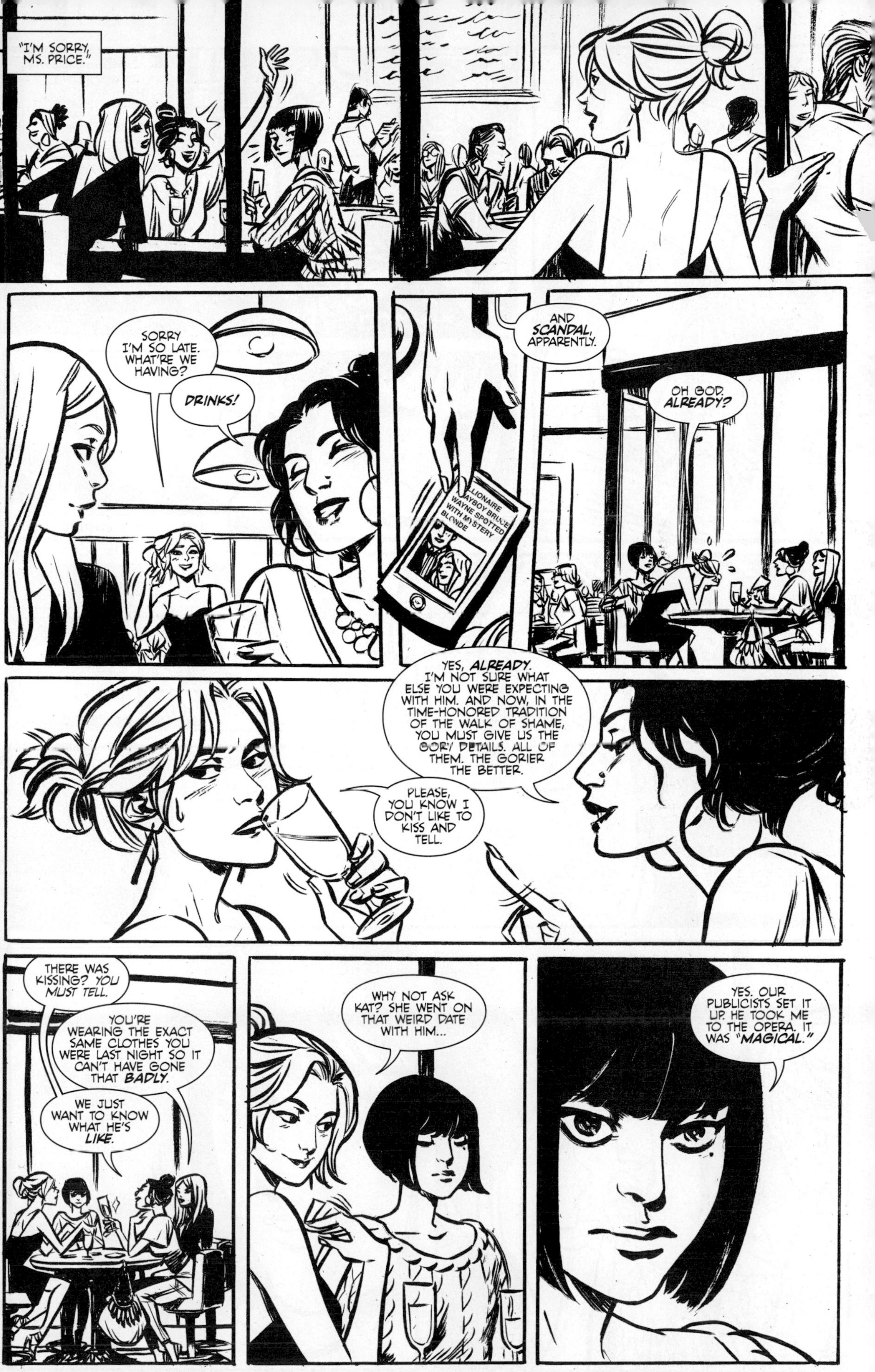
"I'M SORRY, MS. PRICE."
SORRY I'M SO LATE. WHAT'RE WE HAVING?
DRINKS!
AND SCANDAL, APPARENTLY.
LLIONAIRE AYBOY BRUCE WAYNE SPOTTED WITH MYSTERY BLONDE
OH GOD. ALREADY?
YES, ALREADY. I'M NOT SURE WHAT ELSE YOU WERE EXPECTING WITH HIM. AND NOW, IN THE TIME-HONORED TRADITION OF THE WALK OF SHAME, YOU MUST GIVE US THE GORY DETAILS. ALL OF THEM. THE GORIER THE BETTER.
PLEASE, YOU KNOW I DON'T LIKE TO KISS AND TELL.
THERE WAS KISSING? YOU MUST TELL.
YOU'RE WEARING THE EXACT SAME CLOTHES YOU WERE LAST NIGHT SO IT CAN'T HAVE GONE THAT BADLY.
WE JUST WANT TO KNOW WHAT HE'S LIKE.
WHY NOT ASK KAT? SHE WENT ON THAT WEIRD DATE WITH HIM...
YES. OUR PUBLICISTS SET IT UP. HE TOOK ME TO THE OPERA. IT WAS "MAGICAL."

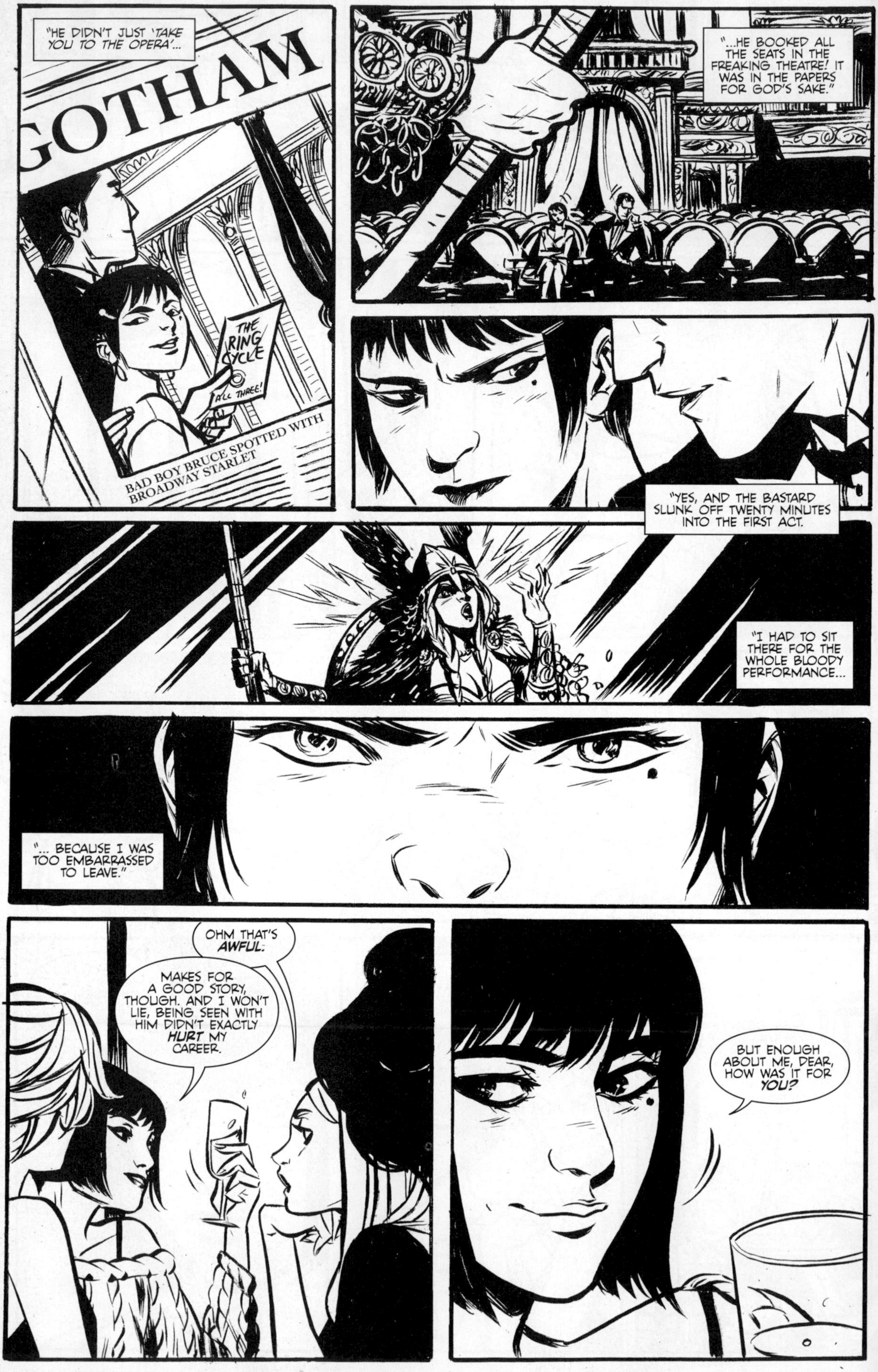
"HE DIDN'T JUST 'TAKE YOU TO THE OPERA'...
GOTHAM
THE RING CYCLE
ALL THREE!
BAD BOY BRUCE SPOTTED WITH BROADWAY STARLET
"...HE BOOKED ALL THE SEATS IN THE FREAKING THEATRE! IT WAS IN THE PAPERS FOR GOD'S SAKE."
"YES, AND THE BASTARD SLUNK OFF TWENTY MINUTES INTO THE FIRST ACT.
"I HAD TO SIT THERE FOR THE WHOLE BLOODY PERFORMANCE...
"... BECAUSE I WAS TOO EMBARRASSED TO LEAVE."
OHM THAT'S AWFUL.
MAKES FOR A GOOD STORY, THOUGH. AND I WON'T LIE, BEING SEEN WITH HIM DIDN'T EXACTLY HURT MY CAREER.
BUT ENOUGH ABOUT ME, DEAR, HOW WAS IT FOR YOU?

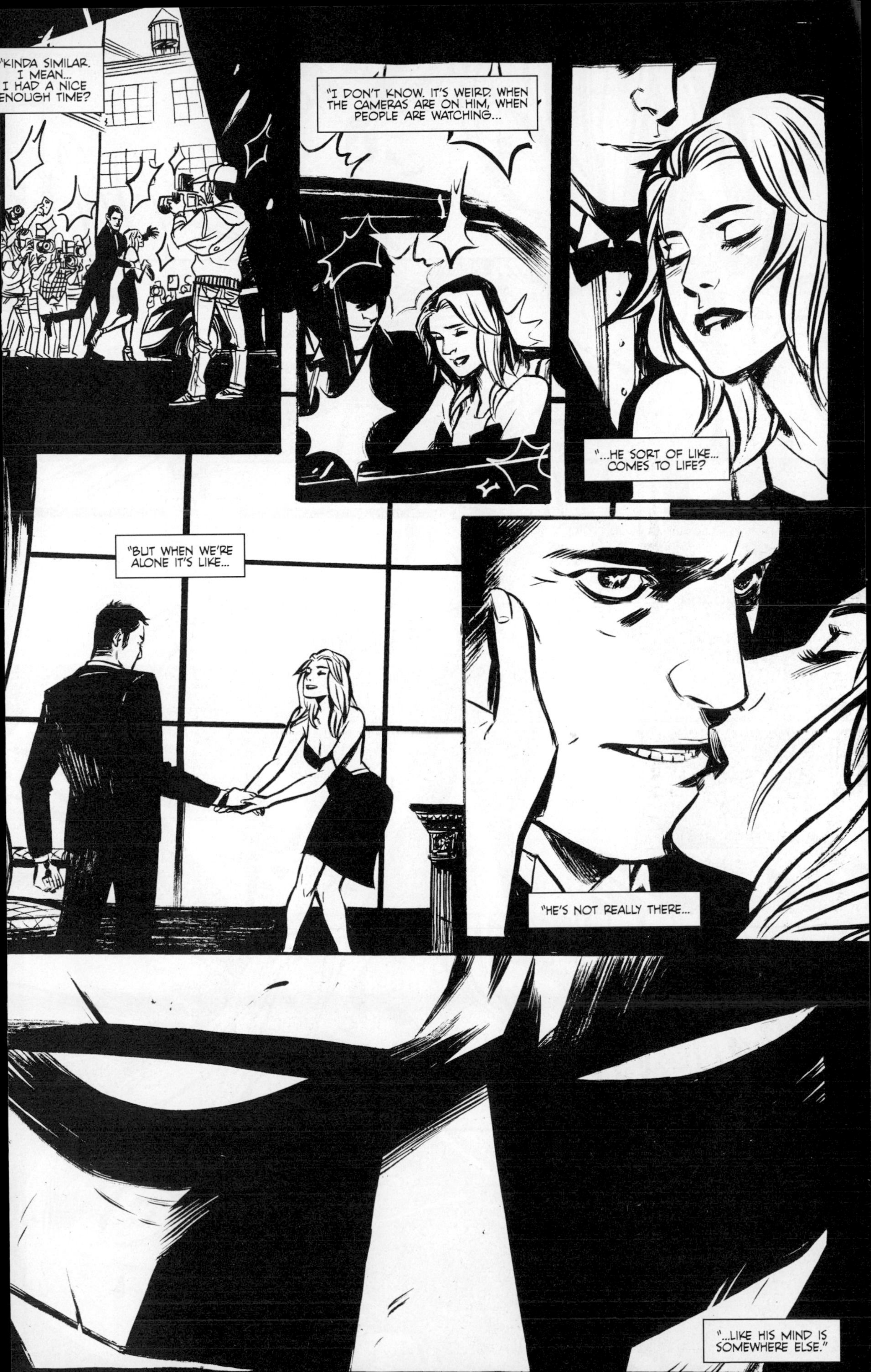
"KINDA SIMILAR. I MEAN... I HAD A NICE ENOUGH TIME?
"I DON'T KNOW. IT'S WEIRD. WHEN THE CAMERAS ARE ON HIM, WHEN PEOPLE ARE WATCHING...
"...HE SORT OF LIKE... COMES TO LIFE?
"BUT WHEN WE'RE ALONE IT'S LIKE...
"HE'S NOT REALLY THERE...
"...LIKE HIS MIND IS SOMEWHERE ELSE."

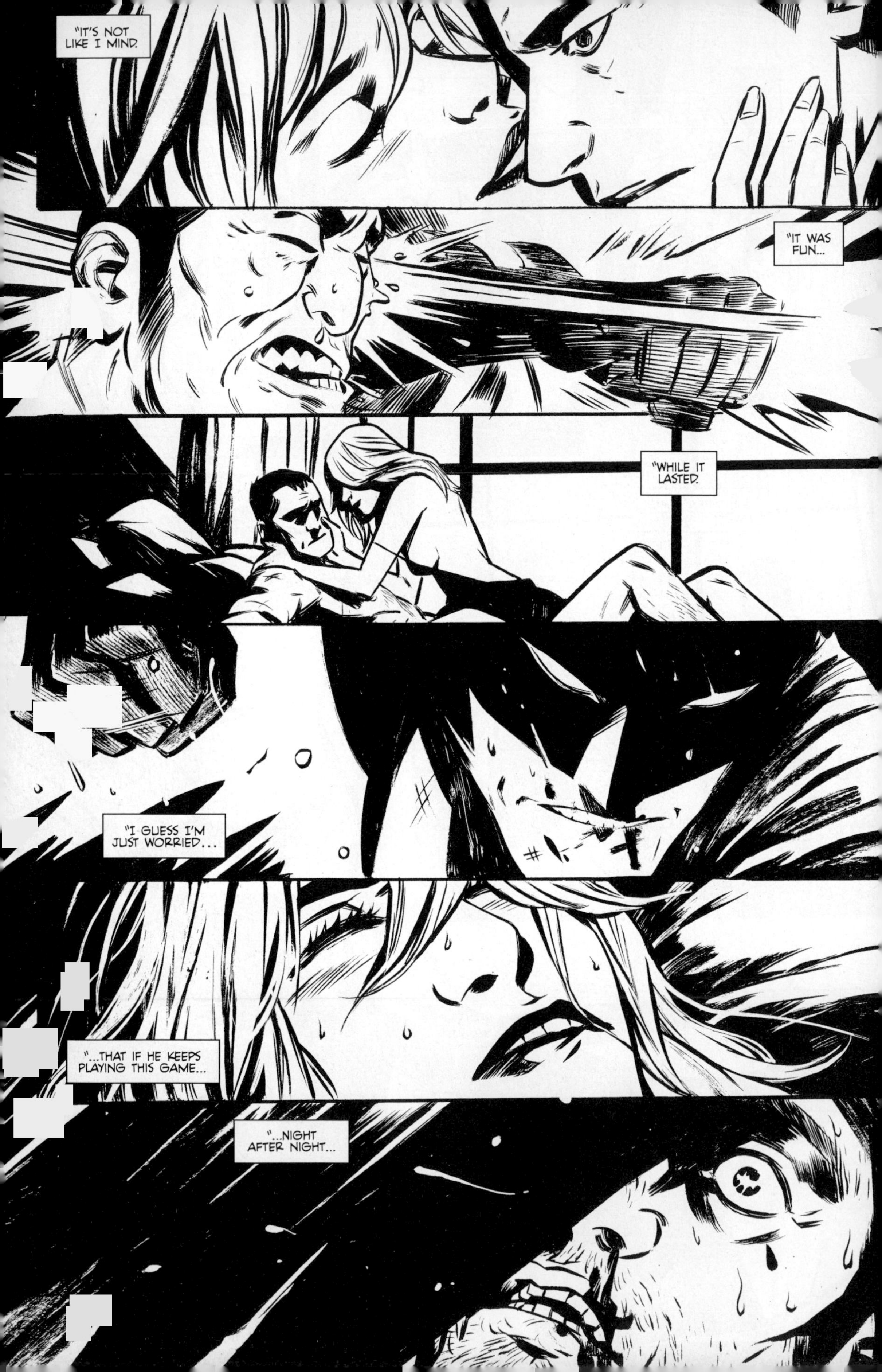
"IT'S NOT LIKE I MIND.
"IT WAS FUN...
"WHILE IT LASTED.
"I GUESS I'M JUST WORRIED...
"...THAT IF HE KEEPS PLAYING THIS GAME...
"...NIGHT AFTER NIGHT...

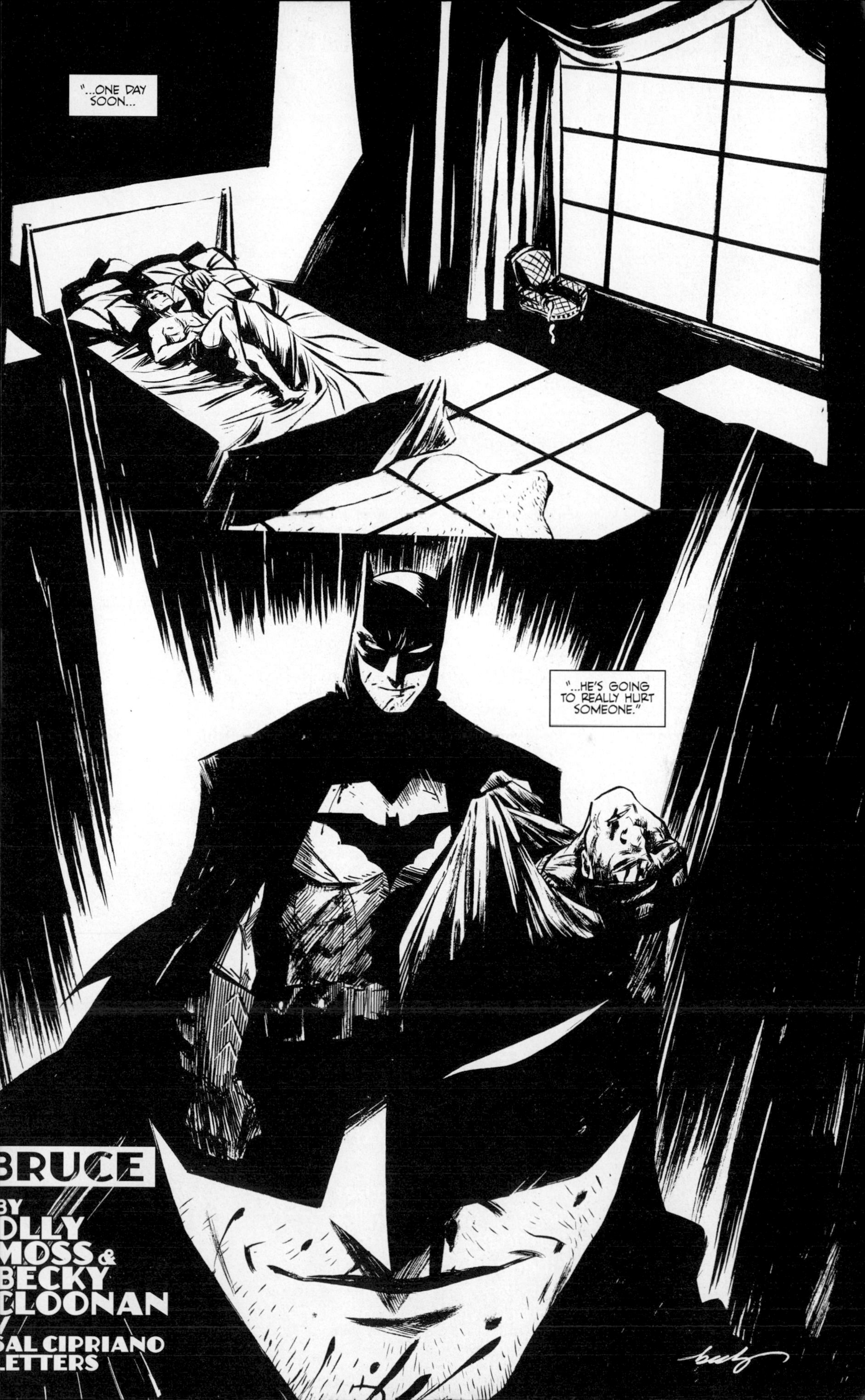
"...ONE DAY SOON...
"...HE'S GOING TO REALLY HURT SOMEONE."
BRUCE
BY
OLLY
MOSS &
BECKY
CLOONAN
SAL CIPRIANO
LETTERS

OLLY MOSS

Olly Moss is one of the leading
poster and print artists in the world. His
astounding visuals can be seen at
Mondo Prints and frequently in the pages of
Empire magazine. This marks the first
time Olly has penned a Batman tale.

BECKY CLOONAN

Becky Cloonan started her career
self-publishing mini comics in 1999. It's
something she still does, but in the years since,
she's become one of the most sought-after
writer/artists in the comics world.
A creator of tales both epic and personal,
Becky is equally at home spinning stories of
tragedy, jealousy, romance, mystery, and horror.

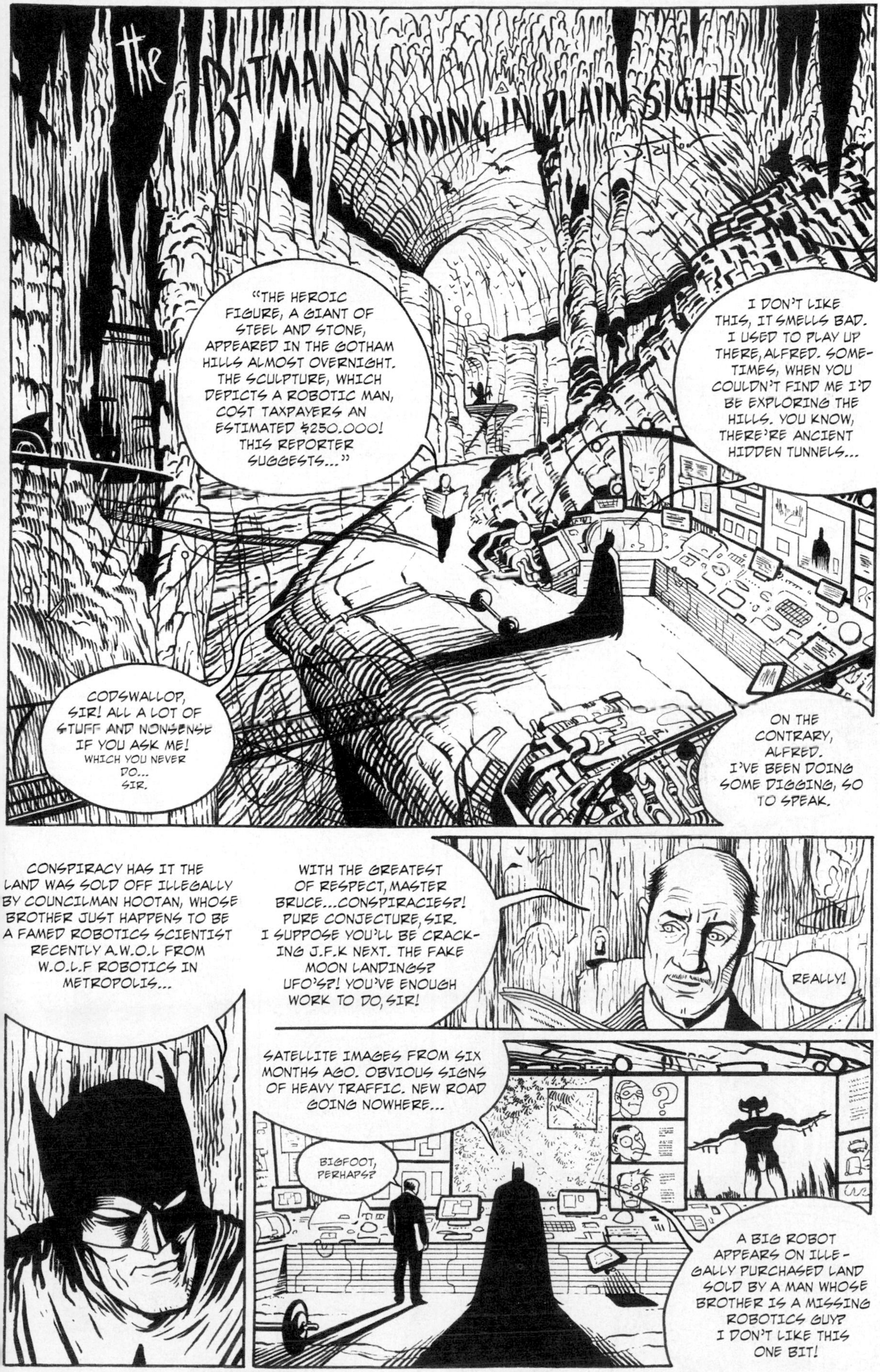

the BATMAN
HIDING IN PLAIN SIGHT
"THE HEROIC FIGURE, A GIANT OF STEEL AND STONE, APPEARED IN THE GOTHAM HILLS ALMOST OVERNIGHT. THE SCULPTURE, WHICH DEPICTS A ROBOTIC MAN, COST TAXPAYERS AN ESTIMATED $250.000! THIS REPORTER SUGGESTS..."
I DON'T LIKE THIS, IT SMELLS BAD. I USED TO PLAY UP THERE, ALFRED. SOMETIMES, WHEN YOU COULDN'T FIND ME I'D BE EXPLORING THE HILLS. YOU KNOW, THERE'RE ANCIENT HIDDEN TUNNELS...
CODSWALLOP, SIR! ALL A LOT OF STUFF AND NONSENSE IF YOU ASK ME! WHICH YOU NEVER DO... SIR.
ON THE CONTRARY, ALFRED. I'VE BEEN DOING SOME DIGGING, SO TO SPEAK.
CONSPIRACY HAS IT THE LAND WAS SOLD OFF ILLEGALLY BY COUNCILMAN HOOTAN, WHOSE BROTHER JUST HAPPENS TO BE A FAMED ROBOTICS SCIENTIST RECENTLY A.W.O.L FROM W.O.L.F ROBOTICS IN METROPOLIS...
WITH THE GREATEST OF RESPECT, MASTER BRUCE...CONSPIRACIES?! PURE CONJECTURE, SIR. I SUPPOSE YOU'LL BE CRACKING J.F.K NEXT. THE FAKE MOON LANDINGS? UFO'S?! YOU'VE ENOUGH WORK TO DO, SIR!
REALLY!
SATELLITE IMAGES FROM SIX MONTHS AGO. OBVIOUS SIGNS OF HEAVY TRAFFIC. NEW ROAD GOING NOWHERE...
BIGFOOT, PERHAPS?
A BIG ROBOT APPEARS ON ILLEGALLY PURCHASED LAND SOLD BY A MAN WHOSE BROTHER IS A MISSING ROBOTICS GUY? I DON'T LIKE THIS ONE BIT!

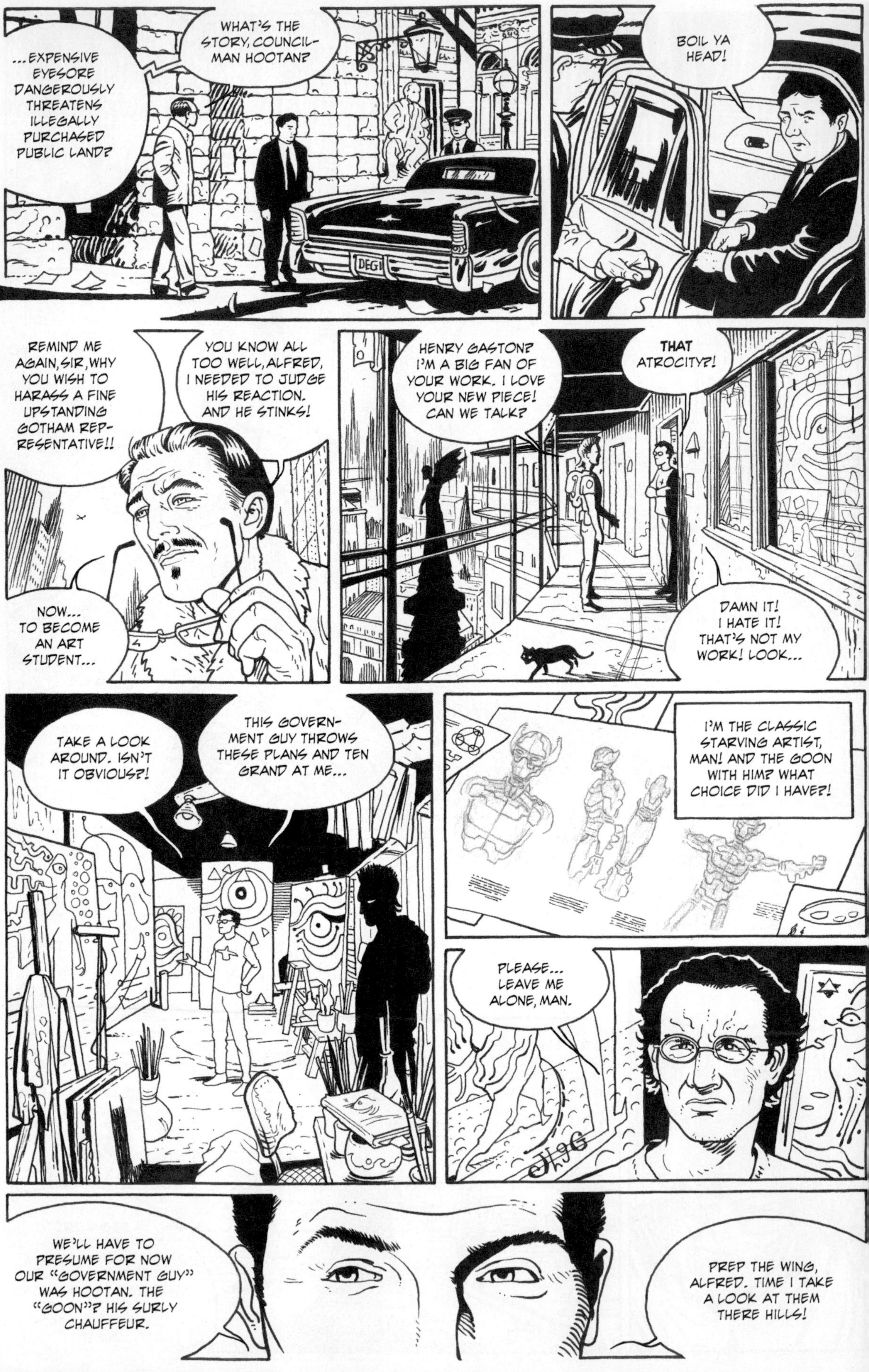
...EXPENSIVE EYESORE DANGEROUSLY THREATENS ILLEGALLY PURCHASED PUBLIC LAND?
WHAT'S THE STORY, COUNCIL-MAN HOOTAN?
DEG1
BOIL YA HEAD!
REMIND ME AGAIN, SIR, WHY YOU WISH TO HARASS A FINE UPSTANDING GOTHAM REP-RESENTATIVE!!
YOU KNOW ALL TOO WELL, ALFRED, I NEEDED TO JUDGE HIS REACTION. AND HE STINKS!
NOW... TO BECOME AN ART STUDENT...
HENRY GASTON? I'M A BIG FAN OF YOUR WORK. I LOVE YOUR NEW PIECE! CAN WE TALK?
THAT ATROCITY?!
DAMN IT! I HATE IT! THAT'S NOT MY WORK! LOOK...
TAKE A LOOK AROUND. ISN'T IT OBVIOUS?!
THIS GOVERN-MENT GUY THROWS THESE PLANS AND TEN GRAND AT ME...
I'M THE CLASSIC STARVING ARTIST, MAN! AND THE GOON WITH HIM? WHAT CHOICE DID I HAVE?!
PLEASE... LEAVE ME ALONE, MAN.
WE'LL HAVE TO PRESUME FOR NOW OUR "GOVERNMENT GUY" WAS HOOTAN. THE "GOON"? HIS SURLY CHAUFFEUR.
PREP THE WING, ALFRED. TIME I TAKE A LOOK AT THEM THERE HILLS!

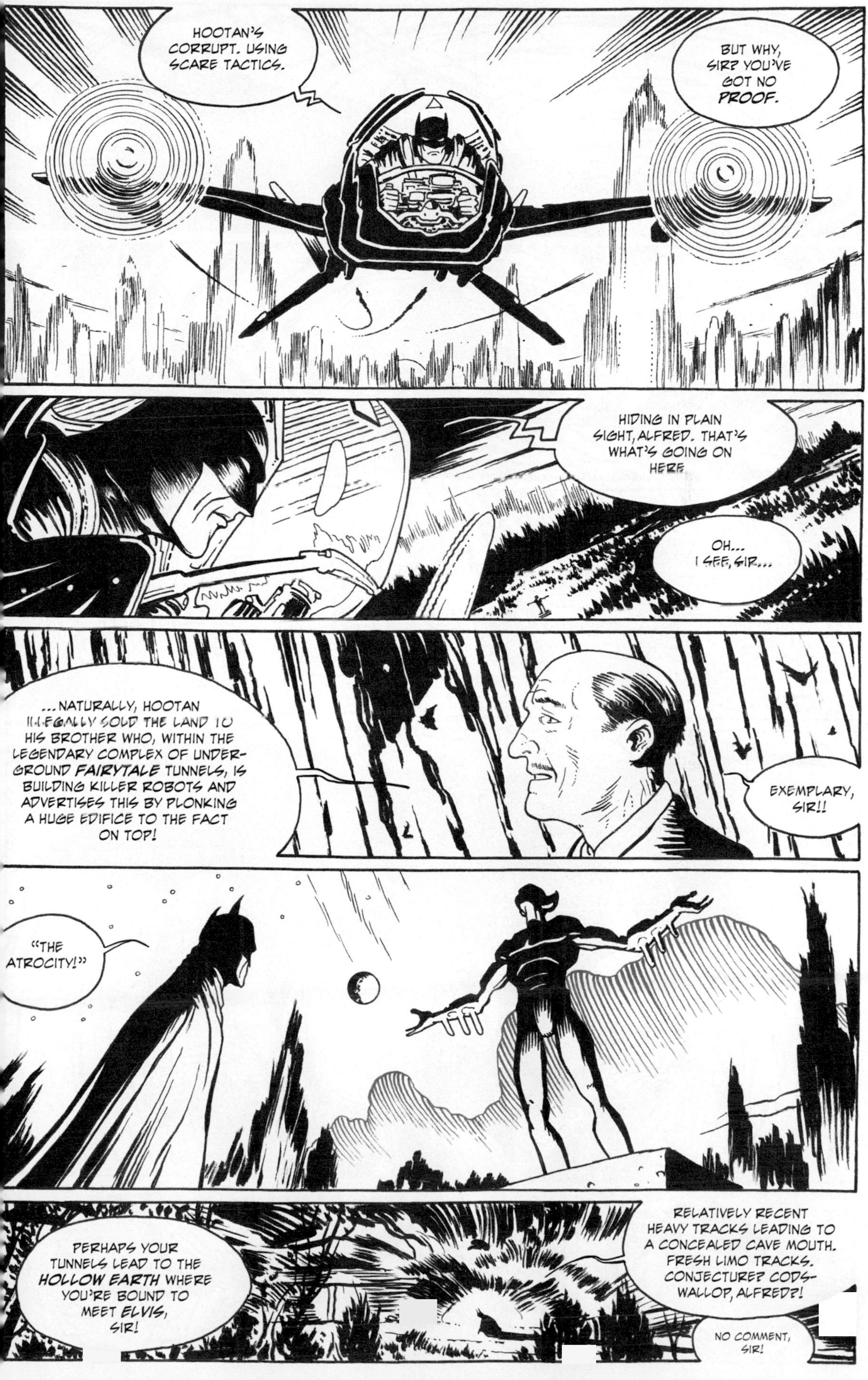
HOOTAN'S CORRUPT. USING SCARE TACTICS.
BUT WHY, SIR? YOU'VE GOT NO *PROOF*.
HIDING IN PLAIN SIGHT, ALFRED. THAT'S WHAT'S GOING ON HERE.
OH... I SEE, SIR...
...NATURALLY, HOOTAN ILLEGALLY SOLD THE LAND TO HIS BROTHER WHO, WITHIN THE LEGENDARY COMPLEX OF UNDERGROUND *FAIRYTALE* TUNNELS, IS BUILDING KILLER ROBOTS AND ADVERTISES THIS BY PLONKING A HUGE EDIFICE TO THE FACT ON TOP!
EXEMPLARY, SIR!!
"THE ATROCITY!"
PERHAPS YOUR TUNNELS LEAD TO THE *HOLLOW EARTH* WHERE YOU'RE BOUND TO MEET *ELVIS*, SIR!
RELATIVELY RECENT HEAVY TRACKS LEADING TO A CONCEALED CAVE MOUTH. FRESH LIMO TRACKS. CONJECTURE? CODSWALLOP, ALFRED?!
NO COMMENT, SIR!

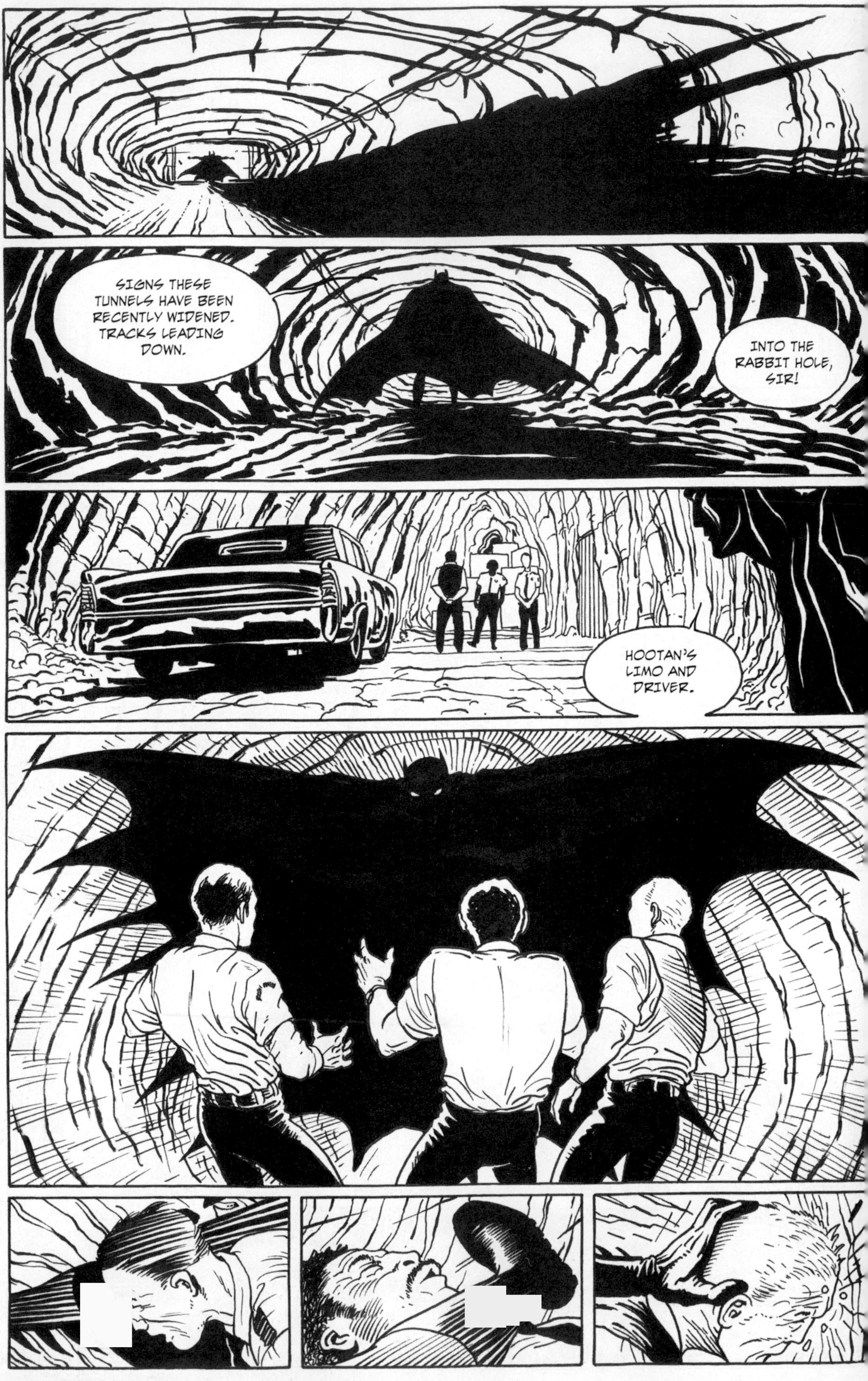
SIGNS THESE TUNNELS HAVE BEEN RECENTLY WIDENED. TRACKS LEADING DOWN.
INTO THE RABBIT HOLE, SIR!
HOOTAN'S LIMO AND DRIVER.

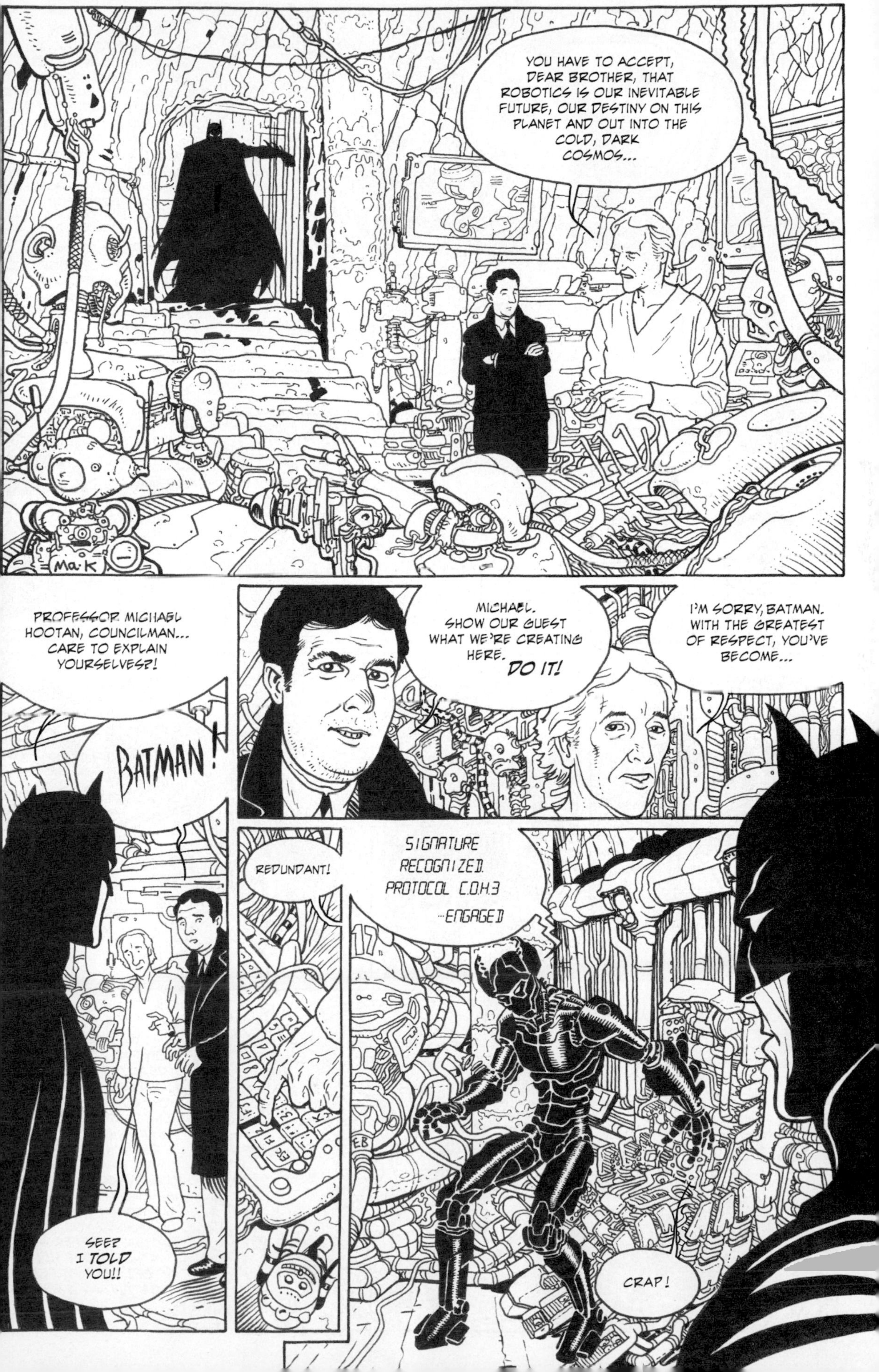
YOU HAVE TO ACCEPT, DEAR BROTHER, THAT ROBOTICS IS OUR INEVITABLE FUTURE, OUR DESTINY ON THIS PLANET AND OUT INTO THE COLD, DARK COSMOS...
PROFESSOR MICHAEL HOOTAN, COUNCILMAN... CARE TO EXPLAIN YOURSELVES?!
BATMAN!
MICHAEL. SHOW OUR GUEST WHAT WE'RE CREATING HERE. DO IT!
I'M SORRY, BATMAN. WITH THE GREATEST OF RESPECT, YOU'VE BECOME...
REDUNDANT!
SIGNATURE RECOGNIZED. PROTOCOL C.O.H.3 ...ENGAGED
SEE? I TOLD YOU!!
CRAP!

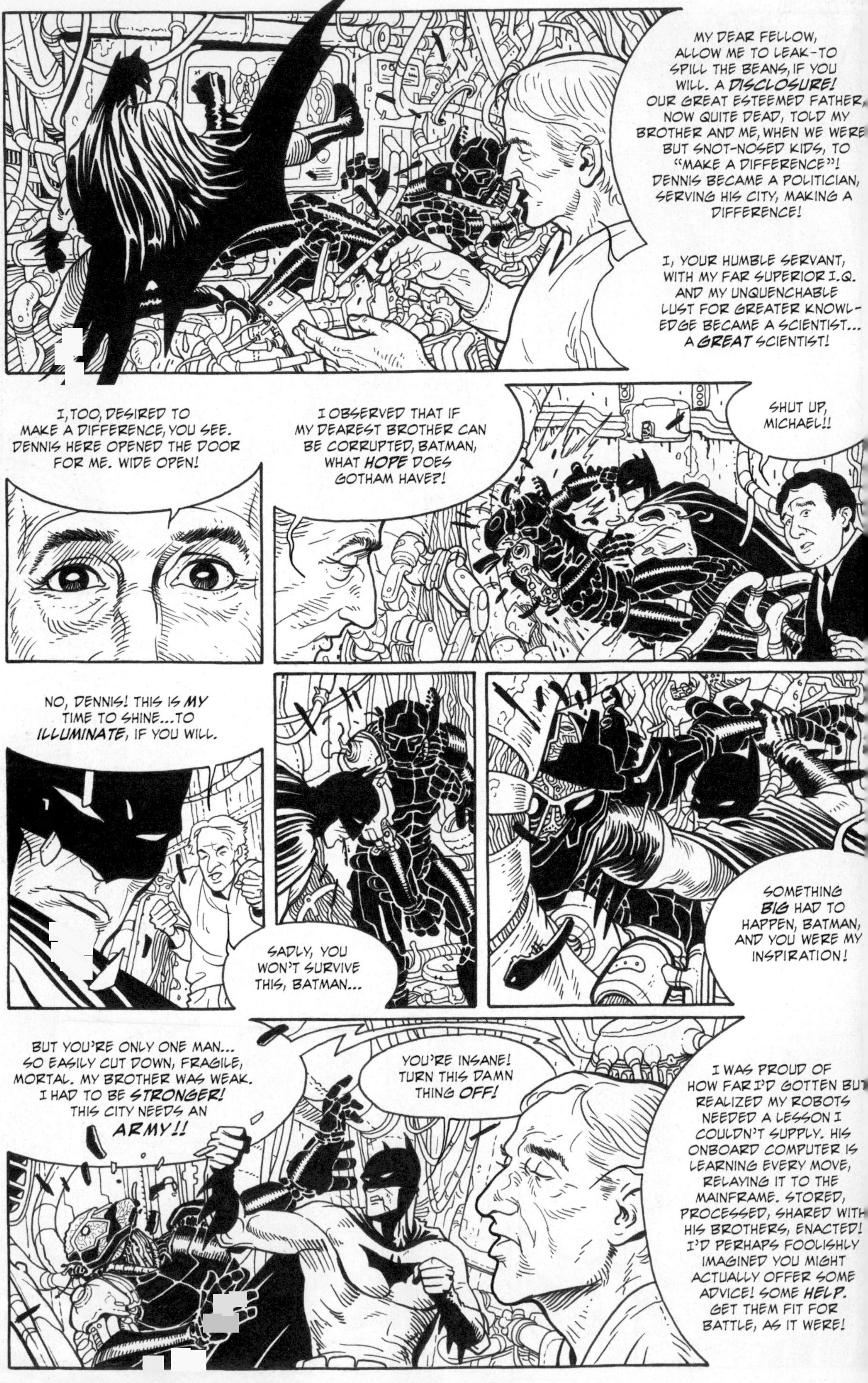
MY DEAR FELLOW, ALLOW ME TO LEAK–TO SPILL THE BEANS, IF YOU WILL. A DISCLOSURE! OUR GREAT ESTEEMED FATHER, NOW QUITE DEAD, TOLD MY BROTHER AND ME, WHEN WE WERE BUT SNOT-NOSED KIDS, TO "MAKE A DIFFERENCE"! DENNIS BECAME A POLITICIAN, SERVING HIS CITY, MAKING A DIFFERENCE!
I, YOUR HUMBLE SERVANT, WITH MY FAR SUPERIOR I.Q. AND MY UNQUENCHABLE LUST FOR GREATER KNOWLEDGE BECAME A SCIENTIST... A GREAT SCIENTIST!
I, TOO, DESIRED TO MAKE A DIFFERENCE, YOU SEE. DENNIS HERE OPENED THE DOOR FOR ME. WIDE OPEN!
I OBSERVED THAT IF MY DEAREST BROTHER CAN BE CORRUPTED, BATMAN, WHAT HOPE DOES GOTHAM HAVE?!
SHUT UP, MICHAEL!!
NO, DENNIS! THIS IS MY TIME TO SHINE...TO ILLUMINATE, IF YOU WILL.
SADLY, YOU WON'T SURVIVE THIS, BATMAN...
SOMETHING BIG HAD TO HAPPEN, BATMAN, AND YOU WERE MY INSPIRATION!
BUT YOU'RE ONLY ONE MAN... SO EASILY CUT DOWN, FRAGILE, MORTAL. MY BROTHER WAS WEAK. I HAD TO BE STRONGER! THIS CITY NEEDS AN ARMY!!
YOU'RE INSANE! TURN THIS DAMN THING OFF!
I WAS PROUD OF HOW FAR I'D GOTTEN BUT REALIZED MY ROBOTS NEEDED A LESSON I COULDN'T SUPPLY. HIS ONBOARD COMPUTER IS LEARNING EVERY MOVE, RELAYING IT TO THE MAINFRAME. STORED, PROCESSED, SHARED WITH HIS BROTHERS, ENACTED! I'D PERHAPS FOOLISHLY IMAGINED YOU MIGHT ACTUALLY OFFER SOME ADVICE! SOME HELP. GET THEM FIT FOR BATTLE, AS IT WERE!

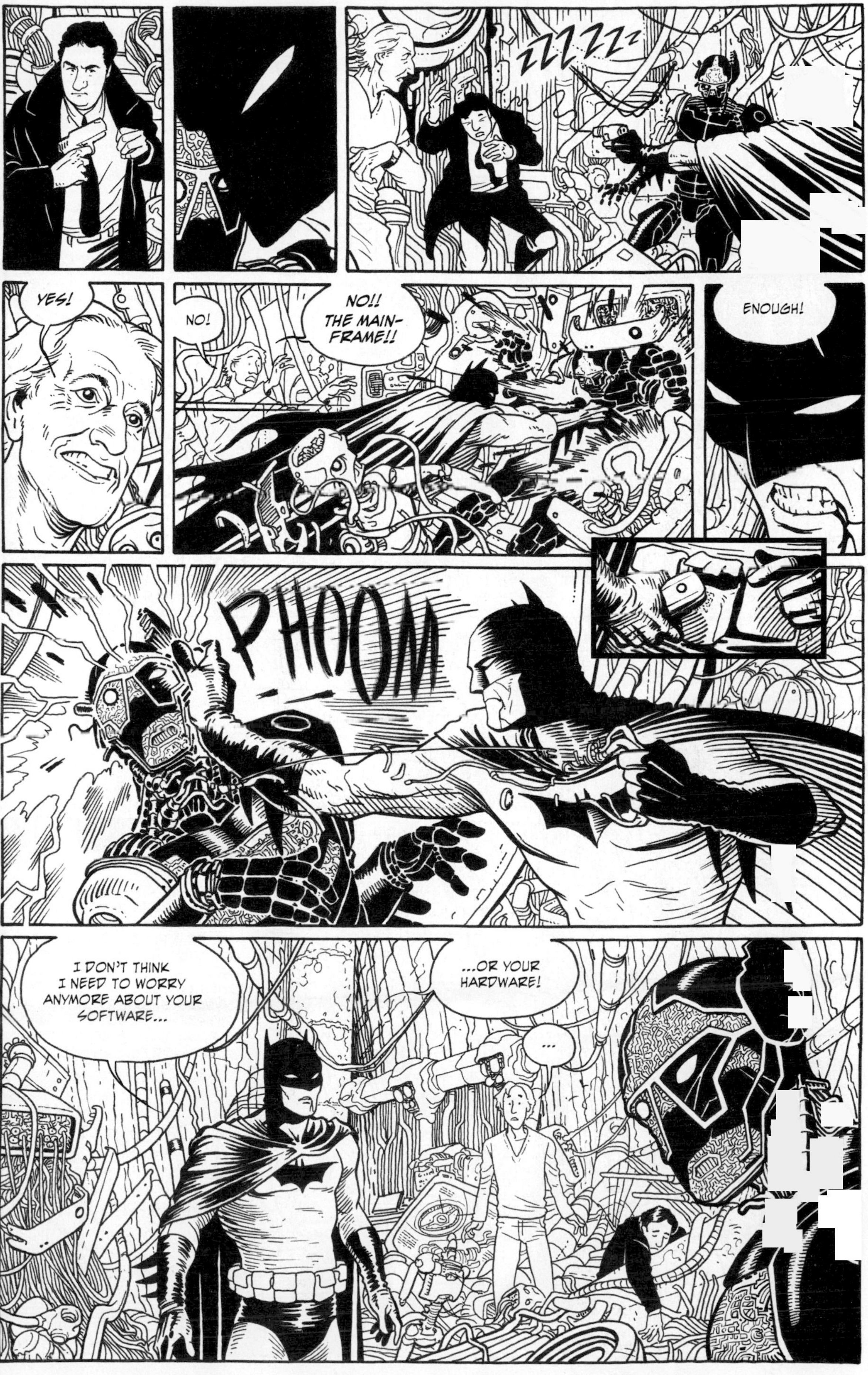
ZZZZZZ
YES!
NO!
NO!! THE MAIN-FRAME!!
ENOUGH!
PHOOM
I DON'T THINK I NEED TO WORRY ANYMORE ABOUT YOUR SOFTWARE...
...OR YOUR HARDWARE!
...

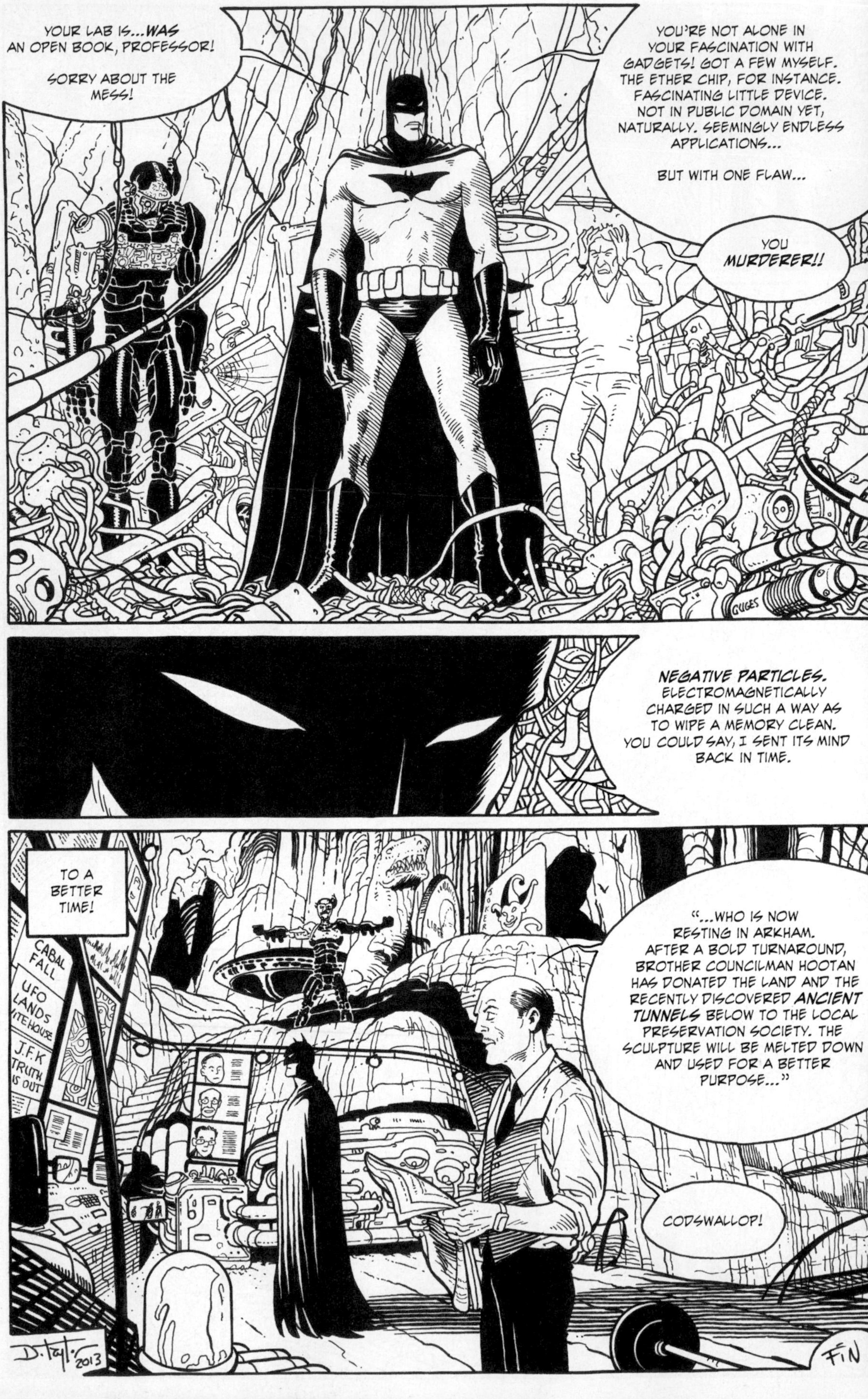
YOUR LAB IS...WAS AN OPEN BOOK, PROFESSOR!
SORRY ABOUT THE MESS!
YOU'RE NOT ALONE IN YOUR FASCINATION WITH GADGETS! GOT A FEW MYSELF. THE ETHER CHIP, FOR INSTANCE. FASCINATING LITTLE DEVICE. NOT IN PUBLIC DOMAIN YET, NATURALLY. SEEMINGLY ENDLESS APPLICATIONS...
BUT WITH ONE FLAW...
YOU MURDERER!!
NEGATIVE PARTICLES. ELECTROMAGNETICALLY CHARGED IN SUCH A WAY AS TO WIPE A MEMORY CLEAN. YOU COULD SAY, I SENT ITS MIND BACK IN TIME.
TO A BETTER TIME!
CABAL FALL
UFO LANDS
J.F.K TRUTH IS OUT
"...WHO IS NOW RESTING IN ARKHAM. AFTER A BOLD TURNAROUND, BROTHER COUNCILMAN HOOTAN HAS DONATED THE LAND AND THE RECENTLY DISCOVERED ANCIENT TUNNELS BELOW TO THE LOCAL PRESERVATION SOCIETY. THE SCULPTURE WILL BE MELTED DOWN AND USED FOR A BETTER PURPOSE..."
CODSWALLOP!
D. Taylor 2013
FIN

DAVE TAYLOR

Having drawn many issues of
BATMAN: SHADOW OF THE BAT,
DETECTIVE COMICS, and WORLD'S FINEST,
as well as the *New York Times* bestseller
BATMAN: DEATH BY DESIGN, artist/writer
Dave Taylor is no stranger to exploits
of the Dark Knight.
Synthesizing European and
American comics styles as well as Victorian
and turn-of-century illustration, Taylor's artwork
is always uniquely and brilliantly his own.

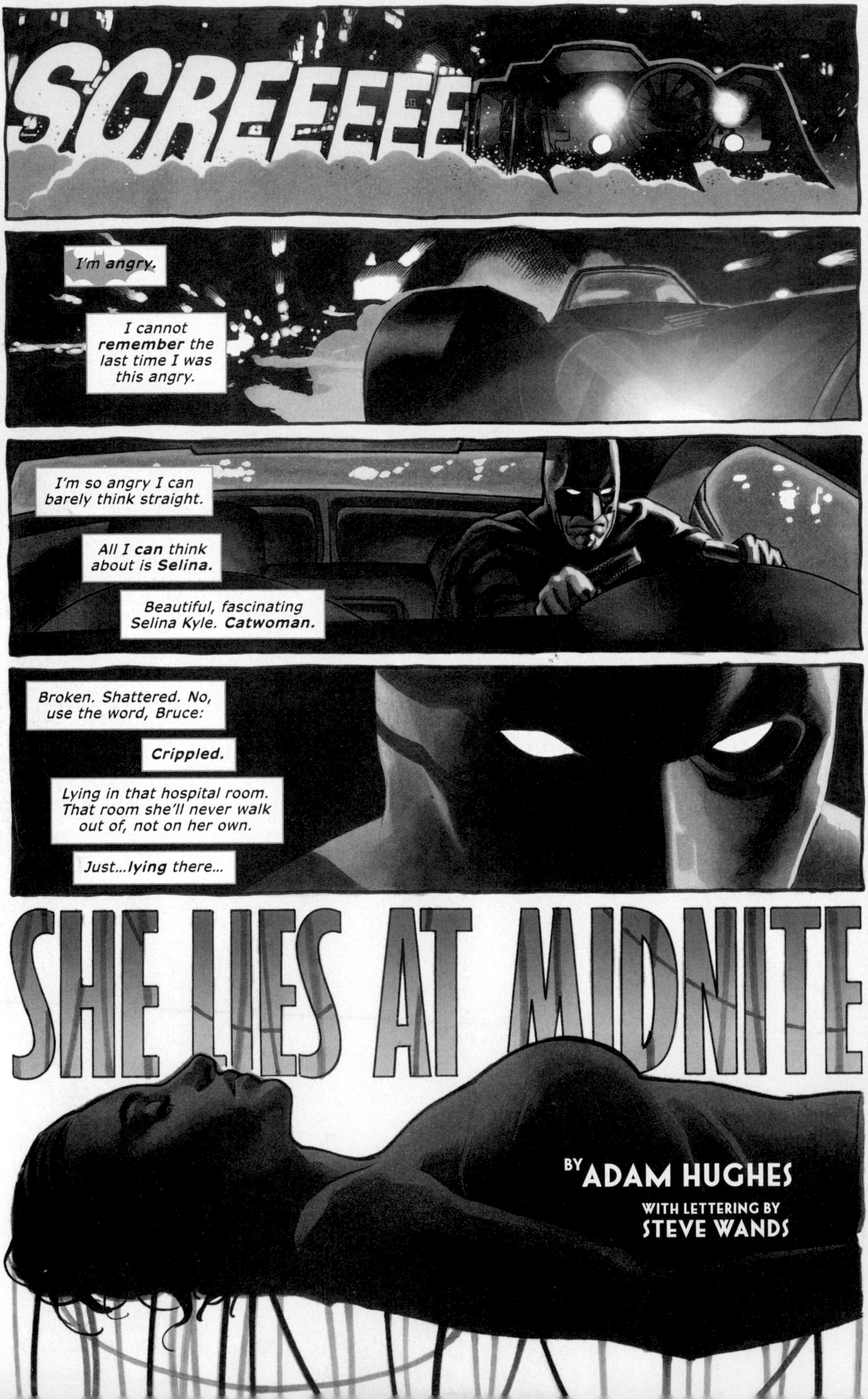
SCREEEEE
I'm angry.
I cannot remember the last time I was this angry.
I'm so angry I can barely think straight.
All I can think about is Selina.
Beautiful, fascinating Selina Kyle. Catwoman.
Broken. Shattered. No, use the word, Bruce:
Crippled.
Lying in that hospital room. That room she'll never walk out of, not on her own.
Just...lying there...
SHE LIES AT MIDNITE
BY ADAM HUGHES
WITH LETTERING BY STEVE WANDS

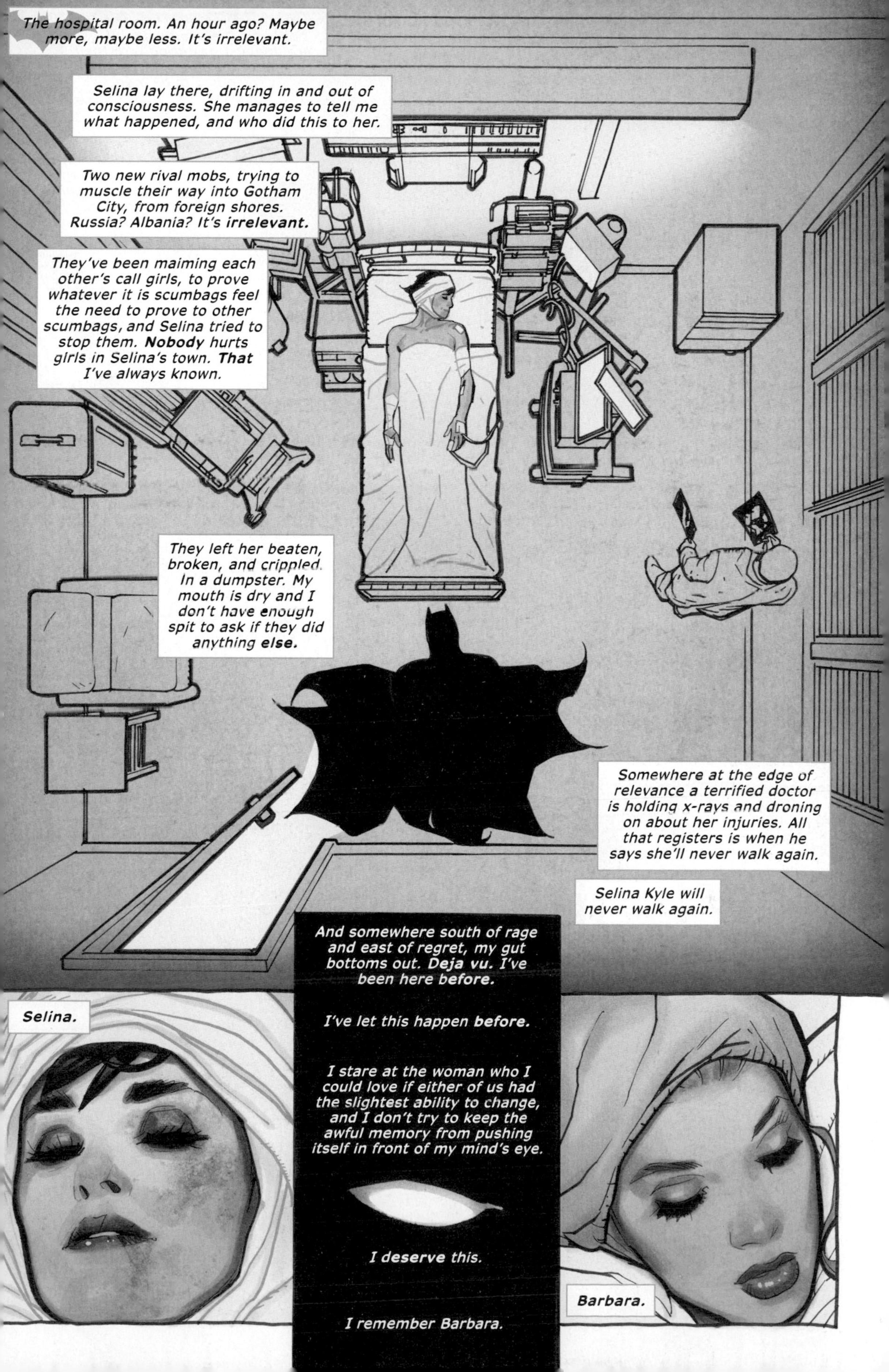

The hospital room. An hour ago? Maybe more, maybe less. It's irrelevant.
Selina lay there, drifting in and out of consciousness. She manages to tell me what happened, and who did this to her.
Two new rival mobs, trying to muscle their way into Gotham City, from foreign shores. Russia? Albania? It's **irrelevant.**
They've been maiming each other's call girls, to prove whatever it is scumbags feel the need to prove to other scumbags, and Selina tried to stop them. **Nobody** hurts girls in Selina's town. **That** I've always known.
They left her beaten, broken, and crippled. In a dumpster. My mouth is dry and I don't have enough spit to ask if they did anything **else.**
Somewhere at the edge of relevance a terrified doctor is holding x-rays and droning on about her injuries. All that registers is when he says she'll never walk again.
Selina Kyle will never walk again.
And somewhere south of rage and east of regret, my gut bottoms out. **Deja vu.** I've been here **before.**
I've let this happen **before.**
I stare at the woman who I could love if either of us had the slightest ability to change, and I don't try to keep the awful memory from pushing itself in front of my mind's eye.
I deserve this.
I remember Barbara.
Selina.
Barbara.

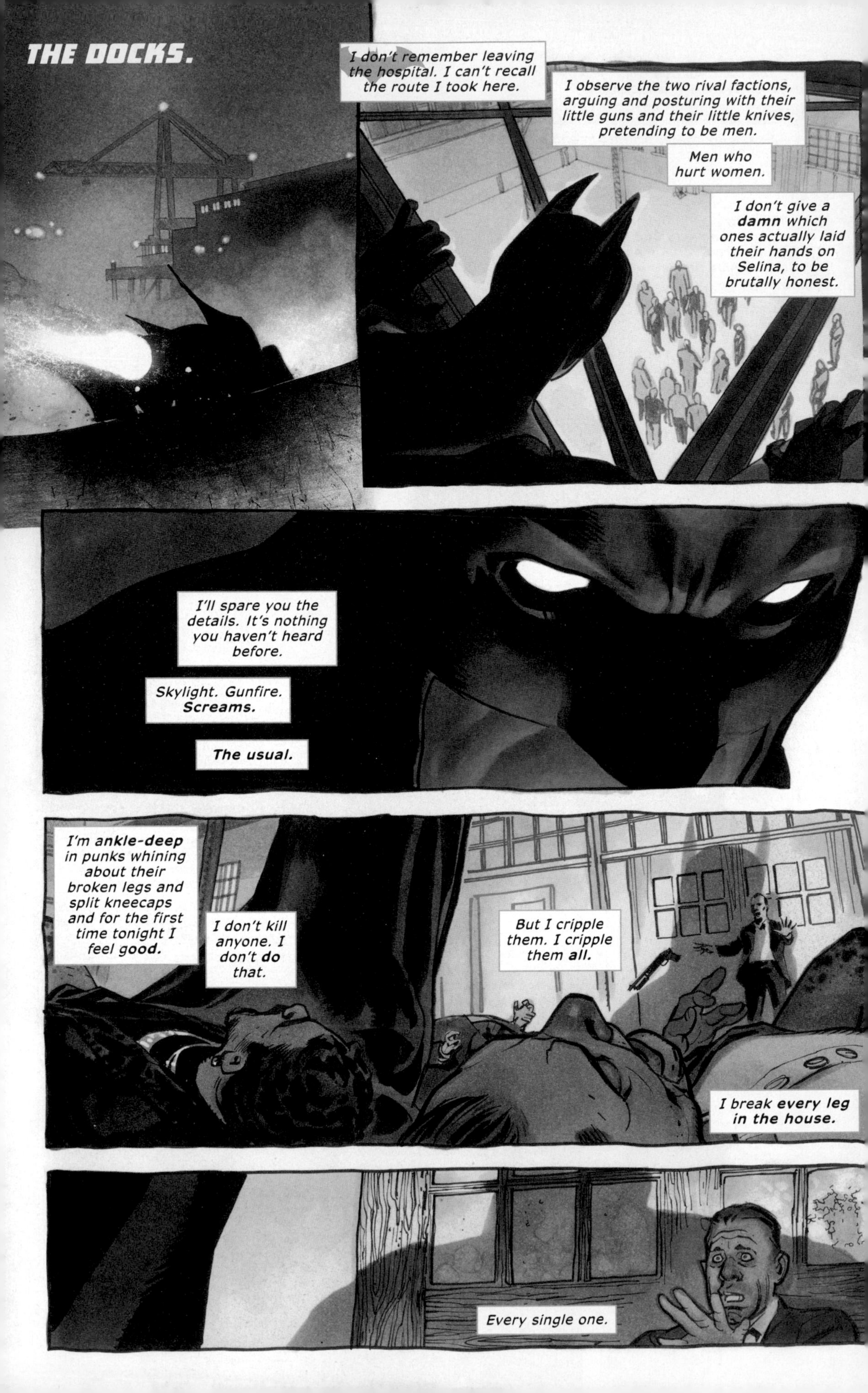
THE DOCKS.
I don't remember leaving the hospital. I can't recall the route I took here.
I observe the two rival factions, arguing and posturing with their little guns and their little knives, pretending to be men.
Men who hurt women.
I don't give a damn which ones actually laid their hands on Selina, to be brutally honest.
I'll spare you the details. It's nothing you haven't heard before.
Skylight. Gunfire. Screams.
The usual.
I'm ankle-deep in punks whining about their broken legs and split kneecaps and for the first time tonight I feel good.
I don't kill anyone. I don't do that.
But I cripple them. I cripple them all.
I break every leg in the house.
Every single one.

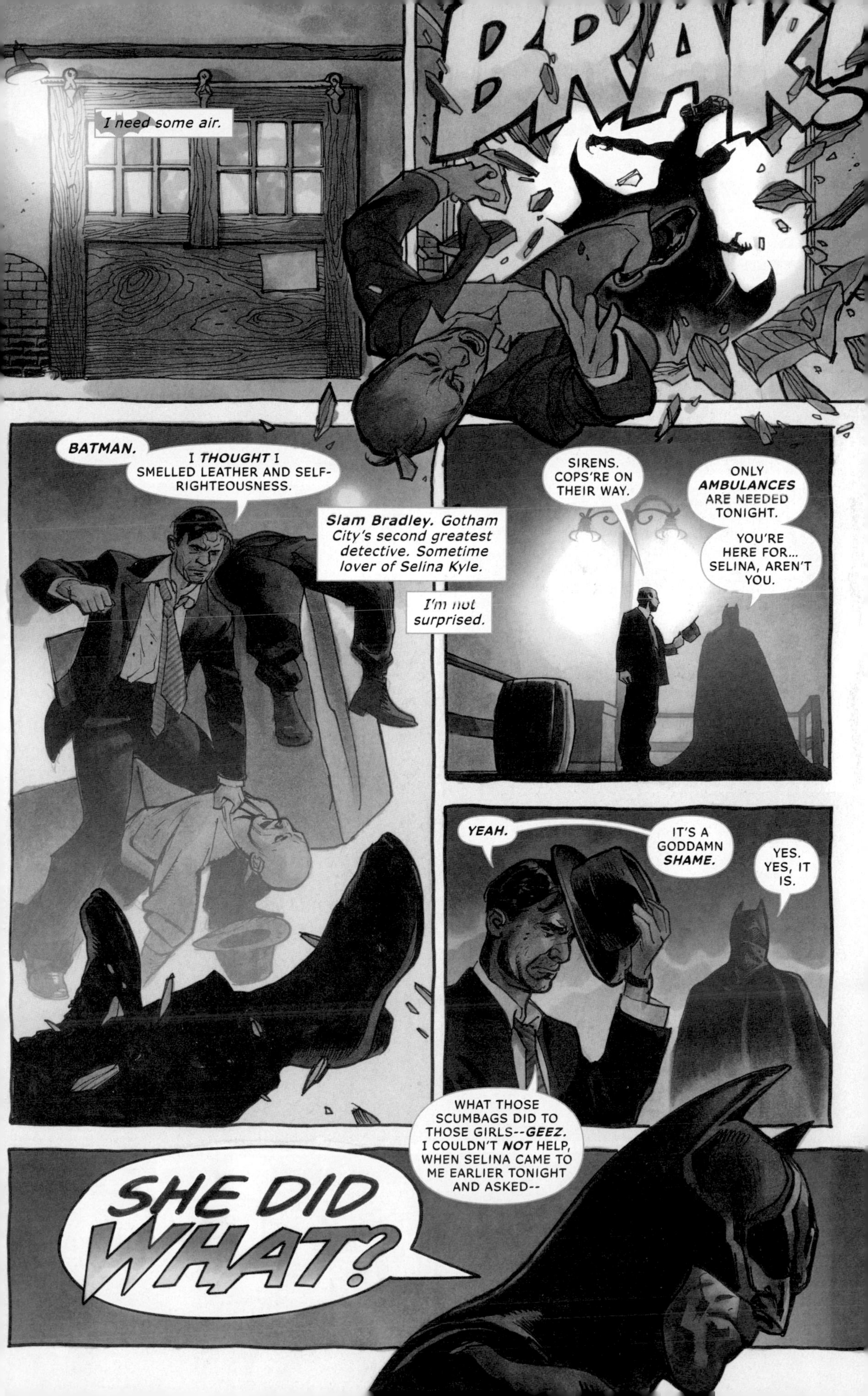
I need some air.
BRAK!
BATMAN.
I *THOUGHT* I SMELLED LEATHER AND SELF-RIGHTEOUSNESS.
Slam Bradley. Gotham City's second greatest detective. Sometime lover of Selina Kyle.
I'm not surprised.
SIRENS. COPS'RE ON THEIR WAY.
ONLY *AMBULANCES* ARE NEEDED TONIGHT.
YOU'RE HERE FOR... SELINA, AREN'T YOU.
YEAH.
IT'S A GODDAMN *SHAME.*
YES. YES, IT IS.
WHAT THOSE SCUMBAGS DID TO THOSE GIRLS--*GEEZ.* I COULDN'T *NOT* HELP, WHEN SELINA CAME TO ME EARLIER TONIGHT AND ASKED--
SHE DID WHAT?

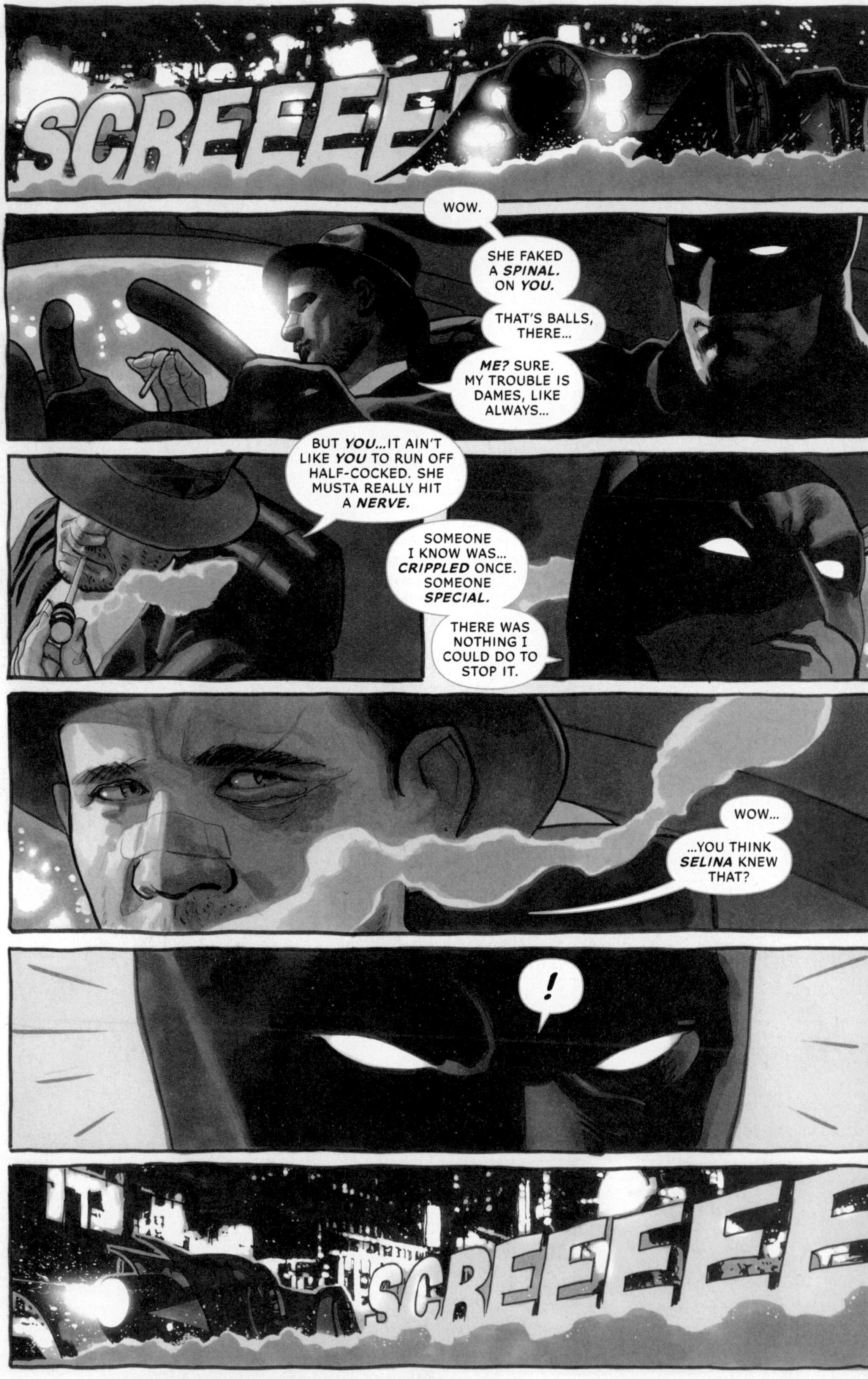
SCREEEEE
WOW.
SHE FAKED A SPINAL. ON YOU.
THAT'S BALLS, THERE...
ME? SURE. MY TROUBLE IS DAMES, LIKE ALWAYS...
BUT YOU...IT AIN'T LIKE YOU TO RUN OFF HALF-COCKED. SHE MUSTA REALLY HIT A NERVE.
SOMEONE I KNOW WAS... CRIPPLED ONCE. SOMEONE SPECIAL.
THERE WAS NOTHING I COULD DO TO STOP IT.
WOW...
...YOU THINK SELINA KNEW THAT?
!
SCREEEEE

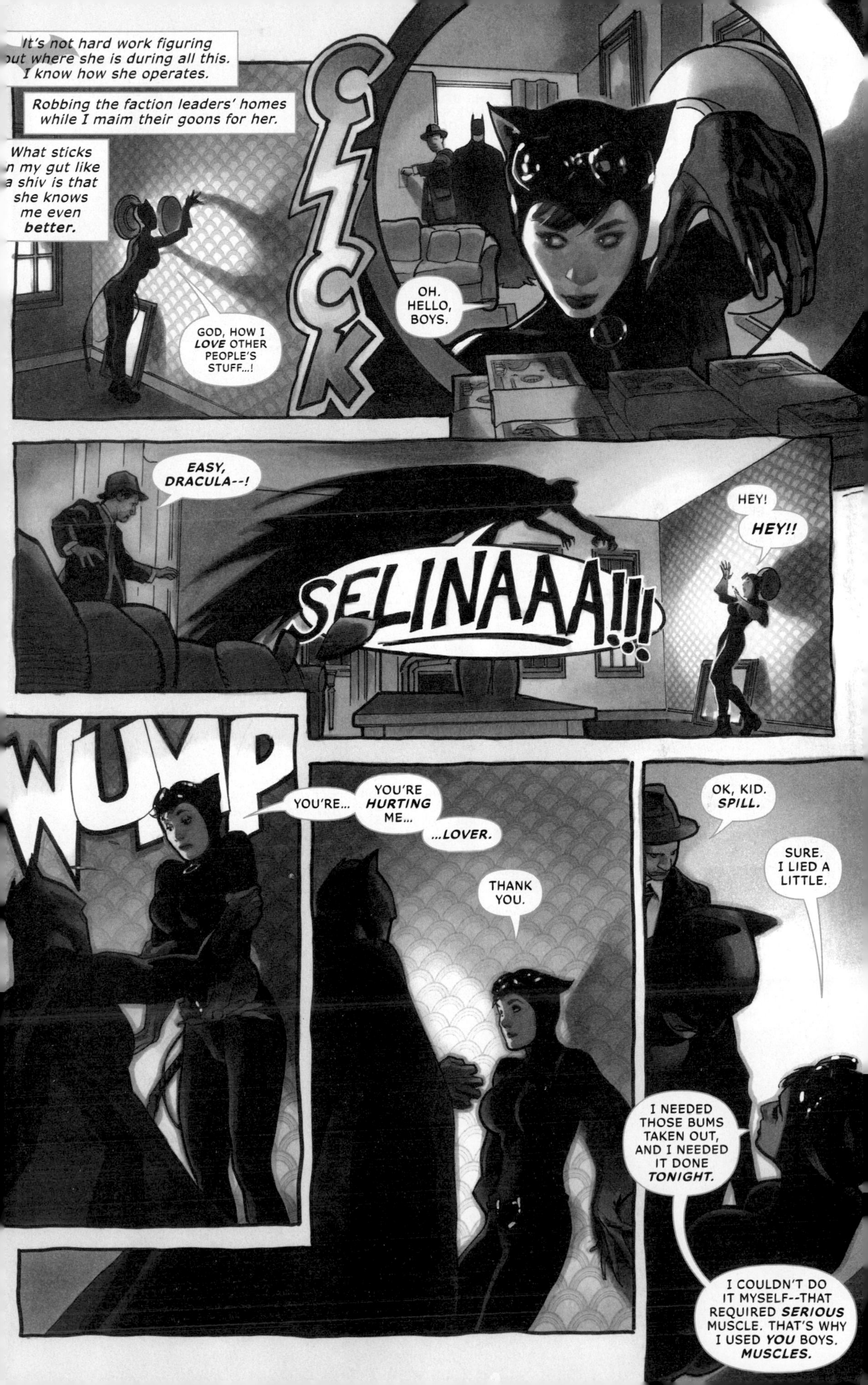
It's not hard work figuring out where she is during all this. I know how she operates.
Robbing the faction leaders' homes while I maim their goons for her.
What sticks in my gut like a shiv is that she knows me even **better.**
GOD, HOW I ***LOVE*** OTHER PEOPLE'S STUFF...!
CLICK
OH. HELLO, BOYS.
EASY, DRACULA--!
HEY!
HEY!!
SELINAAA!!!
WUMP
YOU'RE...
YOU'RE ***HURTING*** ME...
...LOVER.
THANK YOU.
OK, KID. ***SPILL.***
SURE. I LIED A LITTLE.
I NEEDED THOSE BUMS TAKEN OUT, AND I NEEDED IT DONE ***TONIGHT.***
I COULDN'T DO IT MYSELF--THAT REQUIRED ***SERIOUS*** MUSCLE. THAT'S WHY I USED ***YOU*** BOYS. ***MUSCLES.***

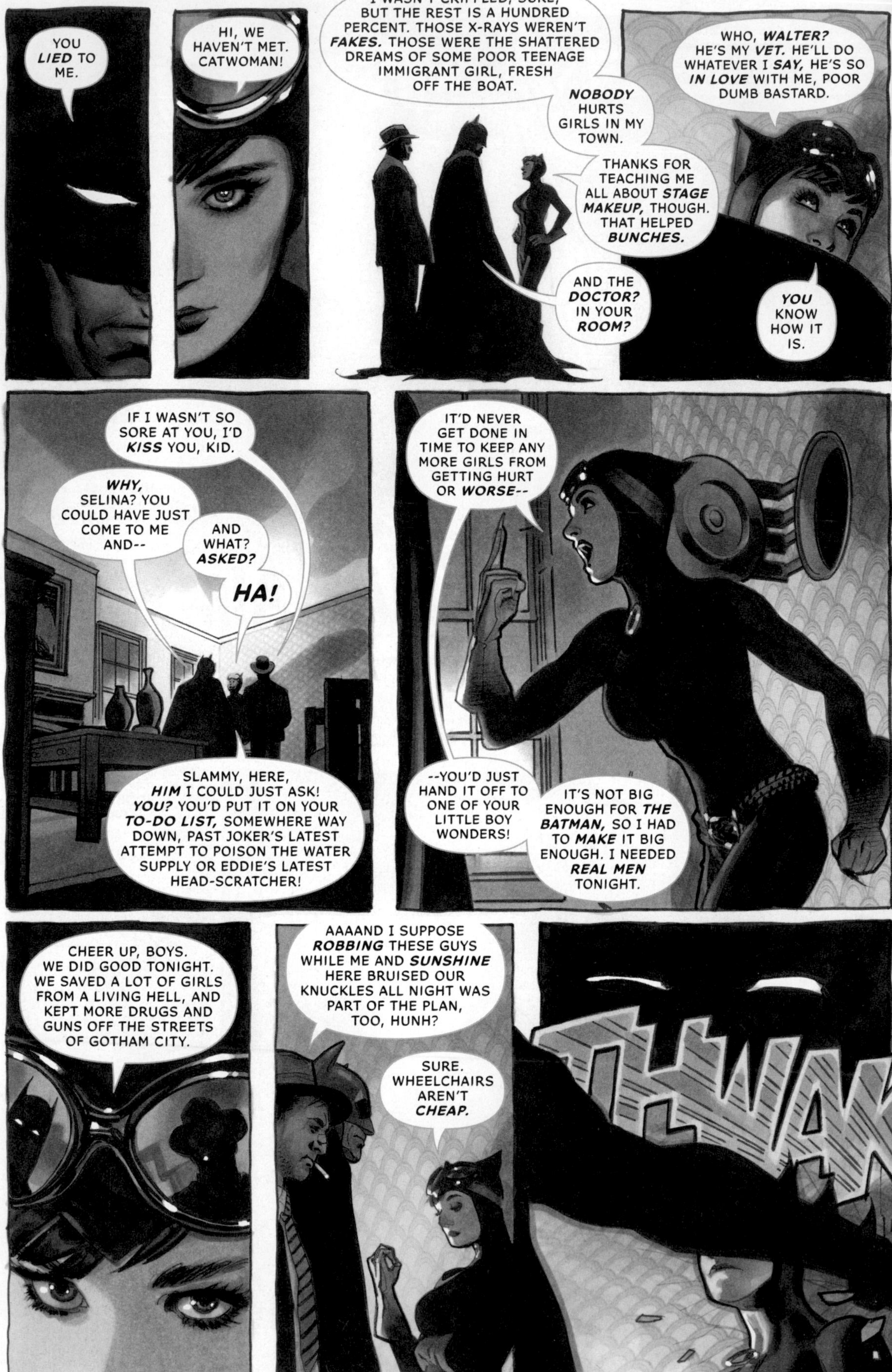
YOU LIED TO ME.
HI, WE HAVEN'T MET. CATWOMAN!
I WASN'T CRIPPLED, SURE, BUT THE REST IS A HUNDRED PERCENT. THOSE X-RAYS WEREN'T FAKES. THOSE WERE THE SHATTERED DREAMS OF SOME POOR TEENAGE IMMIGRANT GIRL, FRESH OFF THE BOAT.
NOBODY HURTS GIRLS IN MY TOWN.
THANKS FOR TEACHING ME ALL ABOUT STAGE MAKEUP, THOUGH. THAT HELPED BUNCHES.
AND THE DOCTOR? IN YOUR ROOM?
WHO, WALTER? HE'S MY VET. HE'LL DO WHATEVER I SAY, HE'S SO IN LOVE WITH ME, POOR DUMB BASTARD.
YOU KNOW HOW IT IS.
IF I WASN'T SO SORE AT YOU, I'D KISS YOU, KID.
WHY, SELINA? YOU COULD HAVE JUST COME TO ME AND--
AND WHAT? ASKED?
HA!
SLAMMY, HERE, HIM I COULD JUST ASK! YOU? YOU'D PUT IT ON YOUR TO-DO LIST, SOMEWHERE WAY DOWN, PAST JOKER'S LATEST ATTEMPT TO POISON THE WATER SUPPLY OR EDDIE'S LATEST HEAD-SCRATCHER!
IT'D NEVER GET DONE IN TIME TO KEEP ANY MORE GIRLS FROM GETTING HURT OR WORSE--
--YOU'D JUST HAND IT OFF TO ONE OF YOUR LITTLE BOY WONDERS!
IT'S NOT BIG ENOUGH FOR THE BATMAN, SO I HAD TO MAKE IT BIG ENOUGH. I NEEDED REAL MEN TONIGHT.
CHEER UP, BOYS. WE DID GOOD TONIGHT. WE SAVED A LOT OF GIRLS FROM A LIVING HELL, AND KEPT MORE DRUGS AND GUNS OFF THE STREETS OF GOTHAM CITY.
AAAAND I SUPPOSE ROBBING THESE GUYS WHILE ME AND SUNSHINE HERE BRUISED OUR KNUCKLES ALL NIGHT WAS PART OF THE PLAN, TOO, HUNH?
SURE. WHEELCHAIRS AREN'T CHEAP.

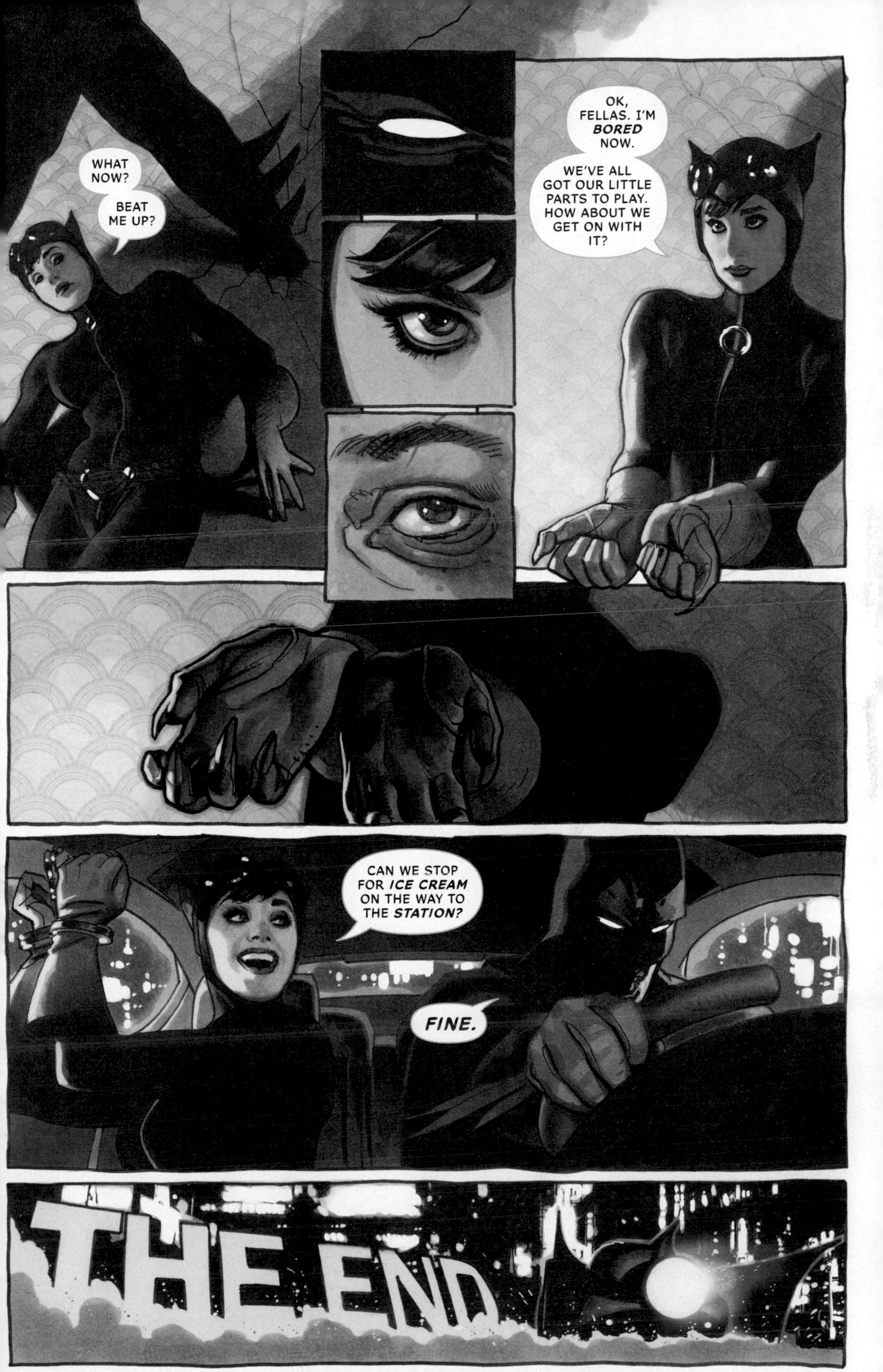
WHAT NOW?
BEAT ME UP?
OK, FELLAS. I'M BORED NOW.
WE'VE ALL GOT OUR LITTLE PARTS TO PLAY. HOW ABOUT WE GET ON WITH IT?
CAN WE STOP FOR ICE CREAM ON THE WAY TO THE STATION?
FINE.
THE END

ADAM HUGHES

A draftsman of extraordinary skill,
Adam Hughes is quite simply a modern master
in the world of comics. His astonishing covers for
WONDER WOMAN, CATWOMAN, FAIREST and
many, many others have set the high water
mark for all other cover artists to follow.

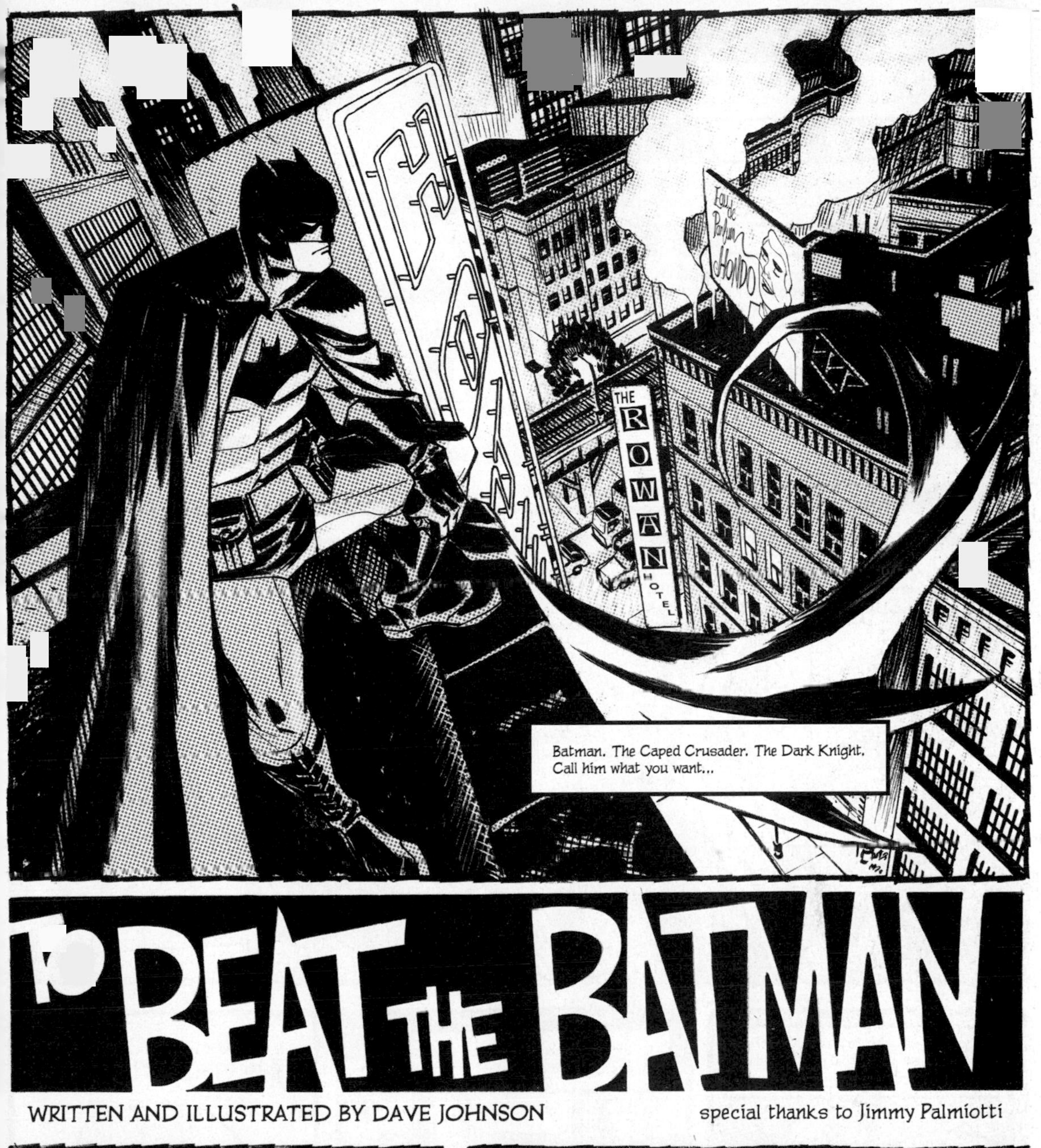
THE ROWAN HOTEL
Batman. The Caped Crusader. The Dark Knight. Call him what you want...

TO BEAT THE BATMAN

WRITTEN AND ILLUSTRATED BY DAVE JOHNSON

special thanks to Jimmy Palmiotti

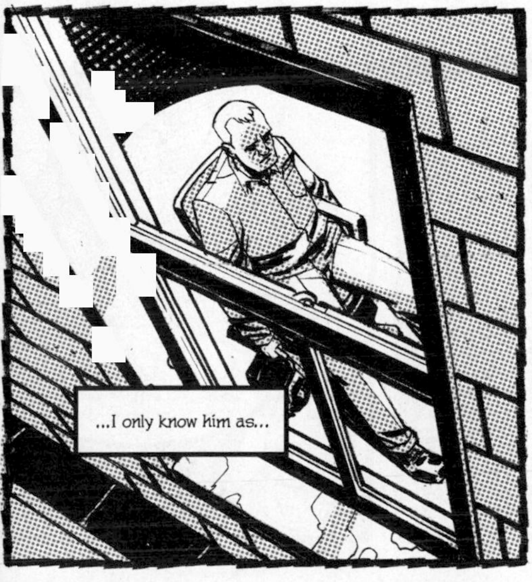
...I only know him as...

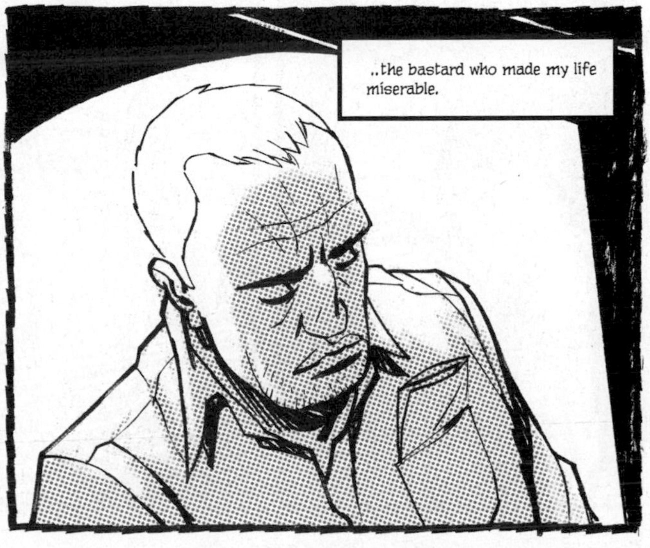
..the bastard who made my life miserable.

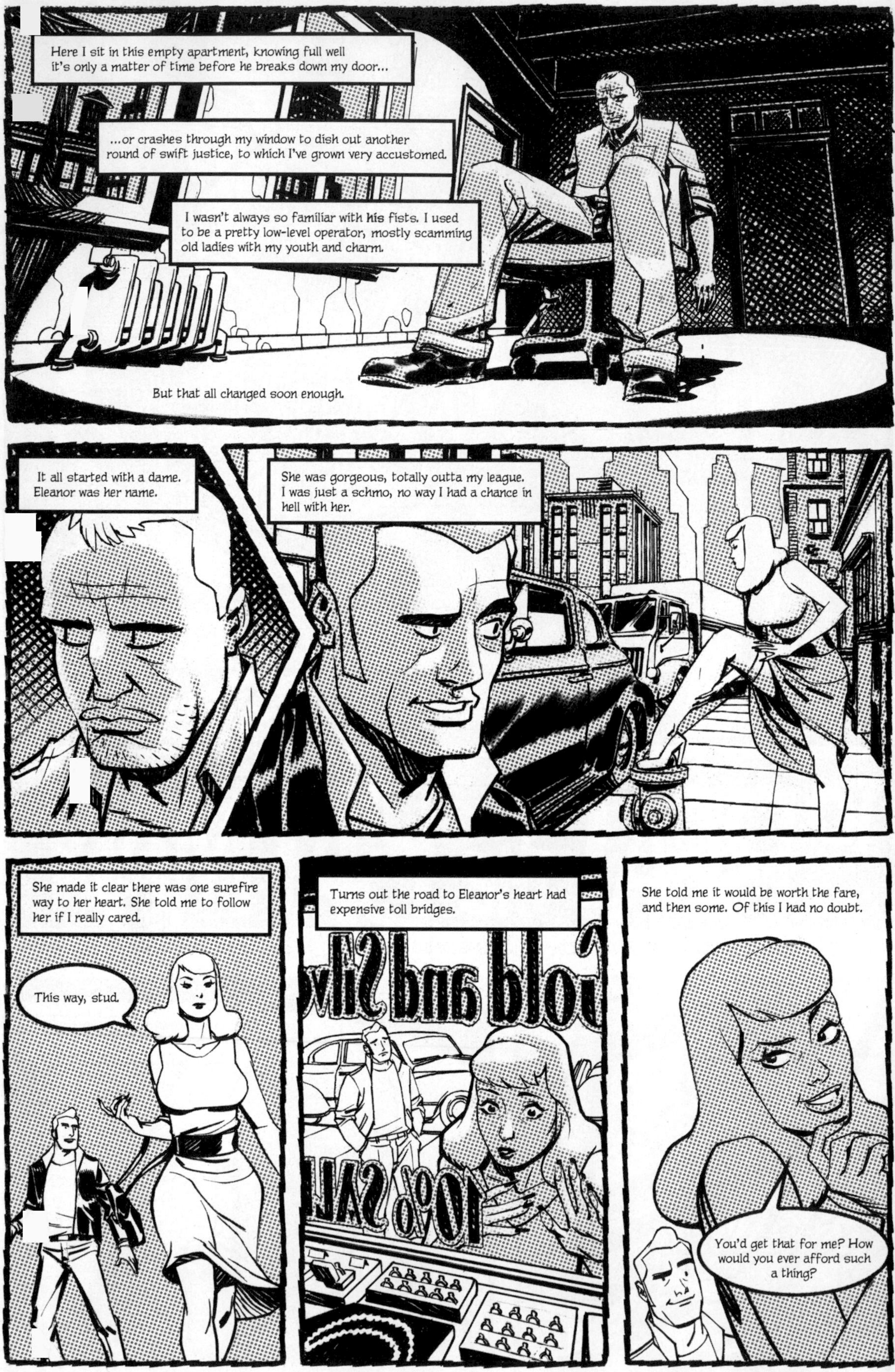

Here I sit in this empty apartment, knowing full well it's only a matter of time before he breaks down my door...
...or crashes through my window to dish out another round of swift justice, to which I've grown very accustomed.
I wasn't always so familiar with his fists. I used to be a pretty low-level operator, mostly scamming old ladies with my youth and charm.
But that all changed soon enough.
It all started with a dame. Eleanor was her name.
She was gorgeous, totally outta my league. I was just a schmo, no way I had a chance in hell with her.
She made it clear there was one surefire way to her heart. She told me to follow her if I really cared.
This way, stud.
Turns out the road to Eleanor's heart had expensive toll bridges.
Gold and Silv
10% SALE
She told me it would be worth the fare, and then some. Of this I had no doubt.
You'd get that for me? How would you ever afford such a thing?

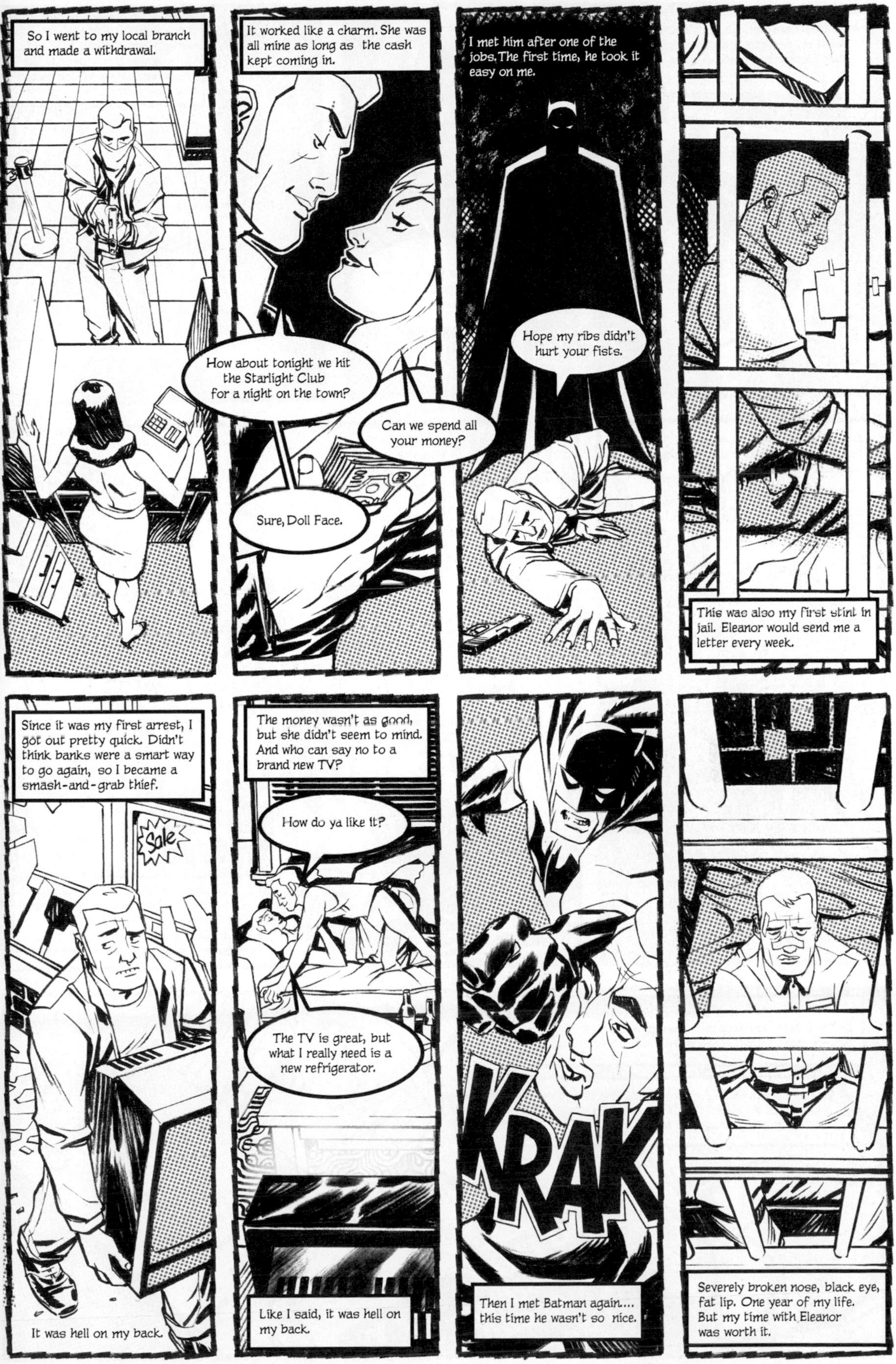
So I went to my local branch and made a withdrawal.
It worked like a charm. She was all mine as long as the cash kept coming in.
How about tonight we hit the Starlight Club for a night on the town?
Can we spend all your money?
Sure, Doll Face.
I met him after one of the jobs. The first time, he took it easy on me.
Hope my ribs didn't hurt your fists.
This was also my first stint in jail. Eleanor would send me a letter every week.
Since it was my first arrest, I got out pretty quick. Didn't think banks were a smart way to go again, so I became a smash-and-grab thief.
Sale
It was hell on my back.
The money wasn't as good, but she didn't seem to mind. And who can say no to a brand new TV?
How do ya like it?
The TV is great, but what I really need is a new refrigerator.
Like I said, it was hell on my back.
KRAK
Then I met Batman again... this time he wasn't so nice.
Severely broken nose, black eye, fat lip. One year of my life. But my time with Eleanor was worth it.

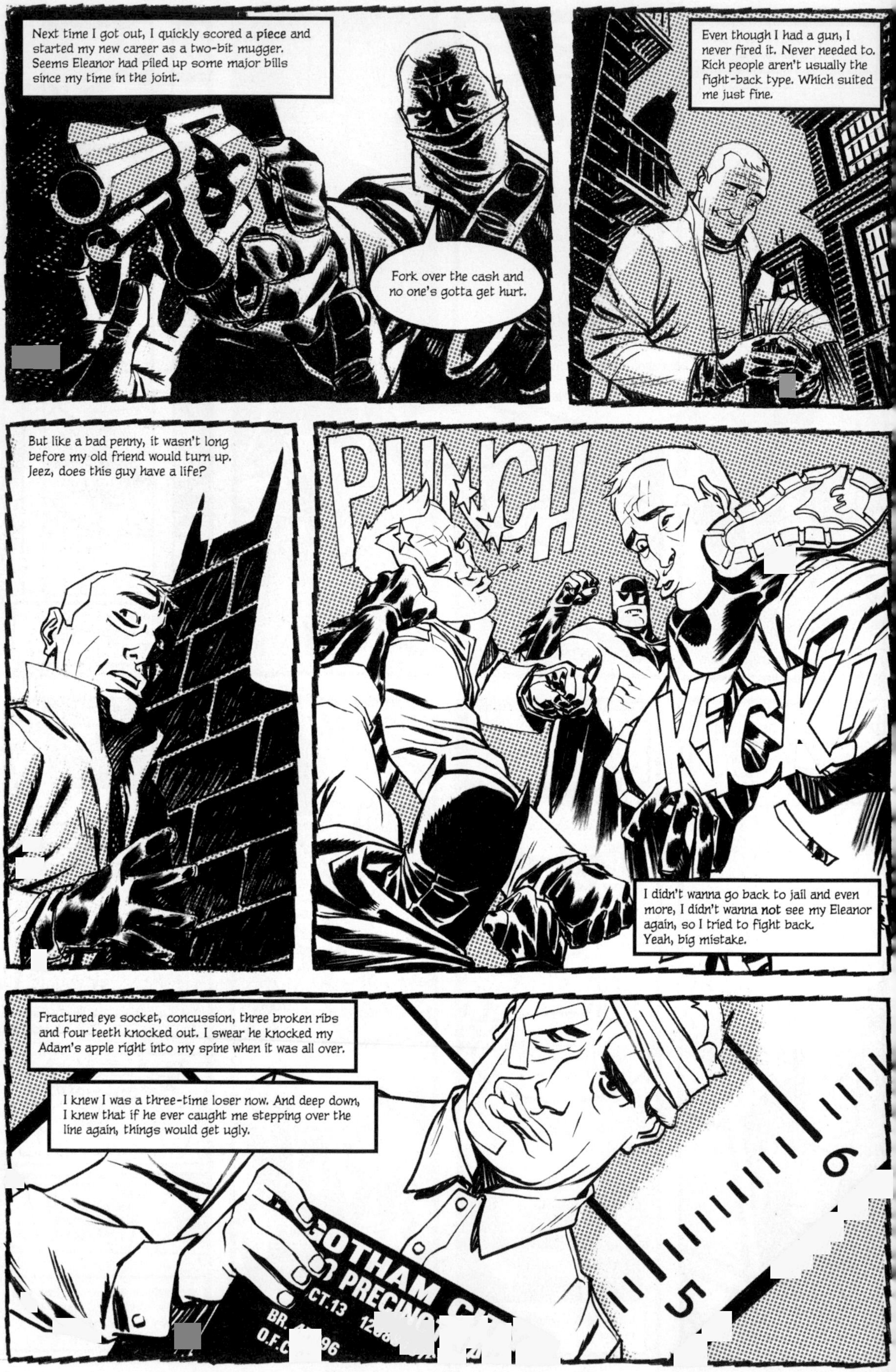
Next time I got out, I quickly scored a **piece** and started my new career as a two-bit mugger. Seems Eleanor had piled up some major bills since my time in the joint.
Fork over the cash and no one's gotta get hurt.
Even though I had a gun, I never fired it. Never needed to. Rich people aren't usually the fight-back type. Which suited me just fine.
But like a bad penny, it wasn't long before my old friend would turn up. Jeez, does this guy have a life?
PUNCH
KICK!
I didn't wanna go back to jail and even more, I didn't wanna **not** see my Eleanor again, so I tried to fight back. Yeah, big mistake.
Fractured eye socket, concussion, three broken ribs and four teeth knocked out. I swear he knocked my Adam's apple right into my spine when it was all over.
I knew I was a three-time loser now. And deep down, I knew that if he ever caught me stepping over the line again, things would get ugly.
GOTHAM

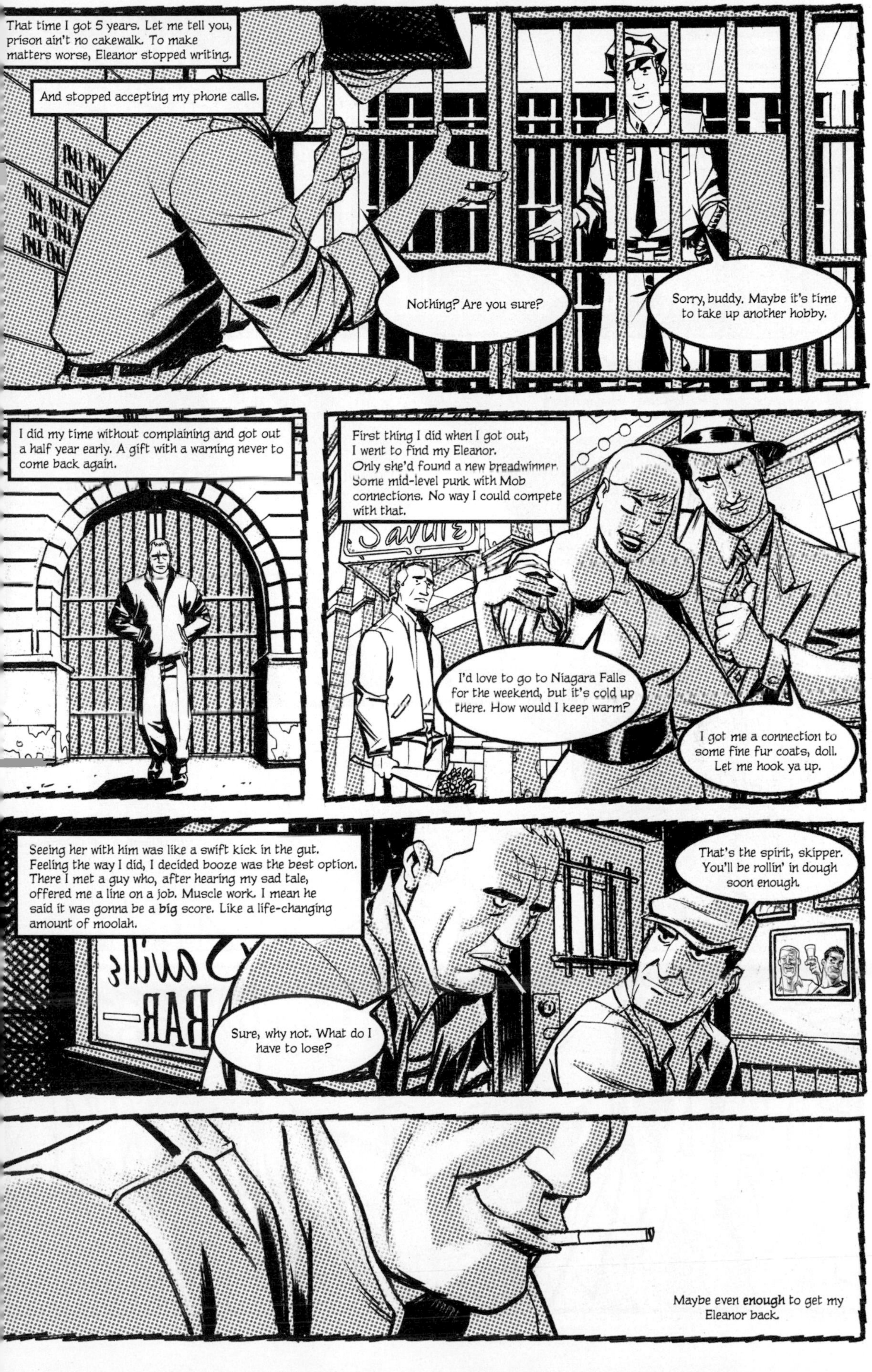
That time I got 5 years. Let me tell you, prison ain't no cakewalk. To make matters worse, Eleanor stopped writing.
And stopped accepting my phone calls.
Nothing? Are you sure?
Sorry, buddy. Maybe it's time to take up another hobby.
I did my time without complaining and got out a half year early. A gift with a warning never to come back again.
First thing I did when I got out, I went to find my Eleanor. Only she'd found a new breadwinner. Some mid-level punk with Mob connections. No way I could compete with that.
I'd love to go to Niagara Falls for the weekend, but it's cold up there. How would I keep warm?
I got me a connection to some fine fur coats, doll. Let me hook ya up.
Seeing her with him was like a swift kick in the gut. Feeling the way I did, I decided booze was the best option. There I met a guy who, after hearing my sad tale, offered me a line on a job. Muscle work. I mean he said it was gonna be a **big** score. Like a life-changing amount of moolah.
That's the spirit, skipper. You'll be rollin' in dough soon enough.
Sure, why not. What do I have to lose?
BAR
Maybe even **enough** to get my Eleanor back.

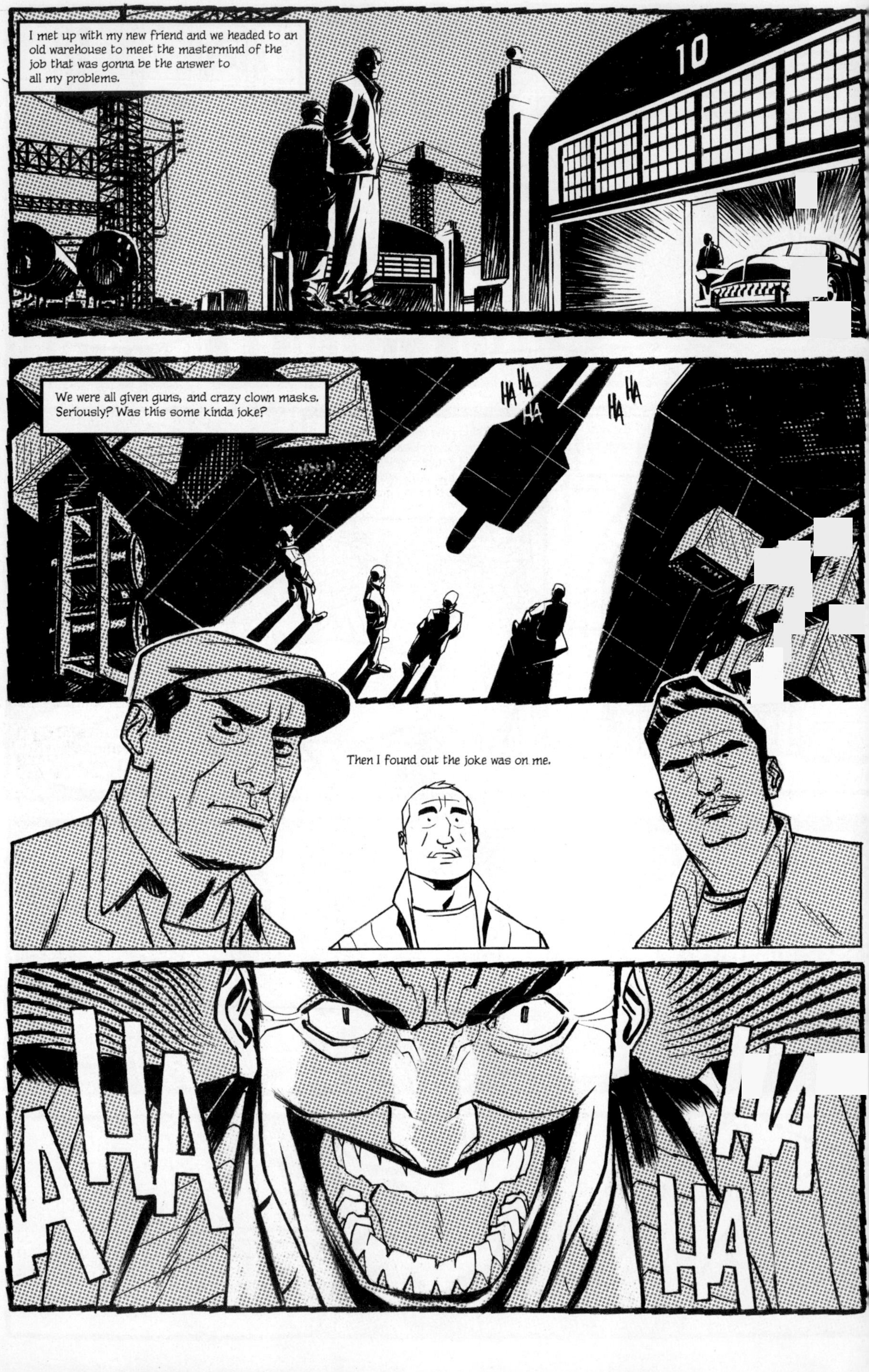
I met up with my new friend and we headed to an old warehouse to meet the mastermind of the job that was gonna be the answer to all my problems.
10
We were all given guns, and crazy clown masks. Seriously? Was this some kinda joke?
HA HA HA
HA HA
Then I found out the joke was on me.
AHAHA
HA
HA

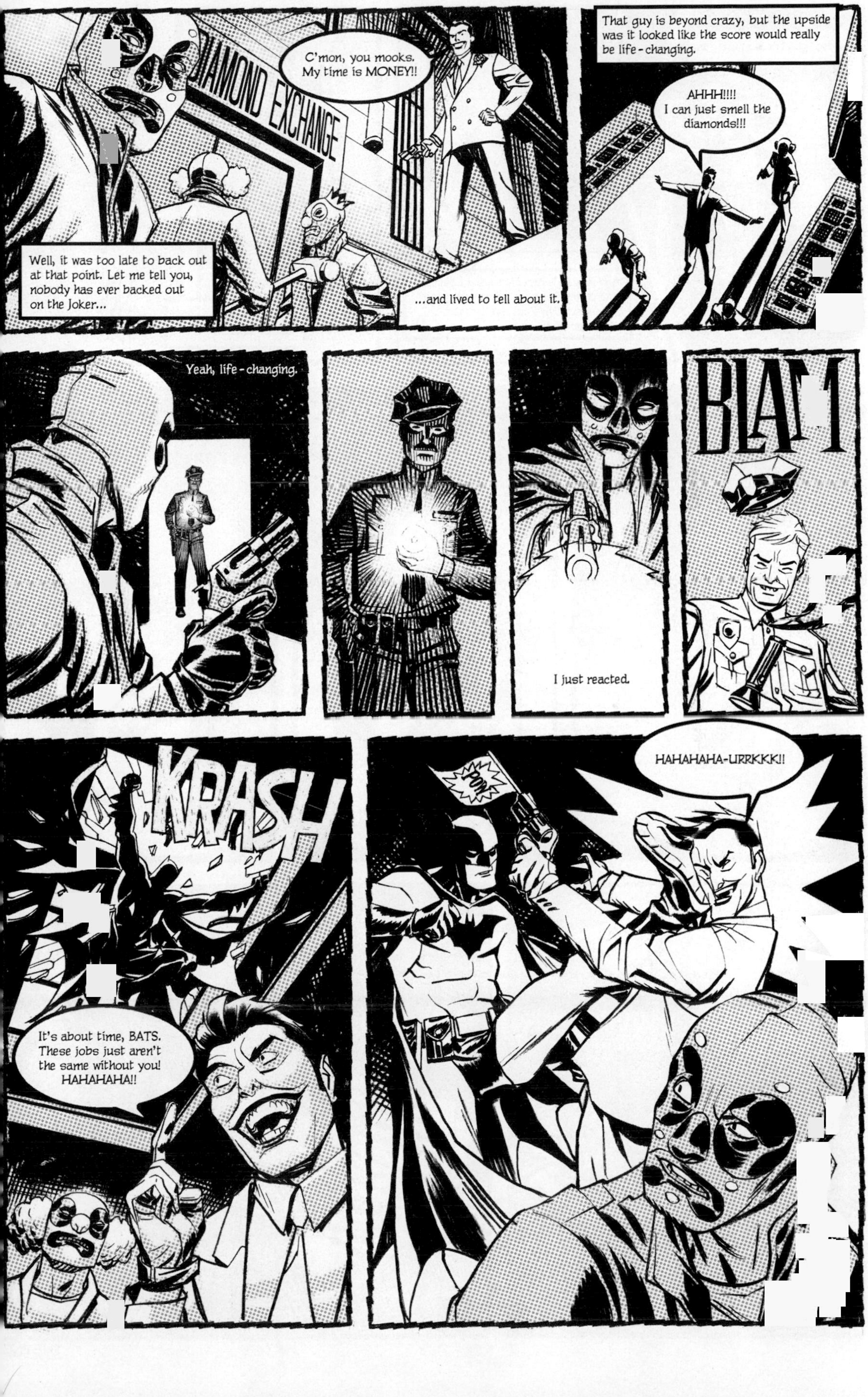

Well, it was too late to back out at that point. Let me tell you, nobody has ever backed out on the Joker...
IAMOND EXCHANGE
C'mon, you mooks. My time is MONEY!!
...and lived to tell about it.
That guy is beyond crazy, but the upside was it looked like the score would really be life-changing.
AHHH!!!! I can just smell the diamonds!!!
Yeah, life-changing.
I just reacted.
BLAM
KRASH
It's about time, BATS. These jobs just aren't the same without you! HAHAHAHA!!
POW
HAHAHAHA-URRKKK!!

I dropped the gun and ran.

And now I sit here. Knowing I deserve everything Batman dishes out. Jeez. Manslaughter. Probably get the chair for that.

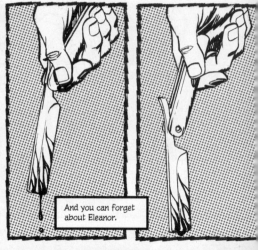

And you can forget about Eleanor.

But here's something about me that I didn't mention yet.

I'm a coward.

And the thought of Batman's wrath is more than I can take.

I've been told that slicing the vein just right will do it pretty painlessly.

So with this.....

...I guess you can say I finally BEAT THE BATMAN.

THE END

DAVE JOHNSON

Possibly the most inventive artist and designer in
all of comics, Dave Johnson never fails to amaze.
His boldly graphic, imaginative and innovative
work has graced many comics covers, including
memorable runs on 100 BULLETS, BATMAN,
UNKNOWN SOLDIER, SPACEMAN, *B.P.R.D.*,
The Punisher, and *Deadpool*.

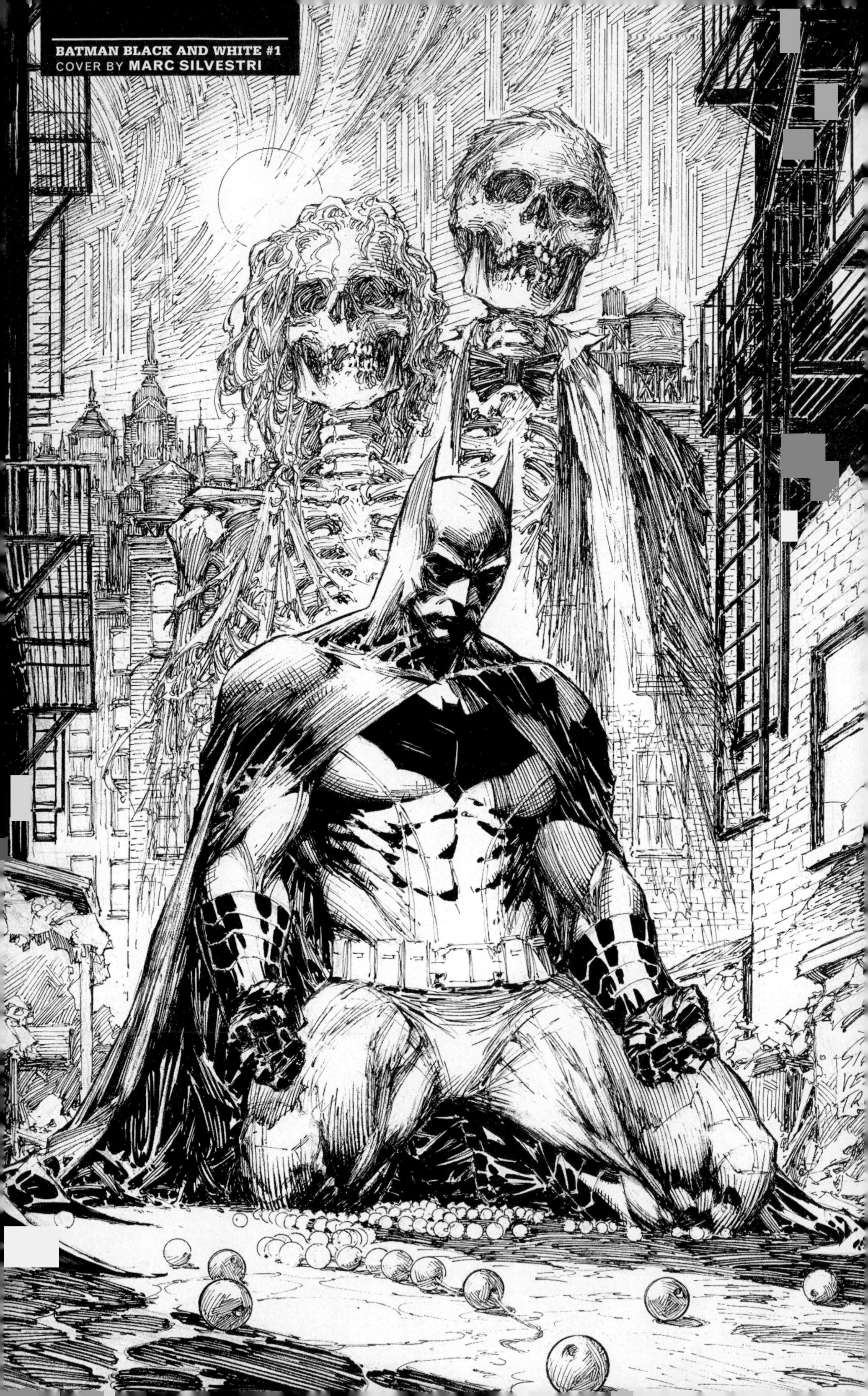

BATMAN BLACK AND WHITE #1
COVER BY **MARC SILVESTRI**

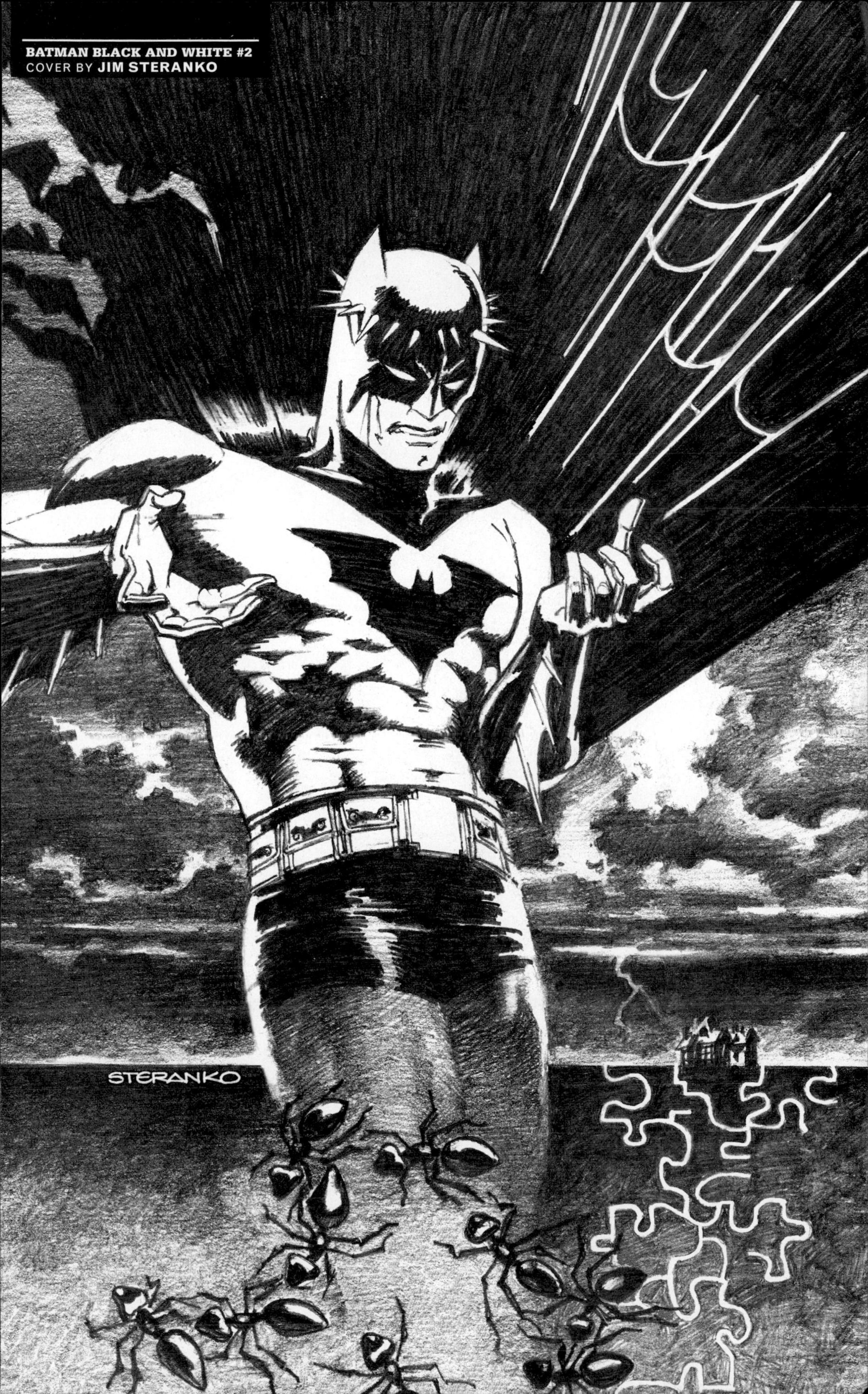
STERANKO

BATMAN BLACK AND WHITE #2
COVER BY **JIM STERANKO**

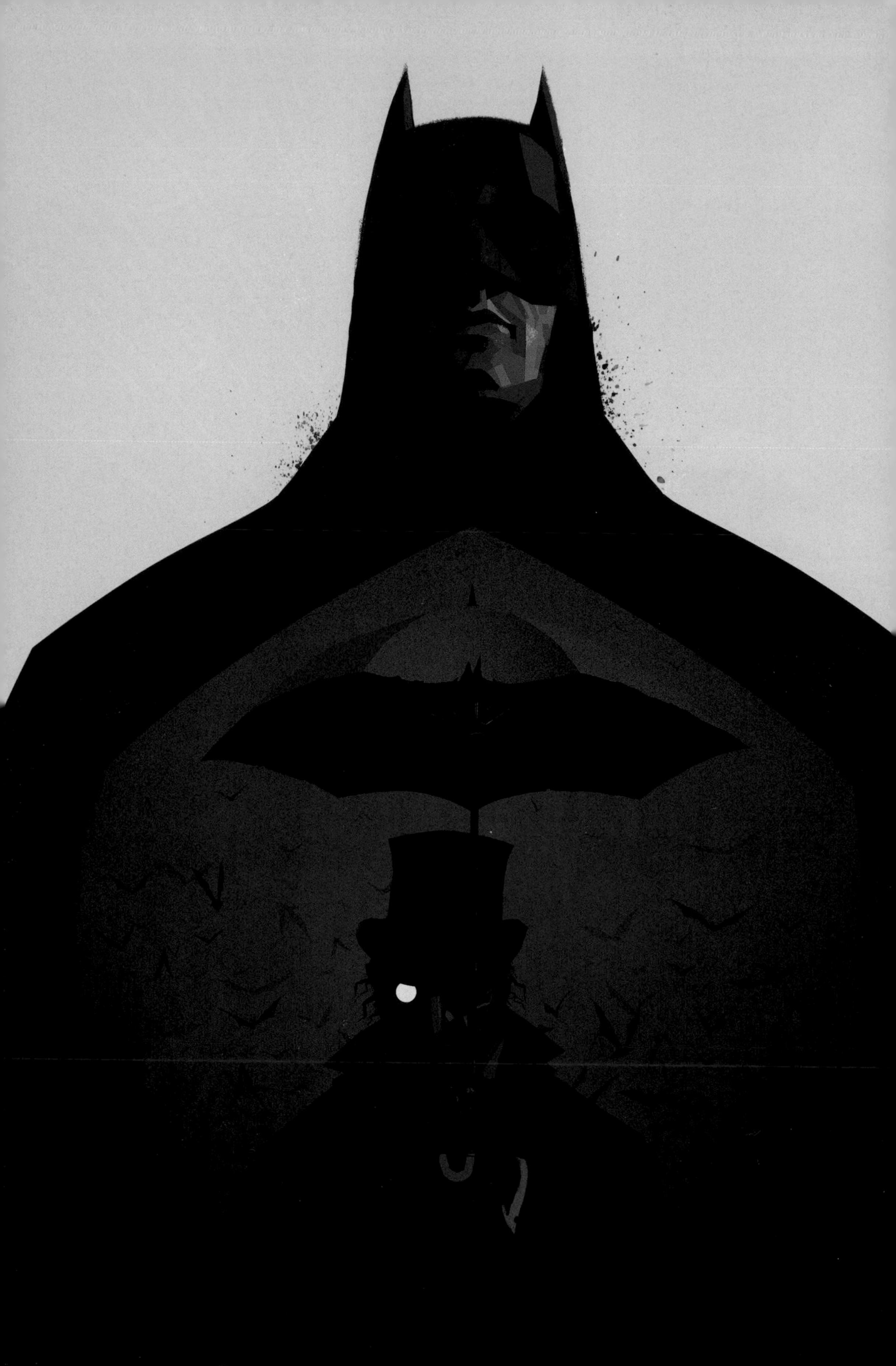

BATMAN BLACK AND WHITE #3
COVER BY **OLLY MOSS**

BATMAN BLACK AND WHITE #4
COVER BY **AMANDA CONNER**

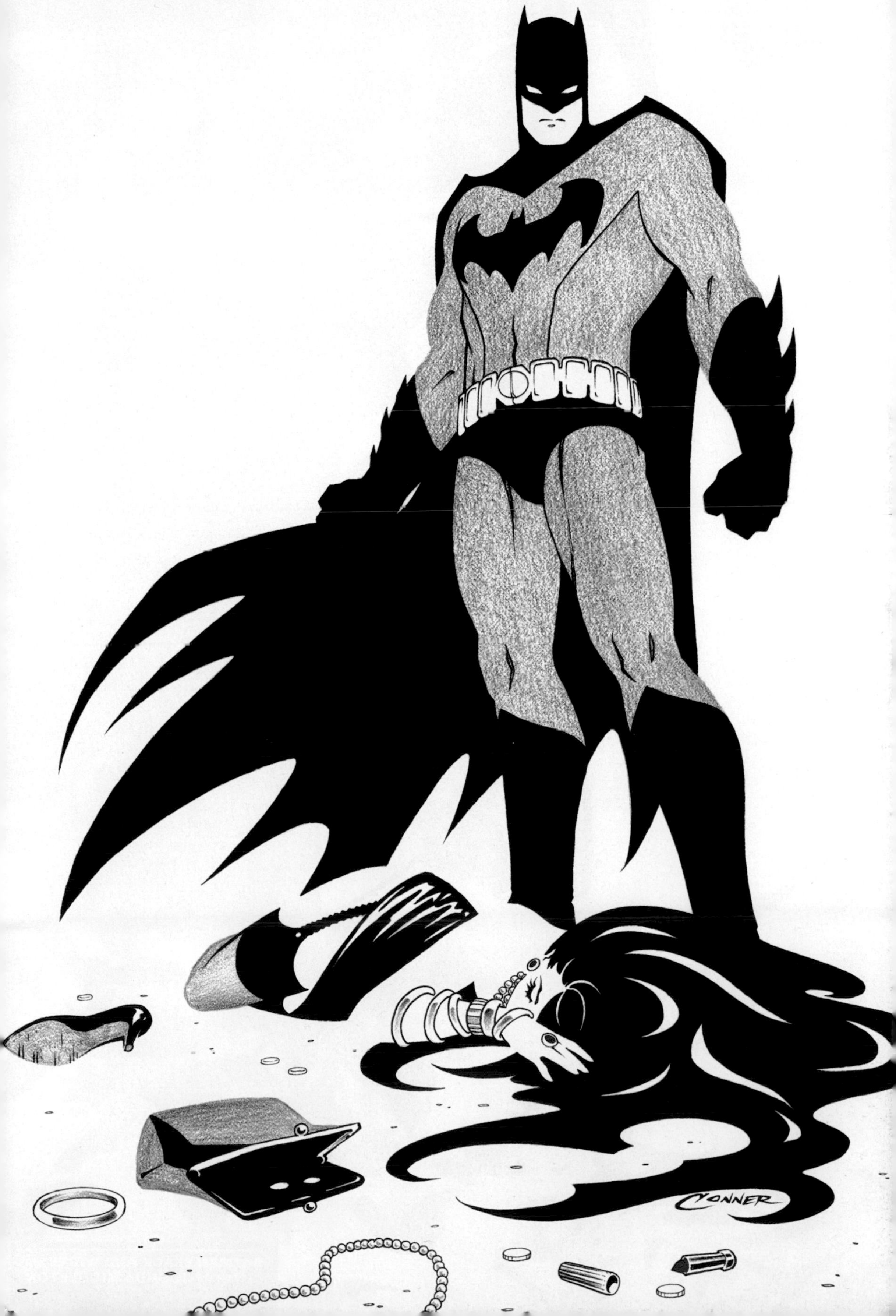
CONNER

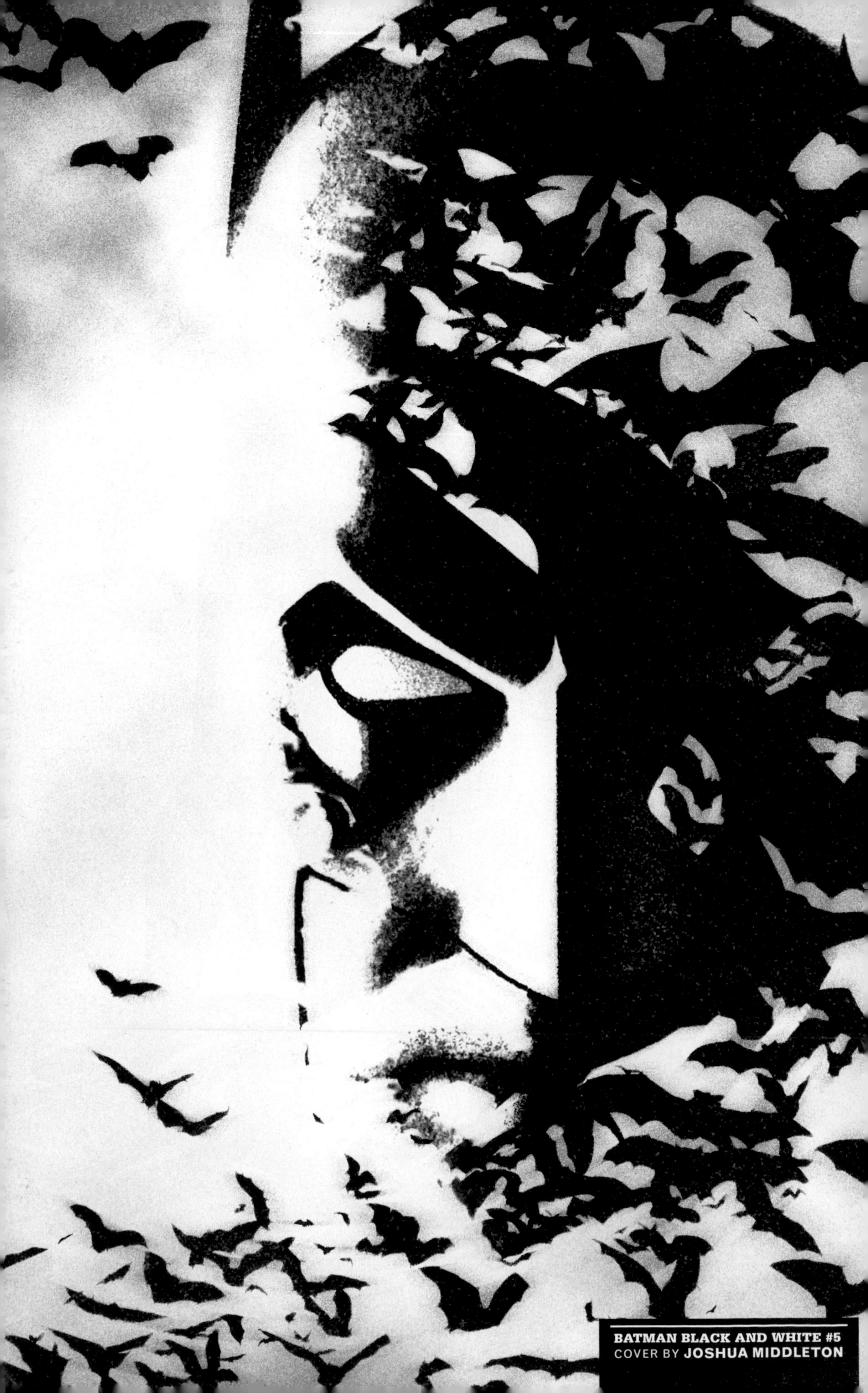

BATMAN BLACK AND WHITE #5
COVER BY **JOSHUA MIDDLETON**

BATMAN BLACK AND WHITE #6
COVER BY **DOUG MAHNKE**

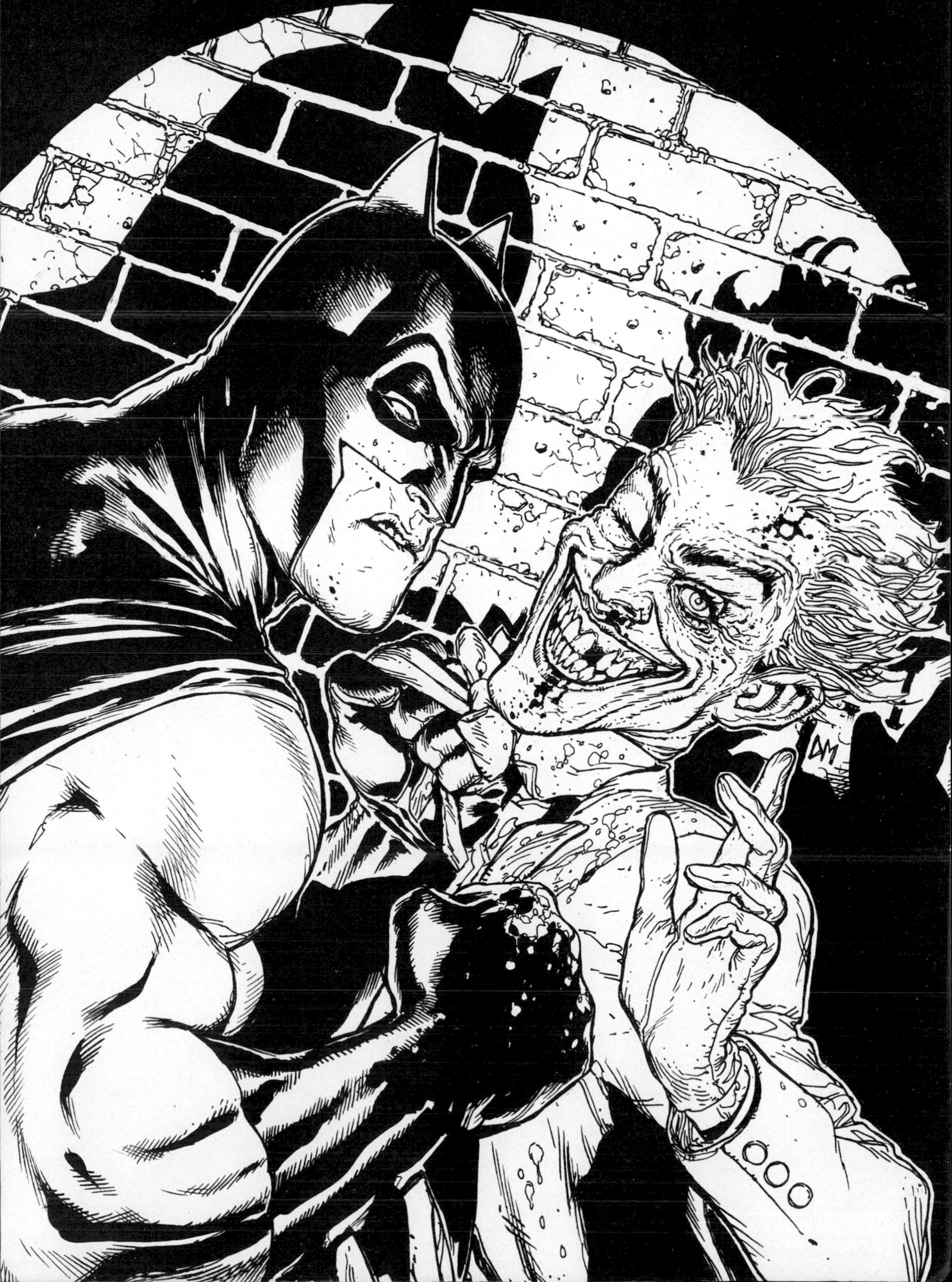

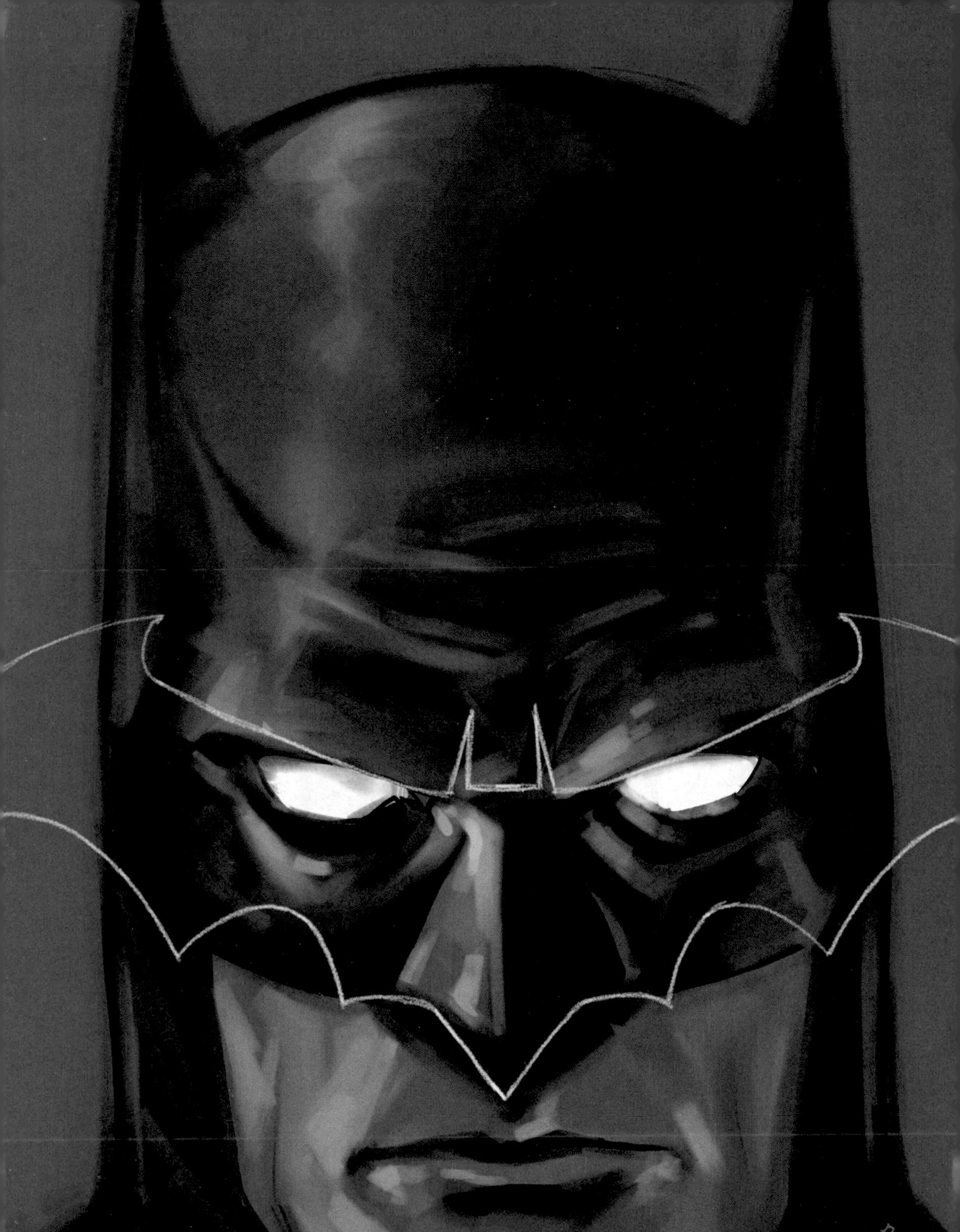
noto

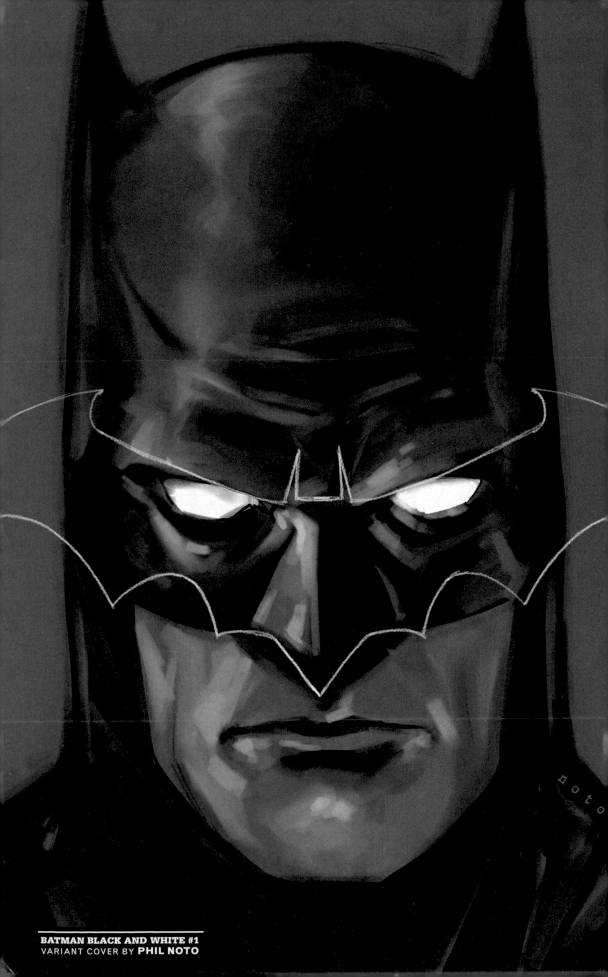

BATMAN BLACK AND WHITE #1
VARIANT COVER BY **PHIL NOTO**

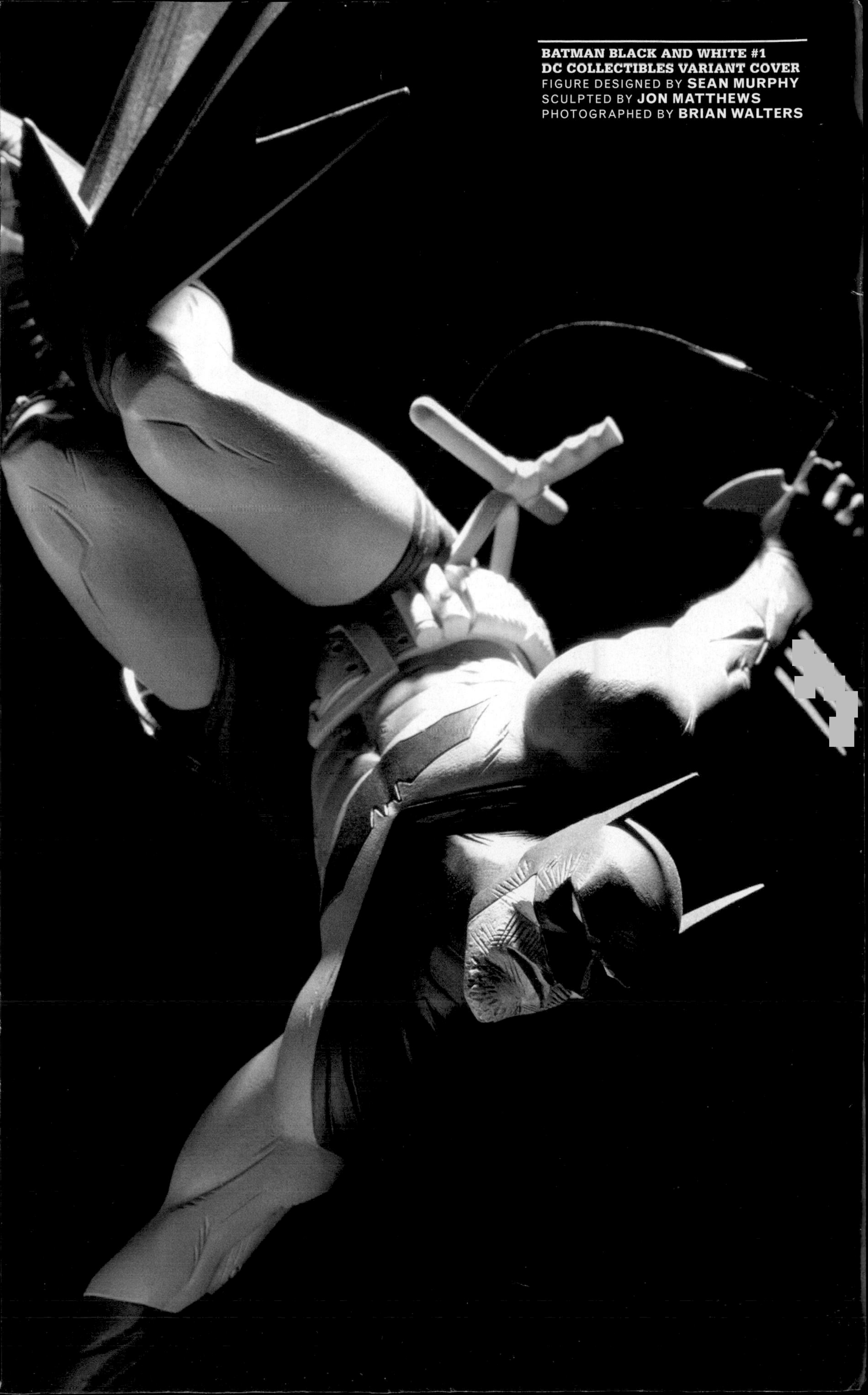

BATMAN BLACK AND WHITE #1
DC COLLECTIBLES VARIANT COVER
FIGURE DESIGNED BY **SEAN MURPHY**
SCULPTED BY **JON MATTHEWS**
PHOTOGRAPHED BY **BRIAN WALTERS**

"[Writer Scott Snyder] pulls from the oldest aspects of the Batman myth, combines it with sinister-comic elements from the series' best period, and gives the whole thing terrific forward-spin."—ENTERTAINMENT WEEKLY

START AT THE BEGINNING!

BATMAN VOLUME 1: THE COURT OF OWLS

BATMAN VOL. 2: THE CITY OF OWLS

with SCOTT SNYDER and GREG CAPULLO

BATMAN VOL. 3: DEATH OF THE FAMILY

with SCOTT SNYDER and GREG CAPULLO

BATMAN: NIGHT OF THE OWLS

with SCOTT SNYDER and GREG CAPULLO

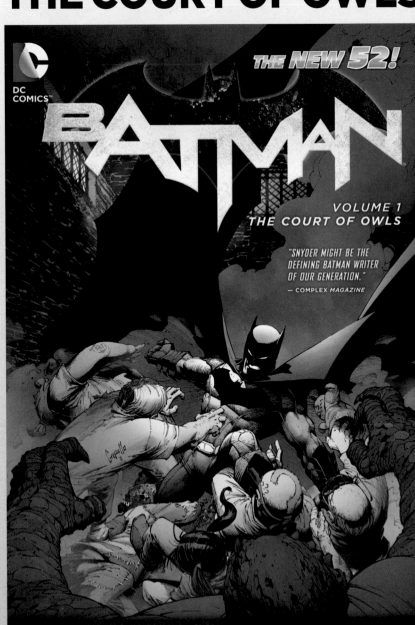

THE NEW 52!

DC COMICS™

BATMAN

VOLUME 1
THE COURT OF OWLS

"SNYDER MIGHT BE THE DEFINING BATMAN WRITER OF OUR GENERATION."
— COMPLEX MAGAZINE

SCOTT **SNYDER**   GREG **CAPULLO**   JONATHAN **GLAPION**

FROM THE CREATOR OF *300* and *SIN CITY*

FRANK MILLER
with KLAUS JANSON

BATMAN:
THE DARK KNIGHT
STRIKES AGAIN

BATMAN: YEAR ONE
DELUXE EDITION

with DAVID MAZZUCCHELLI

ALL-STAR BATMAN
& ROBIN, THE BOY
WONDER VOL. 1

FRANK MILLER + JIM LEE

with JIM LEE

BATMAN: THE DARK KNIGHT RETURNS

FRANK MILLER

with KLAUS JANSON and LYNN VARLEY

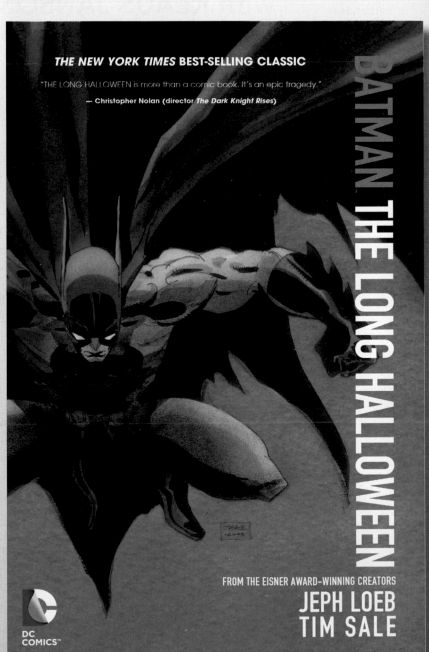